PRAISE FOR THE SIXTH EDITION

Oatley's IPE textbook is simply the best of its kind. It is comprehensive, analytically rigorous, and thoughtfully written for students with no previous background in the field. This latest edition contains a variety of fresh material – on Trump, Brexit, China, migration, and other topics – to keep students and instructors excited about the field.

David A. Singer, *Massachusetts Institute of Technology*

This approachable, accessible new edition of Thomas Oatley's text lays out the foundations of IPE. With constant reference to both historical cases and current policy concerns, it provides both an academic introduction to the issues concerning the field and a vivid application to familiar events. Students reading this book will be empowered to assess the global economy and its effects from a theoretically and empirically informed perspective.

Michael Plouffe, *University College London*

Thomas Oatley's IPE book remains the go-to text for foundational, comprehensive, and rigorous training in the concepts, principles, and major debates in the field. The new sixth edition has been significantly updated for our times, capturing developments of the Trump era and emerging issues like global value chains, the political economy of migration, and the rise of China in global economic governance. Highly recommended!

Soo Yeon Kim, *National University of Singapore*

This is, hands down, the single best textbook I have used for any class in more than two decades of university teaching. It achieves that difficult and elusive goal of conveying complex material at a high level while also making it very accessible and understandable. The result is an invaluable IPE text that brings the students up to the level of the material rather than the reverse.

Strom Thacker, *Union College*

Thomas Oatley succeeds in writing an international political economy text that political science students will find accessible and economics students will find interesting. Incorporating and integrating essential concepts underlying IPE as well as contemporary scholarship, Oatley provides a succinct and effective foundation for understanding the field – and the insights it can provide for current policy issues and dilemmas.

Robert G. Blanton, *University of Alabama-Birmingham*

This book's masterful structural-paradigmatic approach trains students and scholars in the kinds of investigative rigor that must be pursued to gain understanding of the global political economy. Oatley skillfully utilizes the dynamics of position and momentum to demonstrate how competition in global economic exchange creates winners and losers and shapes economic policy.

Hollis M. France, *College of Charleston*

D1293021

Thomas Oatley's *International Political Economy* provides essential background to the interplay of economic behavior and political institutions. It takes seriously the role that economics plays in defining the interests of political actors but also introduces the student to the operation of institutions that govern international trade and finance. In plain language, it describes essential principles of economics and the role that political actors play in governing and negotiating the international political economy.

Paul Rowe, *Trinity Western University*

This is an outstanding introduction to the field of international political economy. Crucially for a textbook, it finds the right balance between theory and context. It provides an engaging and well-written introduction to key developments in world economic history, while also introducing the essential tools that are necessary to interpret these developments. Added to this, students will find it full of engaging real world examples that bring the subject to life. It should be considered as a standard text for all IPE courses at undergraduate level.

Michael Breen, *European University Institute and Dublin City University*

This book is superb: It shows how theories and real-world issues are linked, and provides students with an excellent opportunity to engage in the intellectual exercise of applying theories to pressing questions in international political economy.

Seungjoo Lee, *Chung-Ang University*

Expertly bridging the disciplines of economics and political science, Thomas Oatley's book has inspired, disciplined, and transformed a new generation of scholars and students. With a simple and effective presentation of challenging material, this new sixth edition keeps up not only with the latest developments in IPE but also the very recent changes taking place in the real world. A new chapter on the achievements and challenges to the global capitalist economy provides excellent insight into the causes of the recent emergence of anti-globalization sentiments, once again in a way that is both clear and eye-opening for students.

Andrew X. Li, *Central European University*

This text's most outstanding feature is its deliberate focus on the interactive and reiterative processes that simultaneously shape politics and economics, an approach that makes students more aware of the complexity of IPE and turns them into more critical observers of the world around them. Coming from a wide variety of emphasis areas, my own students love Oatley's straightforward language, ease of access, strong detail, and wide topical coverage.

Leif Hoffmann, *Lewis-Clark State College*

Oatley's textbook represents a masterful introduction to the field of international political economy. The book provides an accessible yet sophisticated overview of the subject for beginners. The society- and state-centered approaches equip students with the theoretical building blocks to understand who wins and who loses from globalization. Each superb new edition gives updated empirical examples, keeping the text timely. I have been using it with students in my classes for a decade.

James Raymond Vreeland, *Princeton University*

INTERNATIONAL POLITICAL ECONOMY

Broadly viewing the global economy as a political competition that produces winners and losers, *International Political Economy* holistically and accessibly introduces the field of IPE to students with limited background in political theory, history, and economics. This text surveys major interests and institutions and examines how state and non-state actors pursue wealth and power. Emphasizing fundamental economic concepts as well as the interplay between domestic and international politics, *International Political Economy* not only explains how the global economy works, it also encourages students to think critically about how economic policy is made in the context of globalization.

New to the Sixth Edition

- Covers the economic impacts of 2016 electoral events, including new Trump administration initiatives related to TPP and NAFTA, the UK and Brexit, and the European populist wave.
- Examines the global financial crisis, EU debt crisis, quantitative easing, global capital flow cycles, and currency wars.
- Probes the death of the Doha Round and explores individual trade preferences, WTO dispute settlement, bilateral investment treaties and global value chains, labor standards, and the role of institutions for economic development.
- Considers how U.S. monetary and fiscal policy shapes the flow of financial capital into and out of emerging market economies with a focus on the "Fragile Five," whether the Chinese Renminbi can displace the dollar as a global currency, and the newly constructed Asian Infrastructure Investment Bank.
- Explores the impact of migration on wages and income inequality, and the growing importance of worker remittances as a source of capital for developing countries.

Thomas Oatley is the Corasaniti-Zondorak Chair of International Politics in the Department of Political Science at Tulane University.

An eResource is available for this book at www.routledge.com/9781138490741

International Political Economy

Sixth Edition

THOMAS OATLEY

Routledge
Taylor & Francis Group

NEW YORK AND LONDON

Sixth edition published 2019
by Routledge
711 Third Avenue, New York, NY 10017

and by Routledge
2 Park Square, Milton Park, Abingdon, Oxon, OX14 4RN

Routledge is an imprint of the Taylor & Francis Group, an informa business

© 2019 Taylor & Francis

The right of Thomas Oatley to be identified as author of this work has been asserted by him in accordance with sections 77 and 78 of the Copyright, Designs and Patents Act 1988.

All rights reserved. No part of this book may be reprinted or reproduced or utilised in any form or by any electronic, mechanical, or other means, now known or hereafter invented, including photocopying and recording, or in any information storage or retrieval system, without permission in writing from the publishers.

Trademark notice: Product or corporate names may be trademarks or registered trademarks, and are used only for identification and explanation without intent to infringe.

First edition published by Pearson 2003
Fifth edition published by Pearson Education, Inc. 2012 and Routledge 2016

Library of Congress Cataloging-in-Publication Data
Names: Oatley, Thomas H., 1962- author.
Title: International political economy / Thomas Oatley, Tulane University.
Description: Sixth edition. | New York, NY : Routledge, 2019. | Includes bibliographical references and index.
Identifiers: LCCN 2018009735| ISBN 9781138490727 (hardback) | ISBN 9781138490741 (pbk.) | ISBN 9781351034661 (ebook)
Subjects: LCSH: International economic relations. | International finance. | Globalization.
Classification: LCC HF1359 .O248 2019 | DDC 337--dc23
LC record available at https://lccn.loc.gov/2018009735

ISBN: 978-1-138-49072-7 (hbk)
ISBN: 978-1-138-49074-1 (pbk)
ISBN: 978-1-351-03466-1 (ebk)

Typeset in Sabon and Bell Gothic by
Servis Filmsetting Ltd, Stockport, Cheshire

Visit the eResources: www.routledge.com/9781138490741

Printed and bound in the United States of America by Sheridan

BRIEF CONTENTS

DETAILED CONTENTS

PREFACE

Local developments reflect global forces, and global forces are in turn shaped by these local developments. Consider the Trump administration that entered office in January 2017. It seems clear that Trump's somewhat surprising victory was due in part to support from workers in key Rust Belt states who had seen their jobs disappear as a consequence of global competition and trade. Trump's promise to "make America great again" held considerable appeal to these voters as the promise seemed to indicate that Trump could revitalize manufacturing employment in the American Midwest. Trump's unlikely victory in the 2016 election is in turn shaping and reshaping the global economy. Since entering office, Trump has been a rather disruptive force for the international trade system. He almost immediately withdrew the United States from the Trans-Pacific Partnership trade agreement, he initiated a sweeping review of the World Trade Organization, and he began to renegotiate the North American Free Trade Agreement with Mexico and Canada. The outcomes from these processes that Trump has initiated will shape the American economy and in doing so will probably have an impact on the outcome of the 2020 presidential election.

More broadly, Trump's election and the subsequent trade policy initiatives he has embraced highlight the extent to which our ability to understand the global economy requires knowledge of politics as well as economics. For globalization is not a spontaneous economic process: it is built on a political foundation. Governments share a broad consensus on core principles; core principles inform the elaboration of specific rules. Specific rules establish international institutions—the World Trade Organization, the World Bank, and the International Monetary Fund. These international institutions in turn facilitate a political process through which governments reduce barriers to global exchange and create common rules to regulate other elements of the global economy. This political system—the foundation and the process—has enabled businesses to construct the network of international economic linkages that constitute the economic dimension of globalization. Understanding the global economy, therefore, requires a political economy approach: we must study its political as well as its economic dimensions.

Studying the political and economic dimensions of the global economy requires us to develop theory that simplifies an inherently complex world. This book develops a theoretical framework in which politics in the global economy revolves around enduring competition between the winners and the losers generated by global economic exchange. As economists since Adam Smith have told us, global exchange raises aggregate social welfare. Yet, global exchange also creates winners and losers. For some, global exchange brings greater wealth and rising incomes; for others, however, the international economy brings job losses and lower incomes. These winners and losers compete to influence government policy. Those who profit from global exchange encourage governments to adopt policies that facilitate such exchange; those harmed by globalization encourage governments to adopt policies that restrict it. This competition is played out through domestic politics, where it is mediated by domestic political institutions, and it is played out through international politics, often within the major international institutions such as the Group of 20 and the World Trade Organization.

NEW TO THIS EDITION

Although this edition maintains the basic structure of previous editions, I have adjusted the book's chapters to incorporate topics that have become increasingly central to IPE scholarship but were absent from the fifth edition. Chapter 2 introduces global supply chains (which is carried forward into Chapters 8 and 9). Chapter 4 incorporates a discussion of international factor mobility and trade politics. Chapter 7 now includes a section on institutions and development, with a specific focus on work by Acemoglu and Robinson. Chapter 8 includes a discussion of Bilateral Investment Treaties as well as a discussion of labor rights and MNCs. Second, I have updated coverage of major substantive issues. Chapters 2 and 3 address the end of the Doha Round and the current uncertainty about trade given the Trump administration's America First policy. The discussion of the financial crisis of 2007–2009 and the EU sovereign debt crisis is brought up to date in Chapter 11. Chapter 14 includes a brief discussion of remittances as a source of foreign capital for developing countries as well as a mention of the newly constructed Asian Infrastucture Investment Bank. A new section of Chapter 15 focuses on the so-called Fragile Five and the currency wars in the broader context of capital flows to emerging markets since 2009. And this edition offers a brand-new concluding chapter that focuses on the achievements of and challenges to the global capitalist economy. As always, I have updated the figures and tables where appropriate to incorporate the most recent data available.

I have changed many of the "Closer Look" and "Policy Analysis and Debate" boxes. In addition to updating recurring features, I added many new topics.

- Chapter 4 includes "Closer Look" boxes that focus on the 2016 British referendum on EU membership (i.e., Brexit), and international factor mobility and trade politics.
- Chapter 6 includes a "Policy Analysis and Debate" focused on the Sustainable Development Goals.
- Chapter 7 includes a "Policy Analysis and Debate" focused on whether development strategies should transition from the Washington Consensus to the Beijing Consensus.
- Chapter 8 includes a "Closer Look" that examines labor and foreign capital in the developing world.
- Chapter 9 includes an updated "Closer Look" that examines the use of incentives to attract Asian auto makers to the U.S. south.

- Chapter 11 includes a "Policy Analysis and Debate" that asks students to consider whether Germany should pursue additional fiscal stimulus to promote economic growth in the EU.
- Chapter 12 includes a "Policy Analysis and Debate" that asks students to discuss the merits and demerits of the Obama administration's effort to double exports in 5 years in part by devaluing the dollar.
- Chapter 15 includes a "Closer Look" that examines debt relief for the Heavily Indebted Poor Countries.
- Chapter 16 is brand new, and traces the remarkable achievements realized within the global capitalist economy and examines how it may also have contributed to rising inequality that is generating an anti-globalization backlash.

FEATURES

This textbook imparts a unique perspective. First, it shows students how domestic politics shape the objectives governments pursue and how interaction between governments shapes the outcomes they achieve. In fact, I dedicate more than one-quarter of the book to the domestic politics of trade and exchange-rate policies. Second, the book shows how the objectives that governments pursue are in turn shaped by interest groups and individuals responding to the impact of the global economy on their incomes. Thus, the book highlights how political processes shape the economic system and how transactions within the global economy in turn shape political dynamics.

The book imparts this perspective by relying on four pedagogical tools. First, each chapter elaborates the logic of the economic models relevant to each issue area in language accessible to the non specialist. Second, each chapter highlights how the distributional consequences of cross-border economic activity shape politics—domestic or international—within that issue area. Third, each chapter uses the models of political competition to explain important historical events. Many chapters contain "Closer Look" boxes to provide in-depth case studies. Finally, each chapter contains a "Policy Analysis and Debate" box to encourage students to relate the theoretical models—political and economic—to contemporary policy debates.

The book applies this approach to the major issue areas in international political economy. The first half of the book is devoted to international trade and production. Chapters 2 and 3 examine the political logic driving the creation and evolution of the international trade system. Chapter 2 traces the historical evolution of the General Agreement on Tariffs and Trade/World Trade Organization. Chapter 3 examines the system through the lens of neoliberal theories of cooperation. Chapters 4 and 5 examine how domestic politics shape government trade policies. Chapter 4 presents a pluralist perspective, while Chapter 5 introduces a statist approach. Chapters 6 and 7 focus on the orientation of developing countries toward the international trade system. Chapter 6 explains why so many governments sought to insulate themselves from the system in the early postwar period. Chapter 7 examines and explains the shift in development strategies from inward to export-oriented. This section concludes with a thorough examination of the political economy of multinational corporations in Chapters 8 and 9.

The second half of the book examines the international monetary and financial systems. Chapters 10 and 11 trace the evolution of the international monetary system. Chapter 10 focuses on core issues of exchange rate systems and balance-of-payments adjustment and traces the creation and collapse of the Bretton Woods system. Chapter 11 focuses on the contemporary floating exchange-rate system, focusing on efforts to manage the system via coordination or to stabilize exchange rates via monetary union. Chapters 12 and 13 examine the domestic politics of monetary and exchange-rate policies. Chapter 12 examines the partisan and sectoral models of macroeconomic and exchange-rate policy; Chapter 13 employs a state-centered approach to explore the impact of central banks as agents independent of governments. Chapters 14 and 15 focus on developing countries' relationships with the international financial system. Chapter 14 examines the emergence and resolution of the Latin American debt crisis. Chapter 15 focuses on the Asian financial crisis and subsequent efforts to manage capital flows to developing countries and to reform the International Monetary Fund. Chapter 16 concludes by drawing on what we have learned to explore some of the major policy debates that have emerged surrounding the global economy.

SUPPLEMENTS

Please visit the online eResource at www.routledge.com/9781138490741.

ACKNOWLEDGMENTS

No book such as this is the work of a single person. I have benefited immensely from the advice and support of many people. Roland Stephen went well beyond the call of duty as friend and colleague in entertaining my many questions, providing suggestions about how to improve the text, and using early versions of the book in his class at North Carolina State University. Eric Reinhardt at Emory University and Jeffry Frieden at Harvard University each offered comments based on their experience with using this text in their courses.

Numerous reviewers provided detailed comments that vastly improved the book in so many ways. It is no light burden to write a thoughtful and constructive review of a book, and I thank them all for taking the time to do so. My thanks, therefore, go to Ali R. Abootalebi, University of Wisconsin–Eau Claire; Frances Adams, Old Dominion University; Andreas Antoniades, University of Sussex; Monica Arruda de Almeida, University of California–Los Angeles; Katherine Barbieri, University of South Carolina; Charles H. Blake, James Madison University; Robert G. Blanton, University of Alabama–Birmingham; Charles Boehmer, University of Texas–El Paso; James Brassett, University of Warwick; Michael Breen, Dublin City University; Terry D. Clark, Creighton University; K. Chad Clay, University of Georgia; Linda Cornett, University of North Carolina–Ashville; Robert A. Daley, Albertson College of Idaho; Charles R. Dannehl, Bradley University; Matthew DiGiuseppe, Binghamton University; Mark Elder, Michigan State University; Hollis France, College of Charleston; Richard Ganzel, Sierra Nevada College; Julia Gray, University of Pennsylvania; Yoram Haftel, DePaul University; Steven Hall, Boise State University; Cullen Hendrix, University of North Texas; Leif Hoffmann, Lewis-Clark State College; Michael Huelshoff, University of New Orleans; Alan Kessler, University of Texas–Austin; Douglas Lemke, Pennsylvania State University; Andrew Long, University of Mississippi; Michael Mastanduno, Dartmouth College; Sean M. McDonald, Bentley University; Daniel McDowell, Syracuse University; Phillip Meeks, Creighton University; Chungshik Moon, Australian National University; Holger Moroff, University of North Carolina; Jeffrey S. Morton, Florida Atlantic University; Layna Mosley, University of North Carolina–Chapel Hill; Gene Mumy, Ohio State University; Clint Peinhardt, University of Texas–Dallas; Jim Peltcher, Denison University; Michael Plouffe, University College London; Leanne Powner, Christopher Newport University; Adrienne Roberts, University of Manchester; Paul Rowe, Trinity Western University; Christina J. Schneider, University of California–San Diego; Roger Schoenman, University of California at Santa Cruz; Herman Schwartz, University of Virginia; Xiaoye She, SUNY Albany; Stuart Shields, University of Manchester; David Andrew Singer, Massachusetts Institute of Technology; Cliff Staten, Indiana University Southeast; Strom Thacker, Boston University; James Raymond Vreeland, Georgetown University; Rachel

L. Wellhausen, University of Texas–Austin; and Christianne Hardy Wohlforth, Dartmouth College.

Finally, I owe a large debt of gratitude to all of those scholars whose research made this book possible. You have taught me much, and I only hope that in writing the book I have treated your work accurately and fairly. Of course, in spite of all this support, I alone am responsible for any errors of fact or interpretation.

Thomas Oatley

International Political Economy

How does the global economy affect my life—and yours? One of the most obvious ways in which the global economy matters is through the impact it has on the items we consume. Because of international trade, grocery stores can keep a wide variety of fresh fruits and vegetables in stock throughout the year. When we shop for clothing, we find that global production and increased trade in the apparel industry have helped to reduce the prices that American shoppers pay for clothing and footwear. The same is true in the technology industries. My smartphone, as well as the notebook computer that I am using to write this book, are "American" products, but they carry lower prices precisely because their production processes have been organized globally—designed in America, manufactured and assembled largely outside of the United States. And when it comes time for me to purchase a new car, the fact that my country participates in the global economy ensures that I have a wide range of brands to choose from—European, Japanese, South Korean, American, and probably soon Chinese. The global economy thus makes the consumers in us better off by reducing the prices of the goods and services we buy and expanding the range of choices we have.

Living in a global economy also means that global economic forces play a much larger role in determining many of our career opportunities today than they did a few decades ago. Twenty-five years ago, manufacturing industries made high-paying jobs available that provided Americans a middle-class life-style. In many southern states, for instance, textile and apparel mills provided jobs for two if not three generations of workers. In the Great Lakes region, steel mills and the huge automobile factories built by Ford, GM, and Chrysler did the same. Today, many of these opportunities have disappeared and much of this loss has occurred as a consequence of international trade. At the same time, the opportunity to find work in a service industry and in high technology has increased dramatically. Medical care, computer design, Internet-based

1

businesses, biotechnology, finance, and high-technology manufacturing industries all have emerged as large growing employers of the American work force since 1980. Thus, the opportunities available today are far different today than they were a quarter-century ago. The global economy has played a central role in bringing about these changes.

International political economy (IPE) studies how politics shape developments in the global economy and how the global economy shapes politics. It focuses most heavily on the enduring political battle between the winners and losers from global economic exchange. Although all societies benefit from participation in the global economy, these gains are not distributed evenly among individuals. Global economic exchange raises the income of some people and lowers the income of others. The distributive consequences of global economic exchange generate political competition in national and international arenas. The winners seek deeper links with the global economy in order to extend and consolidate their gains, whereas the losers try to erect barriers between the global and national economies in order to minimize or even reverse their losses. IPE studies how the enduring political battle between the winners and losers from global economic exchange shapes the evolution of the global economy.

This chapter introduces IPE as a field of study. It begins by providing a broad overview of the substantive issues that IPE examines and the kinds of questions scholars ask when studying these issues. The chapter then briefly surveys a few of the theoretical frameworks that scholars have developed in order to answer the questions they pose. The chapter concludes by looking at the emergence of a global economy in the late nineteenth century in order to provide a broader context for our subsequent focus on the contemporary global economy.

WHAT IS INTERNATIONAL POLITICAL ECONOMY?

IPE studies the political battle between the winners and losers of global economic exchange. Consider, for example, the decision by the Trump administration to raise tariffs on softwood lumber imported from Canada in April 2017. The decision to raise tariffs was prompted by lobbying by American lumber mills and timberland owners. The U.S. Lumber Coalition pressed for higher tariffs on Canadian lumber because they were losing trade. Imported Canadian lumber was capturing a large share of the American market, resulting in mill closings and layoffs, and higher tariffs would protect American lumber from competition, thereby reducing the number of American mills in distress.

The higher tariff on Canadian lumber had negative consequences for other groups in society, however. The tariff hurt American industries that use lumber to produce goods, such as home builders, because these firms had to pay more for wood. Higher lumber prices would cause home prices to rise, higher prices would cause demand for new homes to fall, and as many as 8,200 jobs would disappear. The tariff hurt Canadian lumber producers, who could sell less lumber in their largest market. Groups that suffered from the lumber tariff turned to the political system to try to reverse the decision. In the United States,

The National Association of Home Builders pressured the Trump administration and Congress to reduce and even remove the tariff. The Canadian government responded to pressure from its producers by imposing a tariff on American gypsum (drywall) exported into Canada and is currently considering retaliatory tariffs on American coal and a variety of products made in Oregon (the home to an American Senator who has been a strident advocate of the U.S. tariff on Canadian lumber). As this dispute escalates, it could wind up eventually as an investigation within the World Trade Organization (WTO)—the international organization with responsibility for trade disputes—or become a central component of a renegotiated North American Free Trade Agreement (NAFTA). The story of the U.S. tariff on Canadian lumber thus nicely illustrates the central focus of international political economy as a field of study: how the political battle between the winners and losers of global economic exchange shapes the economic policies that governments adopt.

The softwood lumber tariff dispute also highlights the many distinct elements that IPE must incorporate to make sense of the global economy. To fully understand the dispute, we need to know something about the economic interests of the businesses and workers who produce and consume lumber. Understanding these interests requires us to know economic theory. Moreover, we need to know something about how political processes in the United States transform these economic interests into trade policy. This requires knowledge of the American political system and the American trade policy process. In addition, we need to know something about how a policy decision made by the United States affects businesses and workers based in other countries (more economic theory for this), and we need to know how the governments in those countries are likely to respond to these consequences (which requires knowledge about the political systems in the various countries). Finally, we need to know something about the role that international economic organizations like the WTO and NAFTA play in regulating the foreign economic policies that governments adopt. Thus, understanding developments in the global economy requires us to draw on economic theory, explore domestic politics, examine the dynamics of political interactions between governments, and familiarize ourselves with international economic organizations. Even though such an undertaking may seem daunting, this book introduces you to each of these elements and teaches you how to use them to deepen your understanding of the global economy.

One way scholars simplify the study of the global economy is to divide the substantive aspects of global economic activity into distinct issue areas. Typically, the global economy is broken into four such issue areas: the international trade system, the international monetary system, multinational corporations (or MNCs), and economic development. Rather than studying the global economy as a whole, scholars will focus on one issue area in relative isolation from the others. Of course, it is somewhat misleading to study each issue area independently. MNCs, for example, are important actors in the international trade system. The international monetary system exists solely to enable people living in different countries to engage in economic transactions with each other.

It has no purpose, therefore, outside consideration of international trade and investment. Moreover, problems arising in the international monetary system are intrinsically connected to developments in international trade and investment. Trade, MNCs, and the international monetary system in turn all play important roles in economic development. Thus, each issue area is deeply connected to the others. In spite of these deep connections, the central characteristics of each area are sufficiently distinctive that one can study each in relative isolation from the others, as long as one remains sensitive to the connections among them when necessary. We will adopt the same approach here.

The international trade system is centered upon the WTO, to which some 164 countries belong and through which they have created a nondiscriminatory international trade system. In the international trade system, each country gains access to all other WTO members' markets on equal terms. In addition, the WTO and its predecessor, the General Agreements on Tariffs and Trade (GATT), have enabled governments to progressively eliminate tariffs and other barriers to the cross-border flow of goods and services. As these barriers have been dismantled, world trade has grown steadily. Today, goods and services worth about $7.6 trillion flow across national borders each year. During the last 10 years, however, regional trading arrangements have arisen to pose a potential challenge to the WTO-centered trade system. These regional trade arrangements, such as the NAFTA, are trading blocs composed of a small number of countries who offer each other preferential access to their markets. Scholars who study the international trade system investigate how the political battle between the winners and losers of global economic exchange shapes the creation, operation, and consequences of the WTO-centered system and the emerging regional trading frameworks.

The international monetary system enables people living in different countries to conduct economic transactions with each other. People living in the United States who want to buy goods produced in Japan must be able to price these Japanese goods in dollars. In addition, Americans earn dollars, but Japanese spend yen, so somehow dollars must be converted into yen for such purchases to occur. The international monetary system facilitates international exchange by performing these functions. When it performs these functions well, international economic exchange flourishes. When it doesn't, the global economy can slow or even collapse. Scholars who study the international monetary system focus on how political battles between the winners and losers of global economic exchange shape the creation, operation, and consequences of this system.

Multinational corporations occupy a prominent and often controversial role in the global economy. A multinational corporation is a firm that controls production facilities in at least two countries. The largest of these firms are familiar names such as Ford Motor Company, General Electric, and General Motors. The United Nations estimates that there are more than 82,000 MNCs operating in the contemporary global economy. These firms collectively control about 810,000 production plants and employ about 77 million people across the globe. Together, they account for about one-quarter of the world's economic production and about one-third of the world's trade. MNCs shape politics because they extend managerial control across national borders. Corporate managers based in the United States, for example, make decisions that affect economic conditions in Mexico and other Latin American countries, in Western Europe, and in Asia. Scholars who study MNCs focus on a variety of economic issues, such as why these large firms exist and what economic impact they have on the countries that host their operations. Scholars also study how the political battle between the winners and losers of MNC activity shapes government efforts to attract and regulate MNC activities.

Finally, a large body of literature studies economic development. Throughout the postwar period, developing-country governments have adopted explicit development strategies that they believed would raise incomes by promoting industrialization. The success of these strategies has varied. Some countries, such as the Newly Industrializing Countries (NICs) of East Asia (Taiwan, South Korea, Singapore, and Hong Kong) have been so successful in promoting industrialization and raising per capita incomes that they no longer can be considered developing countries. Other countries, particularly in sub-Saharan Africa and in parts of Latin America, have been less successful. Governments in these countries adopted different development strategies than the NICs throughout much of the postwar period and realized much smaller increases in per capita incomes. Students of the politics of economic development focus on the specific strategies that developing countries' governments adopt and attempt to explain why different governments adopt different strategies. In addition, these students are concerned about which development strategies have been relatively more successful than others (and why), and about whether participation in the international economy facilitates or frustrates development. In trying to make sense of these aspects of development, IPE scholars emphasize how the political battle generated by the distributive consequences of the global economy shapes the development strategies that governments adopt.

Those who study the global economy through the lens of IPE are typically interested in doing more than simply describing government policies and contemporary developments in these four issue areas. Most scholars aspire to make more general statements about how politics shape the policies that governments adopt in each of these issue areas. Moreover, most scholars want to draw more general conclusions about the consequences of these policies. As a result, two abstract and considerably broader questions typically shape IPE scholarship. First, how exactly does politics shape the decisions that societies make about how to use the resources that are available to them? Second, what are the consequences of these decisions? Because these two overarching questions are central to what we cover in this book, it is worth taking a closer look at each of them now.

How does politics shape societal decisions about how to allocate available resources? For example, how does a society decide whether to use available labor and capital to produce semiconductors or clothing? Although this question might appear quite remote from the issue areas just discussed, the connections are actually quite close. The foreign economic policies that a government adopts—its trade policies, its exchange rate policies, and its policies toward MNCs—affect how that society's resources are used. A decision to raise tariffs, for example, will encourage business owners to invest and workers to seek employment in the industry that is protected by the tariff. A decision to lower tariffs will encourage business owners and workers currently employed in the newly liberalized industry to seek employment in other industries. Decisions about tariffs, therefore, affect how society's resources are used. Foreign economic policies are, in turn, a product of politics, the process through which societies make collective decisions. Thus, the study of IPE is in many respects the study of how the political battle between the winners and losers of global economic exchange shapes the decisions that societies make about how to allocate the resources they have available to them.

These decisions are complicated by two considerations. On the one hand, all resources are finite. As a result, choices about how to allocate resources will always be made against a backdrop of scarcity. Any choice in favor of one use, therefore, necessarily implies a choice to forgo another possible use. On the other hand, in every society, groups will disagree about how available resources should be used. Some groups will want to use the available resources to produce cars and semiconductors, for example, whereas others will prefer to use these resources to produce clothing and agricultural products. Societies, consequently, will always confront competing demands for finite resources. One of the important goals of IPE as a field of study is to investigate how such competing demands are aggregated, reconciled, and transformed into foreign economic policies.

The second abstract question asks: What are the *consequences* of the choices that societies make about resource allocation? These decisions have two very different consequences. Decisions about resource allocation have **welfare consequences**—that is, they determine the level of societal well-being. Some choices will maximize social welfare—that is, they will make society as a whole as well-off as possible, given existing resources. Other choices will cause social welfare to fall below its potential, in which case different choices about how to use resources would make society better off. Decisions about resource allocation also have **distributional consequences**—that is, they influence how income is distributed between groups within countries and between nations in the international system.

Welfare and distributional consequences are both evident in the American lumber tariff. Because the tariff makes it more profitable to produce lumber in the United States than it would be otherwise, some investment capital and workers, who might otherwise be employed in highly efficient American industries such as information technology or biotechnology, will be used in the less efficient American softwood lumber industry. The tariff thus causes the United States to use too many of its resources in economic activities that it does less well and too few resources in activities that it does better. As a consequence, the United States is poorer with a high tariff on lumber than it would be without it.

The lumber tariff also redistributes income. Because the tariff raises the price of lumber in the United States, it redistributes income from the consumers of lumber, such as American homebuilders that use lumber in buildings and American consumers who purchase these homes, to the American lumber mills. In addition, because the tariff makes it more difficult for Canadian mills to sell in the American market, it redistributes income from Canadian producers to American producers. The tariff on Canadian lumber, like many economic policies, affects both the level and the distribution of income within a society.

These two abstract questions give rise to two very different research traditions within IPE. One tradition focuses on explanation, and the second focuses on evaluation. **Explanatory studies**, which relate most closely to our first abstract question, are oriented toward explaining the foreign economic policy choices that governments make. Such studies most often attempt to answer "why" questions. For example, why does one government choose to lower tariffs and open its economy to trade, whereas another government continues to protect the domestic market from imports? Why did governments create the WTO? Why do some governments maintain fixed exchange rates whereas others allow their currencies to float? Why do some governments allow MNCs to operate in their economies with few restrictions, whereas other governments attempt to regulate MNC activity? Each of these questions asks us to explain a specific economic policy choice made by a government or to explain a pattern of choices within a group of governments. In answering such questions, we are most concerned with explaining the policy choices that governments make and pay less attention to the welfare consequences of these policy choices.

Evaluative studies, which are related most closely to our second abstract question, are oriented toward assessing policy outcomes, making judgments about them, and proposing alternatives when the judgment made about a particular policy is a negative one. A **welfare evaluation** is interested primarily in whether a particular policy choice raises or lowers social welfare. For example, does a decision to liberalize trade raise or lower national economic welfare? Does a decision to turn to the International Monetary Fund (IMF) and accept a package of economic reforms promote or retard economic growth? More broadly, do current policies encourage society to use available resources in ways that maximize economic welfare, or would alternative policies that encouraged a different allocation result in higher economic welfare? Because such evaluations are concerned with the economic welfare consequences of policy outcomes, they are typically based on economic criteria and rely heavily upon economic theories.

Scholars also sometimes evaluate outcomes in terms that extend beyond narrow considerations of economic welfare. In some instances, scholars evaluate outcomes in terms of their distributional consequences. For example, many nongovernmental organizations are highly critical of international trade because they believe that workers lose and business gains from trade liberalization. Implicit in this criticism is an evaluation of how global trade distributes income across groups within countries. Evaluations may also extend the frame of reference within which outcomes are evaluated beyond purely economic efficiency. For example, even those who agree that international trade raises world economic welfare might remain critical of globalization because they believe that it degrades the environment, disrupts traditional methods of production, or has other negative social consequences that outweigh the economic gains. Explanation and evaluation both play an important role in international political economy. This book, however, focuses primarily upon explanation and, secondarily, upon evaluating the welfare consequences of government policies.

STUDYING INTERNATIONAL POLITICAL ECONOMY

Scholars working within the field of IPE have developed a large number of theories to answer the two questions posed earlier. Three traditional schools of political economy—the mercantilist school, the liberal school, and the Marxist school—have shaped the development of these theories over the last 100 years. Each of these three traditional schools offers distinctive answers to the two questions, and these differences have structured much of the scholarly and public debate about IPE.

Although the three traditional schools remain influential, more and more often, students of IPE are developing theories to answer our two questions from outside the explicit confines of these traditional schools. One prominent approach, and the approach that is developed throughout this book, suggests that the foreign economic policies that governments adopt emerge from the interaction between societal actors' interests and political institutions. We begin our examination of how people study IPE with a broad overview of these alternative approaches. We look first at the three traditional schools, highlighting the answers they provide to our two questions and pointing to some of the weaknesses of these schools that have led students to move away from them. We then examine the logic of an approach based on interests and institutions in order to provide the background necessary for the more detailed theories that we develop throughout the book.

Traditional Schools of International Political Economy

Historically, theories of IPE have been developed in three broad schools of thought: mercantilism (or nationalism), liberalism, and Marxism. **Mercantilism** is rooted in seventeenth- and eighteenth-century theories about the relationship between economic activity and state power. The mercantilist literature is large and varied, yet mercantilists generally do adhere to three central propositions (see, e.g., Viner 1960; Heckscher 1935). First, the classical mercantilists argued that national power and wealth are tightly connected. National power in the international state system is derived in large part from wealth. Wealth, in turn, is required to accumulate power. Second, the classical mercantilists argued that trade provided one way for countries to acquire wealth from abroad. Wealth could be acquired through trade, however, only if the country ran a positive balance of trade, that is, if the country sold more goods to foreigners than it purchased from foreigners. Third, the classical mercantilists argued that some types of economic activity are more valuable than others. In particular, mercantilists argued that manufacturing activities should be promoted, whereas agriculture and other non-manufacturing activities should be discouraged.

"Modern" mercantilism applies these three propositions to contemporary international economic policy:

1. Economic strength is a critical component of national power.
2. Trade is to be valued for exports, but governments should discourage imports whenever possible.
3. Some forms of economic activity are more valuable than others.

Manufacturing is preferred to the production of agricultural and other primary commodities, and high-technology manufacturing industries such as computers and telecommunications are preferable to mature manufacturing industries such as steel or textiles and apparel.

The emphasis on wealth as a critical component of national power, the insistence on maintaining a positive balance of trade, and the conviction that some types of economic activity are more valuable than others leads mercantilists to argue that the state should play a large role in determining how society's resources are allocated. Economic activity is too important to allow decisions about resource allocation to be made through an uncoordinated process such as the market. Uncoordinated decisions can result in an "inappropriate" economic structure. Industries and technologies that may be desirable from the perspective of national power might be neglected, whereas industries that do little to strengthen the nation in the international state system may flourish. In addition, the country could develop an unfavorable balance of trade and become dependent on foreign countries for critical technologies. The only way to ensure that society's resources are used appropriately is to have the state play a large role in the economy. Economic policy can be used to channel resources to those economic activities that promote and protect the national interest and away from those that fail to do so.

Liberalism, the second traditional school, emerged in Britain during the eighteenth century to challenge the dominance of mercantilism in government circles. Adam Smith and other liberal writers, such as David Ricardo (who first stated the modern concept of comparative advantage), were scholars who were attempting to alter government economic policy. The theory they developed to do so, liberalism, challenged all three central propositions of mercantilism. First, liberalism attempted to draw a strong line between politics and economics. In doing so, liberalism argued that the purpose of economic activity was to enrich individuals, not to enhance the state's power. Second, liberalism argued that countries do not enrich themselves by running trade surpluses. Instead, countries gain from trade regardless of whether the balance of trade is positive or negative. Finally, countries are not necessarily made wealthier by producing manufactured goods rather than primary commodities. Instead, liberalism argued, countries are made wealthier by making products that they can produce at a relatively low cost at home and trading them for goods that can be produced at home only at a relatively high cost. Thus, according to liberalism, governments should make little effort to influence the country's trade balance or to shape the types of goods the country produces. Government efforts to allocate resources will only reduce national welfare.

In addition to arguing against substantial state intervention as advocated by the mercantilists, liberalism argued in favor of a market-based system of resource allocation. Giving priority to the welfare of individuals, liberalism argues that social welfare will be highest when people are free to make their own decisions about how to use the resources they possess. Thus, rather than accepting the mercantilist argument that the state should guide the allocation of resources, liberals argue that resources should be allocated through voluntary market-based transactions between individuals. Such an exchange is mutually beneficial—as long as it is voluntary, both parties to any transaction will benefit. Moreover, in a perfectly functioning market, individuals will continue to buy and sell resources until the resulting allocation offers no further opportunities for mutually beneficial exchange. The state plays an important, though limited, role in this process. The state must establish clear rights concerning ownership of property and resources. The judicial system must enforce these rights and the contracts that transfer ownership from one individual to another. Most liberals also recognize that governments can, and should, resolve **market failures**, which are instances in which voluntary market-based transactions between individuals fail to allocate resources to socially desirable activities.

Marxism, the third traditional school, originated in the work of Karl Marx as a critique of capitalism. It is impossible to characterize briefly the huge literature that has expanded on or been influenced by Marx's ideas. According to Marx, capitalism is characterized by two central conditions: the private ownership of the means of production (or capital) and wage labor. Marx argued that the value of manufactured goods was determined by the amount of labor used to produce them. However, capitalists did not pay labor the full amount of the value they imparted to the goods they produced. Instead, the capitalists who owned the factories paid workers only a subsistence wage and retained the rest as profits with which to finance additional investment. Marx predicted that the dynamics of capitalism would lead eventually to a revolution that would do away with private property and with the capitalist system that private property supported.

Three dynamics would interact to drive this revolution. First, Marx argued that there is a natural tendency toward the concentration of capital. Economic competition would force capitalists to increase their efficiency and increase their capital stock. As a consequence, capital would become increasingly concentrated in the hands of a small, wealthy elite. Second, Marx argued that capitalism is associated with a falling rate of profit. Investment leads to a growing abundance of productive capital, which in turn reduces the return to capital. As profits shrink, capitalists are forced to further reduce wages, worsening the plight of the already impoverished masses. Finally, capitalism is plagued by an imbalance between the ability to produce goods and the ability to purchase goods. Large capital investments continually augment the economy's ability to produce goods, whereas falling wages continually reduce the ability of consumers to purchase the goods being produced. As the three dynamics interact over time, society becomes increasingly characterized by growing inequality between a small wealthy capitalist elite and a growing number of impoverished workers. These social conditions eventually cause workers (the proletariat, in Marxist terminology) to rise up, overthrow the capitalist system, and replace it with socialism.

In contrast to liberalism's emphasis on the market as the principal mechanism of resource allocation, Marxists argue that capitalists make decisions about how society's resources are used. Moreover, because capitalist systems promote the concentration of capital, investment decisions are not typically driven by market-based competition, at least not in the classical liberal sense of this term. Instead, decisions about what to produce are made by the few firms that control the necessary investment capital. The state plays no autonomous role in the capitalist system. Instead, Marxists argue that the state operates as an agent of the capitalist class. The state enacts policies that reinforce capitalism and therefore the capitalists' control of resource allocation. Thus, in contrast to the mercantilists who focus on the state and the liberals who focus on the market, Marxists focus on large corporations as the key actor determining how resources are used.

In the international economy, the concentration of capital and capitalists' control of the state are transformed into the systematic exploitation of the developing world by the large capitalist nations. In some instances, this exploitation takes the form of explicit colonial structures, as it did prior to World War II. In other instances, especially since World War II, exploitation is achieved through less intrusive structures of dominance and control. In all instances, however, exploitation is carried out by large firms based in the capitalist countries that operate, in part, in the developing world. This systematic exploitation of the poor by the rich implies that the global economy does not provide benefits to all countries; all gains accrue to the capitalist countries at the top of the international hierarchy.

The three traditional schools of political economy thus offer three distinctive answers to our question of how politics shapes the allocation of society's resources. Mercantilists argue that the state guides resource allocation in line with objectives shaped by the quest for national power. Liberals argue that politics ought to play little role in the process, extolling instead the role of market-based transactions among autonomous individuals. Marxists argue that the most important decisions are made by large capitalist enterprises supported by a political system controlled by the capitalist class.

Each traditional school also offers a distinctive framework to evaluate the consequences of resource allocation. Mercantilists focus on the consequences of resource allocation for national power. The central question a mercantilist will ask is: "Is there some alternative allocation of resources that would enhance the nation's power in the international system?" Liberals rely heavily upon economic theory to focus principally upon the welfare consequences of resource allocation. The central question a liberal will ask is: "Is there some alternative allocation of resources that would enable the society to improve its standard of living?" Marxists rely heavily upon theories of class conflict to focus on the distributional consequences of resource allocation. The central question a Marxist will ask is: "Is there an alternative political and economic system that will promote a more equitable distribution of income?" Thus, liberalism emphasizes the welfare consequences of resource allocation, whereas mercantilism and Marxism each emphasize a different aspect of the distributional consequences of these decisions.

These very different allocation mechanisms and unique evaluative frameworks generate three very different images of the central dynamic of IPE (see Table 1.1). Mercantilists argue that the IPE is characterized by distributional conflict when governments compete to attract and maintain desired industries. Liberals argue that international economic interactions are essentially harmonious. Because all countries benefit from international trade, power has little impact on national welfare, and international economic conflicts are rare. The central problem, from a liberal perspective, is creating the international

TABLE 1.1

Three Traditional Schools of International Political Economy

	Mercantilism	Liberalism	Marxism
Most Important Actor	The State	Individuals	Classes, particularly the capitalist class
Role of the State	Intervene in the economy to allocate resources	Establish and enforce property rights to facilitate market-based exchange	Instrument of the capitalist class uses state power to sustain capitalist system
Image of the International Economic System	*Conflictual:* Countries compete for desirable industries and engage in trade conflicts as a result of this competition	*Harmonious:* The international economy offers benefits to all countries. The challenge is to create a political framework that enables countries to realize these benefits	*Exploitative:* Capitalists exploit labor within countries; rich countries exploit poor countries in the international economy
Proper Objective of Economic Policy	Enhance power of the nation-state in international state system	Enhance aggregate social welfare	Promote an equitable distribution of wealth and income

institutional framework that will enable governments to enter into agreements through which they can create an international system of free trade. Marxists argue that the IPE is characterized by the distributional conflict between labor and capital within countries and by the distributional conflict between the advanced industrialized countries and developing countries within the international arena.

These three traditional schools have structured studies of and debate about the international political economy for a very long time. And although the presence of all three will be felt in many ways throughout the pages of this book, we will spend little more time examining them directly. In their place, we will emphasize an analytical framework developed during the last 15 years or so, which focuses on how the interaction between societal interests and political institutions determines the foreign economic policies that governments adopt.

INTERESTS AND INSTITUTIONS IN INTERNATIONAL POLITICAL ECONOMY

To explain the policy choices made by governments, this book concentrates on the interaction between societal interests and political institutions. Such an approach suggests that to understand the foreign economic policy choices that governments make, we need to understand two aspects of politics. First, we need to understand where the interests, or economic policy preferences, of groups in society come from. Second, we need to examine how political institutions aggregate, reconcile, and ultimately transform competing interests into foreign economic policies and a particular international economic system.

Interests are the goals or policy objectives that the central actors in the political system and in the economy—individuals, firms, labor unions, other interest groups, and governments—want to use foreign economic policy to achieve. In focusing on interests, we will assume that individuals and the interest groups that represent them prefer foreign economic policies that raise their incomes to policies that reduce their incomes. Thus, whenever a group confronts a choice between one policy that raises its income and another that lowers its income, it will always prefer the policy that raises its income. We focus on two mechanisms to explain the formation of these policy interests.

First, people have **material interests** that arise from their position in the global economy. The essence of this approach can be summarized in a simple statement: tell me what you do for work, and I'll tell you what your foreign economic policy preferences are. Consider once again the American softwood lumber tariff. Whether a particular individual supports or opposes this tariff depends on where he or she works. If you work in an American lumber mill or timberland, you favor the tariff because it reduces the likelihood that you will lose your job. If you own an American lumber mill of timberland, you also will favor the tariff, because it helps ensure a market and a relatively high price for the wood you produce. If you are an American homebuilder or you are looking to buy a new home, however, you will oppose the tariff. Higher prices mean that it costs more to produce homes. As homes become more expensive, fewer are sold and, consequently, fewer are produced. The tariff thus increases the chances that construction workers will be laid off and it causes real estate developers to earn smaller profits. These are compelling reasons for builders and their employees to oppose the higher tariff on Canadian lumber. In short, one's position in the economy powerfully shapes one's preferences regarding foreign economic policy. As we shall see, economic theory enables us to make some powerful statements about the foreign economic policy preferences of different groups in the economy.

Second, interests are often based on ideas. **Ideas** are mental models that provide a coherent set of beliefs about cause-and-effect relationships. In the context of economic policy, these mental models typically focus on the relationship between government policies and economic outcomes. Not surprisingly, therefore, economic theory is a very important source of ideas that influence how actors perceive and formulate their interests. By providing clear statements about cause-and-effect economic relationships, economic theories can create an interest in a particular economic policy. The theory of comparative advantage, for example, claims that reducing tariffs raises aggregate social welfare. A government that believes this theory might be inclined to lower tariffs to realize these welfare gains. Alternatively, a government might adopt high tariffs because a different economic theory (the infant industry argument, for example) suggests that under the right conditions, tariffs can raise national income. What matters, therefore, is not whether a particular idea is true or not, but whether people in power, or people with influence over people with power, believe the idea to be true. Thus, ideas about how the economy operates can be a source of the preferences that groups have for particular economic policies.

Understanding where interests come from will enable us to specify with some precision the competing demands that politicians confront when making foreign economic policy decisions. It does not tell us anything about how these competing interests are transformed into foreign economic policies. To understand how interests are transformed into policies, we need to examine political institutions. **Political institutions** establish the rules governing the political process. By establishing rules, they enable groups within countries, and groups of countries in the international state system, to reach and enforce collective decisions.

Political institutions determine which groups are empowered to make choices and establish the rules these "choosers" will use when doing so. In domestic political systems, for example, democratic institutions promote mass participation in collective choices, whereas authoritarian systems restrict participation to a narrow set of individuals. In international economic affairs, governments from the advanced industrialized countries often make decisions with little participation by developing countries.

Political institutions also provide the rules that these groups use to make decisions. In democratic systems, the usual choice rule is majority rule, and policies are supposed to reflect the preferences of a majority of voters or legislators. In international economic organizations, the choice rule is often relative bargaining power, and decisions typically reflect the preferences of the more powerful nations. Political institutions thus allow groups to make collective decisions and, in doing so, determine who gets to make these decisions and how they are to be made.

Political institutions also help enforce these collective decisions. In many instances, individuals, groups, and governments have little incentive to comply with the decisions that are produced by the political process. This is particularly the case for those groups whose preferences diverge from those embodied in the collective choice. And even in cases where a group or a country as a whole does benefit from a particular decision, it may believe it could do even better if it cheated a little bit. If such instances of noncompliance are widespread, then the political process is substantially weakened.

This problem is particularly acute in the international state system. In domestic political systems, the police and the judicial system are charged with enforcing individual compliance with collective decisions. The international system has neither a police force nor a judicial system through which to enforce compliance, however. Consequently, it can be very tempting for governments to attempt to "cheat" on the international economic agreements they conclude with other governments. International institutions like the WTO and the IMF can help governments enforce the international agreements that they conclude.

A focus on interests and institutions will allow us to develop a set of reasonably comprehensive answers to our first question: How does politics shape societal decisions about how to allocate resources? The explanations we construct almost always will begin by investigating the source of competing societal demands for income and then explore how political institutions aggregate, reconcile, and ultimately transform these competing demands into foreign economic policies and a particular international economic system. This approach may not always provide a full explanation of the interactions we observe in the international political economy, but it does provide a solid point of departure.

THE GLOBAL ECONOMY IN HISTORICAL CONTEXT

Although we will focus on how the interaction between interests and institutions shapes government behavior in the post-World War II global economy, the contemporary global economy embodies a deeper historical continuity. Even though the contemporary global economy is distinctive in many ways, this system continues a trend toward deeper international economic integration that began in the nineteenth century. Because the contemporary system has deep roots in the nineteenth century, it is useful to examine the rise, fall, and reconstruction of the global economy in the years before World War II.

People have conducted long-distance trade for hundreds of years, but the first true "global" economy emerged only in the nineteenth century. This "first wave" of globalization was driven by the interaction between technological change and politics. Technological innovation, in particular the invention of the steam engine and the telegraph, made it profitable to trade heavy commodities across long distances. Steam engines dramatically reduced the cost and time involved in long-distance trade. The railroad made it possible to ship large volumes of heavy commodities across long distances—grain from the American plains states to the Atlantic coast, for example—quickly and at low cost. In 1830, it cost more than $30 to ship a ton of grain (or any other commodity) 300 miles; by 1900 the cost had fallen to about $5 (Frieden 2006, 5). The use of steam to power ocean-going vessels further reduced the cost of long-distance trade. Whereas in the early nineteenth century it took a month and cost $10 to ship a ton of grain from the United States to Europe, by 1900 the Atlantic crossing took only a week and cost about $3. Consequently, whereas throughout history high shipping costs discouraged trade of all but the lightest and highest-value commodities, technology had reduced shipping costs so sharply by the late nineteenth century that such trade became very profitable.

Although new technologies made long-distance trade possible, political structures made it a reality. Capitalizing on the new possibilities required governments to establish an infrastructure that facilitated global exchange. This infrastructure was based on a network of bilateral trade agreements and a stable international monetary system. Governments began to reduce barriers to trade in the mid-nineteenth century. Britain was the first to adopt a free-trade policy in the 1840s when it repealed its "Corn Laws" and opened its market to imported grain. The shift to free trade gained momentum in 1860, when Britain and France eliminated most tariffs on trade between them with the Cobden–Chevalier Treaty. The treaty triggered a wave of negotiations that quickly established a network of bilateral treaties that substantially reduced trade barriers throughout Europe and the still-colonized developing world (see Irwin 1993, 97). The United States remained an important exception to nineteenth-century trade liberalization, remaining staunchly protectionist until the 1930s.

Most governments also adopted gold-backed currencies. In this gold standard, each government pledged to exchange its national currency for gold at a permanently fixed rate of exchange. From the late nineteenth century until 1933, for example, the U.S. government exchanged dollars for gold at the fixed price of $20.67 per ounce. Great Britain was the first to adopt the gold standard, shifting from a bimetallic system in which the pound was backed by silver and gold to a pure gold standard in the eighteenth century. Other nations embraced the gold standard during the 1870s. Germany shifted to gold in 1872, and many other governments followed. By the end of the decade most industrialized countries, and quite a few developing countries, had adopted the gold standard. By stabilizing international price relationships, the gold standard encouraged international trade and investment.

Technological innovation and the creation of an international political infrastructure combined to produce a dramatic expansion of global economic exchange in the nineteenth century. Trade grew at an average rate of 3.5 percent per year between 1815 and 1914, three and a half times more rapidly than the previous 300 years. People crossed borders in historic numbers as well. Each year between 1880 and 1900, 600,000 people left Europe to find new lives in the United States, Canada, Australia, and Argentina; the number of such migrants continued to rise, reaching 1 million per year in the first decade of the twentieth century (Chiswick and Hatton 2003). In all, close to 14 million people left Western Europe in this period (Maddison 2001). Although the absolute numbers are large, one gains a deeper appreciation of the scale of late nineteenth-century migration by recognizing that these migrants represented 2 to 5 percent of the total population of the home countries (Baldwin and Martin 1999, 19). Financial capital also poured across borders. In the late nineteenth century British residents invested almost 10 percent of their incomes in foreign markets, and the French, German, and Dutch invested only slightly smaller shares of their incomes. These capital flows constructed railroads and other infrastructure in the lands of recent settlement (Bordo 2002, 23).

By the late nineteenth century, therefore, it was no exaggeration to talk of a global economy. In the passage I paraphrased at the beginning of this chapter, John Maynard Keynes remarked on the extraordinary nature of the global economy in the early twentieth century:

> The inhabitant of London could order by telephone, sipping his morning tea in bed, the various products of the whole earth, in such quantity as he might see fit, and reasonably expect their early delivery on his doorstep; he could at the same moment and by the same means adventure his wealth in the natural resources and new enterprise of any quarter of the world. He could secure forthwith, if he wished it, cheap and comfortable means of transport to any country or climate without passport or other formality .... He regarded this state of affairs as normal, certain, and permanent.
>
> (Keynes 1919, 9–10)

Globalization was not permanent, however. In the first half of the twentieth century governments dismantled the dense international economic networks they had created and retreated into sheltered national economies. World War I triggered the retreat. European governments abandoned the gold standard in order to finance the war. They tightly controlled trade and financial flows in order to marshal resources for the war. Following the war, governments tried to reconstruct the global economy, but were not successful. This failure was a consequence of many factors, a full accounting of which would require more space than we can dedicate here. One of the most critical factors, however, lay in dramatic changes in the global political structure that supported the global economy.

Throughout the nineteenth century Britain stood at the center of the world economy. British manufacturing dominated world trade, and London served as the world's financial center. As the dominant economic power—what many political economists call the hegemon—Britain provided much of the infra-structure of the global economy. By the turn of the century, Britain was ceding ground to the United States and Germany. These two rising nations industri-alized rapidly in the late nineteenth century, taking advantage of science and new forms of corporate organization. By the end of the century both coun-tries were challenging Britain's dominance. World War I accelerated this trend.

American manufacturing output expanded during the war as the United States supplied the European nations. American financial power grew as the belligerents turned to the United States to finance their war expenditures. In contrast, 5 years of fighting weakened the British industrial capacity. Britain borrowed heavily and sold many of its foreign assets to finance its war expenditures, and thus exited the war saddled with a heavy foreign debt. At the war's end, the United States stood as the world's dominant economic power—the world's largest manufacturing economy and its largest creditor.

This power shift meant that postwar global economic reconstruction hinged on American leadership. Yet, the United States refused to accept the responsibilities that hegemonic status carried, preferring instead to retreat into a traditional policy of isolationism. Nowhere was the lack of American leadership more evident than on the war debt question. France and Britain (along with smaller European nations fighting against the Triple Alliance) had borrowed from the United States to finance part of their war expenditures. At the war's end, they asked the United States to forgive these debts. Britain and France had paid a heavy price, measured in terms of human suffering and economic damage, in the war. Was it not reasonable, they argued, for the United States to forgive the war debt as part of its contribution to the common effort? The United States refused, insisting that European governments repay the debt. To further compound the problem, the United States raised tariffs in 1922, making it difficult for Europe to sell products in the American market in order to earn dollars needed to repay the debt.

American war-debt policy held the key to the pace of European economic recovery, and thus had real consequences for the interwar global economy. War debt was linked (at least in the eyes of European governments) to German reparations payments. France insisted that Germany pay for war damages by paying reparations to the Allied powers. The amount of reparations the French sought was, in part, a function of the total demands on French financial resources. The American refusal to forgive French debt, therefore, encouraged France to demand more from Germany. Larger reparations payments in turn delayed economic recovery in Germany. And the delay in German recovery in turn delayed recovery throughout Europe. Had the United States forgiven the war debt, France might have demanded less from Germany. A smaller reparations burden would in turn have enabled Germany to recover more quickly, and German economic recovery would have driven European recovery. No less important, an early settlement would have enabled European governments to move past wartime animosities. Instead, the war debt–reparations mess dominated diplomacy and soured inter-European relations throughout the 1920s.

The failure to resolve these financial issues meant that governments never placed the international economy on a firm foundation. Although governments had re-established a gold standard and had revived international trade by the mid-1920s, lingering war debts and reparations problems rendered the system quite fragile and unable to withstand the shock of the crash of the American stock market in October 1929. The financial collapse depressed economic activity. Consumer demand fell sharply, and as people stopped buying goods, factories stopped production and released their workers. Output fell and unemployment rose. The resulting Great Depression represented the largest collapse of production and employment the industrial world had ever experienced. American production fell by 30 percent between 1929 and 1933; unemployment rose to 25 percent in the United States and as high as 44 percent in Germany.

Governments responded to collapsing output and rising unemployment by raising tariffs in a desperate attempt to protect the home market. The United States led the way, sharply raising tariffs in the 1930 Smoot-Hawley Tariff Act. Countries with colonial possessions created trade blocs that linked the colonial power and its possessions. Great Britain established the Imperial Preference System in 1933 to insulate its trade and investment relationships with its colonies from the rest of the world. France established similar arrangements with its colonial possessions. Powerful countries that lacked colonies began using force to acquire them. Japan invaded Manchuria in the early 1930s and sought to bring much of East Asia into a Japan-dominated Asian Co-prosperity Sphere. Germany exploited its power and position in Central Europe to establish a network of bilateral trade relations with the region. By the mid-1930s, the world economy had disintegrated into relatively insulated regional trading blocs, and governments were moving toward World War II.

The failure to reconstruct the global economy after World War I and the subsequent depression and war had a dramatic impact on American policy. American policymakers drew two lessons from the interwar period. First, they concluded that World War II was caused in part by the failure to reconstruct a stable global economy after World War I. As a result, the construction of a stable and liberal international economy would have to be a centerpiece of post-World War II planning in order to establish a lasting peace. Second, American policymakers concluded that the United States alone controlled sufficient power to establish a stable global economy. America's European allies had been further weakened by World War II, and the Japanese and German economies had been destroyed. The United States, in contrast, emerged in a stronger position. These conclusions encouraged the United States to embrace an internationalist orientation. Working alongside British policymakers in the early 1940s, the United States designed international institutions to provide the infrastructure for the postwar global economy.

The resulting Bretton Woods system—so named because many of its final details were negotiated at an intergovernmental conference held in Bretton Woods, New Hampshire, in late summer of 1944—continues to provide the institutional structure at the center of the global economy. The WTO, the IMF, and the World Bank all have their origins in this concerted period of postwar planning. The contemporary global economy, therefore, was established as an explicit attempt to return to the "golden years" of the late nineteenth century to prevent a recurrence of the economic and political disasters of the interwar period. The post-World War II global economy differed from the classical liberal system of the nineteenth century in important ways. At the broadest level, the difference reflected changed public attitudes about the government's proper economic role. In the nineteenth-century liberal system, governments eliminated trade barriers and made little effort to manage domestic economic activity. The Great Depression encouraged governments to play a more active role in the economy. Governments used macroeconomic policy to promote growth and limit unemployment, and they established safety nets to protect society's most vulnerable from the full force of the market. This more active government role in turn required some insulation between the domestic and the international economies. The rules embodied in the Bretton Woods system provided this insulation. This important difference notwithstanding, the postwar global economy was, in effect, a restoration of the nineteenth-century global economy.

Today, this global capitalist economy faces some significant challenges. During the last 70 years, the global economy has played an important role in helping the world as a whole attain a historically unprecedented standard of living. More people enjoy longer, healthier, and more comfortable lives today than at any prior point in history. The rise of prosperity globally has been associated with rising income and wealth inequalities and heightened economic insecurity for the working classes within societies in North America, Europe, and Asia. These inequalities and insecurities have in turn given rise to populist and anti-globalization political movements in the Europe Union, the United States, and elsewhere. These movements have played an important role in Donald J. Trump's surprising victory in the November 2016 presidential election and in the British decision by referendum in the summer of 2016 to withdraw from the EU. Similar anti-globalization forces and groups are shaping politics and policy in Poland, Hungary, Italy, and elsewhere. In the remainder of this book we will explore how political dynamics created the broad coalition of forces that have supported the global capitalist economy since World War II, and also delineate how the operation of this global capitalist economy can generate distributional inequities that if allowed to accumulate uncorrected can weaken and eventually erode entirely its political foundations.

CONCLUSION

IPE studies the political battle between the winners and losers of global economic exchange. It examines how this political competition shapes the evolution of the international trade and monetary systems, affects the ability of MNCs to conduct their operations, and influences the development strategies governments adopt. Thus, IPE suggests that it is hard to understand anything about the global economy without understanding how political competition unfolds.

IPE scholars traditionally have studied the global economy through the lens of three schools of thought. Each school offers a distinctive window on the global economy, and each emphasizes one aspect of global economic exchange—cooperation, competition between governments, and competition between labor and capital—as the central defining element of politics in the global economy.

This book relies on an approach that emphasizes the interaction between societal interests and political institutions. Such an approach will enable us to develop models that provide insights into how the global economy generates winners and losers, how these groups compete to influence the policies that governments adopt, and how the policies that governments adopt affect the evolution of the global economy.

KEY TERMS

Distributional
  Consequences
Evaluative Studies
Explanatory Studies
Ideas

Interests
Liberalism
Market Failures
Marxism
Material Interests

Mercantilism
Political Institutions
Welfare Consequences
Welfare Evaluation

SUGGESTIONS FOR FURTHER READING

Jeffry A. Frieden's *Global Capitalism: Its Rise and Fall in the Twentieth Century* (New York: W.W. Norton & Company, 2006) offers an excellent discussion of the historical development of the global economy since the late nineteenth century.

For a longer-term perspective see Joerg Baten (editor), *A History of the Global Economy: 1500 to the Present* (Cambridge: Cambridge University Press, 2016).

Benjamin J. Cohen's *International Political Economy: An Intellectual History Paperback* (Princeton: Princeton University Press, 2008) provides an excellent discussion of the development of IPE as a field of study.

The WTO and the World Trade System

E conomic production has gone global during the last 20 years. Not so long ago, world trade involved almost exclusively the exchange of finished goods. Toyota, for instance, produced cars in its Japanese factories and exported these vehicles to, say, the United States. Today, intermediate goods—goods that are assembled together into finished goods—make up a growing proportion of trade. Toyota now sources the components for its autos from producers throughout the world and these components are shipped to factories in the United States (and 15 other countries) where workers assemble them into cars and trucks sold to American consumers as well as exported to more than 20 countries around the world. Global production networks such as these (often called "global value chains") are increasingly common in today's global economy. Consider Nutella, a cocoa-hazelnut spread produced by the Italian Ferrero Group. Ferrero sources the cocoa they use for Nutella in Nigeria and it draws its hazelnuts from Turkey. It sources its sugar from Brazil, while the Vanillin comes from China and the Palm Oil comes from Malaysia. Ferrero transforms these various ingredients into its tasty spread in nine factories located throughout North and South America, Europe, and Australia. The entire production network is managed from corporate headquarters in Alba, Italy.

The fragmentation of production into these global networks (a development we look at more closely in Chapter 8) has been made possible by the dramatic liberalization of and associated rapid growth of world trade flows. Global trade has grown during the last 70 years at an average rate of about 6 percent per year. As a result, annual world merchandise trade has risen from $84 billion in 1953 to $16 trillion in 2016 (World Trade Organization 2017). Never before has international trade grown so rapidly for such a long period. Even more importantly, trade has consistently grown more rapidly than the world's economic output. Consequently, each year a greater proportion of the goods and services produced in the world are created in one country and con-sumed in another. Indeed, globalization is a consequence of these differential growth rates.

None of this has occurred spontaneously. Even though one could argue that the growth of world trade reflects the operation of global markets and the cost-reducing impact of telecommunications technology, all markets rest on political structures. This is certainly the case with international trade. World trade has grown so rapidly over the last 70 years because an international polit-ical structure, the **World Trade Organization** (**WTO**), and its predecessor, the General Agreement on Tariffs and Trade (GATT), has supported and encour-aged such growth. Most political scientists who study the global economy believe that, had governments never created this institutional framework after World War II, or had they created a different one, world trade would not have grown so rapidly. Internationalization, therefore, has been brought about by the decisions governments have made about the rules and institutions that govern world trade.

Because trade plays so important a role in our lives, and because trade is made possible by the political institution that structures trade relationships, understanding the political dynamics of the world trade system is vital. This chapter begins developing that knowledge. It provides a broad overview of the WTO's core components. It then examines how the global distribution of power shapes the creation and evolution of international trade systems. It then explores some contemporary challenges to the WTO, focusing on the rise of developing countries as a powerful bloc within the organization and the rise of civil society groups as powerful critics of the organization from the outside. The chapter concludes by examining regional trade arrangements, considered by many the greatest current challenge to the WTO.

WHAT IS THE WORLD TRADE ORGANIZATION?

The WTO (located on the shore of the beautiful Lac Leman in Geneva, Switzerland) is the hub of an international political system under which gov-ernments negotiate, enforce, and revise rules to govern their trade policies. Between 1947 and 1994 the GATT fulfilled the role now played by the WTO. In 1995, governments folded the GATT into the newly established WTO, where it continues to provide many of the rules governing international trade relations. The rules at the center of the world trade system were thus established initially in 1947 and have been gradually revised, amended, and extended ever since.

The WTO is small compared with other international organizations. Although 164 countries belong to the WTO, it has a staff of only about 640 people and a budget of roughly $200 million (as of late 2017). The World Bank, by contrast, has a staff of about 10,000 people and an operating budget of close to $2.5 billion. As the center of the world trade system, the WTO provides a forum for trade negotiations, administers the trade agreements that governments conclude, and provides a mechanism through which governments can resolve trade disputes. As a political system, the WTO can be broken down into three distinct components: a set of principles and rules, an intergovernmental bargaining process, and a dispute settlement mechanism.

Two core principles stand at the base of the WTO: market liberalism and nondiscrimination. **Market liberalism** provides the economic rationale for the trade system. Market liberalism asserts that an open, or liberal, international trade system raises the world's standard of living. Every country—no matter how poor or how rich—enjoys a higher standard of living with trade than it can achieve without trade. Moreover, the gains from trade are greatest—for each country and for the world as a whole—when goods can flow freely across national borders unimpeded by government-imposed barriers. The claim that trade provides such gains to all countries is based on economic theory we examine in detail in Chapter 3. For our purposes here, it is sufficient to recognize that this claim provides the economic logic upon which the WTO is based.

Nondiscrimination is the second core principle of the multilateral trade system. Nondiscrimination ensures that each WTO member faces identical opportunities to trade with other WTO members. This principle takes two specific forms within the WTO. The first form, called **Most-Favored Nation** (MFN), prohibits governments from using trade policies to provide special advantages to some countries and not to others. MFN is found in Article I of GATT. It states,

> any advantage, favour, privilege, or immunity granted by any contracting party to any product originating in or destined for any other country shall be accorded immediately and unconditionally to the like product originating in or destined for the territories of all other contracting parties.

Stripped of this legal terminology, MFN simply requires each WTO member to treat all WTO members the same. For example, the United States cannot apply lower tariffs to goods imported from Brazil (a WTO member) than it applies to goods imported from other WTO member countries. If the United States reduces tariffs on goods imported from Brazil, it must extend these same tariff rates to all other WTO members. MFN thus assures that all countries have access to foreign markets on equal terms.

WTO rules do allow some exceptions to MFN. The most important exception concerns regional trade arrangements. Governments are allowed to depart from MFN if they join a free-trade area or customs union. In the North American Free Trade Agreement (NAFTA), for example, goods produced in Mexico enter the United States duty free, whereas the United States imposes tariffs on the same goods imported from other countries. In the European Union, goods produced in France enter Germany with a lower tariff than goods produced in the United States. A second exception is provided by the **Generalized System of Preferences** (GSP), enacted in the late 1960s. The GSP allows the advanced industrialized countries to apply lower tariffs to imports from developing countries than they apply to the same goods coming from other advanced industrialized countries. These exceptions aside, MFN ensures that all countries trade on equal terms.

National treatment is the second form of nondiscrimination found in the WTO. **National treatment** prohibits governments from using taxes, regulations, and other domestic policies to provide an advantage to domestic firms at the expense of foreign firms. National treatment is found in Article III of the GATT, which states that

> the products of the territory of any contracting party imported into the territory of any other contracting party shall be accorded treatment no less favourable than that accorded to like products of national origin in respect of all laws, regulations and requirements affecting their internal sale, offering for sale, purchase, transportation, distribution or use.

In plainer English, national treatment requires governments to treat domestic and foreign versions of the same product ("like products" in GATT terminology) identically once they enter the domestic market. For example, the U.S. government cannot establish one fuel efficiency standard for foreign cars and another for domestic cars. If the U.S. government wants to advance this environmental goal, it must apply the same requirement to domestic and foreign auto producers. Together, MFN and national treatment ensure that firms in every country face the same market opportunities and barriers in the global economy.

These two core principles are accompanied by hundreds of other rules. Since 1947, governments have concluded about 60 distinct agreements that together fill about 30,000 pages. These rules jointly provide the central legal structure for international trade. As a group, these rules constrain the policies that governments can use to control the flow of goods, services, and technology into and out of their national economies. Some of these rules are proscriptive, such as prohibition against government discrimination. Others are prescriptive, such as requirements for governments to protect intellectual property. Many of these rules state instances in which governments are allowed to protect a domestic industry temporarily and then delineate the conditions under which governments can and cannot invoke this safeguard. All rules entail obligations to other WTO members that constrain the ability of governments to regulate the interaction between the national and the global economies.

All WTO rules are created by governments through intergovernmental bargaining. **Intergovernmental bargaining** is the WTO's primary decision-making process, and it involves negotiating agreements that directly liberalize trade and indirectly support that goal. To liberalize trade, governments must alter policies that restrict the cross-border flow of goods and services. Such policies include **tariffs**, which are taxes that governments impose on foreign goods entering the country. They also include a wide range of **non-tariff barriers** such as health and safety regulations, government purchasing practices, and many other government regulations. Intergovernmental bargaining focuses on negotiating agreements that reduce and eliminate these government-imposed barriers to market access.

Rather than bargain continuously, governments organize their negotiations in bargaining rounds, each with a definite starting date and a target date for conclusion. At the beginning of each round, governments meet as the WTO **Ministerial Conference,** the highest level of WTO decision making. Meeting for 3 or 4 days, governments establish an agenda detailing the issues

TABLE 2.1

Trade Negotiations within the General Agreement on Tariffs and Trade (GATT)/World Trade Organization (WTO), 1947–2018

Name and Year of Round	Subjects Covered	Participating Countries
1947 Geneva	Tariffs	23
1949 Annecy	Tariffs	13
1951 Torquay	Tariffs	38
1956 Geneva	Tariffs	26
1960–1961 Dillon Round	Tariffs	26
1964–1967 Kennedy Round	Tariffs and Antidumping	62
1973–1979 Tokyo Round	Tariffs	102
	Non-tariff Measures	
	Framework Agreements	
1986–1993 Uruguay Round	Tariffs	123
	Non-tariff Measures	
	Rules	
	Services	
	Intellectual Property Rights	
	Textiles and Clothing	
	Agriculture	
	Dispute Settlement	
	Establishment of WTO	
2002-? The Doha Round	Tariffs	147
	Agriculture	
	Services	
	Intellectual Property Rights	
	Government Procurement	
	Rules	
	Dispute Settlement	
	Trade and the Environment	
	Competition Policy	
	Electronic Commerce	
	Other Issues	

Source: World Trade Organization 1995, 9 and WTO website.

that will be the focus of negotiation and set a target date for the conclusion of the round. Once the Ministerial Conference has ended, lower-level national officials conduct detailed negotiations on the topics embodied in the agenda. Periodic stock takings are held to reach interim agreements. Once negotiations have produced the outlines of a complete agreement, trade ministers meet at a final Ministerial Conference to conclude the round. National governments then ratify the agreement and implement it according to an agreed timetable.

To date, eight of these bargaining rounds have been concluded, and a ninth, the **Doha Round,** began in 2001 (see Table 2.1). These bargaining rounds are usually extended affairs. Although the earlier rounds were typically concluded relatively quickly, the trend over the last 30 years has been for multiyear rounds. Governments launched the Uruguay Round, for example, in 1986 (though they began discussing a new round in 1982) and concluded negotiations in December 1993. Governments launched the Doha Round in 2001 with plans to conclude the round by late 2005. Yet, in late 2017, governments remain unable to reach agreement. The growing length of bargaining rounds reflects the complexity of the issues at the center of negotiations and the growing diversity of interests among WTO member governments.

The rules established by intergovernmental bargaining provide a framework of law for international trade relations. Participation in the WTO, therefore, requires governments to accept common rules that constrain their actions. By accepting these constraints, governments shift international trade relations from the anarchic international environment in which "might makes right" into a rule-based system in which governments have common rights and responsibilities. In this way, the multilateral trade system brings the rule of law into international trade relations.

A Closer Look

The Doha Round

We can gain a better understanding of WTO bargaining by examining the evolution of negotiations in the Doha Round. Governments launched the Doha Round at the WTO's Fourth Ministerial Conference held in Doha, Qatar, in November 2001. In Doha, governments reached agreement on the bargaining agenda: what issues they would address and which they would ignore. Governments agreed to (1) negotiate additional tariff reductions (with a specific focus on developing countries' exports), (2) incorporate existing negotiations in services into the Doha Round, and (3) pursue meaningful liberalization of trade in agricultural products. In agriculture, they agreed to reduce barriers to market access, to eliminate agricultural export subsidies, and to reduce domestic production subsidies. The agenda also called for negotiations on trade-related intellectual property rights, on modifications of existing WTO rules regarding anti-dumping and subsidies' investigations, and on the rules pertaining to regional trade agreements and review of the operation of the dispute-settlement mechanism. Moreover, governments agreed to explore aspects of the relationship between trade and the environment. Finally, members agreed to defer negotiations on trade and investment, competition policy, government procurement, and trade facilitation (four issues known collectively as "The Singapore Issues"). They agreed to treat the agenda as a "single undertaking," meaning that everything must be agreed or nothing is agreed.

The Doha Agenda was just that—an agenda for negotiations. It contained no details about the form an eventual final agreement would take. Negotiations between governments aimed at elaborating these details began at WTO headquarters in Geneva in early 2002. These initial negotiations (conducted for the most part by national delegations staffed by career civil servants or foreign service officers) were not oriented toward making final decisions, but instead explored areas of agreement and disagreement. These negotiations would set the stage for a stock-taking exercise scheduled for the WTO's Fifth Ministerial Conference in Cancún, Mexico, in September of 2003. Even though much of the work proceeded smoothly, it quickly became evident that two issues posed large obstacles. First, developing countries were demanding deeper liberalization of agriculture than the United States and the European Union (EU) were willing to accept. Second, the EU was insisting that negotiations on the Singapore issues be initiated in 2004, but developing countries were unwilling to negotiate on new issues until they had achieved substantial gains in agriculture. In the late summer of 2003, negotiations in Geneva paused as governments prepared for the Cancún Ministerial Conference.

As trade ministers gathered in Cancún in September 2003, they hoped to achieve two broad goals that would push the Doha Round into the home stretch. The first was to bridge the gap concerning agriculture and the Singapore issues. Governments hoped this would be possible in Cancún because trade ministers had the political authority that lower-level officials lacked to make substantial concessions. A simple compromise appeared possible: the United States and the EU would accept substantial liberalization in agriculture, and the developing countries would allow negotiations on some of the Singapore issues. Second, once they had removed this major obstacle, governments would agree on a broad framework for the final agreement. The Geneva-based delegations would then work out the precise details during the following year, and the final agreement would be concluded at the next Ministerial Conference scheduled for Hong Kong in December 2005. Neither goal was achieved. The EU and the United States were unwilling to meet the developing countries' demands regarding agriculture, and the developing countries refused to allow negotiations on the Singapore issues. Unable to reach agreement, the Cancún Ministerial Conference adjourned with negotiations in complete disarray.

It took almost a year to put the negotiations back on track. Finally, on August 1, 2004, governments reached the agreement that had eluded them in Cancún. The EU and the United States accepted broad principles concerning the liberalization of trade in agriculture. In exchange, developing countries agreed to negotiating one of the Singapore issues: trade facilitation. Members hoped that this agreement would allow them to finish negotiations in time to complete the round at the Hong

Kong Ministerial in December 2005. Negotiations progressed slowly, however, as it proved difficult to translate these broad principles into meaningful tariff and subsidy reductions. As a consequence, when governments arrived in Hong Kong in December 2005 there was little chance they would conclude the round. Instead, governments reached a few specific agreements at the Hong Kong Ministerial (the EU agreed to eliminate agricultural export subsidies by 2013; the advanced industrialized countries agreed to eliminate 97 percent of the tariffs on exports of the least developed countries), and they accepted a work program intended to conclude the round by the end of 2006.

Governments ended the Doha Round 9 years later without reaching an overarching agreement. At the 10th WTO Ministerial Conference held in Nairobi, Kenya, members reached limited agreements on agriculture, on trade facilitation, and on information technology, and put aside the broader and more ambitious Doha agenda. Failure has many fathers, but in the case of the Doha Round, the principal culprit was Father Time. As Michael Froman, who was then the United States Trade Representative, argued: "Doha was designed in a different era, for a different era, and much has changed since." It was time "for the world to free itself of the strictures of Doha" in order to make progress along other tracks (Froman 2015). The specific reasons for Doha's failure, which we will look at later in this chapter, raise questions about the role the WTO can play in the international trade system moving forward.

The WTO's **dispute settlement mechanism** ensures that governments comply with the rules they establish. Individual compliance with established rules is not guaranteed. Even though most governments comply with most of their WTO obligations most of the time, there are times when some don't. Moreover, if all governments believed they could disregard WTO rules with impunity, they would comply less often. The dispute settlement mechanism ensures compliance by helping governments resolve disputes and by authorizing punishment in the event of noncompliance.

The dispute-settlement mechanism ensures compliance by providing an independent quasi-judicial tribunal. This tribunal investigates the facts and the relevant WTO rules whenever a dispute is initiated and then reaches a finding. A government found to be in violation is required to alter the offending policy or to compensate the country or countries that are harmed. We will examine the dispute settlement mechanism in greater detail in Chapter 3.

The WTO, therefore, is an international political system that regulates national trade policies. It is based on rules that constrain what governments can do to restrict the flow of goods into their countries and to encourage the export of domestic goods to foreign markets. All of these rules have been created (and can be amended) through intergovernmental bargaining. Because compliance with the rules cannot be taken for granted, governments have established a dispute-settlement mechanism to help ensure that members comply. By creating rules, establishing a decision-making process to extend and revise them, and enforcing compliance, governments have brought the rule of law into international trade relations.

HEGEMONS, PUBLIC GOODS, AND THE WORLD TRADE SYSTEM

The stability of the WTO, and of international trade systems more broadly, is a function of the distribution of power in the international system. In particular, **hegemonic stability theory** is often advanced to explain why the system shifts between periods in which it is open and liberal, and periods in which it is closed and discriminatory.

Hegemonic stability theory rests on the logic of public goods provision. A **public good** is defined by two characteristics: non-excludability and non-rivalry. Non-excludability means that once the good has been supplied, no one can be prevented from enjoying its benefits. A lighthouse, for example, warns captains away from a nearby coast. Once that beacon is lit, no captain can be prevented from observing the light and avoiding the coast. Non-rivalry means that consumption by one individual does not diminish the quantity of the good available to others. No matter how many captains have already consumed the light, it remains just as visible to the next captain.

Public goods tend to be undersupplied relative to the value society places upon them. Undersupply is a result of a phenomenon called free riding. **Free riding** describes situations in which individuals rely on others to pay for a public good (Sandler 1992, 17). My experience with public radio illustrates the logic. My local public radio station uses voluntary contributions from its listeners and businesses to finance 87 percent of its budget. Without these voluntary contributions, the station would go off the air. As a regular listener, I benefit immensely from the station's existence, and my life would be greatly diminished were the station shut down. Yet, I have never contributed to the station. Instead, I rely upon others to pay for the station's operations. In other words, I free ride on other listeners' contributions. Because everyone faces the same incentive structure, contributions to the station are lower than they would be if non-contributors could be denied access to public radio. More broadly, goods that are non-excludable and non-rivalrous tend to be undersupplied.

The severity of the free-riding problem is partly a function of the size of the group. In large groups, each individual contribution is very small relative to the total contribution, and as a result each individual has only a small impact on the ability of the group to achieve its objective. Consequently, each individual readily concludes that the group can succeed without his contribution. In large groups, therefore, the incentive to free ride is very strong. In small groups, sometimes called "privileged groups," each individual contribution is large relative to the total contribution, and therefore each contribution has a greater impact on the group's ability to achieve its common goal. It becomes more difficult for any individual to conclude that the group can succeed without his contribution. As a result, the incentive to free ride is weaker (though not altogether absent) in small groups.

International institutions such as the WTO have public good characteristics. International rules and procedures benefit all governments (though not necessarily all benefit equally). Moreover, it is difficult (though not impossible) to deny a government these benefits once an institution has been established. Moreover, these benefits do not decrease as a function of the number of governments that belong to the institution. Because international institutions have these public good characteristics, their provision can be frustrated by free riding. All governments want global trade rules, but each wants someone else to bear the cost of providing such rules.

Hegemonic stability theory argues that hegemons act like privileged groups and thus overcome the free-riding problem. A **hegemon** is a country that produces a disproportionately large share of the world's total output and that leads in the development of new technologies. Because it is so large and technologically advanced, the benefits that the hegemon gains from trade are so large that it is willing to bear the full cost of creating international trade rules. Moreover, the hegemon recognizes that the public good will not be provided in the absence of its contribution. Hence, the free-riding problem largely disappears, and stable regimes are established, during periods of hegemonic leadership. As a hegemon declines in power, it becomes less willing to bear the cost of maintaining trade rules, and world trade becomes less open.

Historical evidence provides some support for hegemonic stability theory, as world trade has flourished during periods of hegemonic leadership and floundered during periods without it. The two periods of rapid growth of world trade occurred under periods of clear hegemony. Great Britain was by far the world's largest and most innovative economy throughout the nineteenth century. Trade within Europe and between Europe and the rest of the world grew at what were then unprecedented rates. British hegemony, therefore, created and sustained an open, liberal, and highly stable global economy in which goods, capital, and labor flowed freely across borders. The same relationship is evident in the twentieth century. The United States exited World War II as an undisputed hegemon. It played the leading role in creating the GATT, and it led the push for negotiations that progressively eliminated barriers to trade. The result was the most rapid increase in world trade in history. Hence, the two hegemonic eras are characterized by stable trade regimes and the rapid growth of international trade.

The one instance of hegemonic transition is associated with the collapse of the world trade system. The transition from British to American hegemony occurred in the early twentieth century. In 1820, the American economy was only one-third the size of Great Britain's. By 1870, the two economies were roughly the same size. On the eve of World War I, the American economy was more than twice as large as Great Britain's (Maddison 2001, 261). By the end of World War II, the United States produced almost half of the world's manufactured goods (see Table 2.2). During this transition, each looked to the other to bear the cost of reconstructing the global economy after World War I. The British tried to reconstruct the world economy in the 1920s, but lacked the resources to do so (Kindleberger 1974). The United States had the ability to re-establish a liberal world economy, but wasn't willing to expend the necessary resources. Consequently, the Great Depression sparked the profusion

TABLE 2.2

Shares of World Manufacturing Production (Percent)

	1880	1900	1913	1928
United States	14.7	23.6	32.0	39.3
Great Britain	22.9	18.5	13.6	9.9
Germany	8.5	13.2	14.8	11.6
France	7.8	6.8	6.1	6.0

Source: Kennedy 1988, 259.

TABLE 2.3

Collapse of World Trade

	(Average Monthly World Trade, $U.S. millions)
1929	2,858
1930	2,327
1931	1,668
1932	1,122

Source: Kindleberger 1974, 140.

of discriminatory and protectionist trade blocs. As protectionism rose, world trade fell sharply (see Table 2.3). Hence, hegemonic transition has been associated with considerable instability of international trade.

Although these episodes are suggestive, they are too few to support strong conclusions about the relationship between hegemony and international trade. This empirical limitation is of more than pure academic interest, given the emergence of China and India as powerful forces in the global economy. China's emergence, in particular, raises questions about whether we are witnessing a hegemonic transition. Goldman Sachs estimates that China will overtake the United States in total economic production by 2027. Christopher Layne asserts that "economically, it is already doubtful that the United States is still a hegemon" (Layne 2009, 170).

These contemporary developments find parallels in the recent past. During the 1960s, the Japanese economy grew at average annual rates of more than 10 percent, compared with average growth rates of less than 4 percent for the United States. Although Japanese growth slowed during the 1970s and 1980s, Japan continued to grow more rapidly than the United States. Faster growth allowed Japan to catch up with the United States. In the early 1960s, the United States produced 40 percent of the world's manufactured goods, whereas Japan produced only 5.5 percent. By 1987, the United States' share of world manufacturing production had fallen to 24 percent, whereas Japan's share had increased to 19.4 percent (Dicken 1998, 28). In less than 30 years, therefore, Japan transformed itself from a vanquished nation into a powerful force in the world economy.

Many commentators viewed Japan's ascent as a harbinger of hegemonic decline. The United States began running trade deficits in the 1970s, and these deficits continued to grow during the 1980s. American policymakers interpreted these deficits as evidence of declining competitiveness, particularly in high-technology industries. Measures of the United States' comparative advantage in high-technology industries suggested that it was losing ground in critical sectors such as mechanical equipment, electronics, scientific instruments, and commercial aircraft. And what the United States appeared to be losing, Japan appeared to be gaining. Statistics suggested that as the American share of global high-technology markets fell (from 30 percent to 21 percent between 1970 and 1989), Japan's share of this market rose (from 7 percent to 16 percent in the same period) (Tyson 1995, 19). Thus, the trade deficit and the apparent decline in American high-technology industries both pointed to the same conclusion: the United States was losing ground to Japan.

The United States responded to these developments by adopting a more aggressive and protectionist trade policy: it increasingly relied on bilateral initiatives and threatened to protect the American market to force changes in other countries' trade policies (Krueger 1995). Japan was the principal (though not the sole) target of American assertiveness. Many analysts argued that this assertiveness reflected "the syndrome of hegemonic decline." Some argued that the protectionist tendencies generated by hegemonic decline would be reinforced by the end of the Cold War, which deprived the United States of a broader purpose provided by the alliance against the Soviet threat. Robert Gilpin, a political economist at Princeton University, summarized this pessimistic outlook, arguing that "at the opening of the twenty-first century, all the elements that have supported an open global economy have weakened" (Gilpin 2000, 347).

Assertions of hegemonic decline proved premature, however. American unilateralism subsided in the mid-1990s as the United States entered a period of sustained robust growth and Japan struggled to recover from a financial and banking crisis. In this decade, governments strengthened and extended the multilateral trade system. They established the WTO, which enjoyed greater support and attracted a larger membership than the GATT did at the height of American hegemony. As one analyst concluded in looking back on the predictions of hegemonic decline, "the institutions that took hold after World War II continue to provide governance now, and the economic interests and political consensus that lie behind them are more, not less, supportive of an open world economy today than during the Cold War" (Ikenberry 2000, 151).

The open question, therefore, is whether China's emergence today is a hegemonic transition like that which occurred during the early twentieth century or a false alarm like that prompted by Japan during the 1980s. That is, is the global system transitioning from the American century to the Asian century, or will Asia's ascent level off? Moreover, if we are experiencing hegemonic transition, must the global trade system weaken and collapse as it did during the 1920s and 1930s? Might the institutional structures constructed under American leadership help governments transition to a new global power structure without suffering another economic "dark age"?

THE EVOLVING WORLD TRADE ORGANIZATION: NEW DIRECTIONS, NEW CHALLENGES

Although the trade system's core principles and procedures have been stable for roughly 70 years, the past few years have brought substantial change. These changes will probably shape the evolution of the system over the next decade. Two such changes are most important: the emergence of developing countries as a powerful bloc within the organization, and the emergence of NGOs as a powerful force outside the organization. Together these developments have complicated decision making within the WTO and raised fundamental questions about the ability of governments to continue to achieve their goals through the system.

The first substantial change in the WTO arises from the growing power of developing countries within the organization. WTO membership has expanded dramatically since 1985. More than 70 countries have joined, increasing total membership to 164 countries (as of October 2017). Still more countries have applied for membership and are currently engaged in accession negotiations. Assuming all these negotiations are successfully completed, WTO membership will surpass 190 countries during the next few years. Even if all governments have similar interests, more members will make the decision making harder—it is very difficult to gain consensus among 164 countries.

Membership growth reflects the dramatic reorientation of emerging market countries toward international trade. For reasons we explore in greater detail in Chapter 6, governments in most developing countries were skeptical about the ability to foster development through trade. Consequently, most governments participated little in the GATT system. And to the extent that developing countries belonged to the GATT, the industrialized countries accorded them special treatment rather than demanding strict reciprocity. The GATT became, as a result, a rich-country club in which negotiations focused on the areas of interest to the United States, the EU, and Japan, and neglected liberalization in areas of interest to developing countries. Since the mid-1980s, emerging market countries have emphasized development through exports and, as a result, have placed substantially greater importance on the market access that participation in the WTO provides.

Under the leadership of the three largest emerging economies, Brazil, China, and India, developing-country members have constructed a powerful bloc within the WTO. This power has been evident in the past decade. Developing countries stymied the first effort to launch the current round of negotiations in Seattle in 1999 because the proposed agenda dedicated too much attention to issues of interest to the United States and the EU and insufficient attention to the issues developing countries believed important. The current round launched once developing countries were satisfied that the agenda focused sufficient attention on the topics of importance to them, especially liberalization of agriculture and maintaining sufficient policy space to promote development. Since 2003, cooperation among developing countries within the WTO has been institutionalized in the Group of 20.

The emergence of the developing countries as a powerful bloc in the WTO has transformed bargaining. In previous rounds countries with similar economic structures exchanged roughly equivalent concessions. With developing countries on the sidelines, the United States, the EU, and Japan defined the negotiating agenda. As a result, governments liberalized industries in which they all enjoyed relative competitiveness, generally capital-intensive manufactured goods, and continued to protect industries in which they were uncompetitive. Labor-intensive industries and farming thus remained protected in most industrialized countries. In essence, the United States, the EU, and Japan agreed to allow GM, Toyota, and Volkswagen to compete against each other in all three markets. Reducing these barriers challenged national producers in each country by exposing them to global competition, but because all countries were roughly similar in structure, liberalization did not impose substantial adjustment costs.

Current WTO bargaining brings together governments representing countries with very different economic structures. Industrialized countries who are competitive in high-technology products and services bargain with developing countries who are competitive in labor-intensive manufactured goods, in standardized capital-intensive goods such as steel, and in agriculture. For negotiations to succeed, governments in each group must liberalize industries that will not survive full exposure to international competition. As a result, a broad agreement such as that which would have been necessary to conclude the Doha Round would impose hefty adjustment costs, in agriculture for many European Union countries, Japan, the United States, and other developed countries, and in services and manufactured goods for most developing countries.

Changes inside the organization are compounded by changes outside. Of particular importance here is the growing number of nongovernmental organizations (NGOs) striving to influence the organization. Few interest groups (other than businesses) paid much attention to the GATT when negotiations focused solely on tariffs. Since the late 1990s, however, hundreds of groups have mobilized in opposition to what they view as the unwelcome constraints imposed by new WTO rules. In many instances, NGOs worry about how WTO rules affect the ability of governments to safeguard consumer and environmental interests.

WTO rules do not prevent governments from protecting consumers from unsafe foods or protecting the environment from clear hazards. For example, when cattle stricken by mad cow disease were discovered in the United States, nothing in the WTO prohibited other governments from banning the import of American beef. Similarly, when U.S. inspectors found toxic chemicals in toothpaste manufactured in China, WTO rules did not prohibit the United States from banning imports of the afflicted product. Problems arise when governments use health or environmental concerns as an excuse to shelter domestic producers from foreign competition. Such practices can become common in a world in which governments cannot use tariffs to protect indus-try. Suppose the United States wants to protect American avocado growers from competition against cheaper Mexican avocados, and so assert that Mexican avocados contain pests that harm American plants (even though they don't) and on this basis ban Mexican avocados from the American market. This is disguised protectionism—an effort to protect a local producer against foreign competition, hidden as an attempt to protect plant health in the United States.

WTO agreements, such as the Agreement on Sanitary and Phytosanitary Standards, attempt to strike a balance between allowing governments to protect against legitimate health risks and preventing governments from using such regulations to protect domestic producers. This is a difficult balance to strike. It is not easy to determine the real motives behind a government's decision to ban imports of a particular product. Did the EU ban the import of hormone-treated beef because of a sincere concern about potential health consequences or to protect European beef producers from American compe-tition? As a consequence, WTO rules require governments to accept current scientific conclusions about the risks to humans, animals, and plants that such products pose. Governments cannot ban imports of a product on health or safety grounds unless a preponderance of scientific evidence indicates that the product is in fact harmful. Such rules extend deeply into an aspect of national authority: the ability to determine what risks society should be exposed to and protected from.

Civil society groups argue that the balance struck by current WTO rules is too favorable to business and insufficiently protective of consumer and envi-ronmental interests. Moreover, they argue that the bias toward producer inter-ests is a consequence of the nature of the WTO decision making, a process in which producer interests are heavily represented and consumer interests are almost entirely excluded. The mobilization of NGOs around the WTO has thus sought to bring greater attention to consumer interests in order to redress this perceived imbalance.

The growing power of developing countries within the WTO and the greater pressure by NGOs on the outside of the organization have combined to generate questions about whether the WTO can remain relevant under its current decision-making procedures. One dimension of this question concerns effectiveness: Can 164 governments at different stages of economic devel-opment reach agreements that provide meaningful trade liberalization? The failure to reach a broad agreement in the Doha Round highlights the limited effectiveness of consensus-based bargaining among so many states. A second dimension concerns legitimacy: Should rules that constrain national regula-tions be negotiated without the full participation of civil society?

Both dimensions matter, but they point to contradictory conclusions. Concerns about the effectiveness of WTO negotiations highlight the need for reform that limits the number of governments actively participating in nego-tiations. One such proposal advocates the creation of a steering committee, a WTO equivalent of the United Nations Security Council, with authority to develop consensus on trade issues (see Schott and Watal 2000). Such reform would make it easier to reach agreement, but only by making negotiations less inclusive. Concerns about legitimacy highlight the need for reform that opens the WTO process to NGOs. Opening the WTO in this manner, NGOs argue, would ensure that business interests are balanced against other social concerns. Although such reforms might make WTO decision making more inclusive, they would also make it even more difficult to reach agreement within the organization.

Dissatisfaction with current decision-making procedures has yet to produce a consensus about whether and how to change current procedures. The most important consequence of the impasse that prevented major gains in the Doha Round, therefore, has been that governments have found the WTO increasingly less useful as a forum within which to pursue their trade objectives. And as they have reached this conclusion, they have begun to seek alternatives that can be more effective.

THE GREATEST CHALLENGE? REGIONAL TRADE ARRANGEMENTS AND THE WORLD TRADE ORGANIZATION

Regionalism is one alternative that has gained particular appeal. Indeed, many observers believe that regional trade arrangements pose the single greatest challenge to the multilateral trade system. Regional trade arrangements pose a challenge to the WTO because they offer an alternative, and often more discriminatory, way to organize world trade.

A **regional trade arrangement** (RTA) is a trade agreement between two or more countries, usually located in the same region of the world, in which each country offers preferential market access to the other. RTAs come in two basic forms: free-trade areas and customs unions. In a **free-trade area**, like the North American Free Trade Agreement, governments eliminate tariffs on other members' goods, but each member retains independent tariffs on goods entering their market from non-members. In a **customs union**, like the EU, member governments eliminate all tariffs on trade between customs union members and impose a common tariff on goods entering the union from non-members.

Because RTAs provide tariff-free market access to some countries, but not to others, they are inherently discriminatory. Though such discrimination is inconsistent with the GATT's core principle, GATT's Article XXIV allows countries to form RTAs as long as the level of protection imposed against non-members is no higher than the level of protection applied by the countries prior to forming the arrangement. Nevertheless, the discriminatory aspect of RTAs makes many worry about the impact they will have on the nondiscriminatory trade encouraged by the WTO.

Such worries arise because of the rapid proliferation of RTAs. According to the WTO, there are currently 279 RTAs in operation. If all RTAs now planned are created, there may be as many as 445 RTAs in effect. Free-trade agreements constitute the vast majority of these RTAs, for 86 percent of existing RTAs and for 99 percent of arrangements currently being negotiated. More than half of all RTAs are bilateral agreements. The others are "plurilateral" agreements that include at least three countries. RTAs are densely concentrated in Europe and the Mediterranean region. Agreements between countries in Western, Eastern, and Central Europe, and in the Mediterranean account for almost 50 percent of RTAs in operation. North and South America take second place, accounting for about 12 percent. Until quite recently, sub-Saharan Africa and Asia-Pacific states have joined few RTAs.

RTAs have emerged in three distinct waves (see Figure 2.1). The first wave began early in the 1950s and extended to the mid-1970s. This wave began with the construction of the original European Economic Community in 1958 and the Latin American Free Trade Area in 1960, and concluded with the formation of the Economic Community of West African States in 1975. This wave was motivated in part by a desire to promote deeper economic cooperation within particular regions in an attempt to promote peace and achieve more rapid economic development. In this regard, the contribution of the EEC to Franco-German political reconciliation after World War II and to rapid postwar economic recovery encouraged governments in other regions to emulate the approach. This early enthusiasm waned, however, as the economic gains realized in Europe did not materialize in the so-called developing world imitators.

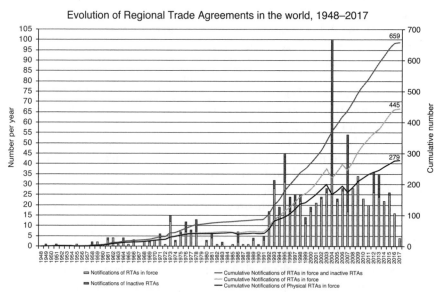

Evolution of Regional Trade Agreements in the world, 1948–2017

Note: Notifications of RTAs: goods, services & accessions to an RTA are counted separately, Physical RTAs: goods, services & accessions to an RTA are counted together. The cumlative lines show the number of notifications/physical RTAs that were in force for a given year.
Source: RTA Section, WTO Secretariat, 20 June 2017.

FIGURE 2.1

Regional Trade Arrangements, 1950–2016

Source: The World Trade Organization, WTO Secretariat, RTA Section, 20 June 2017.

The second wave began in the context of far-reaching trade policy reforms in Eastern and Central Europe, the former Soviet Union, and other developing countries. Governments in former members of the Soviet Bloc, for instance, sought new ways to organize their trade, and sought access to Western European markets. Consequently, a large number of agreements were reached between countries within the region and between these countries and the EU (WTO 2000). Moldova, for example, entered RTAs with eight other newly independent countries formed from the former Soviet Union between 1992 and 1996. Russia entered at least nine RTAs with this same set of countries. Ten Eastern and Central European countries reached bilateral RTAs with the European Union between 1991 and 1997. There were also substantial changes in developing-country trade policies in the late 1980s and early 1990s, which led to a greater willingness to enter RTAs (WTO 2000). Mexico, for example, negotiated RTAs not only with the United States and Canada (NAFTA), but also with Chile, Costa Rica, and Nicaragua. Chile negotiated RTAs with Colombia, Ecuador, and Peru, in addition to completing the agreement it reached with Mexico.

The third wave began in 2008 or so and has been closely associated with the so-called **mega-regional agreements**. The two most prominent of these mega-regional agreements are the Trans-Pacific Partnership (TPP), negotiated between the U.S. and the EU, and the Transatlantic Trade and Investment Partnership (TTIP), which was negotiated by 13 states in Asia and North and South America. A third mega-regional, the Regional Comprehensive Economic Partnership, ties China to 15 other economies throughout Asia and the Pacific. In contrast to previous waves, which tended to focus most heavily on trade liberalization, the mega-regional agreements seek deeper economic integration among their members. To achieve this goal, these agreements are both broader in scope and reach more deeply into domestic arrangements than prior agreements. The TTIP and the TPP were intended to promote cooperation and harmonization on technical barriers to trade, which are domestic rules, regulations, and administrative procedures that can limit trade flows. In addition, these agreements included trade in services, more ambitious rules regarding the protection of intellectual property than are present in the WTO and agreement on the treatment and protection of foreign investment. The TPP included most of these issues as well as an elaborate and enforceable code on labor standards.

Why have RTAs proliferated, especially since 1990? Scholars have advanced a number of general explanations for this trend. Some emphasize a country's desire to gain more secure access to the market of a particularly important trading partner. In the U.S.–Canada Free Trade Agreement concluded in the late 1980s, for example, Canada sought secure access to the U.S. market—the most important destination for Canada's exports. During much of the 1980s, the United States made frequent use of anti-dumping and countervailing duty investigations to protect American producers from Canadian imports. Such measures clearly interfered with the ability of Canadian producers to export to the American market. The Canadian government hoped that the U.S.–Canada Free Trade Agreement would give Canada "some degree of exemption" from these measures (Whalley 1998, 72–73).

Other scholars emphasize a government's need to signal a strong commitment to economic reform. Governments use RTAs to convince foreign partners that they will maintain open markets and investor-friendly policies. This argument has been applied most commonly to Mexico's decision to seek a free-trade agreement with the United States. Mexico shifted from a highly protectionist to a more liberal trade policy in the mid-1980s. The success of that strategy hinged in part on Mexico's ability to attract foreign investment from the United States. The Mexican government feared, however, that American investors would not believe that the Mexican government was committed to its new strategy. What would prevent Mexico from shifting back to protectionism and nationalizing foreign investments? If American businesses didn't believe the Mexican government was committed to this liberal strategy, they would be reluctant to invest in Mexico. Absent American investment, Mexico would be deprived of foreign capital that was critical to the success of its strategy.

A free-trade agreement with the United States allowed Mexico to signal to American investors the depth of its commitment to market liberalization. It did so in part because NAFTA contained very clear and enforceable rules concerning the treatment of foreign investment located in Mexico. A similar argument might be used to understand at least part of the interest that Eastern and Central European governments had in signing free-trade agreements with the EU. These governments were also reorienting their economic policies and were trying to attract foreign investment. Like Mexico, they might have needed an external institution, such as an agreement with the EU, to signal to foreign investors their commitment to market reforms. Notice that these arguments actually place less emphasis on the trade benefits that might result from an RTA and focus more on the need to attract foreign investment.

Other scholars argue that countries enter RTAs to increase their bargaining power in multilateral trade negotiations. A small country bargaining individually in the WTO lacks power because it does not have a large market to offer. By pooling a group of small countries, the market that can be offered to trade partners in WTO negotiations increases substantially. Consequently, each member might gain larger tariff concessions in WTO negotiations. Current American enthusiasm for RTAs might also be seen as an attempt to gain bargaining power in the WTO. As it has become more difficult to reach decisions within the WTO, the United States has explicitly threatened to rely more on free-trade agreements. By doing so, the United States denies its market to countries unwilling to make concessions in the WTO. The fear of losing access to the U.S. market could induce governments to make concessions in the WTO that they would not otherwise make. The threat to rely more on RTAs and less on the WTO, therefore, enhances American power in the organization.

Finally, and clearly relevant to the emergence of the mega-regional agreements, the impasse in the Doha Round encouraged states to find other paths along which to pursue their trade policy goals. These agreements have enabled the EU, the U.S., Canada, Mexico, and South American countries with Pacific ties, as well as a few partners in Asia to pursue economic integration on issues of common interest and concern that they could not address in the WTO, given the resistance by many members to the initiation of negotiations on new issues. Digital trade, for instance, which is commerce in products that are delivered via the Internet (such as music, video, apps, e-books, etc), constitutes an important and growing share of the global economy and international trade. Current estimates indicate that its total value is $4.2 trillion worldwide (U.S. International Trade Commission 2013). Yet, in spite of its growing importance, the issue was kept out of the Doha Round. Within the mega-regionals, governments could negotiate extensive rules to govern this trade. Moreover, the growing importance of global value chains has provided multinational businesses with a strong incentive to pressure their governments to negotiate these deeper agreements in order to better protect their investments, to harmonize product standards across national markets, and to make it easier and cheaper to ship goods across national boundaries (Baldwin 2014).

The rapid growth of RTAs raises questions about whether they challenge or complement the WTO. This is not an easy question to answer. On the one hand, RTAs liberalize trade, a mission they share with the WTO. In this regard, RTAs complement the WTO. On the other hand, RTAs institutionalize discrimination within world trade. In this regard, RTAs challenge the WTO.

Economists conceptualize these competing consequences of RTAs as **trade creation** and **trade diversion**. Consider an RTA between France and Germany. Because the RTA eliminates tariffs on trade between France and Germany, more Franco-German trade takes place. This is trade creation. Because the RTA does not eliminate tariffs on trade between France and Germany on the one hand, and the United States on the other, some trade between the United States and Germany is replaced by trade between France and Germany. This is trade diversion. An RTA's net impact on trade is the difference between the trade it creates and the trade it diverts. If more trade is created than diverted, the RTA has liberalized trade. If more trade is diverted than created, the RTA has pushed the world toward protectionism.

Which of these effects predominates in existing RTAs? Nobody really knows, in large part because it is difficult to evaluate trade creation and trade diversion empirically. It is especially difficult once we begin to think about how RTAs evolve once created. An RTA that originally diverts more trade than it creates might over time create more trade than it diverts. Or an RTA could evolve in the opposite direction. Consider the first case. Some scholars have argued that RTAs exert a kind of gravitational force on countries that are not currently members. Countries that do not belong to the EU, but that engage in lots of trade with it, have a strong incentive to join. So it is no surprise, therefore, that over the last 40 years the EU has expanded from six to 25 member countries. Some see a similar dynamic at work in the Western Hemisphere. Mexico's decision to seek a free-trade agreement with the United States was at least partially motivated by concerns about the cost of being outside a U.S.–Canada Free Trade Area that had been negotiated in the late 1980s (Gruber 2000). The interest of many Latin American countries in a Free Trade Area of the Americas (FTAA) is at least partially a consequence

Policy Analysis and Debate

The United States and the TPP

Question

Should the United States embrace aggressive bilateralism?

Overview

The Trump administration appears committed to a strategy of aggressive bilateralism in its trade relationships with the rest of the world. In its first major outline of trade policy, submitted to Congress in March 2017, the USTR stated that the guiding principle for its policy was to "expand trade in a way that is freer and fairer for all Americans." And it stated that this goal "can be best accomplished by focusing on bilateral trade negotiations rather than multilateral negotiations—and by renegotiating and revising trade agreements" when necessary. Consequently, one of the first steps the Trump administration took upon entering office was to withdraw the U.S. from the TPP. In April of 2017, President Trump called the WTO "another one of our disasters" and ordered the Department of Commerce to undertake an extensive review of WTO rules. One month later, the administration notified Congress of its intention to renegotiate NAFTA, and in September 2017, Trump and other administration officials began to speak publicly about scrapping the U.S.–South Korea Free Trade Agreement. At present, the administration has wavered on its orientation toward TTIP and has yet to state publicly whether it intends to withdraw from this agreement as well.

The administration's stated rationale for these changes is twofold. First, members of the administration assert that existing trade agreements between the United States and other countries put the U.S. at an "unfair advantage in global markets" (USTR 2017). Foreign governments enact unfair trade policies and practices such as subsidies, piracy of intellectual property, and currency manipulation that "harm American workers, farmers, ranchers, services providers, and other businesses" (ibid). And the WTO and other international enforcement mechanisms do not permit the U.S. to take steps to punish such transgressions. Second, the administration asserts that it can negotiate a series of bilateral trade agreements that prevent these unfair practices. It intends to use these bilateral negotiations to "hold our trading partners to higher standards of fairness" and will use American trade law "in response to trading partners that continue to engage in unfair activities."

Policy Options

- The United States should retain its postwar policy based on multilateral cooperation within the WTO supplemented by regional trade agreements.
- The United States should be more aggressive in its trade relationships and the shift to bilateralism is a good way to implement such an approach.

Policy Analysis

- Does the United States derive benefits from the mega-regionals and the WTO that it cannot otherwise enjoy?
- How disadvantaged are American producers by unfair trade practices?

Take a Position

- Which option do you prefer? Justify your choice.
- What criticisms of your position should you anticipate? How would you defend your recommendation against these criticisms?

Resources

Online: Visit the U.S. Trade Representative website (www.ustr.gov) for timely information about current negotiations. The fullest statement of the Trump administration's approach is in the USTR's "The President's 2017 Trade Policy Agenda," which you can find at the Resource Center at USTR.gov

In Print: See Jeffrey J. Schott, *US Trade Policy Options in the Pacific Basin: Bigger is Better, PB17-7* (Washington, DC: Peterson Institute for International Economics, 2017); Doug Irwin, 2017, "The False Promise of Protectionism," *Foreign Affairs* 96 (May/June): 45–56.

of Mexico's entry into NAFTA (Baldwin 1995). Over time, this gravitational pull attracts so many additional members that a regional RTA evolves into a global free-trade area. In this optimistic scenario, RTAs lead eventually to global free trade in which trade creation outweighs trade diversion and RTAs complement the WTO.

By contrast, the creation of a large RTA in one region could encourage the formation of rival and more protectionist RTAs in other regions. In this scenario, NAFTA as well as FTAA could be seen as an American response to the EU. An emerging free-trade area in Pacific Asia could be seen as a response to regionalism in Europe and the Western Hemisphere. In this view, world trade is becoming increasingly organized into three regional and rival trade blocs. Once regional trading blocs have formed, each bloc might raise tariffs to restrict trade with other regions. A tariff increase by one RTA could provoke retaliation by the others, leading to a rising spiral of protection that undermines global trade liberalization (Frankel 1997, 210). In this case, trade diversion outweighs trade creation and RTAs pose an obvious challenge to the WTO.

It is impossible to predict which of these two scenarios is the more likely. The world does seem to be moving toward three RTAs: one in Europe, one in the Western Hemisphere, and one in Asia. At the same time, governments appear to be aware of the challenges RTAs pose to the WTO, as they have created a WTO committee on RTAs that is exploring the relationship between these arrangements and the multilateral system. Only time will tell, however, whether RTAs will develop into discriminatory trade blocs that engage in tariff wars or if instead they will pave the way for global free trade.

CONCLUSION

The multilateral trade system is an international political system. It provides rules that regulate how governments can use policies to influence the cross-border flow of goods and services. It provides a decision-making process through which governments revise existing rules and create new ones. And it provides a dispute-settlement mechanism that allows governments to enforce common rules. By promoting nondiscriminatory international trade, by establishing a formal process for making and revising rules, and by allowing governments to enforce the rules they create, the WTO reduces the impact of raw power on international trade relationships. In short, the WTO brings the rule of law to bear in international trade relations.

Like all political systems, the WTO reflects the interests of the powerful. Its creation reflected the interests of a hegemonic United States; its strengthening during the Cold War era reflected the growing interest of European and Japanese governments that trade liberalization promised real gains. Although one can argue that the WTO reflects only the interests of the advanced industrialized countries, the trends over the last 20 years suggest otherwise. The rapid growth in the number of countries joining the WTO during that period suggests that most of the world's governments believe that they are better off with the WTO than without it. This doesn't mean that the system is perfect. It does suggest, however, that in the contemporary global economy, the majority of the world's governments believe that they do better when world trade is organized by a system based on nondiscrimination and market liberalism than they do in a discriminatory, protectionist, and rule-free environment. The WTO will weaken, and perhaps even crumble, when governments no longer believe this is true.

The largest contemporary challenges to the WTO emerge from the ability of its decision-making process to continue to produce outcomes in a changing world. On the one hand, the growth of WTO membership and the emergence of the G-20 as a powerful bloc within the organization has raised the stakes of trade negotiations and made it more difficult to find packages acceptable to the full membership. On the other hand, the emergence of a vocal NGO movement critical of the WTO's apparent tendency to place business interests before consumer interests has made it even more difficult to reach agreements within the organization. The full consequences of these two challenges remain uncertain. Can governments reform decision making in the system in a way that simultaneously enhances its legitimacy and efficiency? Or will continued decision-making paralysis impart additional impetus to regionalism?

KEY TERMS

Customs Union	The Doha Round	Generalized System
Dispute Settlement	Free Riding	of Preferences
Mechanism	Free-Trade Area	Hegemon

Hegemonic Stability
 Theory
Intergovernmental
 Bargaining
Market Liberalism
Mega-Regional
 Agreements

Ministerial Conference
Most-Favored Nation
National Treatment
Nondiscrimination
Non-tariff
 Barriers
Public Good

Regional Trade
 Arrangement (RTA)
Tariffs
Trade Creation
Trade Diversion
World Trade Organization
 (WTO)

SUGGESTIONS FOR FURTHER READING

A thorough investigation of the WTO and the Doha Round is available in Kent Jones, *Reconstructing the World Trade Organization for the 21st Century: An Institutional Approach* (New York: Oxford University Press, 2015).

The WTO's uncertain future is explored in Judith Goldstein, 2017. "Trading in the Twenty-First Century: Is There a Role for the World Trade Organization?" *Annual Review of Political Science* 20(1): 545–564.

For a more historical treatment, see John H. Barton, Judith L Goldstein, Timothy E Josling, and Richard H Steinberg. *The Evolution of the Trade Regime: Law, Politics, and Economics of the GATT and the WTO* (Princeton: Princeton University Press, 2006).

Finally, a more analytical approach is provided by Bernard Hoekman and Michel M. Kostecki, *The Political Economy of the World Trading System: The WTO and Beyond,* 3rd ed. (New York: Oxford University Press, 2009).

The Political Economy of International Trade Cooperation

The disappointing achievements realized from the Doha Development Round raise serious questions about the WTO's future. The WTO and its predecessor the GATT have been at the center of the international trade system for 70 years. Yet, today, the rise of new issues and the associated emergence of the mega-regionals highlights the willingness of some WTO member governments to pursue their trade policy goals outside the WTO framework, The Trump administration's reliance on aggressive bilateralism and extended review of WTO rules constitutes another challenge to an organization struggling to justify its relevance. Today, perhaps more than at any previous point in time, the centerpiece of the postwar multilateral trade system is under threat. Do the world's governments still need the WTO?

Most analysts would argue, I believe, that the WTO remains an important and perhaps even necessary centrepiece of the global trade system. The claim that governments still need the WTO is typically framed in terms of a somewhat abstract theory of international cooperation. This theory tells us that international cooperation is difficult, even when all states stand to gain from cooperation, because the anarchical international system within which states interact makes it difficult to enforce any agreements that they might make. The challenges associated with enforcing international agreements create opportunities for some states to take advantage of others, and the fear of being exploited by others can make states reluctant to enter cooperative agreements. As a result, cooperation is stymied; states are worse off than they could be. In the specific context of world trade, this logic suggests that countries could gain substantially from cooperation that liberalizes trade. Yet, because some governments may want to exploit others, by choosing to keep their market closed to imports while exporting to economies that have liberalized, for instance, and all governments want to avoid being exploited in this fashion, governments are unwilling to make agreements that would liberalize trade. Consequently, societies are deprived of the benefits that trade confers.

Societies often solve such cooperation problems by creating common institutions that help them enforce agreements. This is how and why the WTO remains important. The WTO helps states enforce trade agreements and in doing so enables states to capture the mutual benefits that trade provides. The WTO performs this role by providing common rules that provide enforceable standards to which states' trade policies must conform. The WTO helps states collect and disseminate information about the degree to which specific trade policies do in fact conform to these standards. And finally, the WTO enables states to sustain cooperation by helping them adjudicate the disputes that do arise. The WTO remains important, therefore, because it enables societies to cooperate and capture the welfare gains that trade offers.

This chapter develops this logic of international trade cooperation in three essential steps. First, we examine trade theory to gain a firm understanding of why trade offers welfare gains to all countries. This examination is important in its own right, but it also highlights the gains available from international cooperation aimed at liberalizing trade. Second, using a standard model of cooperation, the prisoners' dilemma, we examine why cooperation to capture the welfare gains available from trade is difficult. Third, we examine how the WTO helps governments enforce the agreements they reach.

THE ECONOMIC CASE FOR TRADE

Why should countries trade? The standard answer is that countries should trade because trade makes them better off. Grasping why, exactly, trade makes societies better off, however, can be tricky. As the prominent economist Paul Krugman has argued, even many scholars and journalists who spend their lives writing about the global economy don't fully understand why trade makes societies better off (Krugman 1997, 117–125). Because understanding the rationale for trade is central to understanding the global economy but can be difficult to grasp, we develop the logic of comparative advantage in some detail.

We begin by establishing a few core concepts. The first is the production possibility frontier (PPF). Countries are endowed with factors of production in finite amounts. Consequently, any decision to use factors to produce one good, necessarily means that these factors are not available to produce other goods. A decision to allocate capital and labor to the production of computers, for example, necessarily requires the country to forgo the production of some number of shirts. These forgone shirts are what economists call opportunity costs, and the production possibility frontier allows us to measure these opportunity costs quite precisely.

Consider an illustrative PPF for the United States. Let's assume that the United States has a fixed stock of labor and capital that it can use in combination to produce two goods—shirts and computers. Suppose that if the United States allocates all its labor and capital to computer production, it could produce 100 million computers (point *A* in Figure 3.1) and if it allocates all labor and

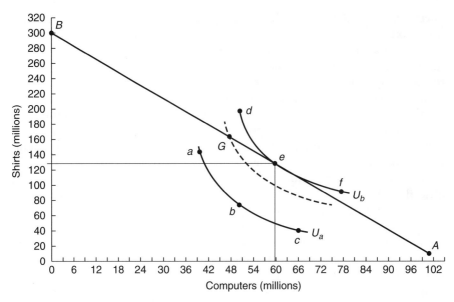

FIGURE 3.1
U.S. Production Possibility Frontier

capital to shirts, it can produce 300 million shirts (point *B* in Figure 3.1). If we connect *A* and *B* with a line, we have defined a production possibility frontier for the United States. Along it lie all combinations of shirts and computers that the United States can produce using all of its factors of production. As we move from *A* to *B*, capital and labor are reallocated away from computer production to shirt production. The slope of the line, called the marginal rate of transformation, tells us exactly how many shirts the United States forgoes for each computer it produces. In this example, every computer the United States produces costs three shirts. Because an autarkic country cannot consume more than it produces, the PPF also defines the limits of possible consumption.

We can draw the PPF either as a straight line, as in our example, or as a curved line. Which we select depends upon the assumption we make about the nature of the opportunity costs that the United States faces. A straight PPF embodies the assumption that the United States faces constant opportunity costs. Every additional computer always costs three shirts. If we assume constant opportunity costs, we also implicitly assume that the United States enjoys constant returns to scale in production. This means that whenever the factors employed in shirt production are increased by some factor, we will increase the number of shirts produced by the same factor. Double the amount of labor and capital employed in shirt production and double the number of shirts produced. Alternatively, we could assume that the United States faces *increasing* opportunity costs and connect points *A* and *B* with a curved line that bends out away from the origin. The shift from producing 49,999,999 computers to 50 million computers costs three shirts. Yet, when the United States moves from producing 89,999,999 to 90 million computers, it costs seven shirts. Thus, the opportunity cost of producing each good rises as the United States dedicates a larger share of its factors to the production of a single good. If we assume the United States faces increasing opportunity costs, we are also implicitly assuming that factors yield diminishing marginal returns. This means that the number of additional computers the United States can produce for each additional worker employed in computer production will fall as the number of workers employed in computer production rises. Most contemporary models assume that factors yield diminishing marginal returns. To keep things simple, we will assume constant marginal returns.

Our second core concept, consumption indifference curves, helps us understand the specific combination of computers and shirts American consumers will purchase. Consumers will acquire shirts and computers in the combination that maximizes their collective utility. Economists conceptualize consumer utility with indifference curves. We assume that consumers prefer more to less, and therefore consumer utility increases as we move away from the origin. Some combinations of shirts and computers, such as those at points *a, b,* and *c* on Figure 3.1, yield the same amount of utility. If asked to choose between these three, our consumer will say, "I like them all the same." If we connect every combination of shirts and computers that provides our consumer with the same amount of utility with a curved line such as U_a, we have drawn an indifference curve. Our consumer enjoys identical utility from every combination of shirts and computers that falls on U_a. We can draw a second indifference curve that links the combinations *d, e,* and *f.* Each of these combinations yield more utility than *a, b,* or *c*, and are thus said to lie on a higher indifference curve. But, our consumer is indifferent between *d, e,* and *f.* We can connect these three combinations with a second indifference curve, U_b. Were we to repeat this exercise for every possible combination of shirts and consumers within this two-dimensional space, we would have a complete indifference map.

Three additional characteristics of indifference curves are important. First, indifference curves typically slope downwards. This slope, called the marginal rate of substitution, tells us how much of one good the consumer is willing to give up to acquire an additional unit of the second good. Second, indifference curves typically bend in toward the origin. This reflects the assumption of diminishing marginal utility. The first computer provides a large improvement in utility. Each successive computer, however, provides a smaller increase of utility. Consequently, even though the consumer might be willing to give up a large number of shirts to acquire her first computer, she will be willing to give up fewer shirts to acquire her sixth computer. Finally, when we focus on production and consumption for an entire country, we construct community indifference curves rather than individual indifference curves. Community indifference curves aggregate utility for all consumers in that society. In this example, then, our community indifference curves embody the aggregated preferences of all American consumers.

Together, the PPF and indifference curves allow us to define equilibrium production and consumption of shirts and computers in this autarkic American economy. Production and consumption will occur at the point where the marginal rate of transformation (the slope of the PPF) is equal to the marginal rate of substitution (the slope of the indifference curve). That is, production and consumption will occur where the PPF and the indifference curve are tangent. This is point *e* on Figure 3.1.

Why must production and consumption occur only at this point? Suppose the United States initially produced and consumed at *G*. Society can gain greater utility than at *G* (consumers can shift to a higher indifference curve) by consuming fewer shirts and more computers. We would therefore expect consumers to demand fewer shirts and more computers and we would expect production to shift in response, producing more computers and fewer shirts. Beyond *e*, consuming additional computers and fewer shirts decreases consumer utility. Consequently, consumers will begin to demand more shirts and fewer computers. Only at *e* is it impossible to achieve higher utility from a different combination of shirts and computers. Consumer utility is thus maximized by producing and consuming at *e*. Under autarky, therefore, equilibrium production and consumption in the United States equals 60 million computers and 120 million shirts.

To see how trade changes this equilibrium, we must introduce a country for the United States to trade with. We will assume that the only other country in the world is China. We construct China's PPF just as we did for the United States (see Figure 3.2). Let's suppose that if China dedicates all its labor and capital to computers, it can produce 20 million computers. If it dedicates all its labor and capital to shirt production, it can produce 400 million shirts.

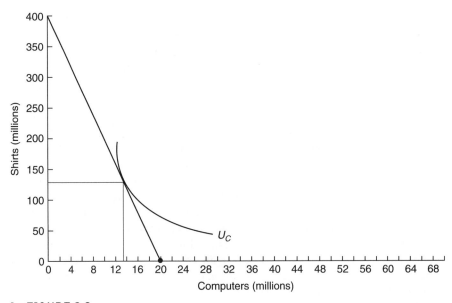

FIGURE 3.2

China's Production Possibility Frontier

Connecting these two points yields China's PPF. Given our assumptions, China's marginal rate of transformation is 20: every computer China produces carries opportunity costs of 20 shirts. We then find the point of tangency between China's consumer indifference curves and the PPF to identify equilibrium production and consumption in an autarkic China. Based on our assumptions, equilibrium production and consumption in autarkic China yields 13 million computers and 140 million shirts under autarky.

We can now see how trade between the United States and China affects equilibrium production and consumption in both countries (see Figure 3.3). Trade changes equilibrium production by causing each country to specialize in the production of one good. The United States specializes in computer production and stops producing shirts. China specializes in shirt production and stops producing computers. Specialization arises from the conclusions each draws from a simple price comparison. The United States acquires more shirts per computer when it buys them from China than when it produces them at home. A computer buys 20 shirts in China whereas at home it buys only three shirts. Why should the United States produce shirts at home when it can acquire them for substantially less in China? The United States thus stops producing shirts, produces only computers, and acquires the shirts it wants from China.

Similarly, China acquires more computers per shirt when it buys them from the United States than when it produces them at home. China can acquire a computer from the United States for only three shirts whereas if it produces computers at home each computer costs 20 shirts. Why should China produce computers when it can acquire them much less expensively from the United States? China therefore stops producing computers, specializes in shirts, and acquires the computers it wants through trade with the United States. Trade thus changes equilibrium production in both countries: the United States specializes in computer production and China specializes in shirt production.

To see how trade affects equilibrium consumption in both countries, we need to know the price at which the United States and China will exchange shirts for computers. We know that this price must fall somewhere between three and 20 shirts per computer. We could solve for the exact price that will arise, but we'll simply assume that the two agree to trade at six shirts per computer. This new price is depicted in Figure 3.3 as the dashed line labeled pt. Now we must find the combination of shirts and computers that maximizes consumer welfare in each country at this new price. To do so, we find the point of tangency between the new price line and our consumer indifference curves. These points are labeled C_{US} and C_C, respectively.

Equilibrium consumption in both countries has thus expanded beyond what was possible under autarky. American consumption expands from 60 million computers and 120 million shirts under autarky to 75 million computers and 150 million shirts. Chinese consumption expands from 13 million computers and 140 million shirts under autarky to 25 million computers and 250 million shirts. At this new equilibrium, both countries consume more shirts and computers than they could under autarky. Consequently, consumers achieve greater utility, which is reflected in the move to higher indifference

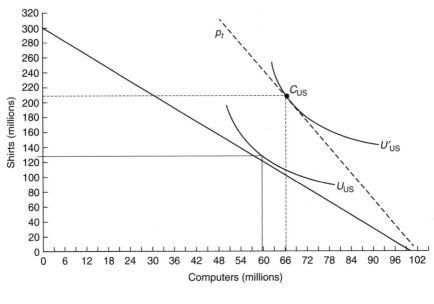

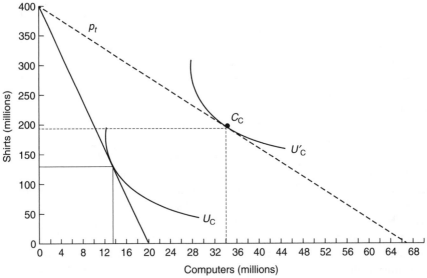

FIGURE 3.3

Equilibrium with Free Trade and Complete Specialization

curves (U'_{US} and U'_C, respectively). This additional consumer utility is the gain from trade. Trade between the United States and China is thus beneficial for both countries.

This specific example illustrates the broader claim that *every* country gains by specializing in goods it produces relatively well and trading them for the goods it produces relatively less well. This is the principle of comparative advantage. These gains are not dependent upon having an absolute cost advantage in a particular industry. The United States does not gain because it produces computers more cheaply than China. It gains because it can acquire more shirts per computer in China than it can at home. And these gains exist even if shirts cost more to produce in China than in the United States. Thus, even countries that produce every good at a higher cost than all other countries gain from trade by specializing in the goods they produce best. This is the logic of comparative advantage.

What determines which goods a particular country will produce relatively well and which it will produce relatively less well? The **Hecksher-Ohlin** (or H-O) **model**, (named after the two Swedish economists, Eli Hecksher and Bertil Ohlin who developed it) provides the standard answer. The H-O model argues that comparative advantage arises from differences in **factor endowments**. Factors are the basic tools of production. When firms produce goods, they employ labor and capital in order to transform raw materials into finished goods. Labor obviously refers to workers. Capital encompasses the entire physical plant that is used in production, including the buildings that house factories and the machines on the assembly lines inside these factories.

Countries possess these factors of production in different amounts. Some countries, like the United States, have a lot of capital but relatively little labor. Other countries, such as China, have a lot of labor but relatively little capital. These different factor endowments in turn shape the cost of production. A country's abundant factor will be cheaper to employ than its scarce factor. In the United States and other advanced industrialized countries, capital is relatively cheap and labor is relatively expensive. In developing countries, labor is relatively cheap and capital is relatively expensive.

Because countries have different factor endowments and face different factor prices, countries will hold a comparative advantage in different goods. A country will have a comparative advantage in goods produced using a lot of their abundant factor and a comparative disadvantage in goods produced using a lot of their scarce factor. In the auto industry, for example, payments to labor account for between 25 and 30 percent of the total cost of production. The much larger share of the costs of production arise from capital expenditures, that is, expenditures on the machines, assembly lines, and buildings required to build cars (Dicken 1998). In contrast, in the apparel industry, wages paid to workers account for the largest share of production costs, whereas capital expenditures account for a much smaller share of the costs of production. It follows that countries like the United States and Japan with a lot of capital and little labor will have a comparative advantage in producing cars and a comparative disadvantage in producing clothing. By the same logic, developing countries with a lot of labor and little capital will have a comparative advantage in producing clothing and a comparative disadvantage in producing cars.

Thus, in our example, the United States has a comparative advantage in computers and not in shirts because the United States is abundantly endowed with physical and human capital and poorly endowed with low-skilled labor. China has a comparative advantage in shirts and not in computers because

China is abundantly endowed with labor and poorly endowed with human and physical capital. Comparative advantage tells us, therefore, that all countries gain from trade by specializing in the goods that rely heavily on the factors of production that they hold in abundance and exchanging them for goods that make intensive use of the factors of production that are scarce in their economy.

TRADE BARGAINING

Although trade liberalization raises the standard of living, governments don't often liberalize trade unilaterally. Instead, governments strive to open foreign markets to the exports of competitive domestic industries and continue to protect less competitive industries from imports. As a result, trade liberalization generally occurs through trade **bargaining** in which governments exchange market access commitments.

We can model trade bargaining using basic spatial theory. To keep things concrete, we will model the central bargaining problem in the Doha Round. We begin by defining the bargaining space. The two issues at the center of the Doha Round are the reduction of barriers to trade in agriculture products that governments in the advanced industrialized countries impose and the reduction of barriers to trade in manufactured goods (called Non-agricultural Market Access (NAMA) in the Doha Round) that governments in developing countries impose. We can depict each of these as a policy dimension (see Figure 3.4a). The horizontal axis depicts all possible levels of agriculture protection in the advanced industrialized countries. Protection of agriculture is zero at the origin and barriers to trade rise as we move out toward the right. The vertical axis captures all possible levels of protection of manufactured goods in developing countries. Again, protection is zero at the origin and increases as we move up from the origin. Each point within the two-dimensional bargaining space represents a combination of trade barriers in industrialized-country agriculture and developing-country manufactured goods.

We can locate the current levels of protection, the status quo, in this bargaining space. The status quo is characterized by a fairly high level of protection in both sectors. The United States, the EU, and Japan excluded agriculture from multilateral trade negotiations until quite recently. Consequently, trade barriers in this sector remain quite high. Similarly, developing-country governments did not participate much in bargaining rounds prior to the Uruguay Round. As a result, they retain high tariffs on manufactured goods. Hence, the status quo, labeled SQ in Figure 3.4a, falls in the northeast quadrant of the bargaining space.

In our next step we locate government ideal points in the bargaining space. An actor's ideal point is its best possible outcome, in this instance the specific combination of barriers to trade in agriculture and manufactured goods that each actor prefers to all other combinations. Rather than depict ideal points for each of the 164 WTO members, we focus on two coalitions at the center of bargaining, the United States/EU and the Group of 20. We locate these ideal points

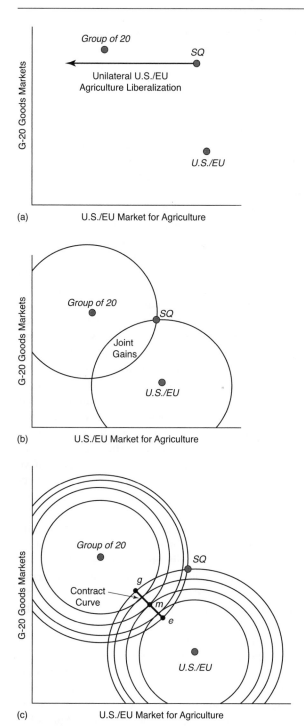

(a)

G-20 Goods Markets

Group of 20

SQ

Unilateral U.S./EU
Agriculture Liberalization

U.S./EU

U.S./EU Market for Agriculture

(b)

G-20 Goods Markets

Group of 20

SQ

Joint
Gains

U.S./EU

U.S./EU Market for Agriculture

(c)

G-20 Goods Markets

Group of 20

SQ

g

Contract
Curve

m

e

U.S./EU

U.S./EU Market for Agriculture

FIGURE 3.4
Tariff Bargaining in the Doha Round

using a simple rule—governments liberalize comparatively advantaged sectors and protect disadvantaged sectors. The United States/EU is relatively poorly endowed with land and relatively abundantly endowed with capital. The ideal outcome from their perspective is a sharp reduction of tariffs on G-20 goods markets and continued protection of their agriculture sector. Their ideal point therefore lies in the southeast quadrant of the bargaining space. Governments in the Group of 20 are abundantly endowed with land and poorly endowed with capital. The ideal outcome for these governments combines low barriers on agricultural markets in the EU and the United States, with high barriers on their goods markets. The ideal point for the Group of 20 thus lies in the northwest quadrant of the bargaining space.

Notice that given these ideal points and the status quo, neither group can improve its utility relative to the status quo from unilateral liberalization. Assume that utility for each actor is a linear function of distance; that is, utility decreases as we move away from the ideal points in any direction. Unilateral reduction of protectionist barriers on United States/EU agriculture shifts the outcome from SQ toward the left along a line parallel to the horizontal axis. Every point on this line is further from the United States/EU ideal point than SQ and thus offers less utility than the SQ. Similarly, any unilateral reduction of tariffs on manufactured goods shifts the SQ down along a line parallel to the vertical axis (not drawn). Every point on this line is further from the G-20 ideal point than SQ. Hence, neither group can realize higher utility by engaging in unilateral liberalization.

What neither is willing to do unilaterally, both are willing to do through international bargaining. To see why, we must first identify all outcomes that each group prefers to the status quo. We can see these outcomes by drawing circular indifference curves centered upon each group's ideal point, with a radius equal to the distance between this ideal point and the status quo (see Figure 3.4b). Each group prefers all outcomes interior to this indifference curve to the status quo. The combinations within the "lens" created by the intersection of the two indifference curves are thus outcomes that the G-20 and the United States/EU both prefer to the status quo. And in the vast majority of these outcomes, each group has liberalized the sector it wishes to protect quite substantially. International bargaining, therefore, enables governments to liberalize domestic sectors that they are unwilling to liberalize unilaterally.

The selection of one outcome from all of those that offer joint gains carries distributional consequences. Some agreements benefit the United States/EU more than the G-20, and some agreements benefit the G-20 more than the United States/EU. We can see this by drawing a series of indifference curves for each group (see Figure 3.4c). We then connect all the points at which the United States/EU and Group of 20 indifference curves are tangent to one another. The result is a **contract curve**—the set of mutually beneficial agreements that exhaust available joint gains. We assume that governments will select an agreement from that set. Now, each agreement on this contract curve carries a different distribution of the joint gains. If the Group of 20 and the United States/EU select the outcome represented by *m*, they divide available joint gains evenly. If they select an outcome between *m* and *e*, the United States/EU realizes larger gains than the Group of 20. If instead they choose an outcome between *m* and *g*, the Group of 20 realizes larger gains than the United States/EU. Hence, governments are not just realizing joint gains, they are also deciding how to distribute these gains between them.

Bargaining power determines which distribution of gains governments ultimately select. Although we often think of power as brute force, bargaining power derives from an array of much subtler characteristics such as patience and outside options. **Patience** refers to the fact that both parties to the negotiation would prefer to settle today rather than tomorrow. Because each side gains from agreement, delaying agreement sacrifices utility for both. But if one government is more patient than another, it can use its willingness to wait to insist on an outcome closer to its ideal point, and thereby capture more of the joint gains for itself. A government may be less patient, and thus willing to concede some of the surplus to other governments in exchange for a quick deal, if it is relatively poor (since economic gains have greater marginal utility for poorer states), or if it has a low tolerance for risking a breakdown in negotiations.

A Closer Look

Bargaining Strategy, Bargaining Power, and the Doha Round

Did the Doha Round fail as a result of a strategic miscalculation on the part of the G-20? Consider the G-20's bargaining strategy as they confronted the U.S. and the EU. The best deal for each government is the one that combines maximum concessions from other members in exchange for minimal concessions. Group of Twenty (G20) governments want large reductions in American and European agricultural protection in exchange for minimal liberalization of their manufacturing and service sectors. American and European governments seek the opposite—maximum G20 cuts in manufacturing and services in exchange for minimal cuts in farm tariffs and subsidies. In bargaining, therefore, governments were tussling over the distribution of the available joint gains, and the agreement best for a G20 government is necessarily less good for the United States and the European Union (EU) (though still better for both than no agreement).

Each government's ability to negotiate the best possible deal for itself is complicated by private information. G20 governments did not know how much American and European governments were willing to reduce farm tariffs and subsidies. Nor did they know how much they had to offer in exchange for such liberalization. Each government held these critical pieces of information about its negotiating position privately, and had no incentive to reveal them to others. If American negotiators told the G20 the maximum cuts in farm tariffs and subsidies the United States would make, then G20 governments would accept nothing less than this maximum. If the United States told the G20 governments the minimal amount of service and NAMA liberalization it expected in return, G20 governments would offer only this minimal amount. Revealing private information about their negotiating positions thus condemns governments to their worst possible deal— minimal gains and maximal concessions.

Negotiating the best deal possible thus requires governments to force each other to reveal information they do not wish to reveal. This is exactly the situation governments faced in Geneva in July 2008. Trade ministers had negotiated for 9 days. By Tuesday, they had reached the point at which each government had to decide whether the resulting package was the best deal it could get. China and India had to decide whether the United States and the EU had made their maximum concessions. Yet, they knew that asking for additional concessions was pointless— they had been asking for 9 days, and asking for more now would simply elicit a quick "No, this is my best offer." China and India could learn if, in fact, the offer on the table was the best offer only by walking away from the negotiations.

Walking away from the table constituted a strategic gambit. Walking out delivered a "costly signal": it transformed cheap talk (we want additional concessions) into costly action (we'll forgo this agreement now to get additional concessions in the future). This costly action, which demonstrated that India and China were patient, could have made American policymakers more likely to believe that additional concessions would be necessary to get a deal. Walking away could have also imposed costs on the United States by denying it an agreement it wanted. By walking out of negotiations, therefore, India and China were trying to gain information about the U.S. bargaining position. If the United States offered additional concessions, India and China would get a better deal and their gamble would have paid off. But even if the United States failed to offer additional concessions, China and India would still gain valuable information that the United States had offered all that it would offer. They could then accept the deal on the table.

This strategic gambit failed, however, because India and its allies neglected to take into full account the outside options available to the U.S. and the EU. A walk-out strategy can work only if one's bargaining partner has no opportunity to achieve its objectives by making deals with other partners. In the absence of outside options, the U.S. and EU would be compelled to reach agreement with the G-20 in the WTO. As it turned out, however, the WTO wasn't the only game in town. After 2008, the U.S. began to pursue its trade policy objectives through mega-regional trade agreements with the EU and in Asia and the Pacific. EU policymakers also began pursuing trade agreements outside of the WTO framework. Moreover, as these mega-regional negotiations progressed it became clear that the U.S. and the EU could realize more of their trade policy goals and make fewer major concessions through the mega-regional framework than by continuing to work within the larger WTO. Consequently, American policymakers came to place greater value upon the outside option and less value on the Doha Round. This made it less and less likely that they would offer major concessions to the G-20.

Of course, I don't know whether the G-20's decision to walk out was a strategic gambit or whether it reflected a sincere preference that the deal on the table didn't offer benefits. Yet, it is interesting to consider the possibility that the Doha Round could have concluded quite differently had key players made different strategic calculations.

If governments are equally patient, one government may gain bargaining power if it has an attractive outside option. An **outside option** is a government's next-best alternative to agreement. For example, if the EU can strike a similar bargain with the United States, then it has little need to make large concessions to the Group of 20: it can leverage its potential deal with the United States to extract concessions from the Groups of 20. If the Group of 20 knows this, it will be willing to allow the EU to capture a larger share of the gains than it would if the outside option of a deal with the United States did not exist. Somewhat paradoxically, therefore, giving one side a good reason to *not* reach agreement often enables governments to find common ground. The U.S. strategy of negotiating regional trade agreements, for example, might be an attempt to demonstrate an outside option in order to gain greater power within WTO negotiations.

In short, governments liberalize trade via trade agreements because they are unwilling to liberalize unilaterally. Given their focus on export expansion, trade negotiations enable governments to exchange market access commitments. Although the resulting trade agreements yield benefits to all parties, they also carry distributional consequences. Some governments will realize smaller gains in market access opportunities in exchange for larger concessions of their own. These distributional consequences reflect differences in bargaining power. Governments that are most willing to wait, that are willing to risk a breakdown of negotiations, and that have outside options are likely to capture a larger share of the available gains from agreement.

ENFORCING AGREEMENTS

The ability of governments to conclude trade agreements is additionally frustrated by the second intervention of politics: the enforcement problem. The **enforcement problem** refers to the fact that governments cannot be certain that other governments will comply with the trade agreements that they conclude (Conybeare 1984; Keohane 1984; Oye 1986). As a result, governments will be reluctant to enter into trade agreements, even when they recognize that they would benefit from doing so. Even though this might seem counterintuitive, we can use a simple game theory model, called the prisoner's dilemma, to see how the enforcement problem can frustrate the efforts of governments to conclude mutually beneficial trade agreements.

Suppose that the Group of 20 and the EU manage to identify an outcome that each prefer to the status quo. In the absence of a mechanism to enforce the agreement, would they be able to conclude the agreement? The prisoner's dilemma tells us that they will be unable to do so. In the prisoner's dilemma, the Group of 20 and the EU each have two strategy choices: each can open its market to the other's exports, which we will call *liberalize*, or each can use tariffs to keep the other's products out of its domestic market, which we will call *protect*. Two governments with two strategy choices each generates the two-by-two matrix depicted in Figure 3.5.

European Union

	Liberalize	Protect
G-20 Liberalize	*L,L* *I*	*L,P* *II*
Protect	*P,L* *IV*	*P,P* *III*

Preference Orders:
G-20: *P,L* > *L,L* > *P,P* > *L,P*
European Union: *L,P* > *L,L* > *P,P* > *P,L*

FIGURE 3.5
The Prisoner's Dilemma and Trade Liberalization

Each cell in this matrix corresponds to a strategy combination, and these strategy combinations produce outcomes. We can describe these outcomes starting in the top left cell and moving clockwise. One word about the notation we use before we proceed. It is conventional to list the strategy choice of the row player (the player who selects its strategy from the rows of the matrix) first and the strategy choice of the column player (the player who selects its strategy from the columns of the matrix) second. Thus, the strategy combination referred to as *"liberalize/protect"* means that the row player, which in this case is Group of 20, has played the strategy *liberalize* and the column player, which is the EU, has played the strategy *protect*.

We can now describe the four outcomes.

- *Liberalize/Liberalize*: Both eliminate tariffs. Group of 20 exports agricultural products to the EU, and the EU exports manufactured goods to Group of 20 countries.
- *Liberalize/Protect*: The Group of 20 eliminates tariffs, but the EU does not. The EU thus exports goods to the Group of 20, but the Group of 20 cannot export farm goods to the EU.
- *Protect/Protect*: Both retain their tariffs. No trade takes place.
- *Protect/Liberalize*: The EU eliminates tariffs, and the Group of 20 does not. The Group of 20 exports farm goods to the EU, but the EU cannot export manufactured goods to the Group of 20.

Now we must determine how each government ranks these four outcomes. How much utility do they realize from each outcome? The Group of 20 ranks them in the following order:

protect/liberalize > liberalize/liberalize > protect/protect > liberalize/protect

where the "greater than" sign means "is preferred to." It is not hard to justify this ranking.

- The Group of 20 gains the most utility from *protect/liberalize*. Here the Group of 20 exports to the EU and protects its producers from EU competition.
- The Group of 20 gains less utility from *liberalize/liberalize* than from *protect/liberalize*. Here the Group of 20 can export to the EU, but must open its market to EU imports.
- The Group of 20 gains still less utility from *protect/protect* than from *liberalize/liberalize*. Here the Group of 20 protects its domestic market, but cannot export to the EU.
- The Group of 20 gains less utility from *liberalize/protect* than from *protect/protect*. Here the Group of 20 opens its market to the EU but does not get access to the EU market.

In other words, the Group of 20's most preferred outcome is unreciprocated access to the EU market. Its second-best outcome is reciprocal tariff reductions, which is in turn better than reciprocal protection. The Group of 20's worst outcome is a unilateral tariff reduction.

The prisoner's dilemma is a symmetric game. This means that the EU faces the exact same situation as the Group of 20. Consequently, the EU's payoff order is identical to the Group of 20's payoff order. The only difference arises from the notation we use. Like the Group of 20, the EU's most preferred outcome is unreciprocated access to the other's market, but for the EU this is the outcome *liberalize/protect*. Also like the Group of 20, the EU's least preferred outcome is granting the other unreciprocated access to its market, which for the EU is the outcome *protect/liberalize*. Thus, the EU's payoff order is identical to the Group of 20's payoff order, but the position of the most and least preferred outcomes are reversed:

liberalize/protect > liberalize/liberalize > protect/protect > protect/liberalize

We can now see how the Group of 20 and the EU will play this game and what outcome will result. The Group of 20 and the EU both have a dominant strategy—a single strategy that always returns a higher payoff than all other strategy choices. *Protect* is this dominant strategy. *Protect* dominates *liberalize* as a strategy choice because each government will always realize higher utility by playing *protect* than by playing *liberalize*.

We can see why *protect* is a dominant strategy by working through the Group of 20's best responses to the EU's strategy choices. Suppose the EU plays the strategy *liberalize*. If the Group of 20 plays *liberalize* in response, the Group of 20 receives its second most preferred outcome (*liberalize/liberalize*). If the Group of 20 plays *protect* in response, the Group of 20 receives its most preferred outcome (*protect/liberalize*). Thus, if the EU plays *liberalize*, the Group of 20's best response—the strategy that returns the highest utility—is *protect*.

Now suppose the EU plays *protect*. If the Group of 20 responds with *liberalize*, it receives its least preferred outcome (*liberalize/protect*). If the Group of 20 responds with *protect*, however, it receives its second least preferred outcome (*protect/protect*). Thus, if the EU plays *protect*, the Group of 20's best response is to play *protect*.

Protect, therefore, "dominates" *liberalize* as a strategy choice—that is, *protect* yields more utility for the Group of 20 than *liberalize* regardless of the strategy that the EU plays. Because the prisoner's dilemma is symmetric, *protect* is also the EU's dominant strategy. Because both governments have dominant strategies to play *protect*, the game always yields the same outcome: the Group of 20 and the EU both play *protect* and the game ends at the *protect/protect* outcome. Governments in both groups retain tariffs and no trade occurs.

This outcome has two important characteristics. First, it is **Pareto suboptimal**. Pareto optimality is a way to conceptualize social welfare. An outcome is Pareto optimal when no single actor can be made better off without at the same time making another actor worse off. Pareto suboptimal refers to outcomes in which it is possible for at least one actor to improve its position without any other actor being made worse off. In the prisoner's dilemma the *protect/protect* outcome is Pareto suboptimal because both governments realize higher payoffs at *liberalize/liberalize* than at *protect/protect*. Thus, rational behavior on the part of each individual government, each playing its dominant strategy *protect*, produces a suboptimal collective outcome. The Group of 20 and the EU are both poorer than they would be if they liberalized trade.

Second, the *protect/protect* outcome is a **Nash equilibrium**. A Nash equilibrium is an outcome at which neither player has an incentive to change strategies unilaterally. If the Group of 20 changes its strategy from *protect* to *liberalize*, the outcome shifts to *liberalize/protect*, the Group of 20's least preferred outcome. Thus, the Group of 20 has no incentive to change its strategy unilaterally. If the EU changes its strategy from *protect* to *liberalize*, the outcome moves to *protect/liberalize*, the EU's least preferred outcome. Thus, the EU has no incentive to change its strategy unilaterally either. Putting these two points together reveals the prisoner's dilemma's central conclusion: even though the Group of 20 and the EU would both gain from reciprocal tariff reductions, neither has an incentive to reduce tariffs. More broadly, the prisoner's dilemma suggests that even when all countries would clearly benefit from trade liberalization, political dynamics trap governments in a protectionist world.

Governments are unable to conclude agreements that make them all better off because each fears getting the "sucker payoff." If the Group of 20 and the EU agree to liberalize trade and then the Group of 20 complies with this agreement but the EU does not, the EU has exploited the Group of 20. The Group of 20 suffers the "costs" of rising imports without getting the "benefit" of increased exports. The gains from trade liberalization could be achieved, of course, if governments could enforce international trade agreements. Governments could agree in advance *to play* strategies if they were confident that cheating would be caught and punished. Moreover, because cheating would be punished, both would comply with the agreement. The international system provides no enforcement mechanism, however. Domestic political systems rely upon the police and the judicial system to enforce laws, but the international system does not have an authoritative and effective judicial system. Instead, the international system is anarchic; that is, it is a political system without an overarching political authority capable of enforcing the rules of the game.

Although the prisoner's dilemma is pessimistic about the prospect for international trade cooperation, cooperation in a prisoner's dilemma is not impossible. Cooperation can emerge if three specific conditions are met. First, cooperation can emerge in an iterated prisoner's dilemma, that is, in a game played repeatedly by the same governments (see Taylor 1976; Axelrod 1984; Keohane 1984; Oye 1986). Iteration changes the nature of the reward structure that governments face. In a one-shot play of the prisoner's dilemma, countries make a one-time choice and receive a one-time payoff. In an iterated game, however, governments make repeated choices and receive a stream of payoffs over time. Assuming that the two other necessary conditions are met, governments will prefer the stream of payments they receive from cooperating over time to the payoff they receive from cheating on an agreement. Iterating the game can therefore make it rational for a government to play the *liberalize* strategy.

Second, governments must use reciprocity strategies to enforce the *liberalize/liberalize* outcome. Although many **reciprocity** strategies exist, the most well known is called **tit-for-tat** (Axelrod 1984). In tit-for-tat, each government plays the strategy that its partner played in the previous round of the game. Trade liberalization by one government in one round of play is met by trade liberalization from the other government in the next round. Should one government play *protect* in one round (that is, cheat on an existing trade agreement), the other government must play *protect* in the next round of play. Playing such tit-for-tat strategies allows governments to reward each other for cooperation and punish each other for cheating.

Finally, governments must care about the payoffs they will receive in future rounds of the game. If governments fully discount future payoffs, the iterated game essentially reverts back to a single play of the prisoner's dilemma; when it does, the threat of punishment in the next round of play can hardly be expected to promote cooperation in the current round. But if governments care about the future and if they use a reciprocity strategy such as tit-for-tat, then cooperation in an iterated prisoner's dilemma becomes rational: each government can realize a larger stream of payoffs by cooperating than it can realize by defecting.

The WTO provides the first two of these three necessary conditions. It helps iterate the game by creating expectations of repeated interaction. Membership in the WTO has been relatively stable. The number of countries that belong to the WTO has increased over time, and very few countries have left the organization after joining. As a consequence, WTO members know that the governments with which they negotiate today will be the governments with which they negotiate tomorrow, next year, and on into the future. In addition, WTO members interact regularly within the organization. Governments have already concluded eight formal bargaining rounds and are now engaged in the ninth such round. In addition to these formal rounds of negotiations, the WTO draws governments together for annual and semi-annual reviews of national trade policies. By bringing the same set of governments together in a regularized pattern of interaction, the WTO iterates intergovernmental trade interactions.

The WTO also provides the information that governments need in order to use reciprocity strategies. In order to use a tit-for-tat strategy effectively, governments must know when their partners are complying with trade agreements and when they are cheating. The WTO makes this easier by collecting and disseminating information on its members' trade policies. Moreover, WTO rules provide clear standards against which governments' trade policies can be evaluated. The WTO's most-favored nation clause, for example, prohibits discriminatory practices except under a set of well-defined exceptions. To give another example, the WTO's rules governing domestic safeguards define the conditions that must be met in order for governments to temporarily opt out of commitments. These detailed rules increase transparency. Transparency means that it is easier for governments to determine whether a specific trade measure adopted by a particular government is or is not consistent with WTO rules. The high-quality information and the transparency provided by the WTO allow governments to monitor the behavior of other WTO members. This in turn makes it easier for governments to use reciprocity strategies to enforce trade agreements.

The ability of governments to use the WTO to enforce trade agreements is most clearly evident in the WTO's **dispute settlement mechanism**. The dispute settlement mechanism follows a standard procedure that was agreed to by all members of the WTO during the Uruguay Round (see Figure 3.6). A dispute is initiated when a government brings an alleged violation of WTO rules to the WTO Dispute Settlement Body (DSB, consisting of all WTO members). The DSB initially encourages the governments involved in the dispute to try to resolve the conflict through direct consultations. If such consultations are unsuccessful, the DSB creates a formal panel to investigate the complaint.

This panel is typically composed of three experts in trade law who are selected by the DSB in consultation with the governments involved in the dispute. The panel reviews the evidence in the case, meets with the parties to the dispute and outside experts if necessary, and prepares a final report that it submits to the DSB. The DSB must accept the panel's final report unless all WTO members, including the government that initially brought the complaint, vote against its adoption.

Both governments can appeal the panel's decision. If an appeal is requested, the DSB creates an appellate body composed of three to five people drawn from a list of seven permanent members. The appellate body can uphold, reverse, or modify the panel's findings, conclusions, and recommendations. The appellate report is given to the DSB for approval, and as with the panel report, the DSB can reject the report only with the consent of all member governments. If at the end of this process it is determined that the disputed trade measure is inconsistent with WTO rules, the government must alter its policy to conform to the rule in question or compensate the injured parties. The entire dispute

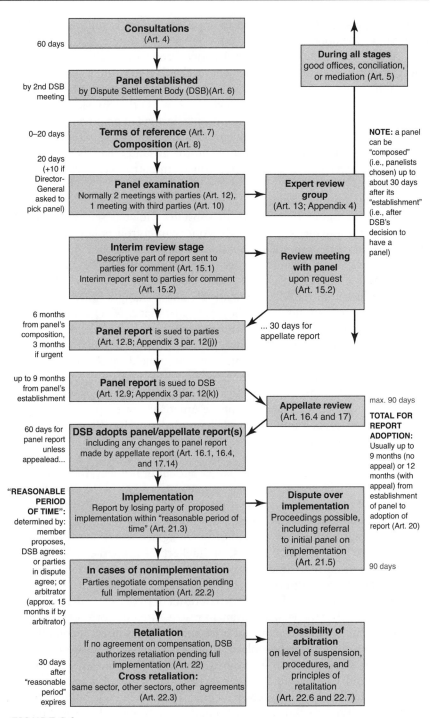

FIGURE 3.6
The Dispute Settlement Mechanism

settlement process, from initiation to appellate report, is supposed to take no longer than 15 months.

An ongoing dispute involving American cotton subsidies illustrates how governments use the dispute-settlement mechanism to enforce compliance with trade agreements (see Schnepf 2010). The cotton subsidy case began in 2002. The Brazilian government complained to the WTO that subsidies paid by the U.S. government to American cotton farmers provided an advantage in global markets that harmed Brazil's cotton growers and violated WTO rules. The Bush administration defended the measures on the grounds that the subsidies represented a "safety net" that protected American cotton growers from volatile global commodity markets. Because the two governments could not settle the dispute through initial discussions, the WTO established a panel in early 2003.

The panel found that American subsidies violated several WTO rules. In particular, the panel ruled that the American cotton policy constituted an export subsidy and domestic production support that harmed Brazilian cotton growers. Although the United States appealed the ruling, the appellate panel upheld it. As a result, the United States modified its policy in an attempt to bring it in line with its WTO obligations. These changes failed to satisfy the Brazilian government, however. They requested that a WTO compliance panel evaluate whether the American adjustment brought the subsidies' regime in line with WTO rules. The compliance panel sided with Brazil; it found that the U.S. policy change was insufficient, a finding upheld by the appellate panel. As a consequence, the WTO authorized Brazil to retaliate against the United States by imposing tariffs on imports of U.S. goods into Brazil up to as much as $823 million per year, the amount the American cotton policy cost Brazil.

Brazil's threatened imposition of these retaliatory tariffs induced the U.S. government to negotiate a less costly solution to the dispute. In April 2010 the two governments announced the results of these negotiations. Arguing that cotton subsidies formed part of its larger agricultural policy, the United States agreed to reform its cotton subsidies regime only as part of the 2012 Farm Bill. Second, until the subsidies regime is reformed, the United States agreed to pay Brazil $147 million per year for capacity-building and technical improvement in Brazilian agribusiness. In exchange, Brazil agreed to not impose retaliatory tariffs against U.S. goods, services, or intellectual property. In other words, Brazil accepted current American policy, even though it violated WTO rules, and the United States agreed to compensate Brazil for doing so.

The dispute finally ended in 2014 as a result of two developments. The most important was that the U.S. government restructured its cotton support in the 2014 Farm Bill. Congress removed price supports and direct income supports for cotton producers. In their place, Congress enacted an insurance program that growers must pay into in order to qualify for payments. Moreover, the insurance fund compensated farmers when they suffered a loss rather than providing benefits to ensure a given income. These changes brought U.S. policy into conformity with WTO rules. Second, once the 2014 Farm Bill was in place, Brazil offered to negotiate a final agreement that would end the dispute. In this agreement, announced on October 1, 2014, Brazil agreed to drop the cotton dispute and refrain from initiating any new WTO actions in return for U.S. commitment to the terms of the Farm Bill and a one-time payment to the Brazil Cotton Institute of $300 million.

The cotton case illustrates how governments can use tit-for-tat strategies to enforce trade agreements. An alleged defection by the United States prompted a WTO investigation. This investigation indicated that U.S. policy violated WTO rules, and when the United States failed to bring its policies into line with its obligations, Brazil was allowed to retaliate by withdrawing concessions it had made previously to the Americans. In the language of the iterated prisoner's dilemma, the United States defected and Brazil, playing a tit-for-tat strategy, defected in response. Moreover, Brazilian retaliation came only after the WTO had determined that it was justified and the scale of the retaliation was proportionate to the injury suffered. Although the WTO's dispute resolution mechanism focuses our attention on a legalistic version of tit-for-tat, it also allows us to see in a very detailed way how the WTO can promote trade cooperation by helping governments enforce trade agreements. The cotton dispute is especially interesting as an illustration of how even (arguably) the most powerful WTO member can be made to bring its policies into accordance with its WTO obligations.

The WTO thus helps governments gain the assurances they need in order to conclude the trade agreements required to capture the gains from trade. The WTO provides this assurance by allowing governments to monitor the behavior of their trade partners and to enforce the trade agreements they reach. By doing so, the WTO enables societies to capture the welfare gains the trade provides. In the absence of the WTO, or an institution that performed similar functions, it is unlikely that governments would be able to reach the agreements required to liberalize trade. Each society, and thus the world as a whole, would be poorer as a result.

CONCLUSION

The WTO exists, therefore, because it facilitates international cooperation, thereby enabling societies to capture the welfare gains available from trade. Trade raises social welfare by enabling consumers to enjoy a higher level of utility than if they could consume only goods produced at home. The principle of comparative advantage tells us that these welfare gains do not require a country to have an absolute advantage in anything. As long as a country is better at doing some things than others, it gains by specializing in what it does relatively well and trading for everything else.

Politics, however, makes it difficult for societies to realize these gains from trade. For reasons we examine in greater detail in the next chapter, governments often neglect consumer interests in favor of producer interests. Consequently, governments can capture the gains from trade only by negotiating agreements in which they exchange market access commitments. In such bargaining, governments strive to gain access to foreign markets for their comparatively advantaged industries in exchange for granting access to their markets in their comparatively disadvantaged industries. Consequently, governments employ bargaining power in an attempt to gain maximum access in exchange for minimal concessions. By providing a forum for bargaining, the WTO enables governments to liberalize trade more than they would be willing to do unilaterally.

Yet, concluding trade agreements is also complicated by the enforcement problem. Governments must believe that cooperation on their part will be reciprocated by cooperation from their partners. They must believe that their partners will not try to take advantage of them. And as the prisoner's dilemma highlights, unless such assurances are provided, governments have little incentive to cooperate. The international trade system lacks the equivalent of a state to enforce agreements, and thus governments face a pervasive enforcement problem when they try to cooperate for mutual gain. Consequently, it is difficult for governments to conclude mutually beneficial agreements, and as a result, societies have lower standards of living.

The WTO helps governments solve this enforcement problem. By enabling governments to feel reasonably secure that their partners will comply with the agreements they enter, the WTO provides the assurances necessary to achieve cooperation. Strictly speaking, the WTO is not an international equivalent of a state because the WTO does not have the authority or the capacity to punish governments that fail to comply with trade agreements. Instead, the WTO facilitates international cooperation by providing an infrastructure that allows governments to enforce agreements themselves. By providing a set of mutually agreed rules, by helping governments monitor the extent to which their partners comply with these rules, and by providing a dispute-settlement mechanism that helps governments resolve those issues of compliance that do arise, the WTO enables governments to enforce effectively the trade agreements that they reach. The WTO thus provides enough assurance that all governments will live up to the agreements that they enter into and that no government will be able to take advantage of the others. By providing this infrastructure, the WTO enables governments to conclude the trade agreements necessary to capture the welfare gains from trade.

KEY TERMS

Bargaining
Contract Curve
Dispute Settlement
    Mechanism
Enforcement Problem

Factor Endowments
Hecksher-Ohlin Model
Nash Equilibrium
Outside Option
Pareto Suboptimal

Patience
Reciprocity
Tit-For-Tat

SUGGESTIONS FOR FURTHER READING

For an approach that emphasizes the intuition of the theory of comparative advantage and downplays explicit theory, see Russell D. Roberts, *The Choice: A Fable of Free Trade and Protectionism*, 3rd edition (New York: Pearson, 2006).

For an excellent account of the theoretical debate over free trade, see Douglas A. Irwin, *Free Trade Under Fire*, 3rd edition (Princeton: Princeton University Press, 2015).

For comprehensive treatment of the WTO dispute settlement system, you should refer to The World Trade Organization, *A Handbook on the WTO Dispute Settlement System*, 2nd edition (Cambridge: Cambridge University Press, 2017).

For an evaluation of the dispute settlement mechanism's effectiveness, see Chad P. Bown and Petros C. Mavroidis, 2017. "WTO Dispute Settlement in 2015: Going Strong after Two Decades." *World Trade Review* 16(2): 153–158.

A Society-Centered Approach to Trade Politics

O ur focus on the international politics of trade has bracketed an important question—what determines the specific trade objectives that governments pursue when bargaining within the WTO, when negotiating regional trade arrangements, or when making unilateral trade-policy decisions? We take up this question in this chapter and the next by examining two approaches to trade politics rooted in domestic politics. This chapter examines a society-centered approach to trade politics. A society-centered approach argues that a government's trade policy objectives are shaped by politicians' responses to interest groups' demands. This approach suggests that the Trump administration's determination to renegotiate NAFTA and other free-trade agreements is a response to specific demands made by important domestic economic groups of workers and firms. Similarly, a society-centered approach argues that the British decision to leave the European Union (Brexit) reflects the economic interests of workers as voters who have been or fear that they will be displaced as a result of trade between Britain and the other European Union economies. Moreover, most of the domestic opposition to Brexit and to the Trump administration's re-evaluation of America's trade deals emerges largely from domestic economic groups that benefit from these trade agreements.

To understand the political dynamics of this competition, the society-centered approach emphasizes the interplay between organized interests and political institutions. The approach is based on the recognition that trade has distributional consequences. In North Carolina, for instance, people who had been employed in the textile and apparel industry—traditionally a large employer of low-skill labor—were hit very hard by trade liberalization. Between 2000 and 2004, 207 textile and apparel factories across the state closed down, and about 44,000 people lost their jobs. In contrast, North Carolinians employed in the pharmaceutical industry or in finance have benefited from trade liberalization. The average wage earned by people employed in these industries rose in the first half of this decade, as did the total number of jobs available in these industries. In North Carolina, therefore, some people have gained from trade, whereas others have lost.

These distributional consequences generate political competition as the winners and losers from trade turn to the political arena to advance and defend their economic interests. The American Textile Manufacturers Institute and the National Council of Textile Organizations, business associations representing textile and apparel firms, pressure American politicians for more stringent controls on textile and apparel imports. They are joined by other business associations representing businesses harmed by trade liberalization. A protectionist coalition gradually begins to form. The Coalition of Service Industries, a business association that represents American financial-services firms (and many other service industry firms), pressures the U.S. government to conclude WTO negotiations aimed at liberalizing world trade in services. As other groups that benefit from expanded trade join them, a pro-liberalization coalition begins to form. Exactly how this competition unfolds—which groups organize to lobby, what coalitions arise, how politicians respond to interest-group demands, which groups' interests are reflected in trade policy and which groups' interests are not—is shaped by the political institutions within which it takes place.

This chapter develops the analytical tools central to a society-centered approach. We focus first on interest-group preferences—which groups prefer protectionism, which groups prefer liberalization, and why? We use trade theory to develop some systematic expectations about trade policy preferences, and we use collective action theory to understand which groups will organize to pursue their interests. We then turn our attention to political institutions, looking at how different institutional frameworks create different kinds of interest representation. We conclude by discussing some of the weaknesses of this approach.

TRADE POLICY PREFERENCES

Because a society-centered approach argues that trade policy reflects interest-group demands, it devotes considerable attention to the source, content, and organization of these demands. Here we examine two standard models of trade policy preferences: the factor model and the sector model. The two models agree that raising and lowering tariffs redistributes income, and they agree that these income consequences are the source of trade policy preferences. The two models offer distinctive conceptions of how trade's income consequences divide society. We examine both models and then turn our attention to the collective action problem that shapes the ability of groups with common interests to organize in order to lobby the government on behalf of their desired policies.

Factor Incomes and Class Conflict

The factor model argues that trade politics are driven by competition between factors of production—that is, by competition between labor and capital, between workers and capitalists. Labor and capital have distinct trade policy preferences because trade's income effects divide society along factor lines. Whenever tariffs are lowered and trade expanded (or tariffs raised and trade restricted), one factor will experience rising income, whereas the other will see its income fall. Trade, therefore, places labor and capital in direct competition with each other over the distribution of national income. To fully understand the reason for this competition, we need to look at how trade affects factor incomes.

To do so, we are going to make some assumptions. First, we will assume that there are only two countries in the world: the United States and China. Second, we will assume that both countries produce two goods: shirts and computers. Third, we will assume that each country uses two factors of production, labor and capital, to produce both goods. Fourth, we will assume that shirt production relies heavily on labor and less heavily on capital, whereas computer production requires a lot of capital and little labor. Finally, we will assume that the United States is endowed with a lot of capital and little labor, whereas China is endowed with a lot of labor and little capital. These assumptions merely restate the standard trade model that we learned in Chapter 3.

These assumptions establish who produces what. First, capital will be relatively cheap and labor will be relatively expensive in the United States, whereas the opposite will be the case in China. Consequently, the United States will export the capital-intensive good (computers) and will import the labor-intensive good (shirts). China will export the labor-intensive good and import the capital-intensive good.

We can now see what happens to factor incomes in the United States and China as they engage in trade. We look first at the United States. When the United States begins to import shirts from China, demand for American-made shirts falls. As demand for American shirts falls, American firms manufacture fewer of them. As shirt production falls, apparel firms liquidate the capital they had invested in shirt factories, and they lay off their employees. At the same time, American computer firms are expanding production in response to the growing Chinese demand for American computers. As American computer production expands, computer firms demand more capital and labor, and they begin to employ capital and labor released by the shirt industry.

There is an imbalance, however, between the amount of labor and capital being released by the shirt industry and the amount being absorbed into the computer industry. The imbalance arises because the two industries use labor and capital in different proportions. The labor-intensive shirt industry uses a lot of labor and little capital, and so as it shrinks, it releases a lot of labor and less capital. The capital-intensive computer industry employs lots of capital and less labor, and so as it expands it demands more capital and less labor than the shirt industry is releasing.

Consequently, the price of capital and labor will change. More capital is being demanded than is being released, causing the price of capital to rise. People who own capital, therefore, now earn a higher return than they did prior to trade with China. Less labor is being demanded than is being released, causing the price of labor to fall. Workers, therefore, now earn less than they did prior to trade with China. For the United States, then, trade with China causes the return to capital to rise and wages to fall.

The same dynamic is taking place in China, but in the opposite direction. As demand for Chinese computers falls, Chinese firms manufacture fewer computers. As computer production falls, Chinese computer manufacturers liquidate the capital they have invested in computer factories and they lay off their employees. Chinese shirt firms are expanding in response to the growing demand in the United States and they demand more capital and labor. The Chinese shirt industry thus absorbs capital and labor released from the computer industry.

Again, however, there is an imbalance between the factors being released and those being demanded. The computer industry uses lots of capital and little labor, and so as it shrinks, it releases lots of capital and only a little labor. Yet, the shirt industry employs a lot of labor and relatively little capital. So, as it expands, it is demanding more labor and less capital than the computer industry is releasing.

Consequently, the relative prices of capital and labor change. More labor is being demanded than is being released, causing the price of labor to rise. Less capital is demanded than is being released, causing the price of capital to fall. Trade with the United States has caused the wages earned by Chinese workers to rise and the return to Chinese capital to fall.

Trade between the United States and China has thus caused changes in the incomes earned by workers and capitalists in both countries. Abundant American capital and abundant Chinese labor both gained from trade. Scarce American labor and scarce Chinese capital both lost. More generally, therefore, trade raises the income of society's abundant factor and reduces the income of society's scarce factor. If we allow this trade to continue uninterrupted, then over time, factor incomes in the United States and China will equalize. That is, wages for American workers will fall and wages for Chinese workers will rise until wages in the two countries are the same. The return to capital in the two countries will also equalize. The return to Chinese capital will fall and the return to American capital will rise until the return to capital in the two countries is the same. The tendency for trade to cause factor prices to converge is known as **factor-price equalization** (or the **Stolper-Samuelson Theorem**).

Trade policy preferences follow directly from these income effects. Because trade causes the scarce factor's income to fall, scarce factors want to minimize trade. Scarce factors thus demand high tariffs in order to keep foreign products out of the home market. Because trade causes the abundant factor's income to rise, abundant factors want to maximize trade. Abundant factors thus prefer low tariffs in order to capture the gains from trade. In the United States and other capital abundant countries, the factor model predicts that owners of capital (the abundant factor) will prefer liberal trade policies, whereas workers (the scarce factor) will prefer protectionist trade policies. In developing countries, the factor model predicts that labor will prefer liberal trade policies, whereas owners of capital will prefer protection. Trade politics are thus driven by conflict between labor and business (or capital). Because this competition pits workers against capitalists, the factor model is often called a class-based model of trade politics.

The **factor model** suggests that the debate over trade policy is a conflict over the distribution of national income between American labor and American business. Because trade reduces the income of American workers, these workers, and the organizations that represent them, have an incentive to oppose further liberalization and to advocate more protectionist policies. And indeed, American labor unions have been very critical of globalization. The AFL-CIO, a federation of 64 labor unions representing 13 million American workers, has been among the most prominent critics of globalization. Although the AFL-CIO does not consider itself protectionist, it has fought consistently to prevent passage of fast-track authority. It is also highly critical of the North American Free Trade Agreement (NAFTA) and was opposed to the Trans-Pacific Partnership (TPP). Moreover, a large body of evidence indicates that support for trade liberalization is lowest among that segment of the American work force with the least amount of formal education, so-called low-skilled workers (see, e.g., Scheve and Slaughter 2001b; Hainmeueller and Hiscox 2006; Bloningen 2008).

Conversely, because trade raises the return to American capital, American businesses should be strong supporters of globalization. And American business has been very supportive of globalization. The Business Roundtable, a business association composed of the chief executives of the largest American corporations, strongly supports globalization. It has been an active lobbyist for fast-track authority, it supports NAFTA and the FTAA, and it strongly supported China's entry into the WTO. The National Association of Manufacturers, which represents about 14,000 American manufacturing firms, also supports the WTO and regional trade arrangements. Trade policy demands from American labor and capital thus reflect the income consequences that the factor model highlights. American trade politics does seem to be shaped by competition over national income between workers and capitalists.

We conclude with an important qualification. The emergence of conflict between workers and capitalists is based on the assumption, embodied in our simple two-factor model, that American labor is homogeneous—all workers are identical. Workers are not homogeneous, however, and at a minimum, we need to divide labor into distinct skill categories, such as low-and high-skill, and treat each category as a distinct factor of production. A model that allows for different skill categories among workers yields different conclusions about trade's impact on the incomes of American workers. Trade still reduces the income of low-skilled American workers; high-skilled workers, however, which are an abundant factor in the United States, would see their incomes rise.

Sector Incomes and Industry Conflict

The **sector model** argues that trade politics are driven by competition between industries. Industries have distinct preferences because trade's income effects divide society along industry lines. Whenever tariffs are raised or lowered, wages and the return to capital employed in some industries both rise, whereas wages and the return to capital employed in other industries both fall. Trade, therefore, pits the workers and capitalists employed in one industry against the workers and capitalists employed in another industry in the conflict over the distribution of national income.

Policy Analysis and Debate

Trade Adjustment

Question

How should governments respond to the economic dislocation caused by trade?

Overview

Most economists believe that trade does not change the number of jobs in the local economy. Instead, trade changes the kinds of jobs that are available. Jobs in import-competing industries disappear as firms shut down or move offshore. In the meantime, jobs are created in export-oriented industries. The jobs created offset the jobs lost.

The jobs being created are quite different from the ones that are eliminated. In North Carolina, for example, trade has eliminated low-skilled jobs in the apparel industry while creating high-skilled jobs in high-technology industries. Society as a whole is much better off over the long run with these high-paying jobs than it is with low-paying jobs.

In the short run, however, the inevitable adjustment creates some real policy dilemmas. It is difficult for workers to move from low-skilled to high-skilled jobs. Typically, low-skilled workers have a high school education at best and in many instances are 40 years old or older. This segment of the population finds it very difficult to become employed in high-technology industries. Moreover, even if it weren't so difficult, many would find it necessary to abandon the communities in which they were born and raised to take a job in a new town. What policies should governments use to manage this trade adjustment problem?

Policy Options

■ *Protectionism*: Governments should raise tariffs or use other means to protect industries threatened by import competition. By protecting industries from import competition, this policy would protect the most vulnerable from the forces of economic dislocation.

■ *Adjustment Assistance*: Governments should establish programs to retrain workers. This policy would help workers move from declining to expanding industries with less difficulty.

Policy Analysis

- What are the costs and the benefits of each policy?
- Who pays the costs for each policy?
- Is one policy more feasible politically than the other? If so, why?

What Do You Think?

- Which policy do you advocate? Justify your choice.
- What criticisms of your position would you anticipate? How would you defend your recommendation against those criticisms?

Resources

Online: Do an online search for U.S. government trade adjustment policy. Compare the U.S. approach with that of another country. (Sweden provides a strong contrast.) Search for the terms *trade adjustment assistance Sweden* and *labor market policy Sweden*.

In Print: Alan V. Deardorff and Robert Stern, *The Social Dimensions of U.S. Trade Policy* (Ann Arbor: University of Michigan Press, 2000); Kenneth F. Scheve and Matthew J. Slaughter, 2007, "A New Deal for Globalization," *Foreign Affairs 86* (July/August); Howard F. Rosen, "Designing a National Strategy for Responding to Economic Dislocation," Testimony before the Subcommittee on Investigation and Oversight House Science and Technology Committee, June 24, 2008. *www.petersoninstitute.org/publications/papers/print.cfm?doc=pub&ResearchID=967*.

The sector model argues that trade divides society across industry rather than factor lines because the assumptions it makes about factor mobility are different from the assumptions embodied in the factor model. **Factor mobility** refers to the ease with which labor and capital can move from one industry to another. The factor model assumes that factors are highly mobile; labor and capital can move easily from one industry to another. Thus, capital currently employed in the apparel industry can be quickly shifted to the computer industry. Similarly, workers currently engaged in apparel production can easily shift to computer production. When factors are mobile, people's economic interests are determined by their factor ownership. Workers care about what happens to labor, whereas capitalists care about the return to capital.

The sector model assumes that factors are not easily moved from one industry to another. Instead, factors are tied, or **specific**, to the sector in which they are currently employed. Capital currently employed in apparel production cannot easily move to the computer industry. What use does a loom or a spinning machine have in the computer industry? Workers also often have industry-specific skills that do not transfer easily from one sector to another. A worker who has spent 15 years maintaining sophisticated automated looms and spinning machines in an apparel plant cannot easily transfer these skills to computer production. In addition, the geography of industry location often means that quitting a job in one industry to take a job in another requires workers to physically relocate. Shifting from apparel production to automobile production might require a worker to move from North Carolina to Michigan. Logistical obstacles to physical relocation can be insurmountable. A worker may not be able to sell his house because the decline of the local industry has contributed to a more general economic decline in his community. Complex social and psychological factors also intervene, as it is difficult to abandon the network of social relations that one has developed over many years. The combination of specific skills, logistical problems, and attachments to an established community mean that labor cannot always move from one industry to another.

When factors are immobile, trade affects the incomes of all factors employed in a given industry in the same way. We can see why by returning to our U.S.–China example. Consider the apparel industry first. Shirt imports from China lead to less shirt production in the United States. Factories are closed, and workers are laid off. As in the factor model, apparel workers see their incomes fall. In contrast to the factor model, however, the owners of capital employed in apparel production also see their incomes fall. Why? Because capital is immobile and therefore capital employed in apparel production cannot move into the computer industry. As demand for American shirts falls, demand for capital employed in the American shirt industry must also fall. As it does, the return to this capital must also fall. Workers and business owners in the apparel sector thus both suffer from trade.

The opposite consequences are evident in the computer industry. Trade's impact on the return to capital employed in the computer industry is similar to the factor model. As computer production expands, increasing demand for capital raises the return to capital employed in the computer industry. Trade's impact on the incomes of workers employed in the computer industry is quite different from the factor model's prediction. The factor model tells us that computer workers see their incomes fall as they compete against the workers released by the apparel industry. With more people chasing fewer jobs, all workers' incomes fall. The sector model argues that computer workers' incomes rise. Because labor is immobile, the workers released by the apparel industry cannot move into the computer industry. Greater demand for labor in the computer industry increases the wages paid to workers already employed in the industry. Thus, capital and labor employed in the American computer industry both gain from trade.

When factors are immobile, it makes little sense to speak of the interests of a unified labor or capital class. The apparel worker loses from trade; the computer worker gains. Roger Milliken (owner of the world's largest privately owned textile firm, Milliken & Company) loses from trade while Michael Dell (founder of Dell Computers) gains. Consequently, trade policy interests are defined in terms of the industry in which people work or have invested their capital. Apparel workers and Roger Milliken will have a common interest in trade policy. Computer workers and Michael Dell will have a common interest in trade policy. Trade politics is then driven by competition between the workers and capitalists who gain from trade and the workers and capitalists who lose. The result is not class conflict, but conflict between industries.

We can be very precise about which industries gain and which lose from trade. Labor and capital employed in industries that rely intensively on society's abundant factor (that is, the country's comparatively advantaged industries) both gain from trade. In the advanced industrialized countries, this means that labor and capital employed in capital-intensive and high-technology industries, such as computers, pharmaceuticals, and biotechnology, gain from trade. As a group, these industries are referred to as the **export-oriented sector**. Conversely, labor and capital employed in industries that rely intensively on society's scarce factor (that is, the country's comparatively disadvantaged industries) lose from trade. In the advanced industrialized countries, this means that the incomes of owners of capital and workers employed in labor-intensive sectors such as apparel and footwear will fall as a result of trade. As a group, these industries are commonly referred to as the **import-competing sector**. Thus, the sector model argues that trade politics is driven by competition between the import-competing and export-oriented sectors.

The sector model adds nuance to our understanding of the political debate over globalization. The factor model suggests that the debate over globalization pits labor against capital, and the sector model suggests that this political debate often pits capital and labor in import-competing industries against capital and labor in export-oriented industries. We might expect therefore that UNITE (the Union of Needletrades, Industrial and Textile Employees), the principal union in the American apparel industry, and the American Textile Manufacturers Institute (ATMI), a business association representing American textile firms, would both oppose globalization. Indeed, this is what we find. UNITE has been a vocal opponent of NAFTA, of the FTAA, and of fast-track authority. For its part, the ATMI has not been critical of all trade agreements, but it has opposed free-trade agreements with South Korea and Singapore, has been very critical of the American decision to grant China permanent normal trade status, and does not support further opening of the U.S. market to foreign textiles through multilateral trade negotiations (American Textile Manufacturers Institute 2001). In general, labor and capital employed in textile and apparel are both skeptical of globalization.

Conversely, the sector model predicts that capital and labor employed in export-oriented industries will both support globalization. It is relatively easy to document such support among American export-oriented firms. A coalition of business associations representing American high-tech firms—including the Consumer Electronics Association, Electronic Industries Alliance, Information Technology Industry Council, MultiMedia Telecommunications Association, and The Semiconductor Industry Association—has supported fast-track authority, the approval of normal trade relations with China, NAFTA, and the FTAA. It is more difficult to document attitudes of workers employed in these industries, in large part because workers in high-technology sectors are not unionized to the same extent as workers in many manufacturing industries. However, workers in high-tech industries are predominantly high skilled, and on average, high-skilled workers are more supportive of trade liberalization than low-skilled workers (Scheve and Slaughter 2001a, 2001b). Although this is indirect evidence, it is consistent with the prediction that both labor and capital employed in American high-technology industries will support globalization.

The factor and sector models thus both argue that trade policy preferences are determined by the income consequences of trade. Trade raises the incomes of some groups and lowers the incomes of others. Those who gain from trade prefer trade liberalization, whereas those who lose prefer protectionism. Each model offers a distinct pattern of trade policy preferences, however, based on distinct conceptions of how the income effects of trade divide society (see Table 4.1). The factor model states that trade divides society across factor lines and that, consequently, trade politics is driven by conflict between labor and capital. The sector model states that trade divides society along sector lines and that, consequently, trade politics is driven by conflict between import-competing and export-oriented industries. These distinct patterns are based on the assumptions each model makes about factor mobility. The factor model assumes that factors are highly mobile, and therefore people define their interests in terms of factor ownership. The sector model assumes that factors are immobile, and thus people define their interests in terms of the industry in which they earn their living.

Some recent research challenges the assumption that trade policy preferences reflect narrowly defined economic self-interest (see, e.g., Mansfield and Mutz 2009, 2013; Mutz and Kim 2017; Mansfield, Mutz and Brackbill 2016; Rho and Tomz 2015, 2017). Rather than base trade policy preferences on their factor ownership or on the sector in which they are employed, this research suggests that people base their trade policy preferences on perceptions or beliefs

TABLE 4.1

Two Models of Interest-Group Competition over Trade Policy

	The Factor Model	The Sector Model
The principal actors	Factors of production or classes	Industries or sectors
How mobile are factors of production?	Perfectly mobile across sectors of the economy	Immobile across sectors of the economy
Who wins and who loses from international trade?	*Winner*: abundant factor—capital in the advanced industrialized countries	*Winner*: labor and capital employed in export-oriented industries
	Loser: scarce factor—labor in the advanced industrialized countries	*Loser*: labor and capital employed in import-competing sectors
Central dimension of competition over trade policy	Protectionist labor versus liberalizing capital	Protectionist import-competing industries versus liberalizing export-oriented industries

about what is good for the country as a whole. Such "sociotropic" concerns might focus on or revolve around attitudes toward out-groups (e.g., foreigners), foreign policy (i.e., isolationism or interventionism), or beliefs about the impact of trade on the national economy rather than specific sectors. As a consequence, people might hold complicated trade policy preferences that change over time. For instance, a person might support trade during economic booms but oppose trade during recessions. If citizens believe that trade enriches their country as a whole, they will be more likely to support open trade. Conversely, if citizens believe that trade causes a loss of jobs to other countries they will be more likely to oppose open trade policies.

What conclusions should we draw from this research about the utility of continuing to rely on the two standard economic models of trade policy preferences? Some scholars argue that the failure to find evidence that individuals' trade policy preferences reflect factor ownership or sector of employment constitutes a fundamental challenge to the open economy politics perspective. Some have argued that this research "shakes the foundations of OEP, threatening to topple the entire superstructure" (Lake 2013, 575). Others suggest that the field should rely less on the assumption that preferences reflect objective reality and focus more on the importance of individual beliefs as models that mediate between the objective material world and individual preferences (Rho and Tomz 2017, S103–4). My own view is that the primary actors that engage in trade politics typically are large organizations rather than individuals. From this perspective, whether United Autoworkers of America's trade policy preferences conform to the expectations of standard trade theory is a more relevant concern than the preferences of the individuals that these associations represent.

A Closer Look

Brexit: A Backlash, but Against What?

On June 23, 2016, voters in the United Kingdom went to the polls to vote on a national referendum that would determine the future of the UK's relationship with the European Union (EU). The question they were asked was remarkably simple: Should the UK Remain a member of the European Union or Leave the European Union? The Brexit referendum had been called by then Conservative Party Leader and Prime Minister David Cameron earlier in the year in order to make good on a promise he had made in 2013: if the Conservative Party were re-elected in the 2015 general election, he would schedule a national referendum on EU membership. Somewhat astonishingly, the Leave vote prevailed (a disappointment for Cameron who resigned the next day), attracting 52 percent of the votes cast.

Is Brexit a backlash against globalization? Is it a retreat from the neoliberalism that has dominated international political economy since the early 1980s? Pressure on the British government to hold a referendum on EU membership arose from a number of sources. First, and most broadly, membership in Europe has always been controversial in British politics. Britain remained outside the European Economic Community (EEC, as it was then called) when it was first established in the late 1950s. And even after it joined the EEC in the early 1970s, Britain remained deeply divided about the terms of its membership. Labour Party leader and Prime Minister Harold Wilson held a first referendum on UK membership in the EEC in 1975, only 2 years after the UK had joined. During the 1980s and 1990s, the Eurosceptics emerged as an influential force within the Conservative Party. Europe, according to a former Conservative Party leader William Hague, served as the Party's "ticking time bomb." Hence, the fact that Britain is deeply divided over its relationship with the EU is hardly a new development generated as a reaction to deepening globalization.

It is true that the more or less constant anti-Brussels refrain in British politics has been amplified since 2006 by a number of factors associated with globalization. In addition, Conservative austerity policies, a slow economic recovery following the 2008 financial crisis, and rising immigration into the UK from the EU's newest members in Central and Eastern Southern Europe added to social dissatisfaction. Nigel Farage exploited this dissatisfaction once he became leader of the stridently anti-Europe United Kingdom Independence Party (UKIP) in 2006. UKIP became a significant actor in the British debate on Europe, winning 24 of the UK's 73 seats in the 2014 European Parliament elections. He began to widen his base by seeking support from the British working class and encouraging defections from the Conservative Party. Cameron's decision to call the referendum in 2016, therefore, constituted a calculated gamble—he hoped that the vote would deliver a majority for Remain and that that would in turn unify the Conservative Party (if not British society) around a common policy (Oliver 2015, 82). So, it is difficult to characterize Brexit as an elite-driven backlash against globalization.

Nor does the evidence on why voters voted as they did provide conclusive evidence that Brexit constitutes a backlash against globalization. On the one hand, polling data offers evidence that British voters' preferences over Brexit reflected their economic interests as the standard trade models we have discussed here would predict (see Owen and Walter 2017; Sampson 2017). In broad terms, these models predict that losers from trade and immigration were likely to vote Leave, while those who gained from Britain's economic interdependence with the EU would vote Remain. And to a considerable extent, this is the pattern we observe. First, voters with a university degree were significantly more likely to support Remain, while voters without a university degree were more likely to vote Leave. This result is consistent with our belief that human capital is comparatively advantaged in the UK, and thus voters who have a university education benefit from and support EU membership, while those without such education are harmed by and wish to exit the EU. Second, higher income households supported continued EU membership, while lower income households supported exit. This result may indicate that households that have done well economically under EU membership are likely to support Remain while households that have done poorly are more likely to support Leave. Finally, young voters (18–24) were significantly more likely to vote for the Remain side and older voters (55 and older) were more likely to vote Leave. This may indicate that individuals with greater mobility and fewer sector-specific skills (the young) are more ready to accept the risks of trade openness than individuals with less mobility. These findings thus reveal that those who gain from EU membership voted Remain, while those who lose voted Leave.

Yet, other evidence confounds this distributive impact of trade interpretation of votes for and against Brexit. We see substantial indication that values and identities played an important role in voter orientation. For instance, people with socially conservative views, as measured by their support for women's rights for instance, were more likely to vote to Leave. Similarly, people who believe that Britain was better off (in some unspecified way) 30 years ago than it was today were more likely to vote Leave. In addition, those who voted Leave reported that the impact of EU membership on immigration and its erosion of British sovereignty were the first and second most important factors in their decision calculus (Owen and Walter 2017, 183). And voters who were most concerned about immigration lived in regions that had among the lowest immigrant populations in aggregate and as a share of total population. Voter support for Leave thus reflected a much more complex configuration of factors—some economic, some social, some individual, some sociotropic—than the standard trade theory models highlight.

So, if Brexit wasn't a backlash against the impact of trade on individual incomes, what was it a backlash against? One might suggest that Brexit constituted a backlash against the broader social, economic and political transformations that have occurred over the last 30 years. Some of these transformations pertain specifically to Britain's experience in the EU, such as a perceived loss of British sovereignty due to EU membership. Many of these transformations are of a more general nature. As Sampson has nicely summarized, Brexit

> succeeded because it received the support of a coalition of voters who felt left behind by modern Britain. People may have felt left-behind because of their education, age, economic situation, or because of tensions between their values and the direction of social change, but, broadly speaking, a feeling of social and economic exclusion appears to have translated into support for Brexit.
>
> (Sampson 2017, 178)

Arguably, this statement applies with equal force to the election of Donald J. Trump in November 2016. And this is deeply troubling, because it isn't clear how one designs policy to address the concerns of those who have been left behind.

ORGANIZING INTERESTS: THE COLLECTIVE ACTION PROBLEM AND TRADE POLICY DEMANDS

Actors' preferences are not transformed automatically into political pressure for specific trade policies. Transforming preferences into political demands requires that the actors who share a common preference organize in order to exert influence on the policy-making process. Organizing can be so difficult that individuals with common interests may not organize at all. This might seem counterintuitive. If trade affects incomes in predictable ways, and if people are rational, then why wouldn't people with common interests join forces to lobby for their desired policy?

Groups often can't organize because they confront a public goods problem or **collective action problem** (Olson 1965). Collective action problems are similar to the problem of public goods provision. Consider consumers and trade policy. As a group, the 200 million or so consumers who live in the United States would all gain from free trade. These 200 million people thus have a common interest in unilateral trade liberalization. To achieve this goal, however, consumers would have to lobby the government. Such lobbying is costly—money is required to create an organization, to pay for a lobbyist, and to contribute to politicians' campaigns, and time must be dedicated to fundraising and organization. Consequently, most consumers will perform the following very simple calculation: my contribution to this campaign will make no perceptible difference to the group's ability to achieve free trade. Moreover, I will benefit from free trade if the group is successful regardless of whether I have contributed or not. Therefore, I will let other consumers spend their money and time; that is, I will free ride. Because all consumers have an incentive to free ride, no one contributes time and money, no one lobbies, and consumer interests fail to influence trade policy. Thus, even though consumers share a common goal, the collective action problem prevents them from exerting pressure on politicians to achieve this goal. The incentive to free ride makes collective action in pursuit of a common goal very difficult.

The logic of collective action helps us understand three important characteristics of trade politics. First, it helps us understand why producers rather than consumers dominate trade politics. Consumers are a large and homogeneous group, and each individual consumer faces a strong incentive to free ride. Consequently, contributions to a "Consumers for Free Trade" interest group are substantially less than the underlying common interest in free trade would seem to dictate. In contrast, most industries are made up of a relatively small number of firms. Producer groups can thus more readily organize to lobby the government in pursuit of their desired trade policy. The logic of collective action helps us understand why producers' interests dominate trade politics, whereas consumer interests are often neglected.

Second, the logic of collective action suggests that trade politics will exhibit a bias toward protectionism. A tariff provides large benefits to the few firms producing in the protected industry. The costs of a tariff, however, are distributed across a large number of individuals and firms. A higher tariff on steel, for example, provides large benefits to the relatively small number of American steel producers and their workers. The costs of a steel tariff fall on everyone who consumes steel, a group that includes most American consumers as well as all firms that use steel as an input in their production processes. The small group of steel producers that benefits from the higher tariff can fairly easily overcome the collective action problem to lobby for protection. The large and heterogeneous group that bears the costs of the tariff finds it much more difficult to organize for collective action. Consequently, trade politics is dominated by import-competing industries demanding protection.

Finally, the logic of collective action helps us understand why governments rarely liberalize trade unilaterally, but have been willing to do so through negotiated agreements. Reciprocal trade agreements make it easier for export-oriented industries to overcome the collective action problem (see Bailey, Goldstein, and Weingast 1997; Gilligan 1997; Milner 1988). Reciprocal trade agreements provide large benefits in the form of access to foreign markets to small groups of export-oriented firms. Reducing foreign tariffs on microprocessors for personal computers, for example, provides substantial gains to the three American firms that dominate this industry (Intel, Advanced Micro Devices [AMD], and Motorola). These three firms will solve the collective action problem they face and lobby for trade liberalization at home in exchange for the removal of foreign barriers to their exports.

Many scholars argue that exactly this effect lies behind postwar trade liberalization in the United States. The Roosevelt administration proposed and Congress passed the **Reciprocal Trade Agreements Act** (RTAA) of 1934. This legislation has continued to structure U.S. trade policy ever since. Under its terms, Congress delegates to the president the authority to reduce tariffs in exchange for equivalent concessions from foreign governments. By linking reductions of American tariffs to the opening of foreign markets to American exporters, the RTAA transformed the large and heterogeneous group favoring liberalization into small groups of export-oriented industries that could more easily organize to pursue common goals. This in turn altered the balance of interest-group pressure that politicians faced. More balanced political pressure made politicians more willing to liberalize trade.

In a society-centered approach, therefore, trade politics are shaped by competition between organized interest groups. This competition sometimes revolves around class conflict that pits workers against business owners, and at other times revolves around industry conflict that pits import-competing industries against export-oriented industries. In all cases, however, the core conflict in, and the ultimate stakes of, this competition remain the same: the distribution of national income. The winners of this political competition are rewarded with rising incomes. The losers become poorer.

POLITICAL INSTITUTIONS AND THE SUPPLY OF TRADE POLICY

While scholars have devoted considerable attention to developing conceptual models of the demand side of trade politics, they have focused less on the supply side of trade politics. Supply-side models strive to say something systematic about who wins the competition over trade policy. Here we find considerable agreement that political institutions play an important role in transforming interest-group demands into actual policies, but substantially less agreement about how exactly they do so.

Political institutions shape how competition between organized interests unfolds. They do so by establishing rules that influence the strategies people adopt in pursuit of their policy objectives. These rules influence how people organize, and thus determine whether interests organize around factor or sectoral interests. Rules influence how organized interests exert pressure on the political process and thus determine whether interest groups lobby the legislature or whether they exert influence through political parties. Rules influence which interests politicians must respond to and thus determine which interests gain representation and which do not. Because political institutions shape the way people behave, they have an important impact on who ultimately wins the battle over national income.

The electoral system is one institution that most political economists agree has an important impact on trade politics. Electoral systems can be classified into two broad categories: majoritarian and proportional. The critical dimension on which the two types are distinguished is the number of legislative seats selected in each constituency. **Majoritarian** electoral systems combine single member districts and first-past-the-post elections. Great Britain, for example, is divided into 650 constituencies, each of which elects a single member of parliament. First-past-the-post voting means that a candidate need only attract a plurality of the vote to win in each district. As a result, British political parties can capture a majority in the House of Commons with only a plurality of the popular vote. In the 2005 election, for example, the Labour Party received 35 percent of the popular vote but won 55 percent of the seats in the House of Commons. In 2010, the Conservative Party captured 47 percent of the seats in the House with only 36 percent of the popular vote. Majoritarian systems also disadvantage smaller third parties. The British Liberal Democrats, for example, earned 23 percent of the popular vote in the 2010 election, but only 9 percent of the seats in parliament.

Proportional representation (PR) electoral systems employ multi-member districts to distribute legislative representation in proportion to the share of the popular vote each party attracts. Norway, for example, is divided into 19 constituencies, each of which elects between 4 and 17 representatives to the Norwegian parliament. Legislators from each district are selected from the political parties in proportion to the party's share of the popular vote in the district. In the 2009 election, the Norwegian Labor Party gained 33 percent of the seats in parliament based on 35 percent of the popular vote, while the second largest party, the Progress Party, captured 22 percent of the seats on 23 percent of the popular vote. In PR systems, therefore, a party's importance in the legislature closely tracks its share of the popular vote.

Electoral systems can affect trade politics in two ways. First, electoral systems may play an important role in shaping how groups organize to pursue their trade policy objectives. In particular, majoritarian systems may encourage organization around the common sector-based interests while PR systems may encourage organization around factors. Consider the incentives created by majoritarian electoral systems. To win elections in such systems, candidates must satisfy the demands of their districts' residents. Each electoral district is relatively small and likely to be dominated by one or two major industries. The wages paid in these industries will in turn play a large role in supporting the rest of the district economy—the retail and service-sector businesses that provide jobs for many other people in the community. Such electoral systems create incentives for elected officials to represent the interests of the owners of and workers in the industries that dominate economic activity in their districts. We expect legislators from Detroit, Michigan, to advance and defend the interests of the auto industry and its employees. Because elected representatives have incentive to reward demands from the industries in their districts, industries have incentive to pursue their narrow interests rather than seek to construct broader coalitions. Consequently, majoritarian electoral institutions may create strong incentives for individuals to organize around narrow industry-specific interests.

In contrast, PR systems do not link political representation tightly to the interests of small and undiversified electoral districts. In the extreme case, for example, a PR system has a single national constituency. In such systems, electoral success requires the construction of electoral coalitions that appeal to broad rather than narrow interests. Consequently, PR systems seem to produce political parties based on class or factor interests. In Norway, for example, the three largest political parties in postwar politics are closely tied to factor-based interests. The labor party is closely linked to Norwegian labor unions, the agrarian party evolved out of the farm movement of the 1920s, and the conservative party has represented the business or capital interest. And with the electoral system creating an incentive to represent factor-based interests, economic actors gain an incentive to pursue their trade policy goals by organizing around factor-based interests. Thus, PR systems may create incentives for individuals to organize for political action around factoral interests.

Electoral systems may also affect the level of protection adopted by governments in the two systems. In particular, we might expect governments in countries with PR systems to maintain lower tariffs (and other trade barriers) than governments in countries with majoritarian electoral systems. The logic behind this hypothesis asserts that the small groups that benefit from protection can more easily influence policy in majoritarian than in proportional systems. As one advocate of this hypothesis explains,

> When automakers or dairy farmers entirely dominate twenty small constituencies and are a powerful minority in fifty more, their voice will certainly be heard in the nation's councils. Where they constitute but one or two percent of an enormous district's electorate, representatives may defy them more freely.
>
> (Rogowski 1987, 208)

Such a logic may help us understand why farmers, who constitute much less than 5 percent of the American population, are able to gain such favorable legislation from Congress. In other words, minority interests can construct legislative majorities more easily in majoritarian than in PR systems.

It has proven difficult to tease out unambiguous empirical support for this electoral system hypothesis (Rickard 2015). The most recent empirical investigation reports substantial evidence that tariffs are higher in countries with majoritarian electoral systems than they are in countries with proportional systems (see Evans 2009). Analyzing the experience of as many as 147 countries (and as few as 30) between 1981 and 2004, this study finds that the average tariff in majoritarian countries stood at 17 percent, while the average tariff in countries with PR systems reached only 12 percent. This five-percentage point difference persists even when the relationship between electoral systems and tariff rates is evaluated with more demanding statistical techniques that control for a large number of possible alternative explanations.

Other research reaches very different conclusions. A study that focuses on the experience of Latin American countries in the 1980s and 1990s finds that tariffs are higher in countries with PR systems than they are in countries with majoritarian electoral systems (Hatfield and Hauk 2004). A study based on variation in non-tariff forms of protection in 14 industrial countries during the 1980s also finds that protectionism was higher in countries with PR systems than in countries with majoritarian systems (Mansfield and Busch 1995). Both of these studies thus find exactly the opposite of what the electoral system hypothesis suggests we should observe. Consistent evidence about how electoral systems shape the level of protection has thus proven difficult to find (see Oatley 2017; Rickard 2015).

One final political institution, the number of veto players present in the political system, may also affect trade policy. A **veto player** is a political actor whose agreement is necessary in order to enact policy (Tsebelis 2002). In the U.S. context, each branch of government might be a veto player. Whether each branch is a veto player in fact depends upon the preferences of the individuals that control each branch. We might count situations of divided government, where one party controls Congress and the other party controls the White House, as two-veto player systems and count unified government as a one-veto player system. Coalition governments in parliamentary systems such as Germany, where two or more parties almost always make up the majority within the legislature and hold cabinet posts, are multi-veto player systems. Britain is perhaps the simplest system (until quite recently). With its majoritarian electoral system and parliamentary government, it has been ruled by single-party majority governments for most of the postwar era. It is typically, therefore, a political system with a single veto player.

The central expectation of veto player theory is that the difficulty of moving policy from the status quo increases in line with the number of veto players in the political system. Applied to trade policy, this suggests that political systems with many veto players will find it difficult to alter tariffs in response to societal pressure for change (Henisz and Mansfield 2006). In contrast, tariffs will be relatively easy to change in political systems with few veto players. Some research that explores how protectionism reacts to changes in macroeconomic conditions supports this expectation. We might expect, for example, that protectionism would rise during recessions and fall during

A Closer Look

International Factor Mobility and Trade Politics

The standard trade theory models that we have looked at in this chapter assume that factors of production are immobile internationally. This means that although capital and labor can shift between uses within a national economy, though at different rates, factors of production cannot move between, say, the United States to Mexico. This assumption is obviously less and less valid in the contemporary global economy. As we shall see in later chapters, capital moves between nations in large amounts and in many forms, while the movement of people has also increased—in 2015, for example, the U.S. accepted 1.4 million new residents. Does international factor mobility force us to alter our approach to the distributional consequences of trade, and thus to the underlying structure of trade politics?

The simplest answer to this question is no: economists tell us that the cross-border flow of factors is fundamentally the same as the cross-border flow of goods (see Blinder 2006; Mankiw and Swagel 2006). As a consequence, cross border factor flows typically reinforce the distributional consequences of trade in goods that the standard H-O and R-V models articulate. For instance, an inflow of low-skilled workers from Latin America to the United States should increase the supply of low-skilled labor in the American economy and thus reduce the return to low-skilled labor in the United States, just as increased imports of labor-intensive goods would. And an inflow of capital from the United States into Mexico would reduce the return to capital in Mexico. Thus, as long as factor flows are typically from areas where they are abundant to regions where they are scarce, cross-border factor flows have the same distributional consequences as the H-O model highlights for trade in goods.

International factor mobility does add some new facets to trade politics, however. First and most prominently, international factor mobility has pushed off-shoring to the center of trade politics. Off-shoring occurs when a firm based in one country moves all or part of its production to a second country and then uses this new location as a platform from which to export back to its original home. American automakers, for instance, have built factories in Mexico but they export a large share of the cars that they build in Mexico back to the American market. A significant element of the Trump administration's trade policy involves arm twisting American corporations in an attempt to get them to move this manufacturing activity back to the American economy. And at least part of the administration's threat to scuttle NAFTA reflects the belief that re-instating tariffs on imports into the U.S. from Mexico would encourage American companies to on-shore production. Perhaps ironically, restricting trade with Mexico could increase migration into the United States from Mexico as American firms pressure the U.S. government to relax controls on such immigration so as to expand the supply of low-skilled labor available in the American economy in order to reduce their labor costs (see Peters 2015, 2017).

Second, international factor mobility pushes class-based conflict to the center of trade politics and pushes sector-based conflict to the side. The increasing importance of factor or class in trade politics arises from the fact that capital is more mobile internationally than labor. Ford or General Motors can shift their production facilities to Mexico, but for a variety of reasons American auto workers typically do not follow these factories to secure jobs in Mexico. Consequently, the commonality of interest over trade policy that the Ricardo-Viner model leads us to expect labor and capital to have when factors are immobile internationally disappears when capital specific to auto manufacturing can exit the American economy and set up shop elsewhere. Thus, as American auto producers increase their production in Mexico they become even stronger supporters of free trade between the U.S. and Mexico, while American auto workers become increasingly protectionist. We might even expect the combination of specific factors and international mobility to aggravate conflict as workers discover that they are trapped in a declining sector at home while their employers can use the same capital to produce the same goods in another location. In this environment, unions might pressure the government to restrict inward migration in an attempt to shore up wages for low-skilled workers (see Peters 2014, 2017).

Third, labor's bargaining power relative to capital weakens with international factor mobility. Labor unions have been able to gain significant concessions from corporations as a result of their ability to threaten to remove workers from the factory. The threat of a strike has thus enabled unions to gain higher wages, good benefits packages (healthcare and pensions especially), and improve working conditions for their members. Union power, however, rests on the assumption that capital is immobile, in both senses of the term. Once capital becomes internationally mobile, corporations can respond to union demands by threatening to move production off shore. The corporate threat to exit when faced with demands by unions thus reduces labor's ability to improve wages and benefits and can allow capital to take back some of the concessions it has already granted. The decline of defined benefit pension plans is one such example of this reversal. Some scholars have suggested that international capital mobility may generate a race-to-the-bottom dynamic in which corporations use the threat of exit to progressively weaken labor standards across the global economy.

Finally, unions have responded to the asymmetry of international factor mobility by pressuring the U.S. government to include enforceable labor standards in the free-trade agreements that it negotiates. All of the FTAs that the U.S. has negotiated since 2000 include a chapter on labor standards. In 2007, the Democrats in Congress reached agreement with the Bush administration that established a new benchmark for the labor chapters that would be included in a number of FTAs then under negotiation (Ciminos-Isaacs 2016, 261). The TPP includes the most ambitious set of labor standards yet (ibid.). Incorporating labor standards in international trade agreements would make it more difficult for corporations to find low-wage and weakly regulated labor markets into which to off-shore production. This would not only strengthen labor rights in emerging market countries but would protect labor standards in the U.S. and Europe by reducing the opportunities for threatening to move production to a low-cost off-shore location.

economic booms. This is surely what occurred during the 1930s as well as to a lesser degree in the 1970s. More recently, policymakers have feared that the recession sparked by the financial crisis would spark a surge of protectionism. However, the extent to which protectionism rises during recessions appears strongly shaped by veto players. Protection rises sharply during recessions in countries with few veto players, but rises substantially less in countries with fewer veto players.

Political institutions thus shape how private-sector trade policy demands are transformed into trade policy outcomes. The rules governing elections can influence whether private-sector groups organize around factors or sectors. These same rules can also shape the level of protectionism. The number of veto players in the political system shapes the government's ability to raise or lower tariffs in response to changes in the relative power of protectionist and liberalizing demands emanating from organized groups. These features of institutions thus play an important role in determining which groups prevail in the distributive competition over trade policy.

CONCLUSION

Although a society-centered approach helps us understand how the interaction between societal interests and political institutions shapes trade politics, it does have weaknesses. We conclude our discussion of this approach by looking at the three most significant weaknesses. First, a society-centered approach does not explain trade policy outcomes. It tells us that trade politics will be characterized by conflict between the winners and losers from international trade, and it does a fine job telling us who the winners and losers will be. It does not help us explain which of these groups will win the political battle. Presumably, a country's trade policy will embody the preferences of society's most powerful interests. To explain trade policy outcomes, therefore, we need to be able to evaluate the relative power of the competing groups. The society-centered approach provides little guidance about how to measure this balance of power. The temptation is to look at trade policy outcomes and deduce that the most powerful groups are those whose preferences are reflected in this policy. Yet, looking at outcomes renders this approach tautological: we assume that the preferences of powerful groups are embodied in trade policy and then infer the power of individual groups from the content of trade policy. Thus, the society-centered approach is better at explaining why trade politics are characterized by competition between organized interests than at telling us why one group outperforms another in this competition for influence.

Second, the society-centered approach implicitly assumes that politicians have no independent trade policy objectives and play no autonomous role in trade politics. This assumption is probably misleading. Politicians are not simply passive recorders of interest-group pressures. As Ikenberry, Lake, and Mastanduno (1988, 8) note, politicians and political institutions "can play a critical role in shaping the manner and the extent to which social forces can exert influence" on trade policy. Politicians do have independent trade policy objectives, and the constellation of interest groups that politicians confront is not fixed. Indeed, politicians can actively attempt to shape the configuration of interest-group pressures that they face. They can, for example, mobilize latent interest groups with a preference for liberalization or protection by helping them overcome their collective action problem. By doing so, politicians can create coalitions of interest groups that support their own trade policy objectives. Political institutions also affect the extent to which societal groups can influence policy. In some countries, political institutions insulate politicians from interest group pressures, thereby allowing politicians to pursue their trade policy objectives independent of interest group demands. We will examine this in greater detail when we look at the state-centered approach in the next chapter.

Finally, the society-centered approach does not address the motivations of noneconomic actors in trade politics. Societal interest groups other than firms, business associations, and labor unions do attempt to influence trade policy. In the United States, for example, environmental groups have played a prominent role in trade politics, shaping the specific content of NAFTA and attempting to shape the negotiating agenda of the Doha Round. Human rights groups have also become active participants in American trade politics. This has been particularly important in America's relationship with China. Human rights groups have consistently sought to deny Chinese producers access to the U.S. market in order to encourage the Chinese government to show greater respect for human rights. The assumption that trade politics are driven by the reactions of interest groups to the impact of international trade on their incomes provides little insight into the motivations of noneconomic groups. The society-centered approach tells us nothing about why groups that focus on the environment or on human rights spend resources attempting to influence trade policy. Nor does it provide any basis with which to make sense of such groups' trade policy preferences. In the past, such a weakness could perhaps be neglected because noneconomic groups played only a small role in trade politics. The contemporary backlash against globalization suggests, however, that these groups must increasingly be incorporated into society-centered models of trade politics.

Although recognizing these weaknesses of the society-centered approach is important, these weaknesses are not reasons to reject the approach. The appropriate measure of any theory or approach is not whether it incorporates everything that matters, nor even whether it explains every outcome that we observe. All theories abstract from reality in order to focus more sharply on a number of key aspects. Consequently, the appropriate measure of any theory or approach is whether it is useful—that is, does it provide us with a deeper understanding of the enduring features of the phenomenon of interest? On this measure, the society-centered approach scores high. By focusing on how trade shapes the fortunes of different groups in society, it forces us to recognize that the enduring features of trade politics revolve around a continual struggle for income between the winners and losers from international trade.

KEY TERMS

Collective Action Problem
Export-Oriented Sector
Factor Mobility
Factor Model
Factor-Price Equalization
Import-Competing Sector

Majoritarian
Proportional
  Representation
Reciprocal Trade
  Agreements Act
Sector Model

Specific Factors
Stolper-Samuelson
  Theorem
Veto Player

SUGGESTIONS FOR FURTHER READING

For an excellent introduction to, and an interesting attempt to resolve the debate over the factor and sector models of trade policy preferences, see Michael Hiscox, *International Trade and Political Conflict: Commerce, Coalitions, and Mobility* (Princeton, NJ: Princeton University Press, 2002).

See Stefanie Walter, 2017. "Globalization and the Demand-Side of Politics: How Globalization Shapes Labor Market Risk Perceptions and Policy Preferences." *Political Science Research and Methods* 5(1): 55–80 for some recent evidence on the material basis of individual trade policy preferences.

The literature on U.S. trade politics is enormous. The best available recent work is probably Douglas A. Irwin, *Clashing Over Commerce: A History of US Trade Policy* (Chicago: University of Chicago Press, 2017).

For a detailed focus on the role of public opinion in trade politics, see Alexandra Guisinger, *American Opinion on Trade: Preferences without Politics* (Oxford: Oxford University Press, 2017) and Sean Ehrlich, *The Politics of Fair Trade: Moving Beyond Free Trade and Protection* (Oxford: Oxford University Press, 2018).

A State-Centered
Approach to
Trade Politics

In the fall of 2017, the United States announced its intention to impose tariffs of 300 percent on the Canadian company Bombardier's new C-Series commercial aircraft. The American move came on the heels of a decision by Delta Airlines in 2016 to purchase 135 of the new jets. Boeing responded to Delta's decision by filing a complaint with the U.S. Department of Commerce and the U.S. International Trade Commission alleging that Bombardier had effectively dumped the C-Series into the American market, selling them less than two-third the cost of production. Moreover, Boeing alleged that Bombardier could afford to offer such steep discounts because the Canadian government had subsidized the airliner's development. In total, Bombardier received a little more than $1.6 billion in various forms from the Canadian government—a significant share of the estimated $6 billion that Bombardier spent to develop the jet. The steep tariff is thus intended to offset this subsidy from the Canadian government. The Canadian government (as well as the British government which hosts some of Bombardier's production) have threatened to retaliate by not purchasing Boeing-made fighter jets.

How do we make sense of this trade conflict? A society-centered approach suggests that we should look at the political influence of the industries concerned. And indeed, there is little doubt that Boeing has substantial influence in American politics. In 2004, the then president, George W. Bush, acknowledged this influence when he promised Boeing workers that he would end EU subsidies to Airbus. Such influence persists today—in the first year of the Trump administration, Boeing management began direct conversations with the president. Yet, the Boeing–Bombardier conflict also raises issues that are not readily incorporated into the society-centered approach. In particular, this isn't an instance of conflict between an American import-competing industry and a foreign export-oriented industry. Instead, the conflict is between two export-oriented firms battling over global market share. Moreover, the conflict does not revolve around one government's use of tariffs to protect domestic producers from foreign competition, but instead focuses on retaliation for one state's use of government subsidies to support the domestic firm as it competes for global market share. To fully understand the trade conflict in the commercial aircraft industry, therefore, we have to broaden our understanding of the economics, and perhaps also the politics, of international trade.

We gain this broader understanding in this chapter by developing a state-centered approach to trade politics. A state-centered approach argues that national policymakers intervene in the economy in pursuit of objectives that are determined independently from domestic interest groups' narrow self-interested concerns. Moreover, this approach suggests that such intervention may (but need not necessarily) raise aggregate social welfare. We examine the state-centered approach with a specific focus on government intervention designed to promote the development of specific national industries. We look first at the broader economic justification for protectionism aimed at creating internationally competitive industries, then narrow our focus to the use of such measures by the advanced industrialized countries in high-technology industries, and then apply the logic of this approach to the current U.S.–EU conflict in the commercial aircraft industry. We conclude the chapter by looking briefly at some of the weaknesses of this approach.

STATES AND INDUSTRIAL POLICY

A state-centered approach is based on two central assumptions, both of which contrast sharply with the assumptions embodied in the society-centered approach. The first assumption concerns the impact of protectionism on aggregate social welfare. The society-centered approach argues that protectionism reduces social welfare by depriving society of the gains from trade and by employing society's resources in comparatively disadvantaged industries, but the state-centered approach argues that under certain circumstances trade protection can raise social welfare.

The second assumption concerns whether governments can operate independently of interest group pressures. The society-centered approach argues that national policy reflects the balance of power among competing interest groups, but the state-centered approach argues that under specific circumstances governments are relatively unconstrained by interest-group demands. As a consequence, a government's trade and economic policies embody the goals of national policymakers rather than the demands of domestic interest groups. The state-centered approach combines these two assumptions to suggest that under a specific set of circumstances, governments will intervene in the domestic economy with tariffs, production subsidies, and other policy instruments in ways that raise aggregate social welfare.

To fully understand this approach, we need to understand the conditions under which such intervention may raise social welfare. We then can examine the institutional characteristics that enable national policymakers to act autonomously from interest groups to capture these welfare gains.

The Infant-Industry Case for Protection

The economic justification for the state-centered approach rests on the claim that targeted government intervention can increase aggregate social welfare. This claim stands in stark contrast to the conclusions drawn from the standard model of trade that we examined in Chapter 3 and extended in our discussion of the domestic adjustments to trade in Chapter 4. The standard model rules out such welfare-increasing government intervention by assumption. In the standard model, society does best by removing all forms of trade protection and by specializing in its comparatively advantaged industry. Maintaining protection merely deprives society of the welfare gains from trade.

Moreover, in the standard trade model, nothing makes it difficult for factors currently employed in comparatively disadvantaged industries to move into the comparatively advantaged sector. Factors of production will move into comparatively advantaged industries because it is profitable to do so—the returns in these industries are higher than the returns in the comparatively disadvantaged industries. Such movement will take time, there will be adjustment costs, and there is a case to be made for government policies that help individuals manage these costs, but such policies are oriented toward shifting workers and resources into sectors where they would go anyway. In this model, tariffs and other forms of protection can only make society worse off by preventing factors from moving out of low-return and into high-return industries. In the world depicted by the standard trade models, therefore, government intervention cannot raise social welfare.

In order to claim that a tariff and other forms of government intervention raise social welfare, one must be able to demonstrate that something prevents factors from shifting into industries that yield higher returns than are available in other sectors of the economy. Historically, this justification has been provided by the infant-industry case for protection. The **infant-industry case for protection** argues that there are cases in which newly created firms (infants, so to speak) will not be efficient *initially* but could be efficient in the long run if they are given time to mature. Consequently, a short period of tariff protection will enable these industries to become efficient and begin to export. Once this point has been reached, the tariff can be removed. The long-run welfare gains created by the now-established industry will be greater than the short-run losses of social welfare imposed by the tariff.

There are two reasons why an industry may not be efficient in the short run, but could be efficient in the long run: economies of scale and economies of experience (Kenen 1994, 279–281). **Economies of scale** arise when the cost of production varies with the size of output, that is, when the unit cost of producing falls as the number of units produced rises. For example, it is quite costly to develop a new commercial aircraft. Estimates put the cost of developing Boeing's new 777 at around $3 billion. The unit cost of production will be very high if Boeing produces only a few of these planes, as we must divide this fixed cost by a small number of final goods. The unit cost falls substantially, however, if Boeing produces 1,000 of these new planes. What we see, then, is that the average cost of each unit falls as the number of units produced rises. Firms in industries with such scale economies face a dilemma, however. They can produce efficiently and begin to export once they produce enough output to achieve the available scale economies. In an open economy, however, these firms must compete immediately against established foreign producers that have already achieved economies of scale. Consequently, a new firm will have a hard time selling its higher-average-cost output in the face of competition from lower-cost firms. Consequently, the new firm will never reach the level of output necessary to achieve economies of scale.

In such cases, a tariff might be welfare improving. By imposing a tariff, the government could effectively deliver the domestic market to the infant domestic firm. With a guaranteed market, the domestic firm could sell its early high-cost output to domestic consumers and eventually produce enough to achieve economies of scale. Once it had done so, it could then compete against foreign producers without the need for tariff protection. The tariff would then be removed.

Economies of experience arise when efficient production requires specific skills that can only be acquired through production in the industry. In many industries, efficient production requires "seasoned managers, skilled workers, and reliable suppliers of equipment and materials" (Kenen 1994, 280). Because these skills are lacking by definition in an infant industry, it will be costly to produce the early units of output. Over time, however, management skills improve, workers learn how to do their tasks efficiently, and reliable suppliers are found and supported. Costs of production fall as experience is gained. For example, when Airbus built its first jet, it took 340,000 person-hours to assemble the fuselage. As Airbus gained experience, however, the time required to assemble the jets fell rapidly. By the time that Airbus had produced 75 aircraft, only 85,000 person-hours were required to assemble the fuselage, and eventually this number fell to 43,000 person-hours (McIntyre 1992, 36). The efficiency gains realized as a result of these dynamics are often called "moving down the learning curve." Again, however, the new firm faces a dilemma. In an unprotected market, it won't be cost competitive in the face of established foreign producers. Consequently, it will never be able to produce enough output to realize these economies of experience. As with economies of scale, a tariff can allow the infant industry to realize the cost savings available from economies of experience and achieve greater efficiency. Once it has done so, it can begin to export, and the tariff can be removed.

A Closer Look

Criticism of the Infant-Industry Case for Protection

Many economists are skeptical about the claim that government intervention is the best response to the problems highlighted by the infant-industry argument (see Kenen 1994, 281). First of all, a tariff is rarely the best policy response to the central problem the infant industry confronts. Economists argue that a subsidy is a much better approach because it is more efficient. Subsidies are a more efficient policy than a tariff because they target the same policy goal—helping the domestic industry cover the gap between its production costs and established foreign producers' costs—but they don't reduce consumer welfare like tariffs do (Kenen 1994, 281). Thus, a subsidy is more efficient.

However, a government subsidy may not improve social welfare either. The case against a subsidy arises from the fact that a firm that will be profitable in the long run but must operate at a loss in the short run should be able to borrow from private capital markets to cover its short-run losses. Such borrowing obviates the need for a subsidy because it enables the firm to sell its goods at the world price and cover its short-term losses with the borrowed funds. Thus, as long as capital markets are efficient and not "strongly averse to risk," infant industries should be able to borrow at an interest rate that reflects the social rate of return on capital. If a firm can't borrow at an interest rate that reflects the social rate of return to capital, then the market is essentially saying that this industry is not the best place to invest society's scarce resources. Consequently, the firm shouldn't be supported with subsidies or tariffs (Kenen 1994, 281). In other words, when capital markets are efficient, the firm should borrow rather than rely on the government; if it can't borrow, the government shouldn't help it either.

This critique of government intervention fails to hold in two circumstances. First, a firm may be reluctant to borrow from private markets when the problem it faces arises from economies of experience. In such instances, borrowed funds yield long-run efficiency by allowing workers employed at a particular firm to gain the skills required to operate efficiently. Yet, once workers have acquired these skills, they may go to work for other firms. If they do, the firm that has paid for their training will be unable to achieve economies of experience and cannot repay the loan. In this instance, government support for the industry might be helpful, but economists argue that government assistance in such cases should take the form of broad government-funded training programs rather than narrow subsidies to a specific firm.

The criticism of subsidies also fails to hold if the private capital market is inefficient and therefore won't loan to a firm entering an infant industry. If this is the case, the firm will have little capacity to gain the financial resources it needs to cover its short-term losses. Even here, however, economists argue that a subsidy or a tariff may not be the right response. If the government is determined to support the development of a specific industry, then it should do what the private capital market won't and extend loans to firms in this industry rather than provide a subsidy. If the government is primarily interested in raising social welfare, however, economists argue that the best thing it can do in this circumstance is strengthen the private capital market so it does operate efficiently (Baldwin 1969). Thus, even though most economists agree that there will be instances in which firms that are not efficient in the short run can become efficient in the long run, there is considerable skepticism about the extent to which government intervention is the only, or the best, solution to this dilemma.

Therefore, tariffs and other forms of government intervention may sometimes improve social welfare, because a disjuncture between the social and private returns from a particular industry may prevent the shift of factors out of relatively low-return industries and into relatively high-return industries (Balassa and Associates 1971, 93). In other worlds, certain industries may offer high social returns over the long run (that is, they will provide large benefits to society as a whole), but the short-run private returns (that is, the profits realized by the person or firm making the investment) are likely to be negative. Consequently, factors don't move automatically into the potentially high-return industry. A tariff, or another form of government intervention, may encourage factors to move into this industry by raising the short-run return above what it would be without a tariff.

The logic of the infant-industry case for protection has been adopted by governments in many late-industrializing countries. A late-industrializing country is one that is trying to develop manufacturing industries in competition with established manufacturing industries in other countries. This term obviously describes most developing countries in the contemporary international economic system. But it once described many of today's advanced industrialized countries, including the United States, as they attempted to develop manufacturing industries in the face of dominant British manufacturing power in the nineteenth century. Indeed, the infant-industry argument was first developed by an American, Alexander Hamilton, in 1791 as an explicit policy for the development of manufacturing industry in the United States. Hamilton's argument was further developed by the Germany political economist Fredrick List in the mid-nineteenth century. Like Hamilton, List was primarily interested in thinking about how the German government could encourage the growth of manufacturing industries in the face of established British dominance. The infant-industry argument continued to have an important impact on government trade policies throughout the twentieth century. Many argue that Japan's postwar trade policies reflect the logic of the infant-industry argument as the Japanese government used a variety of policy instruments to encourage the development of advanced manufacturing industries in the face of American competitive advantages. Many developing-country governments also embraced the logic of the infant-industry argument throughout the early postwar periods, as we will see in greater detail in Chapter 6.

The policies that governments have adopted to promote the development of infant industries are known collectively as industrial policy. **Industrial policy** can be defined as the use of a broad assortment of instruments, including tax policy, subsidies (including the provision of state credit and finance), traditional protectionism, and government procurement practices, in order to channel resources away from some industries and direct them toward those industries that the state wishes to promote. The use of such policies is typically based on long-term economic development objectives defined in terms of boosting economic growth, improving productivity, and enhancing international competitiveness. The specific goals that governments pursue often are determined by explicit comparisons to other countries' economic achievements (Wade 1990, 25–26). In postwar Japan, for example, the explicit goal of Japanese industrial policy was to catch up with the United States in high-technology industries. In much of the developing world, industrial policy was oriented toward creating economic structures that paralleled those of the advanced industrialized countries.

STATE STRENGTH: THE POLITICAL FOUNDATION OF INDUSTRIAL POLICY

The ability of any government to effectively design and implement an industrial policy is dependent on the political institutions within which it operates. The various institutional characteristics that make some states more and others less able to design and implement coherent industrial policies can be summarized by the concept of state strength. **State strength** is the degree to which national policymakers, a category that includes elected and appointed officials, are insulated from domestic interest-group pressures.

Strong states are states in which policymakers are highly insulated from such pressure, whereas weak states are those in which policymakers are fully exposed to such pressures. Strong states are characterized by a high degree of centralization of authority, a high degree of coordination among state agencies, and a limited number of channels through which societal actors can attempt to influence policy. In contrast, weak states are characterized by decentralized authority, a lack of coordination among agencies, and a large number of channels through which domestic interest groups can influence economic policy.

These characteristics of political institutions make it easier for strong states to formulate long-term plans embodying the national interest. In weak states, policymakers must respond to the particularistic and often short-run demands of interest groups. Strong states also may be more able than a weak state to remove protection once an infant industry has matured. In addition, strong states may be more able to implement industrial policies that redistribute societal resources, because policymakers need worry less that policies that redistribute resources from one domestic group to another will have a negative impact on their position in power.

Japan is often depicted as the preeminent example of a strong state that has been able and willing to use industrial policy to promote economic development (see, for example, Johnson 1982). The Japanese state centralizes power and provides limited channels of access to domestic interest groups. Because of this highly centralized state, Japan has been able to pursue a coherent industrial policy throughout the postwar period. The Ministry of International Trade and Industry (MITI: now called the Ministry of Economy, Trade, and Industry or METI) and the Ministry of Finance (MoF) were the principal agencies involved in developing and implementing industrial policy. In the immediate postwar period, these agencies gave priority to economic reconstruction and to improving the prewar industrial economy. Since the 1960s, greater emphasis has been placed on promoting rapid economic growth and developing internationally competitive high-technology industries (Pempel 1977, 732).

With this goal firmly in mind, the Japanese state pursued an active industrial policy (called administrative guidance) through which it channeled resources to those industries it determined critical to Japanese success. Together, the MITI and MoF targeted specific industries for development, starting with heavy industries (steel, shipbuilding, automobiles) in the early postwar period and then shifting to high-technology industries during the 1970s. The state pressured firms to invest in the industries targeted for development, and those that made such investments benefited from tariff and non-tariff forms of protection, tax credits, low-cost financing, and other government subsidies. Some scholars suggest that Japan's remarkable postwar economic performance was a direct result of this state-centered approach to economic development (Johnson 1982).

France also relied heavily upon industrial policies throughout much of the postwar period (Hart 1992). The French state is highly centralized, and French bureaucracies are tightly insulated from societal group pressures, as in Japan. This structure allowed the French government to pursue an industrial policy aimed at developing key industries with little direct influence from domestic interest groups. A former director of the Ministry of Industry described the policy-making process:

> First, we make out a report or draw up a text, then we pass it around discreetly within the administration. Once everyone concerned within the administration is agreed on the final version, then we pass this version around outside the administration. Of course, by then it is a *fait accompli* and pressure cannot have any effect.
> (quoted in Katzenstein 1977, 18)

In the early postwar period, the French state formulated development plans to "establish a competitive economy as an essential base for political independence, economic growth, and social progress" (Katzenstein 1977, 22). French industrial policy in this period was based on a strategy of "National Champions," under which specific firms in industries deemed by the French state to be critical to French economic development received support. In the 1950s and 1960s, for example, two French steel companies and a small number of French auto producers (Renault, Simca, Peugeot) received state support. During the 1960s and 1970s, the French state attempted to develop a domestic computer industry by channeling resources to specific French computer companies such as Machines Bull. Most regard this strategy as relatively unsuccessful, because French national champions failed to become competitive in international markets (Hart 1992). However, the current French government seems poised to revive this approach, announcing in early 2005 the creation of a new industrial policy oriented toward promoting national champions in high-technology industries.

In contrast to Japan and France, the United States typically is characterized as a weak state (Katzenstein 1977; Ikenberry et al. 1988). Political power in the United States is decentralized through federalism, through the division of powers within the federal government, and through independent bureaucratic agencies. This decentralization of power in turn provides multiple channels through which domestic interest groups can attempt to influence policy. Consequently, "American state officials find it difficult to act purposefully and coherently, to realize their preferences in the face of significant opposition, and to manipulate or restructure their domestic environment" (Ikenberry et al. 1988, 11). American trade and economic policy therefore more often reflects the interests of societal pressure groups than the "national interest" defined by state policymakers.

This does not mean that the United States has been unable to support critical industries. American national security and defense policies have channeled substantial resources to maintaining technological leadership over potential rivals. To maintain this lead, the U.S. government has financed the basic research that underlies many high-technology products, including computers, telecommunications, lasers, advanced materials, and even the Internet. In addition, Department of Defense contracts have supported firms that produce both military and civilian items. Thus, even though the United States is a weak state, we do see a form of industrial policy in the U.S. government's support for basic research and in its defense-related procurement practices designed to meet national security objectives.

Policy Analysis and Debate

Green Industrial Policy in the U.S.?

Question

Should the U.S. government employ industrial policy to encourage the development of green technology?

Overview

During the 2008 presidential campaign, Barack Obama pledged to spend $150 billion over 10 years developing new green technologies, and another $60 billion improving energy-related infrastructure. In January 2010, President Obama began a new program that provided $2.3 billion in funding to 183 firms engaged in clean-energy manufacturing, arguing that such programs boost employment while benefiting the environment. At the same time, President Obama has indicated that he will be hesitant to approve of any new trade agreements that do not include environmental protections. On several dimensions, in other words, the Obama administration is attempting to reorient the U.S. economy and trade around environmentally friendly manufacturing and infrastructure. This has generated debate over the government's role in shaping the national economy.

Why is the use of industrial policy controversial? Advocates of green industrial policies—including former Secretary of Labor Robert Reich, the AFL-CIO, and political commentators like Thomas Friedman—claim that government investment is needed to overcome high start-up costs for new industry, boost productivity in high-growth technologies, and maintain competitiveness in globalized markets. Without government involvement, advocates say, the United States will sacrifice the gains from early development of new technologies to other countries. Opponents of green industrial policies—including many economists, business groups, and free-trade advocates—claim that government intervention misdirects investment to less productive industries, that choosing economic winners and losers in the political arena leads to corruption, and that American industry will have an unfair advantage over their foreign competitors. Both sides can point to examples of industrial policies that provide evidence for their claims.

Policy Options

- Use the power of the U.S. government to promote the development of new green technologies by shifting resources into sectors through taxation and redistribution.
- Allow technological development to occur through the market, and resist government interference.

Policy Analysis

- What interest, if any, do other states have in U.S. industrial policy? Why is this the case?
- How might U.S. trading partners react to greater U.S. government involvement? Is this optimal?
- What role does domestic politics play in determining international outcomes in trade and environmental policies?

Take A Position

- What option do you prefer? Justify your choice.
- What criticisms of your position should you anticipate? How would you defend your recommendations against these criticisms?

Resources

Online: Online searches for "industrial policy" and "green jobs."

In Print: For a less rigorous, but best-selling, discussion of this topic, see Thomas L. Friedman, *Hot, Flat, and Crowded: Why We Need a Green Revolution – And How It Can Renew America* (New York: Farrar, Straus, & Giroux, 2008). For a more academic treatment of development and industrial policy, see Dani Rodrik, *One Economics, Many Recipes: Globalization, Institutions, and Economic Growth* (Princeton, NJ: Princeton University Press, 2008).

The state-centered approach, therefore, argues that state policymakers can use industrial policy to improve social welfare. In contrast to the standard model of trade, this approach argues that factors may not move automatically from relatively low-return industries into relatively high-return industries. In such instances, targeted government intervention, in the form of a tariff or a production subsidy, can encourage movement into these industries. Over the long run, the welfare gains generated by this industry are substantially larger than the welfare losses incurred during the period of protection. The ability of policymakers to effectively pursue such policies, however, is strongly influenced by the institutional structure of the state in which they operate. In strong states, such as Japan and France, policymakers are insulated from domestic interest groups and are therefore able to use industrial policy to promote economic development. In weak states, such as the United States, policymakers cannot easily escape interest-group pressures. As a consequence, trade and economic policy is more likely to reflect the particularistic demands of these groups than any broader conceptions of social welfare.

INDUSTRIAL POLICY IN HIGH-TECHNOLOGY INDUSTRIES

High-technology industries have been one area in which governments in many advanced industrialized countries have relied heavily on industrial policies. Boosting the international competitiveness of such industries has been the principal goal of such policies. High-technology industries are highly valued for the contribution they make to national income. These industries tend to earn **rents**; that is, they earn a higher-than-normal return on an investment, and they pay higher wages to workers than do standard manufacturing industries. In addition, relatively recent developments in economic theory that build on the basic insight of the infant-industry case for protection suggest that governments can use industrial policy to create internationally competitive domestic high-technology industries. We examine these issues here, focusing first on the economic theories that justify the use of industrial policy in high-technology industries and then examining two cases in which industrial policy appears to have enabled high-technology firms based in Japan and the EU to become internationally competitive at the apparent expense of high-technology firms based in the United States. We conclude by returning to the current U.S.–EU dispute in commercial aircraft.

Strategic-Trade Theory

Strategic-trade theory provides the theoretical justification for industrial policy in high-technology industries. **Strategic-trade theory** expands on the basic insight of the infant-industry case for protection. Like the infant-industry case, strategic-trade theory asserts that government intervention can help domestic firms achieve economies of scale and experience in order to become efficient and competitive in global markets. In contrast to the classical infant-industry argument, which assumes that markets are perfectly competitive, strategic-trade theory asserts that many high-tech industries are characterized by oligopolistic competition; that is, they feature competition between only a few firms. The combination of economies of scale and experience on the one hand and oligopolistic competition on the other creates a theoretical rationale for government intervention to raise national income.

An **oligopoly** is an industry dominated by a small number of firms. The world auto industry, for example, is dominated by only about eight firms. The world market for long-distance commercial aircraft is dominated by only two firms. Such industries are clearly different from, say, agriculture, in which thousands of farms produce for the world market. Economic dynamics in oligopolistic market structures are quite different from the dynamics we see in perfectly competitive markets. The economic analysis of oligopolistic competition can be quite complex, however, and a detailed analysis of such competition would take us far from our primary concern. Consequently, we will leave a detailed analysis of such competition to the side and simply state that firms operating in oligopolistic markets earn excess returns—profits greater than could be earned in equally risky investments in other sectors of the economy (Krugman and Obstfeld 1994, 282).

Suppose an American firm dominates the world market for commercial aircraft. The United States captures the excess returns available in this industry. As a result, American workers employed in this industry, as well as the people who have invested their savings in this industry, earn higher incomes than they would earn in the next-best use of their labor or savings. American national income is higher than it would be otherwise. If a European firm dominates the world market for commercial aircraft, Europe captures the excess returns and enjoys the higher "national" income. And because an oligopolistic industry is one in which only a limited number of firms can operate, only a small number of countries can capture the available excess returns. It is certainly reasonable to suppose, therefore, that societies would compete over these industries. Strategic-trade theory thus suggests that in some industries global economic interaction gives rise to zero-sum competition over the excess returns available in oligopolistic high-tech industries.

Who is likely to win this competition? In the absence of intervention by any government, the firm that is the first to enter a particular industry will win, and in doing so effectively deter subsequent entry by potential rivals. Thus, such industries offer a first-mover advantage. This first-mover advantage arises from economies of scale and experience. Suppose an American high-tech firm is the first to produce and market a product such as commercial jet aircraft. Because achieving economies of scale and experience is central to the ability to produce commercial jets efficiently, the United States, by virtue of being first into the market, has a production cost advantage over rivals who may want to enter the market at a later time. As a consequence, a European firm that could be competitive once it achieved economies of scale and experience is deterred from entering the industry because the cost advantage enjoyed by the established American firm makes it very difficult to sell enough aircraft to achieve these economies. After all, who will buy the new entrant's higher-cost output? Absent such sales the new firm will never realize the economies of scale and experience essential to long-term success. The U.S. firm, therefore, has an advantage in the industry only because it is the first into the market. Consequently, the United States will enjoy the higher national income yielded by the excess returns in the commercial aircraft industry. Other countries are denied these excess returns, even though were they able to achieve the necessary economies of scale and experience, they would be every bit as successful as the American first mover.

Government intervention may have a powerful effect on the willingness of a latecomer to enter the industry. That is, targeted government intervention may enable late entrants to successfully challenge first movers. By doing so, government intervention shifts the excess returns available in a particular industry from a foreign country to the national economy. The logic of this argument can be illustrated using some fairly simple game theory (Krugman 1987). Let's assume that there are two firms, one American and one European, interacting in a high-tech industry, say commercial aircraft, which will support only one producer. Each firm has two strategies: to produce commercial aircraft or to not produce. The payoffs that each firm gains from the four possible outcomes are depicted in Figure 5.1a. There are two possible equilibrium outcomes in this game, one in which the American firm produces and the European firm does not (cell II), and one in which the European firm produces and the American firm does not (cell IV). Thus, this particular high-tech industry will be based in the United States or in Europe, but never in both. Whichever country hosts the firm earns 100 units in income.

Which country captures the industry depends upon which firm is first to enter the market. Let's suppose that the American firm is first to enter the industry and has realized economies of scale and experience. In this case, the

		European Firm	
		Produce	Not Produce
American Firm	Produce	−5, −5 (I)	100, 0 (II)
	Not Produce	0, 100 (IV)	0, 0 (III)

(a) Payoff Matrix with no Subsidy

		European Firm	
		Produce	Not Produce
American Firm	Produce	−5, 5 (I)	100, 0 (II)
	Not Produce	0, 110 (IV)	0, 0 (III)

(b) Payoff Matrix with European Subsidy

FIGURE 5.1

The Impact of Industrial Policy in High-Technology Industries

European firm has no incentive to enter the industry, because, by doing so, it would earn a profit of 25. If we assume that the European firm is first to enter the market, then it realizes economies of scale and experience. In this case, the American firm has no incentive to enter the market. Thus, even though both firms could produce the product equally well, the firm that enters first dominates the industry. According to strategic-trade theory, therefore, the firm that is first to enter a particular high-technology industry will hold a competitive advantage, and the country that is home to this firm will capture the rents available in this industry.

Against this backdrop, we can examine how governments can use industrial policy to help domestic high-technology firms. Government intervention can help new firms enter an established high-technology industry to challenge, and eventually compete with, established firms. Government assistance to these new firms can come in many forms. Governments may provide financial assistance to help their new firms pay for the costs of research and development. Such subsidies help reduce the costs that private firms must bear in the early stages of product development, thereby reducing the up-front investment a firm must make to enter the industry. European governments participating in the Airbus consortium, for example, have subsidized the development of Airbus aircraft. Governments also may guarantee a market for the early and more expensive versions of the firm's products. Tariffs and quotas can be used to keep foreign goods out, and government purchasing decisions can favor domestic producers over imports. The Japanese government, for example, purchased most of its supercomputers from Japanese suppliers in the 1980s, even though the supercomputers produced by the American firm Cray Industries were cheaper and performed at a higher level. The guaranteed market allows domestic firms to sell their high-cost output from early stages of production at high prices. The combination of financial support and guaranteed markets allows domestic firms to enter the market and move down the learning curve. Once the new firms have realized economies of scale, they can compete against established firms in international markets.

We can see the impact of such policies on firms' production decisions by returning to our simple game (see Figure 5.1b). Suppose that the American firm is the first to enter and dominates the industry. Suppose now that European governments provide a subsidy of 10 units to the European firm. The subsidy changes the payoffs the European firm receives if it produces. In contrast to the no-subsidy case, the European firm now makes a profit of 5 units when it produces, even if the American firm stays in the market. The subsidy therefore makes it rational for the European firm to start producing. Government support for domestic high-technology firms has a second consequence that stems from the oligopolistic nature of high-tech industries. Because such industries support only a small number of firms at profitable levels of output, the entry of new firms into the sector must eventually cause other firms to exit. Thus, government policies that promote the creation of a successful industry in one country undermine the established industry in other countries.

This outcome is also clear in our simple game. Once the European firm begins producing, the American firm earns a profit of 25 if it continues to produce and a profit of 0 if it exits the industry. Exit, therefore, is the American firm's rational response to the entry of the European firm. Thus, the small 10-unit subsidy provided by European governments enables the European firm to eliminate the first-mover advantage enjoyed by the American firm, but ultimately drive the American firm out of the industry. As a consequence, Europe's national income rises by 100 units (the 110-unit profit realized by the European firm minus the 10-unit subsidy from European governments), whereas America's national income falls by 100 units. A small government subsidy has allowed Europe to increase its national income at the expense of the United States.

Strategic-trade theory suggests, therefore, that the location of high-technology industries has little to do with cross-national differences in factor endowments and a lot to do with market structure and the assumptions we make about how production costs vary with the quantity of output. This is a world in which the classical model of comparative advantage doesn't hold. International competitiveness and the pattern of international specialization in high-technology industries are attributed as much to the timing of market entry as to underlying factor endowments.

STRATEGIC RIVALRY IN SEMICONDUCTORS AND COMMERCIAL AIRCRAFT

The semiconductor industry and the commercial aircraft industry illustrate these kinds of strategic trade rivalries between the United States, Japan, and the EU in the contemporary global economy. In the semiconductor industry, American producers enjoyed first-mover advantages and dominated the world market until the early 1980s. The semiconductor industry prospered in the United States in part due to government support in the form of funding for research and development (R&D) and for defense-related purchases. The U.S. government financed a large portion of the basic research in electronics—as much as 85 percent of all R&D prior to 1958, and as much as 50 percent during the 1960s. At the same time, the U.S. defense industry provided a critical market for semiconductors. Defense-related purchases by the U.S. government absorbed as much as 100 percent of total production in the early years. Even in the late 1960s, the government continued to purchase as much as 40 percent of production. These policies allowed American semiconductor firms to move down the learning curve and realize economies of scale. This first-mover advantage was transformed into a dominant position in the global market. In the early 1970s, U.S. semiconductor producers controlled 98 percent of the American market and 78 percent of the European market.

Beginning in the 1970s, the Japanese government targeted semiconductors as a sector for priority development and used two policy measures to foster a Japanese semiconductor industry. First and most importantly, the Japanese government used a variety of measures to protect Japanese semiconductor producers from American competition. Tariffs and quotas kept American chips out of the Japanese market. The Japanese government also approved very few applications for investment by foreign semiconductor firms and restricted the ability of American semiconductor firms to purchase existing Japanese firms. As a direct result, American semiconductor firms were unable to jump over trade barriers by building semiconductor production plants in Japan. The Japanese industrial structure—a structure in which producers develop long-term relationships with input suppliers—helped ensure that Japanese firms that used semiconductors as inputs purchased from Japanese rather than American suppliers. Finally, government purchases of computer equipment discriminated against products that used American chips in favor of computers that used Japanese semiconductors. Second, the Japanese government provided financial assistance to more than 60 projects connected to the semiconductor and computer industry. Such financial assistance helped cover many of the R&D costs Japanese producers faced.

The extent of Japanese protectionism can be appreciated by comparing U.S. market shares in the EU, and Japanese markets. Whereas American semiconductor firms controlled 98 percent of the American market and 78 percent of the EU market in the mid-1970s, they held only 20 percent of the Japanese market (Tyson 1995, 93). By 1976, Japanese firms were producing highly sophisticated chips and had displaced American products from all but the most sophisticated applications in the Japanese market. Success in the Japanese market was followed by success in the global market. Japan exported more semiconductors than it imported for the first time in 1979. By 1986 Japanese firms had captured about 46 percent of global semiconductor revenues, whereas the American firms' share had fallen to 40 percent (Tyson 1995, 104–105). By protecting domestic producers and subsidizing R&D costs, the Japanese government helped Japanese firms successfully challenge American dominance of the semiconductor industry.

A similar dynamic is evident in U.S.–European competition in the commercial aircraft sector. Two American firms, Boeing and Douglas (later McDonnell Douglas), dominated the global market for commercial aircraft throughout the postwar period, in part because of U.S. government support to the industry provided through the procurement of military aircraft (Newhouse 1982; U.S. Congress, Office of Technology Assessment 1991, 345). Work on military contracts enabled the two major American producers to achieve economies of scale in their commercial aircraft operations. Boeing, for example, developed one of its most successful commercial airliners, the 707, as a modified version of a military tanker craft, the KC-135. This allowed Boeing to reduce the cost of developing the commercial airliner. Both jets in turn benefited from the experience Boeing had gained in developing the B-47 and the B-52 bombers (OTA 1991, 345). As Joseph Sutter, a Boeing executive vice president, noted, "We are good ... partly because we build so many airplanes. We learn from our mistakes, and each of our airplanes embodies everything we have learned from our other airplanes" (quoted in Newhouse 1982, 7). The accumulated knowledge from military and commercial production gave the two American producers a first-mover advantage in the global market for commercial airliners sufficient to deter new entrants.

In 1967, the French, German, and British governments launched Airbus Industrie to challenge the global dominance of Boeing and McDonnell Douglas. Between 1970 and 1991, these three European governments provided between $10 billion and $18 billion of financial support to Airbus Industrie, an amount equal to about 75 percent of the cost of developing Airbus airliners (OTA 1991, 354). As a consequence, by the early 1990s Airbus Industrie had developed a family of commercial aircraft capable of serving the long-range, medium-range, large passenger, and smaller passenger routes. Airbus's entry into the commercial aircraft industry had a dramatic impact on global market share. As Table 5.1 makes clear, in the mid-1970s Boeing and McDonnell Douglas dominated the market for large commercial airliners. Airbus began to capture market share in the 1980s, however, and by 1990 it had gained control of 30 percent of the market for large commercial airliners. In 1994 Airbus sold more airliners than Boeing for the first time. And the ensuing 10 years indicates that 1994 was no fluke, as Airbus has firmly established itself as a dominant force in the global market for long-range commercial jets.

As a consequence of Airbus's success, a substantial portion of the rents available from the production and sale of commercial airliners has been transferred from the United States to Europe. Thus, by subsidizing the initial costs of aircraft development, European governments have been able to capture a significant share of the global market for commercial aircraft and the income generated in this sector, at the expense of the United States.

Strategic-trade rivalries of this kind have been a source of conflict in the international trade system. Countries losing high-technology industries as a consequence of the industrial policies pursued by other countries can respond by supporting their own firms to offset the advantages enjoyed by foreign firms or by attempting to prevent foreign governments from using industrial policy. In the United States, which considered itself a victim

TABLE 5.1

Market Share in Global Commercial Aircraft

	Boeing	McDonnell Douglas*	Airbus
1975	67%	33%	0
1985	63%	20%	17%
1990	54%	16%	30%
2005–2007	50.8%	n.a.[†]	49.2%

* Merged with Boeing in 1997; its commercial aircraft fleet is no longer produced.
† n.a., not available.

Source: Data for 1975–1990 are calculated from Tyson 1995, 158–159. Data for 2005–2007 are from Boeing and Airbus.

of the industrial policies adopted by Japan and the EU, the national debate has focused on both responses. Considerable pressure emerged during the 1980s and early 1990s for a national technology policy. Proposals were advanced for the creation of a government agency charged with reviewing global technology and

> evaluating the likely course of key American industries; comparing these baseline projections with visions of industry paths that would be compatible with a prosperous and competitive economy; and monitoring the activities of foreign governments and firms in these industries to provide an early warning of potential competitive problems in the future.
>
> (Tyson 1995, 289)

Many recommended that the U.S. government reduce its R&D support for military and dual-use projects (*dual use* refers to projects with military and commercial applications) and increase the amount of support provided to strictly commercial applications. Proponents of a national technology strategy also encouraged greater cooperation between the public and private sector on precompetitive research in a wide range of advanced technologies. Such proposals played an important role in the first Clinton administration's thinking about international trade, a role reflected in Clinton's selection of Laura D'Andrea Tyson, an economist and one of the most prominent proponents of such policies, to be the chair of his Council of Economic Advisors.

The United States also put considerable pressure on other governments to stop their support of high-technology industries. A series of negotiations with Japan that was conducted during the 1980s and early 1990s were designed to pry open the Japanese market to internationally competitive American high-technology industries. Such negotiations took place in semiconductors, computers, telecommunications, and other sectors. The rationale for these negotiations is evident from the previous discussion about first-mover advantages. If Japanese firms could be denied a protected market for their early production runs, they would never realize the scale economies required to compete in international markets. Opening the Japanese market to American high-technology producers would prevent the emergence of competitive Japanese high-technology firms and thereby help maintain American high-technology leadership. During the 1980s and early 1990s, therefore, the United States responded strategically to the use of industrial policies by Japan and, to a lesser extent, the EU and adopted policies designed to counter them.

It is within this context that we can understand the current U.S.–EU conflict in the commercial aircraft industry. Boeing has long been concerned about the gains Airbus has made in the global market and has long pressured the U.S. government to try to limit the subsidies that European governments offer. In 1992 the United States and the European Union reached agreement that both would not provide subsidies greater than one-third of the total cost of developing a new airliner or greater than 3 percent of the firm's annual revenue. In early summer of 2004 the Bush administration, facing considerable pressure from Boeing, informed the EU that it was time to renegotiate this agreement. The time for such a move looked right, at least to Boeing, for both companies were beginning to develop new aircraft, and Boeing argued that each should do so without government support. As Boeing CEO Henry Stonecipher said, the 1992 agreement "no longer reflected market realities" and had "outlived its usefulness" (King 2004). Given Airbus's current market position, it should stop expecting European governments to give it "truckloads" of money to cover a portion of new aircraft development. "We're saying enough is enough. You're very successful, you're delivering and selling more airplanes than Boeing .... Why don't you go to the bank and borrow money?" It was, Boeing argued, "time for Airbus to accept the financial and marketplace risks that true commercial companies experience" (Casert 2004, p. E.03).

Efforts to renegotiate the 1992 agreement proved unsuccessful. Although EU officials seemed willing to accept the American claim that Airbus had received government support (though they denied that such support amounted to more than a token), they asserted that Boeing had itself been the beneficiary of $23 billion of government subsidies since 1992. These subsidies had come, the EU argued, from U.S. government R&D contracts and from $3.2 billion in tax reductions, tax exemptions, and infrastructure improvements provided by the state of Washington. Consequently, the EU was willing to discuss a reduction of European assistance to Airbus only in conjunction with an American willingness to accept a reduction of such assistance for Boeing. When the United States proved unwilling to either accept the EU claim or to provide information that would dispute the claim, the negotiations broke down. Days later, the United States announced that it was withdrawing from the 1992 agreement and filed a dispute with the WTO alleging that the EU was in violation of its WTO obligations concerning the use of subsidies that cause harm to foreign competitors. The EU responded immediately by initiating its own WTO dispute in which it alleged the same thing of the United States. The stakes are high, as estimates suggest that over the next 20 years sales of large commercial aircraft will generate $2 trillion (Blustein 2004a). It remains to be seen whether American or European producers will capture this income.

CONCLUSION

Even though a state-centered approach directs our attention to the important role that states play in shaping the structure of their domestic economies, it does have some important weaknesses. Three such weaknesses are perhaps most important. First, the state-centered approach lacks explicit microfoundations. The approach asserts that states act in ways that enhance national welfare. A critical student must respond to this assertion by asking one simple question: What incentive does the state have to act in ways that do in fact enhance national welfare? Anyone who has visited the Palace of Versailles in France or has spent any time reading about the experience of other autonomous rulers knows that autonomous states have as much (if not more) incentive to act in the private interests of state officials as they have to act in the interest of society as a whole. Why then would autonomous state actors enrich society when they might just as easily enrich themselves? Answering this question requires us to think about how state actors are rewarded for promoting policies that enhance national welfare and are punished for failing to do so. In answering this question, we develop microfoundations—an explanation that sets out the incentive structure that encourages state officials to adopt policies that promote national welfare. But the state-centered approach currently does not offer a good answer to this question. The reward structure that state policymakers face cannot be elections, for that pushes us back toward a society-centered approach. The reward structure might be security related: one could reasonably argue that states intervene to enhance the power and position of the nation in the international system. We must still explain, however, how these broad concerns about national security create incentives for individual policymakers to make specific decisions about resource allocation. The point is not that such microfoundations could not be developed, but rather, as far as I am aware, that no one has yet done so. As a result, the state-centered approach provides little justification for its central assertion that states will regularly act in ways that enhance national welfare.

Second, the assumption that states make policy independent of domestic interest-group pressure is misleading. Even highly autonomous states do not stand above *all* societal interests. Interest groups need not dictate policy, as the society-centered approach claims, but they do establish the parameters in which policy must be made. Even in Japan, which probably comes closest to the ideal autonomous state, the Liberal Democrat Party's (LDP) position in government was based in part on the support of big business. Is it merely a coincidence that Japanese industrial policy channeled resources to big business, or did the Japanese state adopt such policies because they were in the interest of one of the LDP's principal supporters? Thus, whereas the society-centered approach assumes too little room for autonomous state action, the state-centered approach assumes too much state autonomy. We may learn more by fitting the two approaches together. This would lead us to expect governments to intervene in the economy to promote specific economic outcomes, but often such policies are consistent with and shaped by the interests of the coalition of societal groups upon which the government's power rests.

Finally, strategic-trade theory itself, which provides the intellectual justification for government intervention in high-technology industries, has considerable weaknesses. Strategic-trade theory is as much a prescriptive theory—one used to derive policy proposals—as it is an explanatory theory. As such, it has some important limitations. The claim that government intervention can improve national welfare is not particularly robust. The conclusions one derives from any theory are sensitive to the assumptions one makes when building the theory. If the conclusions change greatly when one alters some of the underlying assumptions, then the confidence one has in the accuracy of the theory must be greatly diminished. Strategic-trade theory has been criticized for producing strong conclusions only under a relatively restrictive set of assumptions. Although the specific criticisms are too detailed to consider here, the bottom line is that altering the assumptions about how one country's established firms respond to a foreign government's subsidy of its firms, about how many firms are in the sector in question, and about where firms sell their products can either weaken the central claim considerably or introduce so much complexity into the model that the policy implications become opaque.

Thus, strategic-trade theory does not provide unambiguous support for the claim that government intervention in high-technology industries can raise national income. In addition, even if we assume that strategic-trade theory is correct, it is not easy for governments to identify sectors in which intervention will raise national income. It is difficult to identify sectors that offer such gains and then to calculate the correct subsidy that will shift this activity to domestic producers at a net gain to social welfare. If governments choose the wrong sectors or provide too little or too much support, intervention can reduce rather than raise national welfare. Thus, the precise policy implications of strategic-trade theory are unclear, in part because the theory itself is weak and in part because it is not easy to translate the theory's simpler conclusions into effective policies.

In spite of these weaknesses, the state-centered approach provides a useful check on the tendency of the society-centered approach to focus exclusively on the interests of societal interest groups. The state-centered approach points our attention to the interests of government officials and underscores the need to think about the ability of these officials to act independent from, and even against, the interests of domestic interest groups. By doing so, it suggests that trade policy may not always reflect the balance of power between interest groups, and tells us that we might need to take into account how state interests intervene in this competition in ways that produce outcomes that no interest groups desire. Yet, in spite of these useful insights, I believe that the absence of clearly specified microfoundations in this approach represents a fatal flaw. Without such foundations, the approach can tell us that autonomous state officials will act, but it cannot tell us *how* they will act. Adding such microfoundations, perhaps by combining the dynamics highlighted by the society-centered approach with the rich institutional environment emphasized by the state-centered approach, would enable us to begin thinking about the conditions under which state officials have the capacity for autonomous action, and about the ends to which such autonomous officials will direct their energies.

KEY TERMS

Economies of Experience	Infant-Industry Case for	Rents
Economies of Scale	Protection	State Strength
Industrial Policy	Oligopoly	Strategic-Trade Theory

SUGGESTIONS FOR FURTHER READING

For a recent and compelling argument for the continuing importance of industrial policy, see Michael Peneder, 2017. "Competitiveness and Industrial Policy: From Rationalities of Failure towards the Ability to Evolve." *Cambridge Journal of Economics* 41: 829–858.

You can find excellent treatments of postwar industrial policy in the advanced industrial economies in Richard D. Bingham, *Industrial Policy American-Style: From Hamilton to HDTV* (New York: Routledge, 2015); Christian Grabas, Alexander Nützenadel, editors, *Industrial Policy in Europe after 1945: Wealth, Power and Economic Development in the Cold War* (London: Palgrave MacMillan, 2014); and Mark Metzler, *Capital as Will and Imagination: Schumpeter's Guide to the Postwar Japanese Miracle* (Ithaca: Cornell University Press, 2013).

Finally, for an argument for using industrial policy to promote sustainable growth, see Dani Rodrik, 2014. "Green Industrial Policy." *Oxford Review of Economic Policy* 30(3): 469–491.

Trade and Development I: Import Substitution Industrialization

Mexico has experienced an economic revolution during the last 20 years. Until the mid-1980s, Mexico was one of the most heavily protected and highly directed nonsocialist economies in the world. Importing anything into the country required formal government approval. Even with such approval, tariffs were very high, averaging over 25 percent and rising as high as 100 percent for many goods. Moreover, Mexico did not belong to the General Agreement on Tariffs and Trade (GATT), and it was hard to imagine any conditions under which Mexico would seek a free-trade agreement with the United States. Behind these high tariff walls, the Mexican government intervened deeply in the domestic economy. Government-owned financial institutions channeled investment capital to favored private industries and projects. The government created state-owned enterprises in many sectors of the economy (about 1,200 of them by 1982) that together attracted more than one-third of all industrial investment (La Porta and López de Silanes 1997). Today, by contrast, Mexico is one of the most open developing countries in the world. Mexico entered the GATT in 1987 and the North American Free Trade Agreement (NAFTA) in the early 1990s. The Mexican government has retreated sharply from involvement in the domestic economy. It has sold state-owned enterprises, liberalized a wide variety of market-restricting regulations, and begun to integrate Mexico deeply into the global economy. In less than 10 years, the Mexican government opened Mexico to foreign competition and drastically scaled back its role in managing Mexican economic activity.

Mexico's experience is hardly unique. Governments in India, China, much of Latin America, and most of sub-Saharan Africa opted out of the global trade system following World War II. Most governments erected very high trade barriers, and to the extent that they participated at all in the GATT, they sought to alter the rules governing international trade. Convinced that the GATT was biased against their interests, developing countries worked through the United Nations to create international trade rules that they believed would be more favorable toward industrialization in the developing world. Like Mexico, most governments intervened extensively in their economies in an attempt to promote rapid industrialization. Drawing on the logic of the infant-industry case for protection, governments used the power of the state to pull resources out of agriculture and push them into manufacturing. And, like Mexico, these policy orientations have changed fundamentally since the late 1980s. Most developing countries have dismantled the protectionist systems they maintained in the first 30 years of the postwar period, have become active participants in the World Trade Organization (WTO), and have abandoned the quest to institute far-reaching changes to international trade rules. Most have greatly reduced the degree of government intervention in the domestic economy.

This chapter and the next examine how political and economic forces have shaped the adoption and evolution of these new trade and development policies. This chapter examines why governments in so many developing countries intervened deeply in their domestic economies, insulated themselves from international trade, and sought changes in international trade rules. The next chapter focuses on why so many governments have dismantled these policies during the last 30 years. We look first at how economic and political change throughout the developing world brought to power governments supported by import-competing interests. We then examine the economic theory that guided policy during those times. As we shall see, this theory provided governments with a compelling justification for transforming the protectionism sought by the import-competing producers that supported them into policies that emphasized industrialization through state leadership. Having built this base, we turn our attention to the specific policies that governments pursued during that period, looking first at their domestic strategy for industrialization and then examining their efforts to reform the international trade system.

DOMESTIC INTERESTS, INTERNATIONAL PRESSURES, AND PROTECTIONIST COALITIONS

Developing countries' trade policies underwent a sea change in the first half of the twentieth century. Until World War I, those developing countries that were independent, as well as those regions of the world held in colonial empires, adopted liberal trade policies. They produced and exported agricultural goods and other primary commodities to the advanced industrialized countries and imported most of the manufactured goods they consumed. Governments and colonial rulers made little effort to restrict this trade. But by the late 1950s, these liberal trade policies had been replaced by a protectionist approach that dominated the developing countries' trade policies until the late 1980s, and whose remnants remain important in many countries today. We begin our investigation of developing countries' trade and development policies by looking at this initial shift to protectionism.

Trade and development policies in developing countries have been strongly shaped by political competition between rural-based agriculture and urban-based manufacturing. Developing countries pursued liberal trade policies prior to World War I because export-oriented agricultural interests dominated politics. In general, developing countries are abundantly endowed with land and poorly endowed with capital (Lal and Myint 1996, 104–110).

The relative importance of land and capital in developing countries' economies can be appreciated by examining the structure of those economies, together with exports, as presented in Table 6.1 and Table 6.2. For the time being, we will focus on 1960, as this will allow us to put to the side the consequences of the development policies that governments adopted during the postwar period. With a few exceptions (particularly in Latin America), between one-third and one-half of all economic activity in developing countries in 1960 was based in agriculture, whereas less than 15 percent was based in manufacturing. By contrast, agriculture accounted for only 5 percent of gross domestic product (GDP) in the advanced industrial economies. If we include the "other industry" category, which incorporates mining, then in all regions of the developing world other than Latin America, agriculture and nonmanufacturing industries accounted for more than half of all economic activity.

A similar pattern is evident in the commodity composition of developing countries' exports (Table 6.2). In 1962, developing countries' exports were heavily concentrated in primary commodities: agricultural products, minerals, and other raw materials. Roughly speaking, in each developing country, primary commodities accounted for more than 50 percent of exports, and in

TABLE 6.1

Economic Structure in Developing Countries (Sector as a Percent of Gross Domestic Product)

	Agriculture			Manufacturing			Other Industry			Services		
	1960	1980	1995	1960	1980	1995	1960	1980	1995	1960	1980	1995
Sub-Saharan Africa	36	24	20	12	12	15	18	24	15	40	38	48
East Asia and the Pacific	46	27	18	16	27	32	7	12	12	31	32	38
South Asia	49	39	30	13	15	17	6	9	10	33	35	41
Latin America	16	10	10	21	25	21	10	12	12	53	51	55

Notes: Figures may not sum to 100 because of rounding.
Other Industry Includes mining, construction, gas, and water.

Sources: Data for 1960 from World Bank, *World Tables,* 3rd ed. (Washington, DC: The World Bank, 1983). Data for 1980 and 1995 from World Bank, *World Development Indicators* (Washington, DC: The World Bank, 1997).

TABLE 6.2

Developing Countries' Export Composition
(Sector as a Percent of Total Exports)

	Fuels, Minerals, and Metals			Other Primary Commodities			Manufactures		
	1962	1980	1993	1962	1980	1993	1962	1980	1993
Sub-Saharan Africa									
Cameroon	21	33	51	75	64	35	4	4	14
Ghana	73	17	25	31	82	52	1	1	23
Kenya	2	36	16	89	52	66	9	13	19
Nigeria	11	97	94	81	2	4	8	0	2
South Africa	23	33	16	47	28	11	26	40	74
Zaire	16	56	69	75	14	13	10	31	18
East Asia and the Pacific									
Hong Kong	2	2	2	3	5	3	93	93	96
Indonesia	37	76	32	63	22	15	0	3	53
Malaysia	n.a.	35	14	n.a.	46	21	n.a.	20	65
Singapore	52	31	14	18	18	6	30	51	80
South Korea	24	1	3	57	9	4	20	90	94
Taiwan	n.a.	2	2	n.a.	10	5	n.a.	88	93
South Asia									
India	9	8	7	47	33	18	44	59	75
Pakistan	0	8	1	75	44	14	25	48	85
Latin America									
Argentina	2	6	11	95	71	57	3	23	32
Bolivia	91	86	56	4	11	25	5	3	19
Brazil	9	11	12	88	50	28	3	39	60
Chile	87	65	43	8	25	38	4	10	19
Mexico	24	73	17	60	15	9	16	12	75

Note: n.a. = not available.

Sources: Data for 1962 from World Bank, *World Tables,* 3rd ed. (Washington, DC: The World Bank, 1983). Data for 1980 and 1993 from World Bank, *World Development Indicators* (Washington, DC: The World Bank, 1997).

more than half of the listed countries, primary commodities accounted for more than 80 percent of exports. In addition, each country exported a narrow range of primary commodities. Some countries were **monoexporters**; that is, their exports were almost fully accounted for by one product. For example, more than 80 percent of Burundi's export earnings came from coffee, and cocoa accounted for 75 percent of Ghana's export earnings (Cypher and Dietz 1997, 339). Similar patterns were evident in Latin America: in 1950, coffee and cocoa made up about 69 percent of Brazil's exports, and copper and nitrates constituted about 74 percent of Chile's exports (Thorp 1999, 346). The structure of their economies and the composition of their exports thus underline the central point: developing countries are abundantly endowed with land and have little capital.

The precise form through which landowners dominated politics prior to World War II differed considerably across regions. In Latin America, an indigenous landowning elite dominated domestic politics. In Argentina and Chile, for example, the landowners controlled government, often in an alliance with the military. Even though these political systems were constitutionally democratic, participation was restricted to the elite, a group that amounted to about 5 percent of the population, in a system that has been characterized as "oligarchic democracy" (Skidmore and Smith 1989, 47). In other Latin American countries such as Mexico, Venezuela, and Peru, dictatorial and often military governments ruled, but they pursued policies that protected the interests of the landowners (Skidmore and Smith 1989, 47). With landowners dominating domestic politics, Latin American governments pursued liberal trade policies that favored agricultural production and export at the expense of manufactured goods (Rogowski 1989, 47). As a result, most Latin American countries were highly open to international trade, producing and exporting agricultural goods and other primary commodities and importing manufactured goods from Great Britain, Europe, and the United States.

In Asia and in Africa, export-oriented agricultural interests dominated local politics through colonial structures. In Taiwan and Korea, for example, Japanese colonization led to the development of **enclave agriculture**—that is, export-oriented agricultural sectors that had few linkages to other parts of the local economy (Haggard 1990). Agricultural producers bought little from local suppliers and exported most of their production. In both countries, agricultural production centered on the production and export of rice; in Taiwan, sugarcane was a staple crop as well. India produced and exported a range of primary commodities, including cotton, jute, wheat, tea, and rice. In exchange, India imported most of the manufactured goods it consumed from Britain. In Africa, colonial powers encouraged the production of cash crops and raw materials that could be exported to the mother country (Hopkins 1979; Ake 1981, 1996). In the Gold Coast (now Ghana), the cocoa industry was a small part of the economy in 1870. Under British rule, Ghana became the world's largest cocoa producer by 1910, and cocoa accounted for 80 percent of its exports. In Senegal, France promoted groundnut (the American peanut) production, and by 1937 close to half of all cultivated land was dedicated to this single product (Ka and Van de Walle 1994, 296). Similar patterns with other commodities were evident in other African colonies (Hopkins 1979).

These political arrangements began to change in the early twentieth century. As they did, the dominance of export-oriented interests gave way to the interests of import-competing manufacturers. In many instances, the most important triggers for this change originated outside of developing societies. In Latin America, international economic shocks beginning with the First World

War and extending into World War II played a central role (Thorp 1999, Chapter 4). Government-mandated rationing of goods and primary commodities in the United States and Europe during the two World Wars made it difficult for Latin American countries to import many of the consumer goods they had previously purchased from the industrialized countries. In addition, falling commodity prices associated with the Great Depression and the disruption of normal trade patterns arising from World War II reduced export revenues. The interruption of "normal" Latin American trade patterns led governments in many countries to introduce trade barriers and to begin producing many of the manufactured goods that they had previously imported. The rise of domestic manufacturing in turn produced a growing urban middle class as workers and industrialists began to move out of agricultural production and into manufacturing industries.

The emergence of manufacturing industries gave rise to interest groups, industry-based associations, and labor unions that pressured the government to adopt economic policies favorable to people working in the import-competing sector. The creation of organized groups to represent the interests of import-competing manufacturing generated its own political logic. On the one hand, the groups that saw their incomes rise from protection had a strong incentive to see protectionist policies continued in the postwar period (see Rogowski 1989; Haggard 1990). On the other hand, the emergence of new organized interests and a growing urban middle class created an opportunity for politicians to construct new political coalitions based on the support of the urban sectors. In Argentina, for example, Juan Perón rose to power in the late 1940s with the support of labor, industrialists, and the military. A similar pattern was evident in Brazil, where Getúlio Vargas was elected to the presidency in 1950 with the support of industrialists, government civil servants, and urban labor. Nor were Argentina and Brazil unique: throughout Latin America, postwar governments were much less tightly linked to landed interests than governments had been before World War I. Instead, governments rose to power on the basis of political support from interest groups whose incomes were derived from import-competing manufacturing (Cardoso and Faletto 1979). Such governments had a clear incentive to maintain trade policies that protected those incomes.

A similar dynamic is evident in India. The global economic collapse of the 1930s forced India to become increasingly self-reliant. Markets for Indian exports constricted sharply, thereby greatly constraining Indian export revenues. Unable to earn foreign exchange, India had to reduce imports of manufactured goods as well. Under this forced self-reliance, India began to create an indigenous manufacturing sector. By the end of World War II, India had emerged as "the tenth largest producer of manufactured goods in the world" (Tomlinson 1979, 31). The indigenous urban manufacturing sector then fused with the burgeoning nationalist movement during the late 1930s to lead the push for Indian independence and to supplant the predominantly foreign-owned export sector at the center of the Indian political system. By the time India achieved independence in 1947, it was committed to a strategy of autonomous industrialization.

In Pacific Asia, the shift in political power came about as a product of de-colonization. In Korea and Taiwan political change resulted from the defeat of Imperial Japan in World War II (see Haggard 1990). In South Korea, Japan's defeat transferred power from a foreign colonizer to indigenous groups. Although the landowners initially dominated postwar politics, the Korean War of the early 1950s and a series of land reforms implemented during that same decade greatly reduced the landowners' power and increased the relative power of the emerging urban sector. On mainland China, Japan's defeat was followed by the defeat of the nationalist Chinese government and the migration of the Chinese nationalists to the island of Taiwan. Once installed in Taiwan, the Chinese nationalists instituted land reforms to assert their authority over indigenous landowners and to prevent a repeat of their experience on the mainland, where the rural sector had supported the Communists. As in South Korea, land reforms reduced the power of landowners and increased the power of the urban–industrial sector.

Africa's transition came later, as decolonization began only in the 1950s, and it took a slightly different form. The push toward decolonization was led by a coalition of indigenous professionals who had been educated by the colonial powers and had then acquired positions in the administration of colonial economic and political rule. One factor motivating Africa's push for independence was dissatisfaction with the discriminatory practices of colonial administration. Colonies were run for the profit of the colonists, with colonial economic enterprises staffed and managed by men from the colonial power. The local population had limited opportunities to participate in these economic arrangements other than as workers. The nationalist struggles for independence that emerged in the 1950s sought to transfer control over existing economic practices from the colonial governments to indigenous elites.

The period demarcated by the start of World War I and the end of decolonization in sub-Saharan Africa thus brought a fundamental change to patterns of political influence in developing countries. Political structures once dominated by export-oriented agricultural interests were now largely under the control of import-competing manufacturing interests. Consequently, governments beholden to the import-competing sector had a clear incentive to abandon liberal trade policies and to continue the protectionist arrangements they had built during the 1930s. As we will see, the political interest in protectionism was reinforced by an elaborate theoretical structure that argued that protectionism was the only path to the establishment of industrialized economies.

THE STRUCTURALIST CRITIQUE: MARKETS, TRADE, AND ECONOMIC DEVELOPMENT

Although protectionism reflected the interests of the politically influential import-competing manufacturing sector, it did not represent a coherent economic development strategy. And most governments were committed, at least rhetorically, to the adoption of policies that would promote economic development. Most governments wanted to shift resources out of agricultural production and into manufacturing industries because they believed that poverty resulted from too heavy a concentration on agricultural production. Higher standards of living could be achieved only through industrialization, and according to what was then the dominant branch of development economics, called **structuralism**, the shift of resources from agriculture to manufacturing would not occur unless the state adopted policies to bring it about (see Lal 1983; Little 1982).

The belief that the market would not promote industrialization provided the intellectual and theoretical justification for the two central aspects of the development strategies adopted by most governments throughout much of the postwar era. Because structuralism played such an important role in shaping developing countries' trade and development policies, understanding the policies governments adopted requires us to understand the structuralist critique.

Market Imperfections in Developing Countries

Structuralists argued that market imperfections inside developing countries posed serious obstacles to the reallocation of resources from agriculture to manufacturing industries. Structuralists argued that markets would not bring about the necessary shift of resources because developing economies were too inflexible.

Most important, according to the structuralists, was the belief that the market would not promote investment in manufacturing industries (Scitovsky 1954). The structuralists pointed to two coordination problems that would limit investment in manufacturing industries. The first problem, called **complementary demand**, arose in the initial transformation from an economy based largely on subsistence agriculture to a manufacturing economy (Rosenstein-Rodan 1943). In an economy in which few people earned a money wage, no single manufacturing firm would be able to sell its products unless a large number of other manufacturing industries were started simultaneously. Suppose, for example, that 100 people are taken out of subsistence agriculture and paid a wage to manufacture shoes, whereas the rest of the population remains in non-wage agriculture. To whom will the new factory sell its shoes? The only workers earning money are those producing shoes, and these 100 workers are unlikely to purchase all of the shoes that they make. In order for this shoe factory to succeed, other factories employing other people must be created at the same time.

Suppose instead, that 500,000 workers are taken out of subsistence agriculture and simultaneously employed in a large number of factories producing a variety of different goods; some make shoes, others make clothing, and still others produce refrigerators or processed foods. With this larger number of wage earners, manufacturing enterprises can easily sell their goods. Shoe workers can buy refrigerators and clothes, workers in the clothing factory can purchase shoes, and so on. Thus, a manufacturing enterprise will be successful only if many manufacturing industries began production simultaneously.

Structuralists doubted that uncoordinated market behavior would produce simultaneous investment in multiple manufacturing industries. No single entrepreneur has an incentive to invest in a manufacturing enterprise unless he or she is certain that others will invest simultaneously in other industries. People willing to invest will thus wait until others invest and, as a consequence, no one will invest in manufacturing unless all potential investors could somehow coordinate their behavior to ensure that all will invest in manufacturing at the same time. The problem of complementary demand thus meant that if investment were left to the market, there would be little investment in manufacturing industries.

The second coordination problem, called **pecuniary external economies**, arose from interdependencies among market processes (Scitovsky 1954). Think about the economic relationship between a steel plant and an automobile factory. Suppose that the owners of a steel factory invest to increase the amount of steel they can produce. As steel production increases, steel prices begin to fall. The automobile factory, which uses a lot of steel, begins to realize rising profits as the price of one of its most important inputs falls. These increasing profits in the automobile industry could induce the owners of the car plant to invest to expand their own production capacity. Such a simultaneous expansion of the steel and auto industries would raise national income.

The two firms face a coordination problem, however. The owners of the steel plant will not increase steel production unless they are sure that the auto industry will increase car production. Yet, the owners of the auto plant will not increase auto production unless they are certain that the steel producer will make the investments needed to expand steel output. Thus, unless investment decisions in the steel and auto industry are coordinated, neither firm will invest to increase the amount it can produce. Once again, structuralists argued, the market could not be expected to solve this coordination problem.

The structuralists' assertion that coordination problems would prevent investment in manufacturing was a serious problem for governments intent on industrialization. Fortunately, the structuralists offered a solution to the problem. Structuralists argued that the way to overcome these coordination problems was with a state-led **big push**. The state would engage in economic planning and either make necessary investments itself or help coordinate the investments of private economic actors. Thus, what the market could not bring about, the state could achieve through intervening in the economy. The structuralist critique of the market therefore provided a compelling theoretical justification for state-led strategies of industrialization.

Market Imperfections in the International Economy

Structuralists also argued that international trade provided few benefits to developing countries. This argument was formulated during the 1950s, principally by Raul Prebisch, an Argentinean economist who worked for the

United Nations Economic Commission for Latin America (ECLA), and Hans Singer, an academic development economist. According to the **Singer-Prebisch theory**, participation in the GATT–based trade system would actually make it harder for developing countries to industrialize by depriving them of critical resources.

The Singer-Prebisch theory divides the world into two distinct blocks— the advanced-industrialized core and the developing-world periphery—and focuses on the terms of trade between them. The **terms of trade** relate the price of a country's exports to the price of its imports. An improvement in a country's terms of trade means that the price of its exports is rising relative to the price of its imports, but a decline in a country's terms of trade means that export prices are falling relative to its import prices. As a country's terms of trade improve, it can acquire a given amount of imports for a smaller quantity of exports. Thus, an improvement in its terms of trade makes a country richer, but a decline in its terms of trade makes it poorer.

The Singer-Prebisch theory argues that developing countries' terms of trade deteriorate steadily over time. When they developed this theory, developing countries exported primary commodities and imported manufactured goods. Singer and Prebisch argued that primary commodity prices steadily fell relative to manufactured goods prices, thereby steadily reducing the incomes of developing countries. The periphery's terms of trade deteriorate, according to this theory, in large part as a result of differences in the income elasticity of demand for primary commodities versus industrial goods (see Lewis 1954; United Nations 1964; Gilpin 1987, 275–276).

The income elasticity of demand is the degree to which a change in income alters demand for a particular product. For a product with a low income elasticity of demand, a large increase in income produces little change in demand for the good. For a product with a high income elasticity of demand, a small increase in income produces a large change in demand for a particular good. Structuralists argued that the income elasticity of demand for primary commodities was quite low, but income elasticity of demand for manufactured goods was relatively high. Thus, as incomes rise in the core countries, a smaller and smaller percentage of those countries' income will be spent on imports of primary commodities. But as incomes rise in the periphery countries, a larger percentage of *those* countries' income will be spent on manufactured imports from the core. Falling demand for primary commodities will cause the periphery countries' export prices to fall, whereas rising demand for manufactured goods will cause the periphery countries' import prices to rise. Rising import prices relative to export prices yields deteriorating terms of trade.

Most research disputes the claim that developing countries face a continuous decline in their terms of trade (see, for example, Borensztein et al. 1994; see also Bloch and Sapsford 2000). Yet, the objective validity of the Singer-Prebisch hypothesis is not the central consideration. What mattered was that governments in developing countries *believed* the hypothesis. Governments of developing countries were convinced that industrialization would not occur if they participated in the GATT–based international trade system. This conviction played an important role in shaping the trade and development policies that developing countries adopted.

DOMESTIC AND INTERNATIONAL ELEMENTS OF TRADE AND DEVELOPMENT STRATEGIES

Structuralism enabled governments to transform the protectionist trade policies that benefited their principal political supporters into comprehensive state-led development strategies. The trade and development policies that most governments adopted following World War II had both a domestic and an international dimension. At home, the desire to promote rapid industrialization led governments to adopt state-led development strategies that were sheltered by high protectionist barriers. In the international arena, concern about the distributional implications of international trade led developing countries to seek far-reaching changes to the GATT–based trade system. We examine each dimension in turn.

Import Substitution Industrialization

Structuralism provided the intellectual justification for a state-led development strategy. Confidence that the state could achieve what markets would not was based in part on evidence of the dramatic industrialization that the Soviet Union had achieved between 1930 and 1950 with an approach based on centralized planning and state ownership of industry. In developing societies outside the Soviet bloc, this state-centered approach to development came to be called **import substitution industrialization,** or ISI. The strategy of ISI was based on a simple logic: countries would industrialize by substituting domestically produced goods for manufactured items they had previously imported.

Governments conceptualized ISI as a two-stage strategy (see Table 6.3). Its initial stage was "wholly a matter of imitation and importation of tried and tested procedures" (Hirschman 1968, 7). **Easy ISI,** as this first stage was often called, focused on developing domestic manufacturing of relatively simple consumer goods, such as soda, beer, apparel, shoes, and furniture. The rationale behind the focus on simple consumer goods was threefold. First, there was a large domestic demand currently satisfied by imports. Second, because these items were mature products, the technology and machines necessary to produce them could be acquired easily from the advanced industrialized countries. Third, the production of relatively simple consumer goods relies heavily on low-skilled labor, allowing developing societies to draw their populations into manufacturing activities without making large investments to upgrade their skills.

Governments expected to realize two broad benefits from easy ISI. Initially, the expansion of manufacturing activities would increase wage-based employment as underutilized labor was drawn out of agriculture and

---

TABLE 6.3

Stages of Industrialization in Mexico and Brazil, 1880–1968

	Commodity Exports, 1880–1930	Primary ISI, 1930–1955	Secondary ISI, 1955–1968
Main Industries	Mexico: Precious metals, minerals, oil Brazil: Coffee, rubber, cocoa, cotton	Mexico and Brazil: Textiles, food, cement, iron and steel, paper, chemicals, machinery	Mexico and Brazil: Automobiles, electrical and nonelectrical machinery, petrochemicals, pharmaceuticals
Major Economic Actors	Mexico: Foreign investors Brazil: National private firms	Mexico and Brazil: National private firms	Mexico and Brazil: State-owned enterprises, transnational corporations, and national private firms
Orientation of the Economy	World market	Domestic market	Domestic market

Note: ISI = import substitution industrialization.
Source: Gereffi 1990, 19.

---

into manufacturing. In addition, the experience gained in these manufacturing industries would allow domestic workers to develop skills, collectively referred to as general human capital, that could be applied subsequently to other manufacturing businesses. Of particular importance were the management and entrepreneurial skills that would be gained by people who worked in and managed the manufacturing enterprises established in this stage. Success in the easy stage would therefore create many of the ingredients necessary to make the transition to the second stage of ISI.

Easy ISI would eventually cease to bear fruit. The domestic market's capacity to absorb simple consumer goods would be exhausted, and the range of such goods that could be produced would be limited. At some point, therefore, governments would need to shift from easy ISI to a second-stage strategy characterized by the development of more complex manufacturing activities. One possibility would be to shift to what some have called an **export substitution strategy,** in which the labor-intensive manufactured goods industries developed in easy ISI begin to export rather than continue to produce exclusively for the domestic market. Many East Asian governments adopted this approach, as we shall see in Chapter 7.

The second alternative, and the one adopted by most governments outside of East Asia, was **secondary ISI.** In secondary ISI, emphasis shifts from the manufacture of simple consumer goods to consumer durable goods, intermediate inputs, and the capital goods needed to produce consumer durables. In Argentina, Brazil, and Chile, for example, governments decided to promote domestic automobile production as a central component of secondary ISI. Each country imported cars in pieces, called complete knockdowns, and assembled the pieces into a car for sale in the domestic market. Domestic auto firms were required to gradually increase the percentage of locally produced parts used in the cars they assembled. In Chile, for example, 27 percent of a locally produced car's components had to be manufactured domestically in 1964. The percentage rose to 32 percent in 1965 and then to 45 percent in 1966 (Johnson 1967).

By increasing the percentage of local components of cars and other goods in this manner, governments hoped to promote the development of backward linkages throughout the economy (Hirschman 1958). **Backward linkages** arise when the production of one good, such as a car, increases demand in industries that supply components for that good. Thus, increasing the percentage of locally produced components of cars, by increasing the demand for individual car parts, would increase domestic part production. The latter would in turn increase demand for inputs into part production: steel, glass, and rubber, for example. Industrialization, therefore, would spread backwards from final goods to intermediate inputs to capital goods as backward linkages multiplied.

Governments promoted secondary ISI with three policy instruments: government planning, investment policy, and trade barriers. Most governments structured their efforts around 5-year plans (Little 1982, 35). Planning was used to determine which industries would be targeted for development and which would not, to figure out how much should be invested in a particular industry, and to evaluate how investment in one industry would influence the rest of the economy. India's second Five Year Plan (1957–1962), for example, sought to generate ambitious growth in manufacturing by targeting the development of capital goods production (Srinivasan and Tendulkar 2003, 8). The plan thus served as the coordination device that governments thought necessary, given their belief that the market itself could not coordinate investment decisions.

With a plan in place, governments used investment policies to promote targeted industries. Most governments either nationalized or heavily controlled the financial sector in order to direct financial resources to targeted industries. Governments also invested directly in those economic activities in which they thought the private sector would not invest. Much of the infrastructure necessary for industrialization—things such as roads and other transportation networks, electricity, and telecommunications systems—it was argued, would not be created by the private sector. In addition, the private sector lacked access to the large sums of financial support needed to make huge investments in a steel or auto plant. Moreover, it was claimed that private-sector actors lacked the technical sophistication required for the large-scale industrial activity involved in secondary ISI.

Governments invested in these industries by creating state-owned and mixed-ownership enterprises. In Brazil, for example, state-owned enterprises controlled more than 50 percent of total productive assets in the chemical, telecommunications, electricity, and railways industries and slightly more than one-third of all productive assets in metal fabrication (Trebat 1983). Indian state-owned enterprises provided 27 percent of total employment and 62 percent of all productive capital (Krueger 1993a, 24–5). In Africa, governments in Ghana, Mozambique, Nigeria, and Tanzania each created more than 300 state-owned enterprises, and in many African countries, state-owned enterprises accounted for 20 percent of total wage-based employment (World Bank 1994b, 101). Throughout developing societies, therefore, the shift to secondary ISI was accompanied by the emergence of the state as a principal, and in many instances the largest, owner of productive capacity.

Finally, governments used trade barriers to control foreign exchange and protect infant industries. Because export earnings were limited, governments controlled foreign trade to ensure that foreign exchange supported their development objectives (Bhagwati 1978, 20–33). After all, many elements critical to industrialization, including intermediate inputs and capital goods, had to be imported. Protection also allowed infant industries to gain the experience needed to compete against established producers. In Brazil and India, for instance, the state prohibited imports of any good for which there was a domestic substitute, regardless of price and quality differences.

The scale and the structure of protection that governments used to promote industrialization are illustrated in Table 6.4, which focuses on Latin America in 1960. In all but two of the listed countries, nominal protection on nondurable consumer goods was well over 100 percent, and for all but three countries, tariffs on consumer durables also were over 100 percent. Mexico and Uruguay stand out as clear exceptions to this pattern, which has more to do with those countries' extensive use of import quotas in place of tariffs than with an unwillingness to protect domestic producers (Bulmer-Thomas 1994, 279). It is also clear that tariffs were lower for semi-manufactured goods, industrial raw materials, and capital goods (all of which were items that developing countries needed to import in connection with industrialization) than they were for consumer goods. This pattern of tariff escalation was common in much of the developing world (Balassa and Associates 1971).

The costs of ISI were borne by agriculture (see Krueger 1993a; Krueger, Schiff and Valdes 1992; Binswanger and Deininger 1997). Governments taxed agricultural exports through marketing boards that controlled the purchase and export of agricultural commodities (Krueger et al. 1992, 16). Often established as the sole entity with the legal right to purchase, transport, and export agricultural products, marketing boards set the price that farmers received for their crops. In the typical arrangement, the marketing board would purchase crops from domestic farmers at prices well below the world price and then would sell the commodities in the world market at the world price. The difference between the price paid to domestic farmers and the world price

TABLE 6.4

Nominal Protection in Latin America, circa 1960 (percent)

	Nondurable Consumer Goods	Durable Consumer Goods	Semi-Manufactured Goods	Industrial Raw Materials	Capital Goods
Argentina	176	266	95	55	98
Brazil	260	328	80	106	84
Chile	328	90	98	111	45
Colombia	247	108	28	57	18
Mexico	114	147	28	38	14
Uruguay	23	24	23	14	27
European Economic Community	17	19	7	1	13

Source: Bulmer-Thomas 1994, 280, Table 9.1.

represented a tax on agricultural incomes that the state could use to finance industrial projects (Amsden 1979; Bates 1988; Krueger 1993a). The trade barriers that protected domestic manufacturing firms from foreign competition also taxed agriculture. Tariffs and quantitative restrictions raised the domestic price of manufactured goods well above the world price. People employed in the agricultural sector, who consumed these manufactured goods, therefore paid more for them than they would have in the absence of tariffs and quantitative restrictions (Krueger 1993a, 9).

Such government policies transferred income from rural agriculture to the urban manufacturing and nontraded-goods sectors. The size of the income transfers was substantial. As a World Bank study summarized,

> the total impact of interventions ... on relative prices [between agriculture and manufacturing] was in some countries very large. In Ghana ... farmers received only about 40 percent of what they would have received under free trade. Stated in another way, the real incomes of farmers would have increased by 2.5 times had farmers been able to buy and sell under free trade prices given the commodities they in fact produced. While Ghanaian total discrimination against agriculture was huge, Argentina, Cote d'Ivoire, the Dominican Republic, Egypt, Pakistan, Sri Lanka, Thailand, and Zambia also had total discrimination against agriculture in excess of 33 percent, implying that in all those cases, farm incomes in real terms could have been increased by more than 50 percent by removal of these interventions.
>
> (Krueger 1993a, 63)

Thus, ISI redistributed income. The incomes of export-oriented producers fell while those of import-competing producers rose.

A Closer Look

Import Substitution Industrialization in Brazil

In the late nineteenth and early twentieth centuries, Brazil was the classic case of a country that exported primary commodities. Its principal crop, coffee, accounted for a large share of its production and the overwhelming majority of its export earnings. This economic structure was supported by a political system dominated by the interests of coffee producers and other agricultural exporters (Bates 1997). Political authority in Brazil was decentralized, and the states used their power in the country's federal system to influence government policy. As a result, Brazil pursued a liberal trade policy throughout the late nineteeth and early twentieth centuries. World War I and the Great Depression disrupted these arrangements. The world price for coffee fell sharply in the late 1920s and early 1930s, generating declining terms of trade and rising trade deficits. The government responded to this crisis by adopting protectionist measures to limit imports. The initial turn to protectionism was accompanied by political change. A military coup in 1930 handed power to Getúlio Vargas, who centralized power by shifting political authority from the states to the federal government. Even though Vargas did not adopt an ISI strategy, this period represented in many respects the easy stage of ISI (Haggard 1990, 165–6). Protectionism promoted the growth of light manufacturing industries at a rate of 6 percent per year between 1929 and 1945 (Thorp 1999, 322). Concurrently, the centralization of power created a state that could intervene effectively in the Brazilian economy. Although the export-oriented interests did not lose all political influence in this new political climate, the balance of power had clearly shifted toward new groups emerging in urban centers: the professionals, managers, and bureaucrats who constituted the emerging middle class and the nascent manufacturing interests. As Brazil moved into the post-World War II period, therefore, the stage was set for the transition to secondary ISI.

A full-blown ISI strategy emerged in the 1950s. The government restricted imports tightly with the so-called law of similars, which effectively prohibited the import of goods similar to those produced in Brazil. In 1952, the Brazilian government created the National Economic Development Bank (BNDE), an important instrument for industrial policy through which the Brazilian state could finance industrial projects. In the late 1950s, the government created a new agency, the National Development Council, to coordinate and plan its industrialization strategy. In taking up its task, the council was heavily influenced by structuralist ideas (Haggard 1990, 174). Studies conducted within these agencies—and, in some instances, in collaboration with international agencies such as the United Nations (UN) Economic Commission on Latin America—focused on how best to promote industrialization (Leff 1969, 46). Most of these studies came to similar conclusions: industrialization in Brazil would quickly run into constraints caused by inadequate transportation networks (road, rail, and sea), shortages of electric power, and the underdevelopment of basic heavy industries such as steel, petroleum, chemicals, and nonferrous metals. Building up those industries thus became the focus of the government's development policies. The Brazilian government had little faith that the private sector would create and expand these critically important industries. Instead, policymakers determined that the state would have to play a leading role. In the early 1950s, the state nationalized the oil and electricity industries and began investing heavily in the expansion of capacity in both. A similar approach was adopted in the transportation sector (in which the government owned the railways and other infrastructure), in the steel industry, and in telecommunications. By the end of the 1950s, the state accounted for 37 percent of all investment made in the Brazilian economy. As a result, the number of state-owned enterprises grew rapidly, from fewer than 35 in 1950 to more than 600 by 1980.

Beyond creating these basic industries, the Brazilian government also sought to create domestic capacity to produce complex consumer goods. To achieve this objective, Brazil, in contrast to many other developing countries, drew heavily upon foreign investment to promote the development of certain industries. The auto industry is an excellent example. In 1956, the Brazilian government prohibited all imports of cars. Any foreign producer that wanted to sell cars in the Brazilian market would have to set up production facilities in the country. To ensure that such foreign investments were not simple assembly operations in which the foreign company imported all parts from its suppliers at home, the Brazilian government instituted local rules that required the foreign automakers operating in the country to purchase 90 percent of their parts from Brazilian firms. In order to induce foreign automakers to invest in Brazil under these conditions, the government offered subsidies; by one account, the subsidies offset about 87 percent of the total investment between 1956 and 1969. Relying on this strategy, Brazilian auto production rose from close to zero in 1950 to almost 200,000 cars in 1962.

Brazil's ISI strategy helped transform the country's economy in a remarkably short time. Imported consumer nondurable goods (the products targeted during easy ISI) had been almost completely replaced with domestic production by the early 1950s (Bergsman and Candal 1969, 37). Imported consumer durables, the final goods targeted in secondary ISI, fell from 60 percent of total consumption to less than 10 percent of total consumption by 1959. Imports of capital goods also fell, from 60 percent of total domestic consumption in 1949, to about 35 percent of consumption in 1959, and then to only 10 percent by 1964. Finally, imports of intermediate goods, the inputs used in producing final goods, also fell continually throughout the decade, to less than 10 percent of total consumption by 1964. Thus, as imports were barred and domestic industries created, Brazilian consumers and producers purchased a much larger percentage of the goods they used from domestic producers and a much smaller percentage from foreign producers. As a consequence, the importance of manufacturing in the Brazilian economy increased sharply: whereas manufacturing accounted for only 26 percent of total Brazilian production in 1949, by 1964 it accounted for 34 percent.

The strategy of ISI promoted rapid economic growth in the 1960s and 1970s: developing countries' economies grew at annual average rates of between 6 percent and 7.6 percent during this period. In many countries, it was the manufacturing sector that drove economic growth. Argentina, Brazil, Chile, Mexico, Mozambique, Nigeria, Pakistan, and India, to select only a few examples, all enjoyed average annual rates of manufacturing growth between 5 percent and 10 percent during the 1960s. A glimpse back at Table 6.1 indicates that, in Latin America, manufacturing's share of the total economy increased substantially between 1960 and 1980. Thus, although the policies that governments adopted had important effects on the distribution of income, they also appeared to be transforming developing societies into industrialized economies.

Reforming the International Trade System

Developing countries also tried to alter the rules governing international trade. For many developing-country governments, these efforts reflected their experience with colonialism. India's perspective was not unique: international trade was "a whirlpool of economic imperialism rather than a positive instrument for achieving economic growth" (Srinivasan and Tendulkar 2003, 13). Consequently, as early as 1947, India, Brazil, and Chile were arguing that the multilateral rules the United States and Great Britain were writing failed to address the economic problems that developing countries faced (Kock 1969, 38–42). Advancing the infant-industry justification for protection, many developing countries argued that their firms could not compete with established producers in the United States and Europe. Yet, GATT rules not only made no provision for the infant-industry justification for protection but indeed, explicitly prohibited the use of quantitative restrictions and tightly restricted the use of tariffs. Developing countries insisted that they be given a relatively free hand in the use of trade restrictions to promote economic development, because the GATT failed to do so.

Developing countries continued to press for GATT reforms throughout the 1950s (see Kock 1969, 238; Finger 1991). By the early 1960s, a coalition of developing countries dedicated to far-reaching reform had emerged. Its first important success was achieved with the formation of the **United Nations Conference on Trade and Development** (UNCTAD) in March of 1964. The UNCTAD was established as a body dedicated to promoting the interests of developing countries in the world trade system. At the conclusion of this first UNCTAD conference, 77 developing-country governments signed a joint declaration calling for reform of the international trade system. Thus was born the **Group of 77**, the leading force in the campaign for systemic reform. During the next 20 years, trade relations between the developing world and the advanced industrialized countries revolved almost wholly around competing conceptions of international trade rules embodied in the GATT and UNCTAD.

During the 1960s, the Group of 77 used UNCTAD to pursue three international mechanisms that would increase their share of the gains from trade (Kock 1969; UNCTAD 1964; Williams 1991). First, the Group of 77 sought commodity price stabilization schemes. Commodity price stabilization was to be achieved by setting a floor below which commodity prices would not be allowed to fall and by creating a finance mechanism, funded largely by the advanced industrialized countries, to purchase commodities when prices fell below the floor. Stabilizing commodity prices would be an important step toward stabilizing developing countries' terms of trade (recall the Singer-Prebisch hypothesis). The Group of 77 also sought direct financial transfers from the advanced industrialized countries to compensate them for the purchasing power they were losing from declining terms of trade (UNCTAD 1964, 80). Developing countries also sought greater access to core-country markets, pressuring the advanced industrialized countries to eliminate trade barriers on primary commodities and to provide manufactured exports from developing countries with preferential access to the core-countries' markets.

These reform efforts yielded few concrete results. Core countries agreed to incorporate concerns specific to developing countries into the GATT charter. In 1964, three articles focusing on developing countries were included in the **GATT Part IV**. Part IV called upon core countries to improve market access for commodity exporters, to refrain from raising barriers to the import of products of special interest to the developing world, and to engage in "joint action to promote trade and development" (Kock 1969, 242). In the absence of meaningful changes in the trade policies pursued by the advanced industrialized countries, however, Part IV provided few concrete gains. The advanced industrialized countries also allowed the developing countries to opt out of strict reciprocity during GATT tariff negotiations. The developing countries that belonged to the GATT were therefore able to benefit from tariff reductions without having to offer concessions in return. Benefits from this concession were more apparent than real, however: GATT negotiations focused primarily on manufactured goods produced by the advanced industrialized countries and excluded agriculture, textiles, and many other labor-intensive goods. Developing countries were therefore exporting few of the goods on which the advanced industrialized countries were actually reducing tariffs. In the late 1960s, the advanced industrialized countries agreed to the **Generalized System of Preferences** (GSP), under which manufactured exports from developing countries gained preferential access to advanced industrialized countries' markets. This concession, too, was of limited importance, because advanced industrialized countries often limited the quantity of goods that could enter under preferential tariff rates and excluded some manufacturing sectors from the arrangement entirely.

Even though their efforts during the 1960s had achieved few concrete gains, the Group of 77 escalated its demands in the early 1970s. Escalated demands were sparked by the 1973 oil shock. The oil shock was a clear illustration of the potential for commodity power. The world's major oil-producing countries, working together in the Organization of Petroleum Exporting Countries (OPEC), used their control of oil to improve their terms of trade. OPEC's ability to use commodity power to extract income from the core countries strengthened the belief within the Group of 77 that commodity power could be exploited to force fundamental systemic change.

Greater confidence in the possibilities that their control of commodities offered led the Group of 77 to develop a set of radical demands dubbed the **New International Economic Order** (NIEO). The NIEO represented an attempt to create an international trade system whose operation would promote development (see Krasner 1985). The NIEO, which the UN General Assembly adopted in December 1974, embodied a set of reforms that would have radically altered the operation of the international economy. In addition to the three mechanisms that developing countries had demanded during the 1960s, the NIEO included rules that would grant developing countries greater control over multinational corporations operating in their countries, easier and cheaper access to northern technology, a reduction in foreign debt, increased foreign aid flows, and a larger role in the decision-making processes of the World Bank and International Monetary Fund (IMF).

Governments in the advanced industrialized countries refused to make significant concessions, and by the mid-1980s the NIEO had disappeared from the international agenda. The failure of the NIEO has been attributed to a number of factors. First, developing countries were unable to establish and maintain a cohesive coalition. The heterogeneity of developing countries' interests made it relatively easy for the advanced industrialized countries to divide the Group of 77 by offering limited concessions to a small number of governments in exchange for defection from the broader group. In addition, the Group of 77 had hoped that OPEC would assist it by linking access to oil to acceptance of the NIEO. But OPEC governments were unwilling to use their oil power to help other developing countries achieve broader trade and development objectives.

Most importantly, however, by the early 1980s, many developing countries were facing serious balance-of-payments problems and turned to the IMF and the World Bank for financial support. The need to obtain IMF and World Bank assistance altered the balance of power in favor of the advanced industrialized countries. This power shift sparked a reform process that changed fundamentally development strategies throughout the developing world.

CONCLUSION

Throughout much of the postwar period, developing countries insulated themselves from the world trade system. The interaction between domestic politics on the one hand, and economic shocks and decolonization on the other, generated governments that were highly responsive to the interests of import-competing manufacturing industries and a growing class of urban workers. Influenced greatly by structuralism, most governments transformed the political incentive to protect these domestic industries into ambitious state-led development strategies. Structuralism's critique of the ability of domestic and international markets to promote industrialization led governments to intervene in domestic markets to overcome the market imperfections that reduced private incentives to invest in manufacturing activities.

Policy Analysis and Debate

The Sustainable Development Goals

Question

Can the Sustainable Development Goals eradicate extreme poverty?

Overview

Members of the UN agreed in 2015 that for the next 15 years they would focus their development policies on 17 **Sustainable Development Goals** (SDGs). The SDGs constitute an ambitious attempt to build on the gains realized through the Millenium Development Goals, and include (among other things) end extreme poverty everywhere (measured as living on less than $1.25 per day) and cut the numbers living in poverty in half by 2030. In addition, the SDGs place greater emphasis on sustainable development—and thus have a variety of environmental goals—and they attach greater importance to protection of human rights. Governments are to achieve these goals through extensive planning at the domestic and international levels. Policies based on these plans will in turn be supported by foreign aid offered by the international community. For that purpose, the UN has called upon rich countries to provide aid equal to 0.7 percent of GDP to developing countries and provide technical assistance and technology transfers where it is useful to do so.

The logic upon which SDGs rest is similar to the thinking that at the broad level shaped the government's role in ISI. The SDGs rest on a diagnosis of poverty that emphasizes structural factors. Rather than emphasize market failure, however, contemporary thinking emphasizes a "poverty trap":

> When poverty is extreme, the poor do not have the ability—by themselves—to get out of the mess ... When [people] are utterly destitute, they need their entire income, or more, to survive ... There is no margin of income above survival that can be invested for the future.
>
> (Sachs 2005, 56)

People can escape the poverty trap with help from the contemporary analogue of the "big push." The international community must provide "a leg up" through well-funded and well-conceived government policy initiatives. Given the logic upon which they are based, do you think the SDGs will be successful?

Policy Options

- An SDG-like strategy is necessary if the world is to eradicate extreme poverty. Governments must embrace these goals.
- The SDGs rest on faulty logic and thus cannot reduce extreme poverty. Governments should re-evaluate their approach to the problem of global poverty.

Policy Analysis

- Do developing-country governments have incentives to implement the policies called for by the SDG strategy? Why or why not?
- Do advanced industrialized countries have incentives to provide the foreign aid that is required to support SDG policies? Why or why not?

Take a Position

- Which option do you prefer? Justify your choice.
- What criticisms of your position should you anticipate? How would you defend your recommendation against these criticisms?

Resources

Online: To learn more about the SDGs and current progress toward achieving them, conduct an online search for the keywords *UN* and *MDGs*. Look especially for the UN's annual progress reports.

In Print: Read the alternative perspectives embodied in Jeffrey Sachs' *Ending Poverty: Economic Possibilities of Our Time* (New York: Penguin Press, 2005), and William Easterly's *The White Man's Burden: Why the West's Efforts to Aid the Rest Have Done So Much Ill and So Little Good* (New York: Penguin Publishers, 2006).

To the extent that developing countries participated in the global trade system, they sought to achieve far-reaching reform of the rules governing the system. Again, the structuralist critique served an important role in this effort, as it suggested that developing countries could not expect to gain from trade with the advanced industrialized countries until they themselves had industrialized. Moreover, structuralism claimed that trade based on GATT rules would only make industrialization harder to achieve. Rather than accept participation in the global economy on what they viewed as vastly unequal terms, developing countries battled to change the rules governing international trade in order to capture a larger share of the available gains. Thus, an international struggle over the distribution of the gains from trade arose as an important counterpart of the domestic strategy of redistributing resources from agriculture to industry embodied in ISI.

KEY TERMS

Backward Linkages
Big Push
Complementary
    Demand
Easy ISI

Enclave
    Agriculture
Export Substitution
    Strategy
GATT Part IV

Generalized System of
    Preferences
Group of 77
Import Substitution
    Industrialization

Monoexporters
New International
  Economic Order
Pecuniary External
  Economies

Secondary ISI
Singer-Prebisch Theory
Structuralism
Sustainable Development
  Goals

Terms of Trade
United Nations
  Conference on Trade
  and Development

SUGGESTIONS FOR FURTHER READING

For a readable introduction to structuralism and development strategies more generally, see Ian Little, Economic Development (New York: Basic Books, 1982). For an in-depth look at Latin America, see Victor Bulmer-Thomas, *The Economic History of Latin American since Independence*, 3rd edition (Cambridge: Cambridge University Press, 2014).

For a comparative study of the role of the state in development, see Atul Kohli, *State-Directed Development: Political Power and Industrialization in the Global Periphery* (Cambridge: Cambridge University Press, 2004).

For a detailed examination of the New International Economic Order, see the recent special issue of *Humanity* (2015 6 (1), http://humanityjournal.org/issue-6-1/), Paul Adler, 2017. "'The Basis of a New Internationalism?' The Institute for Policy Studies and North-South Politics from the NIEO to Neoliberalism." *Diplomatic History* 41(4): 665–93, and the now classic, Stephen Krasner, *Structural Conflict: The Third World against Global Liberalism* (Berkeley: University of California Press, 1985).

Trade and Development II: Neoliberalism and Institutionalism

Whereas structuralism and import substitution industrialization (ISI) shaped development strategies during the first 35 years of the postwar period, the last 30 years have been dominated by neoliberalism and export-oriented industrialization. In contrast to structuralism, with its skepticism about the market and faith in the state, neoliberalism is highly skeptical of the state's ability to allocate resources efficiently and places great faith in the market's ability to do so. And in contrast to structuralism's advocacy of protectionism and state intervention, neoliberalism advocates the state's withdrawal from the economy, the reduction (ideally, elimination) of trade barriers, and reliance on the market to generate industries that produce for the world market. In addition, the current consensus within the development community stresses the critical importance for development outcomes of high-quality political and economic institutions.

Like structuralism, neoliberalism has dramatically affected policy. Across the developing world, governments have reduced tariffs and removed other trade barriers, thereby opening their economies to imports. They have sold state-owned enterprises to private groups. They have deregulated their economies to allow prices to reflect the underlying scarcity of resources. They have shifted their emphasis from producing for the domestic market to producing for the global market. Countries that had never joined the General Agreement on Tariffs and Trade (GATT) sought membership in the World Trade Organization (WTO). Thus, the last 30 years have brought a complete reversal of the development strategies that most governments had adopted. Belief in the power of states has been replaced by belief in the efficacy of the market; skepticism about trade has been replaced by concerted efforts to integrate deeply into the world trade system. Neoliberalism has replaced structuralism as the guiding philosophy of economic development. And as the state retreated from the economy, the development community began to place new

138

emphasis on how important it was to development to have good political and economic institutions.

The shift from structuralism to neoliberalism emerged from the interplay between three developments in the global economy. First, by the early 1970s, ISI was generating economic imbalances. The emergence of these imbalances suggested that economic reform of some type was required, although it did not point to a specific solution. Second, at about the same time, it was becoming apparent that a small group of East Asian economies were outperforming all other developing countries based on what many viewed as a neoliberal strategy. Third, a severe economic crisis in the early 1980s forced governments to embark on reform, and as they did, the International Monetary Fund (IMF) and World Bank strongly encouraged them to base reform on the neoliberal model.

We examine each of these three developments. We look first at the factors that caused ISI to generate economic imbalances. This examination allows us to understand the problems ISI created and the reasons that reform of some type was necessary. We then turn our attention to the East Asian countries. We briefly compare their performance with that of the rest of the developing world. We next examine two contrasting explanations for this remarkable performance, one that emphasizes the neoliberal elements of those countries' strategies and one that emphasizes the role East Asian states played in the development process. We then turn to the economic crisis and reform. We look at how the crisis pushed developing countries to the World Bank and the IMF, and at how these two institutions shaped the content of the reforms governments adopted. In the final section, the chapter explores the relationship between domestic political institutions and economic development.

EMERGING PROBLEMS WITH IMPORT SUBSTITUTION INDUSTRIALIZATION

By the late 1960s, ISI was generating two important economic imbalances, which together suggested that it had reached the limits of its utility as a development strategy. The first imbalance lay in government budgets. ISI tended to generate persistent budget deficits because it prescribed heavy government involvement in the economy. Since governments believed that the private sector would not invest in industries that were important for the success of secondary ISI, governments themselves often made the investments, either in partnership with private-sector groups or alone by creating state-owned enterprises.

Yet, many of these state-owned enterprises never became profitable. By the late 1970s, state-owned enterprises in developing countries were running combined operating deficits that averaged 4 percent of gross domestic product (GDP) (Waterbury 1992, 190). Governments kept these enterprises afloat by using funds from the state budget. Government investment and the subsequent need to cover the losses of state-owned enterprises combined to generate large and persistent budget deficits throughout the developing world.

Domestic politics aggravated the budget deficits generated by ISI. For many governments, urban residents provided critical political support. Governments maintained this support by subsidizing essential items. Electricity, water and sewers, transportation, telephone service, and food were all made available to urban residents at below-market prices. This was possible only by using government revenues to cover the difference between the true cost and the price charged. In addition, many governments expanded the civil service to employ urban dwellers. In Benin, for example, the civil service tripled in size between 1960 and 1980, not because the government needed so many civil servants, but because the government used it to employ urban residents in order to maintain support. Such practices added to government expenditures and added nothing to government revenues, thereby worsening the budget deficit.

ISI also generated a second important imbalance: persistent current-account deficits. The **current account** registers a country's imports and exports of both goods and services. A current-account deficit means that a country is importing more than it is exporting. Import substitution gave rise to current-account deficits because it generated a considerable demand for imports while simultaneously reducing the economy's ability to export. Somewhat ironically, ISI depended on imports. Industrialization required countries to import the necessary machines, and once these machines were in place, production required continued import of parts that were not produced in the domestic economy.

Exports declined for two reasons. First, the manufacturing industries created through import substitution were not competitive in international markets. Production in many of the heavy industries that governments targeted in secondary ISI was characterized by economies of scale. The domestic market in most developing countries, however, was too small to allow domestic producers to realize economies of scale. These inefficiencies were compounded by excess capacity—the creation of more production capacity than the domestic market could absorb (see Little, Scitovsky, and Scott 1970, 98). Consequently, the newly created manufacturing industries could not export to the world market.

Second, the policies that governments used to promote industrialization weakened agriculture. The decline in agricultural production was most severe in sub-Saharan African countries, which, as a region, taxed farmers heavily (Schiff and Valdés 1992). Heavy tax burdens reduced farmers' incentives to produce, hence the rate of growth of agriculture declined. In Ghana, for example, the real value of the payments that cocoa farmers received from the government marketing board fell by about two-thirds between 1960 and 1965. Falling prices gave cocoa farmers little incentive to invest in order to maintain, let alone increase, cocoa output (Killick 1978, 119). In addition, cocoa farmers smuggled much of what they did produce into the Ivory Coast, where they could sell cocoa at world prices (Herbst 1993, 40).

These microeconomic inefficiencies were reinforced by the tendency of most governments to maintain overvalued exchange rates. Ideally, a government should maintain an exchange rate that equalizes the prices of goods in the domestic and foreign markets. However, under ISI, many governments set the exchange rate higher than that, and as a result, foreign goods were cheaper in the home market than they should have been and domestic goods were more expensive in foreign markets than they should have been. Because foreign goods were underpriced in the domestic market, capital goods and intermediate inputs could be acquired from abroad at a lower cost than they could be produced at home. This difference in price created a strong incentive to import, rather than creating the capacity to produce the goods locally. The result was rising imports. Because domestic goods were overpriced in foreign markets, domestic producers, even when efficient, found it difficult to export.

The emergence of budget deficits and current-account deficits indicated that ISI was creating an economic structure that couldn't pay for itself. Many of the manufacturing industries created during secondary ISI could not sell their products at prices that covered their costs of production. Many developing countries could not export enough to pay for the imports demanded by the manufacturing industries they were creating. Such imbalances could not persist forever; some reform was clearly necessary.

Yet, the domestic politics of ISI greatly constrained the ability of governments to implement reforms. The balance of power among domestic interest groups created multiple veto players that limited the ability of governments to alter policies. Because governments depended so heavily on urban residents for political support, they could not easily reduce benefits provided to that group (Waterbury 1992, 192). In 1971, for example, the Ghanaian prime minister devalued the exchange rate in an attempt to correct Ghana's current-account deficit. Concern that devaluation would raise the prices of many imported goods consumed by urban residents contributed to a coup against the government a few days later. Once in power, the new regime quickly restored the currency to its previous rate (Herbst 1993, 22–23). What message did that send to politicians who might be contemplating measures to address the economic imbalances they were facing?

In addition, the administration of ISI had created opportunities for rent seeking and other corrupt practices. Those who engaged in these activities had a vested interest in the continuation of the system. On the one hand, government intervention had established an environment conducive to **rent seeking** (Krueger 1974; Bhagwati 1982)—efforts by private actors to use the political system to achieve a higher-than-market return on an economic activity. Consider, for example, the consequences of government controls on imports. Governments controlled imports by requiring all residents who wanted to import something to first gain the permission of government authorities. Such restrictions meant that imported goods were scarce, thus imports purchased at the world price could be sold at a much higher price in the domestic market. The difference between the world price and the domestic price provided a rent to the person who imported the good. A government license to import, therefore, was valuable. Consequently, people had incentives to pay government civil servants to acquire licenses, and government civil servants had incentives to sell them.

Such behavior was extraordinarily costly. It has been estimated, for example, that rent seeking cost India about 7 percent and Turkey about 15 percent of their national incomes during the 1960s (Krueger 1974, 294). Because so many people inside the government and in the economy were benefiting from the opportunities for rent seeking, they had a very strong incentive to resist any efforts by the government to dismantle the system.

Finally, even if governments could overcome these obstacles, it was unclear what model they should shift to. Far-reaching reforms would require them to re-evaluate the underlying strategy they were using to industrialize. The only available alternative to ISI was a market-oriented development strategy (one we will look at in detail in the next section). In the 1970s, however, it was precisely this strategy that the Group of 77 was fighting against in the UNCTAD and with the NIEO. Even moderate reforms held little appeal. Most governments were unwilling to scale back their industrialization strategies. Instead, they looked for a way to cover the twin deficits without having to scale back their ambitious plans.

Facing economic imbalances, unable and unwilling to change policy, many governments sustained ISI by borrowing from abroad. Yet foreign loans could provide only a temporary solution; foreign lenders would eventually question whether loans could be repaid. When they concluded that they couldn't, they would be unwilling to lend more, and governments would be forced to correct budget and current-account deficits. This point arrived in the early 1980s and ushered in a period of crisis and reform. Before we examine this period, however, we must look at economic developments in East Asia as these developments played a critical role in shaping the content of the reforms adopted throughout the developing world after 1985.

THE EAST ASIAN MODEL

Whereas ISI was generating imbalances in Latin America and sub-Saharan Africa, four East Asian economies—Hong Kong, Singapore, South Korea, and Taiwan—were realizing dramatic gains on the basis of a very different development strategy. The dramatic performance gap is evident in three economic indicators (see Table 7.1).

- Per capita income in East Asia grew almost three times faster than in Latin America and South Asia and more than 26 times higher than in sub-Saharan Africa.
- Manufacturing output grew by 10.3 percent per year between 1965 and 1990. No other developing country came close to this growth for the period as a whole.
- Exports from East Asia grew 8.5 percent per year between 1965 and 1990 while exports from Latin America shrank by 1 percent per year.

TABLE 7.1		
Comparative Economic Performance, Selected Developing Countries (Average Annual Rates of Change)*		
	1965–1990	1985–1995
Growth of per Capita GNP		
East Asia and the Pacific	5.3	7.2
Sub-Saharan Africa	0.2	1.1
South Asia	1.9	2.9
Latin America and the Caribbean	1.8	0.3
Growth of Manufacturing		
East Asia and the Pacific	10.3	15.0
Sub-Saharan Africa	n.a.	0.2
South Asia	4.5	5.3
Latin America and the Caribbean	8.3	2.5
Growth of Exports		
East Asia and the Pacific	8.5	9.3
Sub-Saharan Africa	6.1	0.9
South Asia	1.8	6.6
Latin America and the Caribbean	2.1	5.2

Notes: n.a. = not available.
GNP = gross national product.
Source: World Bank, *World Development Report*, various issues.

As a consequence, manufacturing grew in importance in East Asia, while the importance of agriculture diminished. This differed substantially from ISI countries, where agriculture's importance fell but manufacturing failed to grow (see Table 6.1). The growing manufacturing sector transformed the composition of East Asia's exports (see Table 6.2). By the mid-1990s, manufactured goods accounted for more than 80 percent of East Asian exports. By contrast, only in Brazil, Mexico, India, and Pakistan did manufactured goods account for more than 50 percent of total exports by the 1990s, and most of these gains were realized after 1980. Finally, per capita incomes in East Asia soared above those in other developing countries (Table 7.2). In 1960, per capita incomes in East Asia were lower than per capita incomes in Latin America; by 1990, East Asian incomes were higher than—in some cases twice as large as—per capita incomes in Latin America.

Why did East Asian countries outperform other developing countries by such a large margin? Most people who study East Asian development agree that the countries in the region distinguished themselves from other developing countries by pursuing export-oriented development. In an **export-oriented strategy**, emphasis is placed on producing manufactured goods that can be sold in international markets. Scholars disagree about the relative importance of the market and the state in creating export-oriented industries. One position, the neoliberal interpretation, is articulated most forcefully by the

TABLE 7.2

Gross National Product per Capita, Selected Developing Countries (1996 U.S. Dollars)

	1960	1990	2000	Percent Change 1960–2000
Hong Kong	3,090	20,827	26,699	764
Singapore	2,161	17,933	24,939	1,054
Taiwan	1,430	10,981	17,056	1,093
South Korea	1,495	9,952	15,876	962
Mexico	3,980	7,334	8,762	120
Malaysia	2,119	6,525	9,919	368
Argentina	7,371	7,219	11,006	49
Chile	3,853	6,148	9,926	158
Brazil	2,371	6,218	7,190	203
Thailand	1,091	4,833	6,857	528
Zaire/Congo	980	572	281	−71
Indonesia	936	2,851	3,642	289
Pakistan	633	1,747	2,008	217
India	847	1,675	2,479	193
Nigeria	1,033	1,095	707	−32
Kenya	796	1,336	1,244	56
Zambia	1,207	1,021	892	−26
Tanzania	382	494	482	26

Sources: Penn World Tables; Data for 1996, Data for 1997; Data for 1998.

IMF and the World Bank. This thesis argues that East Asia's success was a consequence of market-friendly development strategies. In contrast, the state-oriented interpretation, advanced by many specialists in East Asian political economy argues that East Asia's success is due in large part to state-led industrial policies.

The IMF and the World Bank contend that East Asia's economic success derived from the adoption of a neoliberal approach to development. This interpretation places particular emphasis on the willingness of East Asian governments to embrace international markets, and their ability to maintain stable macroeconomic environments (see World Bank 1989, 1991, 1993; Little 1982; Lal 1983; for critiques, see Toye 1994 and Rodrik 1999). Most East Asian governments adopted ISI strategies in the immediate postwar period. Unlike governments in Latin America and Africa, however, East Asian governments shifted to export-oriented substitution once they had exhausted the gains from easy ISI. In Taiwan, for example, the government shifted in 1958 from production for the domestic market to a strategy that emphasized production for export markets. South Korea adopted similar reforms in the early 1960s. A second wave of newly industrializing countries (NICs)—a group that includes Indonesia, Malaysia, and Thailand—followed the same path starting in the late 1960s (World Bank 1993). The emphasis on exports forced Asian manufacturing firms to worry about international competitiveness. As a result, the World Bank and the IMF argue, Asian societies invested their resources in domestic industries profitable in world markets.

The shift to export-oriented strategies was followed by selective import liberalization. Asian governments did not engage in wholesale import liberalization. The Taiwanese and South Korean governments continued to rely heavily on tariff and non-tariff barriers to protect domestic markets. In Taiwan, for example, approximately two-thirds of imports were subject to some form of tariff or non-tariff barrier greater than 30 percent, and as late as 1980 more than 40 percent of imports faced protection greater than 30 percent (World Bank 1993, 297). A similar pattern appeared in South Korea, where, as late as 1983, "most sectors were still protected by some combination of tariffs and nontariff barriers" (World Bank 1993, 297). However, selective liberalization helped promote exports by reducing the cost of critical inputs. Reducing tariffs on key intermediate goods, such as looms and yarn in the textile industry, enabled domestic producers to acquire inputs at world prices. This kept exports competitive in international markets.

East Asian governments also maintained stable macroeconomic environments. Three elements of the macroeconomic environment were particularly important. First, inflation was much lower in East Asia than in other developing countries. Between 1961 and 1991, inflation averaged only 7.5 percent in the East Asian economies. By contrast, annual inflation rates in the rest of the developing world averaged 62 percent (World Bank 1993, 110). Second, because governments kept inflation under control, they could maintain appropriately valued exchange rates. In many developing countries, high inflation caused the domestic currency to rise in value against foreign currencies, making exporting difficult. In the East Asian countries, by contrast, governments were able to maintain exchange rates that allowed domestic firms to remain competitive in foreign markets. Third, East Asian governments pursued relatively conservative fiscal policies. They borrowed little, and when they did borrow, they tapped domestic savings rather than turning to international financial markets. This approach was in stark contrast to Latin American governments, which accumulated large public-sector deficits financed with foreign capital.

This stable macroeconomic environment had beneficial consequences for Asian economic performance. Low inflation promoted high savings rates and investment (World Bank 1993, 12). Savings rates in the Asian NICs averaged more than 20 percent of GDP per year, almost twice the level attained in other developing countries, whereas investment rates were 7 percentage points of GDP higher, on average, than in other developing countries (World Bank 1993, 16, 221). A stable macroeconomic environment also made it easier to open the economy to international trade. Because inflation was low and exchange rates were maintained at appropriate levels, trade liberalization did not generate large current-account deficits. Finally, the ability to maintain relatively stable and appropriately valued real exchange rates encouraged private actors to invest in export-oriented industries.

The interaction between the export orientation, the relatively liberal import policy, and the stable macroeconomic environment promoted economic development. As Doner and Hawes (1995, 150) summarize the World Bank perspective, the

> pattern of limited government intervention in the market, coupled with cheap labor and an open economy, [has] guaranteed the private sector stability and predictability, the means to achieve competitiveness on a global scale, and access to the international market so that entrepreneurs could actually discover areas where they have comparative advantage. In shorthand, the model is often reduced to "getting the prices right" and letting market-based prices determine resource allocation. Doing so results in export growth that is in turn positively correlated with broader economic growth.

According to the World Bank and the IMF, East Asia succeeded because markets played a large role, and states played a small role, in allocating resources.

Other scholars have argued that East Asia's success had less to do with allowing markets to work and much more to do with well-designed government industrial policies (see Wade 1990; Amsden 1989; Haggard 1990). In what has come to be called the **East Asian model of development**, economic development is conceptualized as a series of distinct stages. Government intervention in each stage identifies and promotes specific industries likely to be profitable in the face of international competition. In the first stage, industrial policy promotes labor-intensive light industry, such as textiles and other consumer durables. In the second stage, industrial policy emphasizes heavy industries such as steel, shipbuilding, petrochemicals, and synthetic fibers. In the third stage, governments target skill- and research and development (R&D)-intensive consumer durables and industrial machinery, such as machine tools, semiconductors, computers, telecommunications equipment, robotics, and biotechnology. Governments design policies and organizations to promote the transition from one stage to the other (Wade 1994, 70).

These three stages of industrialization are evident in the paths traced by Taiwan and South Korea (see Table 7.3). In Taiwan, industrialization focused initially on light manufacturing, textiles in particular. By the mid-1950s, textiles were Taiwan's most important export. The government also encouraged production of simple consumer durable goods such as television sets. In the late 1950s, the Taiwanese government began to emphasize heavy industries. A joint venture between several Taiwanese firms and an American firm was formed in 1954 to produce synthetic fibers (Wade 1990, 80). In 1957, a plant to produce polyvinyl chloride was constructed under government supervision and then was handed to a private entrepreneur, Y. C. Wang (Wade 1990, 79). The government created state-owned enterprises in the steel, shipbuilding, and petrochemical industries. During the 1970s, attention shifted to skill-intensive industries, with particular emphasis on machine tools, semiconductors, computers,

TABLE 7.3

Stages of Industrialization in Taiwan and South Korea, 1880–1968

	Commodity Exports 1880–1930	Primary ISI* 1930–1955	Primary Export-Oriented Industries 1955–1968
Main Industries	Taiwan: Sugar, rice South Korea: Rice, beans	Taiwan and South Korea: Food, beverages, tobacco, textiles, clothing, cement, light manufactures (wood, leather, rubber, and paper products)	Taiwan and South Korea; Textiles and apparel, electronics, plywood, plastics (Taiwan), wigs (South Korea), intermediate goods (chemicals, petroleum, paper, and steel products)
Major Economic Actors	Taiwan and South Korea: Local producers (colonial Japan)	Taiwan and South Korea: Private national firms	Taiwan and South Korea: National private firms, multinational corporations, state-owned enterprises
Orientation of the Economy	External markets	Internal market	External markets

* ISI, import substitution industrialization.

Source: Gereffi 1990, 19.

telecommunications, robotics, and biotechnology (Wade 1990, 94). By the mid-1980s, electrical and electronic goods had replaced textiles as Taiwan's largest export (Wade 1990, 93).

The South Korean government adopted similar policies (Amsden 1989). In the 1950s, the government emphasized textile production, and textiles became South Korea's first important manufacturing export. During the late 1960s, the South Korean state initiated the development of the chemical and heavy-machinery industries. It created the Pohang Iron and Steel Company, known as POSCO, which subsequently became one of the world's leading steel producers. The government also provided extensive support to Hyundai Heavy Industry, a shipbuilder that subsequently became a world leader in this industry. Then in the late 1970s, the South Korean government began to give priority to skill- and R&D-intensive sectors, and it is during this period that the South Korean electronics and automobile industries began to emerge (Amsden 1989).

In the East Asian model of development therefore, government policy drives industrialization from low-skilled, labor-intensive production to capital-intensive forms of production and from there to industries that rely on high-skilled labor and technology-intensive production. Each stage is associated with particular types of government policies, and as each stage reaches the limits of rapid growth, emphasis shifts to the next stage in the sequence (Wade 1994, 71). Moreover, at each stage, governments stress the need to develop internationally competitive industries.

East Asian governments relied heavily on industrial policies. They used industrial policy to achieve four policy goals: reduce the cost of investment funds in targeted industries, create incentives to export, protect infant industries, and promote the acquisition and application of skills. Taiwan and South Korea created incentives to invest in industries that state officials identified as critical to development. To do so, governments in both countries provided firms investing in these industries with preferential access to low-cost credit. In South Korea, the government nationalized the banks in the early 1960s and in the ensuing years fully controlled investment capital. Control of the banks allowed the government to provide targeted sectors with access to long-term investment capital at below-market rates of interest (Haggard 1990, 132). Although the banking sector was not nationalized in Taiwan, the government did influence banks' lending decisions. During the 1960s, banks were provided with government-formulated lists of industries that were to receive preferential access to bank loans. During the 1970s, the banks themselves were required to select five or six industries to target in the coming year. As a result, about 75 percent of investment capital was channeled to the government's targeted industries (Wade 1990, 166).

Asian governments also implemented policies that encouraged exports. One method linked access to investment funds at low interest rates to export performance. In Taiwan, for example, firms that exported paid interest rates of only 6–12 percent, whereas other borrowers paid 20–22 percent (Haggard 1990, 94). In South Korea, short-term loans were extended "without limit" to firms with confirmed export orders (Haggard 1990, 65). Credit was also made available to exporters' input suppliers and to these suppliers' suppliers (Haggard 1990, 65–66). In addition, "deliberately undervalued exchange rates" improved the competitiveness of exports in international markets (World Bank 1993, 125). Finally, a variety of measures ensured that domestic firms could purchase their intermediate inputs at world prices. These measures often entailed the creation of free-trade zones and export-processing zones—areas of the country into which intermediate goods could be imported duty free as long as the finished goods were exported. Export-processing zones allowed domestic producers to avoid paying tariff duties that would raise the final cost of the goods they produced.

The Taiwanese and South Korean governments also protected infant industries at each stage. In some instances, the measures they used were straightforward forms of protection. The South Korean government, for example, enacted legislation in 1983 that "prohibited the import of most microcomputers, some minicomputers, and selected models of disk drives," in order to protect domestic producers in the computer industry (Amsden 1989, 82). POSCO initially produced steel behind high import barriers. In other instances, protection was less transparent. Hyundai Heavy Industry, for instance, was protected in part through a government policy that required Korean oil imports to be carried in ships operated by a merchant marine that Hyundai Heavy Industry had itself created (Amsden 1989, 273). Taiwan adopted similar policies.

Finally, the Taiwanese and South Korean governments put in place policies that raised skill levels. Investments in education were made to improve labor skills. In Taiwan, enrollment in secondary schools had reached 75 percent of the eligible age group by 1980. Enrollment increases were accompanied by rising expenditures on education; per pupil expenditures increased eightfold in primary schools, threefold in secondary schools, and twofold at the university level between the early 1960s and 1980s (Liu 1992, 369). Similar patterns are evident in South Korea, where enrollment in secondary schools increased from 35 percent in 1965 to 88 percent in 1987 and "real expenditures per pupil at the primary level rose by 355 percent" (World Bank 1993, 43, 45).

Governments also invested in scientific infrastructure to facilitate the application of skills to R&D activities. In Taiwan, the Industrial Technology Research Institute was formed in 1973, and nonprofit organizations were created during the 1970s to perform research and disseminate the results to firms in the private sector. A science-based industrial park designed to realize agglomeration effects was created in 1980 (Haggard 1990, 142). In South Korea, tax incentives were used to induce chaebols, the large South Korean firms, to create laboratories for R&D purposes. An industrial estate for computer and semiconductor production was created, and the Electronics and Telecommunications Research Institute, a government-funded institute oriented toward product development was established there (Amsden 1989, 82). These policies raised skill levels and created an infrastructure that allowed the more highly skilled labor force to work to its full potential. This skill upgrading was critical to the transition to the third stage of the industrialization process.

The two explanations discussed thus present different arguments for East Asia's success. One suggests that East Asia succeeded because governments allowed markets to work. The other suggests that East Asia succeeded because governments used industrial policy to promote economic outcomes that the market could not produce. Which argument is correct? Although we lack definitive answers, we may conclude that both explanations have value. By "getting prices right," the export orientation and the stable macroeconomic environment encouraged investments in industries in which East Asian countries had, or could develop, comparative advantage. By targeting sectors where comparative advantage could be created, by reducing the costs of firms operating in those sectors, by encouraging firms to export, and by upgrading skills, industrial policy encouraged investments in areas that could yield high returns. As Stephan Haggard (1990, 67) has summarized, macroeconomic "and trade policies established a permissive framework for the realization of comparative advantage, and more targeted policies pushed firms to exploit it."

Although the relative importance of the state and the market in accounting for East Asia's success remains in dispute, what is clear is that the experience of the East Asian NICs was vastly different from the experience of

Latin America and sub-Saharan Africa. East Asian governments adopted development strategies that emphasized exports rather than the domestic market, and they realized substantial improvements in per capita income. The development strategies adopted by governments in other developing countries emphasized the domestic market over exports and generated economic imbalances and modest improvements in per capita incomes. Consequently, when economic crises forced governments to adopt reforms, the East Asian example provided a powerful guide for the kind of reforms that would be implemented.

A Closer Look

Economic Reform in China

China's emergence as a global economic power has also been driven by dramatic market reforms. China has followed a distinct path to the global market, however, because it embarked on the journey as a centrally planned economy: all economic activity was conducted by state-owned enterprises in line with targets established by the Communist Party's central plan. China's move to a market economy has followed a strategy of "gradualism" in which it sought to "grow out of the planned economy" (Naughton 1995). Rather than quickly replacing the centrally planned economy with a market economy. China maintained the planned economy while simultaneously encouraging market-based activities. As China's market economy grew, the relative importance of the planned economy shrank. During the last 25 years, therefore, a market economy gradually emerged in place of the previous state-centered economy.

China based reform on three pillars. The first pillar, implemented in the late 1970s, brought market incentives to agricultural production. This Household Responsibility System encouraged farmers to lease land from their agricultural commune. The government required farmers that took advantage of this opportunity to sell some of their crop to the state at state-set prices. They could sell the remainder at market prices and retain the resulting profits. The Chinese government also changed state-set prices to more accurately reflect the supply of and demand for agricultural commodities. In doing so they encouraged farmers to respond to market prices rather than state production targets. By most accounts, the reform was a dramatic success, raising agricultural productivity and farm incomes sharply during the 1980s (Pyle 1997, 10). Agricultural reform also released labor from the Chinese countryside. Consequently, China has experienced substantial rural-to-urban migration of about 10 million people each year.

The second reform pillar, introduced in 1984, brought market incentives to manufacturing. This Enterprise Responsibility System encouraged enterprises to manage themselves like profit-oriented firms. Enterprises were increasingly required to acquire their inputs from and to sell their output in markets at market-determined prices rather than through state agencies at state-set prices. The government reduced production subsidies and required enterprises to turn to banks for working capital. This withdrawal of state financial support forced enterprises to care about profitability. Over time, private contracts based on market prices replaced state-determined targets as the basis for production (Jefferson and Rawski 2001, 247). By 1996, about 9.4 million non-state enterprises were operating in the Chinese economy, accounting for about 75 percent of total industrial output (Shen 2000, 148). Here we clearly see China growing out of the planned economy—each year a larger share of total output is produced by non-state enterprises and a smaller share by the state-owned sector.

The third pillar of reform, the open-door policy, opened China to the global economy by liberalizing foreign direct investment and trade. The government attracted foreign investment by creating Special Economic Zones along China's southern coast. Special Economic Zones (SEZs) allowed more market-based activity than was permitted in the rest of the economy. Tariffs were reduced, labor market restrictions were relaxed, private ownership was allowed, and taxes were reduced in the SEZs. The SEZs thus provided useful "reform laboratories" in which officials could experiment before implementing reforms throughout the country (Shen 2000; Grub and Lin 1991). The decision to locate the SEZs along the southern coast reflected the desire to attract investment by Chinese nationals living abroad. The SEZs in Guangdong province bordered Hong Kong, for example, whereas the SEZ established in Fujian Province faced Taiwan. The policy was extended to the entire coastal region and selectively extended into the interior in 1988. The government also liberalized trade. It expanded the number of companies allowed to conduct foreign trade from 12 to more than 35,000 (Lardy 2002, 41). The government also reduced trade barriers, first shifting from a quota-based to a tariff-based system and then reducing tariffs sharply to the current average rate of 15 percent. In December 2002, China joined the WTO after almost 15 years of negotiations.

These reforms have transformed China from a sleeping dragon into a powerful force in the global economy. China has grown more rapidly than almost all other economies since the early 1980s, with the best estimates suggesting annual growth rates of 6 to 10 percent since the early 1980s. Such rapid growth has raised per capita incomes, which doubled between 1979 and 1990 and then doubled again during the 1990s. Rising incomes have in turn reduced poverty. According to the World Bank, the share of China's population living in extreme poverty fell from 53 percent in 1981 to just 1.9 percent by 2017 (World Bank 2006, 2017c). China has also emerged as an important player in the global economy. It is currently the leading recipient of foreign direct investment in the developing world, and now hosts one-third of all FDI based in the developing world. China's share of world trade has grown from less than 1 percent in the 1970s to 17 percent today (Lardy 2002, 55; WTO 2017). As a consequence, China is now the world's largest exporter of merchandise (WTO 2017).

China's transformation is not yet complete. The state-owned sector remains an important component of China's economy that requires reform. The state-owned sector is composed of a relatively small number (only 106) of very large firms

(47 of these firms are among Fortune Magazine's 500 largest firms in the world). But together these enterprises account for between one-quarter and one-third of China's total output (Leutert 2016). These very large enterprises are (on average) inefficient and require substantial reform. It remains to be seen whether the Chinese government can effectively consolidate these enterprises, or encourage them to operate more efficiently. In late 2015, the Chinese government launched a new reform initiative In addition, rapid growth has widened the income gap between urban and rural regions, as industrial incomes rise more rapidly than agricultural incomes. In fact, farm incomes have even fallen a bit over the last 5 years. Rising inequality has sparked rural protests, which have been met with rather brutal government responses. Thus, China's government continues to face substantial challenges as it transforms its economy.

STRUCTURAL ADJUSTMENT AND THE POLITICS OF REFORM

By the early 1980s, governments in many developing countries were recognizing the need for reform. The imbalances generated by ISI created pressure for reform, and East Asia's success provided an attractive alternative model. It took a massive economic crisis, however, for governments to implement reform. We will examine this crisis in detail in Chapter 14; here, we say a few words about it in order to understand how it produced the wave of reform that swept the developing world during the 1980s.

Economic crises struck developing countries during the early 1980s in large part as a consequence of governments' decision to borrow to finance their budget and current-account deficits. Using foreign loans to finance budget and current-account deficits is not an inherently poor choice. But two factors made this decision a particularly bad one for developing countries in the 1970s. First, many of the funds that governments borrowed were used to pay for large infrastructure projects or domestic consumption, neither of which generated the export revenues needed to repay the loans. As a result, the amount that developing countries owed to foreign lenders rose, but the countries' ability to repay the debt did not.

Second, between 1973 and 1982, developing countries were buffeted by three international shocks: an increase in the price of oil, a reduction in the terms of trade between primary commodities and manufactured goods, and higher interest rates on the foreign debt those countries had accumulated. These shocks increased the amount of foreign debt that developing countries owed to foreign banks, raised the cost of paying that debt, and greatly reduced export earnings. By the early 1980s, a number of developing countries were unable to make the scheduled payments on their foreign debt.

As crisis hit, governments turned to the IMF and the World Bank for financial assistance. The international institutions linked financial assistance to economic reform. The World Bank and the IMF encouraged governments to adopt such reforms under the banner of **structural adjustment programs—** policy reforms designed to reduce the role of the state and to increase the role of the market in the economy. The specific content of the reforms that the IMF and the World Bank advocated were shaped by their belief that East Asia's success had resulted from export-oriented and market-based development strategies (see World Bank 1991, 1993). In the World Bank's own words,

> the approach to development that seems to have worked most reliably, and which seems to offer most promise, suggests a reappraisal of the respective roles for the market and the state. Put simply, governments need to do less in those areas where markets work, or can be made to work, reasonably well.
>
> (World Bank 1991, 9)

To this end, structural adjustment emphasized changing those aspects of developing economies that were most unlike conditions in Asia. Governments were encouraged to create a stable macroeconomic environment, to liberalize trade, and to privatize state-owned enterprises (Williamson 1990, 1994). Macroeconomic stability was to be achieved by transforming government budget deficits into budget surpluses. Governments were encouraged to liberalize imports by dismantling import-licensing systems, shifting from quota-based forms of protection to tariffs, simplifying complex tariff structures, and reducing tariffs and opening their economies to imports.

The IMF and the World Bank also encouraged privatization of state-owned enterprises—that is, selling such enterprises to private individuals and groups. The IMF and the World Bank argued that reducing government involvement in the economy would foster competition and that greater competition would in turn help create a more efficient private sector that could drive economic development. Through structural adjustment, therefore, governments were encouraged to scale back the role of the state in economic development and to enhance the role played by the market.

Many governments implemented structural adjustment programs between 1983 and 1995 (see Table 7.4). They began to liberalize trade in the mid-1980s. In Latin America, average tariffs fell from 41.6 percent prior to the crisis to 13.7 percent by 1990 (Inter-American Development Bank 1997, 42). They began to privatize state-owned enterprises in the late 1980s. In Latin America, "more than 2,000 publicly owned firms, including public utilities, banks, and insurance companies, highways, ports, airlines, and retail shops, were privatized" between 1985 and 1992 (Edwards 1995, 170; see also Corbo 2000). They liberalized investment regimes, thus opening to multinational corporations. They deregulated industries and reduced government intervention in the financial system.

Structural adjustment programs had a dramatic impact on average incomes in the short run and the distribution of income in the long run. The crisis and the reforms brought about a sharp contraction of economic activity. Income fell sharply as a result. In Latin America, income fell by about

TABLE 7.4

Countries Adopting Trade and Domestic Policy Reforms, 1980–1996

Africa		Latin America	
Benin	Malawi	Argentina	Honduras
Burkina Faso	Mali	Bahamas	Mexico
Burundi	Mauritania	Barbados	Nicaragua
Cameroon	Mauritius	Belize	Panama
Central African Republic	Mozambique	Bolivia	Paraguay
Chad	Niger	Brazil	Peru
Congo	Nigeria	Chile	Suriname
Cote d'Ivoire	Rwanda	Colombia	Trinidad
Ethiopia	Senegal	Costa Rica	Uruguay
Gabon	Sierra Leone	Dominican Republic	Venezuela
The Gambia	Tanzania	Ecuador	
Ghana	Togo	El Salvador	
Guinea	Uganda	Guatemala	
Guinea-Bissau	Zambia	Guyana	
Kenya	Zimbabwe	Haiti	
Madagascar			

Sources: World Bank 1994a; Thorp 1999.

8 percent between 1981 and 1984. In sub-Saharan Africa, incomes fell, on average, by about 1.2 percent per year throughout the 1980s (Thorp 1999, 220; World Bank 1993). The dismantling of ISI also redistributed income from urban import-competing sectors to agriculture and emerging export-oriented manufacturing industries. In The Gambia, for instance, structural adjustment tripled the prices farmers received for groundnuts and significantly increased prices that urban residents paid for petroleum products, public transportation, water, electricity, and telecommunications (Jabara 1994, 309). Privatization and civil-service reform resulted in large job losses. In Guinea, for example, the civil service was reduced in size from 104,000 in 1985 to 71,000 in 1989 (Arulpragasam and Sahn 1994, 91). In pursuing structural adjustment, therefore, governments redistributed income: export-oriented producers benefited these policies, whereas people employed in the import-competing and nontraded-goods sectors saw their incomes fall.

The economic consequences of structural adjustment drove the domestic politics of reform (see Nelson 1990; Remmer 1986; Haggard and Kaufman 1992; Oatley 2004). Groups that would lose from structural adjustment attempted to block the reforms, whereas those who stood to gain attempted to promote reform. Governments were forced to mediate between them, and in many countries governments were heavily dependent upon political support from the import-competing and nontraded-goods sectors. Thus, reforms were hard to implement. Over time, however, the economic crisis triggered a realignment of interests, discrediting groups associated with the old policies and giving greater influence to groups that proposed an alternative approach (Krueger 1993a). By weakening key interest groups and by forcing many to redefine their interests, the crisis gradually eroded many of the political obstacles to far-reaching reform. Yet, this process took time, as reforms could be implemented only after new governments responsive to new interests had replaced the governments that presided over ISI.

GETTING INSTITUTIONS RIGHT

As the 1990s progressed, members of the development community began to argue that "getting prices right" by using SAPs to liberalize and marketize developing economies, while perhaps a necessary step toward sustained development, was not sufficient to deliver sustained growth. As a consequence, policymakers and academics began to focus greater attention on the broader context within which states made policy. As attention shifted away from the rather exclusive focus on policy reform, the characteristics and quality of political and economic institutions moved to the center. By the turn of the century there was "widespread agreement among economists studying economic growth that institutional quality holds the key to prevailing patterns of prosperity around the world" (Rodrik 2004, 1).

Thinking about institutions led to the articulation of two broad institutional configurations—inclusive institutions and extractive institutions—that have very different consequences for economic performance (Acemoglu and Robinson 2012). **Inclusive institutions** have political and economic characteristics that encourage individual initiative and sustained economic growth. The most important political characteristics of inclusive institutions include the broad extension of the right to select and constrain governments, adherence to the rule of law and a strong but (by virtue of the rule of law) constrained state. Among the relevant economic characteristics, inclusive institutions have strong property rights and market structures that reward individual talent. Inclusive institutions are likely to provide high-quality public services that are important to growth, such as public education that is available to all and infrastructure investments that facilitate market development. The elaboration of property rights and their defense in the rule of law system encourages investment in productivity-improving activities. The fact that the opportunities for economic activity are open to the broad public rather than restricted to the chosen few creates incentives for individual initiative. Inclusive institutions are thus likely to generate economic growth that is sustained over time.

Extractive institutions, by contrast, lack most of these redeeming qualities. In terms of politics, extractive institutions allocate power very narrowly to a small ruling elite and systematically exclude other segments of society from access to power. In addition, the elite's power is relatively unconstrained by electoral institutions or by a clear rule-of-law-based judicial system. Economic institutions also do little to reward the initiative of individuals. Property rights are often lacking, or where present are unevenly enforced. In such systems, the elite use their power to extract income from those who are excluded from politics and use it to provide benefits to the narrow group that rules or to the subset of society that keeps the government in power. Such systems become characterized by corruption within the state and among the ruling elite, and by rent seeking at the level of the society as a whole. As a consequence, the balance between productive and unproductive activity tips in a direction unfavorable to sustained economic growth.

One might illustrate the importance to economic performance of these institutional differences relative to other possible factors by comparing societies that share common cultures and geographies but have very different institutional characteristics. Consider North Korea and South Korea as one such comparison. South Korea has experienced sustained growth rates and dramatic improvements in the standard of living. North Korea, in contrast, has experienced exceptionally poor economic performance, even to the point of suffering widespread food scarcity. Acemoglu and Robinson's institutional perspective attributes these different economic trajectories to different institutions. They argue that the two countries occupy basically the same geographic space (the Korean peninsula), and thus confront the same climate and geographical constraints and opportunities. The two Koreas share a common language and culture, and (at least through 1940) they had a common history. The two differ primarily in their institutional characteristics, with South Korea benefiting from inclusive institutions and North Korean performance undermined by its extractive institutions. Acemoglu and Robinson offer other comparisons that are similar in nature, such as East and West Germany during and after the Cold War. Perhaps you can think of other comparative cases that either support or confound their institutional hypothesis.

Although the Acemoglu and Robinson institutional hypothesis holds considerable appeal, at least two important questions about the approach have been posed by its critics. The first critique points to potential issues of reverse causality. What we mean by reverse causality is the possibility that economic development outcomes are the underlying cause of institutional configurations rather than the Acemoglu and Robinson hypothesis that institutions cause development outcomes. Concerns about reverse causality arise from a large body of research that had been conducted prior to the more recent work by Acemoglu and Robinson. Indeed, almost 60 years ago Seymour Marin Lipset hypothesized that economic development causes democratization: "the more well-to-do a nation, the greater the chances that it will sustain democracy" (Lipset 1959, 75). Subsequent empirical scholarship has found substantial support for the Lipset hypothesis (Boix 2011; Barro 1996; Przeworski et al. 2000). Indeed, as one highly influential recent study concluded, "the level of economic development, as measured by per capita income, is by far the best predictor of [democratization]" (Przeworski et al. 2000, 88).

The second critique concerns the origins of political institutions. If, as Acemoglu and Robinson claim, different institutional configurations generate different development outcomes, it becomes important to understand what accounts for cross-national variation in institutions. That is, why are some societies fortunate enough to have been endowed with inclusive institutions that promote development while other societies have had the misfortune to be burdened with extractive institutions that do not promote development? Acemoglu and Robinson (2001) have argued that institutions reflected colonial settlement patterns. Where colonial mortality was high, due to climate and disease, colonists did not expect to establish permanent residence. They thus created extractive institutions that maximized their short-run take. Where colonial mortality rates were low, colonists were more likely to establish permanent settlements and thus were more likely to create inclusive institutions that promoted economic development. And these distinct institutions persisted after colonialism ended. For A&R, therefore, contemporary institutions—and thus development outcomes—are reflect developments that occurred hundreds of years ago and continue to exert influence through the social processes that make it very difficult to change institutions. One potential problem with this argument is that it is difficult to isolate the causal significance of institutions from the impact of climate and geography (see Diamond 2012).

Other scholars also have explained institutions by focusing on the interaction between colonialism and resource endowments. Engerman and Sokoloff (2000) focus their attention on explaining divergent development outcomes in South and North America and the Caribbean. They argue that low-quality institutions—essentially the equivalent of extractive institutions—emerged in colonies in which land, climate, and labor endowments encouraged colonists to engage in plantation-based agriculture. On Caribbean islands, for instance, the climate and land were conducive to sugar production, while small indigenous populations forced the colonial powers to rely upon imported slave labor. Colonists built political institutions that enabled them to control sugar production and income and to exclude slaves from participation in politics. The result was high inequality and low political inclusiveness. In contrast, in the northern parts of North America, climatic conditions and land endowments encouraged grain farming organized as small-holdings that relied on family labor rather than slaves. This small holding model generated less economic inequality which carried over into the design of political institutions which were more inclusive. In short, the interaction between geography and colonialism led to the establishment of particular institutional arrangements 250 and more years ago, and these institutions have exerted a powerful influence on development trajectories ever since.

The continued uncertainty about the origins or causes of institutions has important implications. Because different institutions are associated with different development outcomes, a central determinant of success lies in getting institutions right. Yet, this implies that societies stuck with extractive institutions can escape only if they can create more inclusive institutions. But if societies can change from extractive to inclusive institutions at will, then institutions aren't exogenous to state policy—they haven't really been inherited from 200 years ago—and cannot have the substantial independent impact on economic development that institutionalists claim.

Shifting from the Washington to the Beijing Consenus?

Question

Should the "Washington Consensus" be replaced by the "Beijing Consensus" as a development model?

Overview

The 1980s were turbulent for the developing world. The decade began with sovereign debt crises in several Latin American countries, and ended with the collapse of the Berlin Wall and political and market reforms in Eastern Europe. Responding to these events, economist John Williamson identified the "Washington Consensus" on the policies that developing countries must implement to ensure a return to growth. Williamson called this package the Washington Consensus because the World Bank, IMF, and U.S. Treasury Department—all based in Washington D.C.— concurred with these policy recommendations. Key to the Consensus was eliminating government involvement in the economy: "stabilize, privatize, and liberalize."

The recent success of China and other East Asian countries as well as what some characterize as disappointing achievements from the Washington Consensus, have led some to suggest that a so-called "Beijing Consensus" is replacing or should replace the Washington Consensus. If the "Washington Consensus" espoused decentralized market fundamentalism, then the "Beijing Consensus" advocates a return to a state-led development strategy. This new development path appeals to many governments for two reasons: first, it promises rapid results without a loss of sovereignty to Western governments that many developing country governments saw as a major part of the Washington Consensus. Second, it increases the government's power within the country by creating a justification for state intervention and allocation. Advocates for the Beijing Consensus emphasize its potential for delivering rapid development. Critics ask why governments would be expected to have better success with a state-led strategy now than they experienced under ISI.

Policy Options

- Washington-based institutions should continue to promote neoliberal politics. If governments do not comply, Washington-based institutions should withhold aid and consider trade sanctions.
- Governments should be allowed to pursue development as they see fit, and development aid and trade relations should not be contingent upon the adoption of any particular policy orientation.

Policy Analysis

- What differences do you see between the Washington Consensus and the Beijing Consensus? What about between the Beijing Consensus and the ISI strategy?

- What interest, if any, does the United States have in promoting neoliberal reforms like those of the "Washington Consensus"? Why might the United States oppose diffusion of a state-led strategy?
- Why might developing countries resist neoliberal development programs and favor a more state-centric model?

Take A Position

- Should the United States pressure developing countries to pursue neoliberal policies? Should developing countries resist? Justify your answer.
- What criticisms of your position should you anticipate? How would you defend your recommendations against these criticisms?

Resources

Online: Do online searches for "Washington Consensus" and "Beijing Consensus." You might begin with a speech given by John Williamson titled "Did the Washington Consensus Fail?" (located at www.iie.com/publications/papers/paper.cfm?ResearchID=488). Kenneth Rogoff, former head of the IMF, wrote an open letter to Joseph Stiglitz in response to criticisms of IMF neoliberal policies (located at www.imf.org/external/np/vc/2002/070202.HTM). One influential criticism of the "Washington Consensus" is Dani Rodrik, "Goodbye Washington Consensus, Hello Washington Confusion?" (located at www.hks.harvard.edu/fs/drodrik/Research%20papers/Lessons%20of%20the%201990s%20review%20_JEL_.pdf).

In Print: There are many lengthy criticisms of the "Washington Consensus", the best-known of which may be Joseph Stiglitz, *Globalization and Its Discontents* (New York, NY: W.W. Norton & Co., 2002), which prompted Rogoff's reply (linked above).

CONCLUSION

Neoliberalism supplanted structuralism as the guiding philosophy of economic development as a result of the interplay among three factors in the global economy. Import substitution generated severe economic imbalances that created pressure for reform of some type. The success of East Asian countries that adopted an export-oriented development strategy provided an alternative model for development. Finally, the emergence of a severe economic crisis in the early 1980s, a crisis that resulted in part from the imbalances generated by ISI and in part from developments in the global economy, pushed governments to launch reforms under the supervision of the IMF and the World Bank. By the mid-1980s, most governments were implementing reforms that reduced the role of the state and increased the role of the market in economic development.

The implementation of these reforms has been neither quick nor painless. The depth of the reforms brought substantial short-run costs as average incomes fell and as this smaller income was redistributed among groups. The proponents of neoliberal reforms argue that the short-run costs are worth paying, however, for they establish the framework for strong and sustainable growth far into the future. Achieving that outcome will require developing societies to consolidate and build upon the reforms already implemented. In addition, it will require the advanced industrialized countries to accept short-run adjustment costs of their own in order to meet the legitimate demands that developing countries now make about market access.

The adoption of neoliberal reforms in the developing world is also transforming the global economy. For the first time since the early twentieth century, the developing world has integrated itself into that economy. In doing so, developing countries have altered the dynamics of global economic exchange. Standard trade theory tells us to expect trade between capital-abundant and labor-abundant societies. Yet, trade barriers have greatly limited such trade for most of the postwar era. As these barriers have fallen during the last 20 years, trade between countries with different factor endowments has become increasingly important. Businesses are increasingly locating their activities in those parts of the world where they can be performed most efficiently. Labor-intensive aspects of production are being shifted to developing societies, whereas the capital-intensive aspects of production remain in the advanced industrialized countries. The expansion of North–South trade is thus creating a new global division of labor.

KEY TERMS

Current Account
East Asian Model of Development

Export-Oriented Strategy
Extractive Institutions
Inclusive Institutions

Rent Seeking
Structural Adjustment Program

SUGGESTIONS FOR FURTHER READING

On the East Asian Model of Development, see Robert Wade, *Governing the Market: Economic Theory and the Role of Government in East Asian Industrialization* (Princeton: Princeton University Press, 2003), Yin-wah Chu (editor) *The Asian Developmental State: Reexaminations and New Departures* (London: Palgrave MacMillan, 2016), and Dani Rodrik, *One Economics, Many Recipes: Globalization, Institutions, and Economic Growth* (Princeton: Princeton University Press, 2008).

The single best account of China's trajectory is Barry Naughton, *The Chinese Economy: Adaptation and Growth* (Cambridge: MIT Press, 2018).

For a detailed examination of the relationship between institutions and development, see Daron Acemoglu and James Robinson, *Why Nations Fail: The Origins of Power, Prosperity and Poverty* (New York: Crown Business, 2013).

For an application of the institutionalist perspective to contemporary sub-Saharan Africa, see Robert H Bates and Steven Block, 2017. "Political Institutions and Economic Growth in Africa's 'Renaissance.'" *Oxford Economic Papers*, 1–26.

Multinational Corporations in the Global Economy

ultinational corporations highlight—in a very concentrated fashion—the tension that arises when economic production is organized globally while political systems remain organized around mutually exclusive national territories. Multinational corporations often generate tension because they extend managerial control across national borders. This managerial control enables firms based in one country to make decisions about how to employ resources located in a foreign country. Contemporary discussion surrounding the emergence of Chinese firms as a major source of foreign investment in sub-Saharan African economies illustrates these tensions. While African governments have generally welcomed the gains that Chinese investment in infrastructure, natural resources, and manufacturing brings to their societies, many local observers have raised concerns about how these Chinese firms treat African workers, and safeguard the environment. A major American newspaper even went so far as to title a long story about Chinese corporate investment in Africa, "Is China the World's New Colonial Power" (Larmer 2017)? Though investment by Chinese firms raises additional questions about the possibility of state control of these investments, this additional dimension sharpens the issue rather than creating it.

Because multinational corporations operate simultaneously in national political systems and global markets, they have been the subject of considerable controversy among governments and among observers of the international political economy. Some consider multinational corporations to be productive instruments of a liberal economic order: multinational corporations ship capital to where it is scarce, transfer technology and management expertise from one country to another, and promote the efficient allocation of resources in the global economy. Others consider multinational corporations to be instruments of capitalist domination: multinational corporations control critical sectors of their hosts' economies, make decisions about the use of resources with little regard for host-country needs, and weaken labor and environmental standards. About all that these two divergent perspectives agree on is that multinational corporations are primary drivers of, and beneficiaries from, globalization.

This chapter and the next examine the economics and the politics of multinational corporations (MNCs). This chapter focuses on a few of the core economic issues concerning these geographically far-reaching organizations. The first section provides a broad overview of MNCs in the global economy. We define what MNCs are, briefly examine their origins and development, and then examine their rapid growth over the last 30 years. The second section examines standard economic theory developed to explain the existence of MNCs. This theory will both deepen our understanding of the differences between MNCs and other firms and help us understand when we are likely to see MNCs operating and when we are likely to see national firms. The final section examines the impact of MNCs on the countries that host their foreign investments. We look first at the potential benefits that MNCs can bring to host countries and then examine how MNC activities sometimes limit the extent to which host countries are able to realize those benefits.

MULTINATIONAL CORPORATIONS IN THE GLOBAL ECONOMY

For many people, a multinational corporation and a firm that engages heavily in international activities are one and the same thing. Yet, an MNC is more than just a firm that engages in international activities, and many firms that engage heavily in international activities are not MNCs. The standard definition of an MNC is a firm that "controls and manages production establishments—plants—in at least two countries" (Caves 1996, 1). In other words, MNCs place multiple production facilities in multiple countries under the control of a single corporate structure.

The preceding definition does not capture the full range of MNC activities, however. MNCs are engaged simultaneously in economic production, international trade, and cross-border investment. Consider, for example, the U.S.-based company General Electric (GE), which is regularly ranked among the world's largest MNCs. GE controls some 250 plants located in 26 countries in North and South America, Europe, and Asia. Although production in these facilities is obviously important, the ability to engage in international trade is equally critical to GE's success. Many of the goods GE produces cross national borders, either as finished consumer goods or as components for other finished products. Washers, dryers, and microwave ovens that GE produces in Asia and Latin America, for example, are sold in the United States and Europe. To create this global production and trade network, GE has had to make many cross-border investments. Each time that GE establishes a new production facility or upgrades an existing facility in a foreign country, it invests in that country. MNCs are thus also an important source of foreign capital for the countries that host their affiliates. Thus, even though GE certainly controls and manages factories in at least two countries, this does not describe the full range of GE's international activities. Like all MNCs, GE engages simultaneously in production, trade, and cross-border investment.

MNCs are not recent inventions. They first emerged as significant and enduring components of the international economy during the late nineteenth century. This first wave of multinational businesses was dominated by Great Britain, the world's largest capital-exporting country in that century. British firms invested in natural resources and in manufacturing within the British Empire, the United States, Latin America, and Asia. In 1914, British investors controlled almost half of the world's total stock of foreign direct investment, and multinational manufacturing was taking place in a large number of industries, including chemicals, pharmaceuticals, the electrical industry, machinery, automobiles, tires, and processed food (Jones 1996, 29–30). American firms began investing abroad in the late nineteenth century. Singer Sewing Machines became the first American firm to create a permanent manufacturing facility abroad when it built a plant in Glasgow, Scotland, in 1867 (Wilkins 1970, 41–42). By the 1920s, the United States was overtaking Britain as the world's largest source of foreign direct investment (see Jones 1996).

Although MNCs are not a recent innovation, what is novel is the rate at which firms have been transforming themselves into MNCs. We can see the unprecedented growth of MNCs in two different sets of statistics. The first tracks the number of MNCs operating in the global economy. In 1969, just at the tail end of the period of American dominance, there were only about 7,300 MNC parent firms operating in the global economy (Gabel and Bruner 2003). By 1988, 18,500 firms had entered the ranks of MNCs, an impressive growth in 20 years. During the next 20 years, however, the number of MNCs operating in the global economy more than quadrupled, rising to more than 100,000 parent firms by 2010. Together, these parents control almost 900,000 foreign affiliates. Thus, in just over 40 years, the number of firms engaged in international production has increased about elevenfold.

The second set of statistics tracks the growth of foreign direct investment over the same period. **Foreign direct investment** (FDI) occurs when a firm based in one country builds a new plant or a factory, or purchases an existing one, in a second country. A national corporation thus becomes an MNC by making a foreign direct investment. As Table 8.1 illustrates, the total volume of foreign direct investment has grown dramatically since 1990. During the late 1980s, cross-border FDI outflows equalled about $180 billion per year. The figure more than doubled during the 1990s and then doubled again during the first decade of the twenty-first century. Between 2010 and 2016 it averaged about $1.45 trillion per year. As a consequence, the world's stock of FDI, the total amount of foreign investment in operation, has grown from $693 billion in 1980 to $27 trillion in 2016 (United Nations Conference on Trade and Development 2017, 226). The last 30 years have thus brought a dramatic acceleration of the number of firms that are internationalizing their activities.

TABLE 8.1

Foreign Direct Investment Outflows, 1990–2016 ($U.S. Billions)

	1990–1999	2000–2009	2010–2016
World	413.8	1,100.0	1,435.7
Europe	244.2	609.9	482.8
North America	99.8	248.7	369.2
Africa	1.9	11.2	26.5
Asia	33.6	121.8	341.6
Latin America and the Caribbean	4.4	17.7	34.1
Transition Economies	1.1	23.0	49.3

Source: United Nations Conference on Trade and Development, 2017.

As the number of MNCs has increased, the role that they play in the global economy has likewise gained in importance. The United Nations (UN) estimates that MNCs currently account for about a third of global exports (roughly $6.8 trillion in 2016), and much of this is intrafirm trade—that is, trade that takes place between an MNC parent and its foreign affiliates. MNCs and their affiliates employ some 82 million people worldwide (UNCTAD 2017, 26). Much of this activity is concentrated in a relatively small number of firms. The 100 largest MNCs account for more than 9 percent of the total foreign assets controlled by all MNCs, for 16 percent of all MNC sales, and for 11 percent of all MNC employment (UNCTAD 2009, xxi). Together, these 100 firms account for about 4 percent of world gross domestic product (GDP). MNCs thus play an important role in the contemporary global economy, a role that has grown at a rapid pace during the last 30 years.

Although MNCs have a global reach, most of their activities are concentrated in Europe, North America, and (increasingly) in East Asia. We can see just how concentrated MNC operations are by looking at some statistics on the nationality of parent firms and on the global distribution of FDI flows. Ninety-one of the 100 largest MNCs are headquartered in the United States, Western Europe, or Japan, and about 73 percent of all MNC parent corporations are based in advanced industrial countries (see Table 8.2). The advanced industrialized countries historically have been the largest suppliers of FDI as well. During most of the 1980s, the United States, Western Europe, and Japan together supplied about 90 percent of FDI (see Table 8.1). Their share fell to about 80 percent between 1990 and 2009 and then to 60 percent between 2010 and 2016. The biggest underlying change that explains this decrease in developed countries' share has been the emergence of Asian MNCs as important foreign investors.

The advanced industrialized countries and East Asia are also the largest recipients of the world's FDI. Until the late 1980s, Western Europe and the United States regularly attracted a little more than three-quarters of the world's total FDI inflows each year. This share fell to about two-thirds of total inflows

TABLE 8.2

Parent Corporations and Affiliates by Region, 2010

	Parent Corporations Based in the Economy	Foreign Affiliates Based in the Economy
Developed Economies	73,144	373,612
European Union	47,455	310,074
United States	9,692	27,251
Japan	4,543	2,948
Other Developed Economies	3,593	13,472
Developing Economies	30,209	512,531
Africa	621	6,673
Latin America and the Caribbean	4,406	21,634
Asia	25,148	483,715
Southeast Europe and the CIS	433	5971

Source: United Nations Conference on Trade and Development, "World Investment Report 2011, Web Table 34," *http://unctad.org/Sections/dite_dir/docs/WIR11_web%20tab%2034.pdf*.

during the 1990s. The share of inflows that the developed world captures has continued to fall—to an average of 60 percent of the total between 2000 and 2009 and then to slightly less than half of total inflows during the current decade. Asia was on the opposite side of this change, as its share of total inflows rose from 18 percent to 28 percent between 1990 and 2016. Consequently, Asia is now host to 55 percent of all foreign affiliates that MNCs have established in the global economy. Thus, whereas historically most MNC activities have involved American and Japanese firms investing in Europe, European and Japanese firms investing in the United States, and American and European firms investing in Japan, over the last 25 years we see developing Asia becoming an increasingly important player as a source of and host to multinational corporation activities.

MNC activities in other regions have also increased during the last 30 years. Latin America and the Caribbean saw inward FDI increase from an average of $38 billion per year during the 1990s to $172 billion per year in the current decade (see Table 8.3). These investments are heavily concentrated in a small number of economies in the region. Over the last decade, Brazil alone attracted between 40 and 50 percent of all investment in the region. Mexico attracted (on average) another 20 percent of the total inward investment. Africa has also experienced a dramatic increase in foreign direct investment. Indeed, average annual inflows to Africa increased ten-fold between the 1990s and the current decade, rising from $6.6 billion per year to $67 billion per year. During the current decade, Angola has received the largest single share of these investment flows, capturing 22 percent of the total inflows over the period. Most of this

TABLE 8.3

Foreign Direct Investment Inflows, 1990–2016 ($U.S. Billions)

	1990–1999	2000–2009	2010–2016
World	397.6	1,095.2	1,550.7
Europe	167.3	455.0	449.6
North America	99.7	215.5	293.5
Africa	6.6	38.0	67.3
Asia	70.2	224.7	440.8
Latin America and the Caribbean	37.6	81.4	172.1
Transition economies	4.0	42.8	64.9

Source: United Nations Conference on Trade and Development, 2017.

investment has been directed to Angola's oil industry. Egypt and Nigeria also attract a significant share of inward investment. Inward investment increased in the transition economies also, and here the inflows are heavily concentrated in Russia (50 percent of the total on average since 2010) and Kazakhstan (15–20 percent of the total since 2010). Thus, MNC investment in Latin America, Africa, and the transition economies has increased substantially during the last 20 years, but the majority of this investment has been directed to a small handful of countries. And in contrast to Asian economies, these regions have not increased their share of the world's FDI.

The last 30 years also have seen some emerging market countries become home bases for MNC parent firms. To date, however, this development has been limited to a small number of countries, such as Hong Kong, China, South Korea, Singapore, Taiwan, Venezuela, Mexico, and Brazil. Sixty of the top 100 MNCs from developing countries are based in Southeast and East Asia. Another six are based in India. Most of these developing-world MNCs are considerably smaller than the MNCs based in the advanced industrialized world. Only nine developing-country MNCs ranked among the world's 100 largest MNCs in 2017. And as a group, the 100 largest MNCs from developing countries control a combined $1.7 trillion of foreign assets, only one-fifth the value of the foreign assets controlled by the world's 100 largest MNCs (UNCTAD 2017). Even though MNCs based in developing countries remain small relative to the firms based in the U.S. and the EU, the emergence of these MNCs nonetheless constitutes a significant change in the global economy. It indicates that, for the first time in history, some emerging economies are shifting from a position in which they are only the host to foreign MNCs to a position in which they are both host of foreign firms and home to domestic MNCs.

The rapid growth of MNCs during the last 30 years has pushed these firms into the center of the debate about globalization. Indeed, practically every aspect of globalization has been linked to the activities of MNCs. Ross Perot, for example, claimed during his unsuccessful bid for the presidency in 1992 that the North American Free Trade Agreement (NAFTA) would produce a "giant sucking sound" as American MNCs shifted jobs from the United States to their affiliates located in Mexico. Other critics of globalization claim that MNC affiliates based in developing countries are sweatshops engaged in the systematic exploitation of workers in those countries. Still others argue that the ability of MNCs to move production wherever they want is gradually eroding a broad range of government regulations designed to protect workers, consumers, and the environment. We will examine these arguments in greater detail in Chapter 16. For our purposes here, it is sufficient to note that criticism of MNC activities has emerged from the growing sense that the last 30 years have seen a fundamental change in the nature of corporate behavior within the global economy. Falling trade barriers and improvements in communications technology have made it substantially easier for firms to internationalize their activities. Firms have responded to these changes by internationalizing at historically unprecedented rates.

ECONOMIC EXPLANATIONS FOR MULTINATIONAL CORPORATIONS

One might wonder why all of the economic transactions that occur between MNC parent firms and their foreign affiliates are not simply handled through the market. Indeed, the prevalence of MNCs in the contemporary international economy is puzzling to neoclassical economists. When the GAP or the Limited acquire clothes from producers in Bangladesh, they handle most of these transactions through the market. They sign contracts with locally owned Bangladeshi firms that produce clothes and then sell them to the retailer. The GAP and the Limited do not own the firms that produce their clothes. In other instances, however, almost identical transactions are taken out of the market. When Volkswagen decided to assemble some of its cars in Mexico, it could have signed contracts with locally owned Mexican firms, which then could have produced components that met Volkswagen's specifications; assembled them into Jettas, Beetles, and Golfs; and sold the finished cars to Volkswagen. Volkswagen, however, didn't opt for this market-based approach, but instead built an assembly plant in Mexico. Volkswagen thus took the economic transactions that would otherwise have taken place between suppliers of components, assemblers, and corporate headquarters out of the market and placed them under the sole control of Volkswagen headquarters. The rapid growth of MNCs implies that an increasing number of firms have opted to take their international transactions out of the market and to internalize them within a single corporate structure. Why have they done so?

In finding an answer to this puzzle, we deepen our understanding of how MNCs are something more distinctive than simply "large firms." Many MNCs *are* large, but what truly distinguishes them from other firms is the fact that they organize and manage their international activities very differently than other firms do. A firm's decision about whether to conduct international transactions through the market or instead to internalize these transactions inside a single corporation reflects some specific characteristics of the economic environment in which it operates. In conceptualizing how this environment shapes the firm's decision, economists have placed the greatest emphasis on the interaction between locational advantages and market imperfections.

Locational Advantages

As a first step, we need to understand the factors that encourage a firm to internationalize its activities—that is, what factors determine when a firm will stop sourcing all of its inputs and selling all of its output at home and begin acquiring its inputs or selling a portion of its output in foreign markets? At a very broad level, it is obvious that a firm will internationalize its activities when it believes that it can profit by doing so. **Locational advantages** derive from specific country characteristics that provide such opportunities. Historically, locational advantages have been based on one of three specific country characteristics: a large reserve of natural resources, a large local market, and opportunities to enhance the efficiency of the firm's operations. A firm based in one country will internationalize its activities in an attempt to profit from one of these characteristics in a foreign country.

Locational advantages in **natural-resource investments** arise from the presence of large deposits of a particular natural resource in a foreign country. The desire to profit from the extraction of these natural resources was perhaps the earliest motivation for international activities. The American copper firms Anaconda and Kennecott, for example, made large direct investments in mining operations in Chile in order to secure supplies for production in the United States. American and European oil companies have invested heavily in the Middle East because the countries of that region hold so large a proportion of the world's petroleum reserves. The desire to gain access to natural resources remains important today. Indeed, petroleum and mining together account for 17 of the 100 largest MNCs currently in operation.

Locational advantages for **market-oriented investments** arise from large consumer markets that are expected to grow rapidly over time. Firms looking to sell their products in foreign markets clearly prefer countries with large and growing demand to those with small and stagnant demand. In addition, the degree of industry competition within the host country is important. The less indigenous competition there is in a particular foreign market, the easier it will be for the MNC to sell its products in that market. Finally, the existence of tariff and non-tariff barriers to imports is another important consideration for this type of investment. By investing inside the country, firms essentially jump over such barriers to produce and sell in the local market. Countries that have large and fast-growing markets, with a relatively small number of indigenous firms in the particular industry, and that are sheltered from international competition represent attractive opportunities for market-oriented MNC investment.

Much of the cross-border investment in auto production within the advanced industrialized world fits into this category. During the 1960s, many

American automotive MNCs made direct investments in the EU to gain access to the emerging common market. During the 1980s and early 1990s, Japanese and German automotive MNCs, such as Toyota, Nissan, Honda, BMW, and Mercedes, built production facilities in the United States in response to the emergence of voluntary export restraints (VERs) that limited auto imports. Like petroleum and mining, the auto industry is heavily represented among the world's largest MNCs, accounting for 12 of the 100 largest MNCs. Of course, the desire to gain access to foreign markets has not been limited to the auto industry but has been an important motivation for much FDI in manufacturing as well.

Finally, locational advantages in **efficiency-oriented investments** arise from the availability at a lower cost of the factors of production that are used intensively in the production of a specific product. In these efficiency-oriented investments, parent firms allocate different stages of the production process to different parts of the world, matching the factor intensity of a production stage to the factor abundance of particular countries. In computers, electronics, and electrical equipment, for example, the human and physical capital-intensive stages of production, such as design and chip fabrication, are performed in the capital-abundant advanced industrialized countries, whereas the more labor-intensive assembly stages of production are performed in labor-abundant developing countries. Locational advantages thus arise from factor endowments. When the contemplated investment is in low-skilled, labor-intensive production, labor-abundant countries have obvious advantages over labor-scarce countries. When the contemplated investment draws heavily upon advanced technology, the availability of a pool of highly trained scientists is important. American firms in the computer industry, for example, have opted to base many of their overseas activities in East Asian countries, where the average skill level is very high, rather than in Latin America, where, on average, skill levels are lower.

Locational advantages thus provide the economic rationale for a firm's decision to internationalize its activities. These advantages can arise from a country's underlying comparative advantage, as in mineral deposits or abundant labor. They can also be a product of government policies, as in the existence of high tariffs or the creation of a reliable economic infrastructure. Whatever the underlying source, locational advantages create a compelling motivation for a firm based in one country to engage in economic transactions with a foreign country. Locational advantages thus help us understand why a firm elects to engage in economic transactions with one country rather than another, for some countries offer potential benefits from cross-border exchange, whereas others do not.

Market Imperfections

Locational advantages help us understand why some firms opt to internationalize their activities, but they do not help us understand why firms sometimes choose to take the resulting transactions out of the market and place them within a single corporate structure. Why didn't American firms simply buy copper from Chilean firms, rather than establish their own mining operations in Chile? Why didn't American computer firms simply buy semiconductors and other components from indigenous East Asian firms, rather than create their own chip fabrication factories in East Asia? Why didn't American auto firms simply export to the EU and Brazil, rather than build assembly plants in those countries?

To understand why firms sometimes take their transactions out of the market and place them under the control of a single corporate structure, we need to examine the impact of market imperfections. A market imperfection arises when the price mechanism fails to promote a welfare-improving transaction. In the global economy, this means that, under certain conditions, firms will be unable to profit from an existing locational advantage unless they internalize the international transaction. Two different market imperfections have been used to understand two different types of internalization: horizontal integration and vertical integration.

Horizontal integration occurs when a firm creates multiple production facilities, each of which produces the same good or goods. In the international economy, horizontally integrated MNCs produce the same product in multiple national markets. Auto producers are a good example. Ford, General Motors, Volkswagen, and the major Japanese auto producers each produce essentially the same line of cars in factories located in the United States, Western Europe, and Japan. Firms integrate horizontally when a cost advantage is gained by placing a number of plants under common administrative control (Caves 1996, 2). Such cost advantages most often arise when intangible assets are the most important source of a firm's revenue.

An **intangible asset** is something whose value is derived from knowledge or from "a set of skills or repertory routines possessed by the firm's team of human (and other) inputs" (Caves 1996, 3). An intangible asset can be based on a patented process or design, or it can arise from "know-how shared among employees of the firm" (Caves 1996, 3). Intangible assets often give rise to horizontally integrated firms because those assets are difficult to sell or license to other firms at a price that accurately reflects their true value. In other words, markets will fail to promote exchanges between a willing seller of an intangible asset and a willing buyer. The market failure arises because owners of knowledge-based assets confront what has been called the "fundamental paradox of information": "[The] value [of the information] for the purchaser is not known until he has the information, but then he has in effect acquired it without cost" (Teece 1993, 172). In other words, in order to convey the full value of an intangible asset, the owner must reveal so much of the information upon which the asset's value is based that the potential purchaser no longer needs to pay to acquire the asset. If the owner is unwilling to reveal that information, potential buyers will be unsure of the asset's true value and will therefore be reluctant to pay for the asset.

Suppose, for example, that I have developed a production process that reduces by one-half the cost of manufacturing cars. This innovation is purely a matter of how the production process is organized and managed, and has nothing to do with the machines and technology actually used to produce cars. I try to sell this knowledge to Ford Motor Company, but, in our negotiations, Ford's board of directors is skeptical of my claim that I can cut the firm's costs by 50 percent. The board members insist that I disclose fully how I will accomplish this before they will even consider purchasing my knowledge, and they want specifics. Once I disclose all of the details, however, they will know exactly what changes they need to make in order to realize the cost reductions. As soon as they have this knowledge, they have no reason to pay me to acquire it. Like all other owners of intangible assets, I will receive less than my asset's true worth when I sell it to another firm.

Such market failures create incentives for horizontal integration. Suppose an individual owns an intangible asset that can generate more revenue than is currently being earned, because demand for the goods produced with the use of this asset will be greater than can be met from the existing production facility. How can the owner earn the additional revenue that the asset will generate? The only way he or she can do so is to create additional production sites—that is, to integrate horizontally and allow each of these facilities to make use of the intangible asset. Because the same firm owns all of the production sites, it can realize the full value of its intangible asset without having to try to sell it in an open market. Horizontal integration, therefore, internalizes economic transactions for intangible assets.

Vertical integration refers to instances in which firms internalize their transactions for intermediate goods. An intermediate good is an output of one production process that serves as an input into another production process. Standard Oil, which dominated the American oil industry in the late nineteenth century, is a classic example of a vertically integrated firm. Standard Oil owned oil wells, the network through which crude oil was transported from the well to the refinery, the refineries, and the retail outlets at which the final product was sold. Thus, each stage of the production process was contained within a single corporate structure. Why would a single firm incorporate the various stages of the production process under a single administrative control, rather than purchase its inputs from independent producers and sell outputs to other independent firms, either as inputs into additional production or as final goods to independent retailers?

To explain the internalization of transactions within a single vertically integrated firm, economists have focused on problems caused by specific assets. A **specific asset** is an investment that is dedicated to a particular long-term economic relationship. Consider a hypothetical case of a shipowner and a railroad. The shipowner would like to transport the goods he delivers to his dock to market by rail. He contacts the railroad and asks that a rail spur be built from the main line down to the dock so that he can offload goods directly onto railcars. If the railroad agrees to build the spur, then this spur will be dedicated to the transport of that particular shipowner's goods to the main rail line. In other words, this rail spur is an asset that is specific to the ongoing relationship between the shipowner and the railroad owner.

Specific assets create incentives for vertical integration because it is difficult to write and enforce long-term contracts. Returning to our example of the shipowner and the railroad, suppose that, under the terms of the initial agreement, the shipowner agreed to pay the railroad a certain fee per ton to carry goods to market once the spur was built. This initial fee made it profitable for the railroad to build the spur. Once the spur has been built, however, the shipowner has an incentive to renegotiate the initial contract to achieve a more favorable shipping rate. The shipowner recognizes that, because the railroad must incur costs if it decides to reallocate the resources it used to build the spur, the railroad owner will be better off accepting renegotiated terms than refusing to carry the goods. Thus, the existence of a specific asset creates possibilities for opportunistic behavior once the investment has been made: one party in the long-term relationship can take advantage of the specific nature of the asset to extract a larger share of the value from the transaction (Teece 1993, 166–169; Williamson 1985).

The recognition that asset specificity creates incentives for opportunistic behavior after the investment has been made can cause economic actors to refuse to make investments. In our example, the railroad owner will recognize that the shipowner has an incentive to behave opportunistically after the spur is built; therefore, quite rationally, the railroad owner will refuse to build the spur. As a result, a mutually beneficial transaction between the shipper and the railroad will go unrealized.

By incorporating the two parties to the transaction within the same ownership structure, vertical integration eliminates the problems arising from specific assets. If the shipowner also owned the railroad (or vice versa), there would be little incentive for opportunistic behavior once the rail spur had been built. The shipping division of this now vertically integrated firm could pay the firm's railroad division a smaller fee for transporting its goods, but this would simply shift revenues and expenditures between units of the same firm; the firm's overall bottom line would remain constant. By internalizing transactions involving specific assets, therefore, vertical integration enables welfare-improving investments that would not otherwise be made.

Firms thus internalize their transactions—take them out of the market and place them under the control of a single corporate structure—in response to market imperfections. When firms earn a substantial share of their revenues from intangible assets, they face strong incentives to integrate horizontally—that is, to create multiple production facilities all controlled by a single corporate headquarters. When firms earn a substantial share of their revenues from specific assets, they face strong incentives to integrate vertically—that is, to place all of the various stages of production under the control of a single corporate structure. In both cases, the incentive to take transactions out of the market and place them within a single corporate structure arises from the inability of the market to accurately price the value of the asset that generates the firm's income.

Locational Advantages, Market Imperfections, and Multinational Corporations

Although locational advantages and market imperfections often occur independently of each other, we expect to see MNCs—firms that internalize economic transactions across national borders—when both factors are present. Locational advantages tell us that cross-border activity will be profitable, whereas market imperfections tell us that the firm can take advantage of these opportunities only by internalizing the transactions within a single corporate structure.

Table 8.4 illustrates how the interaction between locational advantages and market imperfections shapes the kinds of firms we expect to see in the global economy. When locational advantages and intangible assets are both present, we expect to find horizontally integrated MNCs that have undertaken foreign investment to gain market access. Horizontally integrated MNCs are therefore often present in manufacturing sectors. FDIs by auto producers in the markets of other advanced industrial countries are perhaps the prototypical example of this type of MNC. In the auto industry, intangible assets arising from knowledge about the production process are of great value to individual firms, but are hard to price accurately in the market. Together with important locational advantages—especially the availability of large local markets—intangible assets induce foreign investment. Western Europe and the United States offer large markets for automobiles, and governments in the EU and in the United States have used VERs to restrict imports from foreign auto producers. The combination of market imperfections and locational advantages in the auto industry therefore has led to considerable FDI by all of the major auto producers in the European and American markets.

When locational advantages combine with specific assets, we expect to find vertically integrated MNCs that have invested in a foreign country either to gain secure access to natural resources or to reduce their costs of production. The best example of firms investing to secure access to natural resources is found in the oil industry. An oil refinery must have repeated transactions with

TABLE 8.4

Market Imperfections, Locational Advantages, and Multinational Corporations (MNCs)

		Market Imperfection	
		Intangible Assets	Specific Assets
Locational Advantages	Yes	Horizontally integrated MNC Market based	Vertically integrated MNC Natural resource based; Cost based
	No	Horizontally integrated domestic firm	Vertically integrated domestic firm

the firms that are drilling for oil. The refinery is highly vulnerable to threats to shut off the flow of oil, because an inconsistent supply would be highly disruptive to the refinery and its distribution networks. Thus, we would expect a high degree of vertical integration in the oil industry. This knowledge helps us understand why petroleum companies are so heavily represented in the world's 100 largest MNCs.

The best example of firms investing abroad to reduce the cost of production may be found in the factories built by auto producers in developing countries. The individual components involved in auto production are complex and specific to the final good: one cannot produce a Ford with parts designed for a Nissan. Thus, auto producers must have long-term relationships with their parts suppliers, and these relationships create incentives for vertical integration across borders. It is no surprise, therefore, that the auto industry also is heavily represented in the 100 largest MNCs.

More broadly, MNC investments that combine a quest for efficiency gains with specific or intangible assets have become an increasingly important element of multinational production over the last 20 years. These MNC investment patterns are often called **global value chains** (GVCs). A value chain "describes the full range of activities that firms and workers perform to bring a product from its conception to end use" (Gereffi and Fernandez-Stark 2016, 7). Such activities range from research, development, and design on the one end, to the manufacturing processes in the middle, through the wholesale distribution, marketing, retail sales, and support at the other end. A value chain becomes global when these various stages are allocated to different countries. In the ideal-typical GVC, a lead firm will distribute the stages of production globally in an attempt to realize efficiency gains by matching the factor intensity of each stage of production with the factor abundance of the selected production locations. Stages that rely intensively on human capital, such as R&D and design, would be based in an advanced industrialized economy, the capital-intensive manufacturing activity would be done in a middle-income economy, and labor-intensive manufacturing and assembly would be allocated to low-income labor abundant economies. Marketing and post-sale services would be based in economies with an abundance of human capital.

Global value chains are most common in the consumer electronics and automotive industries. Apple products such as the iPhone are often used as examples of a fairly complex GVC in the consumer electronics industry. Apple is a MNC that has elements of vertical and horizontal integration and also coordinates the activities of hundreds of independent suppliers and assemblers worldwide. Most of the research and design for Apple hardware and software occurs in Apple's campus in California (though it also owns an R&D facility in Austin, Texas, and in 2017 it announced plans to open new R&D facilities in China). At the other end of the chain, Apple retains considerable control of retail distribution via its Apple Stores as well as online sales. To manufacture its products, it coordinates an extensive global supply chain of independent contract manufacturing firms. It sources the hardware components—printed circuit boards, micro-processor chips, memory, storage devices, displays, cases, and so on, from hundreds of independent firms in Asia, the U.S., and Europe. These components are assembled into finished goods at two Foxconn factories in China and Brazil.

The rising importance of GVCs is transforming the nature of international trade. Fifty years ago, the goods and services that entered international trade were predominantly final consumption goods. Sixty years ago, for instance, Sony manufactured transistor radios in its factories in Japan and exported complete radios to the U.S. and Europe in large quantities. FDI often substituted for international trade as corporations created new overseas production sites from which to supply their overseas markets or supported trade by extracting raw materials. Today, in contrast as much as 60 percent of trade consists of intermediate goods and services rather than final goods (UNCTAD 2013, 122) while FDI increases trade as lead firms ever-more finely slice up and disperse their supply chains.

The matrix presented in Table 8.4 also points to those industries in which we would not expect to find a significant amount of MNC activity. When locational advantages exist, but there are neither intangible nor specific assets, we do not expect to find a significant amount of MNC activity. Instead, firms will prefer to purchase their inputs from independent suppliers and to sell their products through international trade, or they will prefer to enter into subcontracting arrangements with firms located in the foreign country and owned by foreign residents. Apparel production fits nicely into this category. Apparel production is a labor-intensive activity and is increasingly done in labor-abundant developing countries. The major retailers in the advanced industrialized world, such as the GAP and the Limited, rely heavily upon producers located in developing countries, but they rarely own the firms that produce the apparel they sell. Instead, they enter into contracting relationships with independent firms.

In sum, MNCs are more than just large firms. MNCs are firms that have responded in predictable ways to the specific characteristics of the economic environment in which they operate. The creation of an MNC is most often the result of a corporate response to a locational advantage and a market imperfection. Locational advantages create incentives to extend operations across borders in order to extract natural resources, sell in foreign markets, or achieve cost reductions. Intangible and specific assets create incentives for firms to shift their economic transactions out of the market and into a single corporate structure. When locational advantages and market imperfections coexist, we expect to find MNCs—firms that have internalized transactions across national borders.

Multinational Corporations and Host Countries

Up to this point, we have focused exclusively on what MNCs are, where they operate, and why they are established. In doing so, we have neglected the impact of MNCs on the countries that host their affiliates. We conclude the chapter by looking at this important dimension of MNC activity. FDI creates a dilemma for host countries. On the one hand, FDI has the potential to make a positive contribution to the host country's economic welfare by providing resources that are not readily available elsewhere. On the other hand, because MNC affiliates are managed by decision makers based in foreign countries, there is no guarantee that FDI will in fact make such a contribution. The politics of host country—MNC relations, a topic that we explore in depth in the next chapter, revolves largely around governments' efforts to manage this dilemma. Here, we look at the benefits that FDI confers on host countries in theory, as well as at a few MNC practices that can erode these benefits.

MNCs can bring to host countries important resources that are not easily acquired otherwise. Three such resources are perhaps the most important. First, FDI can transfer savings from one country to another. Economic growth is dependent on investment in physical capital as well as in human capital. To invest, however, a society needs to save, and in the absence of some form of foreign investment, a society can invest only as much as it is able to save. Foreign investment allows a society to draw on the savings of the rest of the world. By doing so, the country can enjoy faster growth than would be possible if it were forced to rely solely on its domestic savings. Moreover, fixed investments—factories that are not easily removed from the country—are substantially more stable than financial capital flows and thus do not generate the boom and bust cycles we will examine in Chapter 14 and Chapter 15. In addition, because MNCs invest by creating domestic affiliates, direct investment does not raise host countries' external indebtedness. Of the many possible ways that savings can be transferred across borders, direct investment might be the most stable and least burdensome for the host countries.

MNCs also can bring technology and managerial expertise to host countries. Because MNCs control intangible assets based on specialized knowledge, the investments they make in host countries often can lead to this knowledge being transferred to indigenous firms. In Malaysia, for example, Motorola Malaysia transferred the technology required to produce a particular type of printed circuit board to a Malaysian firm, which then developed the capacity to produce these circuit boards on its own (Moran 1999, 77–78). In the absence of the technology transfer, the indigenous firm would not have been able to produce the products.

Such technology transfers can generate significant positive externalities with wider implications for development (see Graham 1996, 123–130). **Positive externalities** arise when economic actors in the host country that are not directly involved in the transfer of technology from an MNC to a local affiliate also benefit from this transaction. If, for example, the Malaysian Motorola affiliate were able to use the technology it acquired from Motorola to produce inputs for other Malaysian firms at a lower cost than these inputs were available elsewhere, then the technology transfer would have a positive externality on the Malaysian economy.

MNCs can also transfer managerial expertise to host countries. Greater experience at managing large firms allows MNC personnel to organize production and coordinate the activities of multiple enterprises more efficiently than host-country managers can. This knowledge is applied to the host-country affiliates, allowing them to operate more efficiently as well. Indigenous managers in these affiliates learn these management practices and can then apply them to indigenous firms. In this way, managerial expertise is transferred from the MNC to the host country.

Finally, MNCs can enable host-country producers to gain access to marketing networks. When direct investments are made as part of a global production strategy, the local affiliates of the MNC and the domestic firms that supply these affiliates become integrated into a global marketing chain. Such integration creates export opportunities that would otherwise be unavailable to indigenous producers. The Malaysian firm to which Motorola transferred the printed circuit board technology, for example, not only wound up supplying Motorola Malaysia, but also began to supply components to 11 Motorola plants worldwide. These opportunities would not have arisen had the firm not been able to link up with Motorola Malaysia.

MNCs provide these benefits at a price, however. To capture the benefits that MNCs offer, a country must be willing to allow foreign corporations to make decisions about how resources will be used in the host country. As long as foreign managers make decisions about how much capital and technology are transferred to the host country, about how the resources MNCs bring to the host country will be combined with local inputs, and about how the revenues generated by the local affiliate will be used, there will be some chance that a particular investment will not enhance, and may even detract from, the welfare of the host country.

MNCs can reduce, rather than increase, the amount of funds available for investment in the host country, as a result of a number of different practices. MNCs sometimes borrow on the host country's capital market instead of bringing capital from their home country. This practice crowds out domestic investment; that is, by using scarce domestic savings, the MNC prevents domestic firms from making investments. MNCs also often earn rents on their products and repatriate most of these earnings. Consequently, the excess profits wind up in the MNC's home country rather than remaining in the host country, where they could be used for additional investment.

In addition, MNCs typically charge their host-country affiliates licensing fees or royalties for any technology that is transferred. When the affiliates pay these fees, additional funds are transferred out of the host country to the MNC's home base. Finally, MNCs often require the local affiliate to purchase inputs from other subsidiaries of the same corporation. These internal transactions take place at prices that are determined by the MNC parent, a practice called transfer pricing. Because such transactions are internal to the MNC, the parent can set the prices at whatever level best suits its global strategy. When the parent overcharges an affiliate for the goods it imports from affiliates based in other countries and underprices the same affiliate's exports, revenues are transferred from the local affiliate to the MNC parent. Sometimes such transfers can be very large: an investigation revealed that Colombia paid $3 billion more for pharmaceutical imports through MNCs than it would have paid in market-based transactions. All of these practices reduce the amount of funds that are available to finance new projects in the host country. In extreme cases, MNCs might *reduce* the total amount of funds available for investment, rather than increase them.

An MNC might also drive established host-country firms out of business. Suppose an MNC enters an industry already populated by local firms. Suppose also that the MNC controls technology or management skills that enable it to produce at a lower cost than the local firms. As the MNC affiliate's local production expands, the established local firms will begin to lose sales to this new low-cost competitor. Some of these businesses will eventually fail. The failure of the local final-good producers may have a secondary impact on local input suppliers. Local firms often acquire their inputs from local firms. In contrast, most MNCs source their inputs from global networks of suppliers. If the new MNC affiliate drives local firms out of business, then the demand for the inputs provided by local firms will fall. The local input suppliers will thus face serious pressure, and many of them will probably go out of business as well. Although such instances may be an example of a more efficient firm replacing less efficient competitors, the dynamic is one in which local firms are gradually replaced by foreign firms and local managers by foreign managers. If the transfer of skills and technology from foreign to local producers is one of the purported benefits of FDI, then a dynamic in which foreign firms drive local firms out of business suggests that very little technology transfer is occurring.

Technology transfers can be further limited by the incentive that MNCs have to maintain fairly tight control over technology and managerial positions. As we have seen, one of the principal reasons for MNC investment arises from the desire to maintain control over intangible assets. Given this desire, it is hard to understand why an MNC would make a large fixed investment in order to retain control over its technology, but then transfer that technology to host-country firms. The transfer of managerial expertise also may be limited because MNCs are often reluctant to hire host-country residents into top-level managerial positions. Thus, the second purported benefit of MNCs—the transfer of technology and managerial expertise—can be stymied by the very logic that causes MNCs to undertake FDI. If this happens, MNC affiliates will function like enclaves, failing to be tightly integrated into the rest of the host-country economy and never realizing any spillover effects.

Finally, the decisions by MNCs about how to use the revenues generated by their affiliates may bear no relationship to the host-country government's economic objectives. In a world in which governments cared little about the type of economic activity that was conducted within their borders, this would be of little consequence. But when governments use a wide variety of policy instruments to try to promote certain types of economic activity, whether it be manufacturing in a developing country or high-technology industries in an advanced industrialized country, foreign control of these revenues can pose serious obstacles to government policy. If, for example, a country's export earnings derive entirely from copper exports, but an MNC controls the country's copper-mining operations, then decisions about how to use the country's foreign exchange earnings will be made by the MNC rather than by the government. Or, if the revenues generated by the local affiliate are sufficient to finance additional investment, decisions about whether this investment will be made in the host country or somewhere else and, if in the host country, then in which sector, are made by the MNC rather than by the government. In short, control by MNCs over the revenues generated by their affiliates makes it difficult for governments to channel resources toward the economic activities they are trying to encourage.

A Closer Look

Labor and Foreign Capital in the Developing World

During the past 25 years, the emergence of off-shoring and global value chains has drawn hundreds of millions of people into the global capitalist economy for the first time. China provides the most spectacular example of this process as estimates suggest that 155 million Chinese residents may have migrated from rural provinces to the industrializing coastal cities between the mid-1990s and 2010 (Chan 2013). And though the Chinese experience is unique in scale—the magnitude of the migration is the largest in human history—other emerging market countries have experienced identical flows. Vietnam and Bangladesh, for example, also experienced substantial internal migration as people abandoned farming in favor of manufacturing. These migrants thus provided the core labor force employed by western multinational corporations and their sub-contractors.

The incorporation of these new urban residents into global production networks raises concerns about how multinational corporations treat workers in developing societies. As we saw in Chapter 4, capital mobility may enable western firms to exploit lower labor standards common in many developing countries in ways that bring harm to indigenous workers. And some of the most serious instances of mistreatment are well known. The Taiwanese firm Foxconn, for instance, which produces Apple products under license in factories in China, has a record of substandard and dangerous working conditions, low wages, and other practices. In 2010, 14 Foxconn workers committed suicide in protest against poor conditions, and in 2012, 150 Foxconn workers threatened to commit suicide by jumping off the roof of a Foxconn factory. In Dhaka, Bangladesh, more than 1,127 people died when a building that hosted a number of garment factories producing for a variety of American retailers collapsed. In this instance, structural weaknesses in the building had been noticed prior to the collapse, but the factories continued to operate—thereby endangering more than 3,000 employees—in spite of these problems.

We might wonder whether the underlying problems that give rise to episodes such as Foxconn and Rana Plaza are common consequences of multinationalized production or whether instead they are exceptional occurrences. In particular, we might want to know whether labor rights—the right to organize into unions, to bargain collectively, and to strike—improve or deteriorate with the arrival of global production. We might also wonder if labor abuses—such things as exposing workers to hazardous conditions, low wages, extremely long hours, gender discrimination, and sexual harassment—are aggravated or lessened by participation in the global economy. It turns out, as two authorities on these issues remark, that the impact of global production on labor in the developing world is complex and depends upon the precise "way in which one's country, industry, or firm participates in the global economy" (Mosley and Singer 2015, 188).

Most generally, workers tend to have more rights and labor abuses are less frequent as the skill-level of the industry increases. Thus, labor-intensive apparel production and general simple assembly operations are characterized by the weakest labor rights and greatest frequency of abuse. Women are often the most exposed to these substandard practices because on the one hand women hold a disproportionate share of jobs in many low-skilled labor-intensive manufacturing jobs, and on the other hand the lack of regard for workers in general in some low-income societies is often reinforced by broader societal norms that deny equal rights to women. As a consequence, women (and especially young women) often bear the burden of labor mistreatment and lack the political rights needed to bring about change.

This general relationship is mediated by at least three other characteristics of multinational production. The first characteristic concerns the specific way that a local factory is connected to the global economy. Generally speaking, labor rights tend to improve when MNCs own the local manufacturing affiliates, and are typically weaker when these local affiliates are independently-owned firms that produce goods under contract with multinational firms (see Mosley 2011; Mosley and Singer 2015). In addition, workers enjoy higher wages, better workplace conditions, and less workplace abuse of other types (such as sexual harassment, long hours without overtime pay) when their employers are affiliates of MNCs than when they work for locally owned firms. It is somewhat challenging to separate the effect of ownership structure on labor standards from the effect of sectoral characteristics because so much of the low-skilled labor performed in developing countries occurs through sub-contract rather than within MNC affiliates.

The second characteristic concerns the specific ways that host states insert themselves in the relationship between foreign capital and domestic labor. On the one hand, host governments might enact labor policies that help protect workers from abusive practices by global capital. In post-liberalization Latin America, for example, governments who were kept in office in part by support from labor had incentive to expand labors' rights vis-à-vis capital as well as social protections more generally. On the other hand, governments in less democratic regimes might be less inclined to align with or support domestic labor. More authoritarian regimes might have greater incentive to suppress labor unions in order to minimize the likelihood that an independent labor movement could organize into a viable political rival and to supply a compliant and complacent labor force that is attractive to potential foreign investors.

Finally, participation in international agreements might affect host country labor standards (see Berliner et al. 2015). As we saw in Chapter 4, the U.S. and the EU have increasingly included labor standards chapters in the free trade agreements they enter with developing countries. A number of recent empirical studies have found that U.S. free-trade agreements have a positive impact on labor standards in the developing country partners, while other studies have found that the EU has been able to influence labor standards in Eastern and Central Europe through the accession agreements it negotiates with these states as they seek EU membership.

Host countries therefore face a dilemma in their relationships with MNCs. On the one hand, MNCs can provide resources to host countries, including access to new sources of capital, innovative technologies, managerial expertise, and market linkages that are not available elsewhere. On the other hand, because FDI extends foreign managerial control into the host country's economy, there is no guarantee that a particular investment will in fact yield the aforesaid benefits. An MNC might consume scarce local savings, replace local firms, refuse to transfer technology, and repatriate all of its earnings. This dilemma has led many to suggest that governments may need to play an active role in structuring the conditions under which MNCs operate within their economies. As we will see in the next chapter, much of the politics of MNCs revolve around government efforts to shape these conditions in order to extract as many benefits from MNCs that they can and to minimize the costs of ceding managerial control to foreign decision makers.

CONCLUSION

The last 30 years have seen rapid growth in the number of MNCs operating in the global economy. By 2008, the number of such corporations was 11 times the number in operation in the early 1980s. As that number has increased, the role these firms play in global production, trade, and cross-border investment has also increased. The activities of contemporary MNCs are heavily concentrated in the advanced industrialized countries. Most FDI in the global economy involves a firm based in one advanced industrialized country establishing a facility in another advanced industrialized country. Although MNCs have recently begun to shift more of their activities to the developing world, only a small number of developing countries have received substantial amounts of investment. It will take many more years of investment before the developing world's share of MNC activities approaches the share of the advanced industrialized countries.

MNCs are more than just large firms. They are firms that organize and manage their activities quite differently than traditional firms do. In particular, they have opted to remove many of their international transactions from the market and to place them within a single corporate structure. Thus, even though many firms engage in international activities, only a subset of these firms—those that own productive establishments in at least two countries—can be classified as MNCs. MNCs have opted for this distinctive organization structure because they face opportunities to profit from international exchange; but, because they earn a substantial share of their income from intangible and specific assets, they can capture these profits only by internalizing the associated transactions. Thus, the modern MNC has emerged as an organizational response to a specific economic problem in the global economy.

Most analysts of MNC activities believe that FDI can benefit the host country as well as the investing firm. Such investments can transfer savings, technology, and managerial expertise to host countries, and can allow local producers to link into global marketing networks. None of these resources are readily available to host countries—especially developing host countries—unless they are willing to open themselves to MNC activity. Yet, opening a country to MNC activity does not guarantee that the benefits will be realized. MNCs are profit-making enterprises, and their activities are oriented toward that end and not toward raising the welfare of their host countries. Consequently, societies that host MNCs face a dilemma: they need to attract MNCs to capture the benefits that FDI can offer, but they need to ensure that activities by MNCs actually deliver those benefits. As we shall see in the next chapter, most of the politics of MNCs revolve around government efforts to manage this dilemma.

KEY TERMS

Efficiency-Oriented Investment

Foreign Direct Investment

Global Value Chains

Horizontal Integration

Intangible Asset

Locational Advantages

Market-Oriented Investment

Natural-Resource Investment

Positive Externalities

Specific Asset

Vertical Integration

SUGGESTIONS FOR FURTHER READING

For a good introduction to the economics of MNCS, see Richard E. Caves, *Multinational Enterprise and Economic Analysis*, 3rd edition (Cambridge: Cambridge University Press, 2007). Another excellent source is John H. Dunning, *Multinational Enterprises and the Global Economy*, 2nd edition (Cheltenham: Edward Elgar, 2008).

The best single source on the history of MNCs is probably Geoffrey Jones, *Multinationals and Global Capitalism: From the Nineteenth to the Twenty-First Century* (Oxford: Oxford University Press, 2005). The most comprehensive treatment of American MNCs is Myra Wilkins, *The Emergence of Multinational Enterprise: American Business Abroad from the Colonial Era to 1914* (Cambridge, MA: Harvard University Press, 1970).

For those interested in the impact of global capital on labor in developing countries, see Layna Mosley, *Labor Rights and Multinational Production* (Cambridge: Cambridge University Press, 2011) and Kimberly Ann Elliott, "Labor Standards," in K. A. Reinhert (ed.), *Handbook of Globalisation and Development* (Cheltenham: Edward Elgar, 2017: Chapter 11).

The Politics of Multinational Corporations

In late 2013 a Chinese company purchased the American pork-processing giant Smithfield Foods for $4.7 billion. The announcement of the deal sparked political backlash in the United States. Senator Debbie Stabenow, Chair of the Senate Agriculture Committee, declared that "food security is national security." She noted that she could not "imagine that the American people will feel comfortable if they wake up one day to discover that half of our food processors are owned by China." She called a special hearing of the Senate Agriculture Committee to look more closely into the Smithfield Foods deal. During that hearing, many Senators voiced concern about how the Chinese acquisition might influence the safety of the American food supply moving forward, while others expressed concern about the long-run implications of the U.S. becoming dependent upon Chinese producers for its food. While the committee lacked the authority to block the deal, the hearing revealed that Chinese acquisitions of American businesses remained a politically sensitive issue.

The sensitivity surrounding the Smithfield Foods deal is hardly unique. MNCs alter the nature of economic decision making in ways that disconnect economic and political geography. Historically, decisions about production have been made by local business owners with reference to local conditions. When MNCs are involved, however, foreign managers make production decisions with reference to global conditions. Yet, whereas the frame of reference for much economic decision making has shifted, the frame of reference for *political* decision making has not. Governments continue to address local concerns in response to the demands of local interest groups. As one prominent scholar of MNCs has written,

> the regime of nation states is built on the principle that the people
> in any national jurisdiction have a right to try to maximize their

well-being, as they define it, within that jurisdiction. The MNC, on the other hand, is bent on maximizing the well-being of its stakeholders from global operations, without accepting any responsibility for the consequences of its actions in individual national jurisdictions.

(Vernon 1998, 28)

The tension inherent in these overlapping decision-making frameworks shapes the domestic and international politics of MNCs. In the domestic arena, most governments have been unwilling to forgo the potential benefits of foreign investment, yet few have been willing to allow foreign firms to operate without restriction. Consequently, most governments have used national regulations and have bargained with individual MNCs to ensure that the operations of foreign firms are consistent with national objectives. Governments' efforts to regulate MNC activities carry over into international politics. Host countries, especially in the developing world, pursue international rules that codify their right to control the activities of foreign firms operating within their borders. Countries that serve as home bases for MNCs—essentially, the advanced industrialized countries—pursue international rules that protect their overseas investments by limiting the ability of host countries to regulate the activity by MNCs.

We examine these dynamics here. We look first at the variety of instruments governments have used to extract as many of the benefits from FDI as they could, while at the same time minimizing the perceived costs arising from allowing foreign firms to control local industries. We then focus on efforts, unsuccessful to date, to negotiate international rules defining the respective rights and obligations of host countries and MNCs.

REGULATING MULTINATIONAL CORPORATIONS

Rather than forgo the potential benefits available from hosting MNC affiliates, most governments have sought to define the terms under which MNCs operate within their borders. Governments have regulated proscriptively and prescriptively—that is, they have prohibited foreign firms from engaging in certain activities, and they have required them to engage in others. All these regulations have been oriented toward the same goal: extracting as many of the benefits from FDI as possible, while simultaneously minimizing the cost associated with ceding decision-making authority to foreign firms. We look first at how developing countries attempted to regulate MNC activity and then turn our attention to practices common in the advanced industrialized world. As we will see, even though both developed and developing countries regulate MNC activities, developing countries have relied far more heavily on such practices. Thus, we conclude this section by examining why the two groups of countries adopted such different approaches toward MNCs.

Regulating Multinational Corporations in the Developing World

In the early postwar period, most developing-country governments viewed MNCs with considerable unease:

The association of foreign companies with former colonial powers, their employment of expatriates in senior positions, their past history (real or imagined) of discrimination against local workers, and their embodiment of alien cultural values all contributed to the suspicion with which foreign [MNCs] were regarded in developing countries.

(Jones 1996, 291)

Governments in newly independent developing countries wanted to establish their political and economic autonomy from former colonial powers, and often this entailed taking control of existing foreign investments and managing the terms under which new investments were made.

Concerns about foreign dominance reflected the continuation of historical practice. Most developing countries entered the postwar period as primary-commodity producers and exporters. Yet, MNCs often controlled these sectors and the export revenues they generated. In the aluminum industry, for example, six MNCs controlled 77 percent of the non socialist world's bauxite output, 87 percent of its alumina output, and 83 percent of its production of aluminum. In agricultural products, the 15 largest agricultural MNCs controlled approximately 80 percent of developing countries' exports (UNCTAD 1983). And although foreign direct investment (FDI) shifted toward manufacturing activity during the 1960s, MNC affiliates also played an important role in these sectors. In Singapore, MNC affiliates currently account for 52 percent of all manufacturing employment, 75 percent of all sales, and approximately 61 percent of all exports. In Malaysia, the figures are comparable: 44 percent of manufacturing employment, 53 percent of sales, and 51 percent of exports (UNCTAD 2001). Although Singapore and Malaysia sit at the high end of the spectrum, MNCs also control large segments of manufacturing activity in other developing countries.

Allowing foreign corporations to control critical sectors raised political and economic concerns. The central political concern was that foreign ownership of critical natural-resource industries compromised the hard-won national autonomy achieved in the struggle for independence. It seemed incongruent to achieve political independence from colonial powers and yet continue to struggle under the economic dominance of the colonial power's multinational firms. Economic concerns arose as governments adopted import substitution industrialization (ISI) strategies. If MNCs were allowed to control export earnings, governments would be unable to use these resources to promote their development objectives. Moreover, if MNCs were allowed to enter the local economy freely, there would be no necessary relationship between the investments they made and the government's development goals. FDIs might remain in the extractive industries, and manufacturing investments might not transfer technology. As a result, economic activities would continue to reflect the interests of foreign actors instead of the government's development objectives.

In general, developing countries responded to these concerns by regulating rather than prohibiting FDI. Rather than shut themselves off completely from the potential benefits FDI promised, governments sought to manage access to their economies to ensure that the benefits were in fact delivered. Governments did block foreign investment in some sectors of the economy. For example, they prohibited MNC ownership of public utilities, iron and steel, retailing, insurance and banking, and extractive industries (Jenkins 1987, 172). When foreign firms already owned enterprises in these sectors, governments nationalized the industries. Through nationalization, the host-country government took control of an affiliate created by an MNC.

Nationalization was common during the late 1960s and the first half of the 1970s (see Figure 9.1). Nationalizations occurred most often in the extractive industries and in public utilities such as power generation and telecommunications. Nationalization served both political and economic objectives. Politically, governments could rally domestic support and silence domestic critics "by taking over the most obvious symbols of 'foreign exploitation'" (Shafer 1983, 94). Nationalization also made "rational economic planning possible for the economy as a whole and enhance[d] the government's financial position sufficiently to make economic diversification and ... balanced economic growth attainable" (Shafer 1983, 93–94).

Governments also created regulatory regimes to influence MNC activities. Many governments required local affiliates to be majority owned by local shareholders, instead of allowing MNCs to own 100 percent of the affiliate. Local ownership, governments believed, would translate into local control of the affiliate's decisions. Governments also limited the amount of profits that MNC affiliates could repatriate, as well as how much affiliates were allowed to pay parent firms for technology transfers. Such measures, governments believed, would help ensure that the revenues generated by MNC activity within the country remained in the country and available for local use.

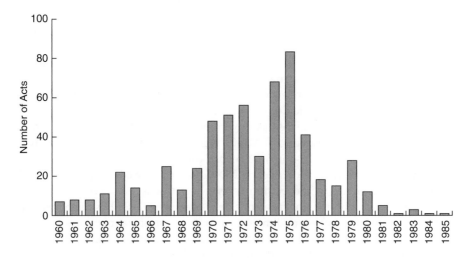

FIGURE 9.1

Expropriation Acts in Developing Countries

Source: Vernon 1998, 6.

Governments also imposed **performance requirements** on local affiliates in order to promote a specific economic objective. If a government was trying to promote backward linkages, for example, it required the affiliate to purchase a certain percentage of its inputs from domestic suppliers. If the government was promoting export industries, it required the affiliate to export a specific percentage of its output. Some governments also required MNCs to conduct research and development inside the host country. Finally, many governments limited the access of MNCs to the local capital market. All these restrictions were aimed at avoiding the downside of MNC involvement, while simultaneously trying to capture the benefits that MNCs could offer.

Of course, not all developing countries adopted identical regimes. Governments that pursued ISI strategies imposed the most restrictive regimes. India, for example, hosted a large stock of foreign investment upon achieving independence. The Indian government was determined, however, to limit the role of MNCs in the Indian economy (Jones 1996, 299). To achieve this goal, the government enacted highly restrictive policies toward new foreign investments and began to "dislodge" existing investments (Encarnation 1989). It forced existing enterprises that owned more than 40 percent of the local subsidiary to either sell equity to Indian firms or leave India. They made exceptions only for MNCs operating in high-priority areas or using sophisticated technologies. As a result, India experienced a net capital outflow during the 1970s when some MNCs, such as Coca-Cola and IBM, left and few new investments arrived.

Other developing countries actively sought FDI in connection with the shift to secondary import substitution, but regulated the terms under which MNCs could invest. Because the Brazilian market was quite large, the Brazilian government could encourage foreign investment on terms that promoted domestic auto production. The government thus banned all auto imports in 1956 and forced foreign auto manufacturers to produce in Brazil in order to sell in Brazil. It imposed high domestic content requirements on MNCs; 35 to 50 percent of cars' parts had to be locally produced in 1956, and the figure was increased to 90–95 percent by the mid-1960s. As a consequence, by the mid-1960s, eight foreign-controlled firms were producing cars in Brazil, and by 1980 over 1 million cars were being produced annually. Thus, even those developing countries that welcomed MNCs sought to ensure that their activities corresponded with the government's development goals.

East Asian governments pursuing export-oriented development strategies were more open to FDI. Singapore and Hong Kong imposed few restrictions; to the contrary, Singapore based its entire development strategy on attracting foreign investment. South Korea and Taiwan were less open to investment than Singapore and Hong Kong: in both countries, the government developed a list of industries that were open to foreign companies, but proposals to invest in these industries were not automatically approved. Each project had to meet requirements concerning local content, the transfer of technologies, the payment of royalties in connection with technology transfers, and the impact on imports (Haggard 1990, 199).

Still, Taiwan and South Korea did more to attract foreign investment than most governments in Latin America or Africa. Beginning in the mid-1960s and early 1970s, both the Taiwanese and the South Korean government created export-processing zones (EPZs) to attract investment. **Export-processing zones** are industrial areas in which the government provides land, utilities, a transportation infrastructure, and, in some cases, buildings to the investing firms, usually at subsidized rates (Haggard 1990, 201). Foreign firms based in EPZs are allowed to import components free of duty, as long as all their output is exported. Taiwan created the first EPZ in East Asia in 1965, and South Korea created its first in 1970. These assembly and export platforms attracted a lot of investment from American, European, and Japanese MNCs. Finally, both countries further liberalized foreign investment during the mid-1970s in an attempt to attract high-technology firms into the local economies (Haggard and Cheng 1987).

Most developing countries have greatly liberalized FDI since the 1980s. Sectors previously closed to foreign investment, such as telecommunications and natural resources, have been opened. Restrictions on 100-percent foreign ownership have been lifted in most countries. Restrictions on the repatriation of profit have been eased. Two factors have encouraged this liberalization. First, restrictive regimes yielded disappointing results (Jones 1996). FDI fell during the 1970s as nationalizations and regulation led MNCs to seek opportunities elsewhere. MNCs that did operate in developing countries were reluctant to bring in new technologies, and the sectors that governments had nationalized performed well below expectations (Shafer 1983). Second, the decision to liberalize FDI came as part of the broader shift in development strategies. Governments intervened less in all segments of the economy, including FDI, as they shifted to market-based strategies.

Developing countries' governments have not abandoned efforts to control MNC activity. Although they have become more open to FDI, they

> continue to look on multinational enterprises from the vantage point of their past experiences. Much as they welcome the contribution of foreign-owned enterprises ... these countries will have grave doubts from time to time about the long-term contribution of such enterprises, especially as they observe that the grand strategy of the enterprise is built on the pursuit of global sources and global markets.
>
> (Vernon 1998, 108)

Regulating Multinational Corporations in the Advanced Industrialized Countries

The typical advanced industrialized country has been more open to FDI and less inclined to regulate the activities of MNCs than the typical developing country. Only Japan and France required explicit government approval for manufacturing investments by foreign firms (Safarian 1993). Most governments have excluded foreign firms from owning industries deemed "critical," but they have not drawn the lists of sectors from which foreign firms are excluded so broadly as to discourage MNC investment (Safarian 1993). In the United States, for example, foreign firms cannot own radio and television broadcasting stations, cannot own a domestic airline, and are prohibited from participating in defense-related industries. Nor are American restrictions unique, as most advanced industrialized countries prohibit foreign ownership in many of these same sectors.

Japan was the clearest exception to this tendency throughout much of the postwar period. Until 1970, Japan tightly regulated inward FDI (see Safarian 1993; Mason 1992). Japanese government ministries reviewed each proposed foreign investment and approved very few. Proposals that were approved usually limited foreign ownership to less than 50 percent of the local subsidiary. Such restrictions were motivated by the Japanese government's economic development objectives. Government officials feared that Japanese firms would be unable to compete with MNCs if FDI was fully liberalized. In particular, the Japanese government feared that unrestricted FDI would prevent the development of domestic industries capable of producing the technologies deemed critical to the country's economic success (Mason 1992, 152–153). Regulations on inward investment thus comprised an important component of Japan's industrial policy.

A Closer Look

Sovereign Wealth Funds

Foreign ownership of local industry has recently generated renewed concern and political activity in the United States and the EU. The trigger has been the visible activities of sovereign wealth funds. **Sovereign wealth funds** (SWFs) are government-owned funds that purchase private assets in foreign markets. Many SWFs, so-called commodity SWFs, are funded with revenues generated by state-owned oil companies in the Gulf states and in Norway. And although commodity SWFs have been around for 50 years (Kuwait established the first in 1953), the recent sharp rise in oil and natural gas prices has stimulated their rapid growth. Non-commodity SWFs are funded via the foreign exchange reserves generated by persistent balance-of-payments surpluses. China's SWF, the China Investment Corporation, for example, was established using some of the foreign exchange reserves the Chinese government has accumulated. Continued growth of these funds is thus directly linked to balance-of-payments positions.

More than 20 governments currently have SWFs, and perhaps six others may be about to create them. The single largest fund, Norway's Government Pension Fund, controls approximately $1 trillion as of September 2017. The second largest, United Arab Emirate's Abu Dhabi Investment Authority, controls approximately $830 billion. As a group, the 20 active SWFs control approximately $6.3 trillion. And though many predicted that the rapid growth seen in the early 2000s would continue, the sharp decline of energy prices after 2009 hit the SWFs hard. To put the size of SWFs in perspective, consider that U.S. gross domestic product (GDP) is more than $17 trillion, and the total market capitalization of the world's 60 largest stock markets is about $69 trillion. SWFs are thus large, but as 10 percent of total global equities, they are not dominant players in global finance.

The recent growth of SWF activity has worried some American and European policymakers. Some fear that governments intend to use their SWFs to achieve political rather than economic objectives. Gal Luft, the Executive Director of the Institute for the Analysis of Global Security, expressed such concerns in testimony to the U.S. House Committee on Foreign Affairs in May of 2008. "Governments," he argued, "have a broader agenda [than private investors]—to maximize their geo-political influence and sometimes to promote ideologies that are in essence anti-Western" (Luft 2008). Luft found particularly worrying the fact that many of the largest SWFs are owned by Gulf states. Persistent high oil prices, he argued, could dramatically increase the size of SWFs and enable them to purchase large segments of the U.S. economy. "At $200 oil," he argued, "OPEC could potentially buy Bank of America in one month worth of production, Apple Computers in a week, and General Motors in just 3 days. It would take less than 2 years of production for OPEC to own a 20 percent stake (which essentially ensures a voting block in most corporations) in every S&P 500 company" (Luft 2008, 4).

Few observers are as worried as Luft about the national security implications of SWFs. But even those who are more sanguine about the security implications of SWFs do raise concerns about SWFs' impact on financial markets (see, for example, Kimmitt 2008). Many of these concerns reflect the lack of transparency in SWF operations and the absence of a common regulatory framework. Few SWFs are open about the strategies that motivate their investment decisions or about the assets that they own. As they grow in size, their investment decisions increasingly will affect markets. In the absence of better information about what they own and what motivates their purchases, other market participants will wind up guessing. Such dynamics could give rise to disruptive and potentially destabilizing trading activity.

American and European policymakers have responded to SWF activity in three ways. One strong impulse has been to welcome SWF investment in the midst of the extended difficulties in the American financial system. SWFs from Gulf states and China have purchased significant stakes in American financial institutions such as Citigroup, Blackstone Private Equity Group, and Merrill Lynch since August of 2007. These investments and others like them (estimated at as much as $69 billion) have helped recapitalize American banks. In this context, then, SWFs have played an important stabilizing role in the global financial system.

Simultaneously, however, policymakers have become a bit more protectionist regarding foreign investment. The German government is currently considering a law, for example, that would review purchases of more than 25 percent of German companies by groups outside the EU. The government also recently blocked a Russian effort to invest in Deutsche Telekom AG and European Aeronautic Defence and Space Company NV (the parent firm for Airbus; Braude 2008). Such moves reflect heightened German concern about foreign government investment in the German economy. In the United States, Congress recently strengthened the scrutiny applied to proposed foreign investments that involve direct control by a government entity.

Finally, American and European policymakers have sought to reconcile these two conflicting tendencies—sometimes welcoming and sometimes blocking investments by foreign governments—by trying to develop international rules, or codes of best practices, to govern SWF activities. Then U.S. Treasury Secretary, Henry Paulson, convened a dinner in October of 2007 that drew together finance ministers from the Group of Seven (G-7); top officials from the International Monetary Fund (IMF), the World Bank, and the Organization for Economic Co-operation and Development (OECD); as well as finance ministers and heads of SWFs from many states with large SWFs. The discussions culminated in the articulation of the Santiago Principles and the creation of the International Forum of Sovereign Wealth Funds (IFSWF) in 2009. The Santiago Principles are designed to promote "good governance, accountability, transparency and prudent investment practices" by SWFs. The IFSWF is intended to help SWFs implement the Santiago Principles as well as provide other services to its SWF members.

Japanese restrictions on inward direct investment were designed to encourage technology transfers (Mason 1992, 151). Japanese officials first pressured foreign firms to license their technologies to Japanese firms. If this strategy proved unsuccessful, the Japanese government would consider a direct investment, but it often attempted to force the foreign firm to create a joint venture with a Japanese firm in order to transfer technology to Japanese firms working in the same industry. Only if a firm was unwilling to license its technology or to form a joint venture—and then, only if that firm controlled technologies that were not available elsewhere—did the Japanese government permit the creation of a wholly owned foreign subsidiary in Japan, and even then the government often attached conditions to the investment. IBM, for example, was forced to license critical technologies to seven Japanese competitors in exchange for being allowed to produce computers in Japan.

Japanese investment restrictions have been greatly liberalized since the late 1960s. In 1967, Japan increased the number of industries open to foreign investment and began to allow 100 percent ownership in some sectors. Additional measures taken in the 1970s and early 1980s further liberalized inward FDI, so that Japan now has no formal barriers to such investments. In spite of this liberalization, however, Japan continues to attract only a small share of the world's foreign investment (see Table 8.2).

Despite the general tendency toward greater openness, governments in the advanced industrialized countries have been sensitive to foreign control of critical sectors. Two instances illustrate such concerns. The China National Offshore Oil Corporation (CNOOC) sought to purchase Unocal in the summer of 2005. In early 2006 the United Arab Emirates-owned Dubai Ports World sought to acquire a British firm that operated American seaports. Both transactions prompted strenuous congressional opposition, and this opposition led both firms to withdraw their offers. Lenovo's acquisition of IBM's personal computer unit was closely scrutinized but ultimately was approved in 2005. These recent cases indicate that American policymakers remain highly sensitive to foreign ownership of critical industries.

In summary, even though the advanced industrialized countries have been more open to FDI than developing countries, they have attempted to manage the terms under which MNCs invest in their countries. Governments that used industrial policies have attempted to protect national firms from competition by restricting foreign investment. Even governments that refrained from promoting active industrial policies restricted foreign ownership of sensitive industries, such as those at the forefront of high-technology sectors as well as industries closely connected to national security.

Bargaining with Multinational Corporations

Many host countries try to restrict MNC activities, but few can dictate the terms under which MNCs invest. Instead, host countries and MNCs often bargain over the terms under which investment takes place. We can think of this bargaining as oriented toward reaching agreement on how the income generated by an investment will be distributed between the MNC parent and the host country. The precise distribution will be determined by each side's relative bargaining power.

Bargaining power arises from the extent to which each side exerts monopolistic control over things valued by the other. To what extent does the host country have monopolistic control over things vitally important to the MNC? Does the host country control natural resources that are not available in other parts of the world? Does the host country control access to a large domestic market? Does the host country control access to factors of production that yield efficiency gains that cannot be achieved in other countries? The more the host country has exclusive control over things of value to the MNC, the more bargaining power it has. Equally critical is the extent to which the MNC exerts monopolistic control over things of value to the host country. Does the MNC control technology that cannot be acquired elsewhere? More broadly, are there other MNCs capable of making, and willing to make, the contemplated investment? The more the MNC has exclusive control over things the host country values, the more bargaining power the MNC has. Bargaining power, therefore, is a function of monopolistic control.

Host countries have the greatest bargaining power when they enjoy a monopoly and the MNC does not. In such cases, the host country should capture most of the gains from investment. In contrast, an MNC has its greatest advantage when it enjoys a monopoly and the host country does not. In these cases, the MNC should capture the largest share of the gains from investment. Bargaining power is approximately equal when both sides have a monopoly. In such cases, each should capture an equal share of the gains from the investment.

The gains also should be evenly distributed when neither side has a monopoly on things the other values. In these cases, neither side has much bargaining power, and they should divide the gains relatively equally. The distribution of the gains from any investment, therefore, will be determined by the relative bargaining power of the host country and the MNC.

We can apply the logic of this kind of bargaining analysis to investments in natural-resource industries and in low-skilled labor-intensive manufacturing industries. In natural-resource investments, bargaining power initially favors the MNC. Few countries enjoy a monopoly over any natural resource; thus, MNCs can choose where to invest. Also, because an MNC often does have a monopoly over the capital, the techniques, and the technology required to extract and refine the natural resources, and because the return on the investment is initially uncertain, the MNC bears all of the risk. The MNC can exploit this power asymmetry to initially capture the larger share of the gains from the investment.

Over time, however, bargaining power shifts to the host country in a dynamic that has been called the **obsolescing bargain** (Moran 1974). The MNC cannot easily remove its fixed investment from the country, so the investment becomes a hostage. In addition, the MNC's monopoly over technology diminishes as the technology is gradually transferred to the host country and indigenous workers are trained. If the investment proves successful, uncertainty about the return on the investment diminishes. Unable to threaten to leave the country without suffering substantial costs, and no longer controlling technology needed by the host country, the MNC sees its earlier bargaining power weaken while the host country's power strengthens. The host country can exploit this power shift to renegotiate the initial agreement and extract a larger share of the gains from the project. Indeed, one might suggest that the widespread nationalizations during the 1960s and 1970s reflected precisely this shift of bargaining power to host countries.

MNCs enjoy more bargaining power than host countries in low-skilled labor-intensive manufacturing investments. On the one hand, no host country enjoys a monopoly on low-skilled labor; thus, MNCs can pick and choose between many potential host countries. Nor are such investments very susceptible to the obsolescent bargain. Often, investments in low-skilled manufacturing entail a relatively small amount of fixed capital that can be readily moved out of a particular country. In addition, technology in many manufacturing industries changes rapidly and therefore is not easily transferred to the host country. Consequently, unlike natural-resource investments, manufacturing investments do not become hostages, and host countries do not gain power once the investment has been made (Kobrin 1987).

Evidence that MNCs enjoy greater bargaining power than do host countries when it comes to manufacturing investment can be seen in the growing competition between host countries to attract such investment. This competition has emerged in the form of **locational incentives**—packages host countries offer to MNCs that either increase the return of a particular investment or reduce the cost or risk of that investment (UNCTAD 1995, 288–289). Host countries offer two types of incentives to MNCs. Most offer tax incentives. In one such incentive, MNCs are granted a reduced corporate income tax rate. Many governments also provide "tax holidays," usually a period of 5 years during which the firm pays no tax. MNCs also are exempted from import duties, are permitted to depreciate their investments at accelerated rates, and are allowed substantial deductions from their gross incomes. Many advanced industrialized countries also offer MNCs direct financial incentives. In some instances, these are provided as a grant from the government to the MNC, in some as a subsidized loan (Moran 1999, 95).

The willingness of governments to offer locational incentives and the size of the typical package have both increased rapidly during the last 20 years. Across the entire OECD, 285 incentive programs offering a total of $11 billion were provided to MNCs in 1989. By 1993—the last year for which comprehensive data are available—362 programs offering incentives totaling $18 billion were provided. Within the United States, the typical package averaged between $50 million and $70 million, but the value of that package has been increasing (Moran 1999). Alabama provided Honda with more than $158 million in the 1990s to attract this auto producer's new plant. In 2005, North Carolina provided incentives totaling $242 million to induce Dell, the personal computer manufacturer, to build a facility in the state. The North Carolina package for Dell, for example, amounted to slightly more than $161,333 per job (Kane, Curliss and Martinez 2004). The growing use of locational incentives suggests that host countries are at a disadvantage when bargaining with MNCs over manufacturing investments.

In sum, few governments have allowed foreign firms to operate without any restrictions, and many have actively managed the terms of their activities, in part by using national regulations and in part by bargaining with MNCs. As we have seen, the typical advanced industrialized country has been less inclined to try to restrict the activities of foreign firms than has the typical developing country. We conclude this section, therefore, by considering a few factors that account for this difference.

Three such factors are probably most important. First of all, developing countries have been more vulnerable to foreign domination than advanced industrialized countries have been. The advanced industrialized countries have larger and more diversified economies than the developing countries; consequently, a foreign affiliate is more likely to face competition from domestic firms in an advanced industrialized country than in a developing country. The lack of diversification is compounded by the fact that, in the early postwar period, most FDI in the developing world was concentrated in politically sensitive natural-resource industries. In contrast, most FDI in the advanced industrialized countries flowed into manufacturing industries. As a result, foreign firms were much more likely to dominate a developing country than an advanced industrialized country, and the advanced industrialized countries have felt less compelled to regulate MNC activity.

There also appears to be a strong correlation between a country's role as a home for MNCs and its policies toward inward FDI. The two largest

A Closer Look

Luring German and Asian Car Producers to the U.S. South

In 1990, no Deep South State manufactured cars. Today, Alabama, Georgia, Mississippi, and South Carolina produce more than 2 million cars per year. This rather extraordinary transformation was achieved through heavy use of investment incentives by state-level governments. In the early 1990s, the German automaker BMW decided to create a new assembly plant outside Germany. Such a move represented a real shift for BMW, which had never previously assembled cars outside of Bavaria. The firm's decision to begin assembling cars outside Germany was motivated by a determination to reduce its costs. German automakers were earning about $28 an hour, far greater than the average of $16 an hour that unionized autoworkers make in the United States. In addition, the persistent strengthening of the German mark against the dollar during the late 1980s had further eroded the ability of BMW to compete in the American market. BMW spent 3 years and looked at 250 different sites in ten countries before deciding in 1992 to build the plant in Spartanburg, South Carolina. In late September 1992, BMW began construction of the $400 million assembly plant that would employ some 2,000 people and produce as many as 90,000 cars a year. In 1998, BMW expanded this production facility from 1.2 million square feet to 2.1 million square feet. The facility remains BMW's only American production site (www.BMW.com).

Why did BMW choose Spartanburg over other potential sites? A range of considerations, including financial incentives offered by the State of South Carolina, shaped BMW's decision to base production in Spartanburg. First, the city had some advantages arising from its location; it is close to Charleston, South Carolina, a deep-water seaport, and is connected to this port by a good interstate highway. This transportation network would allow BMW to transport the cars destined for overseas markets easily. In addition, labor in South Carolina was relatively cheap— averaging about $10 to $15 an hour—and non-unionized. In addition, the state and local government in South Carolina put together a financial package that offset a substantial share of BMW's investment. Officials advanced about $40 million to purchase the 900 acres of land upon which the plant would be built, and they agreed to lease the site to BMW for only $1 per year. In addition, about $23 million was spent preparing the site and improving the infrastructure, including such things as water, sewer, and roads. Another $71 million of tax breaks were offered over a 20-year period. Finally, state, local, and federal money was provided to improve the airport in nearby Greenville (Harrison 1992). Altogether, the incentives offered by South Carolina to BMW totaled about $135 million, an amount equal to $67,500 for each job BMW would create.

The use of financial incentives to attract an investment from a German automaker reached new heights in Alabama's courtship of Mercedes-Benz in the mid-1990s. For reasons identical to those that motivated BMW, Mercedes-Benz decided to build an assembly plant outside of Germany (Myerson 1996). The firm eventually constructed a $300 million plant in Vance, Alabama, employing about 1,200 workers to produce 65,000 sport utility vehicles each year. In its initial search for suitable sites, Mercedes-Benz focused on 62 possibilities, none of which were in Alabama. As Andreas Renschler, who led the search for the site, remarked, "Alabama was totally unknown" (quoted in Myerson 1996). Government officials in Alabama were determined to attract Mercedes to their state, however. The governor, James E. Folsom Jr., flew to Mercedes-Benz headquarters in Stuttgart three times and, working with other state politicians, put together a financial package to attract the German firm to Alabama. The package included $92.2 million to purchase and prepare the site for construction; $75.5 million in infrastructure improvements for water, sewage, and other utilities; $5 million each year to pay for employee training; and tax breaks. In addition, at a cost of about $75 million, the state of Alabama agreed to purchase 2,500 of the sport-utility vehicles that Mercedes-Benz intended to build in the factory. The total package was estimated at between $253 million and $300 million, an amount equal to $200,000 to $250,000 for each job Mercedes-Benz intended to create (Waters 1996).

The state of Alabama built on the lessons it learned during its courtship of Mercedes-Benz to attract other car makers to Alabama. The state offered Toyota Motor Corp. $29 million in 2001 to secure a plant that produced V8 engines. In 2002, Alabama offered Hyundai Motors $234 million to secure a manufacturing plant. And in late 2017, Alabama was competing with (at least) ten other states to attract a new $1.6 billion manufacturing facility that is being planned by Toyota-Mazda as well as a huge $3.1 billion investment by Hyundai-Kia. The state of Mississippi looked at the success Alabama enjoyed in attracting MB, and in the early 2000s offered Nissan almost $300 million to base a manufacturing plant in Canton that opened in 2003. A couple of years later, Mississippi offered Toyota roughly the same amount to build a plant that opened in 2011. Georgia secured a Kia factory with an incentives package worth somewhere in the neighborhood of $400 million. As a consequence of its successful incentives initiatives, Alabama is now the fifth largest producer of cars in the United States. Together, Alabama, Georgia, Mississippi, and South Carolina now produce more than 2 million cars, sport utility vehicles, and light trucks per year.

Although the manufacturers typically deny that the incentive packages they receive play an important role in their decisions to invest in one community rather than another, respectively, it is hard to escape the conclusion that these packages do matter. Because incentive packages do shape the investment decisions that firms make, governments cannot easily opt out of the incentive game. As Harlan Boyles, former treasurer of North Carolina, commented following the Mercedes-Benz–Alabama deal, "All the competition [for investment] has been forced upon the states" by the MNCs. "Until there is meaningful reform and an agreement between states not to participate, very little will change" (quoted in McEntee 1995). Of course, although Boyles's comment was directed at competition for investment among states within the United States, its logic applies equally well to competition among national governments in the international economy.

foreign investors during the last 140 years—the United States and the United Kingdom—have also been the most open to inward foreign investment. Japan began to open itself to inward investment as Japanese firms started to invest heavily in other countries. When countries both host foreign firms and are home base to MNC parents, they are unlikely to adopt policies that reflect purely host-country concerns. Attempts by the United States or Great Britain to regulate inward FDI would invite retaliation that would make it harder for their own firms to invest abroad. Because developing countries have historically hosted foreign investment but rarely have been home bases for MNCs, their concerns are more narrowly based on host-country issues untempered by the fear of retaliation.

Finally, there have been fundamental differences in how governments approach state intervention in the national economy. Although many developing countries pursued ISI strategies that required state intervention, most advanced industrialized countries have been more willing to allow the market to drive economic activity. Different attitudes about the government's role in the national economy translated into different approaches to FDI. Even the exceptions to the non-intervention tendency in the advanced industrialized countries are consistent with this factor: the two governments that were most restrictive toward FDI, Japan and France, were also the two governments that relied most heavily on industrial policies to promote domestic economic activity. Thus, attempts to regulate MNC activity were most likely in countries where governments played a large role in the economy.

All these factors suggest that we are unlikely to see an abrupt shift away from the more liberal attitude toward FDI that has prevailed in the developing world since the late 1990s back to the more restrictive practices that characterized much of the postwar period. Developing countries have become more diversified and now are attracting more foreign investment in manufacturing than in natural resources. As a consequence, some, though certainly not all, of these countries are less vulnerable to foreign domination today than they were in the mid-twentieth century. In addition, some developing countries are gradually moving away from only hosting foreign investment to being a home base for MNC parents as well. This trend, although involving only a small number of East Asian and Latin American countries, will gradually make these governments increasingly reluctant to restrict the activities of foreign firms they host. Finally, there is no evidence of an impending shift back toward interventionist strategies. As long as developing countries continue to pursue liberal strategies, they will continue to make it easier, rather than harder, for foreign firms to participate in the local economy.

THE INTERNATIONAL REGULATION
OF MULTINATIONAL CORPORATIONS

There is no multilateral regime governing FDI and the activities of MNCs. Governments have tried to create a multilateral regime on multiple occasions since 1945. But these efforts have yielded little because conflict between the capital-exporting countries and the capital-importing countries has prevented agreement on such rules. Developing countries have advocated international rules that codify their right to control foreign firms operating within their borders. Advanced industrialized countries have pursued rules that protect foreign investment by limiting how host countries can regulate MNC affiliates operating in their economies. Given these divergent goals, agreement on a multilateral investment regime has proved impossible. Because of the impasse on multilateral rules, capital-exporting states have protected their firms' overseas investments by negotiating thousands of bilateral investment treaties (BITs) with host governments. This BIT-based approach has generated a global FDI regime that is not only decentralized but also highly asymmetric, that is, biased toward the interests of capital-exporting economies.

Historically, international rules governing FDI have been based on four legal principles. First, foreign investments are private property to be treated at least as favorably as domestic private property. Second, governments have a right to expropriate foreign investments, but only for a public purpose. Third, when a government does expropriate a foreign investment, it must compensate the owner for the full value of the expropriated property, or, in legal terminology, compensation must be "adequate, effective, and prompt" (Akehurst 1984, 91–92). Finally, foreign investors have the right to appeal to their home country in the event of a dispute with the host country. Although such principles are designed to protect the property of foreign investors and therefore clearly reflect the interests of the capital-exporting countries, capital-exporting and capital-importing countries alike accepted them throughout the nineteenth century (Lipson 1985). The one exception came from Latin American governments' challenge to the right of foreign governments to intervene in host countries in support of their firms. By the late nineteenth century, Latin American governments were invoking the **Calvo doctrine** (named after the Argentinean legal scholar Carlos Calvo, who first stated it in 1868), which argues that no government has the right to intervene in another country to enforce its citizens' private claims (Lipson 1985, 19).

The capital-importing countries began to challenge these legal principles more intensively following World War I (Lipson 1985). The first challenge came in the Soviet Union, where the 1917 revolution brought to power a Marxist–Leninist government that rejected the idea of private property. The comprehensive nationalization of industry that followed "constituted the most significant attack ever waged on foreign capital" and radically redefined the role of the government in the economy (Lipson 1985, 67). Some Latin American governments also began to expropriate foreign investments during this period, particularly in the extractive industries and public utilities. These acts broadened the notion of "public purpose" that stood behind the internationally recognized right of expropriation, extending it from its traditional association with eminent domain to a much wider association with the state's role in the process of economic development. In addition, such widespread nationalizations posed a challenge to the principle of compensation. The Soviet government linked compensation of foreign investors, for example, to claims on Western governments for damages caused by their militaries during the civil war that followed the revolution (Lipson 1985, 67).

The United States attempted to re-establish the traditional legal basis for investment protection following World War II. As the largest and, in the immediate postwar period, only capital-exporting country, the United States had a clear interest in establishing multilateral rules that secured American overseas investments. But U.S. efforts to achieve this goal by incorporating the historical legal principles into the International Trade Organization (ITO) ran into opposition from the capital-importing countries. Governments from Latin America, India, and Australia were able to create a final set of articles that elaborated the right of host countries to regulate foreign investments within their borders but provided little of the security that American business was seeking (Brown 1950; Lipson 1985, 87). Consequently, American business strongly opposed the ITO's investment components. As the U.S. National Foreign Trade Council commented, "[The investment] article not only affords no protection for foreign investments of the United States but it would leave them with less protection than they now enjoy" (Diebold 1952, 18). Opposition to the investment articles from American business proved a major reason for the ITO's failure to gain congressional support.

The ITO experience is important for two reasons. First, the failure of the ITO meant that there would be no multilateral regime governing FDI. Second, and more broadly, the failure of the ITO reflected a basic conflict that has dominated international discussions about rules regulating FDI to this day. Capital-exporting countries have pursued rules that regulate host-country behavior in order to protect the interests of their MNCs. Capital-importing countries have pursued rules that regulate the behavior of MNCs so that they can maintain control over their national economies. This basic conflict has prevailed for more than 70 years of discussions about international investment rules.

During the 1960s and 1970s, developing countries largely set the agenda for international discussions about FDI. Working through the United Nations (UN), the developing countries sought to create international investment rules that reflected their interests as capital importers. The effort to regulate MNCs became a central element of the New International Economic Order (NIEO), under which developing countries sought two broad objectives that were designed to "maximize the contributions of MNCs to the economic and social development of the countries in which they operate" (Sauvant and Aranda 1994, 99). To this end, states passed the **United Nations Resolution on Permanent Sovereignty over Natural Resources** in 1962. This resolution recognized the right of host countries to exercise full control over their natural resources and over the foreign firms operating within their borders extracting those resources. The resolution affirmed the right of host-country governments to expropriate foreign investments and to determine the appropriate compensation (de Rivero 1980, 92–93; Akehurst 1984, 93). Developing countries also sought to write a code of conduct that would ensure that MNC activities "were compatible with the medium and long-term needs which the governments in the capital importing countries had identified in their development plans" (de Rivero 1980, 96).

The developing countries' efforts to write a code of conduct for MNCs met opposition from the advanced industrialized countries. Although the developing countries wanted the code to be binding, the advanced industrialized countries pushed for a voluntary code; in addition, although the developing countries wanted to regulate only MNCs, the capital-exporting governments insisted that any code that regulated MNC behavior be accompanied by a code that regulated the behavior of host countries (Sauvant and Aranda 1994, 99). Governments worked on both codes throughout the late 1970s and early 1980s, completing drafts of both by 1982. The codes remained in limbo for 10 years until finally in 1992 a UN committee recommended that governments seek an alternative approach (Graham 1996, 78–79).

In the early 1980s, bargaining power in international negotiations shifted back toward the advanced industrialized countries. The capital-exporting countries used this advantage to shift the agenda back toward regulating host-country behavior. Some initial steps were taken during the Uruguay Round. Under pressure from the United States, trade-related investment measures (TRIMs) were placed on the agenda. **A trade-related investment measure** is a government policy toward FDI or MNCs that has an impact on the country's imports or exports. For example, domestic-content or trade-balancing requirements force firms to import fewer inputs or export more output than they would without such government-imposed requirements. Consequently, such requirements distort international trade. In placing TRIMs on the GATT agenda, the United States sought to limit the ability of host countries to use such measures (Croome 1995). Developing countries were reluctant to incorporate TRIMs into the GATT, arguing that "development considerations outweighed whatever adverse trade effects TRIMs might have" (Croome 1995, 258). Not surprisingly, these differing views made it difficult to reach agreement on TRIMs within the GATT.

Failure in the GATT led the principal capital-exporting countries to pursue a **Multilateral Agreement on Investment** (MAI) among OECD members. The OECD appeared to offer at least three advantages. Because the OECD was composed primarily of advanced industrialized countries, all of which shared a commitment in principle to liberal investment rules, negotiations in the OECD seemed more likely to produce agreement. Moreover, because most FDI takes place between advanced industrialized countries, an agreement among OECD members would regulate the majority of international investment. Finally, an OECD-based agreement would not preclude participation by developing countries. Non-OECD governments could accede if they desired.

Governments intended the MAI to liberalize FDI and to provide greater security to MNCs. Liberalization was to be achieved by basing the agreement on national treatment and MFN. National treatment would require states to treat foreign-owned firms operating in their economy no differently than domestic firms. The MFN clause would oblige states to treat the foreign firms from each party to the agreement on the same terms it accorded to firms from all other parties to the agreement. To provide greater security to foreign investors, the agreement incorporated the historical standard of prompt, effective, and adequate compensation in cases of expropriation. In addition, the draft agreement restricted the ability of governments to limit the ability of firms to remit profits, dividends, and proceeds from the sale of assets. The agreement was also to provide for a dispute-settlement mechanism patterned on NAFTA, which would allow for both state-to-state claims and firm-to-state claims.

Governments failed to reach a final agreement on the MAI, however, due to disagreements among OECD governments and to strong and vocal opposition from groups outside the process. By 1997, OECD governments had attached several hundred pages of exceptions to the general obligations they had established. The United States pressed to include labor and environmental standards. Outside the negotiations,

> a coalition of strange bedfellows arose in opposition to the treaty, including the AFL–CIO, Amnesty International, Australian Conservation Foundation, Friends of the Earth, Public Citizen, Sierra Club, Third World Network, United Steelworkers of America, Western Governors' Association, and World Development Movement.
>
> (Kobrin 1998, 98)

In all, some 600 organizations in almost 70 countries spoke out against the proposed treaty (Kobrin 1998, 97). The combination of conflict among OECD governments about the specific content of the treaty and public opposition proved fatal. Negotiations ceased in December 1998 without a final agreement.

In the absence of a broader multilateral framework, states have come to rely heavily on **Bilateral Investment Treaties** (BITs). A BIT is a legally binding agreement between two states that establishes the terms that govern private investment by residents of one state in the national jurisdiction of the other. The typical BIT requires fair and equal treatment, limits expropriation, and protects the repatriation of earnings and assets. In addition, a large number of BITs include arbitration clauses that commit the parties to adjudicate disputes in international forums such as the International Center for the Settlement of Investment Disputes. Though BITs have been part of the global economy since 1959, they emerged as the predominant approach to governing FDI beginning in the late 1980s. In the early 1980s, states had signed fewer than 500 BITs. UNCTAD estimates that in mid-2017 there were 2,360 BITs in force as well as 307 bilateral and plurilateral treaties—such as regional trade agreements—that contain investment provisions quite similar and in some instances identical to those found in the typical BIT. In the absence of a single multilateral regime, therefore, states have created a very decentralized system by negotiating separate agreements with their investment partners.

This system is also highly asymmetric as the typical BIT offers strong protection to MNCs while doing little to expand the rights of host countries. The standard BIT includes a commitment to remain open to FDI from the partner and to adhere to the principles of National Treatment and MFN. In addition, BITs typically restrict the right of states to expropriate foreign investments to a legitimate public purpose and relies upon the historical standard of prompt, effective, and adequate compensation when expropriation does occur. In addition, BITs contain dispute resolution obligations, and many of the treaties obligate the parties to accept binding third-party arbitration within the International Center for the Settlement of Investment Disputes (ICSID) or the United Nations Commission on International Trade Law (UNCITRAL). Indeed, a typical BIT thus reveals the asymmetry inherent in the current FDI regime, as the terms reflect the legal conceptions of capital-exporting states as they have developed during the last 100 years and make little to no effort to protect a conception of host country interests.

The asymmetry is evident also in the distinctive nature of BITs dispute settlement provisions. In practically all other international treaties, states and only states have standing in dispute-resolution proceedings. Under the WTO dispute-settlement mechanism, for instance, states initiate disputes against other states. States might pursue trade disputes in response to pressure from firms, but it is the state and not the firm that has the legal right to file a claim and be heard. Moreover, in the WTO, states are punished for violations; Brazil could remove concessions on American imports until the U.S. government came into compliance with WTO rules on agriculture. In BITs, private firms have standing: a firm based in one country has the right to sue the state of a foreign country in which it has made an investment. Moreover, the firm has the right for that suit to be heard by a third-party arbitrator rather than being required to work through the host-country court system. Finally, when firms are successful in their suits under BITs, they are awarded monetary compensation. BITs thus create a fairly onerous set of obligations for host states, and create an intrusive dispute-resolution system that kicks in when violations of treaty obligations occur. These characteristics lead many to consider the BIT regime asymmetric.

Why do host countries enter into BITs if they are so asymmetric? The standard explanation focuses on the inability of a sovereign state to pre-commit itself to investor-friendly policies. The core logic of this argument harkens back to the obsolescing bargain model: states can have an incentive to renege on the initial agreement once an investment has been made. Moreover, because developing countries are typically host to foreign investments and much less frequently the home of MNC parent firms, developing countries may be less concerned about reciprocity of treatment than they are about trade. In the absence of mechanisms that prevent or at least limit *ex post* opportunism, states will attract less foreign investment than they desire. The challenge of attracting investment without signing BITs is magnified in a world in which all the states with which you are competing to attract investment do sign BITs (see Elkins et al. 2006).

Within this strategic context, BITs can provide a mechanism that helps states commit to investor-friendly policies. BITs provide a stable policy environment by locking states into a set of enforceable international obligations:

> They lock countries in to agreements that offer national or non-discriminatory treatment to foreign investors, allow firms access to dispute-settlement procedures, and promise third-party arbitration of disputes. [And] violating these provisions does seem to be costly ... and hence there is evidence of credible commitments."
>
> (Milner 2014, 4)

Thus, states sign BITs because they believe that on balance the benefits they realize from doing so—benefits that arise from increased FDI inflows—outweigh the costs associated with accepting restraints on their policy choices in the future.

It is growing less clear that the benefits BITs provide do in fact outweigh the costs they carry. On the one hand, it has proven remarkably difficult to find robust evidence to support the proposition that states that sign BITs attract substantially more FDI than states which do not. On the other hand, the frequency of disputes (and thus the cost of litigation for developing countries) has risen dramatically. In 2016 alone the ICSID heard 74 new disputes, with firms from the developed world responsible for 62 of these claims. During the last 6 years, the ICSID has seen 64 new disputes each year on average, up sharply from between 25 and 40 new disputes per year during the first decade of the twenty-first century and fewer than 10 new disputes per year during the 1990s. Since 1990, more than 90 states have been sued under BITS and other IIAs, with more than half of all cases involving a firm from the developed world suing a developing country. And of the 471 ICSID concluded disputes for which we have information, firms win about 27 percent of the time, while states prevail about 36 percent of the time (the remaining suits are either discontinued, settled, or resolved without either party winning). When firms do prevail, the median monetary compensation is about $20 million.

Developing countries, and a few advanced industrialized countries, are beginning to push back against the BIT regime. Bolivia, Ecuador, and Venezuela have opted out of BIT dispute resolution. In 2016, the Indian government withdrew from 57 BITs that it had ratified and was making plans to negotiate new agreements based on its own template—one more favorable to host-country interests. Other states, Indonesia as one prominent example, are renegotiating their BITs as they expire. The UNCTAD reports that more than 350 BITs will be up for renewal between 2014 and 2018, and it will be interesting to observe how much these treaties are restructured in light of the experience with binding arbitration. It does seem that the pendulum is likely to begin to shift back toward the interests of capital-importing countries.

Policy Analysis and Debate

The Race to the Bottom

Question

How should governments respond to the threat of a "race to the bottom" dynamic that weakens public-interest regulation?

Overview

Some scholars have argued that the growth of MNC activity has given rise to a "race to the bottom" dynamic in government regulation. The world's governments maintain different regulatory standards. Some enact stringent regulations concerning how firms can treat workers, how they must handle their toxic waste and other pollutants, and how they must conduct their other business activities. Others maintain less stringent regulatory environments, allowing firms to engage in activities that are illegal in other countries.

Many of these regulations affect production costs. It is more expensive, for example, for a firm to treat chemical waste before it is disposed than simply to dump the raw waste in a landfill. Hence, national regulations that require firms to treat their chemical waste raise production costs. Consequently, even if all other production costs in two countries are the same, different regulatory standards can make it less costly to produce in the country with the lower standard.

MNCs might therefore engage in regulatory arbitrage. That is, they might shift their activities out of countries with stringent regulatory standards and into countries with lax regulatory standards. Governments in high-standard countries will then feel pressure to relax their standards in order to encourage firms to keep production at home. As a consequence, national regulation will increasingly converge on the regulatory practices of the least restrictive country. Governments that refuse to engage in this competition for investment will be left behind, enjoying the benefits of strict regulations but suffering the cost of substantially less investment. How should governments respond to the threat of this race to the bottom?

Policy Options

- Negotiate international rules that harmonize regulations throughout the world. Creating common regulations will prevent regulatory arbitrage and the race to the bottom.
- Restrict foreign direct investment and the activities of MNCs. Such restrictions would limit corporations' mobility, thus enabling governments to maintain distinct national regulations.

Policy Analysis

- Is regulatory arbitrage necessarily a bad thing from the perspective of economic efficiency? Why or why not?
- How easy or difficult will it be for governments to reach agreement about common regulatory standards? How should we weigh these costs?

Take A Position

- Which option do you prefer? Justify your choice.
- What criticisms of your position should you anticipate? How would you defend your recommendation against these criticisms?

Resources

Online: Search for "Race to the Bottom" MNCs. This search will yield more information than you can possibly digest, much of it highly critical of globalization. Miles Kahler's paper, "Modeling Races to the Bottom," surveys many of the issues concerned.

In Print: David Vogel and Robert Kagan, eds., *The Dynamics of Regulatory Change: How Globalization Affects National Regulatory Policies* (Berkeley: University of California Press, 2004); Daniel Drezner, "Bottom Feeders," *Foreign Policy* 121 (November/December 2000): 64–70; Debora Spar and David Yoffie, "Multinational Enterprises and the Prospects for Justice," *Journal of International Affairs* 52 (Spring 1999): 557–581.

Although governments have spent almost 30 years negotiating rules to regulate foreign direct investment—within the UN, within the GATT, and within the OECD—they have yet to agree on a regulatory framework. Conflict between capital-exporting countries and capital-importing countries over the basic purpose of such a regime is the primary reason for this lack of success. Governments have been unable to agree whether such rules should regulate host countries or MNCs. The obvious compromise—that international rules might usefully regulate both—has yet to materialize in a meaningful way.

CONCLUSION

The politics of MNCs emerge from the competing interests of host countries, home countries of the MNCs, and the MNCs themselves. Each group has distinctive interests regarding FDI. MNCs want to operate freely across the globe, with few government-imposed restrictions on their activities. Host countries want to ensure that the MNCs operating within their borders provide benefits to the local economy that offset the loss of decision-making authority that is inherent in foreign ownership. The home countries of the MNCs want to ensure that their firms' overseas investments are secure. The politics of MNCs emerge when these distinct interests come into conflict with each other.

As we have seen, almost all governments impose some restrictions on the activities of foreign firms that operate inside their countries. Many governments, especially in the developing world, have tried to harness multinationals to their development objectives, but even the advanced industrialized countries have been unwilling to allow foreign firms to control critical sectors of the national economy. Similarities arise from the common concern about the local impact of foreign decision making. Differences arise from the fact that most developing countries are only hosts to MNC activities, whereas the advanced industrialized countries are both hosts and home bases. Consequently, developing countries' concerns about foreign domination are not tempered by the need to ensure that foreign governments respect the investments of the developing countries' own MNCs.

The basic conflict between capital-importing and capital-exporting countries is evident also in the international politics of MNCs. In the international arena, politics have revolved around efforts to negotiate comprehensive rules for international investment. Yet, conflict between the capital-exporting and the capital-importing countries has so far prevented agreement on comprehensive investment rules. As we have seen, this conflict reflects a basic disagreement about what the rules should regulate. Should international rules regulate the ability of host countries to control the MNCs that invest in their countries, or should international rules regulate the range of activities that MNCs are allowed to engage in? The inability of the advanced industrialized countries and the developing countries to agree on an answer to this question, as well as the apparent unwillingness of both groups to compromise, has prevented the creation of comprehensive rules to regulate international investment.

KEY TERMS

Bilateral Investment
   Treaties
Calvo Doctrine
Export-Processing
   Zones
Locational Incentives

Multilateral Agreement on
   Investment
Obsolescing Bargain
Performance Requirement
Sovereign Wealth
   Fund

Trade-Related Investment
   Measures
United Nations Resolution
   on Permanent
   Sovereignty over
   Natural Resources

SUGGESTIONS FOR FURTHER READING

For a detailed discussion of the obsolescing bargain model and an application of this model to Chile, see Theodore H. Moran, *Multinational Corporations and the Politics of Dependence: Copper in Chile* (Princeton, NJ: Princeton University Press, 1974). You can trace the subsequent development of state-MNC relations in Jean J. Boddewyn, 2016. "International Business–Government Relations Research 1945–2015: Concepts, Typologies, Theories and Methodologies." *Journal of World Business* 51(1): 10–22.

Rachel Wellhausen's *The Shield of Nationality: When Governments Break Contracts with Foreign Firms* (Cambridge: Cambridge University Press, 2015) offers an excellent analysis of host-country and firm relationships.

For an equally excellent introduction to Bilateral Investment Treaties, see Helen V. Milner, 2014. "Introduction: The Global Economy, FDI, and the Regime for Investment," *World Politics* 66(1): 1–11, and Beth A. Simmons, 2014. "Bargaining over BITs, Arbitrating Awards: The Regime for Protection and Promotion of International Investment." *World Politics* 66(1): 12–46.

The International Monetary System

The sole purpose of the international monetary system is to facilitate international economic exchange. Most countries have national currencies that are not generally accepted as legal payment outside their borders. You wouldn't get very far, for example, if you tried to use dollars to purchase a pint of ale in a London pub. If you want this pint, you have to first exchange your dollars for British pounds. If you are an American car dealer trying to import Volkswagens for your dealership, you will need to find some way to exchange your dollars for euros. If you are an American trying to purchase shares in a Japanese company, you will have to find some way to acquire Japanese yen. International transactions are possible only with an inexpensive means of exchanging one national currency for another. The international monetary system's primary function is to provide this mechanism. When the system functions smoothly, international trade and investment can flourish; when the system functions poorly, or when it collapses completely (as it did in the early 1930s), international trade and investment grind to a halt.

The purpose of the international monetary system is simple, but the factors that determine how it works are more complex. For example, how many dollars it costs an American tourist to buy a British pound, a euro, or 100 Japanese yen (or any other foreign currency) is determined by the sum total of the millions of international transactions that Americans conduct with the rest of the world. Moreover, for these currency prices to remain stable from one month to the next, the United States must somehow ensure that the value of the goods, services, and financial assets that it buys from the rest of the world equals the value of the products it sells to the rest of the world. Any imbalance will cause the dollar to gain or lose value in terms of foreign currencies. Although these issues may seem remote, they matter substantially to your well-being. For every time the dollar loses value against foreign currencies, you become poorer; conversely, you become richer whenever the dollar gains value. This is true whether you travel outside the United States or not.

This chapter and the next develop a basic understanding of the international monetary system. This chapter presents a few central economic concepts and examines a bit of postwar exchange-rate history. Chapter 11 builds on this base while examining contemporary international monetary arrangements. In the current chapter, we explore one basic question: Why do we live in a world in which currency values fluctuate substantially from week to week, rather than in a world of more stable currencies? The answer we propose is that the international monetary system requires governments to choose between currency stability and national economic autonomy. Given the need to choose, the advanced industrialized countries have elected to allow their currencies to fluctuate in order to retain national autonomy.

THE ECONOMICS OF THE INTERNATIONAL MONETARY SYSTEM

We begin by examining three economic concepts that are central to understanding the international monetary system. We look first at exchange rates and exchange-rate systems. We then examine the balance of payments, and conclude by looking closely at the dynamics of balance-of-payments adjustment.

Exchange-Rate Systems

An exchange rate is the price of one currency in terms of another. As I write this sentence, for example, the dollar–yen exchange rate is 107 which means that 1 dollar will purchase 107 Japanese yen. A currency's exchange rate is determined by the interaction between the supply of and the demand for currencies in the **foreign exchange market**—the market in which the world's currencies are traded. When an American business needs yen to pay for goods imported from Japan, for example, it goes to the foreign exchange market and buys them. Thousands of such transactions undertaken by individuals, businesses, and governments each day—some looking to buy yen and sell dollars and others looking to sell yen and buy dollars—determine the price of the dollar in terms of yen and the prices of all of the world's currencies. Imbalances between the supply of and demand for currencies in the foreign exchange market cause exchange rates to change. If more people want to buy than sell yen, for example, the yen will gain value, or appreciate. Conversely, if more people want to sell than buy yen, the yen will lose value, or depreciate.

An **exchange-rate system** is a set of rules governing how much national currencies can appreciate and depreciate in the foreign exchange market. There are two prototypical systems: fixed exchange-rate systems and floating exchange-rate systems. In a **fixed exchange-rate system**, governments establish a fixed price for their currencies in terms of an external standard, such as gold or another country's currency. (Under post-World War II arrangements, for example, the United States fixed the dollar to gold at $35 per ounce.) The government then maintains this fixed price by buying and selling currencies in the foreign exchange market. In order to conduct these transactions, governments hold a stock of other countries' currencies as **foreign exchange reserves**. Thus, if the dollar is selling below its fixed price against the yen in the foreign exchange market, the U.S. government will sell yen that it is holding in its foreign exchange reserves and will purchase dollars. These transactions will reduce the supply of dollars in the foreign exchange market, causing the dollar's value to rise. If the dollar is selling above its fixed price against the yen, the U.S. government will sell dollars and purchase yen. These transactions increase the supply of dollars in the foreign exchange market, causing the dollar's value to fall. The yen the United States acquires then become part of its foreign exchange reserves. Such government purchases and sales of currencies in the foreign exchange market are called foreign exchange market intervention.

In a **floating exchange-rate system**, there are no limits on how much a currency can move in the foreign exchange market. In such systems, governments do not maintain a fixed price for their currencies against gold or any other standard. Nor do governments engage in foreign exchange market intervention to influence the value of their currencies. Instead, the value of one currency in terms of another is determined entirely by the activities of private actors—firms, financial institutions, and individuals—as they purchase and sell currencies in the foreign exchange market. If private demand for a particular currency in the market falls, that currency depreciates. Conversely, if private demand for a particular currency in the market increases, that currency appreciates. In contrast to a fixed exchange-rate system, therefore, a pure floating exchange-rate system calls for no government involvement in determining the value of one currency in terms of another.

Fixed and floating exchange-rate systems represent the two ends of a continuum. Other exchange-rate systems lie between these two extremes. In a **fixed-but-adjustable exchange-rate system**—the system that lay at the center of the post-World War II monetary system and the European Union (EU)'s regional exchange-rate system between 1979 and 1999—currencies are given a fixed exchange rate against some standard, and governments are required to maintain this exchange rate. However, governments can change the fixed price occasionally, usually under a set of well-defined circumstances. Other systems lie closer to the floating exchange-rate end of the continuum, but provide a bit more stability to exchange rates than a pure float. In a **managed float**, which perhaps most accurately characterizes the current international monetary system, governments do not allow their currencies to float freely. Instead, they intervene in the foreign exchange market to influence their currency's value against other currencies. However, there are usually no rules governing when such intervention will occur, and governments do not commit themselves to maintaining a specific fixed price against other currencies or an external standard. Because all exchange-rate systems fall somewhere between the two extremes, one can usefully distinguish between such systems on the basis of how much exchange-rate flexibility or rigidity they entail.

In the contemporary international monetary system, governments maintain a variety of exchange-rate arrangements. Some governments allow their currencies to float. Others, such as most governments in the EU, have opted for rigidly fixed exchange rates. Still others, particularly in the developing world, maintain fixed-but-adjustable exchange rates. However, the world's most important currencies—the dollar, the yen, and the euro—are allowed to float against each other, and the monetary authorities in these countries engage only in periodic intervention to influence their values. Consequently, the contemporary international monetary system is most often described as a system of floating exchange rates. We will examine the operation of this system in detail in Chapter 11.

Is one exchange-rate system inherently better than another? Not necessarily. Rather than rank systems as better or worse, it is more useful to recognize that all exchange-rate systems embody an important trade-off between exchange-rate stability on the one hand, and domestic economic autonomy on the other. Fixed exchange rates provide exchange-rate stability, but they also prevent governments from using monetary policy to manage domestic economic activity. Floating exchange rates allow governments to use monetary policy to manage the domestic economy but do not provide much exchange-rate stability. Whether a fixed or a floating exchange rate is better, therefore, depends a lot on the value governments attach to each side of this trade-off. Fixed exchange rates are better for governments that value exchange-rate stability more than domestic autonomy. Floating exchange rates are better for governments that value domestic autonomy more than exchange-rate stability.

The Balance of Payments

The **balance of payments** is an accounting device that records all international transactions between a particular country and the rest of the world for a given period. For instance, any time an American business exports or imports a product, the value of that transaction is recorded in the U.S. balance of payments. Any time an American resident, business, or government loans funds to a foreigner or borrows funds from a foreign financial institution, the value of the transaction is recorded. All of the government's international transactions also are recorded. When the U.S. government spends money in Iraq supporting the military, or provides foreign aid to Egypt, these payments are recorded in the balance of payments. By recording all such transactions, the balance of payments provides an aggregate picture of the international transactions the United States conducts in a given year.

Table 10.1 presents the U.S. balance of payments for 2016, the latest year for which complete data are currently available. The transactions are divided into two broad categories: the current account and the financial account. The **current account** records all current (non-financial) transactions between American residents and the rest of the world. These current transactions

---

TABLE 10.1

U.S. Balance of Payments, 2016 (Billions of U.S. Dollars)

Current Account

Trade in Goods	
Imports	−2,208
Exports	1,456
Trade in Services	
Imports	−505
Exports	752
Balance on Goods and Services	−505
Primary Income	
Receipts	814
Payments	−641
Secondary Income	
Receipts	135
Payments	−255
Balance on Current Account	−452

Financial Account

Net Acquisition of Financial Assets	
Direct Investment Assets	−312
Portfolio Investment Assets	−40
Other Investment Assets	6
Reserve Assets	−2
New Incurrence of liabilities	
Direct Investment Liabilities	479
Portfolio Investment Liabilities	237
Other Investment Liabilities	25
Financial Derivatives, Net	16
Overall Balance (Statistical Discrepancy)	74

Source: U.S. Bureau of Economic Analysis, www.bea.gov/.

are divided into four subcategories. The *trade account* registers imports and exports of goods, including manufactured items and agricultural products. The *service account* registers imports and exports of service-sector activities, such as banking services, insurance, consulting, transportation, tourism, and construction. The *income account* registers all payments into and out of the United States in connection with royalties, licensing fees, interest payments, and profits.

The **financial account** registers capital flows between the United States and the rest of the world. Any time an American resident purchases a financial asset—a foreign stock, a bond, or a factory—in another country, this expenditure is registered as an acquisition or capital outflow. Each time a foreigner purchases an American financial asset, the expenditure is registered as a liability or capital inflow. Capital outflows (assets) are registered as negative items and capital inflows (liabilities) are registered as positive items in the **capital account**. In 2016, American residents other than the U.S. government purchased about $348 billion worth of foreign financial assets, whereas foreigners (including foreign governments) purchased about $741 billion of American financial assets. Capital outflows are set against capital inflows to produce a capital-account balance. In 2016, the U.S. financial-account balance was approximately $378 billion. To calculate the overall balance-of-payments position, simply add the current account and the capital account together. In 2016, the United States ran an overall balance-of-payments imbalance of $74 billion.

The current and capital accounts must be mirror images of each other. That is, if a country has a current-account deficit, it must have a capital-account surplus. Conversely, if a country has a current-account surplus, it must have a capital-account deficit. Grasping why this relationship must exist is easiest in the case of a country with a current-account deficit. Having a current-account deficit means that the country's total expenditures in a given year—all of the money spent on goods and services and on investments in factories and houses—are larger than its total income in that year. The U.S. case is instructive. American consumers spent a combined total of $12.8 trillion in 2016. The U.S. government spent an additional $3.3 trillion. American firms and households invested an additional $3.1 trillion. Altogether, these expenditures totaled $19.2 trillion. Yet, American residents earned only $18.6 trillion in total income in 2016. The difference between what American residents earned and what they spent is thus equal to $600 billion. Now look back at Table 10.1. The balance on trade in goods and services plus the statistical discrepancy is also approximately $600 billion. (The two would match exactly if we used exact, rather than rounded, numbers.) Hence, the American current-account deficit equals the difference between American income and American expenditures in a given year.

The United States can spend more than it earned in income because the rest of the world was willing to lend to American residents. The U.S. capital-account surplus thus reflects the willingness of residents of other countries to finance American expenditures in excess of American income. If the rest of the world were unwilling to lend to American borrowers, the United States could not spend more than it earned in income. Thus, a country can have a current-account deficit only if it has a capital-account surplus.

The same logic applies to a country with a current-account surplus. Suppose we divide the world into two countries: the United States and the rest of the world. We know that the United States has a current-account deficit with the rest of the world and thus the rest of the world has a current-account surplus with the United States. If the United States can have a current-account deficit only if the rest of the world lends money to the United States, then the rest of the world can have a current-account surplus with the United States only if it lends money to American residents. If it doesn't, Americans can't buy as many of the rest of the world's goods. The rest of the world's current-account surplus (as well as the American current-account deficit) then will disappear. Thus, a country with a current-account surplus must have a capital-account deficit.

In terms of our income and expenditure framework, a current-account surplus means that the country is spending less than it earns in income. The balance—the country's savings—is lent to countries with current-account deficits.

Balance-of-Payments Adjustment

Even though the current and capital accounts must balance each other, there is no assurance that the millions of international transactions that individuals, businesses, and governments conduct every year will necessarily produce this balance. When they don't, the country faces an imbalance of payments. A country might have a current-account deficit that it cannot fully finance through capital imports, for example, or it might have a current-account surplus that is not fully offset by capital outflows. When an imbalance arises, the country must bring its payments back into balance. The process by which a country does so is called **balance-of-payments adjustment**. Fixed and floating exchange-rate systems adjust imbalances in different ways.

In a fixed exchange-rate system, balance-of-payments adjustment occurs through changes in domestic prices. We can most readily understand this adjustment process through a simple example. Suppose there are only two countries in the world—the United States and Japan—and suppose further that they maintain a fixed exchange rate according to which $1 equals 100 yen. The United States has purchased 800 billion yen worth of goods, services, and financial assets from Japan, and Japan has purchased $4 billion of items from the United States. Thus, the United States has a deficit, and Japan a surplus, of $4 billion.

A Closer Look

The Classical Gold Standard

Governments based their exchange rates on the gold standard prior to World War I. In this system, governments exchanged national currency notes for gold at a permanently fixed rate of exchange. Between 1834 and 1933, for example, the U.S. government exchanged dollar notes for gold at the rate of $20.67 per ounce. Because all national currencies were fixed to gold, all national currencies were permanently fixed against each other as well. The gold standard emerged at the center of the international monetary system during the 1870s. Great Britain had adopted the gold standard in the early eighteenth century, but most other currencies remained based on silver or on a combination of silver and gold (a "bimetallic" standard). During the 1870s, most European countries, as well as the United States, abandoned silver as a monetary standard. Much of the rest of the world followed during the 1880s and 1890s. This rapid shift to gold reflected what economists call "network externalities"—the benefit of adopting gold grew in line with the number of countries that had already adopted gold. This exchange-rate stability facilitated the rapid growth of international trade and financial flows in the late nineteenth century.

With exchange rates permanently fixed, prices in each country moved in response to cross-border gold flows; prices rose as gold flowed into the country and fell when gold flowed out. Cross-border gold flows were in turn driven by the relatively autonomous operation of the "price specie-flow mechanism." The price specie-flow mechanism worked in the following way. Suppose the United States experienced a sudden acceleration of economic growth. With the U.S. money supply (its stock of gold) fixed in the short run, the growth spurt would place downward pressure on American prices (with more goods to buy with a fixed amount of money, the average price of goods must fall). As American prices fell, American exports would rise and American imports would fall, thereby generating a balance-of-payments surplus. This payments surplus would pull gold into the United States from the rest of the world. The resulting monetary expansion would push American prices back up to their initial level. The rest of the world would simultaneously experience countervailing dynamics. It would develop a payments deficit as the necessary counterpart to the American surplus. This deficit would generate a gold outflow— the necessary counterpart to the American gold inflow—and this gold outflow would push prices down in the rest of the world. The price specie-flow mechanism thus imposed recurrent bouts of inflation and deflation on the societies linked by gold.

Governments were not supposed to use their monetary policy to counter these price movements. Instead, governments were supposed to follow the "rules of the game." These rules required countries losing gold as a result of an external deficit to raise the discount rate—the interest rate at which the central bank loaned to other banks—to restrict domestic credit and slow domestic investment. Tighter credit would reinforce the deflationary pressure caused by gold outflows. Countries accumulating gold as a consequence of an external surplus were expected to lower the discount rate in order to expand credit and boost investment. Lower interest rates would reinforce the inflationary pressure caused by gold inflows. In essence, therefore, the rules of the game required central banks to set monetary policy in response to developments in their balance of payments rather than in response to conditions in the domestic economy. In this way, the gold standard forced governments to subordinate internal price stability to external exchange rate stability.

The resulting instability of domestic prices was substantial. In the United States, for example, domestic prices fell by 28 percent between 1869 and 1879, rose by 11 percent in the following 5 years, fell by an additional 25 percent between 1884 and 1896, and then gradually rose through the next 15 years (Rockoff 1990, 742). The coefficient of variation provides a more systematic measure of domestic price instability. This coefficient is the ratio of the standard deviation of annual percentage change in domestic prices to the average annual percentage change. Greater price instability generates a larger coefficient of variation. Between 1880 and 1913, the coefficient of variation for the United States was 17. In comparison, the coefficient for the post-World War II era—a period of greater exchange-rate flexibility was 0.8 (Bordo 2002). Thus, even though the gold standard stabilized exchange rates, this external stability came at the price of substantial domestic price instability.

Domestic price instability provoked political conflict. One such episode occurred in the United States in the late nineteenth century. Western grain farmers were hit particularly hard by deflation during 1884–1896. Commodity prices fell more rapidly than did the prices of the manufactured goods and services that farmers purchased, thereby reducing farm purchasing power. In addition, most farmers were in debt and falling commodity prices required them to dedicate more of their income to debt service. The West responded by advocating the return to a bimetallic monetary system. They argued that monetizing silver would expand the money supply and raise commodity prices. The movement peaked in 1896 when the pro-silver wing of the Democratic Party defeated the pro-gold wing at the party's National Convention. This victory was symbolized by the nomination of William Jennings Bryan, who had delivered a passionate speech to the convention in which he avowed that farmers would not be "nailed to a cross of gold," as the party's candidate for the 1896 presidential election. Bryan lost the presidential election to the Republican William McKinley, and the silverites subsequently lost strength as commodity prices rose and remained high until the end of World War I.

This payments imbalance creates an imbalance between the supply of and the demand for the dollar and yen in the foreign exchange market. American residents need 800 billion yen to pay for their imports from Japan. They can acquire this 800 billion yen by selling $8 billion. Japanese residents need only $4 billion to pay for their imports from the United States. They can acquire the $4 billion by selling 400 billion yen. Thus, American residents are selling $4 billion more than Japanese residents want to buy, and the dollar depreciates against the yen.

Because the exchange rate is fixed, the United States and Japan must prevent this depreciation. Thus, both governments intervene in the foreign exchange market, buying dollars in exchange for yen. Intervention has two consequences. First, it eliminates the imbalance in the foreign exchange market as the governments provide the 400 billion yen that American residents need in exchange for the $4 billion that Japanese residents do not want. With the supply of each currency equal to the demand in the foreign exchange market, the fixed exchange rate is sustained. Second, intervention changes each country's money supply. The American money supply falls by $4 billion, and Japan's money supply increases by 400 billion yen.

The change in the money supplies alters prices in both countries. The reduction of the U.S. money supply causes American prices to fall. The expansion of the money supply in Japan causes Japanese prices to rise. As American prices fall and Japanese prices rise, American goods become relatively less expensive than Japanese goods. Consequently, American and Japanese residents shift their purchases away from Japanese products and toward American goods. American imports (and hence Japanese exports) fall, and American exports (and hence Japanese imports) rise. As American imports (and Japanese exports) fall and American exports (and Japanese imports) rise, the payments imbalance is eliminated. Adjustment under fixed exchange rates thus occurs through changes in the relative price of American and Japanese goods brought about by the changes in money supplies caused by intervention in the foreign exchange market.

In floating exchange-rate systems, balance-of-payments adjustment occurs through exchange-rate movements. Let's go back to our U.S.–Japan scenario, keeping everything the same, except this time allowing the currencies to float rather than requiring the governments to maintain a fixed exchange rate. Again, the $4 billion payments imbalance generates an imbalance in the foreign exchange market: Americans are selling more dollars than Japanese residents want to buy. Consequently, the dollar begins to depreciate against the yen. Because the currencies are floating, however, neither government intervenes in the foreign exchange market. Instead, the dollar depreciates until the market clears. In essence, as Americans seek the yen they need, they are forced to accept fewer yen for each dollar. Eventually, however, they will acquire all of the yen they need, but will have paid more than $4 billion for them.

The dollar's depreciation lowers the price in yen of American goods and services in the Japanese market and raises the price in dollars of Japanese goods and services in the American market. A 10 percent devaluation of the dollar against the yen, for example, reduces the price that Japanese residents pay for American goods by 10 percent and raises the price that Americans pay for Japanese goods by 10 percent. By making American products cheaper and Japanese goods more expensive, depreciation causes American imports from Japan to fall and American exports to Japan to rise. As American exports expand and imports fall, the payments imbalance is corrected.

In both systems, therefore, a balance-of-payments adjustment occurs as prices fall in the country with the deficit and rise in the country with the surplus. Consumers in both countries respond to these price changes by purchasing fewer of the now-more-expensive goods in the country with the surplus and more of the now-cheaper goods in the country with the deficit. These shifts in consumption alter imports and exports in both countries, moving each of their payments back into balance. The mechanism that causes these price changes is different in each system, however. In fixed exchange-rate systems, the exchange rate remains stable and price changes are achieved by changing the money supply in order to alter prices inside the country. In floating exchange-rate systems, internal prices remain stable, while the change in relative prices is brought about through exchange-rate movements.

Contrasting the balance-of-payments adjustment process under fixed and floating exchange rates highlights the trade-off that governments face between exchange rate stability and domestic price stability: governments can have a stable fixed exchange rate or they can stabilize domestic prices, but they cannot achieve both goals simultaneously. If a government wants to maintain a fixed exchange rate, it must accept the occasional deflation and inflation caused by balance-of-payments adjustment. If a government is unwilling to accept such price movements, it cannot maintain a fixed exchange rate. This trade-off has been the central factor driving the international monetary system toward floating exchange rates during the last 100 years. We turn now to examine how this trade-off first led governments to create innovative international monetary arrangements following World War II, and then caused the system to collapse into a floating exchange-rate system in the early 1970s.

THE RISE AND FALL OF THE BRETTON WOODS SYSTEM

The **Bretton Woods system** represents both a first and a last in the history of the international monetary system. On the one hand, Bretton Woods represented the first time that governments explicitly made exchange rates a matter of international cooperation. Drawing lessons from their experiences during the interwar period, governments attempted to create an innovative system that would enable them to enjoy exchange-rate stability and domestic economic autonomy. On the other hand, the Bretton Woods system represents the final effort, at least to date, to base the international monetary system on some form of fixed exchange rates. The effort was relatively short lived. The system was not fully implemented until 1959, and by the early 1960s it was beginning to experience the stresses and strains that brought about its collapse into a system of floating exchange rates in the early 1970s.

Creating the Bretton Woods System

American and British policymakers began planning for postwar monetary arrangements in the early 1940s. Harry Dexter White, an economist working at the U.S. Treasury, developed an American plan, and John M. Keynes, an economist who was advising the British Treasury, developed a British plan. Bilateral consultations yielded a joint U.S.–British plan that was published in 1943. This "Joint Statement," as the plan was called, served as the basis for the Articles of Agreement that emerged from a multilateral conference attended by 44 countries in Bretton Woods, New Hampshire, in 1944. The international monetary system they built, the Bretton Woods system, provided an explicit code of conduct for international monetary relations and an institutional structure centered on the International Monetary Fund (IMF).

The Bretton Woods system attempted to establish a system of fixed exchange rates in a world in which governments were unwilling to accept the loss of domestic autonomy that such a system required. Governments had become increasingly reluctant to accept the domestic adjustments imposed by fixed exchange rates as a result of a shift in the balance of political power within European political systems following World War I. We will explore these developments in greater detail in Chapter 12. For now, we note only that the growing strength of labor unions ensured that deficit adjustment would occur through falling output and rising unemployment, while the emergence of mass-based democracies made governments reluctant to accept these costs.

The emergence of political constraints on domestic adjustment ruled out a return to rigidly fixed exchange rates following World War II. Yet, floating exchange rates were viewed as no more acceptable. It was widely agreed that the experiment with floating exchange rates in the 1930s had been disastrous. As an influential study published by the League of Nations in 1944 summarized, "If there is anything that the interwar experience has demonstrated, it is that [currencies] cannot be left free to fluctuate from day to day under the influence of market supply and demand" (quoted in Dam 1982, 61). In creating the Bretton Woods system, therefore, governments sought a system that would provide stable exchange rates *and* simultaneously afford domestic economic autonomy. To achieve these goals, the Bretton Woods system introduced four innovations: greater exchange-rate flexibility, capital controls, a stabilization fund, and the IMF.

First, Bretton Woods explicitly incorporated flexibility by establishing fixed-but-adjustable exchange rates. In this arrangement, each government established a central parity for its currency against gold, but could change this price of gold when facing a **fundamental disequilibrium**. Although governments were never able to define this term precisely, it was generally accepted that it referred to payments imbalances large enough to require inordinately painful domestic adjustment. In such cases, a government could devalue its currency. Exchange rates would thus be fixed on a day-to-day basis, but governments could change the exchange rate when they needed to correct a large imbalance. It was hoped that this element of flexibility would reduce the need for domestic adjustment but still provide stable exchange rates.

Governments were also allowed to limit international capital flows. An important component of the international economy, capital flows allow countries to finance current-account imbalances and to use foreign funds to finance productive investment. Many governments believed, however, that capital flows had destabilized exchange rates during the interwar period. Large volumes of capital had crossed borders, only to be brought back to the home country at the first sign of economic difficulty in the host country. This system resulted in "disequilibrating" capital flows in which countries with current-account deficits shipped capital to countries with current-account surpluses, rather than "equilibrating" flows in which countries with surpluses exported capital to countries with deficits in order to finance current-account deficits. The resulting payments deficits required substantial domestic adjustments that governments were unwilling to accept.

In the early 1930s, most governments began to limit capital flows with **exchange restrictions**—government regulations on the use of foreign exchange. In the most restrictive regimes, the central bank establishes a monopoly on foreign exchange. Any private actor wanting foreign currency or wanting to exchange foreign currency into the domestic currency must petition the central bank, which can then restrict the types of transactions for which it exchanges currencies. It might, for example, refuse to supply foreign currency to a domestic resident who wants to buy financial assets in a foreign country. Alternatively, it might refuse to supply domestic currency to a foreign resident who wants to buy domestic financial assets. By controlling purchases and sales of foreign exchange in this manner, governments can limit financial capital flows into and out of their domestic economies.

Following World War II, the question was whether governments should be allowed to retain these exchange restrictions. American policymakers wanted all restrictions eliminated in order to restore liberal international capital markets. Other governments wanted to retain the restrictions. Keynes, for example, believed that it was "vital" to "have a means ... of controlling short-term speculative movements of flights of currency" (cited in Dam 1982, 98). In the absence of such controls, Keynes argued, exchange rates would be vulnerable to speculative attacks that would force governments to float their currencies. Keynes's position carried the day. The IMF's Articles of Agreement required governments to allow residents to convert the domestic currency into foreign currencies to settle current-account transactions, but they allowed (but did not require) governments to restrict the convertibility of their currency for capital-account transactions. Most governments took advantage of this right, and as a consequence, international capital flows were tightly restricted until the late 1970s.

The Bretton Woods system also created a **stabilization fund**—a credit mechanism consisting of a pool of currencies contributed by member countries. Each country that participated in the Bretton Woods system was assigned a share of the total fund (called a quota), the size of which corresponded to its relative size in the global economy. Each country then contributed to the fund in the amount of its quota, paying 25 percent in gold and the remaining 75 percent in its national currency. As the world's largest economy, the United States had the largest quota, a contribution of $2.75 billion. Britain had the second-largest quota, a contribution of $1.3 billion. Other governments had much smaller quotas; France, for example, had a quota of only $450 million, whereas Panama's was only $0.5 million. In 1944, the stabilization fund held a total of $8.8 billion. A government could draw on the fund when it faced a balance-of-payments deficit. Doing so would obviate the need to respond to a small payments deficit by devaluing currency or by imposing barriers to imports (De Vries and Horsefield 1969, 23–24).

Finally, the Bretton Woods system created an international organization, the IMF, to monitor member countries' macroeconomic policies and balance-of-payments positions, to decide when devaluation was warranted, and to manage the stabilization fund. The IMF was intended to limit two kinds of opportunistic behavior. First, the exchange-rate system created the potential for competitive devaluations. Governments could devalue to enhance the competitiveness of their exports. If one government devalued in an attempt to boost exports, other governments would be likely to devalue in response, setting off a tit-for-tat dynamic that would destroy the exchange-rate system (Dam 1982, 63–64). Second, governments might abuse the stabilization fund. Easy access to this fund might encourage governments to run large balance-of-payments deficits. Countries could import more than they exported and then draw on the stabilization fund to finance the resulting deficit. If all governments pursued such policies, the stabilization fund would be quickly exhausted, and countries would face large deficits that they could not finance. Countries would then float their currencies and perhaps restrict imports as well.

The IMF limited such opportunistic behavior by having authority over exchange-rate changes and access to the stabilization fund. For exchange-rate changes, the Articles of Agreement specified that governments could devalue or revalue only after consulting the IMF, which would then evaluate the country's payments position and either agree or disagree with the government's claim that it faced a fundamental disequilibrium. If the IMF opposed the devaluation, the government could still devalue, but it would not be allowed to draw from the stabilization fund (Dam 1982, 90). The IMF also controlled access to the fund. IMF rules limited the total amount that a government could borrow to 25 percent of its quota per year, up to a maximum of 200 percent of its quota at any one time. It was agreed, however, that governments would not have automatic access to these funds. Each member government's quota was divided into four *credit tranches* of equal size, and drawings from each tranche required approval by the IMF's Executive Board. Approval for drawings on the first tranche was automatic, as these withdrawals represented borrowings against the gold that each member had paid into the stabilization fund. Drawing on the higher credit tranches, however, was conditional. Conditionality required a member government to reach agreement with the IMF on the measures it would take to correct its balance-of-payments deficit before it could draw on its higher credit tranches. Conditionality agreements typically require governments to reduce the growth of the money supply and to reduce government spending. Conditionality thus forces governments to correct the domestic economic imbalances that cause their balance-of-payments problems. The practice of IMF conditionality is controversial, and we will return to it in greater detail in Chapter 14.

Implementing Bretton Woods: From Dollar Shortage to Dollar Glut

Governments had intended to implement the Bretton Woods system immediately following World War II. This proved impossible, however, because European governments held such small foreign exchange reserves (dollars and gold) that they were unwilling to make their domestic currencies freely convertible into foreign currencies. Governments needed to conserve what little foreign exchange they had to import food, capital goods, inputs, and many of the other critical components essential to economic reconstruction. Allowing residents to convert the domestic currency freely into dollars or gold, as the rules of Bretton Woods required, would produce a run on a country's limited foreign exchange reserves. Governments would then have to reduce imports and slow the pace of economic reconstruction.

An aborted British attempt to restore the convertibility of the pound in 1947 starkly illustrated the threat (Eichengreen 1996, 103). Under pressure from the United States, and with the support of a $3.75 billion American loan, the British government allowed holders of the British pound to purchase gold and dollars for current-account transactions. Those who held pounds rushed to exchange them for dollars and, in doing so, consumed the American loan and a large share of Britain's other foreign exchange reserves in only 6 weeks. As its reserves dwindled, the British government suspended the convertibility of the pound. Convertibility—and indeed the implementation of the Bretton Woods system—would have to wait until European governments had accumulated sufficient foreign exchange reserves.

In order for European governments to accumulate foreign exchange reserves, however, dollars had to be transferred from the United States to European governments. The U.S. balance-of-payments deficit provided the mechanism through which this transfer was achieved (see Figure 10.1). Initially, the United States exported dollars through its foreign aid and military expenditures. The Marshall Plan, implemented between 1948 and 1952, is the most prominent example of this American policy. By the late 1950s, however, private capital also was flowing from the United States to Europe (Block 1977). American deficits meant that more dollars flowed out from the United States each year than flowed in. These dollars were accumulated by European governments, which held them as foreign exchange reserves and used them to pay for imports from the United States and other countries. Governments could exchange whatever dollars they held into gold at the official price of $35 an ounce. By 1959, this mechanism had enabled European governments to

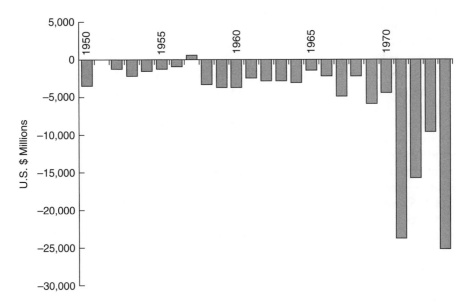

FIGURE 10.1

U.S. Balance of Payments, 1950–1974

Source: Block 1977.

accumulate sufficient dollar and gold reserves to accept fully convertible currencies. In 1959, therefore, the Bretton Woods system was finally implemented, almost 15 years after it had been created.

American policy during the 1950s also had an unintended consequence: the dollar became the system's primary reserve asset. In this role, the dollar became the currency that other governments held as foreign exchange reserves and used to make their international payments and to intervene in foreign exchange markets. This was reasonable: the United States was the largest economy in the world, and at the end of World War II the United States held between 60 and 70 percent of the world's gold supply. The dollar was fixed to gold at $35 per ounce, and other governments were willing to hold dollars because dollars were "as good as gold." As a consequence, however, the stability of the Bretton Woods system came to depend upon the ability of the U.S. government to exchange dollars for gold at $35 an ounce.

The American ability to fulfill this commitment began to diminish as the postwar dollar shortage was transformed into a dollar glut during the 1960s. The dollar glut was the natural consequence of continued American balance-of-payments deficits. Between 1958 and 1970, the United States ran average annual payments deficits of $3.3 billion. These deficits remained fairly stable during the first half of the 1960s, but then began to grow after 1965. Deficits were caused by U.S. military expenditures in connection with the Vietnam War and expanded welfare programs at home, as well as by the unwillingness of the Johnson and Nixon administrations to finance these expenditures with higher taxes. The result was an expansionary macroeconomic policy in the United States that sucked in imports and encouraged American investors to send capital abroad. The dollars accumulated by governments in the rest of the world as the result represented foreign claims on the American government's gold holdings.

The rising volume of foreign claims on American gold led to dollar overhang: foreign claims on American gold grew larger than the amount of gold that the U.S. government held. The progression of dollar overhang can be seen in the evolution of foreign dollar holdings and the U.S. gold stock during the 1950s and 1960s. In 1948, foreigners held a total of $7.3 billion against U.S. gold holdings of $24.8 billion. In this period, therefore, there was no uncertainty regarding the American ability to redeem all outstanding foreign claims on U.S. gold. By 1959, foreign dollar holdings had increased to $19.4 billion, but U.S. gold holdings had fallen to $19.5 billion. By 1970, American gold holdings had fallen to $11 billion, while foreign claims against this gold had risen to $47 billion. Thus, persistent balance-of-payments deficits reduced the ability of the United States to meet foreign claims on American gold reserves at the official price of $35 an ounce.

Dollar overhang threatened the stability of the Bretton Woods system (see Triffin 1960). As long as the dollar remained the system's primary reserve asset, the growth of dollars circulating in the global economy would have to keep pace with the expansion of world trade. This meant that dollar overhang would worsen. Yet, as that happened, people would lose confidence in the ability of the

American government to exchange dollars for gold at $35 an ounce. Once this confidence evaporated, anyone who held dollars would rush to sell them before the dollar was devalued or American gold reserves were exhausted. Declining confidence in the dollar, in other words, would encourage foreign dollar holders to bet against the dollar's fixed exchange rate with gold. Eventually, this dynamic would generate crises that would undermine the system.

Preventing these crises was complicated by the dollar's central role in the system. The United States would have to reverse its balance-of-payments position to eliminate dollar overhang. Rather than run deficits that pumped dollars into the international economy, the United States would have to run surpluses that pulled dollars back in. Yet, because the dollar served as the system's primary reserve asset, reducing the number of dollars circulating in the global economy would reduce the liquidity that financed world trade. As governments defended their fixed exchange rates in the face of this contraction of liquidity, the world economy could be pushed into a deflationary spiral (Eichengreen 1996, 116). The Bretton Woods system therefore faced a dilemma: dollar overhang would eventually trigger crises that undermined the system of fixed exchange rates, but measures to strengthen the dollar could trigger global deflation that might also destroy the system.

This liquidity problem, as it came to be called, was not simply an obscure technical matter. It was also a source of political conflict, particularly between France and the United States. The French argued that the United States gained considerable advantages from the dollar's role as the system's primary reserve asset. No other country could run persistent balance-of-payments deficits, because it would eventually run out of foreign exchange reserves and be forced to eliminate the deficit. But the United States did not face this reserve constraint: it could run deficits as long as other governments were willing to accumulate dollars. The French claimed that this asymmetry enabled the United States to pursue an "imperialistic" policy. In the economic arena, the United States could buy French companies, and in the geostrategic arena, the United States could expand its activities with few constraints, as it was doing in Vietnam (Dam 1982, 144). The French government decried this "exorbitant privilege" and advocated the creation of an alternative reserve asset to provide international liquidity. The French even advocated a return to the gold standard to eliminate the benefits the United States realized from the dollar's role in the system. Efforts to solve the liquidity problem, therefore, became inextricably linked to American power in the international monetary system and in the wider global arena.

Governments did respond to the liquidity problem, creating a new reserve asset to supplement the dollar. Working in conjunction with the IMF, governments created the Special Drawing Right (SDR), a reserve asset managed by the IMF and allocated to member governments in proportion to the size of their quotas. The SDR is not backed by gold or any other standard, cannot be used by private individuals, and is not traded in private financial markets. Its sole purpose is to provide a source of liquidity that governments can use to settle debts with each other arising from balance-of-payments deficits. The intention was that SDRs would supplement dollars as a source of liquidity in the international monetary system. The first allocation of SDRs occurred in 1970. By this time, however, the Bretton Woods system was moving toward its ultimate demise, and the SDR never played an important role.

The End of Bretton Woods: Crises and Collapse

The continued viability of the Bretton Woods system depended upon restoring confidence in the dollar, and this in turn required eliminating the underlying payments imbalances. Adjustment could be achieved through one of three paths: devalue the dollar against gold, restrain economic activity in the United States in order to reduce American imports, or expand economic activity in the rest of the world in order to increase American exports. Governments proved unwilling to adopt any of these measures. Instead, they were paralyzed by political conflict over who should bear the costs of the adjustments necessary to eliminate the imbalances that were weakening the system.

The simplest solution would have been to devalue the dollar against gold. Devaluation was not easily achieved, however. American policymakers believed that they could not change the dollar's exchange rate unilaterally. If they devalued against gold, Europe and Japan would simply devalue in response. As a consequence, the only way to devalue the dollar was to convince European and Japanese governments to revalue their currencies. Europe and Japan were unwilling to revalue their currencies against the dollar, however, because doing so would remove any pressure on the United States to undertake adjustment measures of its own (Solomon 1977, 170). Revaluation, in other words, would let the United States off the hook.

With currency realignment off the table, only two other solutions were left: adjustment through economic contraction in the United States or adjustment through economic expansion in other countries. In the United States, neither the Johnson nor the Nixon administration was willing to adopt the policies required to eliminate the U.S. balance-of-payments deficit. U.S. Secretary of the Treasury Henry Fowler spelled out the two American options in a memo to President Johnson in mid-1966. The United States could either "reduce the deficit by cutting back U.S. commitments overseas," a choice that would entail "major changes in [U.S.] foreign policy," or "reduce the deficit by introducing new economic and balance-of-payments measures at home" (United States Department of State). Neither option was attractive. The Johnson administration was not willing to allow the balance of payments to constrain its foreign-policy goals, and restricting domestic economic activity to correct the deficit was politically inconvenient.

Richard M. Nixon, who assumed the presidency in 1969, was no more willing to adopt policies to eliminate the American deficit. Instead, the Nixon administration blamed other governments for international monetary problems (Dam 1982, 186). The dollar's weakness was not a result of the American balance-of-payments deficit, the administration claimed, but was instead caused by surpluses in Germany and Japan. Because other governments were at fault, the administration began to push these other governments to change policies, acting "like a bull in a china shop," threatening to wreck the international trade and financial system unless other governments supported the dollar in the foreign exchange market and took measures to stimulate imports from the United States (Eichengreen 1996, 130).

Governments in Western Europe and Japan initially supported the dollar, in large part "because [the dollar] was the linchpin of the Bretton Woods system and because there was no consensus on how that system might be reformed or replaced" (Eichengreen 1996, 130). But there were clear limits to their willingness to continue to do so. The case of Germany illustrates both sides. Germany had done more to support the dollar than any other European government. The German government had agreed not to exchange the dollars it was accumulating for American gold, in stark contrast to the French, who regularly demanded gold from the United States for the dollars they acquired. In addition, Germany had negotiated a series of "offset payments" through which a portion of American military expenditures in Germany were offset by German expenditures on American military equipment. Such payments reduced the extent to which American military expenditures in Europe contributed to the U.S. balance-of-payments deficit.

Germany's willingness to support the dollar, however, was limited by that country's aversion to inflation. Germany had experienced hyperinflation during the 1920s, with prices rising at the rate of 1,000 percent per month in 1923. This experience had caused German officials and the German public to place great value on price stability (see Emminger 1977; Henning 1994). Supporting the dollar threatened to increase German inflation. As confidence in the dollar began to erode, dollar holders began to sell dollars and buy German marks. Intervention in the foreign exchange market to prevent the mark from appreciating expanded the German money supply and created inflation in the country, which then made Germany reluctant to support the dollar indefinitely. Continued German support would be based on clear evidence that the United States was adopting domestic policies that were reducing its payments deficit.

Governments, therefore, were unwilling to accept the domestic economic costs arising from the adjustments needed to correct the fundamental source of weakness in the system. As a consequence, the United States continued to export dollars into the system, dollar overhang worsened further, and confidence in the dollar's fixed exchange rate eroded. As confidence eroded, **speculative attacks**—large currency sales sparked by the anticipation of an impending devaluation—began to occur with increasing frequency and mounting ferocity. In the first 6 months of 1971, private holdings of dollars fell by $3 billion, a sign that people expected devaluation (Dam 1982, 187). European governments purchased more than $5 billion defending the dollar's fixed exchange rate. The speculative attacks reached a new high in May as Germany purchased $2 billion in only 2 days, a record amount at that time (Kenen 1994, 500). Such massive intervention breached the limits of German willingness to support the dollar, and the German government floated the mark.

Speculative attacks resumed in the summer of 1971, and in August the Nixon administration suspended the convertibility of the dollar into gold and imposed a 10 percent surcharge on imports (see Gowa 1983). The United States had abandoned the central component of the Bretton Woods system; it would no longer redeem foreign governments' dollar reserves for gold.

Governments made one final attempt to rescue the Bretton Woods system. During the fall of 1971, they negotiated a currency realignment that they hoped would reduce the U.S. payments deficit and stabilize the system. The realignment was finalized in a December meeting held at the Smithsonian Institution in Washington, DC. The dollar was devalued by 8 percent against gold, its value falling from $35 per ounce to $38 per ounce. European currencies were revalued by about 2 percent, thus producing a total devaluation of the dollar of 10 percent. In addition, the margins of fluctuation in the exchange-rate system were widened from 1 percent to 2.25 percent, to give the system a bit more exchange-rate flexibility.

Although Nixon hailed the Smithsonian realignment as "the greatest monetary agreement in the history of the world," it solved neither the economic imbalances nor the political conflicts that were the cause of the system's weakening. The United States refused to adopt measures to reduce its payments deficit. Rather than tighten monetary policy to support the new exchange rate, the Nixon administration loosened monetary policy, "triggering the greatest monetary expansion in the postwar era" (Emminger 1977, 33). German officials remained unwilling to accept the inflation that was the necessary consequence of intervention to support the mark against the dollar. With neither government willing to adjust to support the new exchange rates, speculative attacks quickly re-emerged. A massive crisis in the first months of 1973 brought the system down, as most advanced industrialized countries abandoned their fixed exchange rates and floated their currencies.

Policy Analysis and Debate

Who Should Adjust?

Question

Who should adjust in order to eliminate payments imbalances?

Overview

The payments imbalances at the center of the Bretton Woods system generated a distributive conflict about who should bear the cost of adjustment. The United States ran a large deficit, whereas Europe and Japan ran large surpluses. The elimination of either of these imbalances would necessarily eliminate the other. The situation gave rise to the dispute concerning who should alter its policies in order to adjust. Should the United States restrict its monetary and fiscal policies to shrink its deficit, or should Europe and Japan expand their monetary and fiscal policies to reduce their surpluses? The inability of governments to agree on how to distribute these adjustment costs eventually brought the Bretton Woods system down.

Distributive conflict over the costs of adjusting the balance of payments is of more than historical interest. The contemporary global economy has large current-account imbalances quite similar to those at the center of the Bretton Woods system. The United States runs large current-account deficits. Asian countries, most of which peg their currencies to the dollar, run large current-account surpluses. Asian surpluses finance American deficits. Rather than accumulating claims to American gold, however, as European governments did under Bretton Woods, Asia accumulates U.S. Treasury bills, which represent a claim on future American income.

Distributive conflict over the costs of adjustment has arisen during the last few years as current-account imbalances have expanded. Since 2000 or so, the United States has been pressuring China (one of the largest countries with a surplus) to devalue its currency. China has resisted such pressure thus far. Given the current size of the American deficit, one can imagine that the United States will pressure other Asian countries to adjust as well. Thus, the conflict over who adjusts shapes contemporary international monetary relations, just as it shaped monetary politics in the Bretton Woods system. Who should alter policies to eliminate large payments imbalances?

Policy Options

- The United States should implement the domestic policy changes required to reduce the size of its current-account deficit.
- The United States should pressure Asia to implement the domestic policies required to reduce the size of their current-account surpluses.

Policy Analysis

- What policies would the United States need to implement to eliminate its deficit? What would Asia have to do to eliminate its surplus?
- Is one of the two policy options less painful for the world economy than the other? If so, which one and why?

Take A Position

- Which option do you prefer? Justify your choice.
- What criticisms of your position should you anticipate? How would you defend your recommendation against these criticisms?

Resources

Online: Search for "Are We Back to a Bretton Woods Regime?" and "The Dollar and the New Bretton Woods System."

In Print: To examine past instances of distributive conflict, see Barry J. Eichengreen, *Golden Fetters: The Gold Standard and the Great Depression* (New York: Oxford University Press, 1992), and Barry J. Eichengreen and Marc Flandreau, eds., *The Gold Standard in Theory and History*, 2nd ed. (New York: Routledge, 1997).

Thus, the postwar attempt to create an international monetary system that provided exchange-rate stability and domestic economic autonomy was ultimately unsuccessful. The reasons for its failure are not hard to find. Some argue that the system was undermined by dollar overhang. Others suggest that it was destroyed by the speculative attacks that ultimately forced governments to abandon fixed exchange rates. Even though these factors were important, the fundamental cause of the system's collapse lay in the adjustment problem. To sustain fixed exchange rates, governments had to accept the domestic costs of balance-of-payments adjustment. No government was willing to do so. The United States was unwilling to accept the unemployment that would have arisen from eliminating its deficit, and Germany was unwilling to accept the higher inflation required to eliminate its surplus. This unwillingness to adjust aggravated the dollar overhang, which then created an incentive to launch speculative attacks against the dollar.

CONCLUSION

The creation and collapse of the Bretton Woods system highlights two central conclusions about the workings of the international monetary system. First, even though governments would like to maintain stable exchange rates and simultaneously preserve their domestic economic autonomy, no one has yet found a way to do so. Governments confront this trade-off because each country's balance-of-payments position has a direct impact on its exchange rate. When a country has a payments deficit, the resulting imbalance in the foreign exchange market causes the currency to depreciate. When a country has a payments surplus, the foreign exchange market imbalance causes the currency to appreciate. If the government is pledged to maintain a fixed exchange rate, it must intervene in the foreign exchange market to prevent such currency changes. As governments do so, they alter the money supply, thereby sparking the changes in the domestic economy needed to correct the payments imbalance. If a government is unwilling to accept these domestic adjustments, it will be unable to maintain a fixed exchange rate. The Bretton Woods system collapsed because neither Germany nor the United States was willing to accept the domestic adjustments needed to sustain it.

Second, when forced to choose between a fixed exchange rate and domestic economic autonomy, governments have opted for domestic economic auton-omy. They have done so because domestic adjustment is costly. In the short run, the country with the deficit must accept falling output, rising unemployment, and recession in order to maintain its fixed exchange rate. As American behav-ior in the Bretton Woods system illustrates, governments are rarely willing to do so. The country with the surplus must accept higher inflation, and as Germany's behavior in the Bretton Woods system indicates, surplus govern-ments are not willing to accept these costs. Governments in the advanced indus-trialized countries have been unwilling to pay the domestic economic costs in order to maintain fixed exchange rates against each other. Consequently, the world's largest countries have allowed their currencies to float against each other since the early 1970s.

The shift to floating exchange rates did not reflect agreement among governments that the international monetary system would perform better under floating rates than under fixed rates (although many economists did argue that it would). Instead, the shift to floating exchange rates reflected the political conclusion that fixed exchange rates were too costly. Thus, the answer to the question posed in this chapter's introduction is that we live in a world of floating exchange rates because politics makes governments unwilling to accept the domestic costs imposed by fixed exchange rates.

KEY TERMS

Balance of Payments
Balance-of-Payments
  Adjustment
Bretton Woods System
Capital Account
Conditionality
Current Account
Exchange-Rate System

Exchange Restrictions
Financial Account
Fixed Exchange-Rate
  System
Fixed-but-Adjustable
  Exchange-Rate System
Floating Exchange-Rate
  System

Foreign Exchange Market
Foreign Exchange
  Reserves
Fundamental
  Disequilibrium
Managed Float
Speculative Attacks
Stabilization Fund

SUGGESTIONS FOR FURTHER READING

Perhaps the most readable account of the evolution of the international monetary system during the last 100 years is Barry J. Eichengreen, *Globalizing Capital: A History of the International Monetary System*, 2nd edition (Princeton, NJ: Princeton University Press, 2008).

For an accessible account of the interwar period, see Liaquat Ahamed, *Lords of Finance: The Bankers Who Broke the World* (New York: Penguin Press, 2009).

For further exploration of the origins of the Bretton Woods system, see Francis J. Gavin, *Gold, Dollars, and Power: The Politics of International Monetary Relations, 1958–1971* (Chapel Hill: University of North Carolina Press, 2004), and Ben Steil, *The Battle of Bretton Woods: John Maynard Keynes, Harry Dexter White and the Makings of a New World Order* (Princeton: Princeton University Press, 2014).

Cooperation, Conflict, and Crisis in the Contemporary International Monetary System

In May 2017, U.S. President Donald Trump tweeted that the United States was running a MASSIVE trade deficit with Germany. By late July, news reports suggested that the Trump administration was pressuring the International Monetary Fund to focus more attention on Germany's trade surplus which had surpassed China's as the world's largest. The Commission of the European Union added to the pressure that the German government was feeling, noting that the unprecedentedly large German current account surplus—more than 8 percent of GDP in 2016—was limiting that capacity for growth in other EU economies and calling for Germany to increase public and private investment in order to contribute to stronger growth throughout the EU. German Chancellor Angela Merkel and her economic team have resisted this pressure, and have remained committed to a tight fiscal policy that they had embraced in 2010. Indeed, in October of 2017, the German political parties that were trying to form a coalition agreement made a balanced budget their first priority.

This contemporary conflict between Germany and the U.S. and the broader EU reminds us that the more things change, the more they seem to remain the same. It doesn't take all that much imagination to see that Trump and Merkel are engaged in the same dispute that brought down the Bretton Woods System in the early 1970s. This is somewhat surprising because abandoning Bretton Woods was supposed to provide domestic economic autonomy and relegate such conflicts to the past. Shifting to floating exchange rates was supposed to provide domestic autonomy in two ways. First, governments hoped that a system of floating exchange rates would allow macroeconomic policies to pursue distinct objectives. Any current-account imbalances that emerged would be eliminated automatically through these exchange-rate movements.

No longer would governments be forced to alter their macroeconomic policies to eliminate payments imbalances.

Governments have found, however, that neither the shift to more flexible exchange rates nor the creation of a regional monetary system among deeply integrated European economies has prevented distributive conflicts of the kind that ultimately brought down the Bretton Woods system. The determination to set macroeconomic policy independent of foreign considerations has generated large current-account imbalances that in turn give rise to large cross-border capital flows, disruptive exchange-rate movements, and episodes of financial instability. These economic consequences in turn generate political pressure for policy coordination in order to correct the underlying imbalances. As a result, governments have found themselves engaged in the same types of distributive conflict that brought down the Bretton Woods system in the early 1970s.

This chapter examines how politics generates these imbalances, and how these imbalances drive the politics of cooperation and conflict in the contemporary international monetary system. We look first at the two episodes that have occurred within the broader international monetary system. The first unfolds during the 1980s, while the second begins in the late 1990s and ends with the great financial crisis of 2007–2009. We then turn our attention to monetary cooperation and conflict in the European Union (EU), tracing how disputes over distribution of the costs of exchange-rate stability have shaped the evolution of this regional monetary system.

From the Plaza to the Louvre: Conflict and Cooperation During the 1980s

The 1980s saw the emergence of global imbalances and distributive conflict over the adjustment of these imbalances that echoed the political dynamics that triggered the collapse of the Bretton Woods system. The 1970s had seen relatively small current-account imbalances in the major industrial countries that generally adjusted quickly. This period of relative balance gave way to an extended period of current-account imbalances in the early 1980s (Figure 11.1). After 1980, the United States developed the largest current-account deficit in the global economy. By 1984, the U.S. current-account deficit had widened to a then-record $100 billion. From there it deteriorated further, reaching $150 billion, or about 3.5 percent of GDP, by 1987. American deficits were offset by large current-account surpluses in Japan and Germany. Japan's current-account surplus increased steadily throughout the decade and at its peak equaled close to half of the American current-account deficit. Current-account surpluses emerged in Germany as well, though they lagged behind and were somewhat smaller than the surplus in Japan.

Current-account imbalances were a product of divergent macroeconomic policies in the three major industrial economies. In the United States, the Reagan administration entered office in 1981 and quickly cut taxes and increased military spending. The resulting expansion of the government budget deficit fueled domestic demand and pulled in imports. In contrast, governments placed macroeconomic policy on a more restrictive basis in Germany and Japan. German

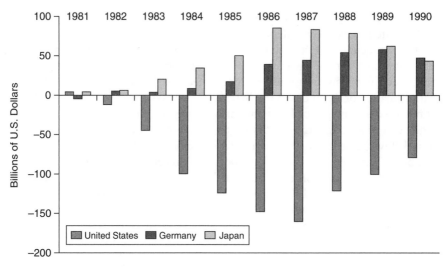

FIGURE 11.1
Current Account Imbalances, 1981–1990

Source: International Monetary Fund, IFS Online.

policymakers embarked on a period of fiscal consolidation beginning in 1981. Confronting large deficits inherited from the 1970s, a new conservative government took steps to return the government budget to balance. At the same time, the Bundesbank tightened monetary policy to combat inflation. The Japanese government also shifted from the rather expansionary policy orientation that had characterized the 1970s to fiscal retrenchment (Suzuki 2000). The government sought to restore its budget to surplus by 1985 and embraced a restrictive monetary policy as well. In both countries, restrictive macroeconomic policies generated large current account surpluses.

A Closer Look

Savings, Investment, and the Current Account

We can deepen our understanding of macroeconomic policy coordination by looking more closely at the relationship between fiscal policy and current-account imbalances. The standard Savings-Investment framework will help us do so. As we learned in Chapter 10, a country's current-account balance is equal to the difference between its national income and expenditures. The Savings-Investment framework builds on and refines this basic relationship to suggest that the current account is equal to the difference between national savings and national investment.

We can see this relationship by manipulating the standard national income identity. The national-income identity states:

$$Y = G + C + I + (X - M) \qquad (1)$$

In words, national income (Y) equals the sum of the government sector (G), private consumption expenditures (C), investment expenditures (I), and the current account (exports [X] minus imports [M]). National savings equals the portion of national income that is not consumed by government and individuals. Thus:

$$Y - (G - C) = I + (X - M) \qquad (2)$$

$$S = Y - (G + C)$$

And substituting

$$S = I + (X - M) \qquad (3)$$

Where S stands for national savings. Finally, we subtract I from both sides:

$$S - I = (X - M) \qquad (4)$$

The difference between national savings and national investment equals the current account. Increased savings or decreased investment improves the current account, while falling savings or increased investment worsens the current account.

Fiscal policy affects the current account via its impact on national savings. We can define private savings and government savings. We can define private savings

$$S_p = Y - C - T \qquad (5)$$

where T is taxes paid to the government. We can define government savings as

$$S_G = T - E \qquad (6)$$

where E is government expenditures. Government savings are thus a function of the budget balance. Tax revenues greater than expenditures (a budget surplus) generate government savings. Tax revenues less than expenditures (a budget deficit) generate government dissavings. Fiscal policy thus affects the current account balance directly. Assuming that all else remains constant, a larger budget deficit (or smaller surplus) worsens the current account. Conversely, a smaller budget deficit (or larger surplus) improves the current account.

It is important to recognize that the relationship between fiscal policy and the current account is indeterminate. Our conclusion that a change in fiscal policy produces an equivalent change in the current-account balance rests on the key assumption that all else remains constant. This means that a change in fiscal policy will affect the current account so long as neither private savings nor investment responds to the change in fiscal policy. Is this always a reasonable assumption? Individuals might recognize that a larger government deficit must eventually generate higher taxes and respond by saving more. Moreover, during the 1990s, the impact on the current account of a smaller budget deficit was offset by an investment boom that may in fact have been a consequence of lower interest rates induced by fiscal consolidation. Hence, although the savings-investment framework is a useful framework, it does not establish deterministic cause-and-effect relationships.

In spite of this qualification, the savings-investment framework helps us better understand the motivation for macroeconomic policy coordination. Governments discuss fiscal policy coordination as a means to adjust global current-account imbalances, because manipulation of tax and expenditures directly alters national savings rates and can affect current-account balances. It is not hard to understand why such coordination has proven difficult to achieve. Few issues pose greater domestic political obstacles to change than taxes and government programs.

Capital flows from Japan and Germany financed the U.S. current-account deficit. Foreign governments purchased an additional $184 billion of U.S. government-issued debt between 1980 and 1989. Foreign institutional investors acquired an additional $150 billion of government debt as well as an additional $400 billion of American corporate securities. By the end of the decade, American foreign debt to the rest of the world had increased from $440 billion to more than $2 trillion. As a consequence, the United States transitioned from a net international creditor to a net international debtor. A net international creditor country is one for which foreign assets owned by residents are greater than the total value of domestic assets owned by foreigners. As Figure 11.2 illustrates, the U.S. position as a net creditor diminishes as the decade progresses. By 1984, the U.S. had shifted into net debtor status and by the end of the decade, the United States net investment position stood at minus $260 billion.

The ability of the United States to attract capital flows from surplus countries depended upon ensuring that the return to investment was greater in the

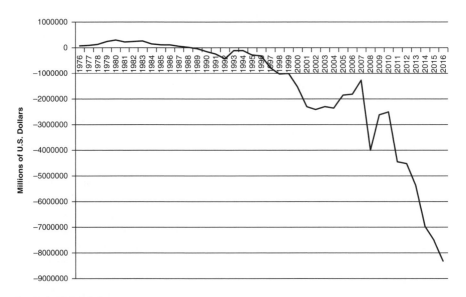

FIGURE 11.2

United States International Investment Position

Source: Bureau of Economic Analysis, 2017.

FIGURE 11.3

Dollar's Exchange Rate, 1980–2017

Source: Federal Reserve Bank, www.federalreserve.gov/releases/h10/Summary.

United States than in other economies. Consequently, in order to pull capital from Japan and Germany, the United States had to maintain relatively high real interest rates. Thus, as the U.S. budget and current-account deficits widened, interest rates rose in the United States. As capital flowed into the American economy in response, the dollar strengthened dramatically. Figure 11.3 depicts the dollar's value, on a trade-weighted basis, since 1980. From a postwar low in 1979, the dollar strengthened sharply after 1980. By 1985, the dollar had appreciated by 50 percent.

The Reagan administration did nothing to reduce the current-account deficit or reverse the dollar's appreciation during its first term in office. Although foreign governments were growing increasingly concerned about the imbalance and the soaring dollar, the Reagan team championed the dollar's rise as evidence of a strong American economy. This policy of benign neglect changed, however, as the series of record current-account deficits and strengthening dollar generated substantial protectionist pressure. Congressional hearing after congressional hearing decried the decline of American international competitiveness. Business and political elite attributed this decline to policies and practices of foreign governments, particularly of the foreign government with which the United States had its largest bilateral trade deficit—Japan. Hence, the trade imbalance generated a wave of Japan bashing that came to define U.S. trade policy for much of the decade (see Chapter 2). On the one hand, Congress pressured the Reagan administration to take steps to force a change in Japanese policy. The desired changes involved eliminating Japanese barriers to American imports and ending Japanese industrial policies perceived to give to Japanese firms an unfair advantage over their American competitors in global markets.

The Senate passed a bill by a 92–0 margin, for example, linking the ability of Japanese automakers to sell in the United States to market-opening initiatives in Japan. At the same time, the congressional and business elite threatened to raise trade barriers to protect American firms from unfair competition. A bill introduced in 1985 threatened to impose a 20 percent tariff rate on Japanese imports, and then reduce this rate by one point for each $1 billion improvement in the bilateral trade balance (Suzuki 2000, 140).

In 1985, the Reagan administration responded to the increasingly protectionist Congress by seeking an international solution to currency misalignments and current-account imbalances. The moment looked favorable. The dollar's appreciation appeared to have peaked, and in the spring of 1985 the dollar had actually begun to depreciate. Secretary of the Treasury James A. Baker III initiated discussions with the German, Japanese, British, and French governments to see whether they would be willing to cooperate in order to realign the dollar, yen, and mark (Funabashi 1988). Initial discussions led to a meeting of the G5 finance ministers at the Plaza Hotel in New York City on September 22, 1985. In a compact known as the **Plaza Accord,** the five governments agreed to reduce the value of the dollar against the Japanese yen and the German mark by 10 to 12 percent. To achieve this realignment, governments consented to intervene in the foreign exchange markets whenever it appeared that the market was pushing the dollar up. In other words, rather than pushing the dollar down, the G5 would try to prevent the market from pushing it up. They agreed to allocate $18 billion to these interventions, with the United States, Germany, and Japan each bearing 25 percent of the total costs, and Britain and France sharing the other 25 percent. Over the next 15 months, governments intervened in the foreign exchange market whenever the dollar's depreciation appeared to be slowing or threatening to reverse.

By early 1987, the dollar had fallen almost 40 percent from its peak. Governments moved to prevent further depreciation. Meeting at the French Ministry of Finance at the Louvre in Paris in February 1987, governments agreed to strive to stabilize exchange rates at their current values. This **Louvre Accord** marked the end of the period of realignment and the beginning of a conversation about whether governments could shift to more institutionalized exchange-rate cooperation moving forward. In particular, policymakers discussed the creation of a variant of fixed-but-adjustable exchange rates called a **target zone,** in which all currencies would have a central parity surrounded by wide margins—one prominent proposal advocated margins of plus or minus 10 percent—within which the exchange rate would be allowed to fluctuate (Williamson 1983; Solomon 1999). When a currency moved outside the margins, governments would be obligated to intervene in the foreign exchange market or to alter domestic interest rates in order to bring it back inside. The idea, which would require substantial and continuous policy coordination, failed to attract sufficient support. As a result, exchange rate cooperation fell off the global agenda.

Governments also embarked on discussions about and accepted some relatively broad commitments to coordinate monetary and fiscal policies in order to promote adjustment of the current account imbalances. The agreement reached in Paris called on the surplus countries to "follow policies designed to strengthen domestic demand and to reduce their external surpluses while maintaining price stability" (Group of 6 1987). For their part, deficit countries agreed to "follow policies designed to encourage steady, low-inflation growth while reducing their domestic imbalances and external deficits" (Group of 6 1987). In practice this meant that Germany and Japan were pressured to adopt more expansionary fiscal policies, largely by reducing taxes, in order to spur domestic demand and increase imports. For its part, the United States would adopt a more restrictive fiscal policy to reduce its budget deficit, thereby decreasing domestic demand and U.S. imports. In conjunction with the dollar's depreciation, the coordination of fiscal policies would promote current-account adjustment.

In practice, however, domestic politics frustrated the implementation of the agreement reached in Paris. In Japan, American pressure to adopt a more expansionary fiscal policy met little success through 1987 (Suzuki 2000). Baker had begun pressuring the Japanese government to adopt a more expansionary fiscal policy as early as 1985. Yet, with a majority of the ruling Liberal Democratic Party committed to fiscal consolidation, the Japanese government could not make substantial concessions to the United States. It took the combination of continued threats of protectionist measures by the U.S. Congress, a yen that continued to appreciate and thus weaken Japan's export competitiveness, and a worrying increase in Japanese unemployment before the Japanese government shifted course. By late 1987, the Japanese government had secured support for a 6 trillion yen fiscal stimulus.

Yet, as reluctant as the Japanese were to alter fiscal policy, they were the most willing and able of all of the governments to make adjustments. In the United States, disagreement between Congress and the administration about how to reduce the deficit blocked progress. The Democrats, who controlled Congress, wanted to reduce the deficit through a combination of higher taxes and reduced military expenditures. The Republican administration, however, preferred to trim other expenditures, with a particular emphasis on social programs. With each party pushing for alternative solutions, the result was deadlock:

> [b]oth parties called the deficits a scandal but could not agree on how to reduce them. The president remained adamantly against any further tax increases and held tenaciously to his defense buildup. The [House] Democrats wanted Social Security shielded from budget cutters and dug in their heels opposing further domestic program cuts.
>
> (LeLoup 2005, 82)

In Germany, macroeconomic stimulus was blocked by continued reluctance to jeopardize price stability. German policymakers pointed to prior experience with international coordination (Greenhouse 1987). During the late 1970s, for example, they had acceded to pressure exerted by the Carter administration and implemented a fiscal stimulus to help pull the world economy out of recession. The initiative had done little to produce growth, they argued, but did generate unwelcome inflation in Germany. Monetary stimulus was blocked by the German central bank, the Bundesbank. Bundesbank policymakers appeared to be split, although a minority recognized the need for German contribution to global adjustment. The majority of members, however, focused on German economic conditions and believed that using German monetary policy to promote global adjustment would merely stimulate inflation at home.

The inability and reluctance to implement the commitments made at Paris concerning macroeconomic policy generated tension between American and German policymakers that eventually spilled out into the public where it triggered financial market turbulence. In late September, policymakers met and agreed to maintain interest rates at then-current levels. Only 2 weeks later, however, the Bundesbank raised interest rates in Germany. The German action angered the Reagan administration. As Baker complained in front of the American press, German interest rate increases "were inconsistent with the spirit of" the agreements they had reached that year (Kilborn 1987). Higher interest rates, Baker argued, would slow the German economy, thereby reducing German demand for American products. The moves would therefore make it more difficult for the United States to reduce its current-account deficit. Baker suggested that the trend of higher interest rates in Germany might force the United States to allow the dollar to depreciate further in compensation.

Baker's remarks annoyed German policymakers. On the one hand, German officials noted that public criticism of currency values and interest rates was dangerous. Disagreement between the United States and Germany in public could easily trigger market unrest (Schmemann 1987). German officials also noted that the American trade deficit was not caused by German monetary policy. Its cause lay squarely in the U.S. government's budget deficit. According to the Germans, therefore, Baker might better focus on reducing the deficit rather than criticizing the Bundesbank. Finally, the Bundesbank noted that its interest rate increases were driven by market developments outside their control.

German concerns about the peril arising from airing grievances in public were prescient, for on the Monday following Baker's public criticism, equity markets around the world registered large, and in many cases, record losses. In Germany, equity markets tumbled by more than 7 percent; in Paris and Italy losses topped 6 percent. In Great Britain, the FTSE 100, the British equivalent to the American Dow Jones, lost 11 percent. The biggest slide came in the United States, however, where the Dow Jones Industrial Index lost 22.6 percent, its largest single-day loss since World War I. And although one should always be cautious when attributing financial sell-offs such as this to specific events, analysts seemed to agree that the financial turbulence was a direct market response to the evident inability of the United States and Germany to find a cooperative solution to global imbalances.

Financial turmoil brought about the policy changes that negotiations alone failed to achieve. The German Bundesbank cut a key interest rate and injected liquidity into the German financial system. In the United States, the deadlock between congressional Democrats and a Republican administration that had blocked meaningful deficit reduction broke. President Reagan announced his willingness to consider any proposal Congress might make. Congress moved quickly to convene a summit that would construct a political coalition around the elements of a deficit-reduction package. Out of this process came the Gramm-Rudman-Hollings Act, legislation that helped the United States place the budget on a deficit-reduction path during the late 1980s and early 1990s.

International monetary politics during the 1980s, therefore, provide neither domestic policy autonomy nor smooth painless adjustment of imbalances via exchange-rate movements. Instead, the decade brought large current-account imbalances as a result of governments pursuing divergent macroeconomic objectives. The large cross-border flows that financed these imbalances generated exchange-rate misalignments that aggravated the problem. And although governments agreed that these imbalances needed correction, they disagreed about who should change policy to correct them. In many respects, these disagreements arose from the impact of domestic politics on macroeconomic policymaking. The United States sought to push the burden of adjustment onto surplus economies. Governments in Japan and Germany resisted and pressed the United States to balance its budget. The conflict over who would adjust persisted until a public spat between the United States and Germany sparked massive turbulence in global equity markets.

GLOBAL IMBALANCES AND THE GREAT FINANCIAL CRISIS OF 2007–2009

The first decade of the twenty-first century saw the emergence of a second episode of large global imbalances, political conflict over the adjustment of these imbalances, and financial crisis. Figure 11.4 depicts the evolution of global current-account imbalances between 1996 and 2010. The improvement of the U.S. current-account position that had been achieved by the early 1990s reversed at the end of the decade. By the middle of the first Bush administration, the American current-account deficit had widened to more than $400 billion. The deficit then widened further, to slightly more than $800 billion in 2006, and then held steady at about $700 billion. As a share of American national income, these current-account deficits were larger than those of the 1980s, rising to 6 percent of GDP at their peak.

American current-account deficits were offset by surpluses in other economies. Japan and Germany were once again important surplus countries. What distinguishes this episode from the 1980s, however, is the emergence of new surplus countries in East Asia, with China assuming particular importance. East Asian economies began to run large current-account surpluses following the severe financial crisis they suffered in 1997 (see Chapter 15). By the turn of

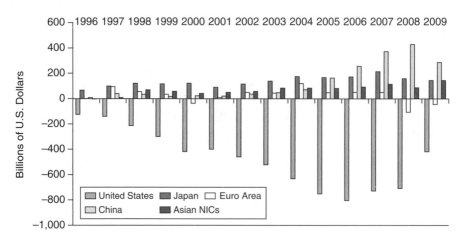

FIGURE 11.4

Current Account Imbalances, 1996–2009

Source: IMF. *World Economic Outlook Database*, April 2010.

the century, these emerging market economies had become some of the most important creditor countries in the global economy. China had emerged as the single largest supplier of credit to the United States.

The need to borrow from surplus economies to finance persistent current-account deficits increased American foreign indebtedness. Foreign government holdings of American government debt increased by 2.5 trillion between 1999 and 2008. Governments in China and other East Asia countries were among the largest purchasers of these assets. China alone accumulated more than $2 trillion of dollar reserves in the course of the decade. Foreign private institutions also accumulated substantial holdings of U.S. government debt and corporate securities. In fact, foreign holdings of non-government securities increased from $2.4 to $6.2 trillion between 1999 and 2007. As a result, the U.S. **international investment position** deteriorated sharply to –$2 trillion by 2007. Indeed, one big puzzle for the decade is why the U.S. international investment position stabilized after 2004 in spite of continued heavy borrowing.

As had been the case during the 1980s, imbalances and capital flows that financed them caused the dollar to strengthen against America's principal trading partners. As Figure 11.3 illustrates, the dollar had remained fairly stable for almost 10 years following the Louvre Accord. It began to strengthen toward the end of the 1990s as the current-account deficit widened. This appreciation continued during the first few years of the twenty-first century and peaked in 2002. Total appreciation approached 50 percent. From its peak in 2002, the dollar then lost value steadily until, by 2010, it had returned to the value it held during much of the 1990s.

Once again, the emergence of large current-account deficits and an appreciating dollar sparked protectionism in the United States. As the dollar peaked in value between 2000 and 2003, American producers faced intensifying import competition and turned to the political system for relief. As Jerry Jasinowski, President of the National Association of Manufacturers, argued,

> the overvaluation of the dollar is one of the most serious economic problems—perhaps the single-most serious economic problem—now facing manufacturing in this country. It is decimating U.S. manufactured-goods exports, artificially stimulating imports and putting hundreds of thousands of American workers out of work.
>
> (Phillips 2002, B17)

Business and political elite focused on the country with which the United States had its largest bilateral trade deficit: China. Congressional leaders focused particular attention on the undervalued Chinese currency. They argued that China's policy of pegging to the dollar at an undervalued rate constituted an unfair trade practice. Congress began considering remedies. Senators Sander Levin of Michigan, Lindsey Graham of South Carolina, and Chuck Schumer of New York championed such efforts. They proposed (though never managed to pass) a variety of trade policy responses, including a surcharge on Chinese imports, and changes to American law to enable producers to gain administered protection (anti-dumping and CVD duties) for currency manipulation. The dollar's appreciation therefore spilled over into trade politics, where it sparked demands for a "get tough on China" trade policy that would include the imposition of tariffs on goods from countries engaged in currency manipulation.

Congressional threats to impose trade barriers in response to the macroeconomic imbalance triggered action from the executive branch. One lever that Congress had over the Executive was the requirement that the Treasury report to Congress on foreign governments' exchange-rate policies twice each year. As the deadline for each report neared, Congress would press the administration to label China a currency manipulator. The process forced the Bush administration to take some action aimed at changing Chinese policy. The action that the Bush administration embraced was an international bargaining process that sought to realign currencies and alter macroeconomic policies to encourage gradual adjustment. The echoes of the Plaza process are clear.

The Bush administration attributed global imbalances, not to U.S. policy, but to what it called a "global savings glut," a reference to very high savings rates in Asia, and to China's determination to stabilize their currency against the dollar. Given this diagnosis, the administration pushed China to expand consumption and allow the RMB to appreciate against the dollar. This pressure came directly from the Bush administration in bilateral negotiations. Pressure came also through American efforts to focus the attention of the IMF on China's exchange-rate policy. The United States also pressed key European governments, especially Germany, to reduce current-account surpluses as part of the broader effort to narrow the global imbalance (Sobel and Stedman 2006).

Governments in surplus countries resisted U.S. pressure and sought changes in American policy. European governments attributed the U.S. current-account deficit to the federal government's budget deficit that emerged following the

Bush administration's large tax cut of 2001. Moreover, European governments (especially the German government) argued that because the euro area as a whole was in current-account deficit (Germany's current-account surplus was offset by deficits in the Mediterranean countries), global imbalances were not an EU issue. For its part, the Chinese government resisted American pressure to allow the RMB to appreciate, though they did shift to a more flexible crawling peg exchange-rate regime in the summer of 2005 (see Bowles and Wang 2008). They too tended to view the U.S. "global savings glut" argument with suspicion and suggested that the United States could adjust by balancing its budget. Because each government sought maximum policy change by others and minimum policy change at home, negotiations failed to generate policy changes that would reduce the magnitude of the imbalances.

Governments' reluctance to alter macroeconomic policies facilitated the development of the financial weaknesses that ultimately sparked the great financial crisis of 2007–2009. The connection between imbalances and the financial crisis lay in the flow of cheap and plentiful credit from the surplus countries to the United States at an unprecedented rate. The ability to borrow large volumes at low interest rates created credit conditions that typically generate asset bubbles. In the U.S. context, this asset bubble emerged in residential real estate. Mortgage lenders in the United States issued more than $1 trillion of new mortgages (and home equity lines of credit) a year in 2002 and 2006. As a result, investment in residential real estate as a share of GDP increased sharply. The surge of investment drove real estate prices up; nationwide, home prices rose by 60 percent between 2000 and the peak in 2006. The magnitude of this housing boom was unprecedented in American history.

Financial institutions channeled about one-third of these funds into real estate with complex financial instruments. Mortgage-backed securities and collateralized debt obligations allowed financial institutions to bundle mortgages with different risks into a single financial instrument and sell them to investors. This slicing and bundling created a single security that was itself a claim on a fairly diverse pool of mortgages. It was believed that these instruments enabled investors to choose how much risk they were willing to hold in their real estate lending. At the same time, credit default swaps, sold by insurers such as AIG, appeared to reduce the risk of mortgage lending even further by promising to repay loans if the original borrowers did not. And although these instruments sheltered investors from risk arising from isolated markets—such as increased loan defaults in one region of the country—they did not shelter investors from a nationwide collapse of real estate prices. Yet, financial institutions discounted the risk of a nationwide collapse of real estate prices because such an event had never before happened—at least not since the 1930s. The worst-case scenario they planned for was a large regional collapse, such as the crisis that occurred during the 1980s.

Yet, real estate prices did collapse nationwide, falling by almost 25 percent during 2007 and early 2008. By the end of 2008, the average price of residential real estate across the United States had fallen back to the pre-bubble price level. As home prices fell, the market value (though not the face value) of the securities issued to purchase real estate fell, too. Consequently, financial institutions that held these securities in large amounts suffered large losses. And because so many of these financial institutions had purchased securities with borrowed funds (called leverage), the losses they suffered as a consequence of falling real estate prices created debt-service difficulties. Debt-service problems extended the negative impact from the collapsing real estate bubble throughout the financial system. Finally, with foreclosures and defaults rising in frequency, AIG and other firms that had insured these assets found themselves on the hook for an amount they couldn't possibly pay out. As a consequence, by late 2007 some of the world's largest banks were reporting multibillion-dollar losses.

The crisis acquired a global dimension for three reasons. First, a few EU countries, such as Great Britain, Ireland, and Spain, experienced their own real estate bubbles that followed the same time line as the American bubble. Second, European financial institutions purchased mortgage-backed securities in large quantities. As a result, European financial institutions also suffered large losses from the collapse of the U.S. real estate bubble. Finally, the freezing of global credit markets following the bankruptcy of Lehman Brothers in the fall of 2008 made it difficult for all financial institutions to secure the credit needed to finance their activities. As credit dried up, interest rates on interbank lending rose sharply, a clear indication that all market participants, wherever they were based, were struggling to roll over their debt and otherwise secure financing.

As the crisis struck, governments and central banks tried to prevent the total collapse of the system. Initially, central banks injected liquidity into the banking system to smooth market turbulence. In August 2007, for instance, the European Central Bank, along with the Federal Reserve and the Bank of England, injected more than $200 billion into markets. Similar operations occurred in December 2007. As the crisis deepened, interventions became more heavy handed. Government regulators closed many banks rendered insolvent by their exposure to real estate. In other instances, policymakers worked feverishly to arrange the sale of large banks about to collapse. The Federal Reserve helped arrange the sale of the American investment bank Bear Stearns to J.P. Morgan Chase. The government helped negotiate the sale of Merrill Lynch to the Bank of America and the sale of Wachovia to Wells Fargo. The government tried, but failed, to find a buyer for Lehman Brothers, a failure that many suggest triggered the worst stage of the crisis during the fall of 2008.

Larger banks deemed "too big to fail" benefited from policies that channeled government funds to them to keep them alive—the so-called bailouts. In September 2008, for example, the U.S. government seized Freddie Mac and Fannie Mae, two government-sponsored agencies that were the largest purchasers of mortgage-backed securities in the United States. Treasury Secretary Henry Paulson noted that the two agencies were of such systemic importance that their failure would severely worsen the crisis and could even destroy the financial system. In November 2008, the U.S. government invested $20 billion in Citigroup in exchange for preferred stock and guaranteed $300 billion of Citigroup's debt. The U.S. government's Toxic Asset Relief Program, passed in late fall of 2008, provided more than $700 billion to purchase risky and hard-to-value assets from the largest banks.

Most broadly, governments held a series of G-20 summits to coordinate their responses to the crisis. Meeting first in Washington, DC, in November 2008 and then in London during April 2009, governments agreed to coordinate fiscal stimulus measures in order to boost economic activity in the wake of the financial turbulence. They also agreed to expand the IMF's lending capacity. Also of great importance, governments agreed to establish a Financial Stability Board charged with coordinating and monitoring efforts on the reform of financial regulation (Nelson 2009, 10–11).

Although this process produced little in the way of policy change, it did prompt a change in process. Following its creation in 1999 as a permanent forum in which developed and emerging market countries discussed issues of common concern, the G-20 remained second in importance as an arena behind the G-7. As imbalances gave way to financial crisis in 2008, however, European and American policymakers shifted management of the crisis as well as macroeconomic policy cooperation out of the G-7 and into the G-20 arena. And while some argue that this development was the natural consequence of the growing importance of emerging market countries, others suggest it reflected efforts by G-7 countries to enhance their bargaining power. European governments, some argue, wanted to bring China into the conversation in order to dilute American influence. The U.S. wanted to bring more countries into the process as a balance against Europe's numeric dominance of the G-7 (Nelson 2009, 5–6). At the G-20 summit in Pittsburgh in 2009, governments created a framework for policy coordination intended to prevent the re-emergence of large imbalances.

Policy Analysis and Debate

German Fiscal Policy and EU Growth

Question

Should Germany Loosen fiscal policy to promote growth in the EU?

Overview

The EU's economic recovery from the financial crisis that hit hard in 2008 has been slow. Initially, the European central bank responded to the financial crisis by lowering interest rates, and some governments, including Germany, embraced the logic of Keynesianism and implemented an expansionary fiscal policy. Meanwhile, the recession accentuated sovereign debt problems in southern European economies such as Greece, Spain, and Portugal. Faced with a possibility of debt default in these countries, EU governments agreed to extend emergency financing on the condition that the recipient governments enact austerity programs to reduce budget deficits through a combination of reduced government expenditures and tax increases.

The German government embraced a conservative fiscal policy at home in order to reinforce austerity in the periphery. Wolgang Schäuble, who was Minister of Finance between 2009 and 2017, was determined to balance the German budget for the first time since 1969, and after he achieved this goal in 2014 he remained committed to this policy of the "black zero." And while Schäuble has since moved to another position in German politics, developments indicate that the CDU remains committed to the black zero moving forward.

While such fiscal conservatism might have been an appropriate EU and German response to the series of sovereign debt crises that occurred in member countries between 2008 and 2010, it seems less appropriate today, almost 10 years after the crisis first struck. Indeed, the continuing commitment to tight fiscal policies by Germany makes it more difficult for other EU economies to realize their growth potential, to generate the export revenues required to service their debt, and thus to realize a full recovery from the extended period of austerity and adjustment. As one prominent economist has noted,

> its neighbors need German demand for their goods and services far more than they need Germany to set an example of fiscal prudence. It is clear—given the risk of a debt-deflation trap in Germany's eurozone partners—that successful adjustment in the eurozone can only come if German prices and wages rise faster than prices and wages in the rest of the eurozone.
>
> (Setser 2016)

As a result, many policymakers and technocrats that work in various international economic institutions are now encouraging Germany to move toward a less conservative fiscal policy.

Policy Options

- Encourage the EU, the IMF, and the U.S. to pressure the German government to embrace a more expansionary fiscal policy in order to reduce its current account surplus.
- Allow Germany to continue to embrace a fiscal policy that it considers best suited to the economic and political pressures in the German economy.

Policy Analysis

- What impact, if any, would a more expansionary German fiscal policy have on the credibility of the euro and the European banking system?
- Why might European governments hesitate to exert pressure on Germany regarding its fiscal policies?
- Does the United States have an interest in having Germany embrace a more expansionary fiscal policy?

Take A Position

- Which option do you prefer? Justify your choice.
- What criticisms of your position should you anticipate? How would you defend your recommendations against these criticisms?

Resources

Online: Do online searches for "European austerity." You can track discussion of
Germany's fiscal policy and its impact on the EU via your library's electronic
news databases. The *Financial Times* will contain particularly detailed coverage.

In Print: It might be useful, however, to read the history of previous financial crises.
A good starting point is Carmen M. Reinhart and Kenneth S. Rogoff, *This
Time Is Different: Eight Centuries of Financial Folly* (Princeton, NJ: Princeton
University Press, 2009). You can read about the impact of austerity in Mark
Blyth, *Austerity: The History of a Dangerous Idea* (New York: Oxford University
Press, 2013). See Yoichi Funabashi, *Managing the Dollar: From the Plaza to the
Louvre* (Washington, DC: Institute for International Economics, 1988) for an
excellent discussion of prior macroeconomic policy disputes.

These post-crisis policy and institutional reforms have not had much of
an impact on international macroeconomic cooperation and coordination.
Global imbalances did narrow in the immediate aftermath of the GFC, but
this reflected the collapses of demand in the global economy rather than far-
reaching international coordination. Global imbalances have remained stub-
bornly large since 2012, averaging close to 2 percent of world GDP each year.
The composition of the imbalance has changed, however. Especially significant has been the re-emergence of Germany as the economy with the world's
largest current account surplus—pushing China into second place in 2016.
We see less significant change on the deficit side, as the United States continues to post the world's largest current account deficits. The persistence of
these global imbalances has led once against to political conflict as the Trump
administration has pressured the German government (as well as China) to
take steps to reduce the German surplus or else face retaliatory measures from
the U.S.

Nor has the international monetary system shifted away from its reliance
upon the dollar as the primary reserve currency in any appreciable degree since
the crisis. And to some extent, the failure for this to occur may be the most
surprising post-crisis development. In the immediate aftermath of the 2008
crisis many observers predicted that the dollar's role as the international monetary system's primary reserve currency were numbered. They saw the euro and
the Chinese renminbi (RMB) as emerging rivals to the dollar's global status.
Arvind Subramanian (2011, 5), for instance, predicted in 2011 that the RMB
"could surpass the dollar as the premier reserve currency well before" 2025.
Many private investment managers share this belief—"I'll eat my hat if the
renminbi isn't the strongest currency on the planet over the next 10 years"
one London-based manager is reported to have said in 2014 (quoted in Cohen
2015, 214). Yet, the dollar has defied such expectations and retained its central
position. The dollar's resilience may have as much to do with the shortcomings
of the existing alternatives as with the inherent strength of the dollar. The eurozone has been mired in crisis since 2008, creating an uncertain future for the

euro; the Chinese financial system requires significant reforms before the RMB can play a large global role (Prasad 2016).

International monetary politics during the last 40 years have been characterized by a recurring pattern of political conflict sparked by large and persistent global imbalances. In general, this pattern is driven by divergent macroeconomic objectives in the world's largest economies that create trade imbalances. The large cross-border capital flows that finance these trade imbalances produce substantial exchange-rate misalignments that aggravate the problem. And although governments have agreed that imbalances are unsustainable and potentially quite dangerous to global economic stability, they disagree about who should change policy to correct them. The United States repeatedly tries to push adjustments onto surplus economies. Governments in the surplus economies resist adjustment and press the United States to adopt policy changes. Because all parties refused to adjust, imbalances generate financial imbalances that increase the chances of suffering a significant financial crisis like the GFC of 2008–2009. Although GFC made governments keenly aware of the risks attached to persistent global imbalances, governments remain very reluctant to coordinate policy to minimize the chances of a repeat.

EXCHANGE-RATE COOPERATION IN THE EUROPEAN UNION

Within the EU, cooperation has been more common than conflict. EU governments in the EU have pursued formal and institutionalized exchange-rate cooperation since the late 1970s. European governments have desired more stable intra-European exchange rates for two reasons. First, exchange-rate instability is costly for the typical EU country, which is highly open to trade and which trades most with other EU countries. As a result, exchange-rate movements within the EU are more disruptive to individual economies in the EU than in the broader international monetary system (see Frieden 1996). In other words, the cost of floating in the EU is so high that European governments are more willing to sacrifice domestic autonomy to stabilize their exchange rates.

Yet, even within this tightly integrated regional economy, governments have found that their willingness to stabilize exchange rates has been a consequence of the extent to which they share common macroeconomic policy objectives. Throughout most of the last 30 years, most European governments did not consider the loss of domestic economic autonomy to be very costly. Meaningful costs arise when governments want to pursue different monetary policies but cannot. During the 1970s, for example, EU governments moved on divergent paths. Some, such as the French and the Italians, pursued expansionary macroeconomic policies that boosted inflation. Others, such as Germany and the Netherlands, were more conservative and emphasized the maintenance of low inflation. With each government committed to different policy objectives, a common exchange-rate system would have been quite costly.

By the late 1970s, most EU governments believed that reducing inflation had to be their chief objective, and as a consequence, almost all governments used monetary policy to restrict inflation. Because all governments were pursuing low inflation, all could participate in a common exchange-rate system without any having to sacrifice the ability to pursue a desired policy objective. Thus, the cost of participating in a fixed exchange-rate system was quite low. As EU government policy objectives converged, therefore, they found it easier to create and maintain a common exchange-rate system. Moreover, and for reasons we explore in detail in Chapter 13, governments thought that participating in a fixed exchange-rate system would help them achieve and maintain price stability. The resulting exchange-rate system, called the **European monetary system** (EMS), began operation in 1979. The EMS was a fixed-but-adjustable system in which governments established a central parity against a basket of EU currencies called the European Currency Unit (ECU). Central parities against the ECU were then used to create bilateral exchange rates between all EU currencies. EU governments were required to maintain their currency's bilateral exchange rate within 2.25 percent of its central bilateral rate.

In practice, the EMS revolved around German monetary policy. The Bundesbank was reluctant to participate in the EMS because it was concerned that it would be forced to continually intervene in the foreign exchange market to support the weaker European currencies. Continued intervention to defend these weaker currencies would raise German inflation, just as intervention to defend the dollar had done under Bretton Woods. German participation in the EMS was secured, therefore, by allowing the Bundesbank to use German monetary policy to maintain low inflation in Germany. Other EU governments would alter their monetary policies in order to maintain the peg to the mark. The burden of maintaining fixed exchange rates therefore fell principally upon the countries with high inflation. Other EU governments accepted this arrangement, in part because they had created the EMS to help them reduce inflation. Pegging their currencies to the German mark, therefore, would force EU governments and central banks to mimic Germany's low-inflation monetary policy stance. Over time, therefore, inflation rates throughout the EU would converge on inflation rates in Germany.

Few observers initially gave the EMS much chance of success. Inflation rates averaged just above 10 percent in EU countries, whereas German inflation stood below 5 percent. Such divergent rates of inflation, reflecting substantially different monetary policies, could easily pull the system apart. Indeed, the EMS got off to a rocky start. Currency realignments were frequent in the system's first year of operation, and a conflict between France and Germany almost destroyed the system in 1981–1983. Conflict arose when newly elected French president, François Mitterrand, adopted an expansionary macroeconomic policy in 1981. This expansion caused French inflation to rise, the French balance of payments to deteriorate, and the franc to weaken in the EMS. Mitterrand blamed the franc's weakness on the restrictive macroeconomic policies pursued in Germany (and the other EU countries), refused to alter French policy, and demanded that Germany loosen its policy in line with France. After 18 months of uncertainty about whether Mitterrand would remove the franc from the system or accept the system's constraints, he reversed course and adopted restrictive macroeconomic policies. The EMS stabilized in the following years. Inflation rates converged, and currency realignments became infrequent. The EMS had defied its critics' expectations. The EMS worked, however, primarily because its member governments placed high value on stable exchange rates and because they all gave priority to the same domestic objective: keeping inflation low. Consequently, participation in the system did not require any government to give up the pursuit of its domestic objectives.

Conflict among EMS participants emerged as perceptions of the cost of participation in the system changed. By the late 1980s, many EU governments were becoming dissatisfied with the Bundesbank's role in the EMS. EU governments were content to place Germany at the center of the EMS as long as they were striving to reduce inflation. They were less content with this asymmetry once inflation had come down. Many governments began to question why the Bundesbank should continue to set monetary policy for the system as a whole. They argued that the Bundesbank should be required to conduct a share of the foreign exchange market intervention necessary to stabilize the mark in the EMU. In addition, because German monetary policy was transmitted by the EMS throughout the EU, the other EU governments argued that they should have some influence over that policy. By 1987, France and Italy, along with some officials in the European Commission, were suggesting that it was time to reform the EMS in order to reduce Germany's privileged role in the system (Oatley 1997). The parallel to French and German criticism of U.S. monetary policy under the Bretton Woods system during the late 1960s is striking.

Dissatisfaction with the distribution of the costs of exchange-rate stability in conjunction with an unwillingness to revert back to more flexible exchange rates created pressures to change EU exchange-rate institutions. Momentum for such institutional reform was reinforced by the reinvigoration of European integration. Apart from the EMS, EU governments had launched few new initiatives during the 1970s, as the oil shock, the collapse of the Bretton Woods system, and economic stagnation made few governments willing to further integrate their economies. EU governments relaunched integration in the mid-1980s by eliminating the remaining barriers to intra-EU flows of products, labor, and capital. The Single European Act, as this initiative was called, gave rise to pressure for **monetary union** because many EU officials believed that the gains from a single market could be realized only with a single currency (see Emerson 1992). Monetary union thus emerged from dissatisfaction with the distribution of costs within the EMS and gained momentum from the broader effort to complete the single market.

Germany, and in particular the Bundesbank, was reluctant to pursue deeper monetary cooperation. The Bundesbank's concerns were fundamentally similar to those that caused it to be reluctant about participation in the

EMS: it feared that EMU would force Germany to accept higher inflation than it desired. The Bundesbank recognized that in a monetary union it would share control of monetary policy with all EU members. It believed that many EU governments were willing to tolerate higher inflation than it considered ideal. Bundesbank policymakers were particularly concerned about joining a monetary union alongside Mediterranean economies. Greece, Italy, Portugal, and Spain all had substantial government budget deficits and large debt burdens as well as persistently high inflation. In addition, the business cycle in these Mediterranean economies was not well synchronized with Northern Europe. As a consequence, Bundesbank policymakers were concerned that participating in a monetary union with the Mediterranean countries would necessarily force Germany to accept monetary policies that were not well suited to the German economy. As a result, Germany would have to accept a higher inflation rate than it considered necessary.

Although the Bundesbank opposed monetary union, it appears that narrow monetary objections were trumped by broader geopolitical considerations. The pressure to create a European monetary union emerged just as the Berlin Wall collapsed. The French government saw the collapse of the Berlin Wall as an opportunity to achieve monetary union. They therefore conditioned French support for German political and economic reunification on German support for monetary union. German Chancellor Helmut Kohl's determination to reunify Germany led him to subordinate the Bundesbank's specific monetary objections to his conception of Germany's broader interests. Germany would thus unify and simultaneously commit itself more deeply to the European integration project.

Once Bundesbank policymakers recognized that they could not prevent German participation in monetary union, they sought to craft monetary institutions that would safeguard its conception of Germany's economic interests. In particular, Bundesbank policymakers pushed for rules to govern the new European Central Bank (ECB) that would insulate its monetary policy decisions from politics. They pushed for a set of convergence criteria that they believed might prevent the Mediterranean countries from qualifying for membership in monetary union. They pushed for rules that required members to pursue relatively conservative fiscal policies. Finally, the Bundesbank insisted that the ECB be prohibited from purchasing government debt, a necessary check that would prevent governments from creating inflation by running large fiscal deficits. In short, Bundesbank policymakers did everything they could to ensure that monetary union would not generate inflation in Germany.

For the first 10 years of monetary union, the Bundesbank's ability to shape EMU institutions appeared to have secured Germany's interests. Inflation remained low across Europe and there were few indications that the Mediterranean countries were impinging on Germany's ability to pursue its economic policy objectives. The only source of disagreement among the system's governments during the euro's first few years involved the currency's external value, and here the ECB refused to actively encourage euro depreciation. This calm collapsed into heated conflict in 2009, however, as severe sovereign debt problems emerged in the Mediterranean countries. Portugal, Ireland, Italy, Greece, and Spain had all borrowed heavily from international lenders between 2000 and 2008. Capital inflows generated robust growth and asset bubbles, very much like the experience of the United States. When these asset bubbles popped in 2008, these economies fell into severe recession and faced mounting debt service problems. As debt service problems emerged, EU governments battled over how the costs of adjustment in the face of this debt problem should be distributed between northern and southern European economies.

The conflict is well illustrated by the case of Greece, the first to experience a severe debt crisis. The Greek government borrowed heavily from foreign lenders to fund budget and current account deficits. Between 2000 and 2008, Greek budget deficits averaged 5 percent of GDP and its current account deficits averaged 9 percent of GDP (Nelson, Belkin, and Mix 2010). Borrowing to cover these deficits pushed Greece's external debt to 115 percent of GDP by 2008. This already precarious financial position worsened in 2009 as the Greek economy moved into recession. With government expenditures rising and government revenues falling, the budget deficit rose to 13 percent of GDP. The announcement of this large deterioration caused markets to question whether Greece could service its debt. Consequently, the Greek government found it more expensive and more difficult to borrow. Indeed, by early 2010 interest rates on Greek government debt were 400 basis points higher than rates on equivalent German government debt—a clear sign of the market's loss of confidence in Greece's ability to service its debt. It looked increasingly likely that the Greeks would be driven to default.

The Greek debt crisis brought into the open for the first time a distributive conflict that had always been implicit in the EU's monetary union. This distributive conflict focused on one central question: who would bear the cost of Greek's excessive debt burden? Would Greece default, thereby pushing the cost onto the institutions and individuals that held Greek debt? Would Greece implement an austerity program to eliminate its budget and current account deficits and thereby generate the funds needed to service its foreign debt? Would other EU governments lend to Greece so it could service its foreign debt without adopting harsh austerity measures? This option would eventually shift the risk of a Greek default from private financial institutions to taxpayers in Germany, France, and other northern European countries. If the Greek government were to default on loans from the EU, residents in these EU countries would have to pay. Would the ECB depreciate the euro, thereby improving Greece's international competitiveness and enabling it to embark on an export-led recovery? Although a weaker euro might benefit Greece, which lacks international competitiveness, a weaker euro would generate inflation in northern Europe.

EU governments have struggled to select among these alternatives. The Greek government asserted that in the absence of financial assistance, it would be forced to default. The so-called troika, the ECB, the EU Commission, and the IMF made it clear that any loans to Greece would necessitate Greek austerity measures. These negotiations unfolded under the shadow of similar sovereign debt problems in Spain, Portugal, and Italy. If Germany went easy on Greece, this would signal other indebted governments that they could expect easy terms as well. This signal would possibly encourage other governments to dump their debt burdens on the broader EU membership. Determined to avoid sending this signal, the Germans bargained hard, demanding stiff austerity measures as the price of EU assistance. By late spring of 2010, Greece and the troika had reached agreement on a package that included a $146 billion loan from the EU and the IMF and a set of fairly stringent austerity measures intended to reduce the budget deficit by 7 percent of GDP.

This first agreement failed to resolve the set of problems that had precipitated the crisis and in fact had the unintended consequence of deepening Greece's economic woes, destabilizing the Greek democracy, and undermining support for the euro throughout the EU. On the one hand, the austerity measures that the troika insisted upon, those in 2010 as well as subsequent measures negotiated in 2011 and 2013, pushed the Greek economy into a debt deflation. As the Greek government cut spending and raised taxes, Greek national income fell sharply. Indeed, according to the World Bank, Greek GDP fell by 45 percent between 2008 and 2011, collapsing from $354 billion to $195 billion. And though Greek debt was written down, the scale of the forgiveness was relatively small. And as a consequence, Greece's debt to GDP ratio rose dramatically, from 126 percent of national income in 2009 to 177 percent in 2014, even though Greek debt had increased by only 6 percent (Krugman 2015). The economic contraction and the dismantling of the Greek public sector undermined public support for the traditional Greek political parties and created an environment that allowed the leftist party Syriza to win the January 2015 election and create a coalition government with a right-wing populist party.

The new Greek government almost immediately sought to renegotiate the terms of Greece's adjustment. The new prime minister, Alex Tsipras, and his Finance Minister, Yanis Varoufakis, demanded a large write down of Greek debt and an easing of the austerity measures. The troika remained committed to the pre-election approach and refused to amend the terms of Greece's agreement or soften the terms of a new agreement under discussion. As negotiations deadlocked in late June, Greece defaulted on a scheduled payment to the IMF and the Greek financial system lapsed back into a crisis environment. The government responded by closing the banks, imposing measures that restricted capital outflows from Greece, and calling for a national referendum on the terms of the troika's new austerity package. The referendum took place on July 5, and about 60 percent of those who turned out voted against the troika plan. Though Tsipras had hoped that a resounding "no" would strengthen his hand in negotiations with the troika, the worsening economic conditions in Greece and a growing impatience among the troika ultimately forced him to accept even more stringent measures than had been on offer in the pre-referendum package. Tsipras was then able to convince a majority of the Greek parliament that exit from the eurozone would be even more of a disaster than austerity, and the parliament approved the new austerity package.

The Greek debt crisis thus raises a set of much broader questions about the viability of the EMU. The core question at the base of the issue is whether it is reasonable for governments to accept the constraints imposed by monetary union or whether they wouldn't be better off with greater exchange rate flexibility. If Greece were not a member of the monetary union, it could devalue its currency to regain export competitiveness. And while this wouldn't eliminate entirely the need for austerity measures, it might enable fiscal policy adjustment to occur in a growing rather than contracting economy. Moreover, more flexible currency arrangements would have obviated the need for other EU member governments to find a solution to the Greek debt problem. Hence, the Greek crisis has regenerated a discussion about whether the EU should be a monetary union and, if so, who should be a member.

CONCLUSION

Developments in the contemporary international monetary system reflect the same dynamics that shaped developments under the Bretton Woods system. In concrete terms, the United States continues to run large current account deficits. American deficits continue to be offset by large surpluses in Germany, Japan, and more recently China. These global imbalances generate conflict. The United States continually pressures its largest creditors, Japan and Germany in the 1980s and Germany and China in the 2000s, to alter policies to promote adjustment. Creditor governments in turn pressure the United States to put its government finances in order. The refusal by all governments to make meaningful policy adjustments generates financial instability—a sharp drop in equity prices in one case and a severe crisis of the global financial system in another. In more abstract terms, developments in the contemporary international monetary system are driven by distributive conflict between governments in creditor and in debtor economies over who should bear the costs of adjustment.

Moreover, the experience of EU governments indicates that distributive conflicts are endemic to international monetary systems rather than a consequence of disagreements among specific governments. For even when governments place great value on exchange-rate stability, exchange rate cooperation has been profoundly shaped by distributive conflict. Indeed, the EU's transition to monetary union was shaped in large part by a desire to redistribute the costs of exchange-rate stability. The ongoing debt problems in Ireland, Greece, and other Mediterranean economies indicate that different macroeconomic policy objectives in northern and southern Europe continue to shape the system's evolution. In the broader international monetary system as well as in the regional systems, the imbalances themselves, as well as the conflict about who should adjust to eliminate them, emerge from the way domestic politics shape macroeconomic policies.

Against the backdrop of these constant characteristics of the international monetary systems, we see substantial change over the past few years. Of particular importance has been China's emergence as a fundamentally important creditor country in the international monetary system. China's emergence in this capacity has affected American policy—shifting American focus from Germany and Japan to China. It has also affected global governance structures. The broadening of the policy coordination process from the Group of 7 to the Group of 20 is symbolic of this change. More fundamentally, China's emergence as a creditor country has placed an emerging market economy in the center of the international monetary system for the first time in its history. It will be interesting to follow the impact of this change in the years to come.

KEY TERMS

European Monetary System

International Investment Position

Louvre Accord

Monetary Union

Plaza Accord

Target Zone

SUGGESTIONS FOR FURTHER READING

For a positive evaluation of how states responded to the 2008–2009 global financial crisis, see Daniel W. Drezner, *The System Worked: How the World Stopped Another Great Depression* (Oxford: Oxford University Press, 2014).

Jonathan Kirshner's *American Power after the Financial Crisis* (Ithaca, NY: Cornell University Press, 2014), evaluates the dollar's future in the wake of the crisis. On the Renminbi's possible increased role in the international monetary system, see Eswar S. Prasad, *Gaining Currency: The Rise of the Renminbi* (Oxford: Oxford University Press, 2017).

For those interested in the European monetary system, see Emmanuel Mourlon-Druol, *A Europe Made of Money: The Emergence of the European Monetary System* (Ithaca: Cornell University Press, 2012). On the EU and the Greek crisis, see Yanis Varoufakis' *Adults in the Room: My Battle with Europe's Deep Establishment* (New York: Farrar Strauss and Giroux, 2017), and C. Randall Henning, *Tangled Governance: International Regime Complexity, the Troika, and the Euro Crisis* (Oxford: Oxford University Press, 2017).

A Society-Centered Approach to Monetary and Exchange-Rate Policies

O ur focus on the international monetary system in the last two chapters hinted at but did not deeply explore an important question—what
determines the specific exchange-rate policies that governments adopt?
Why do some governments fix their exchange rate while others float? Why
do some governments prefer strong, and maybe even overvalued currencies,
whereas others prefer weak and undervalued currencies? We take up this question in this chapter and the next by examining two approaches to monetary
and exchange-rate politics rooted in domestic politics. This chapter develops
a society-centered approach. The society-centered approach argues that governments' monetary and exchange-rate policies are shaped by politicians'
responses to interest-group demands. The European Union (EU)'s willingness
to fix exchange rates reflects EU governments' responses to the demands of
domestic interest groups. The American reluctance to fix the dollar, or even
to do much to stabilize it, reflects American policymakers' responses to the
demands of American interest groups.

To understand the political dynamics of this competition, the society-
centered approach emphasizes the interplay between organized interests and
political institutions. The approach is based on the recognition that monetary policy and exchange-rate movements have distributional consequences.
For example, when the dollar rose in value against America's largest trading
partners by about 30 percent between 2011 and 2017, some groups benefited
and some suffered. American businesses and consumers could import goods at
lower prices. This translated into higher real incomes for consumers, and lower
production costs for businesses. The strong dollar hurt others as American
exporters found it increasingly difficult to sell at profitable prices in foreign

and domestic markets. Eastman Machine, a Buffalo, New York based man-ufacturer of a range of cutting machines, reported that it faced strong pres-sure in its European markets to offer steep discounts on its prices. And in the American market, Eastman found its clients threatening to purchase from its foreign competitors unless Eastman could cut its prices to match. For Eastman Machine and other exporters, the strong dollar reduced earnings and incomes.

These distributional consequences generate political competition as the winners and losers turn to the political arena to advance and defend their economic interests. Businesses that benefit from a weak dollar pressure the government for policies that will keep the dollar undervalued against foreign currencies. Businesses that benefited from a strong dollar, such as the Wall Street firms that gained from importing foreign capital, lobbied to keep the dollar strong. Exactly how this competition unfolds—which groups organ-ize to lobby, what coalitions arise, how politicians respond to interest-group demands, which groups' interests are reflected in monetary and exchange-rate policy, and which groups' interests are not—are shaped by specific characteris-tics of the political institutions within which the competition unfolds.

This chapter develops this society-centered approach to monetary and exchange-rate policy. We focus first on the trade-off between domestic eco-nomic autonomy and exchange-rate stability. We examine how changes in political institutions and innovations in economic theory combined to create incentives for governments to value domestic autonomy more than exchange-rate stability. The chapter then explores three society-centered models of mon-etary and exchange-rate policy. We conclude by considering some weaknesses of this approach.

ELECTORAL POLITICS, THE KEYNESIAN REVOLUTION, AND THE TRADE-OFF BETWEEN DOMESTIC AUTONOMY AND EXCHANGE-RATE STABILITY

We learned in the previous two chapters that governments confront a trade-off between exchange-rate stability and domestic economic autonomy. To main-tain a fixed exchange rate, a government must surrender its ability to manage the domestic economy. To manage the domestic economy, a government must accept a floating exchange rate. Although this trade-off has always been present, it is only since the 1920s that governments have chosen domestic eco-nomic autonomy over exchange-rate stability. Prior to World War I, most gov-ernments sacrificed domestic economic autonomy to maintain fixed exchange rates in the gold standard. Our first goal is to understand how changes in domestic politics and economic theory that occurred during the interwar period led governments to place greater value on domestic economic autonomy and to attach less importance to exchange-rate stability.

The transformation of electoral systems—the rules governing who has the right to vote—throughout Western Europe following World War I fundamentally changed the balance of power in domestic political systems. This new balance of power had tremendous repercussions on government attitudes toward economic management. Prior to World War I, electoral systems in most West European countries were extremely restrictive. The right to vote was generally limited to males, usually aged 25 years or older, who met explicit property or income conditions. In European countries with parliamentary governments, less than one-quarter of the total male population in the relevant age group met these conditions. In Great Britain, for example, only 3.3 percent of the population could vote until 1884; reforms enacted in 1884 extended the right to vote to only about 15 percent of the population. Even in Denmark, where the right to vote was much broader, mass participation was restricted to lower house elections (the *Folketing*), and the monarch did not have to respect lower house majorities in forming governments (Miller 1996).

European electoral systems were substantially reformed after World War I. By 1921, restrictive property-based electoral rules had been eliminated and universal male suffrage had been adopted in all West European countries. Changes in electoral laws had a profound impact on the constellation of political parties in West European parliaments. Table 12.1 displays the share of parliamentary seats held by each of the major political parties in a

TABLE 12.1

Percentages of Seats Held by Parties in Parliament, Pre- and Post-World War I

	1870–1900	1920–1930
Belgium	Catholic (46%–93%)	Catholic (40%)
	Liberals (4%–53%)	Liberals (12%–15%)
		Workers Party (35%–40%)
Denmark	Liberals (60%–75%)	Social Democrats (32%–40%)
	Conservatives (25%–30%)	Liberals (30%–35%)
		Conservatives (16%–20%)
France	Republicans (60%–80%)	Republican Union (30%–35%)
		Socialists (16%–25%)
		Radical Socialists (17%–25%)
Germany	Center (20%)	Social Democrats (20%–30%)
	National Liberals (12%–30%)	National People's Party (20%)
	Conservatives (10%–20%)	Center (13%)
		People's Party (10%)
Netherlands	Liberals Union (35%–53%)	Catholics (28%)
	Catholics (25%)	Social Democrats (20%)
	Anti-revolutionary (15%–25%)	Anti-revolutionary (12%)
Britain	Conservatives (37%–50%)	Conservatives (40%–67%)
	Liberals (26%–48%)	Labour (30%–47%)

Source: Mackie and Rose 1991.

few West European countries before and after World War I to illustrate this political transformation. Prior to World War I, political parties of the right— Conservatives, Liberals, and Catholics—dominated European parliaments. After World War I, leftist parties—Socialists, Social Democrats, and Labour— became large, and in some instances, the largest parliamentary parties in the West European countries. This shift in the balance of political power within European parliaments altered the pattern of societal interests that were represented in the political process. Before World War I, the propertied interests represented by the political parties of the right had a virtual monopoly on political power, whereas the interests of workers were all but excluded from the political process.

Following World War I, however, working-class interests gained an authoritative voice in national parliaments. As a consequence, governments were forced to respond for the first time to the demands of workers in order to maintain their hold on political power. And workers, who on average hold little wealth and whose standard of living thus depends heavily on their weekly pay, have less concern about inflation than propertied interests, whose real value of wealth is eroded by inflation. What workers care about are the employment opportunities available to them and the wages they earn in these jobs. The rise of worker power therefore created political incentives for governments to adopt economic policies that would raise employment and keep wages relatively high. Such policies were not always consistent with a continued commitment to the gold standard. The shift in political power produced by electoral reform, therefore, created political incentives to move away from the rigid constraints of a fixed exchange-rate system to avoid the domestic costs of balance-of-payments adjustment.

The second important change during the interwar period arose from revolutionary ideas in economic theory that emerged during the 1930s. These ideas provided a compelling theoretical rationale for governments to use monetary policy to manage the domestic economy. John Maynard Keynes spurred this revolution in his role as academic economist. Keynes's most influential work was shaped by his observations of the British economy during the 1920s and 1930s. What Keynes focused on in particular was unemployment. British unemployment rose to about 20 percent in the early 1920s and never fell below 10 percent during the remainder of the decade (Skidelsky 1994, 130; Temin 1996). Such persistently high rates of unemployment defied the expectations of the standard economic theory, neoclassical economics.

Neoclassical economics argued that such persistent high unemployment was impossible because markets have equilibrating mechanisms that keep the economy at full employment. High unemployment meant that the demand for labor was lower than the supply of labor at the prevailing wage rate. Because labor markets are no different from any other market, an imbalance between supply and demand should give rise to an adjustment process that eliminates the imbalance. In this case, the excess supply of labor represented by high unemployment should cause the price of labor—wages—to fall. As the price of labor falls, the demand for labor will increase. Eventually such adjustments will guide the economy back to full employment. In neoclassical theory, therefore, unemployment was expected to give rise to an automatic adjustment process that would lead the economy back to full employment.

The persistence of high unemployment in interwar Britain caused Keynes to re-evaluate the neoclassical explanation of unemployment (Lekachman 1966; Skidelsky 1994). Keynes's thinking culminated in a book written in the early 1930s (and published in 1936) called *The General Theory of Employment, Interest, and Money*, which challenged neoclassical economics in two connected ways (Keynes 1936). First, Keynes suggested that neoclassical economists were wrong to think that an economy would always return to full employment automatically. For reasons that we explore in a moment, Keynes argued that an economy could get stuck at an equilibrium characterized by underutilized production capacity and high unemployment. Second, Keynes argued that governments need not accept persistent high unemployment. Instead, governments could use macroeconomic policy—monetary policy and fiscal policy—to restore the economy to full employment.

According to Keynes, economies can get stuck at high levels of unemployment because of the fragility of investment decisions. Investment expenditures typically account for about 20 percent of total national expenditures. Variation in investment expenditures, therefore, can have an important influence on the overall level of economic activity: when investment rises, the economy grows, and when investment falls, the economy stagnates. Investment decisions, in turn, are strongly influenced by firms' expectations about the future demand for their products. When firms expect future demand to be strong, they will invest and the economy will experience robust growth. When firms expect future demand to be weak, however, they will make few new investments and economic growth will slow. If an economy is hit by some sort of shock that causes domestic demand to collapse and unemployment to rise, firms will develop very pessimistic forecasts of the demand for their products in the future. New investments will not be made and the economy will remain stuck at a high level of unemployment. This, according to Keynes, is what had happened to Britain during the 1920s.

Because Keynes believed that the cause of persistent high unemployment ultimately lay in inadequate demand for goods, he proposed that governments use fiscal and monetary policy to manage aggregate demand. Aggregate demand is the sum of all consumption and investment expenditures made by the government, by domestic and foreign consumers, and by producers. Governments manage aggregate demand with fiscal and monetary policies. Fiscal and monetary policies each affect aggregate demand in different ways. Fiscal policy affects aggregate demand directly. When the government cuts taxes without reducing expenditures, aggregate demand increases because private individuals' consumption expenditures increase by some proportion of the tax reduction. When the government increases its expenditures without raising taxes, total government expenditures rise. The additional demand for goods and services that results from these increased expenditures causes firms to hire more workers to produce the additional goods being demanded.

Monetary policy affects aggregate demand indirectly by changing domestic interest rates. An increase in the money supply will cause the domestic interest rate to fall. Lower interest rates make it cheaper to borrow. As the cost of borrowing falls, the demand for investment-related expenditures, such as new homes and high-price consumer items like cars, rises because these are usually purchased with credit and are therefore sensitive to the interest rate. Firms will hire more workers in order to produce the higher level of output being demanded. A monetary expansion, therefore, will lead to falling interest rates, lower interest rates will increase aggregate demand, and increased aggregate demand will cause output and employment to rise.

In short, Keynes argued that by spending when others would not or by increasing the money supply to induce others to spend, the government could increase demand in the economy. By increasing total demand in the economy, investment would rise and unemployment would fall. Thus, by using macroeconomic policy to manage aggregate demand, governments could keep the economy running at full employment. Keynes's *General Theory* therefore represented a substantial challenge to the prevailing wisdom about the role governments could and should play in managing the domestic economy. Neoclassical economists saw the market economy as an inherently stable system that would return automatically to full employment following a shock that raised unemployment. There was therefore no need for active government management of the economy. In contrast, Keynes saw the market economy as potentially unstable and susceptible to large and sustained departures from full employment. Such an unstable economic system needed a stabilizer, and in Keynes's vision governments could perform this stabilizing function by using macroeconomic policy to manage aggregate demand. In one remarkable book, Keynes "rewrote the content of economics and transformed its vocabulary ... [He] informed the world that fatalism toward economic depression, mass unemployment, and idle factories was wrong" (Lekachman 1966, 59).

By the end of World War II many governments had re-evaluated the role they could and should play in the domestic economy. Legislation enacted in the United States and Great Britain illustrates the impact that this re-evaluation had on government policy. In 1945 the U.S. Congress considered "The Full Employment Act" that assigned to the federal government the responsibility for maintaining full employment. Even though Congress did not pass the 1945 act, in 1946 the bill was renamed and passed as the Employment Act. And although the Employment Act replaced the term *full employment* with *maximum employment*, the bill nevertheless symbolized a fundamental change: no longer would the U.S. government leave the operation of the American economy fully to market forces (Stein 1994, 76–77). In Britain, the government published a "White Paper on Employment Policy" in 1944, which stated in its very first line, "the government accepts as one of their primary aims and responsibilities the maintenance of a high and stable level of employment after the war" (cited in Hall 1986, 71). This commitment provided the foundation for the macroeconomic policies of successive British governments until the late 1970s.

Together, electoral reform and the Keynesian revolution had a profound effect on exchange-rate policies. Electoral reform altered the balance of political power, shifting the center of gravity away from the propertied classes toward the workers. This created political incentives to use monetary policy to manage the domestic economy. The Keynesian revolution made governments and publics more aware of the policy measures that could be used to promote employment and at the same time broke the neoclassical strictures on their use. As a consequence, voters have come to expect governments to manage the economy, and governments have responded by becoming more willing to use monetary policy to meet these expectations (Hall 1989, 4).

In this world, exchange-rate politics revolve around competition between groups with very different interests. In some cases, this competition involves factor- or class-based groups pressing the government to adopt their preferred monetary policy. In other cases, this competition involves sector-based groups pressuring the government to adopt their preferred exchange-rate policy. In all instances, monetary and exchange-rate politics are driven by competition between groups pressuring the government to use these policies in ways that advance or defend their economic interests. We turn now to look at three models of this competition.

SOCIETY-BASED MODELS OF MONETARY AND EXCHANGE-RATE POLITICS

Scholars have developed three society-based models of monetary and exchange-rate politics: an institutional model, a partisan model, and a sectoral model. The institutional and partisan models assume that a government's exchange-rate policy reflects its monetary policy decisions. Both models assume that all governments want to retain monetary policy autonomy in order to manage the domestic economy. Sometimes the monetary policy that a government adopts is consistent with a fixed exchange rate and sometimes it is not. These models then examine how politics shape monetary policy in order to understand the government's exchange-rate policies.

The sectoral model assumes that exchange-rate policy is determined by competition between sector-based interest groups. This model does not assume that all governments value monetary-policy autonomy more than exchange-rate stability. Instead, it assumes that each interest group values each side of this trade-off differently. Some groups attach considerable value to exchange-rate stability and little value to monetary autonomy; others attach little value to exchange-rate stability and considerable value to monetary autonomy. Whether the government fixes the exchange rate or whether it retains monetary autonomy is determined by the balance of power among these competing groups. Although the models each provide a distinct perspective, they all agree that exchange-rate policies emerge from political competition.

A Closer Look

The Unholy Trinity

The standard framework used to conceptualize the trade-off between domestic economic autonomy and exchange-rate stability is "the Unholy Trinity." The concept starts from the recognition that governments have three policy goals, each of which is desirable in its own right: (1) a fixed exchange rate, (2) autonomy of monetary policy (using monetary policy to manage the domestic economy), and (3) capital mobility (allowing financial capital to flow freely into and out of the domestic financial system). It then tells us that a government can achieve only two of these three goals simultaneously. If a government wants monetary policy autonomy, it must choose between capital mobility and a fixed exchange rate. If a government wants a fixed exchange rate, it must choose between monetary policy autonomy and capital mobility.

An example illustrates this trade-off in practice. In early 1981, France was maintaining a fixed exchange rate within the European monetary system. In spite of this commitment, it adopted an expansionary monetary policy and cut French interest rates. France was relatively open to capital flows, so financial markets responded to the lower interest rates by selling francs and purchasing foreign currencies. These capital outflows produced an imbalance in the foreign exchange market. Demand for the franc fell, and it began to depreciate within the European monetary system.

If France wanted to maintain the fixed exchange rate, it had to intervene in the foreign exchange market. Intervention would reduce the supply of francs, thereby causing French interest rates to rise and tightening monetary policy. The franc would stabilize once French interest rates again equaled interest rates in foreign countries. Thus, to defend the exchange rate, France would have to reverse its initial monetary expansion. Because France was unwilling to raise interest rates, it was forced to devalue the franc. Given capital mobility, therefore, France was forced to choose between using monetary policy to stimulate the French economy and using monetary policy to maintain a fixed exchange rate.

The French government could have maintained the fixed exchange rate *and* used monetary policy to manage the domestic economy (at least for a while) if it had prevented capital flows. Suppose France implemented capital controls and then cut interest rates and expanded the money supply. The fall in French interest rates would then have created an incentive for capital to move out of France, but the capital controls would have prevented it from actually doing so. Without capital outflows, no large imbalance would develop in the foreign exchange market, and the franc would not depreciate. Thus, a government that prohibits capital flows can maintain a fixed exchange rate and retain monetary policy autonomy.

Restricting capital mobility, however, does not provide complete autonomy: it merely relaxes the trade-off between exchange-rate stability and autonomy. Even if France had prohibited capital flows before embarking on its monetary expansion, it would have been forced eventually to choose between the fixed exchange rate and the monetary expansion. It would have been forced to do so because the monetary expansion would have generated a current-account deficit as greater demand led to rising imports. The current-account deficit would in turn generate an imbalance in the foreign exchange market, causing the franc to depreciate. France would then have to intervene to prevent this depreciation. Continued intervention would eventually exhaust France's foreign exchange reserves. France would then have to either allow the franc to depreciate or tighten monetary policy. Thus, even if capital flows are restricted, France still faces a trade-off between exchange-rate stability and monetary autonomy.

The trade-off is stricter in a world with capital flows, however, than it is in a world without capital flows, for two reasons. First, when capital is mobile, imbalances arise rapidly following a change in monetary policy. In a world without capital flows, imbalances arise slowly as the current account moves into deficit. Second, in a world with capital flows, imbalances can be very, very large. The imbalance equals the difference between large capital outflows and much smaller capital inflows. This difference can be as much as billions of dollars per day. Without capital flows, imbalances remain pretty small. In such a world, imbalances equal the gap between imports and exports, and although this gap might be large over the course of the year, on any given day it will be relatively small and will never approach the multibillion-dollar gaps that characterize a world with capital flows.

Because imbalances are smaller and emerge more slowly in a world without capital flows, a government's foreign exchange reserves last longer than they do when capital is mobile. The large imbalances generated by capital outflows can rapidly exhaust a government's foreign exchange reserves; indeed, a government can run through its reserves in a day or two. France spent $32 billion in a single week defending the franc against a speculative attack in 1992. In a similar vein, Great Britain spent half of its foreign exchange reserves in 2 days. In a world without capital flows, the smaller imbalances generated by current-account deficits do not exhaust a government's foreign exchange reserves nearly so quickly. A government can pursue monetary expansion and spend its reserves defending the exchange rate over the course of the year. Still, reserves will eventually run out, and when they do, the government will be forced to tighten monetary policy or float the currency. Prohibiting capital flows, therefore, doesn't eliminate the trade-off between monetary policy autonomy and exchange-rate stability, but it does relax it substantially.

The Electoral Model of Monetary and Exchange-Rate Politics

The electoral model argues that exchange-rate policy reflects decisions that governments make concerning monetary policy. It assumes that governments care most about monetary-policy autonomy and will maintain a fixed exchange rate only when the monetary policy required to do so corresponds with its domestic economic objectives. In the electoral model, domestic economic objectives are in turn shaped by the need to win elections.

In democratic political systems governments must periodically stand for re-election. In most advanced industrialized societies, domestic economic conditions have an important influence on how voters evaluate incumbent governments, so governments have an incentive to establish their macroeconomic policy objectives with at least one eye on the electoral calendar (see Kramer 1971; Nordhaus 1989; Tufte 1978; Drazen 2000). In particular, politicians may be more likely to adopt expansionary macroeconomic policies in the 18 months prior to an election in order to create strong economic growth and falling unemployment at the time of the election (Tufte 1978, 9). Even if politicians are not inclined to engineer pre-electoral economic booms (and existing research does not provide compelling evidence that there is a systematic electoral cycle in macroeconomic policy), politicians may believe that voters will punish them for poor economic conditions. As an election approaches, politicians might therefore be reluctant to cede monetary authority, choosing to allow exchange rates to fluctuate instead (Bernhard and Leblang 1999). The important point is that because economic performance shapes how people vote, politicians will be less inclined to adopt economic policies that slow economic growth and raise unemployment and more inclined to adopt policies that boost economic growth and lower unemployment.

But politicians operate within a specific institutional context that limits their ability to adjust macroeconomic policies to their benefit. In constitutional democracies politicians must win the approval of veto players, which are actors or organizations whose approval is necessary for enacting policy. Examples of veto players can include opposition political parties and independent government institutions (Bearce 2002; Broz 2002; Tsebelis 2002). For example, in federal democracies, the parties that control the central government may be restricted in their ability to control fiscal policy. They must not only overcome objections from the opposition party, but subnational or supranational governing units also have some influence over economic policy (Hallerberg 2002). In the United States these include the 50 states, which have their own budgets, authority to raise or lower taxes, and other fiscal policy tools. In such cases, where discretion over fiscal policy is limited, a national government may wish to maintain monetary policy autonomy in order to more directly control the national economy. Thus, by limiting fiscal autonomy veto players can heighten the importance of monetary authority and provide incentives to opt for flexible exchange rates.

One of the most widely publicized instances of a government sacrificing a fixed exchange rate to electoral politics occurred in the United States in the early 1970s. The United States ended the convertibility of the dollar into gold in August 1971 and devalued the dollar by 10 percent in the following months. According to one scholar, the decision by President Richard M. Nixon to break the link with gold and devalue was viewed "through a lens that focused on the 1972 presidential election, then fifteen months away" (Gowa 1983, 163). American economic conditions in 1971 were not enhancing the prospects of Nixon's re-election. Early in his first term Nixon had allowed his economic team to reduce inflation, which was at a then-high level of about 5 percent, and by 1970 the American economy had slipped into a recession and unemployment was beginning to rise (Stein 1994, Chapter 5).

The rise in unemployment evoked painful memories for Nixon. In 1960, Nixon, who was at the time vice president, had run for president against John F. Kennedy. The 1960 campaign took place in the context of a recession, and in October unemployment increased by almost half a million. Nixon was convinced that the rise in unemployment just prior to the November election caused him to lose to Kennedy. "All the speeches, television broadcasts, and precinct work in the world could not counteract that one hard fact" of higher unemployment, he later wrote (Nixon 1962, 309). Nixon was determined to avoid again falling victim to an economic slump in the 1972 election.

With economic forecasts predicting that unemployment would rise to 6 percent in 1972, the Nixon administration decided to make the reduction of unemployment the number-one objective of macroeconomic policy (Tufte 1978, 48). As one senior administration official later recounted, "[in 1971] the word went out that 1972, by God, was going to be a good year" (cited in Tufte 1978, 48). Action was taken on both monetary and fiscal policy. The administration made it known that it wanted the Federal Reserve Bank (the Fed) to increase the rate of growth of the money supply, and the Fed obliged (though it remains unclear whether the Fed's expansion was coincidental or a direct response to White House pressure). In addition, government spending was increased through a range of measures. By the middle of 1971, the Nixon administration was using monetary and fiscal policies to reduce unemployment in the run-up to the 1972 presidential election.

The consequences for the dollar's fixed exchange rate against gold were clear and dramatic. The boost to domestic demand caused by the expansionary policy widened the U.S. trade deficit. Interest-rate cuts led to capital out-flows. The combination of a widening current-account balance and capital outflows worsened the United States' overall balance-of-payments position and provoked gold outflows. It quickly became apparent that the Nixon administration would have to choose between its domestic economic expansion and the dollar's fixed exchange rate (Gowa 1983, 170). In an August 1971 meeting at Camp David, therefore, the Nixon administration made two decisions that were inextricably linked: to push forward with its macroeconomic expansion in the hope that this would reduce unemployment in the run-up to the election, and to end the convertibility of the dollar into gold, in effect devaluing the dollar. One might suggest, therefore, that the Bretton Woods system collapsed so that Nixon might win the 1972 presidential election.

The end of dollar convertibility therefore nicely illustrates the logic of the electoral approach to exchange-rate policy. President Nixon's concern that high unemployment would reduce his chances for re-election led him to adopt expansionary macroeconomic policies. When it became apparent that expansionary macroeconomic policies were inconsistent with a fixed exchange rate, the Nixon administration devalued the dollar.

Although the electoral approach highlights an important dynamic driving macroeconomic and exchange-rate policy, it does suffer from two important weaknesses. First, it offers only a limited explanation of exchange-rate policy. It tells us that a government might abandon a fixed exchange rate prior to an election, but it tells us little about exchange-rate policy at other times. If the government wins the election, for example, will it return to a fixed exchange rate? Second, the electoral approach does not provide deterministic predictions. The approach does not claim that all governments will abandon a fixed exchange rate prior to an election. Rather, it suggests only that governments sometimes have an incentive to do so. Thus, the electoral approach offers a quite limited explanation of exchange-rate policy.

The Partisan Model of Monetary and Exchange-Rate Politics

The partisan approach also links exchange-rate policy to the government's monetary-policy decisions. Like the electoral model, the partisan model assumes that every government values monetary autonomy more than exchange-rate stability. All governments will thus maintain a fixed exchange rate only when the monetary policy required to do so is consistent with its domestic economic objectives. In the partisan model, however, different political parties pursue distinct macroeconomic objectives. Some parties use monetary policy to reduce unemployment and are forced to float their currency. Other parties use monetary policy to limit inflation and can more readily maintain a fixed exchange rate.

The partisan model is based on a trade-off between unemployment and inflation called the **Phillips curve**. The Phillips curve is named after British economist A. W. Phillips, who in 1958 was the first to posit such a relationship. It suggests that a government can reduce unemployment only by causing more rapid inflation, and can reduce inflation only by causing higher unemployment. One can clearly see the trade-off between inflation and unemployment that American policymakers faced between 1961 and 1970 (see Figure 12.1). Each data point in Figure 12.1 represents the rate of inflation and unemployment for a single year. Notice how, in the years when inflation was low, unemployment was high, whereas in years when unemployment was low, inflation was high. This relationship produces the negative line on the figure, characteristic of the Phillips curve trade-off.

Political economists have used the apparent trade-off between inflation and unemployment to suggest that different political parties use macroeconomic policy to move the domestic economy to different portions of the Phillips curve. Parties from the political left, such as Socialist parties, Social Democratic parties, Communist parties in Western Europe, the Labour party in Britain, and the Democratic Party in the United States, have traditionally given priority to achieving a low level of unemployment, even though this entails higher inflation. Such parties will try to shift the economy to the upper left portion of the Phillips curve. Parties from the political right, such as the Conservative party in Britain, the Republican party in the United States, Liberal parties, and Christian Democratic parties in Europe, have traditionally given priority to low inflation even though this entails higher unemployment. These parties will

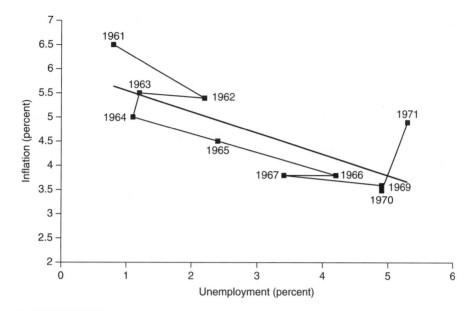

FIGURE 12.1

The Phillips Curve in the United States, 1961–1971

Source: United States Government, *Economic Report of the President* (Washington, DC: Government Printing Office, 2002).

use macroeconomic policy to move the economy to the lower right portion of the Phillips curve.

These distinct partisan macroeconomic policies reflect the interests of the different social groups represented by parties of the left and parties of the right. Leftist parties traditionally have had strong ties to organized labor. Because employment is a central concern of labor unions, the tight link between organized labor and leftist parties creates an incentive for leftist governments to use macroeconomic policy to maintain high levels of employment. Parties of the right have traditionally had closer links to business interests, the financial sector, and the middle class. These social groups are typically less concerned about unemployment and more concerned about protecting the value of their accumulated wealth. Because in modern economies people maintain large portions of their wealth in financial instruments, the desire to protect the value of wealth is transformed into a desire to protect the real value of financial assets. And since inflation erodes the real value of financial wealth, wealth holders have an interest in policies that maintain stable prices. In representing the interests of people with accumulated wealth, therefore, parties of the right have an incentive to adopt macroeconomic policies that maintain stable prices.

A large body of research suggests that leftist and rightist governments in the advanced industrialized countries have in fact pursued distinct macroeconomic policies throughout the postwar period. Research on West European democracies has found that leftist governments have been more willing to tolerate inflation and more inclined to pursue expansionary fiscal and monetary policies than rightist governments (Oatley 1997, 1999; Garrett 1998). Studies of macroeconomic policy and macroeconomic-policy outcomes in the United States have identified similar patterns. Eight of the ten recessions that have occurred in the United States between 1946 and 2002, for example, came under Republican administrations, and only two occurred under Democratic administrations (Keech 1995, 72–73). Moreover, historically, unemployment rates have been 2 percentage points higher, on average, under Republican than under Democratic administrations, whereas the growth of incomes has been 6 percentage points lower under Republican leadership than under Democrats (Hibbs 1987). Republican administrations appear, therefore, to be more willing to tolerate rising unemployment in order to restrain inflation than Democratic administrations. Even though there have certainly been exceptions to this general pattern, research suggests that political parties from the left and right have in fact pursued distinct macroeconomic policies when in office.

Distinct partisan macroeconomic policies can give rise to distinct partisan exchange-rate policies. According to the partisan approach, leftist parties are less likely to maintain a fixed exchange rate. Expansionary policies will reduce domestic interest rates and raise domestic demand. Such policies will in turn cause capital outflows and increasing imports. Capital outflows and a widening current-account deficit will in turn lead to foreign exchange market imbalances and a weakening currency. Committed to the domestic expansion, leftist governments are likely to resist the policy changes required to support a fixed exchange rate against these pressures. Conservative parties are more likely to maintain a fixed exchange rate. Restrictive monetary policies are less likely to generate capital outflows or to increase domestic demand. As a result, conservative governments are unlikely to confront persistent imbalances in the foreign exchange market and therefore will not be forced to change their monetary policies to sustain a fixed exchange rate. Conservative governments are therefore more likely to establish and maintain a fixed exchange rate. Thus, the partisan approach suggests that leftist governments are less likely to maintain a fixed exchange rate than rightist governments.

The politics of macroeconomic policy in France between 1978 and 1982 nicely illustrate how changes in the partisan composition of a government can affect macroeconomic and exchange-rate policies. A center-right government, led by President Valery Giscard d'Éstaing and Prime Minister Raymond Barre, held office in France during much of the 1970s. Giscard and Barre gave priority to reducing inflation (Oatley 1997). This choice was by no means dictated by economic conditions. French inflation was high during the 1970s, rising to 13 percent in 1975 and hovering around 10 percent for the rest of the decade. But French unemployment had also risen steadily throughout the 1970s, from a low of 2.7 percent in 1971 to 6 percent by the end of the decade. The government's decision to give priority to reducing inflation thus reflected a partisan preference.

This emphasis on reducing inflation, along with the associated policy of a fixed exchange rate, was abandoned in the early 1980s when the Socialist Party, led by Francois Mitterrand, defeated Giscard d'Èstaing in presidential elections in May of 1981. Mitterrand quickly abandoned the anti-inflation stance in an attempt to reduce French unemployment. Again, this decision was not dictated by economic conditions. Inflation remained strong, rising to about 13 percent in 1981, despite the previous government's efforts to reduce it. Unemployment had also continued to rise in the late 1970s and early 1980s, reaching what was then a postwar high of 7 percent in 1981. Mitterrand's decision to focus on unemployment and pay less attention to inflation was thus a reflection of this government's close ties to the French working class.

Mitterrand's government implemented expansionary macroeconomic policies. The government budget deficit was increased, pumping more government spending into the economy, and the Bank of France reduced domestic interest rates. This expansion was inconsistent with the franc's fixed exchange rate inside the EMS. Financial capital began flowing out of France in response to the falling interest rates. The French current-account deficit widened as strong domestic demand limited the goods available for export and pulled in imports. The deteriorating balance-of-payments position weakened the franc in the foreign exchange market, generating a series of speculative attacks against the franc's parity in the European Monetary System (EMS). Rather than abandon its effort to reduce unemployment, the Socialist government devalued the franc three times between May 1981 and March 1983. Thus, a leftist government implemented an expansionary policy that was inconsistent with a fixed exchange rate, and when forced to choose between the two objectives, it abandoned the fixed exchange rate.

The French case therefore highlights how partisan politics can shape macroeconomic and exchange-rate policies. A rightist government committed to low inflation tightened monetary policy and embraced a fixed exchange rate. The leftist government that followed gave priority to reducing unemployment, adopted expansionary macroeconomic policies in pursuit of this objective, and repeatedly devalued the currency. Although the partisan approach tells us more about how politics shape monetary and exchange-rate politics than the electoral approach, it too has weaknesses. Its chief weakness is that partisan macroeconomic policies are differentiated too sharply. Not all leftist governments pursue expansionary macroeconomic policies and adopt floating exchange rates. The French Socialists, for example, embraced a fixed exchange rate inside the EMS in mid-1983, and then maintained this fixed rate for the remainder of the decade. Nor do all rightist governments adopt fixed exchange rates. The Conservative Party government led by Margaret Thatcher that governed Britain throughout the 1980s, for example, steadfastly refused to adopt a fixed exchange rate for the pound. And even once the pound was placed in the EMS after John Major replaced Thatcher in 1990, it was a Conservative Party government that took the pound out of the system and returned to a floating exchange rate in 1992. Thus, even though the partisan approach highlights the historical tendency for distinct partisan macroeconomic and exchange-rate policies, it is important to remain sensitive to the specific context when applying this approach to a particular case.

The Sectoral Model of Monetary and Exchange-Rate Politics

The sectoral model links exchange-rate policy choices to competition between sector-based interest groups. Unlike the electoral and partisan models, the sectoral model does not assume that all governments value monetary autonomy more than exchange-rate stability. Instead, government preferences reflect interest-group preferences. And interest groups hold different preferences over the trade-off between domestic economic autonomy and exchange-rate stability. Some interest groups prefer floating, but others prefer fixed exchange rates. Some interest groups prefer a strong currency, but others prefer a weak currency. Each group lobbies the government on behalf of its preferred exchange-rate policy. Exchange-rate policy is determined by the group that has the greatest influence.

The sectoral model splits domestic actors into four domestic interest groups or sectors: import-competing producers, export-oriented producers, nontraded-goods producers, and the financial services industry (see Frieden 1991a, 1997). We have encountered each of these groups previously, so we will not describe their characteristics again here. Each group has preferences over two dimensions of exchange-rate policy. First, each group has a preference regarding the degree of exchange-rate stability. Some groups prefer a fixed exchange rate, but others prefer a floating exchange rate. Second, each group has a preference regarding the level of the exchange rate. Some groups prefer a strong currency, but others prefer a weak currency.

Preferences over exchange-rate stability reflect the importance that each sector attaches to exchange-rate stability and monetary-policy autonomy. Sectors whose economic interests are damaged by exchange-rate movements place considerable value on exchange-rate stability. Those sectors whose interests are not damaged by such movements place less value on exchange-rate stability. Similarly, sectors that conduct most of their business in the domestic economy want to ensure that domestic economic conditions provide adequate demand. They will therefore place considerable value on monetary-policy autonomy. Sectors that conduct most of their business in international markets are less concerned about domestic economic conditions. They therefore place very little value on monetary-policy autonomy. Thus, sector preferences over exchange-rate stability reflect the value that each attaches to exchange-rate stability and monetary-policy autonomy. Sectors that are harmed by exchange-rate movements and that lose little from surrendering monetary autonomy prefer fixed exchange rates. Sectors that are not harmed by exchange-rate movements and that lose from the loss of monetary-policy autonomy prefer floating exchange rates.

This framework generates clear preferences for three of the four sectors. The export-oriented sector prefers a fixed exchange rate. Export-oriented producers are heavily engaged in international trade, and exchange-rate movements damage their economic interests. They therefore place great value on exchange-rate stability. Because export-oriented producers are heavily engaged in foreign trade, they lose very little if the government cannot use monetary policy to manage the domestic economy. They therefore attach little value to monetary-policy autonomy. The export-oriented sector, therefore, is willing to give up monetary-policy autonomy to maintain a fixed exchange rate.

The nontraded-goods and the import-competing sectors prefer a floating exchange rate. Neither of these sectors is deeply integrated into the global economy; both generate their revenues from sales in the domestic market. As a consequence, these sectors are not greatly affected by exchange-rate movements, and they attach little value to exchange-rate stability. Moreover, because producers in these sectors conduct their business in the domestic economy, they have a keen interest in retaining the government's ability to use monetary policy to manage the domestic economy. They therefore assign great value to monetary-policy autonomy. The nontraded-goods and the import-competing sectors therefore want to retain monetary-policy autonomy and accept flexible exchange rates to do so.

The financial services sector's preferences are less clear. Financial services are highly internationalized, and exchange-rate movements can damage their interests. This international exposure creates some interest in exchange-rate stability. At the same time, however, financial institutions profit from exchange-rate volatility. Currency trading has become an important source of profits for the financial services industry. In addition, banks offer services that help businesses engaged in international trade manage their exchange-rate risk (Destler and Henning 1989, 133). Thus, it is not clear how much value the financial services sector attaches to exchange-rate stability. Financial institutions do value monetary-policy autonomy. They depend upon the central bank to maintain the stability of the domestic banking system and to keep domestic inflation in check. Both objectives require monetary-policy autonomy. In addition, financial institutions are damaged by excessive fluctuations in domestic interest rates, and using monetary policy to maintain a fixed exchange rate can produce more volatile domestic interest rates. These crosscutting interests have led many to conclude that on balance, the financial sector prefers monetary-policy autonomy and is willing to accept exchange-rate flexibility (Destler and Henning 1989, 133–134; see Frieden 1991a for an alternative view).

Sectors also have preferences over the level of the exchange rate. These preferences arise from the impact that currency values have on incomes in each sector. The export-oriented and import-competing sectors both prefer a weak or undervalued currency. A weak domestic currency reduces the foreign currency cost of domestic traded goods and raises the domestic currency cost of foreign traded goods. These price levels enhance the competitiveness of export-oriented producers in global markets, thereby allowing them to expand their exports. They also reduce the competitiveness of foreign producers in the domestic market, making it easier for import-competing producers to dominate the home market. Thus, firms in the traded-goods sector prefer an undervalued or weak currency.

The nontraded-goods sector prefers a strong or overvalued currency. A strong currency raises income in this sector. People employed in the nontraded-goods sector consume a lot of traded goods. A strong domestic currency reduces the domestic currency price of traded goods, both those imported from abroad and those produced at home. When the dollar appreciates, for example, foreign goods become cheaper in the American market, and domestic producers must match these falling prices to remain competitive. A strong or overvalued exchange rate, therefore, raises the incomes of people employed in the nontraded-goods sector. For this reason, this sector prefers a strong currency.

The financial services sector again has crosscutting interests. Financial institutions benefit from a strong currency because it allows them to purchase foreign assets at a lower price. But, other factors create an interest in a weak currency. Most financial institutions, even those deeply involved in international business, continue to lend heavily to domestic firms. Because an overvalued exchange rate harms firms in the traded-goods sectors, a strong currency can weaken financial institutions that have loaned heavily to firms in the traded-goods sector. In addition, financial institutions purchase and hold foreign assets for the returns they provide. As these returns are typically denominated in foreign currencies, a weak currency will raise the domestic currency value of these returns. It is not easy for financial institutions to balance these crosscutting considerations. What best suits the interests of financial institutions is the ability to buy foreign assets when the domestic currency is strong and repatriate the returns on these assets when the domestic currency has weakened. Because of these crosscutting interests, financial institutions "tend to be agnostic with respect to the level of the exchange rate" (Destler and Henning 1989, 132).

Bringing these two dimensions of exchange-rate policy together provides a full picture of sectoral preferences over exchange-rate policy (see Figure 12.2). The columns in Figure 12.2 depict the degree of exchange-rate stability. The column labeled "High" denotes a fixed exchange rate (and thus

Preferred Degree of Exchange-Rate Stability

	High	Low
High		Nontradable-goods industry *Financial services*
Low	Export-oriented industries	Import competing industries *Financial services*

FIGURE 12.2

Sectoral Exchange-Rate Policy Preferences

Source: Based on Frieden 1991, 445.

no monetary-policy autonomy), whereas the column labeled "Low" denotes a floating exchange rate (and thus full monetary-policy autonomy). The rows in the table depict the level of the exchange rate. The row labeled "High" denotes a strong currency, whereas the row labeled "Low" denotes a weak currency. Each cell of the table thus represents a combination of the degree of exchange-rate stability and the level of the exchange rate.

We can place each sector in the cell corresponding to its exchange-rate policy preference. The "High–High" cell is empty: no sector desires a strong currency and a fixed exchange rate. The nontraded-goods sector and the financial services industry occupy the "High–Low" cell. Firms in the nontraded-goods sector want a strong currency to maximize their purchasing power, and they want a floating exchange rate so the government can use monetary policy to manage the domestic economy. The financial services industry fits less clearly in this cell. Its preference for a floating exchange rate places it in the left column, but its agnosticism about the level of the exchange rate prevents us from assigning it definitively to the top row.

The export-oriented sector occupies the "Low–High" cell. Export-oriented firms want a weak currency to enhance their export competitiveness, and they want a stable exchange rate to minimize the disruptions caused by exchange-rate volatility. Because these industries are not heavily dependent on the domestic economy, they are willing to sacrifice monetary-policy autonomy to stabilize the exchange rate. Finally, the import-competing sector occupies the "Low–Low" cell. Firms in this sector want a weak currency to enhance their competitiveness against imports in the domestic market, and they want a floating exchange rate so the government can use monetary policy to manage the domestic economy.

Policy Analysis and Debate

A Strong Dollar or a Weak Dollar?

Question

Should the United States pursue a strong dollar or a weak dollar?

Overview

The dollar appreciated sharply in the weeks following the election of President Donald J. Trump. By the time of Trump's inauguration, the dollar had reached levels not seen for more than 10 years. The strong dollar seemingly posed a threat to Trump's campaign promise to reduce and even eliminate America's trade deficit. In pursuit of this goal, the incoming Trump administration threatened to renegotiate existing trade agreements and to label the Chinese government a "currency manipulator." By April of 2017, Trump was giving public voice to his views on the dollar, stating in an interview to the *Wall Street Journal* that he thought that the "dollar is getting too strong" (Baker et al. 2017). Trump's statement, and his continued support for low interest rates, contributed to a weakening of the dollar over subsequent months. By the end of the year, the dollar had fallen by about 10 percent relative to its December 2016 value but remained almost 15 percent above the post-crisis floor that it reached in 2014.

Should the Trump administration strive to weaken the dollar further in pursuit of reducing the trade deficit? Critics of such a policy highlight the costs and potential dangers associated with a weaker dollar. Some analysts argue that market expectations of prolonged dollar weakness could lead to higher interest rates in the United States. Higher interest rates would raise the cost of investment for the private sector and raise the federal government's borrowing costs. Others suggest that a determined policy of undervaluing the dollar will eventually spark foreign retaliation, thereby raising the possibility of another "currency war" like the one Brazil accused American policy of triggering in 2009–2011. More profoundly, a loss of foreign confidence in the commitment by American policymakers to a strong dollar could cause foreign governments to shift from the dollar to the euro as their primary vehicle currency and reserve asset. Such a shift would precipitate a major collapse of the dollar and substantially raise borrowing costs in the United States. For advocates of this position, a strong dollar is a critical American interest. What is the right value for the dollar?

Policy Options

■ Pursue policies to strengthen the dollar against foreign currencies.
■ Pursue policies to keep the dollar relatively undervalued in order to promote exports.

Policy Analysis

■ What are the costs and benefits to the United States of a weak dollar?
■ What are the costs and benefits to the United States of a strong dollar?

Take A Position

■ Which option do you prefer? Justify your choice.
■ What criticisms of your position should you anticipate? How would you defend your recommendation against this critique?

Resources

Online: Do an online search for "strong dollar weak dollar." Look for C. Fred Bergsten's webpage at the Institute for International Economics (www.IIE. com). He writes regularly about dollar policy. See in particular his "The Correction of the Dollar and Foreign Intervention in the Currency Markets." Search also for Barry Eichengreen's home page (at the University of California at Berkeley). He has some interesting papers under his policy section.

In Print: C. Fred Bergsten, "The Dollar and the Deficits," *Foreign Affairs* (November/December 2009); Paola Subacchi and John Driffill. *Beyond the Dollar: Rethinking the International Monetary System* (London: Chatham House, 2010).

The political dynamics surrounding the sharp appreciation of the U.S. dollar in the early 1980s and its subsequent depreciation after 1985 nicely illustrate how these competing interest-group preferences seek to shape exchange-rate policy in the United States (see Destler and Henning 1989; Frankel 1990). The U.S. dollar appreciated by 50 percent between 1980 and 1985. Interest groups mobilized in an attempt to influence the Reagan administration's approach to both the level and the stability of the dollar. Export-oriented producers organized and lobbied for a weaker and more stable dollar. Farmers, for example, argued that the strong dollar was reducing their incomes, and they pressured the Reagan administration to bring the dollar down. Manufacturing industries, led by the Business Roundtable and the National Association of Manufacturers, also pressed for depreciation. The Business Roundtable put together a broad-based coalition of businesses, including representatives from Caterpillar, Ford, U.S. Steel, Honeywell, Motorola, IBM, and Xerox, to pressure the U.S. Treasury, the Federal Reserve, and Congress for policies to weaken the dollar.

This group also advocated measures to increase the stability of the dollar against the other major currencies. Although few suggested that the United States return to a fixed exchange rate, most of the executives in the coalition welcomed the process of coordinated foreign exchange market intervention initiated by the 1985 Plaza Accord and encouraged the Reagan administration to pursue additional coordinated intervention. In addition, the group applauded the 1987 Louvre Accord, under which the United States, Japan, Germany, Great Britain, and France agreed to stabilize exchange rates at their current levels. And finally, they encouraged the U.S. government to explore the possibility of implementing a target zone to bring stability to international monetary arrangements on a more permanent basis. Thus, just as the sectoral approach suggests, export-oriented producers pressured for a weak dollar and for greater exchange-rate stability.

The financial services industry also exhibited the preferences highlighted by the sectoral approach. During the early 1980s, the financial services industry displayed little concern about the dollar's appreciation. For the most part, this industry benefited from the falling prices of foreign assets that the strong dollar implied. To the extent that financial services firms voiced any concerns as the dollar appreciated, they focused on the impact the strong dollar was having on traded-goods industries in the United States (Destler and Henning 1989). Financial institutions also failed to register strong opposition to the Reagan administration's concerted effort to engineer a depreciation of the dollar after 1985. Thus, the financial sector was neither a strong supporter of the strong dollar nor a vocal opponent of a weaker dollar.

Financial services firms did react strongly, however, to the attempt by the traded-goods sector to pressure the Reagan administration to stabilize the dollar. The American Bankers' Association's Economic Advisory Committee argued that the Group of 5 (G5) agreement to stabilize the dollar under the Louvre Accord was a mistake. In addition, the committee opposed broader international monetary reforms that would lead to the adoption of a target-zone system. Monetary policy, they argued, should not be dedicated to maintaining a stable exchange rate, and foreign exchange market intervention should be undertaken only in "exceptional circumstances." As the sectoral approach leads us to expect, therefore, the financial services sector was agnostic about the level of the exchange rate but was opposed to efforts to stabilize the dollar at a fixed exchange rate. American exchange-rate policy during the 1980s thus highlights the dynamics emphasized by the sectoral approach. The interests and power of two prominent sectors of the American economy, export-oriented producers and the financial services industry, shaped American exchange-rate policy.

The sectoral approach provides greater detail about exchange-rate policy than the partisan approach, but it too has weaknesses. Three such weaknesses are most troublesome. First, the sectoral approach may overestimate the importance that export-oriented firms attach to exchange-rate stability. Although exporters may be harmed by exchange-rate volatility, it is also true that businesses can reduce their exposure to volatility by using forward markets to cover the risk they face. As a consequence, exchange-rate volatility may be less damaging in practice. Second, the model may overestimate the importance that the traded-good sector attaches to a weak currency. In an open economy, many firms import intermediate inputs. Because a weak currency raises the domestic currency price of these imports, it raises production costs. As a consequence, a portion of the gains that these firms realize from a weak currency is eliminated. This factor is increasingly important as production is disaggregated and distributed globally in the form of global value chains. Finally, the sectoral model tells us little about exchange-rate policy outcomes. As with the society-centered approach to trade policy, this model does not provide much help understanding which of the competing sectoral demands will ultimately be represented in exchange-rate policy. Insofar as we are interested in explaining policy outcomes, this will remain an important weakness of the sectoral model.

CONCLUSION

The society-centered models thus argue that domestic political pressures determine the monetary and exchange-rate policies that governments adopt. The three approaches presented here suggest that governments face a multitude of social pressures—from voters, from classes, and from sector-based interest groups. These pressures are transmitted to governments through multiple channels, including mass-based elections, class-based party systems, and interest-group lobbying. Social pressures can influence exchange-rate policy indirectly by shaping a government's macroeconomic policy objectives, and they can influence exchange-rate policy directly by shaping the choices that a government makes between a fixed or floating exchange rate and between a strong or weak currency. Rather than suggesting that monetary and exchange-rate policies are determined exclusively by one type of pressure or another, it is probably the case that they are influenced by all of the social pressures discussed here. One approach may be better suited to some countries than to others, or to some time periods than to others. A full understanding of how domestic politics influence monetary and exchange-rate policies, however, will probably require attention to all three approaches.

As a group, however, these society-centered approaches to exchange-rate politics are susceptible to some of the same criticisms that have been directed toward society-centered approaches to domestic trade politics. Chapter 4 pointed to three specific criticisms: they don't explain outcomes, they omit the interests of noneconomic interest groups, and they assume that governments do not have independent preferences. How powerful are these criticisms when applied to a society-centered approach to monetary and exchange-rate policy? Let us look at each of these criticisms in turn. The claim that society-centered models tell us a lot about interests but little about outcomes is less powerful in the context of exchange-rate politics than in the context of trade politics. Two of the three models we looked at provide explicit linkages between societal interests and policy outcomes. In the electoral model, outcomes result from government macroeconomic policy choices taken in reference to electoral concerns. In the partisan model, policy outcomes result from decisions made by the party that controls government. The sectoral approach is more vulnerable to this criticism. As was noted above, the sectoral approach convincingly accounts for interest-group preferences over monetary and exchange-rate policy, but it tells us little about the process through which these competing interests are transformed into policy outcomes.

Society-centered models of exchange-rate and monetary policy are less vulnerable to the claim that they ignore the interests of noneconomic actors. Although these models do exclude noneconomic interest groups, such interest groups appear to have less of a stake in monetary and exchange-rate policies than they may have in trade policy. The exchange rate is a rather blunt policy instrument. A government cannot easily use exchange-rate policy to punish or reward specific foreign governments for their human rights records or for their environmental policies. For example, even though the United States can deny China access to the U.S. market without disturbing its other trade relationships, the United States cannot easily alter the dollar's exchange rate against the yuan (the Chinese currency) without also altering the dollar's exchange rate against other currencies. For this reason, human rights activists, environmental groups, and other noneconomic interest groups have not pressured governments to use exchange-rate policy to achieve specific foreign policy objectives. Thus, the omission of noneconomic interest groups from the society-centered approach may be less worrying in the context of exchange-rate and monetary policies than in trade policy.

Finally, our society-centered models of monetary and exchange-rate policy do overstate the ability of domestic interest groups to influence policy, and they underestimate the importance of independent state action. A fairly large literature suggests that monetary and exchange-rate policies are heavily insulated from domestic pressure groups (see, for example, Krasner 1977; Odell 1982). In the United States, for example, exchange-rate and monetary-policy decisions are made by the Treasury Department, the Federal Reserve, and the White House, all of which are "well insulated from particular societal pressures"

(Krasner 1977, 65). Moreover, in many countries central banks operate with considerable independence from elected officials. Politically independent central banks can pursue monetary and exchange-rate policies free from interest-group pressures and from partisan and electoral politics. In fact, over the last 15 years more and more governments have granted their central banks greater political independence, hoping to insulate monetary policy from social and, more broadly, political pressures. We take up this topic in the next chapter.

KEY TERM

Phillips Curve

SUGGESTIONS FOR FURTHER READING

For a good introduction to the politics of macroeconomic policy, see William R. Keech, *Economic Politics in the United States: The Costs of Democracy*, 2nd edition (Cambridge, UK: Cambridge, University Press, 2013). For a more advanced treatment, see Alan Drazen, *Political Economy in Macroeconomics* (Princeton, NJ: Princeton University Press, 2002).

An excellent source on the sectoral approach to exchange-rate politics is Jeffry A. Frieden, *Currency Politics: the Political Economy of Exchange Rate Politics* (Princeton: Princeton University Press, 2015). For some recent research that evaluates the validity of this approach to exchange rate and monetary policy preferences, see David H. Bearce and Kim-Lee Tuxhorn, 2017. "When Are Monetary Policy Preferences Egocentric? Evidence from American Surveys and an Experiment." *American Journal of Political Science* 61(1): 178–193.

A State-Centered Approach to Monetary and Exchange-Rate Policies

The United States' Federal Reserve System responded to the Global Financial Crisis of 2008 by implementing an unconventional monetary policy called Quantitative Easing, or QE. The European Central Bank (ECB) followed suit and implemented its own version of QE in early 2015. Through QE, central banks purchase government bonds and other securities from private financial institutions such as insurance companies and pension funds in exchange for central bank reserves. These securities transactions wind up increasing deposits in commercial banks, which in turn should encourage banks to increase their lending to private businesses. Increased lending and investment in turn stimulates output and employment. The need for QE arose because interest rates have hovered around 0 percent, rendering traditional monetary policy instruments ineffective.

Two things are rather extraordinary about QE. The first is the sheer magnitude of the initiative. Since QE began in late 2008, the Federal Reserve has purchased on average $30 billion of securities per month. As a consequence, the Fed's balance sheet—its total holdings of assets and the liabilities it has issued to acquire them—quadrupled to $4.5 trillion. For its part, the ECB has been purchasing 60 billion euros worth of securities per month since 2015 and its balance sheet has correspondingly increased by more than 2 trillion euros. As a point of comparison, consider that the American Recovery and Reinvestment Act of 2009—the U.S. government's fiscal policy enacted in response to the financial crisis—approved $831 billion in total spending over 10 years. I am not exaggerating when I suggest that QE has been the central pillar of post-crisis economic policy. The second rather extraordinary aspect of QE is that all of the relevant decisions—whether to continue or suspend the program, how much and what kinds of securities to purchase—have been made by appointed officials who are generally unknown to the public and only weakly accountable to voters and their elected representatives. In the world's two largest economic units, macroeconomic management is the domain of central bankers who operate largely independent from electoral politics.

The increasingly dominant economic role played by independent central banks has not been restricted to the United States and Europe. Governments throughout the world have handed monetary policy to politically independent central banks. Changes in the institutional framework governing monetary policy have in turn altered the way that domestic politics shapes monetary and exchange-rate policies.

This chapter examines the transformation from government to bank control through the lens of a state-centered approach to monetary and exchange-rate politics. Even though the approach is not often called a state-centered approach, it contains the central characteristic of such an approach: insulating policymakers from short-term political pressures that can raise social welfare. We begin by examining contemporary economic theories that argue that political control of monetary policy diminishes social welfare by generating too much inflation. We then consider how, in theory, institutions that insulate monetary policy from politics, such as independent central banks and fixed exchange rates, can eliminate this inflation and thus raise social welfare. We next investigate how the emergence of independent central banks is likely to shape the domestic politics of monetary and exchange-rate policies. Finally, we conclude by looking at some weaknesses of this approach.

MONETARY POLICY AND UNEMPLOYMENT

The state-centered approach is based on economic theories that have increasingly replaced the Keynesian models that dominated macroeconomic policy-making after World War II. The models we examined in Chapter 12, as well as the Keynesian economic theories on which they are based, assumed that governments face a stable trade-off between inflation and unemployment. Governments can exploit this trade-off to guide the economy toward lower unemployment or lower inflation. Contemporary economic theory asserts that no such stable trade-off between inflation and unemployment exists. There is a trade-off in the short run, but a government cannot use monetary policy to reduce unemployment for any extended period without generating an ever-higher rate of inflation (Friedman 1968; Phelps 1968).

At the center of this theory is the claim that all countries have a **natural rate of unemployment,** the economy's long-run equilibrium rate of unemployment. That is, the natural rate of unemployment is the rate of unemployment to which the economy will return after a recession or a boom (Sachs and Larrain 1993). The natural rate of unemployment is determined by the economy-wide real wage, which is the wage at which all workers who want to work can find employment. The natural rate of unemployment is never zero and can in fact be substantially above zero. Every economy will always experience some unemployment. Some people will have left one job and be seeking another. New entrants into the labor market, such as recent high school and college graduates, will not find jobs immediately. Moreover, labor market institutions, such as labor unions, and labor market regulations that govern minimum wages, hiring and firing practices, unemployment compensation, and other social welfare benefits can raise the natural rate of unemployment substantially. These institutions can raise the economy-wide real wage, thereby reducing the demand for labor and raising the natural rate of unemployment. Because such institutions differ from one country to another, each country will have a distinct natural rate of unemployment.

Contemporary economic theory argues that a government cannot use monetary policy to move unemployment below or above the natural rate of unemployment for more than a short time. To understand this claim we must first look at how wage bargaining affects unemployment in the short run. We can then examine how monetary policy affects unemployment in the short run and in the long run. In the short run, such as a 1- or 2-year period, the unemployment rate is determined by the wage agreements concluded between unions and businesses. Suppose that, in the current year, the economy is at its natural rate of unemployment and labor is bargaining with management to determine the real wage for the next year. This wage bargaining is complicated by inflation. Workers care about their real wage—the actual purchasing power of the money they are paid each week—but they are paid a nominal wage—a specific amount of cash per hour or per week. Because wage contracts usually fix wages for a particular period, typically from 1 to 3 years, the nominal wage embodied in a contract will lose purchasing power as prices rise over the life of the agreement. Because workers recognize that inflation will erode the value of their nominal wage, they will take inflation into account when negotiating their wage contracts. In other words, workers will seek nominal wage agreements that protect their desired real wage against the inflation they expect. If labor is seeking stable real wages for the next year, for example, but expects prices to rise by 4 percent in the course of the year, it will seek a 4 percent nominal wage increase.

How does labor know what inflation rate will prevail in the future? The obvious answer is that it doesn't. Instead, labor will formulate expectations about the future rate of inflation, which are essentially its "best guess" about the inflation rate during the period covered by the impending contract. In formulating these expectations, labor unions look at a variety of factors. They may look to the current government's track record; if inflation has persistently run at around 5 percent during the last few years, it might be reasonable to expect 5 percent inflation in the next few years. They may also look for evidence that the government is committed to reducing inflation in the future or, to the contrary, for evidence that the government is likely to produce higher inflation in the future. They may also take into account the partisan composition of the government or its position in the electoral cycle. Irrespective of the source, however, these expectations are likely to be imprecise.

When nominal wage agreements are based on an expected inflation rate that turns out to be mistaken, the real wage will rise or fall. If workers secure a nominal wage increase that is greater than the actual rate of inflation, then the real wage will rise by the difference between the nominal wage increase and the rate of inflation. So, if a wage agreement raises nominal wages by 8 percent, but inflation is only 4 percent, then the real wage will rise by 4 percent. Conversely, if workers secure an agreement that raises their nominal wage by less than the actual rate of inflation, real wages will fall by the difference between the nominal wage increase and the rate of inflation. So, if the wage agreement calls for a 4 percent nominal wage increase, but actual inflation is 8 percent, the real wage will fall by 4 percent.

Changes in the real wage in turn affect the short-run unemployment rate. An increase in the real wage makes labor more costly to employ. The demand for labor therefore falls, causing unemployment to rise. A reduction in the real wage makes labor less costly to employ. The demand for labor therefore rises, causing unemployment to fall. Thus, in the short run, unemployment rises above or falls below the natural rate of unemployment in response to changes in the real wage.

We can now examine how monetary policy affects unemployment in the short run and in the long run. In the short run, an *unanticipated* change in monetary policy that produces a rate of inflation different from the rate that unions expected and incorporated into their nominal wage contract shifts unemployment above or below the natural rate. An unexpected *increase* in the rate of inflation generated by a monetary expansion will lower the real wage and reduce unemployment; an unexpected *reduction* in the rate of inflation caused by monetary contraction will raise the real wage and increase unemployment.

In the long run, however, these changes are reversed by labor market adjustments that push unemployment back to its natural rate. Suppose unanticipated inflation has reduced the real wage. As unemployment falls as a result, fewer people are available to work, and businesses will have to compete against each other to attract new workers and to retain their current employees. This competition will cause real wages to rise, making it more costly to employ workers. As the real wage rises, the demand for labor falls and unemployment gradually returns to its natural rate.

Now suppose that lower-than-anticipated inflation has increased the real wage, causing unemployment to rise above the natural rate. Because unemployment has risen, a larger number of people are now competing for fewer jobs. Competition between workers for scarce jobs will cause real wages to fall, as each worker offers to accept employment at a real wage below those of other workers. As real wages are bid down, the unemployment rate returns to its natural rate. Over time, therefore, labor market adjustments bring the real wage back to the wage that clears the labor market, and the economy returns to its natural rate of unemployment. Thus, even though an unanticipated change in monetary policy can move unemployment below or above the natural rate in the short run, the effects will be reversed over the long run.

Therefore, governments cannot use monetary policy to reduce unemployment over the long run. Any monetary expansion will reduce unemployment for a short while, but eventually labor market adjustments will restore unemployment to its natural rate.

Moreover, a government determined to use monetary policy to keep unemployment below the natural rate for any lengthy period will have to continually increase the rate of inflation to do so. (This is called the **accelerationist principle**.) We can see why from a modified version of the **Phillips curve** (Figure 13.1). In this version, the economy is characterized by multiple Phillips curves. In each short-run period, policymakers face a trade-off between inflation and unemployment—the downward-sloping curves labeled T_1, T_2, and T_3 in the figure. Because there is no long-run trade-off between inflation and unemployment, the long-run Phillips curve is drawn as a vertical line that crosses the horizontal axis at the economy's natural rate of unemployment (U_n).

Now suppose that, from the natural rate of unemployment—point A on Phillips curve T_1—the government expands monetary policy in an attempt to push the rate of unemployment below the natural rate, say, to point U_b. Inflation rises, thereby reducing real wages and boosting employment. This effect in turn pushes the economy along the short-run Phillips curve T_1 to point B. As workers and businesses react to the now-higher inflation, however, the real wage rises back to its initial level and unemployment returns to its natural rate.

The inflation produced by the expansion is permanent, however; consequently, the government now faces a new short-run Phillips curve, labeled T_2. If the government wants to push unemployment below the natural rate again, it must expand the money supply once more. If so, then the resulting inflation

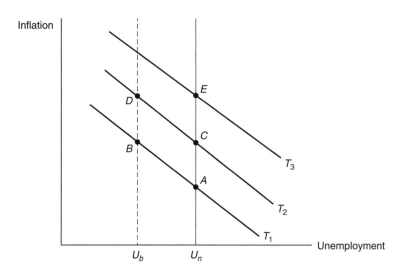

FIGURE 13.1
The Long-Run Phillips Curve

reduces the real wage and causes unemployment to fall to point D. However, adjustments again restore the economy to its natural rate of unemployment at an even higher rate of inflation, point E on short-run Phillips curve T_3. Thus, if a government wants to keep unemployment below the natural rate for any extended period, it must continually increase the rate of inflation.

The experience of the United States since the early 1960s illustrates this dynamic at work. One can identify four distinct short-run Phillips curves for the United States between 1961 and 1999 (see Figure 13.2). During the 1960s, the inflation–unemployment trade-off occurred within a fairly narrow range of relatively low inflation (an average of 3 percent). In the early 1970s, the American economy jumped to a new short-run Phillips curve that persisted until about 1983. The trade-off between inflation and unemployment is apparent on this new Phillips curve, but it occurs at a higher rate of inflation (which averaged about 8.2 percent throughout the period), without a corresponding decrease in the average level of unemployment. In fact, unemployment averaged 7.2 percent during this period, much higher than the level that prevailed during the 1960s.

The American economy moved to a third short-run Phillips curve between 1984 and 1994. Once again, the trade-off between inflation and unemployment is apparent in this period, although now it takes place at a lower rate of inflation. Moreover, the reduction in inflation in this period did not cause unemployment to rise. In fact, average unemployment was lower during these 10 years

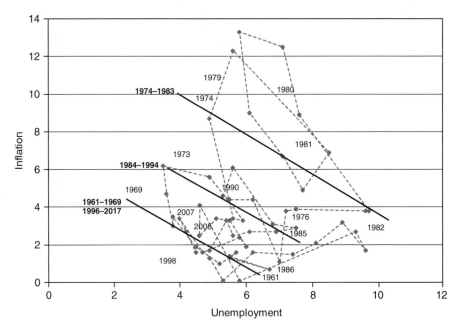

FIGURE 13.2

Phillips Curves in the United States, 1961–2017

Source: FRED: Economic Data, Federal Reserve Bank of St. Louis.

(6.5 percent) than in the previous 10 years, precisely the opposite of what we would expect if a stable long-run Phillips curve trade-off were at work.

Finally, during the 1990s, the United States migrated to a fourth short-run Phillips curve, which coincides well with the curve that held during the 1960s. As was the case during the previous 10 years, falling inflation did not raise unemployment relative to the earlier period. In fact, unemployment throughout this period has again been lower, on average, than it had been during the previous 10 years. The American experience during the last 40 years therefore illustrates the absence of a stable long-run trade-off between inflation and unemployment. Higher inflation during the 1970s did not reduce unemployment relative to the 1960s; lower inflation in the 1980s did not raise unemployment relative to the 1970s; and lower inflation in the 1990s did not raise unemployment relative to the 1980s.

The American experience was not unique, but was instead widely shared by most advanced industrialized countries. Average inflation rates in the EU during the 1970s, rising to 11 percent, were more than twice as high as they had been during the 1960s (see Table 13.1). Some countries experienced much higher inflation than these averages suggest; Italy and Great Britain, for example, saw their inflation rates rise above 20 percent in the mid-1970s. Yet, this higher inflation failed to produce any sustained reduction in unemployment. In fact, unemployment rose almost continuously throughout the decade (see Table 13.1). Unemployment more than doubled in the EU during the 1970s, jumping from 2.3 percent at the end of the 1960s to 5.4 percent in 1980. Thus, economic developments during the 1970s suggested that there was no stable trade-off between inflation and unemployment. Any gains in employment realized from monetary expansion were short term at best and were accompanied by a persistent increase in the rate of inflation.

All of this would be of little concern if inflation were innocuous. Inflation isn't innocuous, however, and may have a large negative impact on a country's economic performance. Inflation raises uncertainty among firms and unions, and this uncertainty can reduce investment and economic growth rates. Less

TABLE 13.1

Inflation and Unemployment, 1964–1990 (period averages)

	1964–1970		1971–1980		1981–1990	
	Inflation	Unemployment	Inflation	Unemployment	Inflation	Unemployment
United States	3.0	4.2	7.4	6.4	7.1	4.2
Germany	3.7	0.7	5.3	2.2	6.0	2.8
France	4.4	2.0	9.9	4.1	9.3	6.3
Britain	4.2	1.7	14.0	3.8	9.7	6.5
Italy	4.5	5.0	14.8	6.1	9.5	0.4
Japan	5.4	1.2	7.6	1.8	2.5	1.4

Source: OECD 1995.

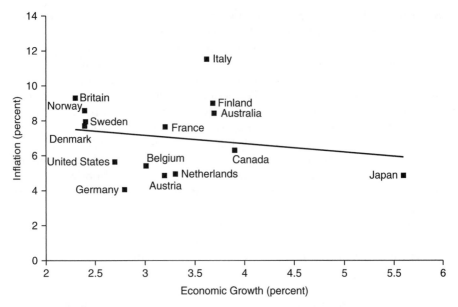

FIGURE 13.3

Inflation and Growth, 1969–1995

Source: OECD 1995.

investment and lower economic growth can in turn raise the natural rate of unemployment. The advanced industrialized countries provide some evidence about how inflation has affected economic performance during the last 26 years. Figure 13.3 illustrates the relationship between inflation and economic growth rates for 15 advanced industrialized countries over that period. Each point on the graph represents the average rate of inflation and the average rate of economic growth for one country between 1969 and 1995. The data suggest that countries with relatively high inflation rates have experienced lower economic growth, whereas countries with relatively low rates of inflation have had higher economic growth. Admittedly, this relationship is not very strong. In fact, Japan, which had one of the lowest rates of inflation and the fastest rate of economic growth of all the countries, is a bit of an anomaly. If we exclude Japan, the negative relationship between inflation and economic growth disappears.

A somewhat stronger pattern is evident when we look at the relationship between inflation and unemployment in these same countries (Figure 13.4). Here, each data point represents the average rate of inflation and the average rate of unemployment for one country between 1969 and 1995. These data suggest that countries with high inflation have had relatively high unemployment rates, whereas countries with low inflation have had relatively lower unemployment rates. At the high end, inflation in Italy averaged just under 12 percent and unemployment just under 8 percent. At the low end, inflation in Japan averaged 4.9 percent, and unemployment only 2 percent. Again, however, the relationship is not terribly strong.

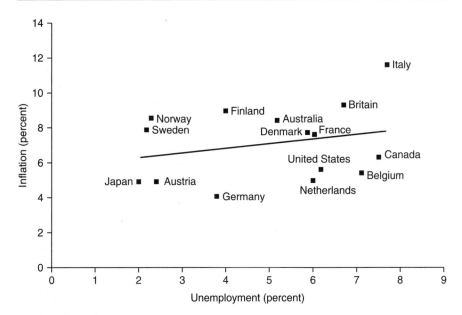

FIGURE 13.4

Inflation and Unemployment, 1969–1995

Source: OECD.

Of course, the determinants of economic growth and unemployment are far more complex than this simple correlation suggests. It may be that once the other factors that determine economic growth and unemployment are taken into account, inflation has no impact at all. What does seem clear, however, is that high inflation has not been associated with *better* economic performance. There is no evidence that countries with higher inflation experienced stronger economic growth or lower unemployment. Consequently, economists argue that, because inflation provides no permanent gains in terms of higher employment or growth and carries potentially large costs in terms of fewer jobs and less growth, society is best served by monetary policies that consistently deliver low inflation.

The apparent collapse of a stable Phillips curve trade-off between inflation and unemployment during the 1970s, combined with innovative economic theories that reconceptualized the relationship between inflation, employment, and monetary policy, altered the way governments thought about monetary policy. The Keynesian strategies that most governments had adopted in the early postwar period were based on the assumption of a stable long-run trade-off between inflation and unemployment. As evidence accumulated that such a trade-off did not exist, and as economists developed new theories to explain why it should not exist, governments began to question the utility of Keynesian strategies. If monetary policy could not be used to maintain full employment, but only produced inflation, and if inflation in turn had a negative impact on economic performance, what good was served by continuing to pursue Keynesian strategies of demand management?

During the 1980s, governments increasingly concluded that the answer to this rhetorical question was "not much." And as they did, they began to abandon the Keynesian approach to macroeconomic management in favor of an alternative approach to monetary policy. In this alternative approach, the only proper objective of monetary policy was to achieve and maintain a very low and stable rate of inflation. The shift from Keynesian strategies to the pursuit of **price stability** occurred first in Great Britain, under the leadership of Margaret Thatcher, and in the United States at the tail end of the Carter administration. Governments in the other advanced industrialized countries adopted similar policies during the 1980s.

THE TIME-CONSISTENCY PROBLEM

Although most governments were determined to achieve and maintain low inflation, few could easily do so. Expectations of high inflation were deeply embedded in society. By the 1980s, the 10-year history of high inflation had convinced workers and businesses to expect similarly high rates of inflation in the future. These expectations in turn shaped wage bargaining, giving inflation a momentum of its own. Expecting high inflation, unions demanded, and business provided, large annual nominal wage increases to keep pace. Governments then faced the unpleasant choice of delivering these high inflation rates or imposing high unemployment. In order to end inflation without generating a sharp increase in unemployment, each government would have to make a **credible commitment** to deliver low inflation. That is, each government would have to convince workers and businesses that it was truly determined to bring inflation down and keep it down.

Governments could not easily make credible commitments to low inflation, however, because they confronted time-consistency problems (Kydland and Prescott 1977). A **time-consistency problem** arises when the best course of action at a particular moment in time differs from the best course of action in general (Keech 1995, 38). Examinations in college courses offer an excellent example of the problem (Drazen 2000, 103). Professors are interested principally in getting their students to learn the material being taught in the course. Examinations are important only because they force students to study more than they would otherwise. As the semester begins, therefore, the professor's optimal strategy—that is, the best course of action in general—is to schedule a final exam. If no final exam is scheduled, most students will study little, but with the threat of a final exam, students will study harder and learn more from the course.

Once exam day arrives, however, the professor's optimal strategy is to cancel the exam. Because students expected an exam, they have studied hard and have learned as much about the material as they can. Giving the exam is pointless. Moreover, the professor is better off if he or she does not give the exam: he or she need not devote time to grading the exam and can use that time for other purposes. The students are also better off, for they are spared the time and the anxiety associated with taking the exam. Thus, the professor's optimal strategy at the beginning of the semester—to declare that a final exam will be given—is not his or her optimal strategy at the end of the semester. The professor, therefore, has time-inconsistent preferences.

Governments often have time-inconsistent monetary-policy preferences. The government's optimal strategy this year is to declare that it will use monetary policy next year to maintain price stability. If workers believe that the government is committed to price stability, they will set nominal wages accordingly. Once next year's nominal wages are set, however, the government can use monetary policy to reduce the rate of unemployment. By raising inflation above the level that it had announced and on which workers had based their nominal wage contracts, the government reduces real wages and raises employment. This decrease in unemployment can boost the government's popularity, making it more likely to win the next election. The government's monetary-policy preferences, therefore, are not consistent over time. It has an incentive to convince wage bargainers that it is committed to low inflation, but then, once it has done so, it has an incentive to expand the money supply to reduce unemployment.

Because the government has time-inconsistent monetary-policy preferences, wage bargainers have little incentive to believe any inflation target that the government announces. Imagine, for example, that you know that in every past semester your current professor has always announced at the beginning of the semester that there will be a final exam but subsequently has always canceled the exam. How credible would you find this professor's current beginning-of-the-semester promise to give a final examination? You would disregard the professor's promise because you recognize that he has an incentive to renege and because you have knowledge that he has reneged in the past. How much work would you then put into the course? Unless you were deeply interested in the subject, it is likely that you would work less hard in that class than in others in which you know that a final exam will be given.

The same logic applies to workers' responses to government statements about inflation. Because workers recognize that the government has an incentive to renege on a promise to deliver low inflation, they will always expect the government to deliver higher inflation than it promises. These expectations of higher-than-announced inflation cause workers to seek nominal wage agreements that protect real wages from the inflation that they expect rather than the amount that the government promises to deliver.

This interaction between wage bargainers and the government has perverse consequences for social welfare. Suppose the government truly intends to keep inflation next year at 2 percent and publicly announces its intention to do so. Workers disregard this promise, however, and expect the government to actually deliver 6 percent inflation during the next year. They then negotiate a nominal wage increase on the basis of this expectation. The government must now choose between two suboptimal monetary-policy responses. On the one hand, the government can refuse to expand the money supply in response to the 6-percent wage increase and stick to its promise to deliver 2-percent inflation. If it does so, however, real wages will rise by 4 percent, and as a consequence, unemployment will rise. On the other hand, the government can expand the money supply in order to deliver the 6-percent inflation that labor anticipated but that nobody really wants. Thus, either inflation or unemployment will be higher than it would be if the government could make a credible commitment to low inflation.

Most European governments faced precisely this situation in the late 1970s. The 10-year history of high inflation generated expectations of continued high inflation in the future. Unions thus sought, and business generally provided, nominal wage increases based on the expectation of annual inflation rates of 8 to 10 percent. With these wage contracts in place, governments faced the unpleasant choice between delivering the high inflation that everyone expected but nobody really wanted, or tightening monetary policy, reducing inflation, and raising unemployment substantially. Unwilling to embrace either option, many governments began to search for some way to make a credible commitment to price stability.

COMMITMENT MECHANISMS

Governments tried to establish a credible commitment to low inflation by creating commitment mechanisms in the form of institutions that tied their hands. Two institutions have been particularly prominent in this quest for a commitment mechanism: independent central banks and fixed exchange rates. In theory, both can provide a credible commitment by preventing the government from using monetary policy to achieve short-term objectives. In practice, however, only central-bank independence has actually done so.

Central-bank independence is the degree to which the central bank can set monetary policy free from interference by the government. More specifically, central-bank independence is a function of three things: the degree to which the central bank is free to decide what economic objective to pursue, the degree to which the central bank is free to decide how to set monetary policy in pursuit of this objective, and the degree to which central-bank decisions can be reversed by other branches of government (Blinder 1999, 54). A fully independent central bank has complete freedom to decide what economic goals to pursue, the capability of determining on its own how to use monetary policy to pursue those goals, and complete insulation from attempts by other branches of government to reverse its decisions.

Switzerland's central bank, the Swiss National Bank, provides a good illustration of a highly independent central bank (Eijffinger and Schaling 1993, 80–81). The National Bank Law that established the Swiss National Bank contains no provision whatsoever for allowing the government to influence monetary policy. In addition, the bank's principal policy-making body, the Bank Committee, is composed of ten members who are selected by the Bank Council, a group of 40 individuals responsible for the management of the bank. Thus, the government has no direct role in selecting the people that make monetary-policy decisions. As a consequence, the Swiss government cannot easily influence the monetary policies adopted by the Swiss National Bank, which thus controls Switzerland's monetary policy independently of the everyday vicissitudes of Swiss politics.

At the other end of the spectrum lies a fully subordinate central bank. Politically subordinate central banks implement monetary policy on behalf of, and in response to, the government, which determines the goals of monetary policy, instructs the central bank how to set monetary policy to achieve those goals, and can reverse the bank's decisions if they are contrary to the ones desired by the government. The Reserve Bank of Australia provides a good illustration of such a central bank (Eijffinger and Schaling 1993, 82–83). The Australian secretary of the treasury, a government minister, has final authority over monetary-policy decisions and must approve any interest-rate changes that the bank proposes. In addition, one government official has a vote on the Reserve Bank Board, the principal monetary-policy decision-making body. The Australian government thus has considerable control over the monetary-policy decisions made by the Reserve Bank. As a result, Australian monetary policy can be strongly influenced by the government's political needs.

Granting the central bank independence solves the time-consistency problem by taking monetary policy completely out of politicians' hands. Monetary policy is no longer set by politicians motivated by short-run political considerations. Instead, appointed officials who cannot easily be removed from office set monetary policy, which is thus insulated from politics. Insulating monetary-policy decisions from short-term political incentives makes it less likely that monetary policy will be directed toward short-term goals, such as a temporary increase in employment, and more likely that it will be oriented toward price stability. An independent central bank, therefore, can make a credible commitment to low inflation even though a government cannot.

The central bank's commitment to low inflation should in turn affect wage bargaining. Because the central bank is not motivated by political objectives, labor unions and businesses will believe that the central bank will deliver the inflation rate it promises to deliver. They will then negotiate next year's wage contract to embody this stated inflation target rather than their best guess of next year's inflation. As a consequence, they are more likely to establish a nominal wage that maintains the appropriate real wage. The result should be lower inflation, as well as less variation in the rate of unemployment and growth. Granting the central bank independence should lead to lower inflation, higher economic growth, and lower unemployment over the long run.

Do independent central banks actually have the economic consequences that are attributed to them in theory? There is some evidence that they do. Figure 13.5 depicts the relationship between central-bank independence and average inflation rates in 15 advanced industrialized countries between 1969 and 1995. The graph shows quite clearly that countries with more independent central banks (the countries located farther to the right along the horizontal axis) have experienced lower rates of inflation, on average, than countries with less independent central banks. Germany, Austria, and the United States, home to three of the most independent central banks in the advanced industrialized countries, have enjoyed substantially lower inflation than Italy and Britain, where politicians controlled monetary policy until quite recently.

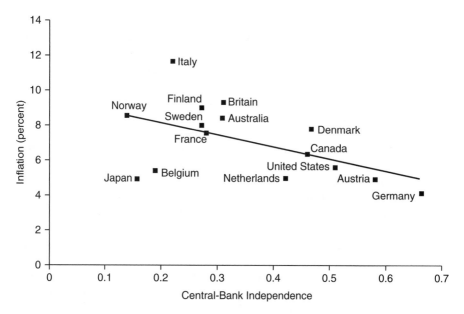

FIGURE 13.5

Central-Bank Independence and Inflation, 1969–1995

Source: OECD 1995 and Cukierman 1992. Higher index values indicate greater independence.

Policy Analysis and Debate

Central Bank Independence and Democracy

Question

Should democracies grant central banks political independence?

Overview

As we have seen, governments have granted their central banks considerable independence since the 1990s. And since 2008, central banks have shaped how societies have responded to and managed the global financial crisis and subsequent great recession. The ECB, for instance, played the leading role in shaping the EU's austerity policies in response to the Greek debt crisis. The justification for doing so lies in theories asserting that, by doing so, governments are able to commit to low inflation, which in turn generates better economic performance. Yet, granting the central bank independence is not costless. One important dimension of these costs is political. As Alan Blinder, former member of the Federal Reserve Board, has asked, "Isn't there something profoundly undemocratic about making the central bank independent of political control? Doesn't assigning so much power to unelected technocrats contradict some fundamental tenets of democratic theory (Blinder 1999, 66)?" Blinder has a point, for monetary policy is perhaps the single most important and single most powerful policy instrument at a government's disposal, and one might reasonably question the legitimacy of conferring such power on people who are not easily held accountable. In fact, it is surprising that democracies confer such independence. Could you imagine voters supporting a decision allowing an institution that was independent of political control to determine income tax rates?

Blinder also highlights two factors that he thinks reduce the inconsistency between democracy and independent central banks. First, legislatures confer independence on central banks; thus, they can withdraw this independence. Accordingly, society retains some influence over monetary policy. Second, central bankers are typically appointed by elected officials and can be removed from office (or not reappointed) if they behave in a manner that is inconsistent with societal interests. Therefore, society sacrifices its ability to influence day-to-day decisions, but retains the ability to set the broad parameters within which monetary policy is made. Should society give up some of its political rights in exchange for the economic benefits that independent central banks are supposed to provide?

Policy Options

- Grant the central bank independence and allow it to set monetary policy without political interference.
- Assert political control over the central bank to ensure that monetary policy reflects the public interest.

Policy Analysis

- How important are the economic benefits that central-bank independence provides?
- How large are the political costs arising from central-bank independence?
- Are any other political institutions granted independence from electoral politics in democracies?

Take A Position

- Which option do you prefer? Justify your choice.
- What criticisms of your position should you anticipate? How would you defend your recommendation against these criticisms?

Resources

Online: Look for two readings focusing on the European Central Bank: Christa Randzio-Plath and Thomas Padoa-Schippo, "The European Central Bank: Independence and Accountability" (www.zei.de/download/zei_wpB00-16. pdf), and Paivi Leino, "The European Central Bank and Legitimacy" (*www. jeanmonnetprogram.org/papers/00/001101.html*).

In Print: Alan Blinder, *Central Banking in Theory and Practice* (Cambridge, MA: MIT Press, 1999); Kathleen MacNamara and Sheri Berman, "Bank on Democracy: Why Central Banks Need Public Oversight," *Foreign Affairs* 78 (March–April 1999); Joseph E. Stiglitz, "Central Banking in a Democratic Society," *De Economist* 142(2), 1998: 199–226.

Other evidence indicates, however, that the lower inflation enjoyed by countries with independent central banks may not have come without cost. Figure 13.6 suggests that countries with more independent central banks have experienced lower rates of economic growth, on average, than countries without independent central banks. Economic growth in Germany, for example, averaged 2.8 percent in the 26-year period from 1969 to 1995, compared with 3.6-percent average annual growth rates in Italy. A similar effect appears to exist for unemployment: countries with independent central banks have had higher rates of unemployment, on average, than countries without independent central banks (Figure 13.7). Germany and the United States, for example, averaged higher unemployment over the 1969–1995 period than did Norway and Sweden, two countries in which governments retained control over monetary policy.

Thus, although independent central banks appear to reduce inflation, there is some evidence that they may also be associated with lower growth and higher unemployment. Once again, however, we should not conclude too much from these simple correlations. Economic outcomes are determined by a complex set of factors. Once these other factors are taken into account, it may turn out that independent central banks do not have a negative impact on economic growth and the rate of unemployment. What does seem clear, however, at least for this set of countries, is that independent central banks have been better able to deliver low inflation than governments have.

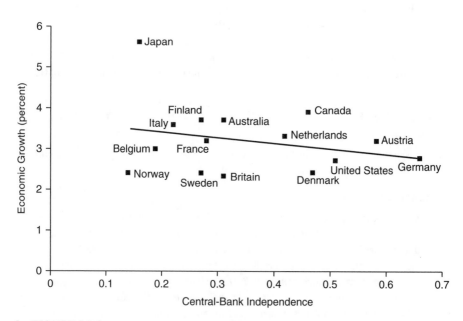

FIGURE 13.6

Central-Bank Independence and Economic Growth, 1969–1995

Note: Higher index values indicate greater independence.

Source: OECD 1995 and Cukierman 1992.

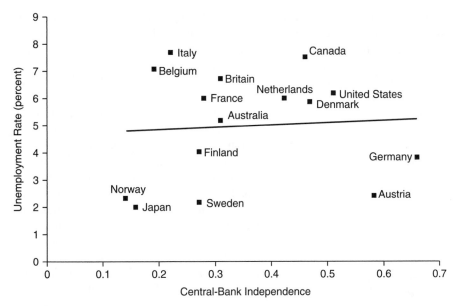

FIGURE 13.7

Central-Bank Independence and Unemployment, 1969–1995

Note: Higher index values indicate greater independence.

Source: OECD 1995 and Cukierman 1992.

In the early 1980s, however, few European governments had independent central banks. Consequently, they sought to establish a credible commitment by using the European monetary system (RMS) as an alternative to central-bank independence (Giavazzi and Giovannini 1989; Oatley 1997). The EMS offered the possibility of a credible commitment to low inflation because it was centered on the German central bank—the Bundesbank—the most independent central bank in the EU. As a result, German monetary policy was little influenced by political pressure, and it could therefore commit to low inflation. Moreover, the Bundesbank had a strong record of delivering low inflation. In fact, German inflation was the lowest among all EU countries, averaging only 4.4 percent between 1975 and 1984 (Oatley 1997, 82). A fixed exchange rate with Germany, therefore, might allow the EU countries with high inflation to "import" both the Bundesbank's low inflation policy and its credible commitment to that policy.

Governments imported German monetary policy by pegging their currencies to the German mark. The Bundesbank used monetary policy to maintain price stability in Germany and was relatively passive toward the mark's exchange rate against other EU currencies. The bank did engage in some foreign exchange market intervention, but only reluctantly and only when required to do so by the system's rules. Other governments used their monetary policies to peg their currencies to the German mark. By pegging to the mark, governments enduring high inflation were forced to mimic the Bundesbank's monetary policy. When the Bundesbank tightened that policy, other governments had to tighten their monetary policies in order to maintain their fixed exchange rates. As long as the Bundesbank continued to maintain low inflation in Germany, a fixed exchange rate inside the EMS would force other EU governments to pursue low-inflation monetary policies, too. By pegging to the mark, therefore, the high-inflation countries could "import" the Bundesbank's low-inflation monetary policy.

In order to "import" the Bundesbank credible commitment to low inflation, however, unions and businesses had to believe that the government was determined to maintain its fixed exchange rate. If these social partners viewed the fixed exchange rate as an irrevocable commitment—one that the government would not alter, regardless of domestic economic developments—they would adjust their wage-bargaining behavior accordingly. Recognizing that their government was committed to the Bundesbank's low-inflation monetary policy to maintain the fixed exchange rate, unions and businesses would reduce their estimates of future inflation rates. As these inflationary expectations fell, unions would seek smaller nominal wage increases. Thus, if a government could make a credible commitment to the fixed exchange rate, it could break the large nominal wage increases that were driving European inflation.

It proved very difficult for governments to demonstrate that they were irrevocably committed to a fixed exchange rate. The EMS did not take control of monetary policy away from the government and place it in the hands of appointed officials insulated from political pressures. Consequently, workers and businesses simply shifted their attention away from whether the government was committed to some inflation target and focused instead on whether the government was truly committed to its fixed exchange rate. Then, because EU governments retained full discretion over their currencies' exchange rates in the EMS, unions and businesses were never convinced that the government would not devalue within the system when it was politically convenient to do so. Governments gave them plenty of reason to be skeptical, as currency devaluations were quite common in the first 7 years of the system's operation. Consequently, even though EU governments did reduce inflation during the 1980s, and though the EMS facilitated this achievement by enabling countries with high inflation to "import" German monetary policy, there is little evidence that the fixed exchange rate provided a credible commitment to price stability. Instead, inflation fell because European governments accepted the higher unemployment that tight monetary policies generated in the context of large nominal wage increases.

EU governments' quest for a credible commitment to low inflation played an important role in the shift to, and the design of, economic and monetary union. The EU's central bank, the ECB, was established in January 1999 and is one of the world's most independent central banks. European governments participating in the EMU no longer have national monetary policies, a factor that greatly reduces their ability to determine national monetary policy. In addition, as a condition for membership in the EMU, EU governments have granted their own national central banks, which have become the operating agencies of the ECB, independence from politics. Finally, the laws governing the ECB and monetary policy in the EU prohibit national governments from attempting to influence the vote of their respective national central-bank governors in the ECB, and they also prohibit the EU's Council of Ministers from attempting to influence ECB decisions. National governments in the EMU, therefore, are three times removed from monetary-policy decisions: once by the EMU itself, a second time by domestic central-bank independence, and yet a third time by the rules governing decision making within the ECB.

The EU's shift to highly independent central banking finds echoes in the rest of the advanced industrialized world. The American central bank, the Federal Reserve, has been highly independent since its creation. Other governments have reformed central-bank laws to grant their banks greater independence. Japan moved to provide its central bank, the Bank of Japan, with greater independence in the mid-1990s. Great Britain granted its central bank, the Bank of England, full independence in 1997, even though it is not yet participating in the EMU. New Zealand granted its central bank greater independence in 1989. Thus, almost all central banks in the advanced industrialized world enjoy substantial independence, and most have gained this independence only recently. Independent central banks have directed monetary policy toward the maintenance of price stability, an objective that is often defined as about 1 to 2 percent inflation per year.

A Closer Look

Explaining Policy Variation Among Independent Central Banks

Most scholarship on central banks assumes that all independent central banks are basically alike. As we have seen, scholars assume that the major policy-relevant distinctions differentiate the behavior of independent central banks from the behavior of central banks that are subordinate to the political system. Freed from the pressures of electoral politics, independent central banks are generally assumed to pursue price stability. Very little energy has been devoted to considering whether and why the behavior and policies of one independent central bank differs substantially from the behavior and policies of another.

Yet, contemporary events suggest that independent central banks are not all cut from the same cloth. Consider how the European Central Bank and the Federal Reserve responded to economic conditions in the summer of 2010. At the time, the global economy appeared to be poised on the brink of a "double dip" recession. Recovery from the post-financial crisis recession had apparently stalled in the summer of 2010 and it looked like a slide into a second recession was possible. This economic environment, common to the U.S. and EU economies, generated very different responses from central banks in the two markets. In the EU, the ECB responded to these developments by calling loudly and repeatedly for fiscal and monetary consolidation (see Trichet 2010). Fearful that its operations to rescue the banking system during the 2009 crisis and those it undertook to prevent default during the Greek crisis of the spring of 2010 injected too much liquidity into the financial system, ECB policymakers began to voice concern about inflation. Such concerns have prompted the ECB to become more cautious about monetary policy, suggesting that inflation is as great a risk in the contemporary environment as deflation. Moreover, in the late spring of 2010, the ECB emerged as the leading advocate for fiscal consolidation in the wake of the EU's coordinated bailout of the Greek government.

In contrast, in the United States the Federal Reserve has evinced much greater concern about a possible stall of the recovery than about potential inflation resulting from the monetary expansion. James Bullard, President of the Federal Reserve Bank of St. Louis and traditionally an anti-inflation hawk, warned that the greatest danger the U.S. economy faced was a Japan-style deflation. He advocated a return to the policy of quantitative easing to supplement the zero-interest rate policy already in place. Although Ben Bernanke, current Chairman of the Federal Reserve Board, did not publicly share Bullard's concern, he has repeatedly noted the uncertainty surrounding current prospects and repeated his determination to use monetary policy to support economic recovery. As he said in his semi-annual appearance before Congress, "We ... will act if the economy does not continue to improve, if we don't see the kind of improvements in the labor market that we are hoping for and expecting" (Bernanke 2010). Bernanke also suggested, in contrast to the ECB, that it was too soon to consider fiscal consolidation: "I believe we should maintain our stimulus in the short term."

The differences between the ECB and the Fed are substantial. The two independent central banks offer very different analyses of the current economic environment and have pursued distinct policy responses. The ECB advocates vigilance against inflation; the Fed views deflation as the greater danger. The ECB advocates monetary and fiscal consolidation; the Fed advocates continued zero-interest rate policies and short-run fiscal stimulus. How do we account for such stark differences in the orientations of these two independent central banks?

One could argue that the differences are a consequence of uncertainty about the state of the economy and disagreement about the correct model of the economy. Given the recent crisis and remaining turbulence in EU sovereign debt markets, it may be especially difficult to forecast future economic conditions. Consequently, perhaps the ECB's focus on inflation and the Fed's relatively greater concern about a second recession or prolonged deflation reflect the extreme bounds of what current forecasts suggest about conditions over the next year. Alternatively, the two central banks might agree on the economic forecast, but disagree about which economic model is correct. The ECB might adhere to an economic model in which fiscal and monetary consolidation are necessary to generate economic recovery. The Fed might adhere to a model that calls for fiscal stimulus and monetary expansion in the current conditions.

Differences might also stem from broader differences in the political institutions within which the two banks operate. The ECB's determination to doggedly pursue price stability and advocate fiscal consolidation might reflect its belief that EU institutions make it exceedingly difficult for EU governments to reduce ECB independence. The EU, after all, is a polity with a large number of veto players. Indeed a treaty change would be required to alter the ECB's charter, and in treaty-making every EU government is a veto player. Hence, changing the ECB's charter would be an exceedingly difficult and extremely long process. This institutional structure might make ECB officials confident that they can pursue potentially unpopular policies without fearing that doing so will have repercussions for their independence. The Federal Reserve is less well protected by institutionalized veto players. In the current environment, the Democrats hold a majority in the Senate and control the Executive, while Republicans control the House. Hence, only three veto players are in play. In conjunction with the extreme criticism leveled at the Fed for failing to prevent the financial crisis might encourage Fed authorities to turn away from what they know will be unpopular policies and positions in order to reduce the likelihood of legislated change.

I am not certain that institutional differences account for the behavioral differences. Perhaps we need to pay attention to differences in policymakers' partisan preferences. Is the ECB being so determined about inflation because it tends to be run by a group with partisan affiliations to conservative parties? Does the Fed's more expansionary orientation reflect affiliation with Democrats on the Fed Reserve Board? Or maybe the differences reflect the way that decision-making rules within each bank aggregate the interests of distinct regional economic entities. Though the explanation is uncertain, striving to understand why similarly structured central banks behave so differently is an interesting question to which current research lacks an answer.

The last 25 years have thus brought fundamental changes to the politics of monetary policy. Throughout the advanced industrialized world, governments have abandoned the Keynesian strategies of demand management that dominated monetary policy in the early postwar period. As governments gradually, and in many cases grudgingly, accepted that there was no stable Phillips curve trade-off between inflation and unemployment that they could exploit for political advantage, they began to look for ways to tie their hands in order to reduce inflation and maintain price stability. The solution they adopted lay in granting political independence to their central banks and allowing those banks to set monetary policy free of daily political interference. As a consequence, throughout the industrialized world, monetary policy is uniformly focused on a single economic objective: maintaining price stability.

INDEPENDENT CENTRAL BANKS AND EXCHANGE RATES

The creation of independent central banks will obviously have an impact on the way that domestic politics shapes monetary and exchange-rate policy. Yet, because the shift to independent central banks is such a recent phenomenon, it is not clear how the dynamics will change. We can, however, draw on the models we developed in Chapter 12 to speculate a bit about how such politics might evolve.

One possibility is that the politics of monetary and exchange-rate policies will be characterized by conflict between elected officials and central banks. Such conflicts may emerge because of three interconnected aspects of monetary and exchange-rate politics in this new institutional environment. First, although the institutional framework governing monetary policy has changed, interest-group preferences over monetary and exchange-rate policies have not. Interest groups, class and sector based, are still affected by monetary and exchange-rate policies in the ways we examined in Chapter 12. As a consequence, interest groups retain incentives to pressure the government and the central bank to adopt the monetary and exchange-rate policies they prefer. The emergence of independent central banks means only that these groups must pursue their goals through different channels.

Second, despite the creation of highly independent central banks, monetary policy is not perfectly insulated from political influence. Even as national governments have relinquished control over monetary policy to independent central banks, they have retained control over exchange-rate policy. In the United States, the Department of the Treasury, an executive-branch agency, takes the lead in setting exchange-rate policy for the dollar (Destler and Henning 1989). Treasury officials are responsible for negotiating currency agreements with foreign governments, and the Treasury makes decisions about when to engage in foreign exchange market intervention (although intervention per se is conducted by the New York Federal Reserve Bank). The Treasury's control over the dollar's exchange rate is not absolute, however. In general, the Treasury is reluctant to act without the consent of, or at least the absence of opposition from, the Federal Reserve. Moreover, although the Treasury can request the Federal Reserve to engage in foreign exchange intervention, it cannot order it to do so on its account. Thus, although the Treasury takes the lead in U.S. exchange-rate policy, it has consistently sought cooperation with the Federal Reserve.

A similar split of authority is evident in the EU (see Henning 2007, 782). The Maastricht Treaty assigns to the ECB control over monetary policy, but to the Council of Ministers it assigns authority over exchange-rate policy (to "conclude formal agreements on an exchange rate system ... in relation to non-Community currencies" and to "formulate general orientations" toward non-EU currencies). In 1999 and 2000, European finance ministers and monetary officials worked out a clearer division of labor at meetings in Turku, Finland, and in Luxembourg. Under the resulting agreements, governments recognized the ECB's sole competence for deciding intervention, but the Eurogroup—the subset of EU finance ministers in the euro area—would set the strategic direction of exchange-rate policy. Moreover, they agreed that key officials would consult and coordinate their public statements. One can be forgiven if this clarification leaves control of exchange-rate policy in the EU a little uncertain.

Because monetary and exchange-rate policies are two sides of the same coin, government control of exchange-rate policy can be used to force the central bank to pursue the monetary policies that the government and its supporters desire. For example, some have argued that Helmut Schmidt, who was the German chancellor in the late 1970s and early 1980s, sought to create the EMS to force the Bundesbank to pursue a more expansionary monetary policy (Oatley 1997). Fixing the German mark to the French franc, the Italian lira, and other EU currencies, Schmidt thought, would force the Bundesbank to intervene in the foreign exchange market. In most instances, this intervention would prevent the mark from appreciating inside the EMS, and would therefore cause an expansion of the German money supply. The exchange-rate commitment would thus force the Bundesbank to pursue a looser monetary policy than it wanted.

An identical logic can be applied to the contemporary international monetary system. A government or, in the case of the EU, a group of governments that want a more expansionary monetary policy than the central bank is willing to adopt might use its control over exchange-rate policy to force the central bank to change its policy. Control over exchange-rate policy, therefore, provides governments with a back door through which they can attempt to influence monetary policy. To the extent that they use this back door, they are likely to come into conflict with the central bank.

Such conflicts are most likely to arise when the central bank wants the exchange rate to move in one direction in order to maintain price stability, but the government wants the exchange rate to move in the other direction to satisfy demands made by important interest groups. Conflicts of this nature arose periodically between the German government and the Bundesbank prior to the creation of the EMU and emerged in the EU in the fall of 1999 and summer of 2000. The euro depreciated sharply against the dollar and the yen in its first 2 years of existence. The ECB became concerned that the depreciation would generate inflation in the union as the price of traded goods rose in response to the euro's weakening. As Matti Vanhala, governor of the Bank of Finland, and therefore a member of the ECB's Governing Council, noted, the euro's weakness is "a bad thing from the point of view of the ECB's goals." The Bank of France's Jean-Claude Trichet echoed these concerns, emphasizing that the ECB needed to be "vigilant about inflation risks" arising from the euro's weakness (Barber 2000b, 9). The ECB tried to stem the euro's depreciation by raising interest rates. European governments were much less concerned about the euro's weakness and criticized ECB efforts to stabilize it. German Chancellor Gerhard Schroder, for example, stated that "the euro's low level [is] a cause for satisfaction rather than concern," because it increased German growth rates by making it easier for German companies to export (Barber 2000a, 8).

Similar dynamics emerged as the euro appreciated in 2007–2008. European business associations began warning that the rapid rise of the euro was harming exporters and slowing EU growth, and called upon EU governments to pressure the United States, Japan, and China to take steps to strengthen their currencies (Echikson 2007). EU finance ministers, including even the usually restrained

German finance minister, began voicing concerns about the ECB's reluctance to cut interest rates in order to stem the rise of the euro. Newly elected French President Nicolas Sarkozy played the lead in this drama, however. Almost immediately upon assuming office, Sarkozy announced his intention to pursue a larger role for the euro group in guiding ECB interest-rate policy (Bennhold and Dougherty 2007). The financial and current account imbalances in the Mediterranean members have generated calls for a weaker euro to facilitate adjustment and reduce the need for domestic austerity measures. Such pressures, if successful, would substantially reduce the ECB's independence.

Such conflicts are not simply between the government and the central bank: interest groups may exert pressures on whichever actor they believe is most likely to pursue their preferred policies. Thus, the sectoral model leads us to expect firms in the traded-goods industries to pressure the government for some form of exchange-rate arrangement because they benefit from a weak currency. Firms in the nontraded-goods sector, which benefit from a strong currency, might in turn become strong supporters of the central bank. Nor will industries in all countries have identical views. Indeed, the most recent euro appreciation has hit French, Italian, and Spanish firms much harder than German firms. In large part this reflects faster productivity growth in Germany than in the other countries, which in turn reflects greater labor market reforms.

Although it remains difficult to distinguish clear patterns in the new institutional environment, the political dynamics of monetary and exchange-rate policy have changed as governments have granted central banks greater political independence. Electoral, partisan, and sectoral interest-group pressures could rather easily have influenced the monetary and exchange-rate policies that governments adopted during the early postwar period. The granting of political independence to central banks makes it much more difficult for these groups to influence policy. Nevertheless, interest groups are still affected by monetary and exchange-rate policies in the ways detailed in the first half of this chapter. Consequently, these groups still have an incentive to try to influence those policies. How they do so and the extent to which they are successful will become clear only as the future unfolds.

CONCLUSION

The state-centered approach to monetary and exchange-rate politics emphasizes the social welfare-enhancing role of independent central banks. By taking monetary policy out of politics and placing it in the hands of officials tightly insulated from the push and pull of politics, society enjoys lower inflation and better overall economic performance than it would enjoy if governments retained control of monetary policy. Governments have embraced this logic, abandoning activist monetary policies and allowing independent central banks to dedicate monetary policy to the maintenance of price stability.

Two principal criticisms can be advanced against this state-centered approach. First, it offers more of a prescriptive framework than an explanatory framework. The approach tells us that social welfare is greater with an independent central bank than with a politically controlled central bank, and on the basis of this claim, it suggests that governments should grant their central banks greater political independence. It tells us very little, however, about what factors motivate elected officials to create independent central banks. One might argue that governments create independent central banks to maximize long-term social welfare. Yet, such an explanation rests uneasily with the central logic of the time-consistency problem. After all, the entire rationale for central-bank independence rests on the claim that elected officials care more about short-term electoral gains than long-run social welfare. We thus need some explanation for why governments that are supposedly unconcerned with long-run welfare gains create central-bank institutions whose sole purpose is to raise long-run social welfare.

Nor does this state-centered approach explain how monetary authorities who are responsible for an independent central bank are likely to behave. Although an independent central bank that gives priority to price stability may raise social welfare, little attention has been devoted to the question of whether the people who run the independent central bank actually have an incentive to give priority to price stability. Consequently, much work remains before this approach offers an explanation for the changes that have taken place in central-banking institutions since the early 1980s.

KEY TERMS

Accelerationist Principle

Central-Bank Independence

Credible Commitment

Natural Rate of Unemployment

Phillips Curve

Price Stability

Time-Consistency Problem

SUGGESTIONS FOR FURTHER READING

Perhaps the most comprehensive work on central-bank independence is Alex Cukierman, *Central Bank Strategy, Credibility, and Independence: Theory and Evidence* (Cambridge, MA: MIT Press, 1992). Pierre L. Siklos' *Central Banks into the Breach: From Triumph to Crisis and the Road Ahead* (Oxford: Oxford University Press, 2017) draws lessons for central banking from the Great Financial Crisis.

Ben S. Bernanke's *The Federal Reserve and the Financial Crisis* (Princeton, NJ: Princeton University Press, 2013) provides an insider's account of the Federal Reserve's response to the global financial crisis.

For current discussion of the euro and the ECB, see Martin Sandbu's *Europe's Orphan: The Future of the Euro and the Politics of Debt* (Princeton: Princeton University Press, 2015), and Joseph E. Stiglitz, *The Euro: How a Common Currency Threatens the Future of Europe* (New York: W.W. Norton, 2016).

Developing Countries and International Finance I: The Latin American Debt Crisis

Developing countries have had a difficult relationship with the international financial system. At the center of these difficulties lies a seemingly inexorable boom-and-bust cycle. The cycle typically starts with changes in international capital markets that create new opportunities for developing countries to attract foreign capital. Wanting to tap into foreign capital to speed economic development, developing countries exploit this opportunity with energy. Eventually, developing countries accumulate large foreign debt burdens and are pushed toward default. Looming default frightens foreign lenders, who refuse to provide new loans and attempt to recover many of the loans they had made previously. As foreign capital flees, developing countries are pushed into severe economic crises. Governments then turn to the International Monetary Fund (IMF) and the World Bank for assistance and are required to implement far-reaching economic reforms in order to gain those organizations' aid. This cycle has repeated itself twice in the last 25 years, once in Latin America during the 1970s and 1980s, and once in Asia during the 1990s. A similar, though distinct, cycle occurred in sub-Saharan Africa. The political economy of North–South financial relations focuses on this three-phase cycle of overborrowing, crisis, and adjustment.

Each phase of the cycle is shaped by developments in the international financial system and inside developing societies. Developments in the international financial system, including changes in international financial markets, in the activities of the IMF and the World Bank, and in government policies in the advanced industrialized countries, powerfully affect North–South financial relations. They shape the ability of developing countries to borrow foreign capital, their ability to repay the debt they accumulate, and the economic reforms they must adopt when crises strike. Events that unfold within developing countries determine the amount of foreign capital that developing societies accumulate and influence how governments and economic actors in those countries use their foreign debt. These decisions in turn shape the ability of governments to service their foreign debt and therefore influence the likelihood that the country will experience a debt crisis.

This chapter and the next examine the evolution of this cycle in North–South financial relations. We begin with a short overview of international capital flows in order to understand why they are important for developing societies and how developing societies gain access to foreign capital. We then briefly examine the relatively stable immediate postwar period during which capital flows to developing countries were dominated by foreign aid and foreign direct investment (FDI). The rest of the chapter focuses on the first major financial crisis of the postwar period: the Latin American debt crisis of the 1980s. We examine how it originated, how it was managed, and its consequences, political and economic, for Latin America.

FOREIGN CAPITAL AND ECONOMIC DEVELOPMENT

If a cycle of overborrowing, crisis, and adjustment has characterized the history of capital flows from the advanced industrialized countries to the developing world, why do developing countries continue to draw on foreign capital? Why do they not simply refrain from borrowing that capital, thus bringing the cycle to an end? Developing countries continue to draw on foreign capital because of the potentially large benefits that accompany its apparent dangers. These benefits arise from the ability to draw on foreign savings to finance economic development.

Investment is one of the most important factors determining the ability of any society to raise per capita incomes (Cypher and Dietz 1997, 239). Yet, investment in developing societies is constrained by a shortage of domestic savings (Bruton 1969; McKinnon 1964). Table 14.1 illustrates average savings rates during the last 40 years throughout the world. The most striking difference that the table highlights is between the high-income Organization for Economic Co-operation and Development (OECD) countries and the world's

TABLE 14.1	
Average Savings Rates as a Percent of Gross Domestic Product, 1970–2006	
High-Income OECD Countries	21.7
Least Developed Countries	13.4
East Asia and the Pacific	34.5
Latin America and the Caribbean	19.9
Sub-Saharan Africa	16.9
South Asia	21.2

Note: OECD = Organisation for Economic Co-operation and Development.

Source: World Bank, *World Development Indicators 2008 CD-ROM* (Washington, DC: World Bank Publications, 2008).

poorest countries. On average, the high-income countries saved slightly more than one-fifth of their national income each year between 1970 and 2006. In contrast, the least developed countries have saved less than 15 percent of their national income per year. Even when a developing country has a high savings rate, as in East Asia and the Pacific and in Latin America, the low incomes characteristic of a developing society mean that the total pool of savings is small. The scarcity of savings limits the amount, and raises the cost, of investment in these societies.

Foreign capital adds to the pool of savings available to finance investment. Many studies have found a one-to-one relationship between foreign capital inflows and investment: one dollar of additional foreign capital in a developing country produces one dollar of additional investment (see, e.g., Bosworth and Collins 1999; World Bank 2001a). Higher investment in turn promotes economic development. Indeed, a considerable body of research suggests that developing countries that have participated in international financial markets during the last 30 years have experienced faster economic growth rates than economies that remain insulated from international finance (see IMF 2001; World Bank 2001a). Although foreign capital does not always yield higher growth (see, for example, Rodrik 1998), a country that draws on foreign capital has the *opportunity* to reach a higher development trajectory. Many other factors, some of which lie inside developing countries and others that inhere in the international financial system, shape the extent to which a developing country can take advantage of this opportunity.

Foreign capital can be supplied to developing countries through a number of channels. The broadest distinction is between foreign aid and private capital flows. **Foreign aid**, or official development assistance, is foreign capital provided by governments and by multilateral financial institutions such as the **International Bank for Reconstruction and Development** (IBRD), known more commonly as the World Bank. In addition to the **World Bank**, a number of regional development banks, including the Inter-American Development Bank, the African Development Bank, and the Asian Development Bank provide concessional loans to support development. These more established institutions were joined in 2016 by the Asian Infrastructure Investment Bank (AIIB). The AIIB is an initiative of the Chinese government intended to foster the construction of transportation, energy, and telecommunciations infrastructure in Asia. The U.S. did not join the AIIB and tried (unsuccessfully) to convince its European allies to remain outside as well. The AIIB thus may be yet another manifestation of the shift in economic power from North America to Asia.

The largest share of foreign aid is provided as bilateral development assistance—that is, foreign aid granted by one government directly to another government. In 2016, the advanced industrialized countries together provided $143 billion of bilateral assistance to developing countries. The World Bank and other multilateral development agencies provided an additional $61 billion. The United States provided the most aid in absolute terms in 2016, about $33.6 billion (Figure 14.1). Japan, France, Germany, and Great Britain were the four next largest donors in absolute terms. China has emerged as

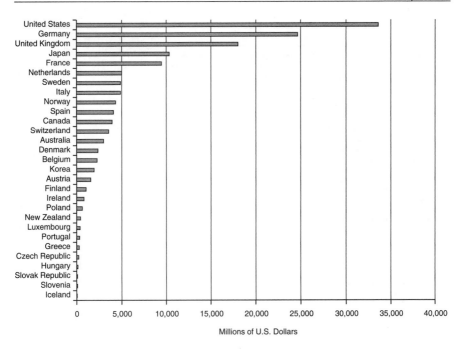

FIGURE 14.1

Foreign Aid Expenditures, 2016

Source: Official and private flows, OECD International Development Statistics (database).

an important source of aid, providing slightly less than $9 billion per year. The rankings change considerably when we measure aid as a share of the donor country's national income (Figure 14.2). By this measure, the smaller northern European countries are the most generous, dedicating between 0.6 and 1 percent of their total national incomes to foreign aid. The United States emerges as one of the least generous of the high-income countries, dedicating only 0.2 percent of its national income to foreign aid.

Private capital flows transfer savings to the developing world through the activities of private individuals and businesses. Private capital can be transferred to developing countries in a number of ways. Commercial banks transfer capital by lending to private agents or governments in developing societies. Private capital is also transferred when individuals and large institutional investors purchase stocks traded in developing-country stock markets. Private capital can also be transferred through bonds sold by developing-country governments and businesses to individuals and private financial institutions in advanced industrialized societies. Finally, multinational corporations (MNCs) transfer capital each time they build a new or purchase an existing factory or other productive facility in a developing country. The relative importance of each type of private capital flow has varied across time, as we shall see as we move through this chapter and the next.

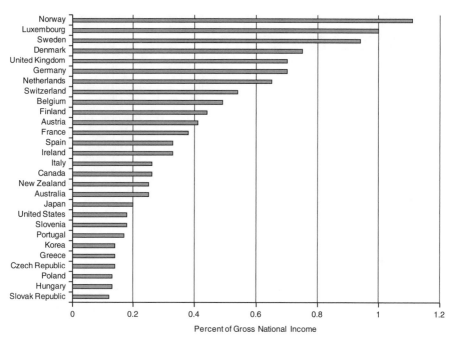

FIGURE 14.2
Foreign Aid Expenditures as a share of National Income, 2016

Throughout the postwar period, private capital flows have been larger than foreign aid flows. In general, private capital flows typically constitute somewhere between two-thirds and three-quarters of all capital flows to the developing world. Yet, developing countries vary substantially in their ability to attract private capital inflows; thus, some countries rely much more heavily than others on foreign aid. These different abilities to attract private capital reflect private lenders' need to balance return against risk when investing in developing societies. On the one hand, because savings are scarce, the return on an investment should be substantially higher in developing societies than in the advanced industrialized world. Consequently, private lenders should earn a higher return on an investment in a developing country than on an equivalent investment in an advanced industrialized country. This pulls in private capital. On the other hand, foreign investment is risky. Private lenders face the risk of default—the chance that a particular borrower will be unwilling or unable to repay a debt. Private lenders also face political risk—the chance that political developments in a particular country will reduce the value of an investment. Political risk arises from political instability—coups, revolution, or civil war— and, less dramatically, from the absence of strong legal systems that protect foreign investment. Large risks substantially reduce an investment's expected return. This risk acts to push private capital away from a country. Indeed, such risks are one of, if not the principal reason why sub-Saharan Africa attracts so little private capital.

More recently, remittances have emerged as an increasingly important third source of capital for developing countries. Remittances are transfers of income earned by migrant workers from jobs in their host countries back to family and friends in their country of origin. Migrant workers typically transfer money back home in small amounts—a couple hundred dollars a month—using international money transfer companies such as MoneyGram, Western Union, and Ria. The countries that receive the largest remittance inflows are those that have the largest number of workers living overseas. Not surprisingly, China and India receive the largest volume of remittances (roughly $65 billion in 2016), and they each receive more than twice as much as each of the next largest recipient countries (the Philippines, Mexico, and Pakistan). The overall volume of remittances has increased dramatically during the last 30 years. The World Bank estimates that total remittances rose from less than $50 billion in 1990 to almost $600 billion by 2017 (World Bank 2017b). This level is four times as large as combined foreign aid flows from the Development Assistance Committee (DAC) countries—the major donor countries. Existing research indicates that remittances are a less volatile source of foreign capital than private capital flows, are often pro-cyclical rather than counter-cyclical, and because remittances flow to individuals rather than to governments or private firms, they have a greater impact on households than other types of capital flow (see, e.g., Grabel 2009).

Developing societies import foreign capital, therefore, because it makes it possible to finance more investment at a lower cost than they could finance if they were forced to rely solely on their domestic savings. And although developing countries can import some capital through foreign aid programs, such programs are limited. Thus, if a developing society is to import foreign savings, it must rely on private capital. The desire to import foreign savings and the need to rely on private capital flows to do so creates difficulties for developing societies, for private capital never flows to developing societies in a steady stream. Instead, financial markets shift from excessive concern about the risk of lending to developing societies to exuberance about the opportunities available in those societies and then back to excessive concern about the risk. As a consequence, a country that is unable to attract private capital one year is suddenly inundated with private capital the next, and then, just as suddenly, is shut out of global financial markets as private investors cease lending. The consequences are often devastating. We turn now to look at the first revolution of this cycle.

COMMERCIAL BANK LENDING AND THE LATIN AMERICAN DEBT CRISIS

The composition and scale of foreign capital flows to the developing world changed fundamentally during the 1970s. In the 1950s and 1960s, foreign aid and FDI were the principal sources of foreign capital for developing countries, and neither was abundant. Only the United States had resources for foreign aid, and these flows were quite limited. World Bank lending was also limited. It perceived its mission as providing loans at "close-to-commercial rates of interest to cover the foreign exchange costs of productive projects" (Mason and Asher 1973, 381). And most of its lending in this period also financed postwar reconstruction in Europe (Mason and Asher 1973).

Development aid increased a little beginning in the late 1950s. The World Bank created the **International Development Association** (IDA) and began to provide concessional loans to many of its member governments. At the same time, a number of **regional development banks,** such as the Inter-American Development Bank, the Asian Development Bank, and the African Development Bank, were created to provide concessional lending on the model of the IDA. Advanced industrialized countries also expanded their bilateral aid programs during the 1960s. As a consequence, the amount of aid provided through multilateral development agencies increased fourfold between 1956 and 1970, whereas bilateral development assistance more than doubled during the same period (see Table 14.2). By the end of the 1960s, official development assistance to developing countries was almost twice as large as private capital flows.

The expansion of foreign aid programs during the 1960s reflected changing attitudes in advanced industrialized countries. These changing attitudes were in turn largely a product of the dynamics of decolonization. World Bank officials recognized that governments in the newly independent countries would have great difficulty borrowing on private capital markets and would be unlikely to qualify for lending under the World Bank's normal terms. The World Bank therefore began to reconsider its resistance to concessional lending. American attitudes toward foreign aid changed in response to political consequences of decolonization. American policymakers believed that the rising influence of developing countries in the United Nations would eventually lead to the creation of an agency that offered development loans at concessional rates. The creation of such a UN agency could undermine the World Bank and weaken American influence over development lending. U.S. officials began to support

TABLE 14.2

Financial Flows to Developing Countries, Millions of U.S. Dollars, 1956–1970

Official Development Assistance	1956	1960	1965	1970
Official Government Aid	2,900.0	4,236.4	5,773.1	6,587.4
Multilateral Organizations	272.5	368.5	312.9	1,176.0
Organization of the Petroleum Exporting Countries (OPEC)				443.5

Private Finance	1956	1960	1965	1970
Foreign Direct Investment	2,500.0	1,847.9	2,207.4	3,557.2
Portfolio Flows	0.0	408.2	836.0	777.0

Source: Wood 1986, 83.

a concessional lending agency within the World Bank, therefore, in order to prevent the creation of a rival within the United Nations, where developing countries had greater influence.

At the same time, during the late 1950s and early 1960s, American policy-makers increasingly came to view foreign aid as a weapon in the battle against the spread of Communism throughout the developing world. Nowhere was this more evident than in the Kennedy administration's "Alliance for Progress," which was designed to use U.S. government aid to promote socioeconomic reform in Latin America in order to prevent the spread of Cuban-style socialist revolutions throughout the region (Rabe 1999). These changes in attitude contributed to the tremendous growth of foreign aid programs during the 1960s.

The paucity of private lending to developing countries changed fundamentally during the 1970s. On the one hand, commercial banks found themselves awash with deposits in the wake of the 1973 oil shock. The oil shock generated large current-account surpluses in the oil-exporting countries. Saudi Arabia's current-account surplus jumped from $2.5 billion in 1973 to $23 billion in 1974 and then averaged about $14 billion during the next 3 years. These surpluses, called **petrodollars**, provided the financial resources that developing countries needed to cover their greater demand for foreign capital. Commercial banks intermediated the flows, accepting deposits from oil exporters and finding places to lend them. The process came to be called **petrodollar recycling**.

It turned out that the growing supply of loanable funds was matched by a growing demand for foreign capital in developing countries. Higher oil prices cost developing countries about $260 billion during the 1970s (Cline 1984). Because most developing countries were oil importers, higher prices for their energy imports required them to reduce other imports, to raise their exports, or to borrow from foreign lenders to finance the larger current-account deficits they faced. Cutting imports was unattractive for governments deeply committed to ISI strategies. Increasing exports was also difficult, as import substitution had brought about a decline in the export sector in most countries. Consequently, the higher cost of oil widened current-account deficits throughout the developing world.

ISI also generated a growing demand for foreign capital. In Latin America, governments were responsible for between one-third and one-half of total capital formation (Thorp 1999, 169). Governments created state-owned enterprises to drive industrialization, and they provided subsidized credit to targeted sectors. These strategies led to an expansion of government expenditures in connection with the initial investment and then in connection with continued subsidies to the unprofitable state-owned enterprises they created (Frieden 1981, 420). Government revenues failed to grow in line with these rising expenditures. As a consequence, budget deficits widened, reaching on average in Latin America 6.7 percent of gross domestic products (GDP) by the end of the 1970s. In some countries, deficits were even larger. Argentina's budget deficit rose to over 10 percent of GDP in the mid-1970s and remained above 7 percent of GDP until the early 1980s. Mexico's budget deficit increased in the early 1970s and then exploded—to more than 10 percent of GDP—in the early 1980s. Governments needed to finance these deficits, which generated a demand for foreign capital.

Commercial banks looking for places to lend and developing-country governments looking for additional funds found each other in the mid-1970s. Commercial banks loaned directly to governments, to state-owned enterprises, and to government-owned development banks. The result was rapid accumulation of foreign debt (see Table 14.3). In 1970, the developing world as a whole owed only $72.7 billion to foreign lenders. By 1980, total foreign debt had ballooned to $586.7 billion. Most was owed by a small number of countries. The 40 most heavily indebted developing countries owed a total of $461 billion in 1980, close to 80 percent of the total. Latin American countries were among the largest borrowers. The foreign debt of the seven most heavily indebted Latin American countries—Argentina, Brazil, Chile, Colombia, Mexico, Peru, and Venezuela—increased by a factor of ten between 1970 and 1982. By the early 1980s, these seven countries accounted for about 80 percent of all Latin American debt and for about one-third of all developing-world foreign debt.

Initially, foreign debt fueled economic growth. The positive impact of commercial bank lending is quite clear in aggregate statistics for the period. In Latin America as a whole, economic growth averaged 5.6 percent per year between 1973 and 1980. Some Latin American countries grew even more rapidly. In Brazil, one of the largest borrowers, the economy grew by 7.8 percent per year between 1973 and 1980; Mexico realized average growth of 6.7 percent over the same period.

Behind this robust economic growth, however, lay some worrying trends. Debt problems emerge when foreign debt grows more rapidly than the country's ability to service its debt. A country's **debt-service capacity**—its ability to make the payments of interest and principal required by the terms of the loan—is a function of how much it needs to pay relative to its export earnings. Thus, as a country increases its foreign debt, it must also expand its export earnings to service the debt comfortably. Exports failed to keep pace with debt service throughout Latin America. Governments invested foreign capital in nontraded-goods. Mexico, Argentina, and Venezuela, for example, created massive hydroelectric projects that added nothing to export revenues (Thorp 1999, 209). Governments borrowed to buy military equipment, to pay for more expensive oil, and to subsidize consumer goods. Even when foreign capital was invested in the traded-goods sector, ISI's focus on capital-intensive projects failed to generate exports. As a consequence, debt service grew faster than export revenues, causing debt-service ratios to rise sharply (Table 14.4). By 1978, debt service was consuming 38 percent of Latin America's export revenues. Debt-service ratios were even higher in Brazil, Chile, Mexico, and Peru.

Rising debt-service ratios rendered Latin American countries vulnerable to international shocks. Three major shocks hit Latin America in 1979 and the early 1980s. First, interest rates began to rise in the United States as the U.S. sought to reduce inflation. Rising American interest rates were transmitted directly to Latin America, because two-thirds of Latin American debt carried variable interest rates. Higher interest rates thus increased debt-service costs. Second, recession

TABLE 14.3

Developing-Country Foreign Debt, Billions of U.S. Dollars, 1970–1984

	All Developing Countries[1]	30 Most Heavily Indebted Countries[2]	7 Most Heavily Indebted Latin American Countries (See also remaining columns)	Argentina	Brazil	Chile	Colombia	Mexico	Peru	Venezuela
1970	72.7	65	28	5.8	5.7	3.0	2.2	7.0	3.2	1.4
1978	391.7	317	142	13.3	54.6	7.4	5.1	35.7	9.7	16.6
1979	480.8	377	174	21.0	61.3	9.4	5.9	42.8	9.3	24.1
1980	586.7	461	214	27.2	71.5	12.1	6.9	57.4	9.4	29.3
1981	703.2	539	261	35.7	81.5	15.7	8.7	78.2	8.6	32.1
1982	809.9	606	294	43.6	93.9	17.3	10.3	86.1	10.7	32.2
1983	880.1	661	316	45.9	98.5	17.9	11.4	93.0	11.3	38.3
1984	921.8	686	328	48.9	103.9	19.7	12.0	94.8	12.2	36.9

Notes:
[1] Developing Countries comprise all 157 low- and middle-income countries as defined by the World Bank.
[2] Most Heavily Indebted Countries comprise Algeria, Argentina, Bolivia, Brazil, Chile, Colombia, Costa Rica, Cote d'Ivoire, Ecuador, Egypt, India, Indonesia, Jamaica, Malaysia, Mexico, Morocco, Nigeria, Pakistan, Peru, Philippines, South Korea, Sudan, Syria, Thailand, Turkey, Uruguay, Venezuela, Yugoslavia, Zaire, Zambia.

Source: World Bank, *World Development Indicators 2001 CD-ROM* (Washington, DC: World Bank Publications, 2001).

TABLE 14.4

Debt-Service Ratios in Latin America [(Payments of Principal plus Interest)/Export Earnings], 1970–1984

	Argentina	Brazil	Chile	Colombia	Mexico	Peru	Venezuela	All Latin American Countries
1970	n.a.	n.a.	n.a.	28	n.a.	n.a.	4	n.a.
1978	42	58	54	12	n.a.	50	9	38
1979	23	63	44	14	66	34	19	38
1980	37	63	43	16	44	45	27	36
1981	46	66	65	22	46	59	23	40
1982	50	82	71	30	51	49	30	47
1983	70	55	54	38	45	34	27	41
1984	63	45	60	30	45	30	25	39

Note: n.a. = not available.

Source: World Bank, *World Development Indicators 2001 CD-ROM* (Washington, DC: World Bank Publications, 2001).

in the advanced industrialized world reduced the demand for Latin American exports and reduced their terms of trade (Cline 1984). Latin America's export revenues thus declined. By 1980, therefore, Latin American governments were facing larger debt-service payments and declining export earnings. As if this wasn't enough, oil prices rose sharply again in 1979, imposing a third shock.

Many governments responded to these shocks by borrowing more. As a result, foreign debt jumped after 1979, rising to $810 billion by 1982. Debt-service ratios also rose sharply (see Table 14.4). For Latin America as a whole, debt service consumed almost 50 percent of all export earnings in 1982. Brazil's position was the most precarious, as debt service consumed more than 80 percent of its export revenues in 1982. These debt problems became an active debt crisis in August of 1982, when Mexico informed the United States government that it could not make a scheduled debt payment (see Kraft 1984). Commercial banks immediately ceased lending to Mexico. Fearing that Mexico's problems were not unique, they stopped lending to other developing countries as well.

The abrupt cessation of commercial bank lending forced governments to eliminate the macroeconomic imbalances that their commercial bank loans had financed. Current-account deficits had to be eliminated because governments could not attract the capital inflows required to finance them. Budget deficits had to be reduced because governments could no longer borrow from commercial banks to pay for them. Rapid adjustment in turn caused economic activity to fall sharply throughout Latin America (Table 14.5). The most heavily indebted countries suffered the worst. Argentina's economy shrank by 6 percent in 1981 and then by another 5 percent in 1982. Brazil's economy shrank by 4 percent in 1981 and then by another 3 percent in 1983. Mexico's economy shrank by 1 percent in 1982 and by another 3 percent in 1983. The end of capital inflows, therefore, ended the economic boom of the 1970s abruptly.

TABLE 14.5

Economic Growth Rates (Percent) in Latin America, 1979–1983

	Latin America	Argentina	Brazil	Chile	Mexico	Peru	Colombia	Venezuela
1979	7	10	7	9	10	6	5	1
1980	9	4	9	8	9	3	4	−4
1981	−1	−6	−4	5	9	7	2	0
1982	−1	−5	1	−10	−1	−1	1	−2
1983	−2	4	−3	−4	−4	−12	2	−4

Source: World Bank, *World Development Indicators 2009 CD-ROM* (Washington, DC: World Bank Publications, 2001).

Commercial bank lending therefore proved a mixed blessing. On the one hand, it allowed many developing countries to finance the large current-account deficits generated by the oil shock. In the absence of these loans, governments would have been forced to reduce consumption sharply to pay for energy imports. Commercial bank loans also allowed developing countries to invest more than they could have otherwise. Private capital flows therefore relaxed many of the constraints that had characterized the foreign-aid-dominated system of the 1950s and 1960s. On the other hand, the rapid accumulation of commercial bank debt rendered developing countries vulnerable to shocks imposed by developments in the U.S. and Europe. The management of this debt crisis dominated North–South financial relations throughout the 1980s.

MANAGING THE DEBT CRISIS

By 1982, the 30 most heavily indebted developing countries owed more than $600 billion to foreign lenders. Few could service that debt. As they defaulted, they turned to governments in the creditor countries for help. As a result, the Latin American debt crisis came to be managed within a framework that reflected the interests of the creditors. This regime was based on a simple, if somewhat unbalanced, exchange between the creditor and debtor governments. Creditor governments offered new loans and rescheduled the terms of existing loans in exchange for policy reform in the indebted countries.

The debt regime was based on the creditors' strongly held belief that developing countries eventually could repay their debt. Creditors initially diagnosed the debt crisis as a short-term **liquidity problem**. The creditors believed that high interest rates and falling export earnings had raised debt service above the debtor governments' current capacity to pay. Once interest rates fell and growth resumed in the advanced industrialized world, developing countries could resume debt service.

This diagnosis shaped the creditors' initial response to the crisis. Because they believed that the crisis was a short-term liquidity problem, they prescribed short-term remedies. They required the debtor countries to implement macroeconomic stabilization programs. **Macroeconomic stabilization** was intended to eliminate the large current-account deficits in order to reduce the demand for external financing. The centerpiece of the typical stabilization program was the reduction of the budget deficit. Balancing the budget has a powerful effect on domestic economic activity, reducing domestic consumption and investment, and thereby the demand for imports. Moreover, the resulting unemployment would reduce wages, making exports more competitive. Exchange-rate devaluation would further improve the balance of trade. The smaller current-account deficits that would follow would require smaller capital inflows. In the ideal world, stabilization would produce current-account surpluses.

In exchange for macroeconomic stabilization, creditor governments provided new loans and rescheduled existing debt to offset the liquidity shortage. New loans were made available by the IMF and by commercial banks through a process called concerted lending. In 1983 and 1984, the IMF and commercial banks provided a total of $28.8 billion to the indebted governments (Cline 1995, 207). Developing countries were also allowed to reschedule existing debt payments. Debt owed to commercial banks was rescheduled in the **London Club,** a private association established and run by the large commercial banks. Rescheduling agreements neither forgave debt nor reduced the interest payments attached to the debt. They merely rescheduled the payments that debtor governments had to make, usually offering a grace period and extending the maturity of the debt. Access to both, however, was conditional on prior agreement with the IMF on the content of a stabilization package.

A Closer Look

The International Monetary Fund

The IMF is based in Washington, DC. It has a staff of about 2,690, most of whom are professional economists, and a membership of 184 countries. The IMF controls $311 billion that it can lend to member governments facing balance-of-payments deficits. Two ruling bodies—the Board of Governors and the Executive Board—make decisions within the IMF. The Board of Governors sits at the top of the IMF decision-making process. Each country that is a member of the IMF appoints one official to the Board of Governors. Typically, the country's central-bank president or finance minister will serve in this capacity. However, the Board of Governors meets only once a year; therefore, almost all IMF decisions are actually made by the Executive Board, which is composed of 24 executive directors, each of whom is appointed by IMF member governments. Each of eight countries (the United States, Great Britain, France, Germany, Japan, China, Russia, and Saudi Arabia) appoints an executive director to represent its interests directly. The other 16 executive directors represent groups of IMF member countries. For example, Pier Carlo Padoan (an Italian) is currently the executive director representing Albania, Greece, Italy, Malta, Portugal, and Spain, whereas B. P. Misra (from India) is currently the executive director representing Bangladesh, Bhutan, India, and Sri Lanka. The countries belonging to each group jointly select the executive director who represents them. A managing director appointed by the Executive Board chairs the Board. Traditionally, the managing director has been a European (or at least non-American).

Voting in the Board of Governors and the Executive Board is based on a weighted voting scheme. The number of votes each country has reflects the size of its quota in the stabilization fund. The United States, which has the largest quota, currently has 371,743 votes (17.14 percent of the total votes). Palau, which has the smallest quota, currently has only 281 votes (0.01 percent of the total votes). Many important decisions require an 85 percent majority. As a result, both the United States, with 17 percent of the total votes, and the EU (when its member governments can act jointly), with more than 16 percent of the total vote, can veto important IMF decisions. As a block, developing countries also control sufficient votes to veto IMF decisions. Exercising this developing-country veto requires a level of collective action that is not easily achieved, however. In contrast with other international organizations, therefore, the IMF is not based on the principle of "one country, one vote." Instead, it is based on the principle that the countries that contribute more to the stabilization fund have a greater say over how that fund is used. In practice, this means that the advanced industrialized countries have much greater influence over IMF decisions than developing countries.

The IMF lends to its members under a number of different programs, each of which is designed to address different problems and carries different terms for repayments:

- Standby arrangements are used to address short-term balance-of-payments problems. This is the most widely used IMF program. The typical standby arrangement lasts 12 to 18 months. Governments have up to 5 years to repay loans under the program, but are expected to repay these credits within 2 to 4 years.
- The Extended Fund Facility was created in 1974 to help countries address balance-of-payments problems caused by structural weaknesses. The typical arrangement under this program is twice as long as a standby arrangement (3 years). Moreover, governments have up to 10 years to repay loans under the program, but the expectation is that the loan will be repaid within 4.5 to 7 years.
- The Poverty Reduction and Growth Facility (PRGF) was established in 1999. Prior to that year, the IMF had provided financial assistance to low-income countries through its Enhanced Structural Adjustment Facility (ESAF), a program that financed many of the structural adjustment packages during the 1980s and 1990s. In 1999, the PRGF replaced the ESAF. Loans under the PRGF are based on a Poverty Reduction Strategy Paper, which is prepared by the borrowing government with input from civil society and other development partners, including the World Bank. The interest rate on PRGF loans is only 0.5 percent, and governments have up to 10 years to repay loans.

■ Two new programs were established in the late 1990s in response to financial crises that arose in emerging markets. The Supplemental Reserve Facility and the Contingent Credit Line provide additional financing for governments that are in the midst of or are threatened by a crisis and thus require substantial short-term financing. Countries have up to 2.5 years to repay loans under both programs, but are expected to repay within 1.5 years. To discourage the use of these programs, except in a crisis, both programs carry a substantial charge on top of the normal interest rate. [H17039]

By 1985, the creditor coalition was revising its initial diagnosis. Latin American economies failed to recover as growth resumed in the advanced industrialized world. Although creditors still believed that countries could repay their debt, they concluded that their ability to do so would require more substantial changes to their economies. Stabilization would not be sufficient. This new diagnosis generated a second, more invasive, set of policy reforms known as **structural adjustment**. Structural adjustment rested on the belief that the economic structures developed under ISI provided too little capacity for export expansion. Governments were too heavily involved in economic activity, economic production was too heavily oriented toward the domestic market, and locally produced manufactured goods were uncompetitive in world markets. This economic structure stifled entrepreneurship, reduced the capacity for economic growth, and limited the potential for exporting. Structural adjustment programs sought to reshape the indebted economies by reducing the government's role and increasing that of the market. Reforms sought substantial market liberalization in four areas: trade liberalization, liberalization of FDI, privatization of state-owned enterprises, and broader deregulation to promote economic competition.

Structural adjustment programs were accompanied by additional lending by the World Bank, new IMF programs, and commercial banks. Commercial banks were asked to provide $20 billion of new loans over a 3-year period to refinance one-third of the total interest coming due in the period. Multilateral financial institutions, particularly the World Bank, were asked to provide an additional $10 billion over the same period. In all cases, fresh loans from commercial banks hinged upon the ability of debtor governments to gain financial assistance from the IMF, and loans from the IMF and World Bank were contingent upon the willingness of governments to agree to structural adjustment programs.

This debt regime pushed the costs of adjustment onto the heavily indebted economies. Table 14.6 illustrates the economic consequences of the crisis for Latin America as a whole. Investment, consumption, and economic growth in the region all fell sharply after 1982. Indeed, by the end of the decade most still had not recovered to their 1980 levels. The economic crisis hit labor markets particularly hard; unemployment rose and real wages fell by 30 percent over the course of the decade. Real exchange rates were devalued by 23 percent,

TABLE 14.6

Economic Conditions in Latin America, 1980–1990

	1980–1981	1982	1983	1984	1985	1986–1990
GDP[1]	100.0	95.6	91.3	92.2	92.7	94.1
Unemployment[1]	77.0	74.0	70.3	70.4	69.9	71.6
Investment[1]	24.4	19.6	14.9	15.2	16.1	15.9
Unemployment[2]	6.7				10.1	8.0
Real Wages[3]	100.0				86.4	68.9
Imports[4]	−12.3	−9.7	−7.5	−8.0	−7.9	−9.2
Exports[4]	12.5	12.6	13.6	14.5	14.2	15.2
Net Transfers[4]	12.2	−18.7	−31.6	−26.9	−32.3	
Fiscal Deficit[5]	3.7	5.4	5.2	3.1	2.7	
Inflation	53.2%	57.7%	90.8%	116.4%	126.9%	

Notes:
[1] GDP, Consumption, and Investment rates as a percentage of 1980–1981 gross domestic product (GDP).
[2] Unemployment rate of open unemployment as a percentage of total labor force.
[3] Real Wages as index of real wages in unemployment.
[4] Imports, Exports, and Net Transfers in $U.S. billions.
[5] Fiscal Deficit as a percent of GDP.
Sources: Thorp 1999; Edwards 1995, 24; Edwards 1989, 171.

on average, and by more substantial amounts in Chile (96 percent), Uruguay (70 percent), and a few other countries (Edwards 1995, 29–30). This adjustment brought a small increase in exports, a sharp reduction in imports, and an overall improvement in trade balances. From an aggregate $2 billion deficit in 1981, Latin America as a whole moved to a $39 billion trade surplus in 1984 (Edwards 1995, 23).

Latin American governments used these current-account surpluses for debt service. Net transfers, which measure new loans minus interest-rate payments, provide a measure of the scale of this debt service. In 1976, net transfers for the 17 most heavily indebted countries totaled $12.8 billion, reflecting the fact that these countries were net importers of capital. Between 1982 and 1986, net transfers for these same 17 countries averaged negative $26.4 billion per year, reflecting the substantial flow of funds from the debtor countries to banks based in the advanced industrialized countries (Edwards 1995, 24). Thus, domestic economic adjustment generated the resources needed to service foreign debt.

The puzzle in the management of this crisis concerns the ability of creditors to push such a large share of the adjustment costs onto the debtor governments. That is, why were creditors so much more powerful than debtors? The short answer is that creditors were better able to solve the free-rider problem than debtors. As a result, creditors could maintain a common front that pushed the costs onto the debtor governments.

Creditor power lay in the ability to condition lending to policy reform. In order to exploit this power, the creditors had to solve a key free-rider problem (see Lipson 1985). Each individual creditor recognized that debt service in the short run required additional financing and in the long run depended on structural reforms that governments would not implement without additional financing. But each individual creditor also preferred that other creditors provide these new loans. Thus, each creditor had an incentive to free ride on the contributions of the other members of the coalition.

Commercial banks had an incentive to free ride on IMF lending. Loans from the IMF would allow the debtor governments to service their commercial bank debt. If the IMF carried the full burden of new lending, commercial banks would be repaid without having to put more of their own funds at risk. Within the group of commercial banks involved in the loan syndicates, smaller banks had an incentive to free ride on the large banks. Smaller banks had much less at stake in Latin America than the large commercial banks had, because the smaller banks had lent proportionately less as a share of their capital. Consequently, default by Latin American governments would not necessarily imperil the smaller banks' survival. Thus, whereas the large commercial banks could not walk away from the debt crisis, the smaller banks could (Devlin 1989, 200–201). Smaller banks could refuse to put up additional funds knowing that the large banks had to do so. Once the large banks provided new loans, the small banks would benefit from the resulting debt service.

The IMF helped creditors overcome this free-riding problem. To prevent large commercial banks from free riding on IMF loans, the IMF refused to advance credit to a particular government until commercial banks pledged new loans to the same government. This linkage between IMF and private lending in turn encouraged the large commercial banks to prevent free riding by the small commercial banks. Because the large commercial banks were unable to free ride on the IMF, they sought to compel the small banks to provide their share of the new private loans. Large banks threatened to exclude smaller banks from participation in future syndicated loans—a potentially lucrative activity for the smaller banks—and threatened to make it difficult for the smaller banks to operate in the interbank market. American and European central-bank officials also pressured the small banks. Free riding thus became costly for the small banks.

Policy Analysis and Debate

International Monetary Fund Conditionality

Question

Should the IMF attach conditions to the credits it extends to developing countries?

Overview

IMF conditionality has long been a source of controversy. Critics of the practice argue that the economic policy reforms embodied in IMF conditionality agreements force governments to accept harsh austerity measures that reduce economic growth, raise unemployment, and push vulnerable segments of society deeper into poverty. Moreover, the IMF has been accused of adopting a "one size fits all" approach when designing conditionality agreements. It relies on the same economic model in analyzing each country, and it recommends the same set of policy changes for each country that comes to it for assistance. Consequently, critics allege, IMF policy reforms are often inappropriate, given a particular country's unique characteristics.

The IMF defends itself by arguing that most developing-country crises share a common cause: large budget deficits, usually financed by the central bank. Such policies generate current-account deficits larger than private foreign lenders are willing to finance. Governments turn to the IMF only when they are already deep in crisis. Because most crises are so similar, the solution to them should also be similar in broad outline: governments must bring spending in line with revenues, and they must establish a stable base for participation in the international economy. And though the short-term costs can be high, the economy in crisis must be returned to a sustainable path, whether the IMF intervenes or not. Should the IMF require governments to implement policy reforms as a condition for drawing from the fund?

Policy Options

- Continue to require conditionality agreements in connection with IMF credits.
- Abandon conditionality and allow governments to draw on the IMF without implementing stabilization or structural adjustment measures.

Policy Analysis

- To what extent are the economic crises that strike countries that turn to the IMF solely a product of IMF conditionality agreements?
- To what extend does conditionality protect IMF's resources? What would happen to these resources if conditionality were eliminated?

Take A Position

- Which option do you prefer? Justify your choice.
- What criticisms of your position should you anticipate? How would you defend your recommendation against these criticisms?

Resources

Online: Do an online search for "IMF conditionality." Follow the links to some sites that defend conditionality and to some that criticize the practice. The Hoover Institution maintains a useful website that examines IMF-related issues. Search for "Meltzer Commission" to find some strong criticisms of the IMF's activities. The IMF explains and defends conditionality in a fact sheet. (Search "IMF facts conditionality.")

In Print: Joseph Stiglitz, "What I Learned at the World Economic Crisis," *The New Republic*, April 17, 2000, and *Globalization and Its Discontents* (New York: W.W. Norton and Company, 2002); Kenneth Rogoff, "The IMF Strikes Back," *Foreign Policy* (January–February 2003): 38–46; Graham R. Bird, *IMF Lending to Developing Countries: Issues and Evidence* (London: Routledge, 1995); Tony Killick, *IMF Programmes in Developing Countries: Design and Impact* (New York: Routledge, 1995).

The ability to solve the free-riding problems produced a united front that effectively controlled financial flows to Latin America. The IMF and the commercial banks advanced new loans to Latin American governments (although the commercial banks did so quite reluctantly), and all accepted a share of the risks of doing so. This united front allowed the creditors to reward governments that adopted a cooperative approach to the crisis with new financing, and to deny additional financing to governments that were unwilling to play by the creditors' rules.

Governments in the debtor countries were unable to exploit their potential power. Debtor power lay in the threat of collective default. Although each of the large debtors owed substantial funds to American banks—in 1982, for example, Mexico's debt to the 9 largest American commercial banks equaled 44.4 percent of those banks' combined capital—no single government owed so much that a unilateral default would severely damage American banks or the American economy (Cline 1995, 74–75). Collective action could provide power, however. If all debtor governments defaulted, the capital of the largest American commercial banks would be eliminated, creating potentially severe consequences for the American economy. A credible threat to impose such a crisis might have compelled the creditors to provide more finance on easier terms, to demand less austerity, and perhaps to forgive a portion of the debt.

Yet, debtor governments never threatened a collective default (Tussie 1988). Latin American governments held a series of conferences early in the crisis to discuss a coordinated response. Governments used these conferences to demand that the creditors "share responsibility in the search for a solution," and they demanded "equity in the distribution of the costs of adjustment," but they never threatened a collective default (Tussie 1988, 291). Argentina was the only country to adopt a non-cooperative stance toward the creditors' coalition, and it tried to convince other Latin American governments to follow suit. Those governments, however, were unwilling to take a hard line; in fact, they encouraged Argentina to adopt a more cooperative stance (Tussie 1988, 288). Thus, instead of threatening collective default, debtor governments played by the creditors' rules.

Debtor governments never threatened collective default because they were caught in a prisoner's dilemma. Even though the threat of collective default could yield collective benefits, each government had an incentive to defect from a collective threat in order to seek a better deal on its own. The incentive to seek the best deal possible through unilateral action, rather than a reasonably good deal through collective action, arose because each debtor government believed that it possessed unique characteristics that enabled it to negotiate more favorable terms than would be available to the group as a whole. Mexico, for example, believed that it could exploit its proximity to the United States and its close ties with the U.S. government to gain more favorable terms. Brazil, which by 1984 was running a current-account surplus, believed that it could use this stronger position to its advantage in negotiations with its creditors (Tussie 1988, 288).

The bilateral approach that the creditors adopted reinforced these fears of defection. Because creditors negotiated with each debtor independently, they could adopt a "divide and conquer" strategy. They could offer "special deals" to induce particular governments to defect from any debtor coalition that might form. If one government did defect, it would gain favorable treatment, whereas the others would be punished for their uncooperative strategy. Punishment could include fewer new loans, higher interest rates and larger fees on rescheduled loans, and perhaps more-stringent stabilization agreements. Thus, even though coordinated action among the debtor countries could yield collective gains, each individual government's incentive to seek a unilateral agreement dominated the strategy of a collective threat of default.

The debt regime pushed the adjustment costs onto debtor governments, therefore, because creditors were able to overcome free-riding problems and develop a coordinated approach to the debt crisis, and debtors were not. The creditors used their power to create a regime that pushed the costs of the debt crisis onto the heavily indebted countries. The regime was based on the dual premises that all debt would be repaid in the long run, but debt service would require the indebted governments to implement far-reaching economic policy reforms. Conditionality thus provided a powerful lever to induce developing countries to adopt economic reforms: few developing countries could afford to cut themselves off completely from external financial flows. After 1982, these governments found that the price of continued access to international finance was far-reaching economic reform.

THE DOMESTIC POLITICS OF ECONOMIC REFORM

Although the creditors established the structure for managing the debt crisis, used conditionality to promote economic reform, and set the parameters on the range of acceptable policies that could emerge from the reform process, the pace at which debtor governments adopted stabilization and structural adjustment programs was determined by domestic politics. Domestic politics caused most governments to delay implementing stabilization and structural adjustment programs.

Economic reform required governments to impose costs on powerful domestic interest groups. The need to impose these costs generated distributive conflict that delayed economic stabilization. Distributive conflict revolved around which domestic groups would bear the costs associated with balancing the budget. Governments had to choose which programs would be cut. Would the government reduce subsidies of food or energy, or would it reduce credit subsidies to industry? In addition, governments had to decide which taxes to raise and who would pay them.

The need to make these decisions generated a war of attrition between veto players. Each veto player pressured to reduce expenditures on programs from which it did not benefit and to tax other groups. Each blocked efforts to cut its preferred programs or tax it at a higher rate (Alesina and Drazen 1991). This war of attrition drove the politics of stabilization throughout the early 1980s. The interest groups that had gained most from import substitution stood to lose the most from stabilization and structural adjustment. Import-competing firms that had benefited from government credit subsidies would be hit hard by fiscal retrenchment. State-owned enterprises would be particularly hard hit, as they would lose the government infusions that had covered their operating deficits during the 1970s. Workers in the urbanized nontraded-goods sector who had benefited from government subsidies of basic services, such as utilities and transportation, and essential food items would also be hit hard by budget cuts. Public-sector employees would suffer as well, as budget cuts brought an end to wage increases and forced large reductions in the number of government employees.

Unwilling to accept the reduction in income implied by fiscal austerity, interest groups blocked large cuts in government expenditures. In Brazil, for example, the military government attempted to implement an orthodox stabilization program in the early 1980s, but "both capitalists and labor in modern industry ... demanded relief from austerity. So too did much of the urban middle class including government functionaries whose livelihood was imperiled by attacks on public spending" (Frieden 1991b, 134). These groups shifted their support to the civilian political opposition, which took power from the military. Once in office, the new civilian government abandoned austerity measures. The Brazilian case was not unique: the import-substitution coalition was well positioned to block substantial cuts in government programs in most heavily indebted countries.

The inability to reduce government expenditures resulted in high inflation throughout Latin America. Many governments financed budget deficits by selling bonds to their central banks. Printing money to pay for government expenditures sparked inflation. Annual average inflation in Latin America rose from about 50 percent in the years immediately preceding the crisis to over 115 percent in 1984 and 1985 (Table 14.6). Worse, these regional averages hide the most extreme cases. In Argentina, inflation averaged 787 percent per year during the 1980s. Brazil fared a little better, enduring average rates of inflation of 605 percent throughout the decade (Thorp 1999, 332). Bolivia's experience was the most extreme, with inflation rising above 20,000 percent in late 1985.

Even rapid inflation was insufficient to induce governments to cut expenditures. In Argentina, Brazil, and Peru, governments responded to high inflation with **heterodox strategies** (see Edwards 1995, 33–37). Advanced as an alternative to standard IMF stabilization plans, heterodox strategies attacked inflation with government controls on wages and prices. The Argentinean and Brazilian plans illustrate the approach. In both programs, the government froze prices and wages in the public sector. Each government also introduced new currencies and established a fixed exchange rate. Initially, the programs appeared to work, as inflation dropped sharply in the first 6 months. Early successes were reversed, however, because neither government was willing to reduce government expenditures. In less than a year, inflation rates rose again and the programs were scrapped (Edwards 1995, 37).

It wasn't until the late 1980s that Latin America governments began to make painful economic adjustments. Governments reduced fiscal deficits and brought inflation under control. Macroeconomic stabilization provided a base upon which to begin structural reforms. Governments began to liberalize trade and privatize state-owned industries. Many governments also began to reduce their role in domestic financial systems and to liberalize capital accounts as well (Edwards 1995, 212).

Three factors induced governments to embark on economic reform. First, the economic crisis altered interest-group politics. Key members of the import-substitution coalition lost strength and faced higher costs from opposing reform. As a result, groups that had once been willing and able to block reform increasingly lost the capacity to do so. The economic crisis also caused "individuals and groups to accept [the fact] that their special interests need[ed] to be sacrificed ... on the altar of the general good" (Williamson 1994, 19). Economic crisis thus created a new political consensus that the old order had failed and that reform was necessary. By weakening key interest groups and by forcing many of these same groups to redefine their interests, the severity of the economic crisis itself removed the political obstacles to reform.

Second, the United States initiated a new approach to the debt crisis in 1989. In March 1989, the United States encouraged commercial banks to negotiate debt-reduction agreements with debtor governments. Under this **Brady Plan** (named after Nicholas J. Brady, the secretary of the U.S. Treasury), debtor governments could convert existing commercial bank debt into bond-based debt with a lower face value. The precise amount of debt reduction that each government realized would be determined by negotiations between the debtor government and its commercial bank creditors. To make the proposal attractive to commercial banks, the advanced industrialized countries and the multilateral financial institutions advanced $30 billion with which to guarantee the principal of these Brady bonds. This guarantee allowed commercial banks to exchange the uncertain repayment of a large bank debt for guaranteed repayment of a smaller amount of bond debt.

The Brady Plan strengthened the incentive to embark on reform by increasing the domestic benefits of reform. Large debt burdens reduced the incentive to adopt structural reforms because a significant share of the gains from reform would be dedicated to debt service. Commercial banks would thus be the primary beneficiary of reform. It is not hard to see why domestic groups would be reluctant to accept costly reforms. Reducing the debt burden ensured that a larger share of the gains from reform would accrue to domestic groups. As a result, the short-run costs of reform would be offset by long-run gains. This plan created a greater incentive to accept the short-term costs that stabilization and structural adjustment entailed.

Mexico was the first to take advantage of the Brady Plan, concluding an agreement in July 1989 (see Cline 1995, 220–221). The deal reduced Mexico's net transfers by about $4 billion, an amount equal to about 2 percent of Mexico's GDP. Reducing debt service allowed the Mexican economy to grow by 2 percentage points more than would have been possible without debt reduction (Edwards 1995, 81). By 1994, Brady Plan agreements covered about 80 percent of commercial bank debt and reduced debt-service payments by about one-third (Cline 1995, 232).

Finally, as the economic crisis deepened, governments became more willing to recognize that the East Asian model offered lessons for Latin America. The Economic Commission on Latin America (ECLA) played an important role in prompting this recognition (see Economic Commission for Latin America and the Caribbean 1985). The ECLA had begun to look closely at East Asia in the mid-1980s and was able to create a new consensus among Latin American governments that the East Asian model was relevant to Latin American development. As an ECLA study recommended in the late 1980s, "[T]he debt problem requires a structural transformation of the economy in at least two senses: the growth strategy needs to be *outward oriented* and largely based on a domestic effort to raise savings and productivity" (cited in Edwards 1995, 148). The ECLA's transformation

> was like "Nixon in China." When the institution that had for decades defended import substitution expressed doubts about its validity and recognized that there were lessons to be learned from the East Asian experience with outward-oriented policies, it was difficult to dismiss those doubts as purely neo-liberal propaganda.
>
> (Edwards 1995, 52)

The Latin American debt crisis was declared over in the mid-1990s (Cline 1995, 39). In hindsight, it is clear that the crisis was more than a financial one: it was a crisis of economic development. The accumulation of foreign debt during the 1970s reflected efforts to rejuvenate the waning energies of ISI. Moreover, the crisis itself, and the debt regime through which it was managed, transformed developing countries' development strategies. Governments abandoned state-led ISI in favor of a market-based and export-oriented strategy. As a consequence, developing countries fundamentally altered their relationship with the international economy.

CONCLUSION

The Latin American debt crisis illustrates the tragic cycle at the center of North–South financial relations. A growing demand for foreign capital generated in part by international events and in part by domestic developments combined with a growing willingness of commercial banks to lend to developing societies in order to generate large capital flows to Latin American countries during the 1970s. The resulting accumulation of foreign debt rendered Latin American societies extremely vulnerable to exogenous shocks. When such shocks hit in the late 1970s and early 1980s, governments found that they could no longer service their commercial bank debt, and commercial banks quickly ceased lending fresh funds. As the supply of foreign capital dried up, Latin American economies were pushed into crisis.

The Latin American debt crisis also forced governments in the advanced industrialized world to establish an international regime to manage the crisis. In the resulting debt regime, the IMF, the World Bank, and commercial banks provided additional financial assistance to the heavily indebted countries on the condition that governments implement stabilization and structural adjustment packages. This approach pushed most of the costs of the crisis onto Latin America. Moreover, the reforms it encouraged provoked far-reaching changes in Latin American political and economic systems. With a few changes that we will examine in the next chapter, this debt regime remains central to the management of developing-country financial crises.

Although the Latin American debt crisis is unique in many respects, in others it is all too typical. And though this crisis was the first of the postwar period, it would not be the last. In fact, crises have become increasingly common during the last 20 years, and the more recent ones share many of the central characteristics of the Latin American crisis and have been managed in much the same way. They have also generated much discussion about whether and how the international financial system should be reformed in order to reduce the number and severity of such crises. We examine these issues in Chapter 15.

KEY TERMS

Brady Plan
Debt-Service Capacity
Foreign Aid
Heterodox Strategies
International Bank for
    Reconstruction and
    Development

International Development
    Association
Liquidity Problem
London Club
Macroeconomic
    Stabilization
Petrodollar Recycling

Petrodollars
Regional Development
    Banks
Structural Adjustment
World Bank

SUGGESTIONS FOR FURTHER READING

For a detailed treatment of the relationship between development and the international
    financial institutions, see Eric Helleiner, *Forgotten Foundations of Bretton Woods:
    International Development and the Making of the Postwar Order* (Ithaca: Cornell
    University Press, 2016).
On the 1980s debt crisis, see Robert Devlin, *Debt and Crisis in Latin America: The
    Supply Side of the Story* (Princeton, NJ: Princeton University Press, 2016).
For the politics of IMF lending, see James Vreeland, *The International Monetary Fund:
    Politics of Conditional Lending* (New York: Routledge, 2007), and Erica Gould,
    *Money Talks: the International Monetary Fund, Conditionality, and Supplementary
    Financiers* (Palo Alto: Stanford University Press, 2006).
On the IMF and neoliberalism, see Sarah Babb and Alexander Kentikelenis, 2018.
    "International Financial Institutions as Agents of Neoliberalism," in D. Cahill, M.
    Cooper, M. Konings, and D. Primrose (eds.), *The SAGE Handbook of Neoliberalism*
    (Thousand Oaks, CA: SAGE Publications, 2018: 16–27).

Developing Countries and International Finance II: The Global Capital Flow Cycle

G lobal investors became nervous in the summer of 2017 in the face of discussion about tightening monetary policy in the United States and European Union. At the center of investor concern was the fear that tighter policy in the U.S. would spark a substantial outflow of capital from emerging markets. Large and sustained capital outflows would force governments in emerging market economies to raise interest rates, erode their accumulated foreign exchange reserves, and possibly spark currency crises and broader balance-of-payments crises. Such fears arose in the summer of 2017 because memories of the way markets reacted to the U.S. decision to tighten monetary policy in 2013 and 2014 remained fresh. In that period, stock markets in emerging economies fell and interest rates rose sharply as investors shifted back into dollar-denominated assets in response to rising interest rates in the U.S. The episode angered many emerging market policymakers, who accused the Federal Reserve of showing little concern for how its policy affected emerging market economies.

This episode constitutes the most recent manifestation of a broader dynamic in the global financial system, called the global capital flow cycle, that has come into sharp relief since 1990. The global **capital flow cycle** is characterized by two central components. One component is a two-phase cycle in the distribution of cross-border capital flows. In one phase, financial capital flows into emerging market economies in large volumes, where it strengthens currencies and inflates asset prices. In the second phase, investors sell their emerging market assets in favor of dollar-denominated assets, thereby depressing asset prices, raising interest rates, and creating the risk of banking and currency crises. The second component is the role of American monetary policy in shifting the cycle from one phase to the other. When interest rates fall in the U.S., capital flows to emerging markets in search of higher returns. When interest rates in the U.S. rise, capital flows out of emerging markets and back into dollar-denominated assets. American policy thus generates a capital flow cycle that increases financial volatility in the emerging market economies.

Although this global capital flow cycle was an important factor in the evolution of the Latin American debt crisis, the cycle has become more pronounced since 1990. Since 1990, the capital flow cycle has gone through two full rotations. The first rotation began in the early 1990s with large and sustained capital inflows to a small number of Asian economies, Argentina, Brazil, Mexico, Russia, and Turkey. This phase of the cycle ended with a series of crises that began in the late 1990s and widespread calls for reform of the global crisis management regime. The second revolution began in the wake of the 2008 U.S.-centered financial crisis as loose monetary policy in the U.S. encouraged investors to search for higher returns in emerging market economies. The shift to a more restrictive monetary policy in the U.S. since 2014 has created substantial volatility for emerging markets, but has not yet produced a major banking or currency crisis. The challenges governments face in managing their economies in the face of the volatilities generated by this capital flow cycle has caused the International Monetary Fund to become more forgiving of capital controls.

We examine this global capital flow cycle in this chapter. We look first at the series of crises that struck during the 1990s, focusing deeply on the largest of them: the 1997 Asian crisis. We then examine how that crisis subsequently prompted considerable discussion about reforming the international financial system in order to alter how crises are managed and to try to reduce the frequency of such crises in the future. We then look at the most recent revolution of the cycle, which began in the wake of the U.S. financial crisis of 2008. The chapter concludes by drawing some more general lessons.

THE ASIAN FINANCIAL CRISIS

The first revolution of the global capital flow cycle occurred between 1990 and 1999. Developing countries attracted little new private capital during the 1980s. It was not until the end of the decade and after reform had taken root that private capital began flowing again. Private capital flows resumed in a changed environment, however. On the one hand, policies toward private capital flows were radically different. Although most governments had restricted capital flows in connection with import substitution, many dismantled these controls in connection with policy reforms implemented during the 1980s and early 1990s. Consequently, it became much easier for private individuals to move capital into and out of emerging markets. On the other hand, financial liberalization in advanced industrialized countries had increased the importance of securities—stocks and bonds—as sources of financing. The growing importance of nonbank capital flows was reinforced by the lingering effect of the Latin American debt crisis: few banks were willing to lend to countries that had so recently defaulted.

These changes combined to alter the composition, as well as the scale, of private capital flows to the developing world. The importance of commercial bank lending diminished, whereas that of bond and equity flows increased. Most private capital flows to Latin America during the 1990s, for example, financed government and corporate bonds and purchased stocks in newly liberalized stock markets. By the mid-1990s, private capital flows to the entire developing world had risen to about 3 percent of these countries' gross domestic product (GDP) (see Figure 15.1). Asia was the largest recipient of capital inflows prior to 1997, accounting for almost 50 percent of total flows to all developing countries in the first half of the decade. Latin America was the second-largest recipient, obtaining between one-quarter and one-third of all flows to developing countries (IMF 2000).

The resumption of private capital flows generated one crisis after another. The growing importance of bond and equity flows, often referred to as **hot money** because it can be withdrawn at the first hint of trouble, increased the volatility of private capital flows to these "emerging market" countries.

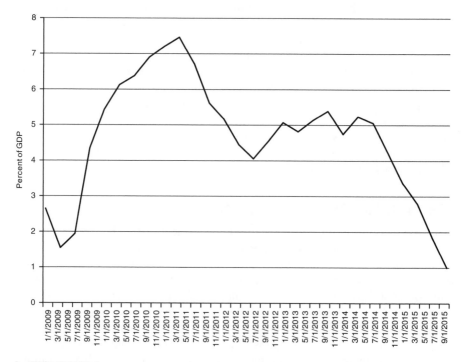

FIGURE 15.1

Gross Private Capital Inflows to Emerging Market Economies, 2009–2015

Note: Excludes foreign direct investment flows.

Sources: Clark et al., 2016; World Bank, *Global Development Finance 2004 CD-Rom*, Table 1.1 (Washington, DC: World Bank Publications, 2004); World Bank, *Global Development Finance 2005 CD-Rom*, Table 1.1 (Washington, DC: World Bank Publications, 2005) and World Bank, *Global Development Finance 2008 CD-Rom*, Table 1.1 (Washington, DC: World Bank Publications, 2008).

Although developing countries have struggled with such volatility throughout the last 100 years, volatility increased during the 1990s compared with earlier periods (IMF 2001, 163; World Bank 2001a). Historical evidence suggests that more volatile capital flows have been associated with lower economic growth rates over the long run (World Bank 2001a, 73). In addition, the record of the 1990s indicates that increased volatility of private capital flows is associated with more frequent financial crises that substantially reduce economic growth for a year or two.

Such financial crises became all too common during the 1990s. Mexico experienced the first one in late 1994. Four Asian countries—Indonesia, Malaysia, South Korea, and Thailand—had severe crises in the summer and fall of 1997. Brazil and Russia both experienced crises in 1998. Turkey and Argentina were struck by crises in 2000 and 2001. Each crisis was distinctive in some way, and yet all shared important similarities (see Table 15.1). First, each country struck by a crisis maintained some form of fixed exchange rate. In most instances, governments maintained a crawling peg or the slightly less restrictive crawling band. Second, each country developed a heavy reliance on short-term foreign capital.

The combination proved perilous. Heavy dependence on short-term capital required the continual rollover of foreign liabilities. The ability to roll over these liabilities depended critically on the government's ability to maintain foreign investors' confidence in its commitment to the fixed exchange rate. In each crisis, foreign investors lost confidence in that commitment. The trigger for crisis varied. Sometimes it was a political shock, as in Mexico; sometimes it was an economic shock, as in Russia and Argentina; sometimes it was contagion from crises in other regions. In all instances, however, the evaporation of foreign investors' confidence in the government's commitment to the fixed exchange rate triggered massive capital outflows that forced governments to devalue and (with the lone exception of Brazil) pushed the country into deep economic crisis. In many instances, the economic crisis toppled governments as well.

The Asian financial crisis of 1997 provides the clearest illustration of the challenges these countries faced. The Asian crisis originated in political and economic dynamics in four countries: Thailand, Indonesia, South Korea, and Malaysia. During the late 1980s and early 1990s, the government in each country liberalized their financial markets to make it easier for domestic banks and firms to borrow on international financial markets. In Thailand, for example, the government created the Bangkok International Banking Facilities in 1992 in an attempt to make Thailand an Asian banking center. The government hoped that Thai banks would borrow on international markets and then lend the funds obtained to borrowers across Asia. Financial liberalization thus enabled Asian banks to intermediate the flow of funds from international lenders to domestic borrowers. The incentive for such intermediation was powerful. Interest rates in international markets were considerably lower than interest rates inside Asian economies. Asian banks could thus borrow money at a relatively low rate of interest, such as 9 percent, from foreign commercial

TABLE 15.1

A Chronology of Crises, 1994–2002

Mexico (December 1994–January 1995)

Exchange Rate: Crawling band pegged to the dollar.

Financing Problem: The Mexican government began issuing short-term debt linked to the U.S. dollar in April 1994 *(Cetes,* analogous to U.S. Treasury bonds) to reduce its interest rate. The value of the *Cetes* issued soon exceeded the central bank's foreign exchange reserves.

Trigger: Unrest in Chiapas province generated a speculative attack in early December.

IMF Support: Mexico secured credits for $48.8 billion, including $17.8 billion from the IMF and $20 billion from the U.S. government.

Fallout: The government devalued the peso by 15 percent on December 20 and then floated the peso on December 22. The peso depreciated from 3.64 per dollar to more than 7 per dollar. Mexico suffered a depression and severe banking problems that prompted government rescues.

Contagion: Speculative attacks spread throughout Latin America and Asia.

East Asia (July 1997–January 1998)

See details in this chapter.

Russia (August 1998)

Exchange Rate: Crawling band pegged to the dollar.

Financing Problem: The Russian government was paying very high interest rates on large short-term debt.

Trigger: Falling prices for oil (the country's major export) and weak growth generated speculative attacks. The government widened the *ruble's* band by 35 percent in August and then floated the *ruble* in early September. The *ruble* depreciated from 6.2 per dollar to more than 20 per dollar.

IMF Support: Russia secured IMF credits of $11.2 billion in July 1998.

Fallout: The government defaulted on its ruble-denominated debt and Soviet-era foreign debt and imposed a moratorium on private-sector payments of foreign debt. The economy fell into recession. Many Russian banks became insolvent.

Contagion: Speculative attacks spread to Latin America, hitting Brazil especially hard. The U.S. hedge fund Long Term Capital Management was pushed to the brink of bankruptcy and was rescued in an effort coordinated by the Federal Reserve Bank of New York.

Brazil (January 1999)

Exchange Rate: Crawling band pegged to the U.S. dollar.

Financing Problem: Growing government debt and a sizable current-account deficit generated large short-term external debt.

Trigger: The Russian crisis and the subsequent collapse of Long Term Capital Management generated speculative attacks between August and October of

(Continued)

TABLE 15.1 (Continued)

1998. Attacks resumed in early 1999 when a state government defaulted on payments to the federal government. The *real* was devalued by 9 percent on January 13, 1999, and then floated on January 18. The currency depreciated from 1.21 per dollar to 2.18.

IMF Support: Brazil secured an IMF credit of $18 billion on December 2, 1998.

Fallout: Mild; growth strengthened in 1999 and 2000. The financial system suffered little.

Contagion: Brazil's devaluation contributed to recessions in Argentina and Uruguay and generated speculative attacks that forced Ecuador to float in February 1999.

Turkey (February 2001)

Exchange Rate: Crawling peg against the dollar and the German mark.

Financing Problem: Large government short-term debt and a large current-account deficit generated heavy dependence on short-term foreign capital.

Trigger: Concern about a criminal investigation into ten government-run banks in late November 2000 generated a speculative attack. Eight banks became insolvent and were taken over by the government. Investors lost confidence in February 2001 when conflict between the president and prime minister weakened the coalition government. The government floated the lira on February 22, and it depreciated from 668,000 per dollar to 1.6 million per dollar by October 2001.

IMF Support: Turkey secured an IMF credit of $10.4 billion on December 21.

Fallout: The Turkish economy contracted by 7.5 percent in 2001.

Contagion: None.

Argentina (2001)

Exchange Rate: Fixed to the U.S. dollar.

Financing Problem: Large government short-term debt.

Trigger: Speculative attacks against this peg emerged in 2000 and continued sporadically into 2001. The government introduced some exchange-rate flexibility in mid-2001, generating new speculative attacks. The government floated the peso in January 2002 and defaulted on its foreign debt.

IMF Support: Argentina secured a total of $40 billion in credits from the IMF and the advanced industrialized countries.

Fallout: Argentina's economy collapsed into deep depression.

Contagion: None.

Sources: Compiled from information in Eichengreen 2001; Joint Economic Committee 2003; and material on the IMF website (www.IMF.org).

banks and then lend it to domestic borrowers at a much higher rate of interest, such as 12 percent.

Such intermediation was risky. Asian banks contracted short-term loans denominated in dollars and other foreign currencies from foreign banks and then offered these funds as long-term loans denominated in the domestic currency to local borrowers. Asian banks thus confronted two kinds of risk. First, they faced exchange-rate risk, which arose from the possibility that the government would devalue the local currency. Were this to happen, the domestic currency cost of servicing the dollar-denominated loans would rise substantially. At the extreme, the domestic currency cost would rise above the payments that Asian banks were receiving from the businesses to which they had lent money. Asian banks were also exposed to the risk that foreign lenders would stop rolling over their short-term loans. Because Asian banks had borrowed on a short-term basis and then made long-term loans, they needed foreign lenders to renew the loans every 6 or 12 months. If foreign commercial banks became unwilling to rollover loans, Asian banks would be forced to repay all of their short-term debt at once. Yet, because these funds were tied up in the long-term loans that the Asian banks had made to local borrowers, the Asian banks would be unable to raise the funds needed to repay their debts to foreign banks.

The ability of Asian banks to intermediate safely between international and domestic financial markets was compromised by flaws in Asian countries' financial regulations. The central weakness was a problem called **moral hazard,** which arises when banks believe that the government will bail them out if they suffer large losses on the loans they have made. If banks believe that the government will cover their losses, they have little incentive to carefully evaluate the risks associated with the loans they make. If borrowers repay, banks earn money. If borrowers default, the government—and society's taxpayers—pick up the tab. In such an environment, banks have an incentive to make riskier loans than they would make in the absence of a promise of a government bailout. This incentive arises because banks charge higher interest rates to high-risk borrowers. As a result, higher-risk loans, when they are repaid, yield higher returns than low-risk loans. A government guarantee thus creates a one-way bet for banks: lend heavily to risky borrowers and they will profit greatly if the loans are repaid, yet they will suffer little if they are not, because the government will bail them out. The danger is that the practice of lending heavily to high-risk borrowers makes a systemic financial crisis more likely. Banks will lend too much to risky borrowers, and too many of these high-risk borrowers will default. Banks will therefore lose money, forcing the government to step in and bail them out. The government guarantee thus makes a financial crisis more likely.

Moral hazard was particularly acute in many Asian countries. Financial institutions had close ties to governments, sometimes through personal relationships and sometimes through direct government ownership. In Indonesia, for example, seven state-owned banks controlled half of the assets in the banking system (Blustein 2001, 94), and relatives and close friends of Indonesian President Suharto controlled other financial institutions. In the past, such relationships had led governments to rescue banks and other financial institutions in distress. In Thailand, for example, the government rescued the Bangkok Bank of Commerce in 1996 at the cost of $7 billion (Haggard 2000, 25). In Indonesia, two large corporate groups rescued Bank Duta (which held deposits from President Suharto's political foundations) after it had lost

$500 million in foreign exchange markets. The corporate rescuers were in turn rewarded by the Suharto regime (Haggard 2000, 26). Given this recent history, foreign and domestic financial institutions participating in the Asian market had reason to believe that Asian governments would not allow domestic financial institutions to fail. This belief in turn led international investors to lend more to Asian banks, and Asian banks to lend more to Asian businesses, than either would have been willing to lend had Asian governments not rescued banks in the past.

In principle, governments can design financial regulations to prevent the risky lending practices to which moral hazard so often gives rise. Banking regulation can limit the activities that financial firms engage in and thereby confine the overall risk in lending portfolios. In the Asian-crisis countries, however, such financial regulation was underdeveloped, and where it did exist, it was not effectively enforced. In Indonesia, for example, any regulator "who attempted to enforce prudential rules ... was removed from his position" (Haggard 2000, 33). Nor was this kind of treatment restricted to civil servants: the managing director of the central bank was fired in 1992, and the minister of finance was fired in 1996 (Haggard 2000, 33). As Haggard notes, the more general problem lay in the "influence that business interests exercised over legislation, regulation, and the legal process" (Haggard 2000, 38). In other words, the same network of business–government relations that created the moral hazard problem in the first place also weakened the incentives that governments had to develop and enforce effective prudential regulations. As a consequence, there were few regulatory checks on the lending practices of Asian financial institutions.

This regulatory framework enabled Asian banks to accumulate financial positions that could not easily withstand exogenous shocks. Asian economies were hit by shocks in late 1996 and early 1997. First, Asian countries' exchange rates began to appreciate against the Japanese yen in the mid-1990s. Most Asian governments pegged their currencies to the dollar. As the dollar appreciated against the yen in the mid-1990s, Asian currencies appreciated too. Exchange-rate appreciation made it difficult for domestic firms to export to Japan, one of their major export markets, which in turn created debt-service problems for export-oriented firms. Second, real-estate prices began to fall in late 1996, creating debt-service problems for real-estate developers. In March, the Thai government purchased $4 billion of debt that property developers owed but were unable to pay to domestic banks. By 1997, therefore, many of the Asian banks' largest domestic borrowers were struggling to service their debts. As a consequence, the number of non-performing loans—loans on which interest payments had not been made for 6 months or more—held by Asian banks began to grow. Because domestic borrowers could not repay domestic banks, the domestic banks could not easily repay foreign banks. Domestic debt-service difficulties thus began to generate international debt-service difficulties.

Weaknesses in Asian financial systems became a source of general concern in the spring of 1997. The trigger was the discovery that one of Thailand's largest financial institutions, Finance One, was insolvent. The discovery caused foreign banks to look much more closely at banks throughout Asia.

Close inspection indicated that Finance One's situation was not unique; banks across Asia were facing similar problems as a result of appreciating currencies and popping real estate bubbles. Deteriorating conditions in Asian financial systems and shifting international market sentiment combined to produce a panicked withdrawal of funds from Asian markets in the summer of 1997. Foreign banks that had loaned heavily to Asian banks refused to roll over existing loans and demanded repayment of whatever loans they could. Funds also started flowing out of Asian stock markets.

The panic began in Thailand in May 1997, where it quickly consumed the Thai government's foreign exchange reserves and forced the government to float the baht. The panicked withdrawal of funds from Asia over the next 6 months struck practically every country in the region. After their experience with Thailand, financial markets shifted their attention to the Philippines, forcing the government to abandon its fixed exchange rate after only 10 days. Attention shifted to Indonesia and Malaysia in July and August, and governments in both countries responded to massive capital outflows by abandoning their fixed exchange rates and allowing their currencies to float. From there, speculation targeted Taiwan, forcing a devaluation of the Taiwanese dollar, and Hong Kong, where capital flight caused the Hong Kong stock market to lose about one-quarter of its value in only 4 days. The crisis moved to South Korea in November, forcing the government to float the won by the middle of the month. A total of $60 billion was pulled from the region in the second half of 1997, roughly two-thirds of all the capital that had flowed into the region the year before. An additional $55 billion was pulled out in 1998 (IMF 1999, 92).

As the crisis struck, Asian governments turned to the IMF for financial assistance. The Philippines was the first to do so, gaining a $1.1 billion credit on July 14. The Thai government turned to the IMF 2 weeks later and was provided $16 billion from the IMF and other Asian countries. Indonesia held out longer, turning to the IMF only in October and receiving a $23 billion package. South Korea received the most support from the international community, acquiring a $57 billion package in early December. In all, the four hardest-hit countries—South Korea, Indonesia, Thailand, and Malaysia—received $117.7 billion.

As in earlier crises, IMF assistance was conditional upon economic reform. The reforms incorporated into IMF conditionality agreements in the Asian crisis targeted three broad areas: macroeconomic stabilization, reform of the financial sector, and structural reform. Macroeconomic stabilization programs were necessary, the IMF argued, to restore market confidence in the crisis countries and to stem capital outflow. Governments tightened monetary policy to stem the depreciation of their currencies. They tightened fiscal policies to generate the financial resources needed to rebuild the financial sector. Finally, the IMF required Asian governments to implement structural reforms, including trade liberalization, elimination of domestic monopolies and other uncompetitive practices and regulations, and privatization of state-owned enterprises. In Thailand, structural reforms targeted the civil service and state-owned

TABLE 15.2

Economic Growth and Current-Account Balances in Asia

	1995	1996	1997	1998
Economic Growth (annual percent change)				
Thailand	8.8	5.5	−0.4	−5.0
Indonesia	8.2	8.0	4.6	−13.7
South Korea	8.9	7.1	5.5	−5.8
Current-Account Balance (percent of gross domestic product)				
Thailand	−7.8	−7.9	−2.0	6.9
Indonesia	−3.2	−3.3	−1.8	1.6
South Korea	−1.9	−4.7	−1.9	7.3

Source: International Monetary Fund (IMF), *IMF Annual Report* (Washington, DC: IMF, 1999).

enterprises. In Indonesia, the IMF pressed the government to deregulate agriculture and reduce the monopoly position of the national agriculture marketing board. The IMF pressed the Indonesian government to privatize 13 state-owned enterprises and to suspend the development of auto and commercial aircraft industries.

The crisis had severe economic and political repercussions. The financial crisis and macroeconomic stabilization precipitated deep recessions throughout Asia. Indonesia experienced the biggest downturn, with economic output contracting by more than 13 percent in 1998. In most countries, the economic crisis hit the poor the hardest, and as a consequence, poverty rates rose sharply. In Indonesia, the number of people living below the poverty line grew from 11 percent of the population to 19.9 percent in 1998. In South Korea, the poverty rate rose from 8.6 percent to 19.2 percent in 1998. Deteriorating economic conditions sparked protest and political instability. In Indonesia, economic crisis sparked large-scale opposition to the Suharto government's corruption, nepotism, and cronyism. As the crisis deepened, regime opponents demanded fundamental political reform and a reduction of basic commodity prices, particularly of energy and rice. Protests and opposition peaked in May 1998. Four students were killed by the military during an anti-Suharto demonstration at Triskati University, sparking even larger protests during the days that followed. By late May, Suharto had stepped down from office.

The economic crisis sparked political change in Thailand as well. Thailand had begun constitutional reform in the early 1990s but had stalled under competing visions of how the new political institutions should be structured. Acceptance of the new constitution by the major societal groups was "propelled forward" by the economic crisis. As Haggard (2000, 94) notes, it is "highly doubtful that [this political reform] would have occurred in the way that it did in the absence of crisis circumstances." In addition, the government that had presided over the economy in the years leading up to the crisis was unable to maintain a majority coalition. It was replaced in November 1997 by a new government based on a 5-party coalition dominated by the

Democrat Party, the oldest political party in Thailand. The Democrat Party was "free of the more egregious patronage, pork-barrel spending, and corruption of its opponents" (Haggard 2000, 94). In Indonesia and Thailand, therefore, economic crisis provoked a reaction against the corruption of previous governments, mobilized societal support for far-reaching constitutional reform, and brought to power groups committed to economic and political reform.

A Closer Look

Cancelling the Debt for the World's Poorest Nations

By the late 1990s, the world's poorest countries, most of which are located in sub-Saharan Africa, owed about $200 billion to foreign creditors. Most of this debt was owed to official lenders—to the World Bank and the IMF or to governments in the advanced industrialized world. Payments to service this debt in 1999 (before the latest debt-relief initiative had taken effect) amounted to slightly more than $3 billion, a sum equal to 21 percent of government revenue and 15 percent of export earnings. The indebted countries are very poor. Roughly half of their combined population of 615 million people were living on less than $1 per day, and for at least ten of these countries, per capita income in 1999 had fallen below the level of 1960.

Such heavy debt burdens depressed economic growth in sub-Saharan Africa. Facing large debt payments, governments were forced to devote a sizable share of their available domestic resources to debt service. Large debt burdens also make it impossible to attract new foreign capital. Private lenders are unwilling to lend to countries that are unable to service their existing debt, so private capital flows are not an option. Official lenders also are increasingly reluctant to offer new loans. As the scale of the debt problem grew, the World Bank and the IMF, as well as many of the bilateral donors, became increasingly focused on restructuring existing debt rather than on providing new loans, and any new loans that were forthcoming were typically offered primarily to facilitate debt service. As a consequence, large debts essentially forced countries to forgo access to fresh foreign capital.

The creditor governments managed the African debt crisis by using essentially the same negotiation and rescheduling process that they had employed to manage the Latin American debt crisis. African governments negotiated stabilization and structural adjustment packages with the IMF and the World Bank, which then provided additional financial support, and existing debt was rescheduled. By the late 1980s, official creditors were concluding that the heavily indebted countries would never be able to repay their debts and that the level of debt service was having seriously deleterious consequences on those countries' economic performance. As this recognition took hold, creditor governments began to offer debt-reduction packages to the most heavily indebted poor countries.

The results from debt-reduction programs provided during the 1990s were disappointing. In spite of reducing foreign debt by around $60 billion, debt-service burdens actually increased for the poorest countries (IMF 2000; Easterly

2002, 125–126). Consequently, and partly in response to pressure from a coalition of nongovernmental organizations and religious groups, the World Bank and the IMF launched the **Heavily Indebted Poor Countries (HIPC)** debt initiative in September 1996. The most novel aspect of the HIPC initiative was that, for the first time, creditors would reduce the debt owed to multilateral lenders. All previous debt-relief measures had focused on debt owed to other governments, or bilateral debt. With HIPC, officials finally recognized that they would have to reduce the debt owed to the World Bank, the IMF, and the regional development banks.

Eligibility for the HIPC initiative was limited to the world's poorest countries. Moreover, in its initial design, the program was not intended to eliminate all foreign debt in these countries, but to reduce this debt to sustainable levels (Van Trotsenberg and MacArthur 1999). The IMF and the World Bank estimated that the typical country that completed the program would see its debt reduced by two-thirds and its debt-service ratio cut in half. Like other IMF and World Bank programs, the HIPC initiative incorporated conditionality. The initiative was structured around a two-stage process. In stage one, governments worked with domestic groups, the IMF, and the World Bank to develop Poverty Reduction Strategy Papers (PRSP). The PRSP described the macroeconomic, structural, and social policies the government would adopt in order to foster growth and reduce poverty. The idea was for governments to establish track records of implementing the strategy presented in the PRSP. At the end of the stage, countries would reach the "decision point," at which time the IMF and the World Bank conducted a debt-sustainability analysis to determine the country's eligibility for debt forgiveness. In stage two, the government continued to adhere to the PRSP targets until the IFIs were satisfied that it was committed to the program. Once the IMF and the World Bank concluded that the government had satisfactorily implemented its program, the country reached the "completion point" and gained the full amount of debt relief committed at the decision point.

The HIPC initiative was an important step in the management of the debt burden. However, critics charged that HIPC would not fully resolve the debt crisis, and that a full resolution required 100-percent forgiveness (see, for example, Roodman 2001; Birdsall and Williamson 2002). By the fall of 2004 some governments in the advanced industrialized countries were reaching the same conclusion (Blustein 2004b). The Group of Eight (G-8) initially discussed 100-percent forgiveness for the HIPC countries during the IMF–World Bank meetings in October 2004; by early June of 2005, the G-8 finance ministers had officially proposed that the World Bank, the IMF, and the African Development Fund (ADF) forgive all of their claims on the countries in the HIPC process. This first official call for 100-percent cancellation was reaffirmed by the G-8 heads of state 1 month later at the G-8 Summit in Gleneagles, Scotland. Governments announced the final details of this initiative, christened the **Multilateral Debt Relief Initiative** (MDRI), at the IMF World Bank meetings in March 2006. The cost of cancellation, estimated at the time at $50 billion, was financed through contributions to the multilateral lenders by the advanced industrialized countries.

By 2017, the HIPC initiative and the MDRI had eliminated practically all of the accumulated foreign debt burden for the 36 heavily indebted developing countries that had reached the completion point (World Bank 2017a). In all, the programs relieved these 36 countries of $101.4 billion of debt, shrinking their combined foreign debt burden to only $5 billion at the end of 2015. Consequently, the debt-to-GDP ratios had fallen from 114 percent in 1999 to 22 percent in 2015. Encouragingly, current indicators suggest that now that they are no longer burdened by large foreign debts, governments in these societies are dedicating at least a portion of the resources previously directed to debt service to critical social programs such as health and education.

BRETTON WOODS II

Perhaps the most profound consequence of the Asian crisis concerned not just East Asia but the entire international financial system. Arguably the roots of the 2008–2009 global financial crisis lie in East Asian governments' responses to the 1997 crisis. East Asian governments drew one overarching lesson from the crisis and crisis management: don't allow the economy to become vulnerable to shifts in market sentiment or subject to IMF intervention. As we have seen, crises induced by capital flows were politically destabilizing; IMF conditions reflected American interests and, as a consequence, carried deeply intrusive and often inappropriate policy demands. Thus, the central lesson governments drew from the crisis was, "never again."

East Asian governments relied on two mechanisms to reduce the likelihood that they faced future crises that pushed them to the IMF. The first line of defense was self-insurance through the accumulation of large stocks of foreign exchange reserves. Starting from less than zero in the crisis countries, and not substantially above zero in other countries, East Asian governments as a group accumulated more than $4 trillion in foreign exchange reserves between 1998 and the end of 2009. This amount constituted slightly more than half of global reserve holdings (U.S. Department of the Treasury, 2010). China accumulated the largest stock of foreign exchange reserves by far, holding about $2.4 trillion by the end of 2009. Japan, with the second largest stock, held just less than $1 trillion.

Asian governments accumulated foreign exchange reserves by running persistent and large current account surpluses. Up until the 1997 crisis, most economies ran current account deficits in most years. These deficits were financed by the capital inflows that eventually triggered the crisis. These deficits disappear in 1998, however, and from 1998 until the crisis hit in 2009, East Asian economies ran large current account surpluses. Indeed, as we saw in Chapter 11, East Asian economies emerged as important creditor countries after 2000.

East Asian economies have been able to run persistent current account surpluses in part because they have pegged their currencies to the dollar at competitive (many analysts argue undervalued) exchange rates. The competitive exchange rates encourage exports and discourage imports. Of equal importance, however, has been the dominant tendency to engage in sterilized intervention to maintain these exchange-rate pegs. Under sterilized intervention, a government with a current account surplus will exchange local currency for foreign currency at the fixed rate and then subsequently offset the impact of these purchases on the domestic money supply. Consequently, government foreign exchange reserve holdings increase, but the money supply does not. The currency thus remains competitively valued. In East Asian countries, the government then used the foreign exchange reserves (largely dollars) to purchase U.S. government securities and government-backed securities.

Policy Analysis and Debate

Does China's Creditor Status Confer Political Power?

Question

Does the Chinese government's status as a large lender to the United States government confer creditor power that China can exploit to alter American policy?

Overview

During the last decade, the Chinese government has emerged as the single largest foreign lender to the United States government. China's current account surpluses have generated an increase in the Chinese government's official dollar holdings. Rather than hold these reserves in the form of dollars, which pay no interest rates, China has used them to purchase relatively safe financial instruments that do pay interest. U.S. government debt is the safest instrument available. Hence, China's current account surpluses have transformed China into a major foreign funder of U.S. government debt. At the end of May 2010, China owned $868 billion worth of U.S. government securities (United States Department of the Treasury, 2010). This constitutes about 6.5 percent of total U.S. debt, but about 22 percent of total foreign-owned U.S. debt. Hence, a substantial share of U.S. government debt is controlled by a single foreign government that is not closely allied with the United States. Moreover, the ability for the United States to run deficits rests, in part, on the continued willingness of the Chinese government to acquire and hold U.S. government debt.

China's emergence as an important creditor to the U.S. government has raised questions about financial power. Some argue that its creditor status confers upon China substantial power. China's creditor position might make it difficult to defend American interests in Asia. As President Obama remarked during the campaign, "It's pretty hard to have a tough negotiation when the Chinese are our bankers" (cited in Drezner 2009, 15). China might also gain leverage over

U.S. policy at home. A threat to dump U.S. debt or to refuse to purchase more could sharply increase the cost of funding the debt. The desire to avoid these costs could encourage the U.S. to change policy in line with China's interests. Other analysts argue that creditor status does not confer much power. They emphasize the interdependent nature of the relationship. China buys U.S. debt so that the United States can buy Chinese goods. Moreover, because China holds so much U.S. debt, a massive sell-off would be quite painful.

Policy Options

- China's status as a major creditor to the U.S. government confers power that China can exploit and that must be a source of concern for the U.S. government.
- China's status as a major creditor results from economic interdependence and thus does not generate exploitable power.

Policy Analysis

- What factors determine whether creditor status confers political power?
- How does China's trade relationship with the United States influence its orientation toward the acquisition of additional U.S. debt?
- What if anything could China do to exploit its status without reducing the value of its assets?

Take A Position

- Which option do you prefer? Justify your choice.
- What criticisms of your position should you anticipate? How would you defend your recommendation against these criticisms?

Resources

Online: Visit the U.S. Department of the Treasury's "Treasury International Capital System" to update the data on foreign ownership of U.S. government debt. www.treasury.gov/tic/fpis.shtml

In Print: Daniel Drezner. 2009. "Bad Debts: Assessing China's Financial Influence in Great Power Politics." *International Security*, 34(2): 7–45, and Brad Setser, *Sovereign Wealth and Sovereign Power: The Strategic Consequences of American Indebtedness* (New York: Council on Foreign Relations, 2008).

The system that results from these arrangements has come to be called "**Bretton Woods II**" (Dooley, Folkerts-Landau and Garber 2004). East Asian governments peg to the dollar because the United States is their most important trade partner. East Asian economies run persistent trade surpluses with the United States (and with the world as a whole). East Asian governments finance exports in excess of imports by using the dollars they earn from their export surplus to purchase and hold U.S. government debt instruments. These arrangements are a modern-day Bretton Woods for two reasons. First, the U.S. trade deficit drives growth in East Asia, just as the U.S. current-account imbalance drove early postwar growth in Europe. Moreover, the system is stable as long as East Asian countries are willing to accumulate claims on the U.S. government, just as the original Bretton Woods system was stable as long as European governments were willing to accumulate claims on U.S. gold.

As a second line of defense, East Asian governments created a regional framework for financial cooperation (see Henning 2002 and Chey 2009). Called the **Chiang Mai Initiative**, this regional body provided framework within which governments could pool their foreign exchange reserves to assist each other in the event of market turbulence. The idea of an Asian mechanism first emerged in the fall of 1997. Wary of American and IMF objectives in the conditionality agreements, Japan proposed an Asian Monetary Fund that would effectively supplant the IMF in the region. The proposal drew strong opposition from the United States, who viewed it as a challenge to American interests in the region, and indifference from many East Asian governments, who were a bit wary of Japanese ambitions in the region. The proposal also failed to attract support from China. Consequently, the Japanese stepped back from the initiative.

The push for regional financial cooperation re-emerged in late fall 1997. Still fuming at their treatment by the IMF, ASEAN governments invited China, Japan, and South Korea to their summit to explore financial cooperation. By 1998, the ASEAN + 3 finance ministers had begun discussion about creating a system of bilateral swap arrangements to provide liquidity to governments facing balance-of-payments problems. In May of 2000, while meeting in Chiang Mai, Thailand, the governments announced that they had reached agreement on the basic framework. Through the CMI, governments pledge to make available a total of $120 billion. China and Japan are the two largest contributors, each contributing $38 billion. South Korea contributes approximately $19 billion, and the balance of contributions comes from governments in the ten smaller ASEAN countries. Each participant in the Initiative would be entitled to swap its currency for U.S. dollars in the amount equal to its contribution times its "purchasing multiplier."

Bretton Woods II arguably played a key role in the development of the global financial crisis of 2008–2009. The global savings glut, the favored term of many U.S. policymakers, is another name for the huge stock of foreign exchange reserves East Asian governments accumulated. East Asian societies saved as much as 50 percent of their income after 1997, and used an important share of these funds to purchase U.S. government securities. The plentiful demand for U.S. government debt instruments drove down interest rates, and this cheap credit arguably sparked the asset bubbles that popped in 2007 and 2008. Somewhat ironically, therefore, policies that East Asian governments adopted to reduce the likelihood that they would experience another crisis at home contributed to the development of an even larger crisis abroad.

CURRENCY WARS, TAPER TANTRUMS, AND THE GLOBAL CAPITAL FLOW CYCLE

For the developing world as a whole, though, the early 2000s were a period of financial stability. Because investors focused their attention on the American property market capital flows to emerging markets remained relatively low. Moreover, governments in developing countries took advantage of the period to stabilize their economies and accumulate reserves. By 2008, the financial situation in the developing world had improved greatly. Outstanding IMF credit had fallen to less than $10 billion, the lowest level in almost 30 years, an indication that developing countries had not only avoided new crises after 2000 but also that they had repaid the loans they had acquired in the late 1990s.

This decade of financial stability in the emerging markets was brought to a close by U.S. policy as the Federal Reserve sought to induce economic recovery in the wake of the global financial crisis. The first political manifestation of the emerging financial volatility came in the fall of 2010 when Brazilian Finance Minister Guido Mantega accused the United States—and the Federal Reserve specifically—of sparking an international currency war. Mantega's allegation came in midst of a series of rather complex reactions of capital markets and currency markets to America's monetary policy as the Federal Reserve transitioned from restoring financial stability to fostering post-crisis economic recovery. As an attempt to promote economic activity, the Federal Reserve implemented a second round of quantitative easing, known as QE2, in November 2010. Under QE2, the Fed announced that it would purchase $600 billion worth of U.S. Treasury securities by the middle of 2011. Such purchases would keep U.S. interest rates low. Low interest rates would encourage private investment that would in turn boost economic output and employment. The Fed extended its policy of quantitative easing in 2012 (which became QE3), as it committed to purchasing $40 billion worth of Treasury securities every month.

The Fed's expansionary monetary policy had unintended consequences (spillovers) for the global economy in general and for emerging market economies in particular. Most fundamentally, low interest rates in the U.S. economy encouraged investors to search for higher returns in other countries. Investors thus sold dollar-denominated assets and purchased financial assets in Asian and Latin American economies that had been relatively unaffected by the 2008 financial crisis. As a result, financial capital poured out of dollar-denominated assets and into emerging market assets, causing the dollar to depreciate rather sharply between May 2010 and May 2011. Policymakers in some countries, including in Japan and China, appeared to be intervening in currency markets in an attempt to devalue their currencies against the sinking dollar in order to retain export competitiveness. As a consequence, other emerging market economies with fixed exchange rates were losing export competitiveness and facing strong pressure from domestic industry to devalue. The Brazilian Real was especially hard hit as foreign capital flowed into the

Brazilian economy. By late 2010, Goldman Sachs proclaimed the Brazilian currency the world's most overvalued currency (Reuters 2010). It was in this context that Mantega accused the Federal Reserve of triggering an international currency war.

The large influx of foreign capital triggered by the Fed's QE2 had consequences for emerging market countries that stretched beyond currency values. Easy access to credit triggered investment booms in many emerging market countries, while overvalued currencies encouraged this investment to flow into nontraded activities such as real estate and construction. As a result, asset prices began to rise rapidly in emerging market countries from 2011, generating fears of an emerging market housing bubble. Governments in many emerging market economies responded to these developments by introducing capital controls in an attempt to divert the inflow. Moreover, and perhaps somewhat surprisingly, this return to capital controls was supported by the International Monetary Fund as it moved toward a new "Institutional View" on capital flows that recognized the potential utility of capital controls in the face of large and possibly destabilizing cross-border flows (see IMF 2011). By late 2012, markets had stabilized.

Stability was short lived however, as the tempers of many emerging market policymakers flared again as the Federal Reserve began to shift away from quantitative easing in the middle of 2013. In May 2013, in the context of his semi-annual testimony to Congress' Joint Economic Committee, Federal Reserve Board Chairman Ben Bernanke suggested that the Fed might begin to reduce the amount of these purchases—Fed purchases of Treasury Securities would taper off—sometime in the near future. Such a shift in Fed policy would cause interest rates to rise in the U.S. In early 2014, the Federal Reserve began to taper.

The shift in American monetary policy hit emerging market economies very hard. Investors that had only months previously been too eager to acquire assets in emerging market economies now rushed to liquidate their assets as fast as they could. Equity markets slumped, governments' foreign exchange reserves eroded, and currencies depreciated. Moreover, the suddenness of the shift in investor sentiment was dramatic—practically overnight. The destabilizing consequences for emerging market economies that resulted from the Federal Reserve's policy shift generated substantial and often very outspoken anger (which was rather patronizingly termed a "taper tantrum") among policymakers in emerging market countries. Raghuram Rajan, who at the time was the Governor of the Reserve Bank of India, was among the most vocal critics of American policy. He accused the Fed of refusing to take into account the impact its policy shift had on the rest of the world. In a speech delivered at the Brookings Institution in Washington, DC, Rajan asked rhetorically, "If the policy hurts the rest of the world more than it helps the United States, should this policy be pursued" (Caruso-Cabrera 2014). Rajan's critical perspective was not welcomed by the engineer of the Fed policies, Ben Bernanke, who was in attendance (though no longer the Chairman of the Federal Reserve Board) and challenged Rajan's claim during the question and answer session that followed Rajan's speech.

Rajan's concerns were hardly unique. Indeed, by early 2014 global policy-makers, investment banks, and media outlets were becoming increasingly concerned about the financial health of five emerging maret economies—India, Brazil, Turkey, South Africa, and Indonesia. Foreign capital had driven an economic boom in each of these economies and as a consequence continued growth had become highly exposed to changes in market sentiment. Of particular concern was the possibility of a sudden change in market sentiment that would trigger a large sell-off, a run on central bank foreign exchange reserves, and a systemic banking crisis. In this case, however, governments moved proactively in an attempt to stem the sell-off. In January, the Turkish central bank responded to market speculation against the Turkish lira by increasing interest rates by 4.25 percentage points—a massive one-time rise. South Africa's central bank pushed its main rate up the next day, though by a much smaller amount. India had also pushed up its lending rate to reassure nervous investors. To this point, however, the tapers have generated substantial volatility, considerable uncertainty, but have not precipitated a major banking or currency crisis.

This episode highlighted once again two enduring characteristics of the global financial system. First, the system is characterized by a recurring two-phase global cycle in which capital flows between the center of the system in one phase and then to the emerging markets in the other phase. Second, the transition between phases is triggered by changes in U.S. monetary and fiscal policy. And though the specific details of this most recent capital flow cycle are unique, in broad outline the same systemic dynamic generated the Latin American debt crisis and the Asian crisis that we explored earlier in this chapter. The most distinctive aspect of this most recent manifestation of the capital flow cycle is that neither systemic banking nor sovereign debt crises have materialized. Perhaps this indicates that the lessons that governments in the emerging market economies drew from the Asian crisis helped their financial systems withstand the most recent period of volatility. Nevertheless, moving forward, we again confront the realization that reducing the amplitude of the capital flow cycle will require closer macroeconomic cooperation than we have observed during the last 30 years.

CONCLUSION

At the beginning of the twenty-first century, developing countries are facing new challenges in managing their relationship with the international financial system. On the one hand, international financial integration over the last 20 years has greatly expanded developing countries' opportunities for attracting foreign capital. Yet, those countries seem incapable of escaping from a repeating cycle of overborrowing, crisis, and adjustment that lies at the center of their difficulties. As we have seen, this cycle typically starts with changes in international capital markets. Petrodollars increased the supply of foreign capital to many developing countries during the 1970s, and the dynamics of international financial integration increased the supply of foreign capital to

Asian countries during the 1990s. Developing countries have exploited the opportunities presented by changes in international financial markets with great enthusiasm. By reducing the constraints imposed by limited savings and limited foreign exchange, foreign capital allows developing countries to invest more than they could if they were forced to rely solely on domestic resources. The problem, however, is that developing countries eventually accumulate large foreign currency exposures that they cannot service and are pushed to the brink of default. Impending default causes foreign lenders to refuse additional loans to developing countries and to recall the loans they had made previously. Now shut out of international capital markets, developing countries experience severe economic crises and implement stabilization and structural adjustment packages under the supervision of the IMF and the World Bank. This cycle has repeated three times in the last 40 years, once in Latin America during the 1970s and 1980s, once in Asia during the 1990s, and most recently across a geographically diverse set of emerging market economies.

These cycles are driven by the interaction between developments in the international system and those within developing countries. The cycle is driven in part by interests and institutions in the international system over which developing-country governments have little control. The volume and composition of capital flows from the advanced industrialized countries and the developing world have been shaped in large part by changes in international financial markets and changes in American monetary policy. The build-up of debt in Latin America during the 1970s was made possible by the growth of the Euromarkets and the large deposits in these markets made by OPEC members. The buildup of large foreign liabilities by many Asian countries resulted in part from the more general increase in international financial integration during the late 1980s. The ability to service foreign debt is also influenced by international developments. In the Latin American debt crisis, rising American interest rates and falling economic growth in the advanced industrialized world made it more difficult for Latin American governments to service their foreign debt. In the Asian crisis, the dollar's appreciation against the yen made it more difficult for Asian borrowers to service their debt. Finally, the advanced industrialized countries, the IMF, and the World Bank have established the conditions under which developing countries experiencing crises can regain access to foreign capital.

Interests and institutions within developing countries have also played an important role. Domestic politics influence how much foreign debt is accumulated and the uses to which it is put. In the 1970s, Latin American governments made poor decisions about how to use the foreign debt they were accumulating, thereby worsening their situation when the international environment soured. In Asia, governments failed to regulate the terms under which domestic banks intermediated between foreign and domestic financial markets, thereby weakening domestic financial systems and sparking an erosion of investor confidence in Asia. A country's ability to return to international capital markets following a crisis is contingent on policy reform. Domestic politics often prevents governments from speedily implementing such reforms. Thus, even though it might be tempting to place the blame for the cycle solely on the international financial system or solely on developing-country governments, a more reasonable approach is to recognize that these cycles are driven by the interaction between international and domestic developments.

KEY TERMS

Bretton Woods II
Capital Flow Cycle
Chiang Mai Initiative

Heavily Indebted Poor
  Countries (HIPC)
Hot Money

Moral Hazard
Multilateral Debt Relief
  Initiative

SUGGESTIONS FOR FURTHER READING

On the Asian financial crisis, see Stephan Haggard, *The Political Economy of the Asian Financial Crisis* (Washington, DC: Institute for International Economics, 2000).

For a broader examination of emerging market strategies in the global financial system, see the contributions in Leslie Elliott Armijo and Saori N Katada, eds., *The Financial Statecraft of Emerging Powers: Shield and Sword in Asia and Latin America.* (London: Palgrave Macmillan, 2014).

For the global financial cycle, see Obstfeld, Maurice, and Alan M. Taylor, 2017. "International Monetary Relations: Taking Finance Seriously." *Journal of Economic Perspectives* 31(3): 3–28, Sarah Bauerle Danzman, W. Kindred Winecoff, and Thomas Oatley, 2017. "All Crises Are Global: Capital Cycles in an Imbalanced International Political Economy." *International Studies Quarterly* 61(4): 907–923, and Atish R. Ghosh, Jonathan D. Ostry, and Mahvash S. Qureshi, *Taming the Tide of Capital Flows: A Policy Guide* (Cambridge, MIT Press, 2017).

The Achievements of and Challenge to the Global Capitalist Economy

Twenty years ago, the politics of globalization were relatively straight-forward. At the time, capitalist democracy and the political coalition upon which it rested faced no serious challenges. The Soviet economic model, the Soviet Bloc, and even the Soviet Union itself had collapsed more than 10 years previously, taking with it the only serious post-World War II global rival to capitalist democracy. And as the Soviet model collapsed, capitalism spread to Eastern and Central Europe, into Central Asia and the Caucuses, and even into Russia itself. China had just joined the World Trade Organization and appeared well on its way toward the more gradual transition to a market-based and eventually fully capitalist economy. In the so-called Third World, inward-looking and state-led development strategies had been abandoned in Latin America, India, and Turkey. And though many developing countries found fault with some of the rules of the world trade system, their solution emphasized reform from within the structure of the system rather than a more profound restructuring or replacement. By the dawn of the millennium, global capitalism and its international institutional manifestations—the World Trade Organization, free-trade agreements such as NAFTA and the EU, the International Monetary Fund—had appeared to have prevailed in the twentieth-century battle over global economic organization.

The primary challenges to globalization at that time arose from a campaign generated by a set of loosely allied non governmental organizations (NGOs). Yet even this social movement was not, at least among at its dominant centrist elements, anti-globalization as much as it constituted an effort to redress perceived imbalances between the economic interests of business relative to those of labor, consumers, and the environment. The more radical currents of this social movement produced the Battle in Seattle at the WTO Ministerial Conference in the fall of 1999. The more centrist groups gave us the so-called "trade and ..." agenda in which governments (and especially the

U.S. government) linked trade liberalization in FTAs to specific and often narrowly framed details on labor rights and environmental objectives

Today, the politics of globalization are far more complex. This complexity arises in part because globalization itself is more complicated today than it was 20 years ago. Not only are national economies more interdependent today than they were 20 years ago, but also the nature of economic interdependence has changed. As we have seen, economic production has become more global via the articulation of global value chains that distribute the discrete stages of manufacturing to different regions of the world. Simultaneously, the global economy has become increasingly financialized, with cross-border capital flows increasing to unprecedented levels. The changing nature of economic interdependence has in turn generated a substantial backlash that poses a major challenge to globalization. Globalization is challenged from within by neo-populist movements that are stridently anti-trade, anti-immigrant, and often xenophobic and racist, anti-elite, and nationalist. The surprise election of Donald J. Trump to the Presidency of the United States in November 2016 as well as the British electorate's majority support to leave the European Union provide two good examples. Globalization also is challenged from the outside by old foes and more recent adversaries who exploit the network infrastructure of the capitalist democratic global order to attempt to undermine its political foundations. Putin's Russia offers one obvious example of this challenge.

We don't yet have a good understanding of these "new" politics of globalization. Many of the various dimensions of these new politics are such recent developments that we have not yet had time to fully work through their logic. And because these dimensions are so varied, scholars and other observers of the international economy haven't yet had time to work through how these various threads are woven together into a more cohesive cloth. It might be useful, therefore, to conclude our exploration of international political economy by stepping back to examine what the post-World War II global economy has achieved, what is the primary challenge that it confronts, and what solutions to this challenge might exist.

THE ACHIEVEMENTS OF THE GLOBAL CAPITALIST ECONOMY

We begin by looking at the positive achievements of the postwar global capitalist economy. To grasp fully the nature of these achievements I think that one must zoom out a bit from the specific details of contemporary trade and financial markets and focus on these economic arrangements as one component of a broader international order put in place after World War II. It is relatively easy to forget how fragile was the status of the global capitalist economy in the first half of the twentieth century. The destruction and dislocation that resulted from World War I brought to an end the nineteenth-century experiment with globalization, and the Great Depression not only destroyed the results of governments' efforts to rebuild global trade and finance after WWI, but also eroded societies' faith in markets. The Marxist–Leninist regime in the Soviet Union offered one attractive alternative model to capitalist democracy, and the fascist regimes that emerged in Southern Europe, Germany, and Asia seemed to provide yet another option. In 1937, with the world in the midst of the Great Depression and sliding toward World War II, it was far from obvious that capitalist democracy would survive, much less win this three-way competition over how to organize the global political economy.

But not only did capitalist democracy survive this competition, it prevailed. The challenge posed by fascism ended with the destruction of Nazi Germany and Imperial Japan in 1945. And while Soviet-style Marxism–Leninism persisted on into the postwar era, it too had largely ceased to offer an appealing alternative model by the 1970s and had disappeared entirely by 1990. By the mid-1990s, the global capitalist economy had succeeded beyond the wildest expectations of the postwar planners who helped construct its foundations. As Francis Fukuyama famously wrote on the eve of the Soviet Collapse: "The triumph of the West, of the Western idea, is evident … in the total exhaustion of viable systematic alternatives to Western liberalism," (Fukuyama 1989, p. 3).

But the achievements of the postwar global capitalist economy lie not in the failures of the alternative models, but in the impact that the global capitalist economy has had on the material conditions of human life. And by this measure, the postwar global capitalist economy has provided the foundation for unprecedented improvements in practically every material facet of the human condition. First, humanity enjoys a higher material standard of living today than at any previous time in history. Bradford de Long, an economic historian at the University of California at Berkeley, estimates that worldwide per capita income only doubled in the 12,000 years that spanned 10,000 bce and 1800 ce, rising from about $100 at the time humans settled into agrarian lives to $195 in 1800 (measured in today's money) (De Long 1998). Over the next 100 years, per capita income increased by a factor of 3, reaching $679 by 1900. Between 1900 and 2000, global per capita income increased an additional ten times, reaching $6,539 in 2000. And somewhat remarkably, according to World Bank data, per capita income subsequently increased by an additional 86 percent since 2000, reaching more than $10,000 by 2017. And as per capita income rose, the share of the world's population living in extreme poverty diminished. In 1950, almost three-quarters of the entire global population lived in extreme poverty. By 2013, this number had fallen to only 10.7 percent (Bourguignon and Morrison 2002; World Bank 2016), which in absolute numbers equals 767 million (World Bank 2016). Indeed, since 1990, the number of people who live in extreme poverty has fallen by about 1.1 percent per year—which means that each year 114 million fewer people in the world live in extreme poverty. And this historically unprecedented reduction in the number of people who live in extreme poverty has occurred even as the size of the global population has continued to increase to its current level of 7.3 billion.

Second, and perhaps largely because of the unprecedented level of prosperity we have achieved during the last 70 years, we have been living through what has come to be called "the long peace" (Pinker 2011). Over the last 75 years, humans have been significantly less prone to engage in organized violence than at any prior time in history. International politics featured almost continuous warfare among the major powers between 1500 and 1750. And though the frequency of major war lessened somewhat after 1750, the first half of the twentieth-century featured the bloodiest and most destructive war in all of human history. In contrast, the world has not experienced a single great power conflict since 1953. Other forms of organized violence are also in abeyance. Between 1492 and 1945, the European powers invaded and conquered four continents (North America, South America, Africa, Australia) and captured significant portions of another (Asia). By the late nineteenth century, 36 percent of the world's population—more than one-third—lived under colonial rule. In contrast, the post-World War II era has been characterized by decolonization such that by 1990 nobody lived under colonial rule. The postwar global capitalist economy has thus contributed to a remarkable and to some extent unprecedented era of peace and prosperity.

And at the level of the individual, these aggregate achievements mean that the material conditions of life for the typical person are better today than ever before in human history. The average person lives twice as long today as in 1913 and 50 percent longer than in 1950. People enjoy more secure access to better food and are thus unlikely to be malnourished as a child and as an adult. The water they drink is clean and unlikely to make them sick. They have better access to a vastly improved healthcare system and are thus unlikely to suffer from (much less die from) treatable medical conditions. Moreover, improvements in medical science and technology have greatly expanded the set of conditions that are treatable. They have far greater opportunity to acquire an education and as a consequence are better able to provide for their own and their family's economic needs. And, they are more likely to live in a democratic society where they can enjoy political rights and liberties and are less likely to be subject to state sanction for their beliefs.

It is certainly true that we owe many of these improvements to the way that science has expanded our understanding of medicine, agriculture, and industry. But the potential benefits that science has generated have had a greater impact in societies that participated in the global capitalist economy than in those societies that stood outside this system. Consider as an illustration of this difference the gap in the improvements in life expectancy that has arisen between North and South Korea since the Korean War. Both societies started at the same point in 1955, with a life expectancy of approximately 55 years. During the next 60 years South Korea embedded itself into the global capitalist economy while North Korea remained aloof, associating instead with the Communist economic bloc through the 1980s and then becoming increasing insular ever since. Life expectancy in the more isolated North Korea peaked at 70 years in 1994 and has subsequently receded to 68 years where it stands today. In contrast, by 2011 life expectancy in South Korea had increased to 81 years. Similarly, consider the trajectory of life expectancy in the former Soviet Union. There, life expectancy peaked in the early 1960s at 70 years.

Life expectancy then declined over the next two decades as the Soviet political economy stagnated and stood at 67.5 years in the mid-1980s. In the midst of the political and economic instability that characterized the dissolution of the Soviet Union, life expectancy fell further to between 64 and 65 years. We can find exceptions to this pattern. Cuba, for instance, has remained largely outside the liberal international economy since its revolution in 1961 and yet experienced a sustained improvement in life expectancy, which increased from 65 to 78 years during the period. The global capitalist economy has thus proven better able to deliver sustained improvements to humanity than other political and economic systems that we have tried.

GLOBALIZATION AND THE POLITICS OF INEQUALITY

As is usually the case, however, global aggregate statistics obscure a considerable amount of individual variation. In this case, what we begin to see as we start to disaggregate these statistics is that although global per capita incomes have increased and income inequality globally has fallen, wealth and income have become increasingly unequal *within* many societies. And many observers argue that the greatest challenge the contemporary global economy faces arises from the impact that this rising **inequality** has on political support for continued participation in the global economy.

Income and wealth inequality in the United States and in European Union member countries has been rising for the past 25 years. Rising inequality reflects that fact that some people have realized gains from globalization that are orders of magnitude greater than the average improvement, while others have seen their material situation stagnate or even decline relative to the average. For instance, at the end of 2017 there were approximately 5 billion adults alive in the world. About 36 million of these adults—about 0.7 percent of the world's adult population—each had wealth of $1 million or more. In contrast, 3.5 billion adults—70 percent of the world's adult population—each held wealth of 10,000 dollars or less (Credit Suisse 2017). A similarly large gap is evident when we look at household incomes in the advanced industrial economies. In the United States in 2015, for instance, people in the top 1 percent of the income distribution earned on average roughly $1.4 million; in contrast, the people in the bottom 90 percent of the income distribution earned, on average, approximately $35,000 (Saez 2016). The gap between the top earners and the rest of the work force has widened over the last 40 years. In the mid-1970s, the top 10 percent of incomes in the U.S. accounted for about one-third of all income earned in the American economy. This share rose steadily after 1980 such that by 2015, the top 10 percent of households accounted for half of all income earned in the U.S. (Saez 2016). And although the income inequality in the U.S. is greater than in other societies, the trend of rising inequality that we see in the U.S. is not unique. Income and wealth inequality have increased significantly in Russia, China, Latin America, in more than half of the countries in sub-Saharan Africa, and in most of the members of the European Union (Novokmet et al. 2017; Piketty 2017; World

Bank 2016). Inequality has even risen in Taiwan, South Korea, and Japan, where until the mid-1980s, "growth with equity" had constituted a prominent element of the development model (World Bank 2016).

This rising inequality is, at least in part, a consequence of the globalization of economic activity. From the stand point of theory, the Stolper-Samuelson Theorem tells us that in the American economy we would expect free trade to increase the return to physical and human capital and reduce the return to labor, precisely what we observe. And this effect of trade on inequality was increased in the 2000s by the entry of China into the WTO, a development that appears to have been associated with a substantial reduction of manufacturing jobs in the American economy (Autor et al. 2016). The impact of trade is accentuated by the emergence of global supply chains and the shift of low- and medium-skill jobs in many manufacturing industries out of the United States and Western Europe and into emerging economies in Eastern and Central Europe, Latin America, and Asia. Globalization isn't the only culprit, of course. Technological change has also been an important cause of rising inequality. Advanced economies have experienced what economists call "**skill biased technological change**", a process wherein technology substitutes for low-skilled workers. This process includes things ranging from the self-service checkout lanes that are now common in grocery stores, ATMs and online banking more broadly, to robots that have been installed on assembly lines in modern manufacturing facilities. This technological change has reduced the demand for low-skilled workers and therefore contributed to the failure of income among this group to keep pace (Acemoglu and Restrepo 2017). Of course, trade and technological change are not entirely independent of one another—increased international competition via trade can be an important factor that causes firms to incorporate new technologies into their production process (Bloom et al. 2016).

Somewhat more broadly, by encouraging economic reorganization, globalization is also bringing about social reorganization. Peter Temin, an economic historian who has spent much of his career at MIT, has recently argued that the U.S. economy has evolved into a **dual economy**: one high-wage economy and one low-wage economy and very few connections between them (2017). The emergence of a dual economy is mirrored by the emergence of a dual society, a society characterized increasingly by two distinct groups of "insiders" and "outsiders." Insiders are those individuals who have been rewarded economically by globalization. These insiders are college educated and often (at least in the U.S. and the EU) have post-graduate degrees and typically reside in a major metropolitan area. Insiders embrace globalization because their investment in human capital and their enthusiasm for life in the metropolis puts them in a position to command jobs in industries that are rewarded by globalization. Outsiders, by contrast, are those who have not benefited directly from globalization. Outsiders have less education than insiders; the typical person in this group will have a high school education; many will have less than a high school diploma (and a few will have had a few years in college). Outsiders also typically live outside major metropolitan areas. As a category, this covers a lot of ground, including residents of cities and small towns, suburban communities, and rural areas. Globalization is more likely to constitute a threat to multiple facets of the outsider's life, eliminating his job at the local factory and enabling an influx of foreign workers that seemingly "take jobs" from citizens and contribute to downward pressure on incomes paid to low skilled workers. And just as the two sectors of the dual economy have little interaction with each other, so the two segments of contemporary society increasingly function without much interaction with each other. The economic polarization that is occurring within the global capitalist economy thus generates a social and political polarization as well.

The social impact of trade- and investment-induced economic restructurings has been amplified, I think, by a couple other economic shocks. First, the world has suffered through a rather extended and very partial recovery from the 2008–2009 global financial crisis. The last 10 years have brought austerity measures throughout the European Union that have suppressed economic growth. The American economy recovered relatively more quickly, but manufacturing employment in the industrial Great Lakes region of the U.S. has still not fully regained its pre-crisis levels. Arguably, this financial crisis and the policy response imposed new burdens on the segment of society that were already most exposed to the downsides of globalization. Second, and especially in Europe, societies have experienced large inflows of refugees as people have fled from the horrors of civil war in Syria as well as significant migrant worker flows into Germany, the United Kingdom, Switzerland, Spain, and France from countries in southern, eastern, and central Europe (European Commission 2017). These inflows of people seem to have created resentment among some segments of the host societies as refugees attract scarce financial resources from the government in an era of fiscal austerity, and migrant workers compete with locals for a shrinking number of low-skilled jobs.

Thus, although the postwar global capitalist economy has generated unprecedented global prosperity, income and wealth have been unevenly distributed within societies, and those who have realized the fewest gains seem to be most exposed to the series of negative shocks. As we have seen, such inequalities are beginning to influence electoral politics and governments' foreign economic policies. In the summer of 2016, a (small) majority of British voters instructed their government via a referendum to withdraw the United Kingdom from the European Union. During his 2016 campaign for the presidency, Donald J. Trump pledged to "Make America Great Again" in part by implementing a neo-mercantilist and unilateralist trade policy. Since entering office, the Trump administration has withdrawn the U.S. from the Trans-Pacific Partnership, began to renegotiate the North American Free Trade Agreement, and launched a comprehensive review of the terms of America's participation in the World Trade Organization USTR, 2017). Not only does the Trump administration policy clash with America's postwar support for the global liberal international economy, but a decision to reduce foreign access to the American market makes it unlikely that other societies would keep their markets open to American exports.

How serious a challenge to the global capitalist economy do these current political developments represent? To be frank, nobody knows. But Dani Rodrik's concept of the "Political Trilemma" offers a useful lens through which to view how these developments fit together (see Figure 16.1). The **Political Trilemma** is similar to the Unholy Trinity we learned about in our discussion of exchange rates in Chapter 12. Rodrik suggests that governments face three desirable objectives: globalization, democratic decision making, and national autonomy. Yet, at any given time, they can realize only two of these three goals. If states want globalization, they must choose between national autonomy and democracy. If they want democracy and national autonomy, they must give up globalization. In the late nineteenth century, states accepted what Rodrik calls the "Golden Straightjacket," embracing globalization and national autonomy but sacrificing democratic decision making. The Bretton Woods compromise that states crafted after World War II combined national political autonomy and democratic decision making but sacrificed globalization. One might argue that members of the EU have embraced globalization and democratic decision making by agreeing to give up a substantial degree of national autonomy by shifting economic governance to the supranational EU forum. From this perspective, contemporary societies are reacting against globalization in order to reassert national autonomy and re-establish democratic decision making (perhaps excessively so in its populist mode). The reassertion of national autonomy and British democracy were certainly central elements of the pro-Brexit Leave campaign of 2016. Reducing globalization is a necessary consequence of achieving these other goals.

And while many observers question many of the specific details contained in Trump's mercantilist approach to trade and the UK's decision to withdraw completely from the EU, we are seeing a growing number of calls to reform and rebalance globalization. As Dani Rodrik wrote recently, "The rise of populism

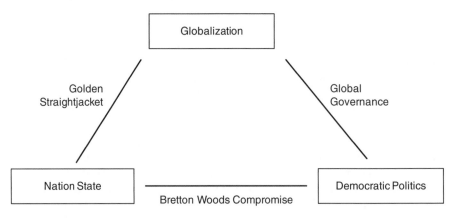

FIGURE 16.1
The Political Trilemma of the World Economy

Source: Rodrik, *The Globalization Paradox* (2011), 201.

forces a necessary reality check. Today the big challenge facing policymakers is to rebalance globalization so to maintain a reasonably open world economy while curbing its excesses" (Rodrik 2017, 27). And what would a rebalanced globalization look like? Rodrik and others have supported a twenty-first-century version of the Bretton Woods compromise. Suzanne Berger, a political economist at MIT, for instance, suggests that

> open borders must once again be linked to a broad program of social and fiscal reforms. There are many obvious candidates: raising minimum wages, consolidating national health insurance, lowering financial barriers to post-secondary education for working- and middle-class children, tax reforms, and tackling the sources of inequality.
>
> (Berger 2018)

Implementing these measures would most likely require governments to increase tariffs, restrict cross-border capital flows, and probably also limit the flow of migrant workers. And though these barriers would be in many cases the same as those threatened by Trump's mercantilism and Brexit, a new **Bretton Woods compromise** would rebalance globalization through coordinated multilateral cooperation—a collective reform process based around commonly agreed rules—rather than through unilateral and nationalist initiatives.

A decision to rein in globalization by crafting a twenty-first-century version of the Bretton Woods compromise would certainly be a better outcome than the destruction of globalization by unilateralism. But, such an endeavor would still confront major unknowns, not least of which are whether states could agree on the elements of a new Bretton Woods compromise, whether, if they could, such an approach would successfully address the central issues driving the political backlash, and finally, what a new Bretton Woods compromise would cost in terms of global prosperity and peace moving forward. More fundamentally, if we are to save globalization in order to build upon the unprecedented achievements of the last 70 years, and I believe we must preserve globalization for these reasons, then we need to commit to a broader and more equitable distribution of the gains from globalization across all segments of society.

KEY TERMS

Bretton Woods Compromise	Inequality	Skill-Biased Technological Change
Dual Economy	Political Trilemma	

SUGGESTIONS FOR FURTHER READING

On the remarkable achievements realized over the last 70 years, see Angus Deaton's *The Great Escape: Health, Wealth, and the Origins of Inequality* (Princeton: Princeton University Press, 2016).

For a detailed study of contemporary inequality, see Branko Milanovic's *Global Inequality: A New Approach for the Age of Globalization* (Cambridge: Harvard University Press, 2016).

For an exploration of the social impact of economic change in contemporary America, see Peter Temin's *The Vanishing Middle Class: Prejudice and Power in a Dual Economy* (Cambridge: MIT Press, 2017). J. D. Vance's *Hillbilly Elegy: A Memoir of a Family and Culture in Crisis* (New York: Harper Collins, 2016) offers a more personal account.

GLOSSARY

absolute advantage   The principle upon which Adam Smith first claimed that free-trade benefits all countries. It holds that a country benefits from trade when it produces a particular good at a lower cost (in terms of labor input) than it costs to produce the good in any other country. By specializing in the production and export of this good and importing goods whose production costs are higher than in other countries, the country can consume more of both goods. In trade theories, this principle was later replaced by the principle of comparative advantage. (*See* comparative advantage.)

accelerationist principle   A central component of monetarist theories and first stated by Milton Friedman in the 1960s, it claims that a government can keep unemployment below the natural rate of unemployment only if it is willing to accept a continually increasing rate of inflation. That is, the principle claims that there is no long-run Phillips curve trade-off between inflation and unemployment. Such a trade-off exists only in the short run. This principle became widely accepted by governments and central bankers in the advanced industrialized countries during the 1980s, leading to the demise of Keynesian strategies of macroeconomic management. (*See* Keynesianism; Phillips curve.)

antidumping   Government investigations to determine whether a foreign firm is selling its products in international markets at a price that is below its cost of production. Under the rules of the international trade system, a positive finding in such an investigation allows the government to impose tariffs to offset the margin of dumping. (*See* dumping.)

backward linkages   A term applied to the industrialization process that refers to instances when the creation of a domestic industry increases demand in domestic industries that supply inputs to the original industry. For example, the creation of a domestic auto industry may increase the demand for domestic auto parts such as batteries, glass, tires, etc.

Baker Plan   Proposed in 1985 by Secretary of the U.S. Treasury James A. Baker III, this plan attempted to resolve the developing-country debt crisis through a combination of economic adjustment and additional lending. Of particular significance, the plan linked access to financial assistance from the International Monetary Fund, World Bank, and private lenders, to the willingness of debtor governments to adopt structural adjustment programs.

balance of payments   An accounting device that records a country's international transactions. The balance of payments is divided into two broad categories: the current account and the capital account.

balance-of-payments adjustment   The use of government policies to correct a balance-of-payments deficit or surplus.

big push   The state would plan and coordinate a substantial large investment to solve the market failures that structuralists believed inhibited rapid industrialization in developing societies.

bilateral investment treaty (BIT)   A legally binding agreement between two states that establishes the terms that govern private investment by residents of one state in the national jurisdiction of the other. The typical BIT requires fair and equal treatment, limits expropriation, and protects the repatriation of earnings and assets. In addition, a large number of BITs include arbitration clauses that commit the parties to adjudicate disputes in international forums such as the International Center for the Settlement of Investment Disputes.

Brady Plan   Proposed in 1989 by Secretary of the U.S. Treasury Nicholas J. Brady, this plan attempted to bring the developing-country debt crisis to a close. It encouraged commercial banks to negotiate debt reduction agreements with debtor governments. To make the proposal attractive to commercial banks, the advanced industrialized countries and the multilateral financial institutions advanced $30 billion with which to guarantee the principal of the Brady bonds, as the new debt instruments came to be called.

Bretton Woods compromise   A broad agreement among labor, business, and governments in the U.S. and Europe in which it was agreed to limit the extent of global market liberalism in order to provide greater economic security to industrial workers. Also known as embedded liberalism.

Bretton Woods system The international monetary system that was created in 1944 at Bretton Woods, New Hampshire. It was based on fixed-but-adjustable exchange rates in an attempt to provide a stable international monetary system and at the same time allow governments to use monetary policy to manage the domestic economy. The system collapsed in 1973 and represented the last time that governments attempted to create and maintain an international monetary system based on some form of fixed exchange rates.

Calvo doctrine Named after the Argentinean legal scholar Carlos Calvo who first stated it in 1868, this doctrine argues that no government has the right to intervene in another country to enforce the private claims of that government's citizens. The doctrine was invoked by Latin American governments during the late nineteenth and early twentieth century to challenge the right of governments to use diplomatic pressure and military force to protect foreign investments made by their citizens.

capital account One of the two principal components of the balance of payments, it records all financial flows into and out of a particular country. Such financial flows include bank loans, equities (stocks and bonds), and foreign direct investment.

central bank independence The degree to which a country's central bank can set monetary policy free from interference by the government. Typically considered to be a function of three things: the degree to which the central bank is free to decide what economic objective to pursue, the degree to which the central bank is free to decide how to set monetary policy in pursuit of this objective, and the degree to which central-bank decisions can be reversed by other branches of government. Contemporary economic theory argues that independent central banks are better able to deliver low inflation than are central banks controlled by the government.

collective action problem Applies to instances in which the action of a number of individuals is required to achieve a common goal. The problem arises because people will not voluntarily invest time, energy, or money to achieve a common goal, but will instead allow others to bear these costs. That is, each free rides on the efforts of others. Because all members of the interested group act in the same way, insufficient time, energy, and money are dedicated to the achievement of the goal, and the goal is therefore not achieved. In international political economy, it has been used to understand interest-group formation, and in particular, why consumer interests are under-represented in trade policy.

Common Agricultural Policy (CAP) A set of policies used by the European Union (EU) to protect European farmers from farm products produced outside the union. These policies include production and export subsidies to support European farmers, as well as tariffs and quotas to limit imports of foreign agricultural products. The CAP is one of the most controversial aspects of the U.S.–EU trade relationship.

comparative advantage First fully stated by David Ricardo in the early nineteenth century, this concept holds that a country has a comparative advantage in a good if it can produce that good more cheaply than it can produce other goods. By specializing in the production of goods in which it holds a comparative advantage and importing the other goods, the country can consume more of all goods. In contrast to Adam Smith, therefore, this principle states that a country need not have an absolute advantage in any good to benefit from trade. The principle provides a powerful justification for liberal international trade by asserting that all countries benefit from such trade.

complementary demand A market failure structuralists believed would limit automatic industrialization. In an economy in which few people earn a money wage, no single manufacturing firm can sell its products unless other manufacturing activities are started simultaneously.

conditionality Property applied to the terms governing transactions between the International Monetary Fund and member governments. In order to gain access to International Monetary Fund financial resources, a government must agree to a set of policy changes designed to correct its balance-of-payments deficit. Typically, governments must tighten the money supply and reduce government spending. In more extreme cases, governments are also required to undertake structural reforms. (*See* macroeconomic stabilization; structural adjustment.)

core labor standards Principles elaborated by the International Labour Organization that include the freedom of association, the right to bargain collectively, abolition of forced labor, non-discrimination in the workplace, and minimum employment age.

countervailing-duty investigation A government investigation used to determine whether a foreign government is subsidizing its national firms' exports directly or indirectly. Under the rules of the international trade system, a positive finding in such an investigation allows the government to impose tariffs to offset the subsidy.

credible commitment When the cost to an individual of changing a current policy or policy position is greater than the benefits conferred to that same individual by the new policy or policy position. A credible commitment is typically seen as a solution to a time-consistency problem.

current account One of the two principal components of the balance of payments. It records all payments between the country and the rest of the world in connection with goods, services, income earned on foreign investments, royalties, licenses, unilateral transfers by private individuals, government expenditures on foreign aid, and overseas military spending.

customs union A form of regional trading arrangement in which member governments eliminate all tariffs on trade between members of the union and create a common tariff that is imposed on goods entering any member country of the union from countries outside the union.

debt-service capacity The ability of a country to make payments of interest and principal on foreign debt. Because debt service, especially in developing countries, must be made with foreign currencies, export earnings are a good measure of a country's debt-service capacity.

debt-service ratio The percentage of a country's export earnings that must be devoted to payments of interest and principal on foreign debt. A high debt-service ratio means that a large share of the country's total export revenues must be used to make debt payments.

devaluation A reduction in a currency's value within a fixed or fixed-but-adjustable exchange-rate system. Should be distinguished from depreciation, which is a change in a currency's value caused by foreign exchange market transactions. Thus, a floating currency may depreciate, but cannot be devalued.

dispute settlement mechanism A quasi-judicial tribunal that is used to resolve trade disputes between WTO member governments.

dollar overhang Foreign holdings of dollars and dollar-denominated assets in excess of U.S. holdings of monetary gold necessary to redeem foreign dollar holdings. In other words, outstanding claims on U.S. monetary gold greater than the stock of monetary gold the United States held. Many argue that dollar overhang lay at the base of the instability of the Bretton Woods system.

domestic safeguards Clauses in the General Agreement on Tariffs and Trade that allow governments to temporarily suspend tariff reductions they have made previously when a domestic industry is being threatened by a sudden surge of imports.

dual economy An economy that is organized into two distinct sectors, one being a high-wage economy and one being a low-wage economy, that have very few connections between them. Traditionally thought to characterize pre-industrial economies that combined an industrialized export sector and traditional subsistence-based agriculture.

dumping The act of selling a good in a foreign market at a price that is either below the cost of production of the good or below the price at which the good sells for in the home market. Dumping is illegal under General Agreement on Tariffs and Trade rules, and governments are allowed to counter the practice by raising tariffs. (*See* antidumping investigation.)

East Asian model A model in which economic development is conceptualized as a series of distinct stages of industrialization. In the first stage, industrial policy promotes labor-intensive light industry, such as textiles and other consumer durables. In the second stage, the emphasis of industrial policy shifts to heavy industries, such as steel, shipbuilding, petrochemicals, and synthetic fibers. In the third stage, governments target skill-intensive and R&D-intensive consumer durables and industrial machinery, such as machine tools, semiconductors, computers, telecommunications equipment, robotics, and biotechnology. Governments design policies and organizations to promote the transition from one stage to the other.

easy import substitution industrialization The first stage of import substitution industrialization that focused on developing domestic capacity to produce consumer nondurable manufactured goods.

economies of experience The cost of producing a good fall as workers and managers gain the specific skills as a consequence of producing the good. Often referred to as "moving down the learning curve."

economies of scale Reductions in the unit cost of producing a good caused by increases in the number of goods produced. Economies of scale often arise from knowledge acquired in production. The existence of economies of scale in certain industries can provide a justification for welfare-enhancing industrial policy, as well as a rationale for strategic trade theory.

efficiency-oriented investment One of the three types of foreign direct investment by a foreign firm in the local economy made in order to use the locally abundant factor in production oriented toward the global market.

enclave agriculture Export-oriented agriculture that has few linkages to the rest of the local economy. Examples might include cocoa production in Ghana.

enforcement problem In the anarchic international state system, governments cannot be certain that other governments will comply with the trade agreements that they conclude. As a consequence, governments are reluctant to enter into such agreements. This problem complicates all forms of international cooperation and has been used to understand the need for the World Trade Organization.

Engel's Law Law asserting that people spend smaller percentages of their total income on food and other primary commodities as their incomes rise. It was a central component of the Singer-Prebisch theory that formed a part of structuralism.

environmental Kuznets curve A posited inverted *U*-shaped relationship between per capita income and environmental degradation. Low- and high-income societies both have relatively low environmental impacts. The most severe environmental damage occurs in middle-income rapidly industrializing societies.

eurodollars Literally, dollar-denominated bank accounts and loans managed by banks outside of the United States. More broadly, the term refers to bank accounts denominated in currencies other than the currency issued by the government in the country in which the account is held.

European monetary system (EMS) Founded by European Community governments in 1979, the EMS was a fixed-but-adjustable exchange-rate system in which governments established a central parity against a basket of European Union (EU) currencies called the European Currency Unit (ECU). Central parities against the ECU were then used to create bilateral exchange rates between all EU currencies. EU governments were required to maintain their currency's bilateral exchange rate within 2.25 percent of its central bilateral rate. In January 1999, monetary union replaced the EMS.

exchange rate misalignment Large and persistent gaps between the "correct" or equilibrium exchange rate and the actual (or market-determined) exchange rate.

exchange-rate system A set of rules that together specify the amount by which currencies can appreciate and depreciate in the foreign exchange market. Under a fixed exchange-rate system, the rules require governments to restrict currency movements to a narrow range around some central rate. In a floating exchange-rate system, governments can allow their currencies to move by as much as they desire.

exchange restrictions Government regulations controlling the private use of foreign exchange. Used extensively by governments in the advanced industrialized countries under the Bretton Woods system to limit capital outflows.

Exon-Florio Amendment An amendment to the United States 1988 Omnibus Trade Act that allows the executive to block foreign acquisitions of American firms for reasons of national security. More broadly, it highlights government concerns about the role foreign corporations play in the domestic economy.

export-oriented strategy A development strategy in which emphasis is placed on producing manufactured goods that can be sold in international markets. Adopted by the East Asian newly industrialized countries in the late 1950s to early 1960s after the gains from easy import substitution industrialization had been exhausted. During the late 1980s, this strategy and the apparent Asian success based on it provided the foundation for the "Washington Consensus."

export-processing zones   Industrial estates where the government provides land, utilities, transportation infrastructure, and, in some cases, buildings to the investing firms, usually at subsidized rates. They are often established by developing countries to attract foreign direct investments by multinational corporations.

export substitution strategy   A development stage in which labor-intensive manufactured goods produced as a consequence of easy import substitution industrialization take the place of primary commodities in exports.

externality   Market failures that arise when the parties to a given transaction do not bear the full cost of or realize the full benefit from their transaction. Externalities can be negative (when you hire a DJ to play loud music at your all-night party, your early-to-bed roommate suffers costs) or positive (when you hire a service to clean your room, your never-clean-up roommate realizes some of the benefits). When individuals do not bear the full costs of their transactions, they will engage in more of that activity than society desires. (You could afford to hire fewer DJs if you had to pay for your roommate's hotel room each time you had a party.) When individuals do not capture all benefits from a transaction, they engage in less of that activity than society desires. (You could afford more frequent visits by the cleaning service if your roommate paid for the benefit she gained from cleaning.)

factor endowments   The amount of land, labor, and capital a country has available. Countries have different relative factor endowments, and in the Hecksher-Ohlin model of international trade, these differences are the source of comparative advantage.

factor mobility   The ease with which factors of production can move from one industry to another. All factors are mobile in the long run, but many are relatively immobile in the short run. Different assumptions about the mobility of factors underlie two different political theories of trade politics. The factor model assumes a high degree of factor mobility, whereas the sectoral model assumes

that at least one factor is immobile in the short run.

factor model   A political model that argues that the politics of trade policy is characterized by competition between labor and capital. Each of these two groups has a distinct trade policy preference because international trade has a differential effect on the groups' incomes. The scarce factor will be harmed by trade and therefore lobbies for protection. The abundant factor will benefit from trade and therefore lobbies for trade liberalization.

factor-price equalization (Stolper-Samuleson theorem)   In open economies, international trade will cause the price of the factors of production to equalize. In a two-country world, the price of each country's scarce factor will fall, whereas the price of each country's abundant factor will rise. Eventually, the price of labor will be the same in both countries and the price of capital will be the same in both countries.

factors   The basic tools of production, including labor, land, and capital.

fast track   The domestic political process setting the terms under which the United States participates in international trade negotiations and ratifies the resulting agreements. Congress first grants the executive the authority to negotiate international trade agreements. Congress must then approve (by a simple majority and within 90 days) any trade agreement the executive concludes before the agreement can become law. Congress cannot amend the trade agreement. The 1974 Trade Act first instituted this procedure.

fiscal policy   The use by the government of tax and spending policies to manage domestic demand. An expansionary fiscal policy will boost domestic demand, thereby raising economic output; a restrictive fiscal policy will reduce domestic demand, thereby lowering economic output.

fixed-but-adjustable exchange-rate system   A system in which governments establish a central or official rate for their currency against some standard, as in a fixed exchange-rate system, but are also allowed to change the official rate occasionally, usually under a set of well-defined circumstances.

fixed exchange-rate system   A system in which governments establish a central or official rate for their currency, usually expressed in terms of some standard, such as gold or another currency. Governments are required to use monetary policy and foreign exchange market intervention to maintain their currency within a band around the official rate.

floating exchange-rate system A system in which governments do not establish a central or official rate for their currency and are under no obligation to engage in foreign exchange market intervention to influence the value of their currency. In this system, the value of one currency in terms of another is determined purely by the interaction between supply and demand in the foreign exchange market.

foreign aid (official development assistance) Financial assistance provided to developing countries' governments by the advanced industrialized countries and by multilateral financial institutions such as the World Bank and the regional development banks in order to finance development projects. Foreign aid can be supplied as a grant (requiring no repayment) or a loan (requiring repayment). Loans can be offered on concessional terms (below market rates of interest) or non-concessional terms (at market rates of interest).

foreign direct investment (FDI) A form of cross-border investment in which a resident or corporation based in one country owns a productive asset located in a second country. Such investments are made by multinational corporations. FDI can involve the construction of a new, or the purchase of an existing, plant or factory.

foreign exchange market The market in which national currencies are traded. It is through transactions in this market that the market exchange rates of the world's currencies are established. According to the Bank of International Settlements, more than $1 trillion worth of currencies are traded each day.

foreign exchange reserves Government holdings of other countries' currencies.

free riding *See* collective action problem.

free-trade area A regional trading arrangement in which governments eliminate all tariffs on goods imported from other members, but retain independent tariffs on goods imported from non-members. (*See also* customs union and regional trading arrangements.)

fundamental disequilibrium Imprecisely defined, the balance-of-payments conditions that must pertain in order for a government to alter its central parity against gold in the Bretton Woods system. The balance of payments had to be so imbalanced as to make adjustment through fiscal and monetary policy too costly.

GATT Part IV Added to the General Agreement on Tariffs and Trade in 1964, in part as a result of developing countries' pressure. Contains three articles that focus on developing countries' trade problems. The three articles call upon the advanced industrialized countries to improve market access for commodity exporters, to refrain from raising barriers to the import of products that are of special interest to the developing world, and to engage in "joint action to promote trade and development."

General Agreement on Tariffs and Trade (GATT) An international agreement concluded in 1947 establishing rules that regulate national trade policies. Between 1947 and 1995, the GATT also was the principal international trade organization, providing a forum for trade negotiations, administering trade agreements, helping governments settle trade disputes, and reviewing national trade policies. In 1995, the last role was taken over by the World Trade Organization. Today, the GATT continues to provide the core rules regulating national trade policies.

Generalized System of Preferences (GSP) Part of the General Agreement on Tariffs and Trade (GATT) concluded in the late 1960s under which advanced industrialized countries can allow manufactured exports from developing countries to enter their markets at preferential tariff rates. The GSP is therefore a legal exception to the GATT principle of non-discrimination.

Gini coefficient A metric employed to estimate income inequality. It ranges from 0 to 1, with higher values reflecting greater inequality. In the contemporary era, Sweden has the least inequality, as measured by a Gini coefficient of .25, whereas Brazil is among the most unequal, as measured by a Gini coefficient of .57.

global division of labor One of the economic consequences of an open international trade system. Over time, trade will cause countries to specialize in producing goods that make intensive use of their abundant factors of production. Eventually, each country will produce goods in which it has a comparative advantage and shed industries in which it has a comparative disadvantage.

Group of 77 A coalition of developing countries established at the conclusion of the first United Nations Conference on Trade and Development (UNCTAD) conference in the early 1960s. Seventy-seven developing-countries' governments signed a joint declaration that called for reform of the international trade system. The Group of 77 subsequently led the campaign for reform of the multilateral trade system during the next 20 years. (*See* UNCTAD and New International Economic Order.)

Heavily Indebted Poor Countries (HIPC) initiative A plan initiated in September 1996 to reduce the debt owed by the world's poorest countries to multilateral lenders; linked debt reduction to a two-stage conditionality process. The goal was to bring a country's total foreign debt down to sustainable levels, defined as less than 150 percent of export earnings. HIPC was succeeded by the Multilateral Debt Relief Initiative in 2006. (*See* multilateral debt relief initiative.)

Hecksher-Ohlin model A model of the determinants of comparative advantage that argues that comparative advantage arises from cross-national differences in factor endowments. A country's comparative advantage will lie in goods produced through heavy reliance on its abundant factors. Capital-abundant countries have a comparative advantage in capital-intensive goods, and labor-abundant countries have a comparative advantage in labor-intensive goods. (*See* factor endowments.)

hegemonic stability theory A model that hypothesizes that the global economy will be open and stable when a hegemon exists and will tend toward protectionism, instability, and crisis when no hegemon exists.

hegemony A particular distribution of power in the international state system characterized by the existence of one country (a hegemon) whose power capabilities are substantially greater than the next-most-powerful country or countries. The relevant capabilities include economic power, measured as the size and technological sophistication of the economy, and military power. A prominent hypothesis, called

hegemonic stability theory, links the openness and stability of the international economic system to the presence or absence of a hegemon.

heterodox strategies An approach to macroeconomic stabilization adopted by some Latin American governments during the 1980s. Seen as an alternative to the orthodox approach advocated by the International Monetary Fund, these strategies attempted to reduce inflation through government controls on wages and prices, rather than by restricting aggregate demand by reducing government budget deficits and slowing the rate of growth of the money supply. In most instances, they failed to stabilize the economy.

horizontal integration A form of industrial organization that occurs when a corporation creates multiple production facilities, each of which produces the same good or goods. Many multinational corporations are horizontally integrated firms, producing the same product or product line in multiple factories based in different countries. Firms integrate horizontally to capture the full value of the intangible assets they control.

hot money Financial capital held in short-term instruments that can be quickly liquidated at the first sign of financial trouble. Seen by many to be a source of volatility and instability in contemporary capital markets.

import substitution industrialization (ISI) An economic development strategy adopted in many developing countries after World War II in which states attempted to industrialize by substituting domestically produced goods for manufactured items that had previously been imported. The strategy proceeded in two stages. Under easy ISI, the focus was on creating simple consumer goods. In the second stage, the focus shifted to consumer durable goods, intermediate inputs, and the capital goods needed to produce consumer durables. Most governments have abandoned this approach since the mid-1980s in favor of an export-oriented strategy.

industrial policy An assortment of government policies, including tax policy, government subsidies, traditional protectionism, and government procurement practices, used to channel resources away from some actors and industries and direct them toward those actors and industries the government wishes to promote. The use of such policies is typically based on long-term economic development objectives defined in terms of boosting economic growth, improving productivity, and enhancing international competitiveness. The specific goals are often determined by explicit comparisons to other countries' economic achievements.

income inequality Broad term used to characterize how income generated by market activity is distributed across a given population. In current discourse, typically used to refer to the pattern in which incomes have risen significantly for people in high income segments of the population but have stagnated for people in the middle- and low-income parts of the income distribution.

infant-industry case for protection A theoretical justification for protection that applies to cases in which a country's newly created firms (infants) could not *initially* compete against foreign producers in an established industry, but would be able to do so eventually if they were given time to mature.

intangible asset Something whose value is derived from knowledge or from skills or production processes of a firm. An intangible asset can be based on a patented process or design, or it can arise from production-specific knowhow shared by workers in the firm. The inherent difficulty of selling or licensing this kind of asset provides an important rationale for horizontal integration.

intellectual property Creations of the mind, such as inventions, literary and artistic works, symbols, names, images, and designs, used in commerce. The protection of intellectual property is the subject of the Trade Related Intellectual Property Rights agreement negotiated as part of the Uruguay Round.

intergovernmental bargaining The process through which governments negotiate the agreements with which they regulate their interaction in the global economy.

International Bank for Reconstruction and Development (IBRD or World Bank) Established in 1944 at the Bretton Woods conference, the IBRD extends long-term loans to developing countries to finance physical and social infrastructure needed to reduce poverty and promote development. These loans are financed by bonds that the IBRD sells in private bond markets.

International Development Association (IDA) Part of the World Bank group, the IDA was established in the early 1960s as a separate development lending agency. The IDA is a concessional loan agency; its loans have a longer time to maturity than standard International Bank for Reconstruction and Development loans have, and they carry 0 percent interest rates. These loans are financed by member government contributions. To be eligible for IDA lending, a country must have a per capita income of less than $885 per year.

international investment position The difference between the value of a country's holdings of foreign assets and the value of its foreign liabilities. This position can be positive (the country owns more foreign assets than it has foreign liabilities), negative (the country's foreign assets are less than its liabilities to foreigners), or balanced (foreign assets exactly equal foreign liabilities).

International Monetary Fund (IMF) Established at the Bretton Woods conference in 1944, the IMF was initially charged with helping governments finance and ultimately eliminate balance-of-payments deficits in order to maintain stable exchange rates. Since the shift to floating exchange rates in 1973, the IMF has become increasingly focused on the management of debt and balance-of-payments crises in developing countries. (*See* conditionality.)

Keynesianism An approach to macroeconomic policy that places primary emphasis on using fiscal and monetary policies to manage domestic demand in order to maintain full employment. Named after John Maynard Keynes, who was the first to demonstrate that governments could use macroeconomic policies for this purpose. The approach was widely adopted by governments in the advanced industrialized countries following World War II, but lost favor during the 1980s.

liberalism A traditional school of political economy that emerged in Britain during the eighteenth century as a challenge to mercantilism. Liberalism asserts that the purpose of economic activity is to enrich individuals, and that the state should thus play little role in the economic system. Liberalism gave rise to the theory of comparative advantage. It suggests that international political economy is cooperative rather than conflictual.

liquidity problem (or crisis) Situation that arises in financial markets in which a financial institution or other actor is solvent (assets are greater than liabilities) but cannot readily trade its assets for the cash required to settle a liability.

locational advantage   Country characteristics, such as its factor or natural resource endowments or market size, that create incentives for a foreign corporation to invest in the country.

locational incentives   Offered by governments to multinational corporations (MNCs), locational incentives are designed to reduce the costs of, and thereby increase the return from, a particular investment. Governments offer them to induce MNCs to invest in their country rather than another.

London Club   A private association established and run by the large commercial banks engaged in international lending. Developing countries' governments that want to reschedule their commercial bank debt must work out the terms of a rescheduling agreement with the London Club.

macroeconomic policy   The use of fiscal and monetary policy to influence aggregate economic activity in the national economy, such as the rate of economic growth, the rate of inflation, and the level of unemployment. (*See* Keynesianism.)

macroeconomic stabilization   The correction, through various policy programs, of macroeconomic imbalances that are producing high and rising inflation. Most programs involve the reduction of a government budget deficit and a tight monetary policy. Most conditionality agreements with the International Monetary Fund contain such a program.

managed float   A form of floating exchange-rate system in which governments occasionally intervene in foreign exchange markets to try to influence the value of their currency. Such interventions are voluntary and sometimes involve coordinated intervention by more than one country.

maquiladora program   An export-processing zone in northern Mexico established by the government in an attempt to encourage American manufacturing multinational corporations to create assembly operations.

market liberalism   A core principle of the World Trade Organization that asserts that an open or liberal international trade system raises the world's standard of living. Every country gains from liberal trade, and these gains are greatest when cross-border trade is not restricted by tariffs and other barriers.

market-oriented investment   One of the three types of foreign direct investment by a foreign firm in the local economy made in order to gain access to consumers (the market) within the host country.

Marxism   A school of political economy originating in the nineteenth century work of Karl Marx. It asserts that politics is dominated by distributional conflict between social groups, and that social groups are defined by economic structure. In capitalism, politics is dominated by conflict between capitalists and workers. Marxist theories of international political economy often emphasize distributional conflict between advanced industrialized and developing countries.

mega-regional   Mega-regional agreements seek deeper economic integration among their members. To achieve this goal, these agreements are both broader in scope and reach more deeply into domestic arrangements than prior agreements. The TTIP and the TPP were intended to promote cooperation and harmonization on technical barriers to trade, which are domestic rules, regulations, and administrative procedures that can limit trade flows. In addition, these agreements included trade in services, more ambitious rules regarding the protection of intellectual property than are present in the WTO, and agreement on the treatment and protection of foreign investment.

mercantilism   A traditional school of political economy dating from (at least) the seventeenth century. It asserts that power and wealth are inextricably connected. Accordingly, it argues that governments structure their international economic transactions in order to enhance their power relative to other states and domestic society. Mercantilism thus depicts international political economy as inherently conflictual.

Ministerial Conference   The highest level of World Trade Organization decision making. They draw top-level officials together for a 3- or 4-day session at least once every 2 years. Typically used to establish an agenda for forthcoming negotiations or bridge remaining differences in ongoing negotiations.

monetary policy   Changes in the country's money supply undertaken in an attempt to manage aggregate economic activity. An expansionary monetary policy is typically associated with rising inflation, a restrictive monetary policy with falling inflation and rising unemployment.

monetary union   An exchange-rate system in which governments permanently fix their exchange rates and introduce a single currency. The European Union created a monetary union on January 1, 1999, and introduced a single currency—the euro—on January 1, 2002.

moral hazard   A consideration that arises when banks believe that the government will bail them out if they suffer large losses on the loans they have made. If banks believe that the government will cover their losses, they have little incentive to carefully evaluate the risks that are associated with the loans they make. If the loans are repaid, banks earn money. If the loans are not repaid, the government—and hence society's taxpayers—picks up the tab. In such an environment, banks have an incentive to make riskier loans than they would make in the absence of a guarantee from the government, thereby raising the likelihood of a crisis.

most-favored nation   The central principle upon which the World Trade Organization (WTO) is based, this rule requires that any advantage extended by one WTO member government to another also be extended to all other WTO members. The principle therefore prevents trade measures that discriminate between countries.

Multilateral Agreement on Investment (MAI)   A document negotiated by the advanced industrialized countries in the Organization for Economic Cooperation and Development between 1995 and 1997 that laid out international rules governing the treatment of multinational corporations by governments. Designed to promote investment liberalization based on the principles of national treatment and most-favored nation, the MAI was never concluded, because negotiations proved fruitless.

Multilateral Debt Relief Initiative (MDRI)   A plan for 100-percent debt forgiveness announced by the Group of eight governments, the World Bank, and the International Monetary Fund in March of 2006. MDRI is based on the same conditionality program as the Heavily Indebted Poor Countries Initiative, but provides full forgiveness of all debt to multilateral lenders for eligible countries. Funding for the program, and thus initial debt forgiveness, began in July 2006. (*See* Heavily Indebted Poor Countries Initiative.)

multilateral environmental agreements   International agreements between three or more governments dedicated to the achievement of a specific environmental objective.

multinational corporation (MNC)   A company that has ownership and manages production facilities in two or more countries. There are approximately 63,459 parent firms that together own a total of 689,520 foreign affiliates. These parent firms and their foreign affiliates account for about 25 percent of the world's economic production and employ some 66 million people worldwide.

Nash equilibrium   An outcome in a game theoretic model in which none of the players has an incentive to change their strategy unilaterally.

national treatment   The second component of non-discrimination in the General Agreement on Tariffs and Trade (GATT) embodied in GATT Article III, as well as in the General Agreement on Trade in Services and Agreement on Trade-Related Aspects of Intellectual Property Rights. National treatment requires governments to impose identical tax and regulatory policies on foreign and domestic like products. This principle thus prohibits governments from using taxes and regulatory policies to provide advantages to domestic producers over foreign producers.

natural rate of unemployment   The economy's long-run equilibrium rate of unemployment, or the rate of unemployment to which the economy will return after a recession or a boom. The natural rate of unemployment is never zero, and can in fact be substantially above zero.

natural resource investment   One of the three types of foreign direct investment by a foreign firm in a local economy made in order to gain access to the local economy's natural resources.

neoliberalism   *See* Washington Consensus.

New International Economic Order (NIEO)   A reform effort driven by the Group of 77 and adopted by the United Nations General Assembly in December 1974. It embodied a set of reform objectives that, if implemented, would have radically altered the nature and operation of the international economy by creating "development-friendly" trade rules and giving developing countries a larger role in the decision-making processes of the World Bank and International Monetary Fund. The New International Economic Order was abandoned in the early 1980s.

non-discrimination A core principle of the World Trade Organization (WTO) that ensures that each WTO member faces identical opportunities in trade with other WTO members. Embodied in the "most favored nation" and in "national treatment."

non-tariff barrier (NTB) Any of a number of policy or structural impediments to trade other than tariffs. NTBs include such things as health and safety regulations, government purchasing practices, and retail and distribution networks. As quotas have been eliminated and tariffs reduced, NTBs have become one of the most important remaining obstacles to international trade and are thus an increasingly important issue in the World Trade Organization.

nontraded-goods sector Sector containing all economic activities that do not enter into international trade, either because the good is too costly to transport (e.g., houses or concrete) or because in some cases the good or service must be performed locally (e.g., the railway system, many public utilities, healthcare, auto repair, and the retail sector more generally). In addition, government employees, such as civil servants, teachers, and military personnel, also work in the nontraded-goods sector.

obsolescing bargain Explains how a multinational corporation (MNC) and a host country government divide the income generated by an MNC investment in the host country. It asserts that the MNC has a bargaining advantage in the pre-investment negotiations. Consequently, the initial investment agreement will direct a larger share of the resulting income to the MNC and a smaller share to the government. Once the investment is made, however, the government gains bargaining power at the expense of the MNC. The government uses its enhanced bargaining power to renegotiate the initial agreement and claim a larger share of the investment income. The initial bargain is thus rendered obsolete by post-investment changes in relative bargaining power.

official development assistance *See* foreign aid.

oligopoly In contrast to perfectly competitive markets, oligopoly defines a market dominated by a few producers. As a consequence, each firm has some influence over the price of the good it makes, whereas in perfectly competitive markets each producer is a price taker.

Pareto suboptimal A status quo in which at least one member of society can be made better off without making any other member of society worse off.

Paris Club An informal group composed of 19 permanent members, all of which are governments that hold large claims on other governments. Its primary role is to negotiate the rescheduling of these debts.

pecuniary externality A market failure structuralists believed would limit automatic industrialization that arises from the interdependence of economic activities. Investment in industry A that supplies inputs to industry B will not occur unless industry B expands output. Industry B will not expand output unless industry A expands its output. Hence, investments in each are dependent upon decision in the other.

performance requirement A target imposed on the local affiliate of an MNC by the host-country government in order to promote a specific economic objective. If the government is trying to promote backward linkages, for example, it will require the local affiliate to purchase a specific percentage of its inputs from domestic suppliers. The use of these measures was somewhat constrained by the agreement on Trade Related Investment Measures negotiated during the Uruguay Round.

petrodollars The revenues earned by Organization of Petroleum Exporting Countries' (OPEC) governments in the wake of the 1973 oil price rise. These funds were channeled by commercial banks to some developing-country governments to finance their current account deficits in a process that came to be called petrodollar recycling.

Phillips curve Curve that posits a trade-off between inflation and unemployment: governments can reduce unemployment only by causing higher inflation and can reduce inflation only by causing higher unemployment. Named after British economist A. W. Phillips, who was the first to pose such a relationship in 1958. The trade-off between inflation and unemployment is now seen to hold only in the short run. (*See* accelerationist principle.)

Plaza Accord   A pact reached in September 1985 under which the Group of Five agreed to reduce the value of the dollar against the Japanese yen and the German mark by 10 to 12 percent. This agreement is the most recent episode of a concerted attempt by the Group of Five to manage exchange rates.

pocketbook voter   A person whose vote for or against an incumbent (or sitting government) depends upon their economic condition. A voter whose income has risen will vote for the incumbent; a voter whose income has fallen will vote against the incumbent. Contrast with sociotropic voting.

political institutions   The formal and informal rules that structure collective decision making (politics). These rules establish who can legitimately participate in the political process, how these participants will make collective decisions, and how they will ensure compliance with the decisions they make. Such rules thus enable groups in countries and groups of countries in the international state system to reach and enforce collective decisions.

Political Trilemma   A concept developed by Dani Rodrik that asserts that although societies might value the three goals of globalization, democratic decision making, and national autonomy, in any historical era they can attain only two of them. In an era of globalization, societies must thus choose between national autonomy and democratic decision making.

price stability   Now commonly considered by governments to be the appropriate objective for monetary policy, it connotes a low and stable rate of inflation—about 1–2 percent per year.

prisoners' dilemma   A game-theoretic model often used to depict the difficulties that governments face when trying to cooperate in the global economy. Emphasizes the incentives that governments have to "cheat" on any international agreements into which they enter and shows how those incentives make governments reluctant to enter into cooperative agreements.

process and production methods (PPMs)   A concept central to the relationship between trade and the environment. Under World

Trade Organization (WTO) law, goods that are identical in all senses other than how they are produced (PPM) are considered like goods and must be treated the same. This prevents WTO members from discriminating between versions produced with green and non-green PPMs.

Reciprocal Trade Agreements Act   American trade legislation passed in 1934 under which Congress allowed the executive to reduce tariffs by as much as 50 percent in exchange for equivalent concessions from foreign governments. Created the institutional framework for reciprocal tariff reductions achieved under GATT following World War II.

reciprocity   The central principle upon which bargaining within the World Trade Organization is based. The concessions that each government makes to its partners in multilateral trade negotiations are roughly the same size as the concessions it gains from its trading partners.

regional development banks   Created in the 1960s to provide concessional lending on the model of the International Development Association. They include the Inter-American Development Bank, the Asian Development Bank, and the African Development Bank.

regional trading arrangements (RTAs)   Trade agreements in which tariffs discriminate between members and non-members. Although inherently discriminatory, RTAs are recognized as a legitimate exception to this principle under General Agreement on Tariffs and Trade Article XXIV. Sometimes called preferential trade arrangements. (*See also* customs union and free-trade area.)

rent   A higher-than-normal return on an investment. Rents are created by barriers to entry, which can result from monopolistic or oligopolistic market structures or government policies.

rent seeking   Efforts by private actors to convince politicians to enact policies that create rents they can capture. (*See* rent.)

secondary import substitution industrialization   The second stage of ISI strategies in which emphasis shifts to production of consumer durables, intermediate inputs such as steel and chemicals, and capital goods.

sectoral model   A political model that argues that the politics of trade policy is characterized by competition between import-competing and export-oriented industries. Each industry has a distinct trade policy preference because international trade has a differential effect on the industries' incomes. Industries that rely heavily on the economy's scarce factor will be harmed by trade and therefore lobby for protection. Industries that rely heavily on the economy's abundant factor will benefit from trade and therefore lobby for trade liberalization.

service An economic activity, such as financial services, transportation, consulting and accounting, and telecommunications, that does not involve manufacturing, farming, or the extraction of resources.

Singer-Prebisch theory Developed during the 1950s by Raul Prebisch and Hans Singer, it claimed that, because developing countries faced a secular decline in their terms of trade, participation in the General Agreement on Tariffs and Trade-based multilateral trade system would hamper their industrialization. The theory provided an intellectual justification for import substitution industrialization.

skill-biased technological change A change in the nature of economic production that results from innovation (technological change) that has the consequence of decreasing the overall demand for low-skilled workers. This is often seen to be an important reason for the rising income inequality that has characterized advanced industrialized economies during the last 30 years.

Smoot-Hawley Act Trade legislation passed by the U.S. Congress in 1930 that raised the average American tariff to a historic high of almost 60 percent. Widely regarded to have contributed to the collapse of the world trade and monetary systems and deepened the global depression during the 1930s.

sociotropic voting Votes for or against an incumbent reflect voters' evaluations of the general state of the economy. Voters are likely to vote against incumbents that preside during periods of low income growth and high unemployment and likely to vote for incumbents whose time in office corresponds with high income growth and low unemployment. Contrast with pocketbook voters.

sovereign wealth fund (SWF) A government-owned fund that purchases private assets in foreign markets. Many SWFs, known as commodity SWFs, are funded with revenues generated by state-owned oil companies.

specific asset An investment dedicated to a particular economic use or particular long-term economic relationship. Alternatively, an asset that cannot be shifted from one use to another without losing a substantial portion of its value.

specific factor A factor of production (labor, capital, or land) that is tied to a particular industry or sector and that cannot be easily or quickly moved to another sector. Indicates a low level of factor mobility. (*See* factor mobility.)

speculative attack A spate of very large sales of one country's currency by private financial institutions, sparked by the belief that the government is about to devalue the currency. The huge volume of currency sales in recent speculative attacks has led some officials to conclude that fixed-but-adjustable exchange rates are no longer a viable policy option. Instead, governments must choose between a permanently fixed exchange rate and a floating exchange rate.

stabilization fund The credit mechanism controlled by the International Monetary Fund (IMF) created by contributions from IMF member governments. The pool of liquidity thus established is in turn loaned to member governments when they face balance-of-payments problems.

state strength The degree to which policymakers are insulated from interest-group pressures when making policy decisions. Typically seen to range from weak states, wherein policy making is easily influenced by interest groups to strong states, where interest groups cannot readily access policymakers.

sterilized intervention Foreign exchange-market intervention that is not allowed to have an impact on the country's money supply. If a government sells foreign exchange to buy its own currency, thereby reducing the money supply, it will then buy government securities, thereby expanding the money supply. If a government sells its own currency and buys foreign currencies, thereby expanding its money supply, it will then sell government securities and buy its own currency, thereby reducing the money supply.

Stolper-Samuelson theorem *See* factor-price equalization.

strategic-trade theory Expands on the infant-industry case for protection by asserting that government intervention can help domestic firms gain international competitiveness in high-technology industries by providing means whereby those firms can overcome the competitive advantages enjoyed by established firms. The theory also suggests that governments can use trade policy to compete for valued industries. (*See* infant-industry case for protection.)

structural adjustment Policy reforms designed and promoted by the World Bank and the International Monetary Fund (IMF) that seek to increase the role of the market and reduce the role of the state in developing-countries' economies. First emerged in connection with the Baker Plan, but have subsequently become a standard component of IMF conditionality agreements.

structuralism A body of development economics that dominated the field in the early postwar period. It held that the shift of resources from agriculture to manufacturing associated with industrialization would occur only if the state adopted policies explicitly designed to bring it about. Structuralism provided the intellectual and theoretical justification for a large role for the state in the development process and for import substitution industrialization.

Sustainable Development Goals (SDG) A set of objectives adopted by UN member states in September 2015 as part of a larger commitment to sustainable development. The SDG is the successor to the Millennium Development Goals that were put in place between 2000 and 2015. The SDG goals are intended to end poverty, protect the environment, and deliver prosperity to all by achieving a set of more specific targets by 2030.

syndicated loan A loan in which hundreds of commercial banks each take a small share of a large loan made to a single borrower. This arrangement allows commercial banks to spread the risk involved in large loans among a number of banks, rather than requiring one bank to bear the full risk that the borrowing country will default.

target zone An exchange-rate system in which all currencies have an official rate surrounded by very wide margins within which the rate is allowed to fluctuate. When a currency moves outside the margins, the government is obligated to intervene in the foreign exchange market or alter domestic interest rates in order to bring the currency back inside. Such a system was discussed in connection with the Plaza Accord, but was never implemented.

tariff escalation The practice of imposing higher tariffs on goods involving more processing. This practice, common in the advanced industrialized countries, makes it difficult for developing countries to export processed food to the industrialized countries. This barrier in turn makes it difficult for developing countries to diversify their exports away from commodities, while still capitalizing on their comparative advantage.

tariff peaks Tariff rates above 15 percent. Such rates apply to about 5 percent of the advanced industrialized countries' imports from all developing countries and to about 10 percent of their imports from the least-developed countries.

tariffs Taxes that governments impose on foreign goods coming into the country. This tax raises the price of the foreign good in the domestic market of the country imposing the tariff. Even though tariffs distort international trade, they are the least distortionary of all trade barriers.

terms of trade The ratio of the price of a country's exports to the price of its imports. An improvement in a country's terms of trade means that the price of the goods it exports is rising relative to the price of the goods it imports, whereas a decline in a country's terms of trade means that the price of the goods it exports is falling relative to the price of the goods it imports. An improvement in its terms of trade makes a country richer, whereas a decline in its terms of trade makes it poorer.

time consistency problem Situations in which the best course of action in the present is not the best course of action in the future.

tit-for-tat A strategy often associated with iterated play of the prisoners' dilemma in which each actor plays the strategy its partner played in the prior round of play. If I play cooperation in the current round, you play cooperation in the next round. Tit-for-tat was found to support cooperation in an iterated prisoners' dilemma.

Tobin tax A small tax on foreign exchange market transactions that is high enough to discourage short-term capital flows, but not high enough to discourage long-term capital flows or international trade. By discouraging short-term capital flows, countries gain a degree of macroeconomic policy autonomy.

trade openness A standard measure of the degree to which a particular country is integrated into the world trading system. Openness is typically measured by dividing a country's total trade (its imports plus its exports) by its gross domestic product.

trade-related investment measure (TRIM) A government policy toward foreign direct investment or multinational corporations that has an impact on the country's imports or exports. For example, domestic content or trade-balancing requirements force firms to import fewer inputs or export more output than they would in the absence of such regulations. The result is a distortion of international trade. Such measures are regulated under the World Trade Organization.

unholy trinity Highlights the trade-offs that governments face when making decisions about fixed exchange rates, monetary policy, and international capital flows. Governments have three policy goals, each of which is desirable in its own right: (1) maintaining a fixed exchange rate; (2) having the ability to use monetary policy to manage the domestic economy, which we refer to as monetary policy autonomy; and (3) allowing financial capital to flow freely into and out of the domestic financial system, or capital mobility for short. The unholy trinity states that any government can achieve only two of these three goals simultaneously.

United Nations Conference on Trade and Development (UNCTAD) First established in March 1964 in response to developing countries' dissatisfaction with the General Agreement on Tariffs and Trade, this is a permanent United Nations body dedicated to promoting the developing countries' interests in the world trade system.

United Nations Resolution on Permanent Sovereignty over Natural Resources Adopted by the United Nations General Assembly in 1962, this document recognizes the right of host countries to exercise full control over their natural resources and over the foreign firms operating within their borders extracting those resources. The resolution affirmed the right of host-country governments to expropriate foreign investments and to determine the appropriate compensation in the event of expropriation.

U.S. Trade Representative Established as the Special Trade Representative by Congress in the 1962 Trade Expansion Act and given its current name by Congress during the 1970s, this office sets and administers U.S. trade policy, is the nation's chief trade negotiator, and represents the United States in the World Trade Organization and other international trade organizations.

vertical integration A form of industrial organization in which a single firm controls the different stages of the production process, rather than relying on the market to acquire inputs and sell outputs. A single corporation, for example, might own oil wells, the associated oil pipeline, the oil refinery, and a chain of gas stations. Difficulties inherent in long-term contracting create incentives for vertical integration.

voluntary export restraints A form of protectionism under which one country (or a number of countries) agrees to limit its exports to another country's market. Adopted by governments in order to circumvent General Agreement on Tariffs and Trade restrictions on the use of other types of protectionism, such as tariffs and quotas.

Washington Consensus, The The collection of policy reforms advocated by U.S. officials and by the International Monetary Fund and World Bank staffs as the solution to the economic problems faced by developing countries. The emphasis is on stabilization, structural adjustment, privatization, and market liberalization.

World Bank *See* International Bank for Reconstruction and Development.

World Trade Organization The principal international trade organization today that began operation in 1995. Located in Geneva, Switzerland, the World Trade Organization is a relatively small organization whose role includes administering trade agreements, providing a forum for trade negotiations, helping governments settle trade disputes, and reviewing national trade policies.

REFERENCES

Acemoglu, Daron, Simon Johnson, and James A. Robinson. 2001. The colonial origins of comparative development. *American Economic Review* 91: 1369–401.

Acemoglu, Daron, Simon Johnson, and James A. Robinson. 2012. *Why nations fail: The origins of power, prosperity, and poverty*. New York: Crown Business.

Acemoglu, Daron, and Pascual Restrepo. 2017. *Robots and jobs: Evidence from US labor markets*. NBER Working Paper no. 23285 Cambridge, MA: National Bureau of Economic Research (March).

Airbus. *Airbus results*. www.airbus.com.

Ake, Claude. 1981. *A political economy of Africa*. London: Longman.

Ake, Claude. 1996. *Democracy and development in Africa*. Washington, DC: Brookings Institution.

Akehurst, Michael B. 1984. *A modern introduction to international law*, 5th ed. Boston: Allen & Unwin.

Alesina, Alberto, and Alan Drazen. 1991. Why are stabilizations delayed? *American Economic Review* 81 (*December*): 1170–89.

American Textile Manufacturers Institute. 2001. *Statement of the American textile manufacturers institute to the committee on ways and means, U.S. house of representatives on President Bush's trade agenda*. www.atmi.org/NewsRoom/test030701.pdf (site now discontinued).

Amsden, Alice H. 1979. Taiwan's economic history: A case of etatisme and a challenge to dependency theory. *Modern China 5* (*July*): 341–80.

Amsden, Alice H. 1989. *Asia's next giant: South Korea and late industrialization*. Oxford, UK: Oxford University Press.

Arulpragasam, Jehan, and David E. Sahn. 1994. Policy failure and the limits of rapid reform: Lessons from Guinea. In *Adjusting to policy failure in African economies*, ed. David E. Sahn. Ithaca, NY: Cornell University Press, 53–95.

Autor, David H., David Dorn, and Gordon H. Hanson. 2016. The China shock: Learning from labor-market adjustment to large changes in trade." *Annual Review of Economics* 8 (*1*): 205–40.

Axelrod, Robert. 1984. *The evolution of cooperation*. New York: Basic Books.

Bailey, Michael, Judith Goldstein, and Barry Weingast. 1997. The institutional roots of American trade policy: Politics, coalitions, and international trade. *World Politics* 49 (*April*): 309–38.

Baker, Gerard, Carol E. Lee, and Michael C. Bender. 2017. "Trump says dollar 'getting too strong,' won't label China a currency manipulator." *The Wall Street Journal*, April 12. www.wsj.com/articles/trump-says-dollar-getting-too-strong-wont-label-china-currency-manipulator-1492024312 (accessed April 12, 2018).

Balassa, Bela, and Associates. 1971. *The structure of protection in developing countries*. Baltimore: Johns Hopkins University Press.

Baldwin, Richard. 2014. WTO 2.0: Governance of 21st century trade. *Review of International Organization* 9: 261–83.

Baldwin, Richard E. 1995. A domino theory of regionalism. In *Expanding membership in the European Union*, ed. Richard E. Baldwin, Pentti Haaparanta, and Jaako Jiander. Cambridge, UK: Cambridge University Press.

Baldwin, Richard E., and Phillipe Martin. 1999. *Two waves of globalization: Superficial similarities, fundamental differences*. NBER Working Paper no. 6904. Cambridge, UK: NBER.

Baldwin, Robert. 1969. The case against infant-industry protection. *Journal of Political Economy* 77 (*May–June*): 295–305.

Barber, Tony. 2000a. Germans at odds over the euro. *Financial Times*, September 6, 8.

Barber, Tony. 2000b. Rift emerges over ECB's euro policy. *Financial Times*, September 5, 9.

Barro, R. 1996. Democracy and growth. *Journal of Economic Growth 1* (*1*): 1–27.

Bates, Robert. 1988. Governments and agricultural markets in Africa. In *Toward a political economy of development: A rational choice perspective*, ed. Robert H. Bates. Berkeley: University of California Press.

Bates, Robert. 1997. *Open-economy politics: The political economy of the world coffee trade*. Princeton, NJ: Princeton University Press.

Bearce, David H. 2002. Monetary divergence: Domestic political institutions and the monetary autonomy-exchange rate stability trade-off. *Comparative Political Studies 35* (2): 194–220.

Bennhold, Katrin, and Carter Dougherty. 2007. French push euro countries to confront ECB. *International Herald Tribune*, July 17. www.iht.com/articles/2007/07/17/business/euro.php.

Berger, Suzanne. 2018. Globalization survived populism once before—and it can again. *Boston Review* (January 30). http://bostonreview.net/class-inequality/suzanne-berger-globalization-survived-populism (accessed February 2, 2018).

Bergsman, Joel, and Arthur Candal. 1969. Industrialization: Past success and future problems. In *The economy of Brazil*, ed. Howard S. Ellis. Berkeley: University of California Press.

Berliner D., A. R. Greenleaf, M. Lake, M. Levi, J. Noveck. 2015. Governing global supply chains: What we know (and don't) about improving labor rights and working conditions. *Annual Review of Law and Social Science 11* (1): 193–209.

Bernanke, Ben S. 2010. *Semiannual Monetary Policy Report to the Congress*. Testimony by Ben S. Bernanke, Chairman of the Board of Governors of the US Federal Reserve System, before the Committee on Banking, Housing, and Urban Affairs, U.S. Senate, Washington, DC, February 24, 2009.

Bernhard, William, and David Leblang. 1999. Democratic institutions and exchange rate commitments. *International Organization 53* (1): 71–97.

Bhagwati, Jagdish. 1978. *Anatomy and consequences of exchange control regimes*. Cambridge, MA: Ballinger Publishing Company.

Bhagwati, Jagdish. 1982. Directly unproductive, profit-seeking (DUP) activities. *Journal of Political Economy 90* (*October*): 988–1002.

Binswanger, Hans P., and Klaus Deininger. 1997. Explaining agricultural and agrarian policies in developing countries. *Journal of Economic Literature XXXV* (*December*): 1958–2005.

Birdsall, Nancy, and John Williamson. 2002. *Delivering on debt relief: From IMF gold to a new aid architecture*. Washington, DC: Institute for International Economics.

Blinder, Alan. 2006. "Offshoring: The next industrial revolution?" *Foreign Affairs* (*March/April*).

Blinder, Alan S. 1999. *Central banking in theory and practice*. Cambridge, MA: MIT Press.

Bloch, H., and D. Sapsford. 2000. Whither the terms of trade? An elaboration of the Prebisch-Singer hypothesis. *Cambridge Journal of Economics 24* (4): 461–81.

Block, Fred. 1977. *The origins of international economic disorder: A study of United States international monetary policy from World War II to the present*. Berkeley: University of California Press.

Blonigen, Bruce. 2008. *New evidence on the formation of trade policy preferences*. Working Paper no. 14627. Cambridge, MA: National Bureau of Economic Research.

Bloom, Nicholas, Mirko Draca, and John Van Reenen. 2016. Trade induced technical change? The impact of Chinese imports on innovation, IT and productivity. *The Review of Economic Studies 83* (1): 87–117.

Blustein, Paul. 2001. *The chastening: Inside the crisis that rocked the global financial system and humbled the IMF*. New York: Public Affairs.

Blustein, Paul. 2004a. U.S. files grievance over Airbus with WTO; E.U. responds with Boeing complaint. *Washington Post*, October 7, E.01.

Blustein, Paul. 2004b. U.S. wants to cancel poorest nations' debt. *Washington Post*, September 14, A6.

Boix, C. (2011). Democracy, development, and the international system. *American Political Science Review, 105* (4): 809–28.

Bordo, Michael D. 2002. Globalization in historical perspective. *Business Economics*, January: 20–39.

Borensztein, Eduardo, Mohsin S. Khan, Carmen Reinhart, and Peter Wickham. 1994. *The Behavior of Non-Oil Commodity Prices*. IMF Occasional Paper 112. Washington, DC: The International Monetary Fund.

Bosworth, Barry, and Susan M. Collins. 1999. Capital flows to developing economies: Implications for saving and investment.

Brookings Papers on Economic Activity 1: 143–69.

Bourguignon, François, and Christian Morrisson (2002). Inequality among world citizens: 1820–1992. *The American Economic Review 92 (4):* 727–44.

Bowles, Paul, and Baotai Wang. 2008. The rocky road ahead: China, the US and the future of the dollar. *Review of International Political Economy 15 (3):* 335–53.

Braude, Jonathan. 2008. *New German foreign investment law faces challenges.* Law.com. www.law.com/jsp/article. jsp?id=1202424321685.

Brown, William A. 1950. *The United States and the restoration of world trade: An analysis and appraisal of the ITO charter and the general agreement on tariffs and trade.* Washington, DC: The Brookings Institution.

Broz. J. Lawrence. 2002. Political system transparency and monetary commitment regimes. *International Organization 56* (4): 861–87.

Bruton, Henry J. 1969. The two gap approach to aid and development: Comment. *American Economic Review 59 (June):* 439–46.

Bulmer-Thomas, Victor. 1994. *The economic history of Latin America since independence.* Cambridge, MA: Cambridge University Press.

Cardoso, Fernando, and Enzo Faletto. 1979. *Dependency and development in Latin America.* Los Angeles: University of California Press.

Caruso-Cabrera, Michelle. 2014. Banker showdown: Bernanke tells off India's rajan. CNBC.com (April 10). www.cnbc. com/2014/04/10/banker-showdown-bernanke-tells-off-indias-rajan.html (accessed December 8, 2017).

Casert, Raf. 2004. Little progress in aircraft talks; U.S., E.U. butt heads over Boeing and Airbus subsidies. *The Washington Post*, September 17, E.03.

Caves, Richard E. 1996. *Multinational enterprise and economic analysis.* Cambridge, MA: Cambridge University Press.

Chan, Kam Wing. 2013. China, internal migration. In *The Encyclopedia of Global Migration*, ed. Immanuel Ness, and Peter Bellwood. Chicester, UK: Blackwell Publishing.

Chey, Hyoung-kyu. 2009. The changing political dynamics of East Asian financial cooperation: The Chiang Mai Initiative. *Asian Survey 49 (3):* 450–67.

Chiswick, Barry R., and Timothy J. Hatton. 2003. International migration and the integration of labor markets. In *Globalization in historical perspective*, ed. Michael D. Bordo, Alan M. Taylor, and Jeffrey G. Williamson. Chicago: University of Chicago Press.

Ciminos-Isaacs, Cathleen. 2016. Labor standards in the TPP. In *Trans-Pacific Partnership: An Assessment*, ed. Cathleen Cimino-Isaacs, and Jeffrey J. Schott. Washington, DC: Peterson Institute of International Economics, 261–97.

Clark, John, Nathan Converse, Brahima Coulibaly, and Steve Kamin. 2016. "Emerging Market Capital Flows and U.S. Monetary Policy." International Finance Discussion Paper Notes. Washington, DC: Board of Governors of the Federal Reserve System (October). www. federalreserve.gov/econresdata/notes/ifdp-notes/2016/files/emerging-market-capital-flows-and-us-monetary-policy-20161018. pdf (accessed December 15, 2017).

Cline, William R. 1984. *International debt: Systemic risk and policy response.* Washington, DC: Institute for International Economics.

Cline, William R. 1995. *International debt reexamined.* Washington, DC: Institute for International Economics.

Cohen, Benjamin J. 2015. *Currency power: Understanding monetary rivalry.* Princeton: Princeton University Press.

Conybeare, John. 1984. Public goods, prisoners' dilemmas and the international political economy. *International Studies Quarterly 28:* 5–22.

Corbo, Vittorio. 2000. Economic policy reform in Latin America. In *Economic policy reform: The second stage*, ed. Anne O. Krueger. Chicago: University of Chicago Press.

Credit Suisse. 2017. *Global Wealth Report 2017.* http://publications.credit-suisse.com/tasks/render/file/index. cfm?fileid=12DFFD63-07D1-EC63-A3D5F67356880EF3 (accessed January 3, 2018).

Croome, John. 1995. *Reshaping the world trading system: A history of the Uruguay round.* Geneva: World Trade Organization.

Cukierman, Alex. 1992. *Central bank strategy, credibility, and independence: Theory and evidence*. Cambridge, MA: MIT Press.

Cypher, James M., and James L. Dietz. 1997. *The process of economic development*. London: Routledge.

Dam, Kenneth W. 1982. *The rules of the game: Reform and evolution in the international monetary system*. Chicago: University of Chicago Press.

de Rivero, Oswaldo. 1980. *New economic order and international development law*. Oxford: Pergamon Press.

De Long, Bradford. 1998. *Estimates of world GDP, one million B.C.–present*. http://delong.typepad.com/print/20061012_LRWGDP.pdf (accessed October 31, 2017).

De Vries, Margaret G., and J. Keith Horsefield. 1969. *Analysis. Vol. II of the international monetary fund 1945–1969*. Washington, DC: International Monetary Fund.

Destler, I. M., and C. Randall Henning. 1989. *Dollar politics: Exchange rate policymaking in the United States*. Washington, DC: Institute for International Economics.

Devlin, Robert. 1989. *Debt and crisis in Latin America: The supply side of the story*. Princeton, NJ: Princeton University Press.

Diamond, Jared. 2012. What makes countries rich or poor? *The New York Review of Books* (June 7): www.nybooks.com/articles/2012/06/07/what-makes-countries-rich-or-poor/ (accessed December 27, 2017).

Dicken, Peter. 1998. *Global shift: Transforming the world economy*, 3rd ed. New York: Guilford Press.

Diebold, William Jr. 1952. *The end of the ITO*. Princeton, NJ: Princeton Essays in International Finance, no. 16.

Dollar, David. 2004. *Globalization, poverty, and inequality*. World Bank Research Working Paper no. 3333. http://econ.worldbank.org/files/39000_wps3333.pdf.

Doner, Richard, and Gary Hawes. 1995. The political economy of growth in southeast and northeast Asia. In *The changing political economy of the third world*, ed. Manochehr Dorraj. London: Lynne Rienner, 145–85.

Dooley, Michael P., David Folkerts-Landau, and Peter Garber. 2004. "The revived Bretton Woods system." *International Journal of Finance and Economics 9*: 307–13.

Drazen, Allan. 2000. *Political economy in macroeconomics*. Princeton, NJ: Princeton University Press.

Drezner, Daniel. 2009. Bad debts: Assessing China's financial influence in great power politics. *International Security 34* (2): 7–35.

Easterly, William. 2002. *The elusive quest for growth: Economists' adventures and misadventures in the tropics*. Cambridge, MA: MIT Press.

Echikson, William. 2007. Politics and economics: Strong euro stirs fresh jitters; European group calls for dialogue over currencies. *Wall Street Journal*, October 4, A.7.

Economic Commission for Latin American and the Caribbean. 1985. *External debt in Latin America: Adjustment policies and renegotiation*. Boulder, CA: Lynne Rienner Publishers, Inc.

Economic Report of the President. 2006.

Edwards, Sebastian, ed. 1989. *Debt, adjustment, and recovery: Latin America's prospects for growth and development*. New York: Basil Blackwell.

Edwards, Sebastian. 1995. *Crisis and reform in Latin America: From despair to hope*. Oxford, UK: Oxford University Press.

Eichengreen, Barry J. 1996. *Globalizing capital: A history of the international monetary system*. Princeton, NJ: Princeton University Press.

Eichengreen, Barry J. 2001. "Crisis Prevention and Crisis Management: Any Lessons from Argentina and Turkey?" Background paper for the World Bank's Global Development Finance 2002. http://emlab.berkeley.edu/users/eichengr/policy/crisis101901.pdf.

Eijffinger, Sylvester, and Eric Schaling. 1993. Central bank independence in twelve industrial countries. *BNL Quarterly Review 184* (March): 49–89.

Elkins, Z., A. T. Guzman, and B. A. Simmons. 2006. Competing for capital: The diffusion of bilateral investment treaties, 1960–2000. *International Organization*, 60(Fall), 811–46.

Emerson, Michael. 1992. *One market, one money: An evaluation of the potential benefits and costs of forming an economic and monetary union*. Oxford, UK: Oxford University Press.

Emminger, Otmar. 1977. *The D-mark in the conflict between internal and external equilibrium, 1948–1975*. Princeton, NJ: Essays in International Finance.

Encarnation, Dennis J. 1989. *Dislodging multinationals: India's strategy in comparative perspective*. Ithaca, NY: Cornell University Press.

European Commission. 2017. *2016 Annual Report on intra-EU Labour Mobility*, 2nd ed. Brussels: European Commission.

Evans, Carolyn L. 2009. A protectionist bias in majoritarian politics: An empirical investigation. *Economics & Politics 21* (2): 278–307.

Faith, Nicholas. 1993. Nothing finer than a plant in Carolina. *The Independent*, May 9, 14. www.frbsf.org/publications/economics/letter/2002/el2002-31.pdf.

Finger, J. Michael. 1991. Development economics and the general agreement on tariffs and trade. In *Trade theory and economic reform: North, south, and east. Essays in honor of Bela Balassa*, ed. Jaime de Melo, and Andre Sapir, 203–23. Oxford, MA: Basil Blackwell.

Frankel, Jeffrey A. 1990. *The making of exchange rate policy in the 1980s*. NBER Working Paper no. 3539. Cambridge, MA: National Bureau of Economic Research.

Frankel, Jeffrey A. 1997. *Regional trading blocs in the world economic system*. Washington, DC: Institute for International Economics.

Frieden, Jeffry A. 1981. Third world indebted industrialization: International finance and state capitalism in Mexico, Brazil, Algeria, and South Korea. *International Organization 35* (*Summer*): 407–31.

Frieden, Jeffry A. 1991a. Invested interests: The politics of national economic policies in a world of global finance. *International Organization 45* (Autumn): 425–51.

Frieden, Jeffry A. 1991b. *Debt, development, and democracy: Modern political economy and Latin America, 1965–1985*. Princeton: Princeton University Press.

Frieden, Jeffry A. 1996. The impact of goods and capital market integration on European monetary politics. *Comparative Political Studies 29* (April): 193–222.

Frieden, Jeffry A. 1997. Monetary populism in nineteenth-century America: An open-economy interpretation. *Journal of Economic History 57* (June): 367–95.

Frieden, Jeffry A. 2006. *Global capitalism: Its fall and rise in the twentieth century*. New York: W.W. Norton & Company.

Friedman, Milton. 1968. The role of monetary policy. *American Economic Review 58* (*March*): 1–17.

Froman, Michael. 2015. We are at the end of the line on the Doha Round of trade talks. *The Financial Times online* (December 13) www.ft.com/content/4ccf5356-9eaa-11e5-8ce1-f6219b685d74 (accessed September 22, 2017).

Fukuyama, Francis. 1989. The end of history? *The National Interest 16*: 3–18.

Funabashi, Yoichi. 1988. *Managing the dollar: From the Plaza to the Louvre*. Washington, DC: Institute for International Economics.

Gabel, Medard and Henry Bruner. 2003. *Global Inc: An atlas of the multinational corporation*. New York: W.W. Norton.

Garrett, Geoffrey. 1998. *Partisan politics in the global economy*. Cambridge, MA: Cambridge University Press.

Gereffi, Gary. 1990. Paths of industrialization: An overview. In *Manufacturing miracles: Paths of industrialization in Latin America and East Asia*, ed. Gary Gereffi and Donald L. Wyman. Princeton, NJ: Princeton University Press.

Gereffi, Gary, and Karina Fernandez-Stark. 2016. *Global value chain analysis: A primer*, 2nd ed. Durham, NC: Duke Center on Globalization, Governance, and Competitiveness.

Giavazzi, Francesco, and Alberto Giovannini. 1989. *Limiting exchange rate flexibility in Europe*. Cambridge, MA: MIT Press.

Gilligan, Michael. 1997. *Empowering exporters: Reciprocity, delegation, and collective action in American trade policy*. Ann Arbor: University of Michigan Press.

Gilpin, Robert. 1987. *The political economy of international relations*. Princeton, NJ: Princeton University Press.

Gilpin, Robert. 2000. *The challenge of global capitalism: The world economy in the 21st century*. Princeton, NJ: Princeton University Press.

Gowa, Joanne. 1983. *Closing the gold window: Domestic politics and the end of Bretton Woods*. Ithaca, NY: Cornell University Press.

Grabel, Ilene. 2009. Remittances: Political economy and developmental implications. *International Journal of Political Economy 38* (4): 86–106.

Graham, Edward M. 1996. *Global corporations and national governments.* Washington, DC: Institute for International Economics.

Greenhouse, Steven. 1987. Allies urge German rate cuts. *The New York Times,* October 30, D7.

Group of 6. 1987. *Statement of G6 finance ministers and Central Bank governors (Louvre Accord),* Paris, February 22. www.g8.utoronto.ca/finance/fm870222. htm (accessed December 4, 2010).

Grub P., and J. Lin. 1991. *Foreign direct investment in China.* Westport, CT: Quorum Books.

Gruber, Lloyd. 2000. *Ruling the world.* Princeton, NJ: Princeton University Press.

Haggard, Stephan. 1990. *Pathways from the periphery: The politics of growth in the newly industrializing countries.* Ithaca, NY: Cornell University Press.

Haggard, Stephan. 2000. *The political economy of the Asian financial crisis.* Washington, DC: Institute for International Economics.

Haggard, Stephan, and Robert Kaufman, eds. 1992. *The politics of economic adjustment: International constraints, distributive conflicts, and the state.* Princeton, NJ: Princeton University Press.

Haggard, Stephan, and Tun-jen Cheng. 1987. State and foreign capital in the East Asian NICs. In *The political economy of the new Asian industrialism,* ed. Frederic C. Deyo. Ithaca, NY: Cornell University Press.

Hainmueller, Jens, and Hiscox, Michael J. 2006. Learning to love globalization: Education and individual attitudes toward international trade. *International Organization* 60 (2): 469–98.

Hall, Peter A. 1986. *Governing the economy: The politics of state intervention in Britain and France.* Oxford: Oxford University Press.

Hall, Peter A. 1989. *The political power of economic ideas.* Princeton, NJ: Princeton University Press.

Hallerberg, Mark. 2002. Veto players and the choice of monetary institutions. *International Organization* 56 (4): 775–802.

Harrison, Barbara. 1992. Survey of locating in North America. *Financial Times,* October 20, 38.

Harrison, Christopher S. 2004. *The politics of international pricing of prescription drugs.* Westport, CT: Praeger.

Hart, Jeffrey. 1992. *Rival capitalists: International competitiveness in the United States, Japan, and Western Europe.* Ithaca, NY: Cornell University Press.

Hatfield, John W., and William R. Hauk Jr. 2004. "Electoral Regime and Trade Policy." In SIEPR Discussion Paper. Palo Alto: Stanford.

Heckscher, Eli. 1935. *Mercantilism.* London: Allen & Unwin.

Henisz, W. J., and E. D. Mansfield. 2006. Votes and vetoes: The political determinants of commercial openness. *International Studies Quarterly 50* (1): 189–212.

Henning, C. Randall. 1994. *Currencies and politics in the United States, Germany, and Japan.* Washington, DC: Institute for International Economics.

Henning, C. Randall. 2002. *East Asian financial cooperation.* Washington, DC: The Institute for International Economics.

Henning, C. Randall. 2007. Democratic accountability and the exchange-rate policy of the euro area. *Review of International Political Economy 14* (5): 774–99.

Herbst, Jeffrey. 1993. *The politics of reform in Ghana, 1982–1991.* Berkeley: University of California Press.

Hibbs, Douglas R. 1987. *The American political economy: Macroeconomics and electoral politics.* Cambridge, MA: Harvard University Press.

Hirschman, Albert O. 1958. *The strategy of economic development.* New Haven, CT: Yale University Press.

Hirschman, Albert O. 1968. The political economy of import-substitution industrialization in Latin America. *Quarterly Journal of Economics LXXXII* (February): 1–32.

Hoekman, Bernard M., and Michel M. Kostecki. 1995. *The political economy of the world trading system: From GATT to WTO.* Oxford: Oxford University Press.

Hopkins, Anthony G. 1979. *Two essays on underdevelopment.* Geneva: Graduate Institute of International Studies.

IADB. *See* Inter-American Development Bank.

Ikenberry, G. John. 2000. Don't panic: How secure is globalization's future? *Foreign Affairs 79* (May/June): 145–51.

Ikenberry, G. John, David A. Lake, and Michael Mastanduno. 1988. Introduction: Approaches to explaining American foreign economic policy.

International Organization 42 (*Winter*): 1–14.

IMF. *See* International Monetary Fund.

Inter-American Development Bank. 1997. *Latin America after a decade of reforms.* Washington, DC: Inter-American Development Bank.

International Monetary Fund. 1999. *International capital markets: Developments, prospects, and key policy issues.* Washington, DC: International Monetary Fund.

International Monetary Fund. 2000. *International capital markets: Developments, prospects, and key policy issues.* Washington, DC: International Monetary Fund.

International Monetary Fund. 2001. International financial integration and developing countries. *World Economic Outlook* (*September*): 143–71.

International Monetary Fund. 2002. *World economic outlook.* Washington, DC: International Monetary Fund. www.imf. org/external/pubs/ft/weo/2002/02/index. htm.

International Monetary Fund. 2003. Lessons from the crisis in Argentina. *Policy Development and Review Department.* www.imf.org/external/np/pdr/ lessons/100803.pdf.

International Monetary Fund. 2004. *Classification of exchange rate arrangements and monetary policy frameworks.* www.imf.org/external/np/ mfd/er/2004/eng/1204.htm.

International Monetary Fund. 2008. *Impact of high food and fuel prices on developing countries.* www.imf.org/external/np/exr/ faq/ffpfaqs.htm#q3.

International Monetary Fund. 2011. *IMF Develops Framework to Manage Capital Inflows.* IMF Survey Online (April 5), www.imf.org/en/News/ Articles/2015/09/28/04/53/sonew040511b (accessed December 8, 2017).

Irwin, Douglas. 1993. Multilateral and bilateral trade policies in the world trading system: An historical perspective. In *New dimensions in regional integration*, ed. Jaime de Melo, and Arvind Panagariya. New York: Cambridge University Press.

Jabara, Cathy. 1994. Structural adjustment in a small, open economy: The case of Gambia. In *Adjusting to policy failure in African economies*, ed. David E. Sahn.

Ithaca, NY: Cornell University Press, 302–3.

Jefferson, Gary H., and T. G. Rawski. 2001. Enterprise reform in Chinese industry. In *Growth without miracles*, ed. Ross Garnaut, and Yiping Huang. New York: Oxford University Press, 244–62.

Jenkins, Rhys. 1987. *Transnational corporations and uneven development: The internationalization of capital and the third world.* London: Methuen.

Johnson, Chalmers. 1982. *MITI and the Japanese miracle: The growth of industrial policy, 1925–1975.* Stanford, CA: Stanford University Press.

Johnson, Leland L. 1967. *Economic development and cultural change.* Chicago: University of Chicago Press.

Joint Economic Committee, United States Congress. 2003. *Argentina's economic crisis: Causes and cures.* www.house.gov/ jec/imf/06–13-03long.pdf.

Jones, Geoffrey. 1996. *The evolution of international business: An introduction.* London: Routledge.

Ka, Samba, and Nicolas Van de Walle. 1994. Senegal: Stalled reform in a dominant party system. In *Voting for reform: Democracy, political liberalization and economic adjustment*, ed. Stephan Haggard, and Steven B. Webb. *Washington, DC*: World Bank.

Kane, Dan J., Andrew Curliss, and Amy Martinez. 2004. North Carolina lawmakers approve $242 million in incentives to lure Dell. *News and Observer*, November 5, 1.

Katzenstein, Peter J. 1977. International relations and domestic structures: Foreign economic policies of advanced industrialized states. *International Organization* 31 (*Autumn*): 1–45.

Keech, William R. 1995. *Economic politics: The costs of democracy.* Cambridge, MA: Cambridge University Press.

Kenen, Peter B. 1994. *The international economy*, 3rd ed. Cambridge, MA: Cambridge University Press.

Kennedy, Paul. 1988. *The rise and fall of the great powers.* New York: Random House.

Keohane, Robert O. 1984. *After hegemony.* Princeton, NJ: Princeton University Press.

Keynes, John Maynard. 1919. *The economic consequences of the peace.* London: MacMillan.

Keynes, John Maynard. 1936. *The general theory of employment, interest and money.* London: Macmillan and Co., Ltd.

Kilborn, Peter T. 1987. U.S. cautions Bonn it may force the dollar lower. *New York Times,* October 16, A1.

Killick, Toy. 1978. *Development economics in action: A study of economic policies in Ghana.* London: Heinemann.

Kim, Soo Yeon, 2015. Deep integration and regional trade agreements. In *The Oxford Handbook of the Political Economy of International Trade,* ed. Lisa L. Martin. Oxford: Oxford University Press.

Kimmitt, Robert M. 2008. Public footprints in private markets: Sovereign wealth funds and the world economy. *Foreign Affairs* (January/February). www.foreignaffairs.org/2008010/faessay87109/robert-m-kimmitt/public-footprints-in-private-markets.html.

Kindleberger, Charles P. 1974. *The world in depression, 1929–1939.* Berkeley: University of California Press.

King, Neil Jr. 2004. U.S., Europe sue each other at WTO over aircraft subsidies; Boeing and Airbus spar for dominance in sales; Brawl could rattle industry. *Wall Street Journal,* October 7, A.2.

Kobrin, Stephen. 1987. Testing the bargaining hypothesis in the manufacturing sector in developing countries. *International Organization 41 (Autumn):* 609–38.

Kobrin, Stephen. 1998. The MAI and the clash of globalizations. *Foreign Policy 98 (Fall):* 97–112.

Kock, Karin. 1969. *International trade policy and the GATT, 1947–1967.* Stockholm: Almqvist & Wiksell.

Kraft, Joseph. 1984. *The Mexican rescue.* New York: Group of Thirty.

Kramer, Gordon. 1971. Short-term fluctuations in U.S. voting behavior, 1896–1964. *American Political Science Review 65:* 131–43.

Krasner, Stephen D. 1977. United States commercial and monetary policy: Unraveling the paradox of external strength and internal weakness. *International Organization 31 (Autumn):* 635–71.

Krasner, Stephen D. 1985. *Structural conflict: The third world against global liberalism.* Berkeley: University of California Press.

Krueger, Anne O. 1974. The political economy of the rent-seeking society.

American Economic Review 64 (June): 291–303.

Krueger, Anne O. 1993a. *Political economy of policy reform in developing countries.* Cambridge, MA: MIT Press.

Krueger, Anne O. 1995. *American trade policy: A tragedy in the making.* Washington, DC: The AEI Press.

Krueger, Anne O., Maurice Schiff, and Alberto Valdes. 1992. *The political economy of agricultural price intervention in Latin America.* San Francisco: ICS Press.

Krugman, Paul. 1987. Is free trade passé? *Journal of Economic Perspectives 1 (Autumn):* 131–44.

Krugman, Paul. 1997. In praise of cheap labor: Bad jobs at bad wages are better than no jobs at all. *Slate,* March 21.

Krugman, Paul. 2015. Debt deflation in Greece. *New York Times,* July 7. https://krugman.blogs.nytimes.com/2015/07/07/debt-deflation-in-greece/?_r=0 (accessed November 24, 2017).

Krugman, Paul R., and Maurice Obstfeld. 1994. *International economics: Theory and policy,* 4th ed. Reading, MA: Addison Wesley.

Krugman, Paul R., and Maurice Obstfeld. 2003. *International economics: Theory and policy,* 6th ed. Reading, MA: Addison Wesley.

Kydland, Finn, and Edward C. Prescott. 1977. Rules rather than discretion: The dynamic inconsistency of optimal plans. *Journal of Political Economy 83:* 473–91.

Lake, David. 2013. Theory is dead, long live theory: The end of the great debates and the rise of eclecticism in international relations. *European Journal of International Relations 19:* 567–87.

Lal, Deepak. 1983. *The poverty of "development economics."* London: The Institute of Economic Affairs.

Lal, Deepak, and Hla Myint. 1996. *The political economy of poverty, equity, and growth: A comparative study.* Oxford: Clarendon Press.

La Porta, Rafael, and Florencio López de Silanes. 1997. *The benefits of privatization: Evidence from Mexico.* NBER Working Paper no. W6215. Cambridge, MA: National Bureau of Economic Research.

Lardy, Nicholas. 2002. *Integrating China into the global economy.* Washington, DC: The Brookings Institution.

Larmer, Brook. 2017. "Is China the world's new colonial power?" *The New York Times*, May 2. www.nytimes.com/2017/05/02/magazine/is-china-the-worlds-new-colonial-power.html (accessed October 6, 2017).

Layne, Christopher. 2009. The waning of U.S. hegemony: Myth or reality? A review essay. *International Security 34 (1)*: 147–72.

Leff, Nathaniel H. 1969. *Economic policy-making and development in Brazil, 1947–1964*. New York: John Wiley & Sons, Inc.

Lekachman, Robert. 1966. *The age of Keynes*. New York: Vintage.

LeLoup, Lance T. 2005. *Parties, rules, and the evolution of Congressional budgeting*. Columbus: Ohio State University Press.

Leutert, Wendy. 2016. Challenges ahead in China's reform of state-owned enterprises. *Asia Policy, 21 (January)*: 83–99.

Lewis, Arthur. 1954. Economic development with unlimited supplies of labor. *Manchester School of Economic and Social Studies 22*: 139–91.

Lipset, Seymour Martin. 1959. Some social requisites of democracy: Economic development and political legitimacy. *American Political Science Review 53 (1)*: 69–105.

Lipson, Charles. 1985. *Standing guard: Protecting foreign capital in the nineteenth and twentieth Centuries*. Berkeley: University of California Press.

Little, Ian. 1982. *Economic development*. New York: Basic Books.

Little, Ian, Tibor Scitovsky, and Maurice Scott. 1970. *Industry and trade in some developing countries: A comparative study*. London: Oxford University Press.

Liu, Paul K. C. 1992. Science, technology, and human capital formation. In *Taiwan: From developing to mature economy*, ed. Gustav Ranis. Boulder: Westview Press, 357–93.

Luft, Gal. 2008. *Sovereign wealth funds, oil, and the new world economic order*. Testimony before the House Committee on Foreign Affairs. http://foreignaffairs.house.gov/110/luf052108.htm.

Mackie, Thomas T., and Richard Rose, eds. 1991. *The international almanac of electoral history*. Washington, DC: Congressional Quarterly.

Maddison, Angus. 2001. *The world economy: A millennial perspective*. Paris: Organization for Economic Cooperation and Development.

Mankiw, Gregory and Swagel, Phillip. 2006. "The Politics and Economics of Offshore Outsourcing." NBER Working Paper no. 12398.

Mansfield, Edward D., and Diana C. Mutz. 2009 Support for free trade: Self-interest, sociotropic politics, and out-group anxiety. *International Organization 63 (03)*: 425–57.

Mansfield, E., D. Mutz, and D. Brackbill. (2016). Effects of the Great Recession on American attitudes toward trade. *British Journal of Political Science*, 1–22.

Mansfield, Edward D., and Marc L. Busch. 1995. The political economy of nontariff barriers: A cross-national analysis. *International Organization 49 (4)*: 723–49.

Mason, Edward S., and Robert E. Asher. 1973. *The World Bank since Bretton Woods*. Washington, DC: Brookings Institution.

Mason, Mark. 1992. *American multinationals and Japan: The political economy of capital controls, 1899–1980*. Cambridge, MA: Harvard University Press.

McEntee, Christopher. 1995. Trends in the region: States evaluating cost of enticing industry. *Bond Buyer (May 25)*: 20.

McIntyre, Ian. 1992. *Dogfight: The transatlantic battle over Airbus*. Westport, CT: Praeger.

McKinnon, Ronald L. 1964. Foreign exchange constraints in economic development and efficient aid allocation. *Economic Journal 74 (June)*: 388–409.

Miller, Kenneth E. 1996. *Friends and rivals: Coalition politics in Denmark, 1901–1995*. Lanham, MD: University Press of America.

Milner, Helen V. 2014. Introduction: The global economy, FDI, and the regime for investment. *World Politics 66 (1)*: 1–11.

Milner, H. 1988. *Resisting protectionism: Global industries and the politics of international trade*. Princeton: Princeton University Press.

Montiel, Peter and Eduardo Fernández-Arias. 2001. Reform and growth in Latin America: All pain and no gain? *IMF Staff Papers 48 (3)*: 522–46.

Moran, Theodore H. 1974. *Multinational corporations and the politics of dependence: Copper in Chile.* Princeton, NJ: Princeton University Press.

Moran, Theodore H. 1999. *Foreign direct investment and development: The new policy agenda for developing countries and economies in transition.* Washington, DC: Institute for International Economics.

Moran, Theodore H. 2002. *Beyond sweatshops: Foreign direct investment in developing countries.* Washington, DC: The Brookings Institution.

Mosley, Layna. 2011. *Labor rights and multinational production.* New York: Cambridge University Press.

Mosley, Layna, and David A. Singer. 2015. Migration, labor, and the international political economy. *Annual Review of Political Science, 18 (1):* 283–301.

Muhleisen, Martin, and Christopher Towe. 2004. *U.S. fiscal policies and priorities for long-run sustainability.* Washington, DC: The International Monetary Fund.

Mutz, Diana and Eunji Kim. 2017. The impact of in-group favoritism on trade preferences. *International Organization 71 (4):* 827–50.

Myerson, Allen R. 1996. O governor, won't you buy me a Mercedes plant? *New York Times,* September, Section 3, 1.

Naughton, Barry. 1995. *Growing out of the plan: Chinese economic reform, 1978–1993.* New York: Cambridge University Press.

Nelson, Joan, ed. 1990. *Economic crisis and policy choice: The politics of adjustment in the third world.* Princeton, NJ: Princeton University Press.

Nelson, Rebecca M. 2009. *The G-20 and international economic cooperation: Background and implications for Congress.* Washington, D.C: Congressional Research Service.

Nelson, Rebecca M., Paul Belkin, and Erik E. Mix. 2010. *Greece's debt crisis: Overview, policy responses, and implications.* Washington, D.C: Congressional Research Service.

Newhouse, John. 1982. *The sporty game.* New York: Knopf.

Nixon, Richard M. 1962. *Six crises.* New York: Doubleday.

Nordhaus, William. 1989. Alternative approaches to the political business cycle. *Brookings Papers on Economic Activity* 2: 1–68.

Oatley, Thomas. 1997. *Monetary politics: Exchange rate cooperation in the*

European Union. Ann Arbor: University of Michigan Press.

Oatley, Thomas. 1999. How constraining is capital mobility? The partisan hypothesis in an open economy. *American Journal of Political Science 43 (October):* 1003–27.

Oatley, Thomas. 2004. Why is stabilization sometimes delayed? Re-evaluating the regime type hypothesis. *Comparative Political Studies 37 (April):* 286–312.

Oatley, Thomas. 2017. Open economy trade politics and trade policy. *Review of International Political Economy 244 (4):* 699–717.

Odell, John S. 1982. *U.S. international monetary policy: Markets, power, and ideas.* Princeton, NJ: Princeton University Press.

OECD. *See* Organization for Economic Cooperation and Development.

Oliver, Tim. 2015. To be or not to be in Europe: Is that the question? Britain's European question and an in/out referendum. *International Affairs 91 (1):* 77–91.

Olson, Mancur. 1965. *The logic of collective action.* Cambridge, MA: Harvard University Press.

Organization for Economic Co-operation and Development. 1994. *The OECD jobs study: Evidence and explanations.* Paris: Organization for Economic Cooperation and Development.

Organization for Economic Co-operation and Development. 1995. *Historical statistics.* Paris: Organization for Economic Cooperation and Development.

Organization for Economic Co-operation and Development. 2005. *Economic survey of China 2005.* Paris: Organization for Economic Cooperation and Development.

OTA. *See* U.S. Congress, Office of Technology Assessment.

Owen, Erica, and Stefanie Walter. 2017. Open economy politics and Brexit: Insights, puzzles, and ways forward. *Review of International Political Economy 24 (2):* 179–202.

Oye, Kenneth A., ed. 1986. *Cooperation under anarchy.* Princeton, NJ: Princeton University Press.

Peters, Margaret. 2017. *Trading barriers, immigration and the remaking of globalization.* Princeton: Princeton University Press.

Peters, Margaret E. 2015. Open trade, closed borders immigration in the era of globalization. *World Politics* 67 (1): 114–54.

Peters, Margaret E. 2014. Trade, foreign direct investment, and immigration policy making in the United States." *International Organization* 68 (4): 811–44.

Pempel, T. J. 1977. Japanese foreign economic policy: The domestic bases for international behavior. *International Organization* 31 (*Autumn*): 723–74.

Phelps, Edmund S. 1968. Money-wage dynamics and labor-market equilibrium. *Journal of Political Economy* 76 (*July–August*): 678–711.

Phillips, Michael M. 2002. O'Neill defends dollar. *The Wall Street Journal*, May 2, B17.

Piketty, Thomas Li Yang Gabriel Zucman. 2017. *Capital accumulation, private property and rising inequality in China, 1978–2015.* NBER Working Paper no. 23368. Cambridge: National Bureau of Economic Research

Pinker, Stephen. 2011. *The better angels of our nature: Why violence has declined.* New York: Penguin.

Prasad, Eswar. 2016. *Gaining currency: The rise of the renminbi.* Oxford: Oxford University Press.

Przeworski, Adam, Michael E. Alvarez, Jose Antonio Cheibub, and Fernando Limongi. 2000. *Democracy and development: Political institutions and well-being in the world, 1950–1990.* New York: Cambridge University Press.

Pyle, David J. 1997. *China's economy: From revolution to reform.* New York: St. Martin's Press.

Rabe, Stephen G. 1999. *The most dangerous area in the world: John F. Kennedy confronts communist revolutions in Latin America.* Chapel Hill: University of North Carolina Press.

Remmer, Karen L. 1986. The politics of economic stabilization: IMF standby programs in Latin America, 1954–1984. *Comparative Politics* 19 (*October*): 1–24.

Reuters 2010. Brazil Warns of World Currency War. *The Telegraph*, September 28. www.telegraph.co.uk/finance/economics/8029560/Brazil-warns-of-world-currency-war.html (accessed December 8, 2017).

Rho, Sungmin and Tomz, Michael. 2015. Industry, Self-Interest and Individual Preferences over Trade Policy. Unpublished manuscript.

Rho, Sungmin and Tomz, Michael. 2017. Why don't trade preferences reflect economic self-interest? *International Organization* 71 (*Supplement*): S85–S108.

Rickard, Stephanie J. 2015. Electoral systems and trade. In *The Oxford Handbook of the Political Economy of International Trade,* ed. Lisa L. Martin. Oxford: Oxford University Press.

Rockoff, Hugh. 1990. The Wizard of Oz as a monetary allegory. *Journal of Political Economy* 98 (4): 739–60.

Rodrik, Dani. 1998. Who needs capital account liberalization? In *Should the IMF pursue capital-account convertibility?* ed. Stanley Fischer, Essays in International Finance, 207. Princeton, NJ: Department of Economics, Princeton University.

Rodrik, Dani. 1999. *Making openness work: The new global economy and the developing countries.* Washington, DC: Overseas Development Council.

Rodrik, Dani. 2004. "Getting Institutions Right," unpublished manuscript, https://drodrik.scholar.harvard.edu/files/dani-rodrik/files/getting-institutions-right.pdf (accessed April 9, 2018).

Rodrik, Dani. 2011. *The globalization paradox: Democracy and the future of the world economy.* New York: W.W. Norton & Company.

Rodrik, Dani, 2017. *Populism and the economics of globalization. NBER Working Paper* no. 23559. Cambridge: National Bureau of Economic Research (July).

Rogowski, R. 1987. Trade and the variety of democratic institutions. *International Organization* 41 (2): 203–23.

Rogowski, R. 1989. *Commerce and coalitions.* Princeton, NJ: Princeton University Press.

Roodman, David Malin. 2001. *Still waiting for the jubilee: Pragmatic solutions for the third world debt crisis.* Washington, DC: Worldwatch Institute.

Rosenstein-Rodan, Paul. 1943. Problems of industrialization of eastern and south-eastern Europe. *Economic Journal* 53 (*June–September*): 202–11.

Sachs, Jeffrey. 2005. *The end of poverty: Economic possibilities for our time.* New York: Penguin Press.

Sachs, Jeffrey, and Felipe B. Larrain. 1993. *Macroeconomics in the global economy*. Englewood Cliffs, NJ: Prentice Hall.

Saez, Emmanuel. 2016. Striking it richer: The evolution of top incomes in the United States (updated with 2015 preliminary estimates). https://eml.berkeley.edu/~saez/saez-UStopincomes-2015.pdf (accessed January 3, 2018).

Safarian, A. E. 1993. *Multinational enterprises and public policy: A study of industrial countries*. Brookfield: Edward Elgar.

Sampson, Thomas. 2017. Brexit: The economics of international disintegration. *Journal of Economic Perspectives 31 (4)*: 163–84.

Sandler, Todd. 1992. *Collective action: Theory and applications*. Ann Arbor: University of Michigan Press.

Sauvant, K. P., and V. Aranda. 1994. The international legal framework for transnational corporations. In *Transnational corporations: The international legal framework*, ed. A. A. Fatouros. London: Routledge.

Scheve, Kenneth, and Matthew Slaughter. 2001a. What determines individual trade-policy preferences? *Journal of International Economics 54 (2)*: 267–92.

Scheve, Kenneth E., and Matthew J. Slaughter. 2001b. *Globalization and the perceptions of American workers*. Washington, DC: Institute for International Economics.

Schiff, Maurice, and Alberto Valdés. 1992. *The plundering of agriculture in developing countries*. Washington, DC: World Bank.

Schmemann, Serge. 1987. West Germans irritated by Baker's rate stance. *New York Times*, October 17, 41.

Schnepf, Randy. 2010. Brazil's WTO Case Against the U.S. Cotton Program. *CRS Report for Congress*. Washington, D.C.: Congressional Research Service.

Schott, Jeffrey J., and Jayashree Watal. 2000. Decision-making in the WTO. *Institute for International Economics Policy Brief 00–2*. http://iie.com/publications/pb/pb00–2.htm.

Scitovsky, Tibor. 1954. Two concepts of external economies. *Journal of Political Economy 62 (April)*: 143–51.

Setser, Brad. 2016. Germany is running a fiscal surplus in 2016 after all. Follow the Money blog (Council on Foreign Relations). August 25. www.cfr.org/blog/germany-running-fiscal-surplus-2016-after-all (accessed November 21, 2017).

Shafer, Michael. 1983. Capturing the mineral multinationals: Advantage or disadvantage? *International Organization 37 (Winter)*: 93–119.

Shen, Raphael. 2000. *China's economic reform: An experiment in pragmatic socialism*. Westport, CO: Praeger.

Skidelsky, Robert. 1994. *John Maynard Keynes: The economist as savior, 1920–1937*. London: Allen Lane, Penguin Press.

Skidmore, Thomas E., and Peter H. Smith. 1989. *Modern Latin America*, 2nd ed. New York: Oxford University Press.

Sobel, Mark, and Louellen Stedman. 2006. The Evolution of the G-7 and Economic Policy Coordination. In *Office of International Affairs Occasional Paper*. Washington, D.C.: Department of the Treasury.

Sokoloff, Kenneth. L. and Stanley. L. Engerman. 2000. History lessons: Institutions, factors endowments, and paths of development in the new world. *The Journal of Economic Perspectives, 14 (3)*: 217–232.

Solomon, Robert. 1977. *The international monetary system, 1945–1976: An insider's view*. New York: Harper & Row Publishers.

Solomon, Robert. 1999. *Money on the move: The revolution in international finance since 1980*. Princeton, NJ: Princeton University Press.

Soltwedel, Rudiger, Dirk Dohse, and Christiane Krieger-Boden. 2000. European labor markets and EMU: Challenges ahead. *Finance and Development 37 (June)*: 37–40.

Srinivasan, T. N., and Suresh D. Tendulkar. 2003. *Reintegrating India with the world economy*. Washington, DC: Institute for International Economics.

Stein, Herbert. 1994. *Presidential economics: The making of economic policy from Roosevelt to Clinton*. Washington, DC: American Enterprise Institute.

Subramanian, Arvind. 2011. *Eclipse: Living in the shadow of China's economic dominance*. Washington, DC: Peterson Institute for International Economics.

Suzuki, Takaaki. 2000. *Japan's budget politics: Balancing domestic and international interests*. Boulder: Lynne Rienner.

Taylor, Michael. 1976. *Anarchy and cooperation*. New York: Wiley.

Teece, David J. 1993. The multinational enterprise: Market failure and market power considerations. In *The theory of transnational corporations*, ed. John Dunning. New York: Routledge, 163–82.

Temin, Peter. 2017. *The vanishing middle class: Prejudice and power in a dual economy*. Cambridge: MIT Press.

Temin, Peter. 1996. *Lessons from the Great Depression*. Cambridge, MA: MIT Press.

Thorp, Rosemary. 1999. *Progress, poverty, and exclusion: An economic history of Latin America in the 20th Century*. Baltimore: Johns Hopkins University Press.

Todaro, Michael P. 2000. *Economic development*, 7th ed. Reading, MA: Addison-Wesley.

Tomlinson, B. R. 1979. *The political economy of the Raj, 1914–1947: The economics of decolonization in India*. London: Macmillan Press.

Toye, John. 1994. *Dilemmas of development*, 2nd ed. Oxford, UK: Blackwell.

Trebat, Thomas J. 1983. *Brazil's state-owned enterprises: A case study of the state as entrepreneur*. Cambridge, UK: Cambridge University Press.

Trichet, Jean-Claude. 2010. Stimulate no more—it is now time for all to tighten. *The Financial Times*, July 22. www.ft.com/cms/s/0/1b3ae97e-95c6-11df-b5ad-00144feab49a. html?dbk#axzz17FmZbW5i (accessed December 4, 2010).

Triffin, Robert. 1960. *Gold and the dollar crisis*. New Haven, CT: Yale University Press.

Tsebelis, George. 2002. *Veto players: How political institutions work*. Princeton: Princeton University Press.

Tufte, Edward R. 1978. *Political control of the economy*. Princeton, NJ: Princeton University Press.

Tussie, Diana. 1988. The coordination of the Latin American debtors: Is there a logic behind the story? In *Managing world debt*, ed. Stephanie Griffith-Jones. New York: St. Martin's Press.

Tyson, Laura D'Andrea. 1995. *Who's bashing whom? Trade conflict in high technology industry*. Washington, DC: Institute for International Economics.

UNCTAD. *See* United Nations Conference on Trade and Development.

UNEP. *See* United Nations Environment Programme.

United Nations. 1964. *Towards a new trade policy for development*. New York: United Nations.

United Nations Conference on Trade and Development. 1964. *Towards a new trade policy for development*. New York: United Nations.

United Nations Conference on Trade and Development. 1983. *World investment report*. Geneva: United Nations Conference on Trade and Development.

United Nations Conference on Trade and Development. 1995. *World investment report: Transnational corporations and competitiveness*. Geneva: United Nations.

United Nations Conference on Trade and Development. 2000. *World investment report: Cross-border mergers and acquisitions and development*. Geneva: United Nations.

United Nations Conference on Trade and Development. 2001. *World investment report: Promoting linkages*. Geneva: United Nations.

United Nations Conference on Trade and Development. 2004. *World investment report: The shift toward services*. Geneva: United Nations.

United Nations Conference on Trade and Development. 2007. *World investment report*. Geneva: United Nations Conference on Trade and Development.

United Nations Conference on Trade and Development. 2009. *World investment report*. Geneva: United Nations Conference on Trade and Development.

United Nations Conference on Trade and Development. 2013. *World investment report*. Geneva: United Nations Conference on Trade and Development.

United Nations Conference on Trade and Development. 2017. *World investment report*. Geneva: United Nations Conference on Trade and Development.

United States Department of State. Memorandum from Secretary of the Treasury Fowler to President Johnson, May 10, 1966. *Foreign relations of the United States 1964–1968, Volume VIII: International monetary and trade policy*.

Washington, DC: U.S. Government Printing Office.

United States Department of the Treasury. 2010. *Major foreign holders of Treasury securities.* www.ustreas.gov/tic/mfh.txt (accessed July 21, 2010).

United States Government. 2006. *Economic report of the President.* Washington, DC: U.S. Government Printing Office.

U.S. Congress, Office of Technology Assessment. 1991. *Competing economies: America, Europe, and the Pacific Rim.* OTA-ITE-498. Washington, DC: U.S. Government Printing Office.

U.S. International Trade Commission. 2013. *Digital trade in the U.S. and global economies, Part 1.* Washington, DC: Government Printing Office.

USTR. 2017. The President's 2017 trade policy agenda. https://ustr.gov/sites/default/files/files/reports/2017/AnnualReport/Chapter%20I%20-%20The%20President%27s%20Trade%20Policy%20Agenda.pdf (accessed September 25, 2017).

Van Trotsenberg, Axel, and Alan MacArthur. 1999. *The HIPC initiative: Delivering debt relief to poor countries.* www.worldbank.org/hipc/related-papers/hipc-initiative-feb99.pdf.

Vernon, Raymond. 1998. *In the hurricane's eye: The troubled prospects of multinational enterprises.* Cambridge, MA: Harvard University Press.

Viner, Jacob. 1960. *Studies in the theory of international trade.* London: Allen & Unwin.

Vogel, David. 2000. International trade and environmental regulation. In *Environmental policy: New directions for the twenty-first century*, ed. Norman J. Vig, and Michael Kraft. Washington, DC: CQ Press.

Wade, Robert. 1990. *Governing the market: Economic theory and the role of government in East Asian industrialization.* Princeton, NJ: Princeton University Press.

Wade, Robert. 1994. Selective industrial policies in East Asia: Is the East Asian miracle right? In *Miracle or design? Lessons from the East Asian experience*, ed. Albert Fishlow, Catherine Gwin, Stephan Haggard, Dani Rodrik, and Robert Wade, 55–79. Washington, DC: Overseas Development Council.

Walter, Stefanie. 2017. Globalization and the demand-side of politics: How globalization shapes labor market risk perceptions and policy preferences. *Political Science Research and Methods* 5 (*1*): 55–80.

Waterbury, John. 1992. The heart of the matter? Public enterprise and the adjustment process. In *The politics of economic adjustment: International constraints, distributive conflicts, and the state*, ed. Stephen Haggard and Robert R. Kaufman, 182–217. Princeton, NJ: Princeton University Press.

Waters, Richard. 1996. Bidding war reaches new heights. *Financial Times*, November 20, 5.

Weinstein, Michael M., and Steve Charnovitz. 2001. The greening of the WTO. *Foreign Affairs*, 80 (*November/December*): 147–56.

Whalley, John. 1998. Why do countries seek regional trade agreements? In *The regionalization of the world economy*, ed. Jeffrey A. Frankel. Chicago: University of Chicago Press.

Wilkins, Myra. 1970. *The emergence of multinational enterprise: American business abroad from the colonial era to 1914.* Cambridge, MA: Harvard University Press.

Williams, Marc. 1991. *Third world cooperation: The Group of 77 in UNCTAD.* London: Pintner Publishers.

Williamson, John. 1983. *The exchange rate system.* Washington, DC: Institute for International Economics.

Williamson, John. 1990. *The progress of policy reform in Latin America.* Washington, DC: Institute for International Economics.

Williamson, John, ed. 1994. *The political economy of policy reform.* Washington, DC: Institute for International Economics.

Williamson, Oliver. 1985. *The economic institutions of capitalism.* New York: Free Press.

Wood, Robert E. 1986. *From Marshall plan to debt crisis: Foreign aid and development choices in the world economy.* Berkeley: University of California Press.

World Bank. 1983. *World tables,* 3rd ed. Washington, DC: World Bank.

World Bank. 1989. *Sub-Saharan Africa: From crisis to sustainable growth.* Washington, DC: World Bank.

World Bank. 1991. *World development report: The challenge of development.* Oxford, UK: Oxford University Press.

World Bank. 1993. *The East Asian miracle: Economic growth and public policy.* Washington, DC: World Bank.

World Bank. 1994a. *Adjustment in Africa: Lessons from country case studies.* Washington, DC: World Bank.

World Bank. 1994b. *Adjustment in Africa: Reform, results, and the road ahead.* Oxford, UK: Oxford University Press.

World Bank. 1995. *World development report.* Washington, DC: World Bank.

World Bank. 1997. *Global development finance.* Washington, DC: World Bank.

World Bank. 1999. *The Philippines: The case of economic Zones.* Washington, DC: World Bank.

World Bank. 2001a. *Global development finance.* Washington, DC: World Bank.

World Bank. 2004. *HIPC at a Glance.* http:// siteresources.worldbank.org/INTDEBT DEPT/DataAndStatistics/20263217hipc- pages.pdf.

World Bank. 2006. *Global monitoring report 2006: Strengthening mutual accountability—Aid, trade & governance.* http://go.worldbank.org/9UNL7FRYC0 (accessed December 16, 2008).

World Bank. 2016. *Poverty and shared prosperity, 2016: Taking on inequality.* Washington, DC: The World Bank Group.

World Bank. 2017a. *Heavily indebted poor countries initiative and multilateral debt relief initiative statistical update* (August 4). http://pubdocs.worldbank.org/ en/175131505738008789/WB-HIPC-stat- update-2017.pdf (accessed December 8, 2017).

World Bank. 2017b. Migration and Remittances: Recent Developments and Outlook. *Migration and Development Brief* 28 (October). www.knomad.org/ sites/default/files/2017-10/Migration%20 and%20Development%20Brief%2028. pdf (accessed November 28, 2017).

World Trade Organization. 1995. *Trading into the future.* Geneva: World Trade Organization.

World Trade Organization. 2000. *Mapping of regional trade arrangements.* WT/ REG/W/41 11 October. Geneva: The World Trade Organization.

World Trade Organization. 2017. *World trade statistical review.* Geneva: World Trade Organization.

WTO. *See* World Trade Organization.

INDEX

Note: Page numbers in *italic* type refer to *figures*. Page numbers in **bold** type refer to tables.